THE RUGBY LEAGUE ALMANAC 2012
John Harms • Nick Tedeschi

THE EDITORS

John Harms is a writer and broadcaster.
He lives in Melbourne. His books include:

Confessions of a Thirteenth Man
Memoirs of a Mug Punter
Loose Men Everywhere
The Pearl
Play On (omnibus)
The Footy Almanac 2007
The Footy Almanac 2008
The Footy Almanac 2009
The Footy Almanac 2010
The Footy Almanac 2011
The Footy Almanac 2012

Nick Tedeschi is a sportswriter and rugby league analyst.
He is the managing editor of *Making The Nut* and the
rugby league and betting editor at *Back Page Lead*.

His books are:

Chasing Greatness
Punters' Guide to the NRL Season

The Rugby League Almanac 2012

---◆◇◆---

Edited by John Harms
and Nick Tedeschi

With forewords by Roy Masters,
John Stanley and William McInnes

malarkey

PUBLICATIONS

First published in Australia in 2012
by Malarkey Publications Pty Ltd
PO Box 1402, Fitzroy North, Victoria 3068
ABN 80 127 972 025

EMAIL

footyalmanac@bigpond.com
j.t.h@bigpond.net.au
nicktedeschi@hotmail.com

ISBN 978 0 9874343 1 9

Cover image by Martin Tighe

Book design by John Kingsmill

Typeset in 11/16 point Stone Print
by Tabloid Pty Ltd. 85 Halifax Street,
Adelaide SA 5000

Printed and bound in Australia
by McPherson's Printing Group,
Maryborough, Victoria

Ode to Rugby League

We go to the cupboard;
we take out club colours
and the air sings.

The season's close.
This season, this season ...
this is our season.

Kids paint signs,
and I am seven again.
I know I will see heroes soon.

I feel the excitement.

Blow that whistle, ref.
Send that ball soaring.
Blow that whistle, ref.

THOMAS KENEALLY

AN EXPLANATION

This is a book by fans for the whole rugby league community.

Some are professional sportswriters and rugby league analysts but most are everyday people who follow the football and enjoy writing about it.

What they have in common is their love for rugby league and a passion for their team and for the game.

This book tells the story of the 2012 season with a game-by-game account and, in the appendices, a simple summary of the important statistics.

We want to start an annual tradition. We invite you to become a part of it as a reader and, next season, as a contributor.

COVER ART

The portrait of Ben Barba was painted by Melbourne artist Martin Tighe.

www.martintighe.com.au

SPONSORS

Malarkey Publications appreciates the support of TattsBet, Dixon Advisory, Momentum, Brimar Electrical Services, Murrindindi Vineyards, Diskman and Tabloid Pty Ltd.

CONTENTS

ROUND TEN

146 Broncos/Sea Eagles.................LINDSEY CUTHBERTSON
148 Bulldogs/Titans ....MARK SEYMOUR
149 Warriors/Roosters ....STEVE MASCORD
152 Knights/Cowboys ....JOHN HARMS
154 Raiders/Eels ....MICK PEARSON
156 Sharks/Storm ....MARK NICHOLS
158 Panthers/Dragons ....PETER ABELA

BYES *Tigers, Rabbitohs*

ROUND ELEVEN

160 Tigers/Warriors ....STU WARREN
162 Cowboys/Panthers ....PETER HULTHEN
164 Sea Eagles/Roosters ....MICHAEL GROSVENOR
166 Dragons/Rabbitohs...........................JOHN CAMPBELL
168 Bulldogs/Sharks.....................................NATHAN BOSS

BYES *Raiders, Storm, Knights, Titans, Eels, Broncos*

STATE OF ORIGIN I

New South Wales/Queensland

171 PAUL DALLIGAN   173 LIAM HAUSER

ROUND TWELVE

175 Storm/Broncos....................................PAUL CONNOLLY
177 Rabbitohs/Raiders ....DOUG ROWETH
179 Knights/Titans.....................................MATT O'HANLON
181 Dragons/Eels.................................GLEN HUMPHRIES
183 Panthers/Sea Eagles...............................MIKE WILSON
185 Tigers/Cowboys ....CLIFF BINGHAM
187 Roosters/Bulldogs.................................NICK TEDESCHI

BYES *Warriors, Sharks*

ROUND THIRTEEN

189 Sea Eagles/Dragons.........................PAUL CONNOLLY
191 Titans/Cowboys ....IAN HAUSER
193 Raiders/Tigers.....................................DOUG ROWETH
195 Bulldogs/Rabbitohs ....LUKE CHARLTON
197 Warriors/Storm...JACK MUIR
199 Broncos/Knights ....HUW FOWLES
201 Eels/Sharks.....................................MICHAEL KENNEDY

BYES *Panthers, Roosters*

ROUND FOURTEEN

203 Storm/Tigers..NICK McGRATH
205 Knights/Raiders.................................MATT TEDESCHI
207 Sharks/Titans......................................DANIEL DWYER
209 Roosters/Broncos ....BRETT OATEN
211 Panthers/Warriors ....PETE ABELA

BYES *Sea Eagles, Bulldogs, Dragons, Cowboys, Eels, Rabbitohs*

STATE OF ORIGIN II

New South Wales/Queensland

214 NICK TEDESCHI   216 HUW FOWLES

ROUND FIFTEEN

219 Dragons/Bulldogs........................... MICHAEL ADAMS
221 Cowboys/Broncos...............................DAVE FLETCHER
222 Sharks/Warriors .... JOHN HARMS
224 Eels/Rabbitohs.....................................ANDREW RYAN
226 Titans/Panthers .... ALEX MADGE
228 Tigers/Roosters............................GREG OBERSCHEIDT
230 Sea Eagles/Storm ....MARK SHANNON

BYES *Raiders, Knights*

ROUND SIXTEEN

232 Broncos/Rabbitohs...........................DOUG ROWETH
234 Dragons/Titans...............................PAUL ROBERTSON
236 Cowboys/Raiders............................MICHAEL PEARSON
238 Panthers/Eels .... PETER ABELA
240 Bulldogs/Storm ....JUSTIN McILVEEN
241 Roosters/Sea Eagles ....MICHAEL GROSVENOR
243 Knights/Tigers..................................... LUKE JAMIESON

BYES *Warriors/Sharks*

ROUND SEVENTEEN

246 Broncos/Sharks .... MARK NICHOLS
248 Eels/Knights ....MICHAEL KENNEDY
250 Rabbitohs/Panthers...........................JOHN CAMPBELL
252 Warriors/Cowboys...............................ANDREW SMITH
254 Raiders/Dragons ....TIM NAPPER

BYES *Sea Eagles, Bulldogs, Storm, Roosters, Tigers, Titans*

STATE OF ORIGIN III

New South Wales/Queensland

257 CLIFF BINGHAM   259 LINDSEY CUTHBERTSON

ROUND EIGHTEEN

261 Tigers/Bulldogs.......... MICHAEL HARRISON-FORD
263 Storm/Raiders ....CHRIS PARKINSON
264 Titans/Warriors ....MATT O'HANLON
266 Rabbitohs/Knights...........................MARTY SPENCER
269 Sea Eagles/Eels..................................ANDREW BOMM
271 Sharks/Roosters...................................DANIEL KEARY

BYES *Broncos, Panthers, Dragons, Cowboys*

ROUND NINETEEN

273 Bulldogs/Eels... NICK TEDESCHI
275 Broncos/Warriors....................................WILL EVANS
277 Storm/Cowboys .... LUKE JAMIESON
279 Knights/Sea Eagles ....LINDSEY CUTHBERTSON
280 Tigers/Panthers ....GREG OBERSCHEIDT
282 Raiders/Titans ....TIM NAPPER
284 Dragons/Sharks .... GLEN HUMPHRIES
286 Roosters/Rabbitohs...........................DANIEL KEARY

ROUND TWENTY

288 Sea Eagles/Bulldogs ....HUW FOWLES

Ben Barba

by ROY MASTERS

HE RUNS LIKE MERCURY ACROSS A MARBLE TABLE. Trap him here and he'll escape you there. Send a straight line of defence in his direction and, akin to a ruler sliding across a surface seeking to capture quicksilver, he'll find a way to slip around the corners.

Mercurial is a word often used in sport to describe the evasive and the instinctive but Ben Barba, rugby league's 2012 Dally M winner, defines it.

The diminutive Canterbury fullback has probably scored more long-range tries in a single season than any player in history. He is the NRL's top try scorer in 2012 with 22.

No one has been able to pick up a ball on the ground in his in goal and reach full stride as speedily as Barba.

While he has superb reflexes, breathtaking acceleration and the evasive skills of a step, a swerve and the new one – a jink – his strength is vastly under-estimated. Barba pushes away much bigger opponents, shocking them with his power.

But can he add anticipation to his arsenal?

Anticipation is a learned skill, where players calculate what a defender, or a multiple of them, will do in advance and then exploit it. Anticipation requires thought. Most of Barba's play involves no thought.

He's more the work of French existentialist philosopher Jean Paul Sartre than his junior coaches. One of Sartre's characters in the play *No Exit* said:

Only actions determine intentions.

Barba might not know what he intends doing, until he does it.

This is not to say Bulldogs coach Des Hasler has played no role in the rise of Barba who was forced to wait his time with Hasler's predecessors, Steve Folkes and Kevin Moore.

Barba credits Hasler with significant improvement in his defence and catching the high ball.

And, while most of the signature plays on a football field are those moments where no thought, or all thought, is required, Barba claims some of his recent tries were scored because he calculated what he should do.

A classic example, he says, was in a Round 6, 2011 match against Parramatta when he selected a single blade of grass to force the ball near the corner post after deliberately swinging his legs in the air over the sideline in order to position his arms infield.

In a match against the Storm in his home town of Mackay this year, he beat a frightening defensive rush to escape his own in-goal, sprinted downfield and then kicked for centre Josh Morris who gathered the ball and scored.

A couple of years earlier, oblivious to the cries of "hog" from his teammates, Barba would have taken on the Melbourne fullback, gambling he could score the try on his own.

The Bulldogs, in their sometimes brutal educative process, didn't do little Benny any early favours. His first Sydney home was a tiny one bedroom flat at Campsie with a mattress on the floor and he worked at a $13 an hour car wash. But, like many players who come to Sydney from the bush, Barba didn't deserve any early favours.

Unlike two other great Olympians, Cathy Freeman and Susie O'Neill who were also born in Mackay, Barba soon succumbed to the bright lights. He teamed up with the Bulldogs' then giant centre, Jamal Idris, for a few late nights close to matches.

Significantly, when Idris moved to play with the Titans, Barba blossomed. However, paralleling his increasing on-field maturity, Barba is now aware of his responsibilities as a role model. Proud of his indigenous heritage, he seeks to emulate other small-of-stature Aboriginal players, such as the Titans' retired Preston Campbell.

With a ready, engaging smile, he is a marketer's dream. He's popular with the fans. And he has two daughters with partner, Ainslee.

I watched him outside the Sydney Town Hall after he had won the Dally M Medal as the game's best player. He signed autographs until his smile must have ached, except that it is natural.

On the field, he is yet to play structured football, reacting only to what is in front of him.

He is certainly capable of playing first receiver but, given the game-breaking role of fullbacks in today's football, Hasler would not want to script him.

Unlike movies, books and plays, we never know how a game of football will end and the mercurial Barba adds romance to the mystery.

Renaissance man Roy Masters is the doyen
of rugby league writers.

The mind of the fan

by JOHN STANLEY

FANS ARE FASCINATING CREATURES. My mate, Ando, is a glass half-empty footy man. A couple of losses and this most miserable of supporters goes to work. The coach is no good. Players are over the hill, overrated, overpaid.

Conversations with Ando after an early-season loss are typically: "Surely you don't think that garbage was good enough?"

"No, but I saw some good signs."

"Well, I'm sick of this mob – they've lost me."

"Ok, I'll buy you a Roosters membership and jumper."

One or other will then hang up.

Half-empty fans are especially annoying for those of us with a more optimistic approach; we view open criticism of the team as disloyalty but readily agree, once a player or coach has left, that he wasn't much good and that now he's someone else's problem.

The half-empties are at every club and in every code but the Dragons' half-empty edition had been hardened by a quarter of a century of unfulfilled expectation. Finalists most years. A string of Grand Finals, but no title. The long drought didn't deter the optimists. Merely wearing the famous Dragons jumper made a player tougher, stronger, faster.

The Premiership was an entitlement, forged in the legend of 11 successive premierships in the '50s and '60s; we were like religious zealots who predict the second coming and, when it doesn't happen, just revise the date.

This blind faith was summed up by a sign on the Kogarah hill. Josh, one of the two identical Morris twins, had left for the Bulldogs. These identical twins play identically. Same skills. Same speed. Same everything. But the sign on our hill was WE HAVE THE BETTER MORRIS, simply because ours, Brett, was still wearing red and white.

Then, in 2008, the second coming: The Messiah was on his way. The game's greatest-ever coach, Wayne Bennett, had signed up with the Dragons. The half-empties were still murmuring. No big-name signings, just a couple of bench players from Canberra and a winger from Brisbane who was learning to play fullback. Would Bennett succeed away from his geographical comfort zone? He's commuting! Family still living in Brisbane. How committed can he be?

It took one game, an opening round golden point loss to the Storm in Melbourne, and the murmuring stopped. Polished, tough and disciplined, the Dragons moved to the top of the table within a few rounds and stayed there.

On the hill a large sign emerged. IN WAYNE WE TRUST. And that's how it was, for three glorious years. Two minor premierships. The 2010 title.

The Messiah had delivered.

For the first time in decades the culture of supporters turning on their own was put aside. Even a run of losses, after a wonderful start to 2011, were the Premiership/Origin hangover or injuries. When the great coach himself admitted he didn't know how to turn it around even the most cynical gave him the benefit of the doubt, remembering his early proclamation: "I know what I'm doing."

And when the premiership defence ended in a golden point in Brisbane, Bennett had extracted one of the best performances of the year, only going down through a Darren Lockyer miracle.

And no one was glad that the coach was leaving.

Except the fans at Newcastle. The Messiah missed the finals with the Knights in 2012 but the good judges know big things will start happening in the Hunter in 2013.

Most clubs have had their messiahs, but messiahs are rarely obvious. Bennett at the Dragons and Jack Gibson at Parramatta were standouts, but when Des Hasler or Craig Bellamy or Phil Gould started they were young, untried rookies. This is the great hope that drives all fans of clubs not coached by Bennett or Bellamy or Hasler: that their baby-faced, no-name coach will be the next Bellamy or Gould, that the next kid that emerges from nowhere will be wearing your colours.

As for Ando and me and the Dragons?

It was Round 3, 2012, and the angry phone calls were back.

"It looks like we're back to the rubbish of the past."

"Does this bloke have any idea?"

In fairness to Ando, in the midst of his tirades he often drops in: "I've backed them at 25/1 – there's money down the drain."

So, deep down, he's a believer too. As for me, well, let me put it this way: there are a couple of young blokes coming into first grade this year that you'll all be talking about by the end of the season ...

John Stanley is a Sydney journalist and broadcaster with a lifelong passion
for the St George, now St George Illawarra Dragons.
He is a much more peaceful soul since October, 2010.

Oh, you beauty!

by WILLIAM McINNES

WHY DO PEOPLE GET FUSSED OVER THE NEW SOUTH WALES bias in the Channel Nine coverage of the State of Origin series? I love it. I love that the commentators are so one-eyed that discretions made by the Blues are just not shown, or even referred to and that any cheap shot or behind-the-play incident is ignored.

It adds to the glorious retro idea that Queensland is forever under the pump and, in some way, not in the same league as The Cockroaches. I love how these wise old men cling to their old-world belief.

In days gone by, New South Wales was that mythical other Queensland; the place that had things we Queenslanders never had. Important things like double-decker trains and political corruption (none of that in Queensland) and even a prince of the Church, Cardinal Norman Gilroy, whom my father always referred to as *Our Man Norm* because he was a Labor supporter. New South Wales also had that curse of all league lovers in the '70s: the poker machines. Glittering avenues of them created so much wealth for the league clubs down there that they could lure and poach Queensland's best league talent with big money.

They tempted stars like Steve Rogers, Artie Beetson and Rod Reddy with coin and these players returned the favour by flogging Queensland year in, year out in interstate matches.

Today there is no reason for anybody in Queensland to feel envious about one thing in New South Wales.

Although the Channel Nine stalwarts serve their purpose, I do miss the commentators of the old Brisbane league scene, especially come State of Origin time.

Channel Nine commentators are entertainers as well as people who know the game. Gus Gould's supremely over-the-top pre-match soliloquy is pure fun. He struts between the goalposts in his ill-fitting suits and with his mic shoved in front of his great cunning, broken face.

So, too, Ray Warren's out-of-time *Newsreel* voice and his purple descriptions which border on the poetically insane, my favourite being, "That pass wasn't forward; I suggest it was acutely flat."

To be honest, it wouldn't be the same if they were impartial. Wouldn't be fun feeling that silly outrage at their smug tone when they win, or the joy (and smiling amusement) at their strangled congratulations to victorious Maroons.

Dear old late Rex Mossop was the same. The Channel Seven call of the first State of Origin game in 1980 was a delight. Nothing so entertaining as a patronising club-tongued ex-New South Wales dual international murdering the English language and having a Blues defeat shoved down his gullet.

Or is there? On my way through Brisbane Airport recently, I thought I spotted a familiar face. It was Billy J. Smith. Made me think of those few years in the 1970s when the Brisbane Rugby League competition had a collection of volcanic callers whose commentary ricocheted round the local airwaves like cannon fire.

George Lovejoy, Ripper Doyle, Billy J. Smith, John McCoy, Fonda Matassa ,George Doniger and Mick Vievers.

George and Mick were great. Accurate, passionate and they'd rabbit on like the best of mates. George's great cry was: "*Oh, you beauty!*" and the immortal "*That's champagne football, that is!*"

I can still quote the George Symons Suit Factory ad starring the helmet-haired Norths goal-kicking winger Bruce Warwick.

Video of Bruce with an impossible kick from the sideline.

Mick: "Here's Warwick's kick."

George: "He's put it over! *Ohhhhhh, yes!*"

Cut to Bruce smiling in a caramel suit.

For truly colossal callers nobody beat Fonda Matassa, The Golden Greek. He was loud . And he, too, had a catch-cry that was bellowed like a bull in a rut: "*Oh, what a dooooozy!*" In fact Fonda may have been a tad too loud for some. I saw him once at Lang Park screaming from his box while, next door, a journalist banged the wall with all his might yelling: "For Christ's sake, shut-up!"

One of Fonda's great claims to fame was the night he got hiccups calling a game. One football broadcasting's great digestively effected moments. Brothers versus Redcliffe. He sounded like the noise the neighbour's dog Penny made when she got run over by the baker one morning. Lots of screeching and howling.

So maybe somebody should grab George and Mick and Billy and Fonda and even John 'Around the Grounds with Wymps Tyre Service' McCoy and let them loose on the microphones. Twenty minutes each calling the game.

Now that would be champagne football.

With seven years of Origin rule, surely we have earned the right to bring some of our cultural light to the philistine world of the South.

William McInnes is an actor, writer and rugby league fan. His book *A Man's Got To Have A Hobby* highlights the place of rugby league in the cultural life of the Redcliffe Peninsula and helps us to understand why there should be a fund established to immortalise Peter Leis in bronze on Crash Corner.

A rugby league match between Queensland and New South Wales in Brisbane, ca. 1920.

FOREWORD

State of Origin I, 2012

by JOHN HARMS

I AM ON THE 112 TRAM, HEADING DOWN BRUNSWICK STREET, FITZROY. That would be Fitzroy, the first suburb of Melbourne; the suburb immediately north of the CBD; the once working class suburb situated between Collingwood and Carlton; the suburb of the great Maroons, indeed the first Maroons, who dominated the VFL before rugby league was invented. Yes, Melbourne.

State of Origin rugby league is back in Melbourne Town.

When I got on at Merri Creek (which once provided the sticky, silty black soil for the MCG wicket), there was one maroon scarf on the whole tram worn by a young woman as nothing more than a fashion accessory. But near the Brunswick Street Oval a trio of visiting (bescarfed) Queenslanders jump on with a six-pack.

"Them cameras work, mate?" says the young bloke, nodding at the big-brother domes in the tram's ceiling.

"I reckon they would be," I say. He cracks open a stubby. And points at the camera, "Cheers!" And they all laugh the laugh of the free.

More rugby league fans get on along Brunswick Street and especially along Collins Street as we head towards Docklands. A Kiwi Queensland contingent (*Hey bro, you fuckin' got no colour on, bro ...What's fuckin' wrong with you, bro? ... I got maroon jocks on, bro*) jump on. And more and more, including some blue. But a lot of maroon.

"Cane toads and cockroaches off hear," says the driver before the tram turns left to South Melbourne.

The throng is full of boys on tour, and families on tour, and expats and (I suppose) a few locals. There's some rough heads among them all too. Looks like every second bastard has been a prop forward and spent time in the tattoo parlour. There's an Ormeau jumper. And a Townsville tracksuit.

On the footbridge I can smell rugby league: the waft of weed, just like the old days at Lang Park when it was still shoulder to shoulder on the terrace and it could occasionally get like the English soccer; where blokes drank XXXX cans and peed into them and the atmosphere was wild. Loyal and wild. Brisbane felt like a frontier town still. With a tropical madness and a rage against anything south.

What rage there was in that first game in 1980. When we wondered whether this State of Origin caper had any merit, any substance. Whether it meant anything at all. What rage, too, the following year: New South Wales led 15-0 when a Son of the North called Rover assured us the Maroons would come storming home, and they did, and there wasn't enough rum in Bundaberg for the party.

You can almost see the wavy-line waft of the weed like the smell of apple pie in the cartoons and thinking of that makes me giggle as does the busker dressed as a penguin and playing the bagpipes. The tune is known to no one, and I can't find another penguin to ask.

But it has that sort of atmosphere. That we're-here-so-look-out atmosphere. And we're in Melbourne.

I speak on the phone to my Brisbane mates who have gathered together in Indooroopilly, parts of which went under in the flood. They are with their kids, who possess a new generation of Queensland rage that sits alongside the Queensland laid-backness. They also love the game, and they love Origin night because that's what they've known. It is big now; it has replaced Cracker Night, and Easter, but I doubt it will replace Christmas. It's as much-loved as an RDO. My mates are eating spag bol, drinking red and trying to think of ways Queensland can lose.

I keep walking and I am surprised at the sea of maroon and the number of jumpers with 6 and Lewis on their backs. Ah, Wally. Had he been a soccer player the world would know him. But in this quaint game played in a small radius around Huddersfield, a smaller one around Auckland and in two Australian states he is as ordinary as the sago cannister.

Of the many things about State of Origin, and about rugby league, it is the game's ordinariness I love the most. The sheer naivete of those involved. Blokes who, if they ever read *The Grapes of Wrath*, would be talking about how they could have fixed the motor on the old tilly when the dislocated were on the move. I love how you can still see the links between *The Footy Show* and Miss O'Connell's Grade 3 classroom at Lutwyche Primary. It's all so real in a way that Australian footy at the highest level is not anymore. And blokes like Alfy (who'll be running the water) and Kevvy and Wal can just wander down to Stones Corner to get the paper and buy a custard apple or a mango or a Weis's Fruito.

I get inside and it's chockers. Just in time for the players to run out, and the anthem. Annie Hall is ready on the podium and there isn't a house north of the Murray where those watching haven't said: "It's Fatty's girl."

Bizarrely I feel like I am at a school swimming carnival. There are two major sections on the city side: a maroon section and a blue section. It is very odd in an Australian crowd.

There's Phil Gould looking more and more like a polar bear, heading back upstairs to commentate; to maybe agree with Rabs Warren for once. Even the callers wear their colours.

I've been doing this for over 30 years. I have thought about it, analysed it, written about it and tried to explain it. I have been distant from it, yet I am happy to acknowledge that at this moment, as the Maroons stand together, I feel like a Queenslander. I feel like an insider: like the bloke from Melbourne near me wouldn't know who Jackie MacDonald was, or wouldn't have been on the brewery tour at XXXX, or had in their kitchen's second draw an opener that pierced the top of those big cans of Golden Circle pineapple juice.

The ten days of build-up is released with the kick-off. Origin is alive in Melbourne. The first crunching tackles rattle the pylons.

It's a wild beast, Origin. Raw. Powerful. The big blokes matter. They're all big blokes, but the *biggest* blokes *really* matter. Petero and Matt Scott for Queensland. The inspirational Paul Gallen and James Tamou for the Blues.

In the early minutes the Blues have all the football, but the contest, while robust, lacks fire. It soon hots up with the New South forwards making good yards while the Maroons are back-pedalling. Someone yells: "Put 'em on-side." Which is quintessentially time-honoured insofar as calls from a rugby league crowd are concerned.

The Queenslanders look a little stunned as the Blues continue to come at them. The Maroons' sets are pedestrian, lacking sparkle. They are one out. No hands. Flat. Get-back-into-it football.

The game has just settled into a rhythm (New South Wales') when Farah puts up a kick. From the scrambled contest Uate takes possession and falls over the line. The ball has hit arms and heads and backs which means the video ref has a bit to sort out. He awards the try. Carney misses. 4-0.

Again, New South Wales attack and only frantic defence holds them out, the most frantic of which is a last-ditch tackle to hold a Blue up.

Queensland still can't get into the game, but the Blues aren't able to take advantage. Until a few things facilitate a change. The two Queensland props are replaced by Hannant and Shillington who start to win metres in what has been known for a century as 'up the guts'. It is clear they are fresh and their impact lasts for a good while. This allows Thurston to throw the ball around, and the Maroons look more dangerous.

Origin would not be Origin without a donnybrook when the hotheads come from everywhere to throw a punch. Having watched his teammate suffer the gross indignity of being donged on the head with a gently lobbed football, and watched further as those nearby turned and raised their fists to defend the honour of their violated man, Michael Jennings runs, jumps, and launches a haymaker which sort-of connects, but is so ridiculously melodramatic that the refs are smirking as they point him at the sin bin.

Now Queensland have the numbers. A beautiful backline move sends Tate down the right. He's half a stride from scoring, but Jarryd Hayne bumps him into the corner post. Minutes later, quick hands to the left find Slater, whose even quicker hands send Darius Boyd on his way. Over! Slater has been quiet but has worked his way into the game with a series of runs. But this is the first time he has really challenged the Blues – and he's successful. Thurston slots the goal with his hook foot. Queensland 6-4.

The Queenslanders are making good ground now. The tone has changed and now you feel New South Wales are vulnerable. Fifteen out and it's, in 1970s terms, 'backs ball'. Sam Thaiday is in the wrong spot and JT almost taps him on the shoulder to get him to move to be a flat decoy. Thaiday, having found the right place, plays his role by doing nothing, and a scintillating passing sequence finishes with Boyd who again sprints for the corner. Over! Quality stuff. Thurston again kicks the difficult conversion and Queensland lead 12-4 at halftime.

Jennings wishes he were back in the Penrith reserve grade.

"How far Queensland?" they whisper around the Docklands.

I have hardly noticed Todd Carney. Farah seems to be in everything and the skipper has led from the front.

After the break New South Wales look the better side. Slater, who is not having his best game, misses a high ball by one-and-a-half cubits (Is it the roof?) and Jennings snaffles the crumbs to go over. Carney converts and it's 12-10.

This is a surprise to many. Now pressure is a factor.

Queensland look flakey and it takes the wise head of Brent Tate to make some darting yards. The Maroons attack up the middle with some nice inside balls.

But really it's the Blues who retain the authority. Strangely they take a penalty shot to level the scores when they have the momentum, and Carney misses anyway.

They still have field position but they lack penetration as they get near the Maroons' line. They keep opting for the high ball, partly because it has worked. Tate takes a beaut mark to hold the Blues out again.

A couple of New South Wales errors and some very good kick-chases (one where Cronk makes a crazy kamikaze tackle in front of the posts) put Queensland on the attack. They pin New South down and there is a telling moment when Uate, returning a kick, is absolutely hammered by Nate Myles and Cam Smith. Uate is shaken. He is slow to his feet and the Queensland skipper stands over him while behind him they salivate, crouched, and ready to take the advantage.

Thurston, who has looked dangerous all night, moves the ball about, and the

Queenslanders have the Blues on the back foot. A high ball is batted back by Slater, to Inglis who, to the naked eye, goes over for a simple try. However the replay shows he had lost the ball initially and then pressed it. But hang on, word spreads across the terrace that it has been kicked out. Played at by Farah. The this-is-a-try camp is bullish. And the longer it goes the more chance it is. The deliberations take minutes until finally the try is awarded.

Thurston converts, and that's the ball game.

I am quietly pleased. It has been a good game without ever reaching great heights – sort of the Mt Gravatt of Origin fixtures.

But with the right result.

On the Epping train, through Richmond and Collingwood, I am pensive. I read a little of Ron Powers' Mark Twain biography. I am sure Twain would have loved Origin. He'd have made a lot of it. Of the carnivale. Of the two tribes. Of combat. Of what it means to live north of the Tweed.

I wish we had his observations.

Season review

by NICK TEDESCHI

A RUGBY LEAGUE SEASON IS ALIVE FROM THE MOMENT Tom Keneally, somewhere in Manly, screams: "Blow that whistle, ref" to that moment on Grand Final day when the sweaty, the bloodied, the battered hoist the premiership trophy aloft. Some moments are season-defining; some are inconsequential. Some are lamentable. Some are memorable.

The last moment of this home-and-away season was one that won't be forgotten. It typified rugby league. For all the theorising, all the commerce, all the celebrity and all the hype, rugby league is still two teams running out to do battle in what is ultimately a game. It's more than just knockabout fun – rugby league is too brutal for that - but it's still a game.

Nothing highlighted that more than the very last moment of the regular season.

It happened at ANZ Stadium. In the dying minutes of the game, with the score at 29-6 to the Dragons, the Eels were awarded a penalty. Nathan Hindmarsh, gruff and rough and much-loved, a country bloke who'd made a name for himself in the big smoke, raised two fingers and pointed to the posts. It was the first kick of his career. Fans, until then going through the motions, started to notice what was happening.

The champion Eel, old school to the end, waved the kicking tee away. He wanted the sand. Out jogged the ball-boy, who'd obviously been worded up. Perhaps he'd brought the sand to the ground himself in a neopolitan icecream container. Hindmarsh placed the football and pulled up his socks. All eyes were by then on him. His famous backside was barely contained by his shorts. Calmly, he walked back to his mark. He stepped in. The shot flew straight over the crossbar.

There wasn't a footy fan anywhere who wasn't smiling.

It wasn't the finale Hindmarsh had hoped for, though. The toughest of competitors, he could never imagine a team of his taking home the wooden spoon. At the other end of proceedings it had been a year of ebb and flow.

From the outset fans were puzzled by what might unfold. You could find a reasonable argument for each club. Bookmakers were just as puzzled.

Defending premiers Manly spent about a week at the top of the board after the 2011 Grand Final, before Des Hasler swapped maroon and the beach for blue and the suburban sprawl.

Wayne Bennett's arrival at Newcastle, along with Darius Boyd and the return of Danny Buderus, had Novocastrians convinced that they were right in it.

The Wests Tigers had been knocking on the door for a few seasons. Tim Sheens decided the club needed to get bigger so the Tigers cut an almighty cheque for the Storm's Adam Blair. It was a move that soon drew ire from the faithful.

Melbourne had never been far away under Craig Bellamy and with the triumvirate of Slater, Smith and Cronk, few were willing to put a line through them. By March they were the popular elect.

Hopes were certainly high at Redfern. A hard taskmaster, rookie coach Michael Maguire had Greg Inglis and Dave Taylor as fit as Black Caviar. It was the dawning of a new age for the pride of the league.

The Warriors had made the Grand Final in all three grades in 2011 and despite losing their coach were again expected to be a force of big boppers and scything ballplayers. They were led by Shaun Johnson, precocious and brilliant.

Brisbane champion Darren Lockyer was absent from the Broncos for the first time since 1994. Petero returned, though. Until 2012, the Broncos had never gone into a season without an international six or seven.

Up north in Townsville, there was a quiet confidence. The Cowboys were jam-packed with talent and the tough attitude brought in by Dallas Johnson and Brent Tate had them confident of a good run.

Canterbury were giddy at Hasler's arrival but weren't sure how long it would take for him to have an impact given his late entrance. It was the same story at Penrith, though fans of the Panthers knew the road back was long, to borrow a line from The Hollies and an old punter who used to sing the tune on a Saturday afternoon when the ponies had left him in a hole.

The Titans had splurged, signing Nate Myles, Luke Douglas, and both Jamal Idris and his spare tyre. The Raiders had Terry Campese back from injury.

And the Sharkies – still with the porch light on, waiting for Harold Holt to return with the honey chicken – had gone all-in on Todd Carney, hoping the talented-yet-troubled half could finally provide The Shire with a legitimate match-winner.

Hope, of course, was not limited to on-field deeds and it was like V-Day when it was announced in February that rugby league was free of News Limited's involvement. Some 17 years after the Super League war had begun, they were out, and an Independent Commission was in. There was no dancing in the street but there was an air of optimism around the game not seen since Tina Turner winked saucily at Cliffy Lyons.

The saddest moment of the break came in December when Immortal Arthur Beetson passed away at just 66. The game mourned a man whose unique style and unwavering principles gave so much to rugby league.

It was a year of change in the coaching ranks with seven clubs appointing new mentors. They call it the coaching merry-go-round but it moves with the speed of The Cyclone and the brutality of a Greg Inglis shoulder charge.

Four more were spun off by September.

The season opened with great drama when Jamie Soward kicked the winning field goal in golden point as the Dragons rolled their former coach Wayne Bennett.

It wasn't the only drama of the opening weekend. Benji Marshall sent a full Leichhardt into delirium when he landed the winning drop goal in extra-time, capping off a controversial win over a feisty Cronulla side while the Roosters came from eight down in the last minute to down rivals Souths.

Only one week of the season had passed when it was announced Beau Scott would be moving from the Dragons to the Knights in 2013. The day the announcement was made, Canterbury flogged a distracted St George Illawarra.

After his side dropped the opening two games of the season, Souths coach Michael Maguire shook the dice and moved Greg Inglis to fullback. The Bunnies suddenly looked electric, decimating the Panthers 40-24. Soon after, however, behemoth forward Dave Taylor announced he would be moving to the Titans. It was an interesting acquisition by the Gold Coast, considering they owed creditors the better part of $35 million.

After four rounds, the evenness of the premiership was obvious with just Melbourne undefeated and Parramatta the only team still to register a win. Pressure was mounting on coach Stephen Kearney. More so when Nathan Hindmarsh announced that 2012 would be his last season.

The Eels broke their duck that weekend, downing premiers Manly.

Billy Slater was the undisputed star of the opening month, becoming the first player in the history of the premiership to open the season with four consecutive doubles.

The big disappointments early were one-time premiership favourites, the Wests Tigers. After a fortunate first-up win, the Tigers dropped five straight and were labelled "soft" by *Fox Sports* analyst Matthew Johns. Robbie Farah claimed he was ambushed when Johns confronted him about his team's lack of gumption. But most agreed with Johns.

The Broncos were showing that life after Darren Lockyer was not all bleak. With Peter Wallace steering a tight ship, Brisbane won six of their first seven heading into the rep weekend break, concerns over the halves forgotten.

Canterbury marked their emergence as a legitimate contender with a gripping 12-6 loss to Melbourne at AAMI Park. There was a new way about the Bulldogs, a sizzling competitiveness combined with some big-man skill that was subtly changing the way the game was played. Props were now ballplayers, halves ball runners. Sam Kasiano was labelled the biggest halfback in premiership history.

After Round 7, for the first time, clubs received a bye for the annual Anzac Test and the City-Country fixture. New Zealand hosted the Anzac Test (which hadn't happened in over a decade) but the Kiwis went down 20-12. City pipped Country 24-22 in Mudgee.

Nine decided to show neither game live. *Two and a Half Men* must be very good.

Anzac Day itself saw the Sydney Roosters all but home against St George Illawarra in front of a packed Sydney Football Stadium before Jason Nightingale inspired the Red V to a comeback win that won't be forgotten.

Newcastle suffered an almighty blow to a campaign that was quickly spiralling out of control, losing Kurt Gidley for the season in Round 8 with a shoulder injury. Without The Butcher, the Knights dropped five.

Cronulla emerged as the early bolters. Todd Carney was providing the club with plenty of confidence. The Storm were undefeated through nine rounds but that didn't worry a hammer-headed Cronulla side – sans Paul Gallen – on a spectacular Sunday afternoon at Shark Park, handing Melbourne its first defeat. The Sharks had pushed to second and took confidence in their ability to win without their leader.

The excitement surrounding Origin was as great as it had ever been with the Blues really believing they could stop the Maroons at six successive series wins. Ricky Stuart can talk a big game. The inspiration to go seven straight was Petero Civoniceva, who was set for his last Origin campaign.

Game one was a disaster for the Blues, who had made a number of selection blunders - including unknown Jamie Buhrer - and sold the game to Melbourne. Befuddled Victorian sports minister Hugh Delahunty, obviously a big fan of The Greatest Game of All, called it "State of *the* Origin" between "Queensland and New Zealand". Blues skipper "Paul Callen" was less than amused. The match was overshadowed by the horrid video refereeing call to award Greg Inglis a try off a clear knock on. The ramifications were not inconsiderable.

It would take a major story to simmer the sizzle over refereeing but that's what the game got when NRL CEO David Gallop 'resigned' after ten years at the helm. No seeing out the year. No grand tribute. The Commission chairman John Grant – a former international centre and IT business guru - had made his first power play. On that rainy Sydney day, the game was hopeful of a new dawn yet saddened to see the back of a man who had given so much.

The Blues held off a seventh straight series victory in Sydney with the rub this time going their way but Cooper Cronk's field goal in the Suncorp decider sent Petero out a winner and gave Queensland the sweet seven. South of Goondiwindi there was stunned devastation. North, there was talk that the run could last longer than Joh.

The Maroon and Blue may have been the main course during the Origin period but there was still plenty to feast on in club football.

Canterbury started a winning streak in Round 11 against Cronulla that lasted until Round 25. The Bulldogs lured three-quarters Krisnan Inu and Sam Perrett while Ben Barba emerged as the most exciting player in the game, pulling off the tackle of the year in Round 15 against Souths before setting up the try of the year a week later in his hometown of Mackay with a memorable 70-metre run from his own in-goal.

A lack of enterprise in attack and an ageing roster hurt the Dragons, who failed to win three on the trot all year. An extra-time field goal loss at the hands of Souths' reliable rookie Adam Reynolds was perhaps their cruellest defeat.

Canberra's season reached a low point when they were belted 40-0 at home by the Tigers. David Furner was gone. Ricky Stuart, the mill suggested, was in. Miraculously though, kick started by yet another victory over the Dragons in Round 18, they won eight of their last ten to save Furner's bacon. The turning point came when Furner decided to house the Raiders in a hotel, even for home games. Expertise in pop psychology is a handy tool for a coach.

Robbie Farah was a late withdrawal before the Tigers' Round 15 clash with the Sydney Roosters after his mother had passed away. Tim Sheens' side had won seven straight to that point. They won just three more.

Popular Penrith veteran Luke Lewis was forced out of the Panthers after coach Ivan Cleary took the captaincy from him in a move clearly designed to shake up the club. It did. Phil Gould had taken the sledgehammer to the joint and was acting to redefine the culture and rebuild the foundations. Fans are yet to be convinced. Lewis will join a priory of Panthers in The Shire in 2013.

The Storm, so dominant over the opening two months of the season, lost their way after winning the 'Battle of Brookvale II', losing five straight for the first time in the Bellamy era. The coach believed his voice wasn't resonating with the players. Cooper Cronk told Bellamy to get over himself and start coaching the players again.

Manly's premiership defence also looked in disarray after being thumped 32-6 by Newcastle in Round 19 but then they fired off six straight wins heading into the finals and entered September title favourites.

Souths were another team who had built some momentum helped when they snuck under the Tricolours' guard like Rocky against Apollo Creed in the second film. Down 22-12 with just two minutes to play, the Rabbitohs went the length of the field twice to shock a gutted Roosters team.

After copping a trouncing at the hands of Canterbury in Round 19 – the eighth time in 17 games the Eels had conceded 30-plus points – Parramatta became the first club of 2012 to fire its coach. Stephen Kearney was axed after winning just nine of 41 games at the club.

Ricky Stuart was announced as his replacement. Since Brad Fittler retired, Stuart's record is only marginally better than Kearney's. Stuart resigned as NSW boss. Laurie Daley, who has coached exactly zero NRL games, was named his successor. Blues fans will watch that closely.

Kearney wasn't the only coach looking for a new gig. The Warriors' form had been tumultuous under Brian McClennan. An eight-game losing streak closed their season.

Tim Sheens' decade-long reign at the Tigers came to an end after the season, as did

Brian Smith's tenure at the Roosters; some 1,270 games gone in an instant.

Round 22 was telling for teams battling to sneak into the eight. Just one win separated eighth to thirteenth. Only the Raiders and Tigers won. It was the Waterloo weekend for many. In their fifteenth year in the premiership, the Melbourne Storm unveiled their first local junior in Round 23 when promising winger Mahe Fonua made his debut against the Titans.

The most anticipated day of the year came on August 21 when details of the new television deal were announced. It was worth in excess of $1 billion, a big result for the game. Fans groaned, however, at five more years of delayed free-to-air coverage.

Ben Barba capped an astonishing year by winning the Dally M Medal. At the beginning of the season the Bulldogs were reportedly chasing a big-name fullback. By the end of the year Barba was the most thrilling player in the game.

The NRL had mercifully done away with the dreaded McIntyre Final Eight System and, for the first time in the NRL era, the final four teams were the best four teams. The new system gives more credits to those who shine in the season proper.

Brisbane and Cronulla slunk out of the race in the first week, Petero Civoniceva's career drawing to a disappointing finale. It was North Queensland and Canberra who dropped out in week two, the former in controversial circumstances when Kieran Foran's 'Hand of God' play led to a key Manly try and a Sea Eagles win.

Poor video refereeing – not helped by confusing and complex rules and their interpretation, and difficulties in working out what can be deduced when a three-dimensional situation is represented by a two-dimensional TV screen – caused anguish all season and it reached critical mass in the finals. Angst over benefit-of-the-doubt and obstruction interpretations had fans edgy. There had been so many disputed decisions all year and there was a fear after some controversial calls that another big game would be tainted by yet another controversial verdict from the man in the box. And it was.

The Storm ended the Sea Eagles' season in the first preliminary final but only after Melbourne had received an early helping hand from video referee Sean Hampstead. The frustrated public called for Bill Harrigan's head again. Anthony Watmough had earlier in the week admitted to using Stillnox. Manly played as if they were all on it.

Sydney was gripped by the second prelim between Canterbury and South Sydney, providing the second largest crowd for a prelim in the history of the game. The Bunnies held the upper hand early but when Adam Reynolds' hamstring snapped, so too did the Rabbitohs' fairytale.

Nearly ten months after rugby league had lost Immortal Arthur Beetson, it gained another when Andrew Johns became the eighth member of the exclusive club. A tough-as-nails halfback whose skill reshaped the way rugby league was played, Joey was a popular and deserving choice.

The return to a fairer finals system had provided the game with the Grand Final it deserved: minor premiers Canterbury against second-placed Melbourne, Des Hasler against Craig Bellamy, a new style that excited against an old one that worked.

Experience proved telling. The Storm played a conservative yet tactically astute game. Bellamy instructed his men to give the Bulldogs no room. Cooper Cronk pounded the ball into the corners and forced drop-out after drop-out. Centres Dane Nielsen and Will Chambers played an aggressive up-and-in defence that smashed Ben Barba and Josh Reynolds. Cameron Smith controlled the ruck.

Deep in the first half, scores were level at 4-4 after a wild brawl that saw British Bulldog James Graham – known around the club as 'Cow's Head' – Mike Tyson Billy Slater's ear. The Bulldogs faithful knew the scoreboard was flattering and, if they could weather the invading force until the break, they would come out with renewed confidence.

They couldn't. Billy Slater scored, and then Justin O'Neill. It was 14-4 at the break. It could have been more, such was the Storm's dominance.

The second stanza played out the same as the first. The Storm had all the momentum, all the field position, all the aces. When the fulltime siren sounded, it was the best team who had won. Melbourne had dominated Canterbury in every facet.

Cronk was a standout for the Churchill Medal.

Melbourne had played as well in a Grand Final as any team ever has. They were near flawless.

Craig Bellamy has always taught perfection. He has arguably never been closer to it than on the final Sunday of September.

It was a murky picture finding the winner at season's beginning. By Grand Final night that picture was crystal clear.

Round 1

Golden start

Newcastle Knights *versus*
St George Illawarra Dragons
7.30pm, Thursday, 1 March
Hunter Stadium, Newcastle

LUKE JAMIESON

WHEN YOU ENDURE A LONG, HARD SOUL-CRUSHING SUMMER OF CRICKET, you get pretty damned excited about the start of footy season. So when you get to one of the few Melbourne pubs that has both the ability and the want to show rugby league and you find out somewhere along the line there has been a breakdown in proceedings, anger doesn't begin to describe the feeling.

Three beers, one inhaled parma, a fast cab, and finally, 12 minutes into the game, NRL season 2012 has arrived!

I will have to fast forward three hours before I finally get to see those lost 12 minutes: Hornby getting season 2012 under way by putting the pigskin out on the full. Three hours and one minute later I will see the Knights open the scoring for 2012 courtesy of a penalty goal that Gidley banks off the upright.

There are then several minutes before that fast cab arrives at venue No.2 to see, live, the Dragons with their first real opportunity to test the Newcastle line courtesy of a penalty in the Knights red zone. Three tackles later and Brett Morris crosses in the corner after several sets of hands. Soward converts from the sideline. *Dragons 6-2.*

In the following exchanges the Dragons look keen and fit, the Knights perhaps a half yard off the pace, but trying hard. Naiqama spills the Knights' best chance before the Dragons go 100 metres in a set. Some end-to-end sets follow as both teams start to tire before the Knights put The Bennett Blueprint into play with Boyd wrapping around out wide to link up with McManus, only to be let down by a forward pass at the end.

The youngsters on both sides are really looking to make their mark on the game with Jack de Belin for the Dragons making some hard yards early and Joel Edwards for the Knights out to prove a point.

The Dragons extend their lead to six points courtesy of a Soward penalty, and they start to look like they're getting on top of the arm wrestle. They apply more pressure on the Knights goalline to no avail. Shortly afterwards Jarrod Mullen senses an opportunity and makes Beau Scott pay for some lazy marker defence to go 30 metres for a great individual try for the Knights. *Dragons 8-6.*

Some good forward thrust and then some side to side passing ensues before Cooper opens the scoring in the second half, barging across against some indifferent Knights defence. Soward converts. *14-8.*

The Knights press the Dragons in attack for a few sets before Timana Tahu proves that his return to the Knights may not have brought him the peace he seeks. Tahu trips, and then knees Matt Prior after a harmless facial and then plays windmills with Jason Nightingale, who takes offence. It is a silly overreaction from Tahu that results in a penalty to the Dragons and relief from deep within their own 20 metre zone.

Two minutes later Tahu goes from complete flog to complete flog with a try assist after he stands up Hornby and passes to McManus, who makes a wonderful pick up and dives over in the corner. Gidley converts. *Dragons 14-12.*

The match takes on a new urgency and it is seemingly anybody's game. The Knights have hung in, and The Red V is feeling the pressure. The final minutes are made up of play after play, each of which is sure to be singled out as a turning point. But after each one, there is another. And another. Knock ons from dummy-half. Big defence forcing errors. A penalty allows the Knights to tie it up at 14-all. Missed field goal attempts. Both sides seem sure to rue turnovers.

Even with the commencement of golden point, the opportunity for a game changing play is apparent. Richie Fa'aoso's shot on Prior to force the ball loose could have been play of the game but the Knights could not capitalise.

In the end, field position, a penalty and a Jamie Soward field goal all combined to hand the Dragons a thrilling one-point win. Sensational game. More please!

St George Illawarra 15		REFEREES	Matt Cecchin
			Ashley Klein
TRIES	Morris, Cooper	CROWD	29,189
GOALS	Soward 3/3	VOTES	**3. Merrin**
FIELD GOAL	Soward		Dragons
Newcastle 14			**2. De Belin**
			Dragons
TRIES	Mullen, McManus		**1. McManus**
GOALS	Gidley 3/3		Knights

Here come the Broncs

Parramatta Eels *versus* **Brisbane Broncos**
7.30pm, Friday, 2 March
Parramatta Stadium, Sydney

MATT O'HANLON

SEASON OPENERS ARE ALWAYS DANGEROUS AFFAIRS for the better-credentialed side and tonight the Broncos are clearly favourites although it's bucketing down, and the rain narrows the gap between the sides.

There are similarities between the teams. Both have second-year coaches though they do face different challenges. Griffin: confident, but lacking Lockyer. Kearney: confident, but without key pre-season signing Tonga and star Hayne.

Brisbane: enjoying the aura built on six titles in 20 years and a dominant recent record over the Eels. Parramatta: dreaming of the glory days of the four titles in the 1980s, which seem to act as something of a burden.

The Broncos: looking to Corey Norman, the kid from Beenleigh, to don the club's most revered jersey, the No.6 in the shadow of Lewis, Walters and, now, Lockyer. How will they go without him? The Eels: looking to Sandow, the highly paid kid from Cherbourg, to wear the club's most revered but troubled jersey, the No.7, with the curse on all who have followed Peter Sterling.

This is the topic of discussion for the assembled crew prior to kick-off. It's a discussion held in the finest tradition of Friday night football and especially a season opener: fuelled by fine food (*tick*) and plenty of the brewer's finest (*tick*). The beauty of modern television and the comfort of the lounge room are a guiltless pleasure, but we spare a thought for the hardy fan doing it tough at Parramatta Stadium.

It's belting down.

Hang on! We're on the wrong channel. The boys think it is Hawthorn with the Broncos in a bright yellow strip. No, that's Sam Thaiday leading them out. The Broncos away jersey may take a while to grow on the collection of armchair experts awaiting kick-off.

No sooner has the ref blown proceedings on and the unbelievable happens. Sandow has scored. A seemingly innocuous kick is muffed by Beale and Sandow, chasing hard, cleans up the crumbs. Parra are up 6-0 with the Burt kick. Four minutes into the match and the most talked about off season signing in the league has, according to all reports, delivered half his pay cheque.

The rest of the first half is a dour affair. The special pasta is a highlight washed down with the Nine Tales Amber Ale. I check in with the Golden Girl, who is home alone, hamstrung by work commitments on Saturday. Her view: Parramatta seem to be defending better than last year but the Broncos have bombed some. All concur. G-squared, as per normal, is on the money. Parramatta have shown a greater resolve in defence with a memorable tackle on Te'o in the 21st minute by a number of Eels followed up by desperation in the 26th minute to hold up Reed. Evidence that was lacking last year. *Halftime, 6-0 Eels*.

The wet and cold Eels faithful can only hope the second half will produce some stronger attack to match the defensive resolve. The Broncos on the other hand are starting to develop an ominous look. Their attack, albeit rusty, looks dangerous and barring the fourth-minute blunder the Bronco defence is well-organised, tight and working.

In the 51st minute we are served up the classic Bronco try. Hooker to half, half to Lewis, I mean Walters, no I mean Lockyer – sorry, I mean the new kid, Norman, who feigns a ball to the lead runner before hitting Hodges and on to Yow Yeh, who has spreadeagled the defence in front of him.

The Parker touchline conversion spells doom for the Eels as the armchair assortment all feel that here-come-the-Broncs feeling. And they do. The knock on from the kick-off was a glimmer of hope for the Eels. Not for long. Wallace burrows over and a few minutes later Hannant capitalises on a lack of coordination in the Eels defence to score a relatively soft try.

The fulltime score makes me think the Broncos, as usual, will run deep into this competition. The Eels will be better (and they will need to be) when key attackers Hayne and Tonga are back engaged with Sandow, and Maitua is fit.

Brisbane 18			REFEREES	Shayne Hayne
				Gavin Morris
TRIES	Yow Yeh, Wallace, Hannant		CROWD	11,331
GOALS	Parker 3/3		VOTES	**3. Thaiday**
				Broncos
Parramatta 6				**2. Hannant**
				Broncos
TRY	Sandow			**1. Allgood**
GOAL	Burt 1/1			Eels

Capital classic

Canberra Raiders *versus* **Melbourne Storm**
5.30pm, Saturday, 3 March
Canberra Stadium

JOHN HARMS

THE WEATHERMEN HAD PROMISED TORRENTIAL RAIN across southern New South Wales in the days leading up to the Raiders' opening fixture forthe 2012 season, and they were right. Creeks flowed, paddocks were sodden, towns prepared for the worst flooding in years. Cooma, up the road, was in strife.

And just as the players ran onto Canberra Stadium in the sort of gloom you get at the home of rugby league in Yorkshire, the rain got heavier, and the fans sat under ponchos and in drizabones with drips falling from their noses. I was happy to be on the couch in Melbourne with a beer and a packet of Burger Rings, and the kids in the bath.

The Canberra faithful had endured an awful 2011 season with off-field upset, ill luck with injuries, and a defence that couldn't hold. But this was a fresh start.

The expectant mood lasted all of two minutes. On the 20, Smith distributed to Cronk, who flipped it back to his skipper, who found Slater on the fly. Billy burst through the hole that had opened at the ruck and stepped around Dugan who was no chance on the slippery ground. *6-0* and you could just about hear the groan.

It got louder minutes later when Cronk's grubber bobbled about on the tryline and somehow the halfback got his arm around behind the somnambulant Canberra defenders. 12-0 after six minutes. I nearly turned it off.

But the Raiders rallied encouragingly. Terry Campese, back after a year out with injury, was as lippy as ever, stirring his own, and whinging to the referees. Indeed, he was grumpy all afternoon. Although playing in the No.6 jumper, he acted as first receiver with his big blokes running off him. Shillington, Learoyd-Lahrs and Fensom did a power of battering. McCrone, playing wider, fed his outside backs, who looked dangerous at times.

With the attack set deep to his left, McCrone attacked the line, giving a short pass to Shillington, whose offload in the tackle found Fensom. The workhorse juggled before going over under the posts. *12-6*.

Then Smith slotted a penalty to give the Storm a handy break. The football was pretty good given the conditions and surprisingly both sides were happy to throw the ball around.

Canberra continued to play the game in Melbourne's half until Campese's spinning grubber created a shemozzle on the Storm line and McCrone scored. *14-12*.

Campese got even grumpier just before halftime. McCrone, having a solid game, moved to his right to find runners and threw a long cut-out pass to Ferguson on the touchline. The winger picked up the half-volley brilliantly and sprinted over. It was a marginal pass but the refs deemed it had travelled forward.

The rain kept tumbling down after oranges, but the football remained engaging. O'Neill scored for Melbourne. But soon after McCrone put Buttriss over. Croker's kick levelled the scores. The crowd stirred to the point where you could no longer hear individual voices. The pressure mounted. That don't-make-a-mistake nervousness descended on the game.

Canberra had their chances and when the ball came to Dugan, 25 out, directly in front, he produced a drop kick so ill-bred it was barely recognisable. But the mongrel wobbled in the direction of the posts, belted into the crossbar and climbed over. Canberra by a point with just minutes to go.

The Raiders maintained possession and looked to be hanging on when Campese shaped to hoof the football downfield. The colour drained from his face as the ball slipped from his grasp. From the next set, Cronk chipped the sort of dinky drop punt that kids south of the Barassi Line put up at lunch time so that one of their mates can take a speccie. Billy Slater must have seen plenty of these in Melbourne. Ignoring his inner-Innisfail he soared early, got the ride off a Canberran, which pushed him even higher, and pulled down a classic mark that would have made Jezza nod in approval.

The Raiders and their fans cried in disapproval. They had played well, but had paid for their sleepy start. It was a ripper match in tough conditions. Again Smith, Cronk and Slater built on the slavish work of the Storm plodders, and somehow won the day.

Melbourne 24			REFEREES	Gavin Badger Brett Suttor
TRIES	Slater 2; Cronk, O'Neill			
GOALS	Smith 4/5		CROWD	7,862
			VOTES	**3. Slater** Storm
Canberra 19				**2. Fensom** Raiders
TRIES	Fensom, McCrone, Buttriss			**1. Cronk** Storm
GOALS	Croker 3/3			
FIELD GOAL	Dugan			

Shouldering the load

Penrith Panthers *versus* **Canterbury Bulldogs**
7.30pm, Saturday, 3 March
Centrebet Stadium, Sydney

MARK SEYMOUR

NO MATTER HOW MANY SEASONS COME AND GO, no matter how my team played last year, there is always something about the opening round of the NRL fixture that puts a spring in my step. It's like the first evidence of spring after a long winter. Time to emerge from the darkness and take in the sights, sounds and expectations that come just before the kick-off.

Adding to the intrigue of this fixture was the place of both coaches who had been involved in the 2012 Grand Final but with different teams.

Much had happened at Belmore over the summer to give Bulldog supporters some optimism, and the hope that 2012 would be a season where the potential of the team would finally be realised. The question was whether all the changes would gel for the opening game against the Panthers at Centrebet Stadium, a fixture that has always troubled Canterbury, even in its winning years.

Would Des Hasler bring his premiership ways with him? Or was he only successful because he had terrific Manly sides? There is no doubt Hasler had much work to do in the offseason. Defence, first and foremost. The Bulldogs had the ignominy of being the team that conceded the most yards of turf in season 2011 so clearly, something in the philosophy had to change there.

As with all opening games, players took time to dust off the cobwebs, and in this case to come to grips with the wet, greasy conditions and the increased tempo not seen in practice matches. Of concern to me was that the Bulldogs did not seem to be able to complete a set of six without conjuring some way to lose the ball. They were particularly creative in this regard. Penalties were also making life difficult, giving field position to the Panthers. In contrast, Penrith were doing a fine job of holding on to the ball, completing 19 of 23 sets in the first half.

With stats like that it was certainly no surprise that the Panthers opened the scoring in the 12th minute via Travis Burns. An errant pass that should have been cut out by the Bulldogs defence was fumbled and the prowling Burns swooped, scooped and crossed the tryline. Worse was to come for Canterbury five minutes later when Michael Jennings scored under the posts. The only thing missing was the Benny Hill music.

Although the tide of possession was against the Bulldogs, a pivotal moment came when the Penrith scoring machine, Michael Gordon, sustained a broken leg in a tackle while trying to make another assault on the Canterbury line. This seemed to affect the Panthers' momentum and they struggled to score after that. Against the run of play the Bulldogs, through Josh Reynolds, scored just on the half-hour to give the scoreboard some respectability.

Ben Barba, who had been in everything for Canterbury in the first half, evened up the match when he opened the scoring six minutes into the second half. Barba, who scored 23 tries in season 2011, may well surpass that figure in 2012 if his form holds. Although the Panthers moved into the lead via a penalty goal from Luke Walsh, the Bulldogs would not be denied and further tries to Josh Morris and Bryson Goodwin in a five-minute spree made it look like a comfortable win for the visitors.

A big hit by ex-Panther Frank Pritchard on winger Dave Simmons became one of the talking points of the round. Simmons was knocked out by the shoulder charge and Pritchard was placed on report.

By far the best player for the Bulldogs was James Graham, who was leading the stats for hit-ups, metres gained, and tackles, clearly showing why the Bulldogs fought to get him to Belmore.

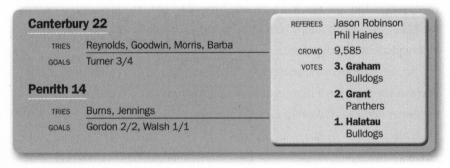

Canterbury 22		REFEREES	Jason Robinson
			Phil Haines
TRIES	Reynolds, Goodwin, Morris, Barba	CROWD	9,585
GOALS	Turner 3/4	VOTES	**3. Graham**
			Bulldogs
Penrith 14			**2. Grant**
			Panthers
TRIES	Burns, Jennings		**1. Halatau**
GOALS	Gordon 2/2, Walsh 1/1		Bulldogs

The month of hope

North Queensland Cowboys *versus* **Gold Coast Titans**
8.30pm, Saturday, 3 March
Dairy Farmers Stadium, Townsville

CLIFF BINGHAM

MARCH IS A LEGITIMATE CONTENDER FOR MY FAVOURITE MONTH OF THE YEAR. In no other month does the concept of hope resonate more strongly. Hope that my tipping competition exploits and ongoing duels with bookmakers will prove successful over the winter months; that victory will be mine. Hope that via another skill-based medium, fantasy football, in its multiple guises, I can be one up on my mates. Hope that the Maroons win the State of Origin series for a seventh straight year. And last, but far from least, hope that this is the year for my beloved North Queensland Cowboys.

Changes up Townsville way had been relatively minor in the offseason. Halfback Robert Lui and promising centre Kane Linnett were the biggest signings; Willie Tonga the biggest departure. The new(ish) player I was most interested to see though was boom youngster Jason Taumalolo (who sadly was a late withdrawal from the game). Tariq Sims proved a wrecking ball in 2011; I was hoping for lightning to strike twice.

The transfer lounge at Robina, however, was a hive of big-market activity. The Titans opened the chequebook and snapped up Jamal Idris, Nate Myles, Luke Douglas and Beau Champion among others. Mat Rogers and Preston Campbell retired. Anthony Laffranchi joined St Helens.

Nathan Friend was the most perplexing Titans departure of all, heading to the Warriors after an injury-plagued year where his sharp playmaking from dummy-half was desperately missed. I can't remember the last premier to have a poor 1-6-7-9 combination, so to spend big but be a net loser across those four positions seemed an odd move for a side coming off the wooden spoon. It was the complete antithesis of recruitment during the Craig Bellamy era at Melbourne – never a good sign.

I therefore felt confident going in, the good feeling tempered somewhat though by the tradition of crazy opening rounds.

Unfortunately though, the die was cast early in this one from Dairy Farmers.

Matt Scott dropped the ball in the opening set of six. The next possession concluded with another failure to complete the set, as did the third. Jamal Idris opened the scoring for the Titans, but even that failed to sting the Cowboys into securing the pill. At one point the completion rate read as three out of 13, but even that was a misnomer; the three 'completed' sets had involved receiving a penalty before the inevitable dropped ball came along.

The siren for halftime blew, mercifully, with the 6-0 margin masking how lopsided the first half had been. I assured myself that the Titans would be made to pay for failing to take the game away when they had the chance.

Alas, the second half mirrored the first. Anger turned into ironic amusement and finally amazement. The great Johnathan Thurston failed to find touch from a penalty in the first half, but put one out on the full during the run of play in the second. Ashton Sims played the ball at a 90° angle to the intended target. More dropped ball. More forward passes. And so it went.

The Titans put the game away via tries to Michaels and a second to Idris. It's hard to get a gauge on them in light of the cacophony of Cowboys errors, but a convincing road win is a convincing road win, no matter how you cut it.

As for my Cowboys, much like a batsman who keeps getting out before you can work out if he's in good touch or not, it's hard to evaluate the implications of this performance for the season's prospects.

I hope it was an aberration. I hope to laugh about it come September.

That's the beautiful thing about hope, and why March is a great time of year for it.

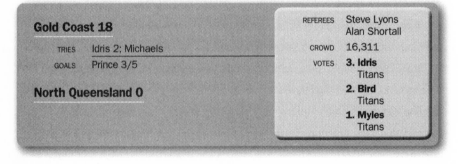

Gold Coast 18		REFEREES	Steve Lyons
			Alan Shortall
TRIES	Idris 2; Michaels	CROWD	16,311
GOALS	Prince 3/5	VOTES	**3. Idris**
			Titans
North Queensland 0			**2. Bird**
			Titans
			1. Myles
			Titans

A postcard for the Greatest Game

New Zealand Warriors *versus* **Manly Sea Eagles**

2pm, Sunday, 4 March

Eden Park, Auckland

LINDSEY CUTHBERTSON

I F THE ADVERTISING FOLK OF THE NRL WERE ASKED TO CREATE A POSTCARD to promote this great game and they didn't choose this afternoon's setting – the cloudless blue sky, the lush green of the field and the colourful mixture of a large, passionate crowd – then they should be asked to find another job. This was Sunday afternoon footy at its most picturesque ... and I haven't even started on the quality of the game itself.

Grand Final rematches like the one between the Manly Sea Eagles and the New Zealand Warriors don't come along very often. Two teams with a point to prove, both to themselves and to others, were given a dry track to demonstrate their talent. They didn't disappoint.

After a scratchy performance in the World Club Challenge two weeks before, Manly hit the ground running, playing an expansive style that saw them get on the outside of the Warriors defence and consistently march up the field. In the eighth minute it saw the Sea Eagles claim a try in the corner to David Williams, but the skill by the winger to set up the second was even more thrilling to watch.

After backing up Jamie Lyon down the right-hand side, 'The Wolfman' was able to get a kick back infield with his foot only centimetres from the touchline. The kick was caught on the full by halfback Daly Cherry-Evans, who proceeded to score underneath the posts. There will be plenty of breathtaking moments on the footy field this year, but Williams and Cherry-Evans have set the bar very high.

The Warriors weren't looking too out of shape though, not even when Steve Matai pushed through some soft defence off a scrum to give the Sea Eagles a 16-0 lead. And looks weren't deceiving: the home side hit back a few minutes later with two quick tries to make the score at halftime a more respectable 16-10.

These two Warriors tries came from a brilliant period of play by halfback Shaun Johnson. For the first he jinked and sputtered across the Sea Eagles' right edge before somehow bounce-passing to winger Manu Vatuvei to score. The second was a solo effort utilising a couple of right foot steps and some great strength to get the ball down under the posts despite the best efforts of Manly fullback Brett Stewart.

It was a seesawing first half, and the second followed along the same trajectory. Tony Williams bulldozed over from short range in the 44th minute to open the Sea Eagles' lead to 12 points; in the 52nd Kevin Locke collected the spoils of a contested bomb on the Manly tryline to bring the lead back to eight.

The crowd was getting louder the longer the half went on. While Manly hooker Matt Ballin was sin-binned for a professional foul with only 13 minutes to go, Manu Vatuvei scored off a beautifully spiralled torpedo pass by Johnson that was almost intercepted by Williams of the David variety. The crowd found another level of volume again.

But just like they were able to quell the Warriors' fightback in the Grand Final last year, the Sea Eagles were able to rally with only 12 men and score to give themselves some breathing space. It started with a break against the run of play by Jamie Lyon and finished with a try to Glenn Stewart to give the game its final score of 26-20.

For Manly, Jamie Lyon was outstanding in the Sea Eagles' blitzkrieg opening and their gutsy, backs-to-the-wall end. Tony Williams was a big performer on the left-hand side, making more metres than any player on the field besides the Warriors boom rookie Konrad Hurrell, who announced himself as a player to watch in a very big way. And while both teams' halves were classy, Shaun Johnson simply shone.

You can't ask for a more exciting way to kick off Sunday footy for 2012.

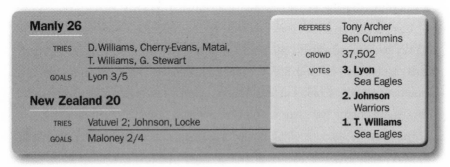

Manly 26

TRIES	D. Williams, Cherry-Evans, Matai, T. Williams, G. Stewart
GOALS	Lyon 3/5

New Zealand 20

TRIES	Vatuvei 2; Johnson, Locke
GOALS	Maloney 2/4

REFEREES	Tony Archer Ben Cummins
CROWD	37,502
VOTES	**3. Lyon** Sea Eagles
	2. Johnson Warriors
	1. T. Williams Sea Eagles

The Boss Bowl

Wests Tigers *versus* **Cronulla Sharks**
2pm, Sunday, 4 March
Leichhardt Oval, Sydney
NICK TEDESCHI

ARRIVED AT THE ORANGE GROVE HOTEL in Leichhardt around midday. I had been awake since 7am, champing at the bit, ready for the first real footy action of 2012. I had soaked up most of the wet and wild Round 1 on the box. Now we were getting into it.

The Orange Grove was packed to the brim with the faithful. A few game Sharkies fans found their way in but this was Tigers heartland, a place where Laurie Nicholls once sat. You wouldn't know how many of the old-timers at the main bar had pulled on the orange and black.

Knocking back schooner three with rugby league diehard Robbo, waiting for Parko and the Boss family, I got that overwhelming feeling that God had a soft spot for the Tigers. The sun was shining brightly, the only time anywhere south of Townsville it had during these opening days of the season.

The Boss family soon arrived, as did Parko. Parko was a late call-up, in town for matters of business and otherwise. I was a late call-up with the Boss family. I grew up with that lot, playing rugby league in the Boss family backyard with Nathan and sometimes Dan, then we'd go inside to watch the TV games with Pete and Jenny. Jenny's name is not actually Jenny. It's Leanne. She has a twin sister called Jenny and many years ago a number of us thought it was amusing to call her Jenny as well. It has stuck.

This clash had actually been called the Boss Bowl. Nathan was a long-suffering Sharks fan and Dan a Tigers diehard. I enjoy asking Nathan at the beginning of every season: "35th year lucky? 40th year lucky? 45th year lucky?" It never gets old.

By the time we got to Leichhardt, it was blistering. I was served well by my penchant for shorts and thongs in all situations. Parko and Dan weren't so lucky.

There is no more old-school ground in the game. There was no scanning of tickets, just some old birds ripping them in two. I certainly couldn't pull away from the lure of the footy double. It was certainly an indication that the day was not going to be my day.

Double 10. Keith Galloway and Ben Ross. Galloway, eight tries in 142 games and just four in the last six seasons. Ross, seven in 132 games with just three meat pies since 2004. The only way the ticket could have been worse was if I'd pulled 'Away – Eight' and got to ride Bryce Gibbs' 114-game tryless streak. Either way, the 100-1 on offer was severe unders. It also had me concerned for the minus and the over, both of which I had plonked on.

The Tigers jumped out of the blocks early and the pulsating crowd went ballistic. Popular Tigers winger Beau Ryan collected Benji Marshall's chip and crossed before the Sharks had touched the ball. The Sharks scored through hooker Isaac De Gois. Benji was brilliant in putting the Tigers up 14-4 at the break.

That all meant little though as the story was the second half: the Sharks' dominance and the series of horrid refereeing blunders that cost them the match. I rarely feel much sympathy for those from The Shire but, after a courageous effort, they were stitched up by some shockers.

The game, of course, ended in extra-time with a Benji Marshall field goal. It came after the Sharks kicked off and collected it off the crossbar and attempted a field goal. That was charged down by two offside Tigers and then the rebound was knocked on by Benji. The result, of course, was a Tigers penalty, the biggest hometown decision in many years and one that should see referee Jared Maxwell in reserve grade next week.

The game was a real dandy and many will remember it for its fine winning field goal but for mine, it was some incredibly one-sided officiating that will forever taint the game.

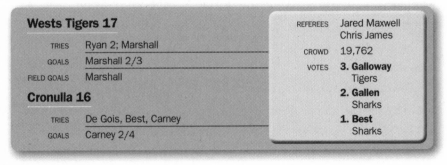

Wests Tigers 17			REFEREES	Jared Maxwell
TRIES	Ryan 2; Marshall			Chris James
GOALS	Marshall 2/3		CROWD	19,762
FIELD GOALS	Marshall		VOTES	**3. Galloway**
				Tigers
Cronulla 16				**2. Gallen**
				Sharks
TRIES	De Gois, Best, Carney			**1. Best**
GOALS	Carney 2/4			Sharks

Mini's miracle

South Sydney Rabbitohs *versus* **Sydney Roosters**
7pm, Monday, 5 March
ANZ Stadium, Sydney

ANDREW RYAN

THE JERSEYS HAD BEEN UNPACKED from a dusty garbage bag in the garage – a new coach, new recruits, fresh hope born again with the new season. The first round of the season really is the perfectly clean slate, all teams equal, only separated by their alphabetic prowess.

Footy is back.

Unfortunately for me, an unavoidable clash meant that I wouldn't be at ANZ stadium for the local derby between my beloved Bunnies and the mortal enemy the Sydney Roosters. SMS updates had been teed up with a mate at the ground, and a suitably tragic pub open late enough on a Monday night to watch the 10.30pm replay pencilled in. But while being a South Sydney supporter can be trying in itself, even I wasn't masochistic enough to ever want to watch this particular replay.

Apart from the game, I really missed seeing that shine of the fresh jerseys. Faces familiar enough, not quite acquaintances, yet not perfect strangers, just people you only ever see at the footy, and who are also along for the feat of endurance that is the 26 rounds of the NRL season.

Most of all though I really missed an annual gesture of ours; a new season 'good luck' handshake just before kick-off amidst my footy friends. It carries one part hope, one part desperation, and a great whack of mateship. It almost serves as our commitment to subjecting ourselves to another season of supporting the Bunnies.

The Rabbitohs can find ways to lose football games in the most enigmatic manner possible.

The Roosters scored their first try after six minutes from a turnover caused by a ball being passed into the head of a Souths decoy runner, for instance.

Souths hit back after conceding that calamitous early try with a soft one to Crocker from a quick tap. In the 20th minute a perfectly placed cross kick from rookie half Adam Reynolds found Chris McQueen, who escaped the clutches of the Roosters defenders to score. A similar try from a kick for the Roosters' Aidan Guerra saw the scores locked at 12-12.

After oranges, John Sutton took on the line and stepped his way over in the 47th minute. The conversion and a penalty soon after saw Souths lead by eight with half-an-hour to go. They still had that lead with three minutes to go.

As soon as I read the text message, ROOSTERS TRY. KICK IN FRONT. WE HAVE A NERVOUS MINUTE AND A HALF, I had that sinking feeling. Souths have been making the easy difficult for decades. Snatching implausible defeats from comfortable leads with mere minutes remaining has been one of their more exasperating, yet enduring, specialties.

DON'T WATCH IT, DO SOMETHING MORE FUN LIKE PULLING YOUR FINGERNAILS OUT.

I hit the computer as soon as I got home, hoping against hope, and reason, for a less shocking ending to the story. Of course, one wasn't coming. Phrases like HOUDINI were being thrown around in headlines. STUN, STOLE, SCARCELY BELIEVABLE and MIRACULOUS all described the result, though sadly for most Bunnies fans, the right word was probably INEVITABLE.

For the record, the Roosters managed two tries within the last two minutes to win 24-20. The 78th minute of the game saw Jared Waerea-Hargreaves, a name more suited to rugby, score a try akin to a rolling maul as he dragged four Rabbitoh defenders over the line to take the score to 20-18. The match-wining try came with 13 seconds remaining on the clock, after 80 metres of innovation and desperation, as the ball was spread across the field, kicked ahead and ultimately regathered and grounded by Anthony Minichiello after a footrace and a valiant last-ditch effort by Matt King to hold him up. I could only commiserate from afar.

NUMB WITH DISAPPOINTMENT ended the SMS updates for the evening.

Sydney Roosters 24				
TRIES	Tasi, Guerra, Waerea-Hargraves, Minichiello	REFEREES	Adam Devcich Chris Sutton	
GOALS	Mortimer 4/4	CROWD	18,278	
		VOTES	**3. Mortimer** Roosters	
South Sydney 20			**2. S. Burgess** Rabbitohs	
TRIES	Croker, McQueen, Sutton		**1. Sutton** Rabbitohs	
GOALS	Reynolds 4/4			

Round 2

You got me again, Bomber

Manly Sea Eagles *versus* **Wests Tigers**

7.30pm, Friday, 9 March
Bluetongue Stadium, Gosford

GREG OBERSCHEIDT

THE PHYSICALITY OF RUGBY LEAGUE is the basis for the underlying beauty of the code. The element of the game that allows it to stand above its rivals is the brutality of the contest. The biggest and the toughest men go head to head in a battle for supremacy. Over time many of these contests have gained a certain amount of momentum.

Every rugby league pundit knows about the rivalry that existed between Manly and Wests throughout the '70s and '80s. The war between the Fibros and the Silvertails was the cause of some of the most brutal contests of the era. It transcended sport and went straight to the heart of class distinctions that had emerged throughout Sydney – the haves and the have-nots.

It's fair to say Manly have a similar relationship with the majority of their opponents. Perhaps not as deep-seated as the Western Suburbs revulsion but they are certainly the team all others love to hate. Their continued (begrudged) success and (nauseating) air of superiority have been enough to fuel the flames for a generation.

I'll confess that my own hatred of Manly stems from a more personal rivalry. My best mate in high school was a Manly supporter and I was a Tiger through and through. Balmain didn't get across the line too many times during the '90s while Manly were a powerhouse, so I was on the receiving end of the usual barbs. I was able to take this in my stride however; sticks and stones and all that.

My real hatred of Manly and my ensuing hatred of my mate 'Bomber' stemmed from our one on one matches in the backyard. Aping our heroes. Getting a timely shepherd from the trampoline, getting coat-hangered by the Hills Hoist. Bomber, at about 6'2" and 80 kegs had convinced himself he was Matthew Ridge; however, given the mismatch he only needed to have been channelling 'Spud' Carroll.

Bomber was a talented ball-runner and a solid defensive player given to overt acts of aggression when faced with a weaker opponent. In other words, he was a big bully jerk. There wasn't much of me in those days and I had even less ability. As such, Michael Gillett always seemed like an appropriate avatar. Needless to say the battles between us all had similar results, generally about 40-6 before medical necessity forced a close. Much the same as the Manly-Balmain encounters of the time.

I managed to grow a bit over the next few years. Unfortunately, so did Bomber. One on one football soon gave way to beers and birds and our rivalry was now firmly fixed around our chosen teams and, thankfully, it has progressed in a loosely civilised manner. Think Joseph Conrad.

The last few years have allowed me to share the spoils to some degree and even though Manly are the defending premiers I approached Round 2 of 2012 with plenty of optimism. I was savouring the chance to get one back on the old foe.

Both sides went into the match missing key personnel. Would the Tigers' young forwards be able to stand up to the experience of the Manly pack? Despite having the best of the early play, the Sea Eagles found themselves trailing 8-0 after some creative counterattack from the Tigers. A late penalty got Manly on the board and saw the halftime siren sound.

Manly capitalised on their chances in the second half and got themselves out to a 14-point lead on the back of some solid work from Foran and some brilliance from Cherry-Evans.

Benji Marshall and Robbie Farah tried to spark the Tigers and managed a couple of late tries to add some respectability to the score but in the wash-up the Tigers were outplayed by a superior outfit and will need to put together some strong performances to justify their early favouritism.

You got me again, Bomber. But the mighty Tigers will be back.

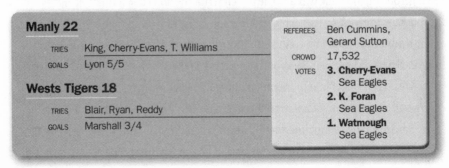

Manly 22

TRIES	King, Cherry-Evans, T. Williams
GOALS	Lyon 5/5

Wests Tigers 18

TRIES	Blair, Ryan, Reddy
GOALS	Marshall 3/4

REFEREES	Ben Cummins, Gerard Sutton
CROWD	17,532
VOTES	**3. Cherry-Evans** Sea Eagles
	2. K. Foran Sea Eagles
	1. Watmough Sea Eagles

Read the script

Brisbane Broncos *versus* **North Queensland Cowboys**
7.30pm, Friday, 9 March
Suncorp Stadium, Brisbane
IAN HAUSER

HERE WAS ONLY EVER GOING to be one winner of this game. The unveiling of Broncos legend Darren Lockyer's statue; Petero Civoniceva's homecoming appearance; the Broncos' first home game of the season; Captain Thaiday playing his (supposed) 150th match for Brisbane ... they all pointed to one thing.

The Broncos were hot favourites after their solid win in Round 1 while the Cowboys had been just plain awful in their home defeat by the Titans.

The lead changed six times in the course of the match as both teams demonstrated a willingness to throw the ball around. A frantic pace, a warm evening, some crunching defence and the pressure of a derby ensured that fatigue would play a part sooner or later and, in the end, that was the difference.

The Broncos had more possession, advanced more metres, had more hit-ups and were called on to complete fewer tackles. How clear can a script be?

The Cowboys scored early with a good cut-out ball to Dallas Johnson who went in, untouched, under the posts. The Broncos replied with a spread to the right where a fortunate bounce gave Jharal Yow Yeh an easy run to the line. An overenthusiastic Ashton Sims gave the Broncos two points after some silly carry-on in the tackle and the Broncos were in front and in charge. Thaiday led from the front, Ben Hannant was in everything, Peter Wallace schemed away at halfback and Justin Hodges ran dangerously from dummy-half. The match script was intact.

Little things change matches though.

Broncos fullback Josh Hoffman fumbled a rebound off the goal post allowing James Segeyaro to score. The Broncos lost focus and conceded three penalties in three minutes. The Cowboys found some rhythm and drive through Matt Scott and James Tamou up front while Johnathan Thurston and Ray Thompson hustled at the back.

This all culminated in another Cowboys try to Brent Tate. Tate, whose injuries have made him the unluckiest player in the NRL in the last five years, hauled in a rebound off a cross-field kick to scamper over on his old home ground. 16-8 to the Cowboys could easily have been 22-8 but Ashley Graham dropped an easy pass with the line open just before the hooter.

Those pesky Cowboys were doing a round-up on a disorganised herd of Broncos. Read the script, boys, read the script!

Whatever coach Anthony Griffin said at halftime worked a treat with the Broncos eliminating the deficit and taking the lead within seven minutes of the restart.

Josh McGuire benefitted from a Matt Bowen fumble to score at the end of the first set before back-to-back penalties gave Brisbane field position. A Jack Reed round-the-corner pass allowed Beale to score untouched. Order was restored and the big crowd settled down to see the script play out.

Someone forgot to tell Thurston that he had flown to Brisbane to play bridesmaid for the occasion. JT and 'Mango' Bowen worked a special through the middle for Bowen to score a trademark try. Cowboys back in front.

I could almost hear Sundance ask Butch, "Who are those guys anyway?" as the North Queensland posse refused to give up.

Wallace, Corey Norman and Hodges wouldn't give in and, with players tiring all over the field, a two-tackle surge ended with Ben Te'o scoring less than 10 minutes from time. Parker, probably Brisbane's best player, booted his fifth from five attempts to put the Broncos four points ahead and settle a few Bronco nerves.

A bloke can't play on his 30th birthday and not have something to go home to celebrate. And so it was that, two minutes from time, Matt Bowen packed down at lock, picked up the ball at the back of the scrum, dummied, stepped, outran the wrong-footed defence and scored under the posts to give the Cowboys a last minute win.

End of script – the outcome was never in doubt.

North Queensland 28			REFEREES	Jason Robinson, Gavin Reynolds
	TRIES	Bowen 2; Johnson, Segeyaro, Tate	CROWD	43,171
	GOALS	Thurston 4/5	VOTES	**3. Thurston** Cowboys
Brisbane 26				**2. Parker** Broncos
	TRIES	Yow Yeh, McGuire, Beale, Te'o		**1. Scott** Cowboys
	GOALS	Parker 5/5		

By Jack

Gold Coast Titans *versus* Canberra Raiders

4.30pm, Saturday, 10 March

Skilled Park, Gold Coast

CHRIS PARKINSON

IT'S NOT ALWAYS EASY BEING A RAIDERS FAN – it seems like a lifetime ago the Green Machine was at the peak of its powers. Canberra was a different place back then: buses were painted in the team colours and school tuckshops served up lime-green milk. Since that time, success has been fleeting, there have been consistent finals appearances, but the grand prize has not been attained.

One thing that a Raiders supporter can take heart in is that the playing roster consistently boasts one of the highest percentages of junior players in the NRL. The lure of big city lights and pop star lifestyles has not made it easy to retain some of this talent over the years, but there has always been more prodigious talent coming through to lessen the hit.

It brought a big smile to my face when I heard the news a couple of weeks ago that local junior Josh Dugan had re-signed. To secure the services of possibly the best attacking fullback in the league is fantastic news for Canberra. He joins other former juniors such as Campese, Fensom, Papalii and Croker in committing to the future of the Green Machine.

To follow on the same line, it was exciting to see the debut of Jack Wighton on Saturday night. While I am weary of putting too much of a wrap on him after only one game, his strong defence and smart attack gave indications of another exciting product of the Raiders' under-20s program. The knock back try assist from Wighton to Jarrod Croker was the highlight of the weekend for mine.

The Raiders had never won at Skilled Park and, in recent encounters, the Titans have had the wood over them. Add to this the good form shown by the Titans in comprehensively beating the Cowboys in the first round and the bookies had the Titans favourites. Although the Raiders had lost in Round 1 to the chin-strapping Storm, they did get close in atrociously wet conditions. So I was happy to take the bookies on.

At the end of the first half, the scores were tied at 12-12. In the first 20 minutes the

Raiders surged to a two-try lead through the individual brilliance of Josh Dugan who showed his kicking skills with a 40/20 and backed up in the next set with a try. Then a bomb to the left-hand corner by Terry Campese was knocked back by Wighton for Croker to score a four-pointer. The Titans got their act together in the last 20 and showed that if you can control the ball, the points will follow, with the tries to Jordan Rankin and Dominique Peyroux.

The second half was a slightly different matter. The Raiders dominated possession in the early part, but great defensive efforts from the likes of Nate Myles kept the Raiders from adding to their score. But eventually errors and too many missed tackles started to creep into the Titans' game and tries from Joel Thompson and then another from Croker gave the Raiders a comfortable lead. The Titans rallied and had a couple of opportunities to reduce the margin, but it was all a little too late to have an impact on the final result.

It was an encouraging win for coach David Furner. There has been a marked improvement in the ball-handling and discipline across the board for the Raiders this year. The return of Campese has also had a positive impact on the direction of the team. As for the Gold Coast, they had their opportunities, but were not able to capitalise.

Maybe the win against the Cowboys in the first round was more a reflection on how bad North Queensland was. It could be a long and frustrating year for Coach Cartwright.

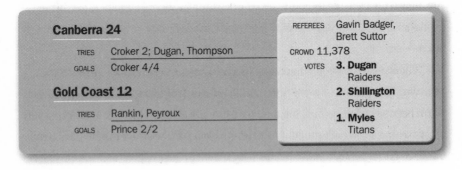

Canberra 24

TRIES	Croker 2; Dugan, Thompson
GOALS	Croker 4/4

Gold Coast 12

TRIES	Rankin, Peyroux
GOALS	Prince 2/2

REFEREES	Gavin Badger, Brett Suttor
CROWD	11,378
VOTES	**3. Dugan** Raiders
	2. Shillington Raiders
	1. Myles Titans

Will the real Dragons please stand up?

Canterbury Bulldogs *versus* **St George Illawarra Dragons**
7.30pm, Saturday, 10 March
ANZ Stadium, Sydney

GLEN HUMPHRIES

RIGHT UP TO THE MORNING OF THE GAME I figured we were morals to knock over the Dogs. That's because their first round effort against Penrith was pretty ordinary – a woeful 64 per cent completion rate and 11 fewer sets of six than the Panthers. They were just lucky the Panthers were even more ordinary and allowed themselves to lose 22-14.

The Dragons, on the other hand, played tough in a tight matchup with a Knights side coached by some guy whose name escapes me. We fought it out all the way to our first golden point victory.

That confidence took a nosedive when I saw the Saturday papers, which carried news that Dragon Beau Scott had signed with the Knights. Scott has been providing the mongrel our side has lacked for God knows how many years. He was the first Dragon in ages that opposition players feared, because of both his defence and his disinclination to take a backward step in the "push me-push you" displays that substitute for punch-ups these days.

When I read that story I figured my Saturday couldn't get any worse. But, Lordy, I was wrong. It got worse to the tune of a 30-4 shellacking at the hands of those Dogs who'd been so ordinary (did I mention that?) a week earlier. And if the shellacking and Scott's scarpering wasn't enough, there was the icing on the cake – the Dragons giving away not one, not two, but three (three!) penalties for incorrectly playing the ball. Jeez, not even the kiddies teams that play at halftime during NRL matches would screw up the play the ball that many times (if only out of fear that the coach won't take them to McDonalds after the game).

It didn't take the Dogs long to start the shellacking, even if they were a bit lucky. On the last tackle Aiden Tolman was about to die with the ball when he desperately flung it out the back. The Dogs pounced and spread left to Josh Morris who had a four-metre run to cross the line in just the eighth minute.

Soon after came the first of that trio of unforgiveable play-the-ball penalties, committed by hooker Mitch Rein. Fortunately it didn't lead to points but the next one by Matt Prior, looking permanently like a guy who's just woken up and is trying to work out where he is, did. A few tackles after giving the Dogs the ball, Josh Morris embarrassed a slow Ben Hornby by running around him to score (not dissimilar to the way Timana Tahu posted him up last week).

The Dragons finally got on the board in the 28th minute through some brilliant work by Brett Morris and Kyle Stanley. A metre from the line, Morris got his arm free and offloaded to Stanley, who managed to pick the ball up from the ground at pace and plant it over the line without knocking on. But that was all she wrote, for the Dragons. A few minutes later, Josh Morris crossed for his – and his team's – third try to make it 18-4 at halftime.

Nine minutes into the second half, Bryson Goodwin kicked for himself and beat everyone to the ball for another Dogs try. That was the signal for the wheels to fall off for the Dragons. A side noted for its discipline got increasingly frustrated by an inability to score or even hold onto the ball. That only led to more dropped ball, a few questionable hits and, late in the game, Rein's second play-the-ball penalty.

That second indiscretion led to the Dogs' last try of the night, an embarrassing effort where Eastwood ran ten metres straight through four Dragon defenders to score under the posts for a final score of 30-4.

I was left wondering one thing. Which team was the real 2012 Dragons? Was it the one that muscled up against the Knights last week or the one that just got done by the Dogs?

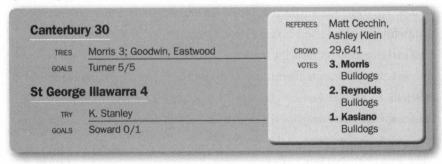

Canterbury 30			REFEREES	Matt Cecchin, Ashley Klein
TRIES	Morris 3; Goodwin, Eastwood		CROWD	29,641
GOALS	Turner 5/5		VOTES	**3. Morris** Bulldogs
St George Illawarra 4				**2. Reynolds** Bulldogs
TRY	K. Stanley			**1. Kasiano** Bulldogs
GOALS	Soward 0/1			

The ultimate battle of good and evil

Cronulla Sharks *versus* **Newcastle Knights**
2pm, Sunday, 11 March
Toyota Stadium, Sydney

NATHAN BOSS

IFE AS A CRONULLA SUPPORTER is difficult to explain to the uninitiated. Actually, it's just plain difficult to explain. Actually, it's just plain difficult.

There can be few other ventures in life where one puts in so much for so little return. But one of the startling features of any Cronulla fan is the ability to put aside the failures of seasons prior and convince oneself that this will be the year that Harold Holt finally wanders up to that eerily vacant porch in Portsea.

Over the years Cronulla supporters have placed great hope in many false idols.

Tommy Bishop. Norm Provan. Arthur Beetson. Johnny Lang. Chris Anderson. Brett Kimmorley. Ricky Stuart. David Peachey. Jack Gibson. Andrew Ettingshausen. Trent Barrett. Don Tweddle. Shaun Wessels.

While these idols achieved varying amounts of success at the club, they were not able to make any impression on the Sharks' trophy cabinet.

And so it came to 2012. Sharks supporters, having spent the past few years worrying about developments, flood plains and out-of-touch councillors, had become rejuvenated. The source of that renewed enthusiasm would be the enigmatic Todd Carney. The faith shown in Carney as the almighty lord and saviour appeared to be somewhat warranted after a brilliant second half in torrid conditions at Leichhardt Oval in the opening round of the season.

So it was with this backdrop that I arrived at Melbourne's Limerick Arms Hotel to watch the Sharks' first home game of season 2012 against the Nathan Tinkler-assembled Newcastle Knights. The ultimate battle of good and evil. The boys from The Shire taking on Tinky Winky's Millionaires. I took my seat feeling somewhat intimidated by the wave of Newcastle supporters in attendance (well, four people passively watching the contest, drinking cider).

Regardless, I was in high spirits early on in the contest as Isaac De Gois made a clean break down the middle of the field. With Nathan Gardner looming up on the outside I was getting ready to belt out another version of Feede Le Grande's *Put Your Hands Up For De Gois*.

Then it happened. The moment that reminded me that it was the Cronulla Sharks that I was watching. De Gois magically managed to throw the ball directly into the outstretched arms of Darius Boyd and the Knights went on to score moments later.

And with that moment, my hopes and aspirations for 2012 were dashed quicker than you can say super-profits mining tax.

The remainder of the contest was like an awful flashback to Sharks moments past. Balls were dropped with the line wide open. Simple two-on-ones were butchered. The part of Ben Pomeroy's brain that allows him to focus on catching the ball had disappeared once again. Nathan Gardner was attempting ridiculous tap-ons. Then there was the obligatory ridiculous refereeing decision.

I can only assume that the conversation to award the Junior Sau try in the second half went something like this:

Pat Reynolds: "Tony, it's a clear knock on."

Tony Archer: "Are you sure, remember it's the Sharks?"

Pat: "Oh, sorry Tony. I'll make it a ref's call so you can find some way to award it."

After an excruciating 80 minutes, the Newcastle faithful attempted to comfort me by noting that they felt really sorry for the Sharks and hoped the boys from The Shire would win a few more games this season.

Another season of the Sharks as the NRL's poor little orphan has commenced.

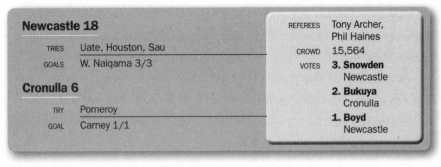

Newcastle 18		
TRIES	Uate, Houston, Sau	
GOALS	W. Naiqama 3/3	
Cronulla 6		
TRY	Pomeroy	
GOAL	Carney 1/1	

REFEREES	Tony Archer, Phil Haines
CROWD	15,564
VOTES	**3. Snowden** Newcastle
	2. Bukuya Cronulla
	1. Boyd Newcastle

I should have stayed at the beach

Sydney Roosters *versus* **Penrith Panthers**

3pm, Sunday, 11 March

Allianz Stadium, Sydney

BRETT OATEN

I HAVE SAT THROUGH SOME TERRIBLE ROOSTER PERFORMANCES against Penrith in my time. They have tended to involve lots of rain and Craig Gower, the 2003 Grand Final being a particularly painful case in point. Today involved neither, and yet may have been worse as a result.

This should have been a good day for the Roosters. Perfect weather, the first home game of the year, only a few days after a miracle victory against the arch-enemy. What did we get? The Roosters served up a shocker.

I spent most of the summer convincing myself that the Roosters had such quality among their young players that they were the new 2005 Tigers. I could put this delusion down to heat but we had the worst summer ever. I also seemed to have forgotten we don't have a Benji. Or a Farah. Is it possible we have 17 Daniel Fitzhenrys? On today's evidence, sadly, yes.

Today, the Roosters forwards – our great hope – went missing, Jared Waerea-Hargreaves and Anthony Mitchell excepted. No punch, no drive, no mongrel and, after 45 minutes, no Jake Friend, who surely played his worst game in the Tricolours. Mitchell Pearce, definitely the only Origin halfback who can't pass to the right, was woeful, as was five-eighth Braith Anasta.

Anasta, like John Sutton at Souths, would rather be a very limited five-eighth than a very skilful backrower. His ego demands that he be the playmaker rather than an important cog. Take it from me: he should be a cog. He was a great one in 2010, and Brian's Smith's indulgence of him will prove costly.

But full credit to the Panthers (did I really just say *full credit*?). Penrith is no one's tip for a contender but the Panthers looked like they had inflatable muscles underneath those pink jumpers and were stronger, faster and far sharper all day. They had a plan and they executed it.

Michael Jennings should spend 16 straight hours at the Star Casino more often on this showing – the Roosters couldn't touch him all day.

Kevin Kingston ran the game around the rucks – that Parramatta sent him away and kept Matt Keating comforts me that the Roosters do not have the sole mortgage on moronic decision making. Penrith's largely anonymous forward pack bullied the Roosters. Sam McKendry scored a magnificent 30-metre try, shrugging off four Rooster defenders in a run that is destined to be his career highlight. Dayne Weston, Luke Lewis and Cameron Ciraldo were tough. Clint Newton used to go out with Jennifer Hawkins.

You could argue that Penrith didn't have much to beat, but they did what they had to do cleanly, and the result was never in doubt. It is a mark of Sydney's charms that in mid-March you can go to the beach in the morning and the footy in the arvo.

I wish I'd stayed at the beach.

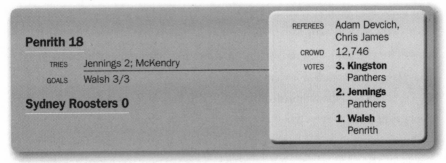

Penrith 18

TRIES	Jennings 2; McKendry
GOALS	Walsh 3/3

Sydney Roosters 0

REFEREES	Adam Devcich, Chris James
CROWD	12,746
VOTES	**3. Kingston** Panthers
	2. Jennings Panthers
	1. Walsh Penrith

Hope springs eternal

Melbourne Storm *versus* South Sydney Rabbitohs

7pm, Sunday, 11 March

AAMI Park, Melbourne

PAUL CONNOLLY

NOBODY LOVES THE MELBOURNE STORM. Even in their own city the Storm are as overlooked as the models' shoes in a Victoria's Secret lingerie parade. Okay, sure they have *some* fans. There's Molly, of course, and a hardy and hardened cadre (you'd have to be to wear purple and endure cow bells as your clarion cry) of northern ex-pats, Kiwis, and, yes, bewitched locals who've had their heads turned. But until the AFL admits it's all just a joke and stops doing what it's been doing for far too long, they are resigned to be forever swimming against the cultural tide.

Outside of Melbourne, the Storm have even fewer friends. The salary cap scandal hasn't helped matters one bit – just like throwing petrol on a burning house doesn't exactly improve things – but no one was sending them Christmas cards before that.

You can speculate all you like about some of the reasons for the animosity. I'd suggest Craig Bellamy's chicken wings, Billy Slater's knees and Cameron Smith's face, but their main crime has been success. *Relentless* success.

Instead of remaining chained in the attic, the ugly bastard child of the NRL has instead imposed itself on the League. They won a comp in their second season, for God's sake, and since 2006 – operating mostly out of Olympic Park, Dante's little known 10th circle of Hell – they've remained at or near the top. That's an eternity for the haters.

Even last season, without much of their vaunted lineup (though not, tellingly, any of the Holey Moley Trinity –Smith, Slater and Cooper Cronk), the Storm just kept on keeping on. Like British Paints. In eggplant.

Few teams know this as well as Souths, a kind of anti-Storm. At times resembling a team even a rabble wouldn't want to be associated with, the relentlessly *unsuccessful* Rabbitohs had beaten the Storm just three times in 18 outings before Sunday night's affair.

But the Bunnies entered the evening matchup with some hope and insider knowledge, what with a squad including Greg Inglis, Michael Crocker and, back from England, Matt King (sporting a hairdo that has come to resemble an Ewok thrown in a wet ditch and beaten half to death with a shovel).

And Souths looked up for the fight when they admirably fought back from 10-0 down to level up by halftime; their two tries (to winger Chris McQueen and Sam Burgess) owing much to giant Dave Taylor's ability to offload and Burgess' ability to resemble a Panzer tank rampaging through a church fete. Souths may have even hit the lead early in the second half but for winger Fetuli Talanoa's boot grazing the chalk when a try seemed on the cards.

But that wouldn't have been enough to win it anyway. Souths showed the previous week against the Roosters that no lead is too big to blow, while the Storm have been demonstrating for six years that winning is a habit they've no intention of kicking.

To be fair to Souths, they looked sharp at times and they forced the Storm into some uncharacteristically sloppy play, but the Storm have the ability to flick a switch when they need to.

So it was with a sense of inevitability that they regained the lead with a 55th minute try, a sweeping right-to-left set-piece that saw Cronk wrap around Ryan Hoffman and float a wobbly one out to Slater who flirted with the sideline – all but buying it a drink – but still found a way to score.

Less than 10 minutes later a similar move ended up in the hands of centre Dane Nielsen, who stepped inside for his second try of the night.

And then, with a minute remaining, the coup de grâce. A break on the halfway line ended up with Cronk, then Nielsen, who deftly kicked inside for anyone backing up.

Anyone, of course, means Slater, who picked up the grubbering ball and dived over for his 128th career try.

Nobody loves the Storm (well, nobody except Molly and the almost 16,000 fans in attendance) but you've *got* to admire them.

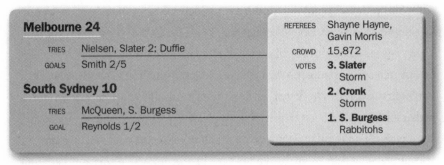

Melbourne 24		REFEREES	Shayne Hayne, Gavin Morris
TRIES	Nielsen, Slater 2; Duffie	CROWD	15,872
GOALS	Smith 2/5	VOTES	**3. Slater** Storm
South Sydney 10			**2. Cronk** Storm
TRIES	McQueen, S. Burgess		**1. S. Burgess** Rabbitohs
GOAL	Reynolds 1/2		

The man on the grassy knoll

Parramatta Eels *versus* **New Zealand Warriors**
7pm, Monday, 12 March
Parramatta Stadium, Sydney

BRUNO BRAYOVIC

THERE WAS GOOD AND BAD NEWS for Parramatta in the lead-up to kick-off of this Monday night fixture against the Warriors, with Jarryd Hayne and Willie Tonga named as late inclusions to the run-on side and skipper Nathan Hindmarsh ruled out with a virus. Judging by what it usually takes to floor Hindmarsh, one can only assume he is suffering from the flesh-eating Ebola virus.

This was to be Hayne's first appearance since injuring his knee in a trial match, while Tonga was returning to Parramatta after a 10-year absence, no doubt as part of Parramatta's recruitment and retention practice of nurturing a player, then selling him off to another club where he has his best years before re-signing him in the twilight of his career.

Casey McGuire has benefited from this program and Parramatta fans can look forward to the day Tony Williams re-joins them in 2020.

The Warriors started slowly last week against Manly and they repeated the dose this week, letting in two early tries to Eels wingers Ken Sio and Cheyse Blair. The tries came about courtesy of some enterprising play.

There were good signs for the home team with the new halves combination of Sandow and Roberts taking on the defensive line and combining well with Hayne. Supercoach in the making, Stephen Kearney, would have felt vindicated after copping a spray from Eels fans for his inclusion of Sio and Blair at the expense of the legendary Luke Burt and other regular first-grader, Ryan Morgan.

They joined Justin Horo and Shane Shackleton as the most expensive things to ever come out of Wentworthville, slugging it out in the NSW Cup.

Parramatta's defence was the highlight of their loss to the Broncos in Round 1 but unfortunately this week they buckled at the first whiff of a Warriors attack. Just like old times. Some very handy ball work from Elijah Taylor presented Feleti Mateo with a try against his old club. Entertaining stuff with the scoreboard reading 8-6 after only 12 minutes.

A minor detail, before I forget – Hayne was stretchered off with a knee injury. Yep. Attempting a trademark pounce-and-run from a Warriors kick, Hayne seemed to be brought down by a sniper after only running a few metres. Was Luke Burt the man on the grassy knoll?

Apparently the injury will keep him out for weeks, not months, but it was of little comfort as Parramatta had effectively lost the match as soon as he was carted off.

They well and truly dropped their bundle and when Bill Tupou crossed over in the 19th minute and then new powerhouse runner Konrad Hurrell played the part of Mum's-four-wheel drive to Ben Roberts' toddler-in-the-driveway 10 minutes later, it looked like the Warriors might be there to put on a show. The Tupou try was especially difficult to take as Maloney converted from the sideline and I then copped a full screen view of three members of my touch football team (go the Germs!), all in their Warriors jerseys, clapping and gesturing madly at the cameras. Thanks guys. The teams went to the break 14-18 after some Sandow cockiness created an error, which led to the first of his two tries.

The second half was lacklustre in comparison, with the only exception being the Kiwi lot scoring a superb try through Maloney, who capitalised on some incredible offloading from 14 other pairs of hands.

The Warriors scored twice in the last seven minutes but more as a result of Parramatta's desperation turning to dust than any Kiwi magic.

Only some Sandow zip kept Parramatta in the hunt.

The Warriors deserved their win. They started slowly but ground their way back into the match, much the same way they did against Manly, with the major difference being that Parramatta is not Manly. Parramatta showed some good signs in the form of the new halves, but consistency from the pair and the forwards cost the Eels dearly.

It could be a long season.

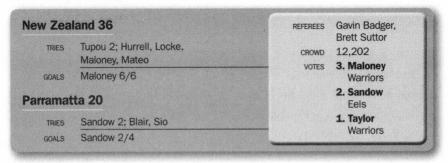

New Zealand 36		REFEREES	Gavin Badger, Brett Suttor
TRIES	Tupou 2; Hurrell, Locke, Maloney, Mateo	CROWD	12,202
GOALS	Maloney 6/6	VOTES	**3. Maloney** Warriors
Parramatta 20			**2. Sandow** Eels
TRIES	Sandow 2; Blair, Sio		**1. Taylor** Warriors
GOALS	Sandow 2/4		

Round 3

You are with us or you are against us

St George Illawarra Dragons *versus* **Wests Tigers**

7.30pm, Friday, 16 March
WIN Jubilee Oval, Sydney

PAUL ROBERTSON

AFTER ROUND 2, 2012		
1	**Bulldogs**	**2-0**
2	**Storm**	**2-0**
3	**Sea Eagles**	**2-0**
4	**Knights**	**1-1**
5	**Broncos**	**1-1**
6	**Panthers**	**1-1**
7	**Warriors**	**1-1**
8	**Raiders**	**1-1**
9	Titans	1-1
10	Tigers	1-1
11	Roosters	1-1
12	Cowboys	1-1
13	Dragons	1-1
14	Sharks	0-2
15	Rabbitohs	0-2
16	Eels	0-2

J ACK STRAW IS A RECLUSE, BUT NOT COMPLETELY. The house he bought on Jubilee Avenue in the early fifties sits dilapidated but now he rarely leaves the comfort of it. He walks down to his beloved ground, Jubilee Oval, five or six times a year to watch the "mighties", as he calls them, go around.

"I attended all eleven Grand Finals," he announces rubbing his ghostly white stubble, as I help him to his seat on the south-western corner-post. "But I couldn't make it to the more recent ones."

"It's a bit of a circus now," he adds regretfully.

I ask him what it felt like to be a St George supporter during the golden era – Provan, Gasnier, Langlands, Raper.

"We were the chosen ones," he says. "Rugby League is the greatest game, don't get me wrong, but it felt like we were chosen for something great back then."

As I gaze across at the eastern hill on this humid March Friday evening, our first home game of the year, I see the spirit of Jack Straw infused in the chanting and singing of the thousand-strong Dragon Army. Tonight we're home.

It's been a slightly tumultuous week in the Dragon camp. After the controversy of Beau Scott's announcement over his exit to Bennett's Newcastle and a shameful loss to local rivals Canterbury-Bankstown, tonight we welcome our very own Judas figure, Tim Moltzen. It is his first trip to Kogarah since he bailed out of a contract with us.

To people like Jack and the emboldened Dragon Army, the actions of

Moltzen amount to sacrilege. "How could an individual so publicly not want to be one of us?" Jack exclaims as the Tigers run out.

The crowd waits in anticipation to death-ride the man who knocked back an offer to wear the much-blessed Red V.

There is a ten-minute sorting out period and then Adam Blair dishes out a cheap shot. Penalty. Mitch Rein scores from a dummy half double show-and-go. 6-0, Dragons.

With discipline, particularly around the ruck, letting them down again, the Tigers allow Brett Morris to break through via an angled run. Morris looks like he will be held upright one metre out but miraculously fires an offload to Dan Hunt who goes over under the posts. 12-0 after 15.

The Tigers hit back with a dubious try to Beau Ryan, from Benji Marshall's grubber kick in the far north-east corner of the ground. 12-6, Dragons.

Moltzen's fumble at the scrum base 10 metres out from the Dragons' line adds to the Shakespearean tragedy of the Tigers' performance. The local faithful are seeing it more as a comedy of errors. Jack chuckles.

We are five minutes out from halftime when Trent Merrin busts through a missed shoulder charge from Blair, sending Nathan Fien over for a try. The Red V leads 18-6.

With the Tigers defending the field goal, Fien exploits another soft Tiger middle to send Ben Hornby over for the final try of the first half and right on halftime the Dragons surely have the game sewn up at 24-6.

The Tigers come back, after half-time, with a dicey try to Joel Reddy, but their rally is ended by Daniel Vidot's try in the 69th minute.

The Dragons finish off the Tigers with a try in the final minute. Soward's bomb is cleaned up by Morris, who deftly sends Ben Creagh over.

Brett Morris has been the standout and could very easily be the answer to the important fullback question for the Dragons this year.

The Dragons were very close to their best in this dominant performance against fancied opposition. After a last round thrashing where their attitude was questioned, they returned to the ruthless mindset of 2010.

Many will pontificate on the rights and wrongs of ex-coaches like Bennett poaching players and other players like Moltzen reneging on contracts and turning their back on history.

The antidote to all this is realising that players play. Tonight the Dragons players played for themselves with the right attitude and the right execution and in the right spirit of competition.

This is all I ask for and I'm sure, if pressed, Jack would agree.

Jack waddles back behind his crumbling brick fence that separates him from the ecstatic horde which skips along. This is the mood that surfaces with the thrashing of an old rival. The empty disappointment of last week is forgotten.

St George Illawarra 36		REFEREES	Tony Archer, Phil Haines
TRIES	Creagh, Fien, Hornby, Hunt, Rein, Vidot	CROWD	18,726
GOALS	Soward 6/7	VOTES	**3. Morris** Dragons
Wests Tigers 12			**2. Soward** Dragons
TRIES	Reddy, Ryan		**1. Fien** Dragons
GOALS	Marshall 2/2		

No match for the past

Newcastle Knights *versus* Brisbane Broncos
7.30pm, Friday, 16 March
Hunter Stadium, Newcastle

WILL EVANS

FROM THE PERSPECTIVE OF A BRISBANE BRONCOS DIEHARD, matches against the Newcastle Knights have traditionally incorporated an extra bit of spark. Many clashes between the two sides who entered the competition in 1988 are secure in the memory including:

- the Broncos' 37-12 victory in the club's 1992 farewell to the old Lang Park;
- the Knights' resounding maiden success against the Broncos at their 12th attempt, 24-10 in 1994;
- Brisbane's Allan Langer-inspired come-from-behind 24-19 win in a Monday night classic in 1996;
- Newcastle's 44-0 drubbing in 2001 – a then-record defeat for the Broncos;
- the Knights' 32-30 victory in 2006 as Andrew Johns and Darren Lockyer duelled spectacularly in one of the finest contests of the NRL era; and
- the Broncos' emphatic 50-6 win at the semi-final stage in 2006, the only post-season showdown between the proud clubs.

The media focussed on Wayne Bennett's first clash against his former club as coach of Newcastle – which was predictable, and understandable – as well as the absence of injured captain Kurt Gidley. Brisbane entered the clash with its own problems, with lock Corey Parker pulling out due to a thumb complaint thereby sending the Fantasy NRL fraternity into a tailspin.

The jury is still out on the 2012 prospects of both clubs – the early incarnation of the post-Lockyer Broncos swept aside Parramatta in the opening round before suffering an almighty choke against North Queensland, while the Knights went down in golden point to St George Illawarra (another ex-Bennett empire) and eased to victory over a bumbling Cronulla outfit.

Broncos backrower Alex Glenn powered through flimsy goalline defence to post the first try after just four minutes. But the home side reduced the deficit to two points in the twelfth minute courtesy of a sweeping backline shift; Kangaroos Test winger Akuila Uate was on the end of it and unleashed two giant right-foot steps to score his fifteenth try in his last ten first grade appearances. Try-saving tackles by Newcastle half Jarrod Mullen on Jack Reed and Glenn prevented Brisbane from extending its lead inside the opening quarter, before the Broncos' marquee centre Justin Hodges scythed through the defensive line and cantered 40 metres for a four-pointer. The 12-4 halftime scoreline barely reflected Brisbane's dominance and wealth of possession.

Fundamental errors and the failure to capitalise on gift-wrapped try-scoring opportunities had me wondering aloud whether the Broncos had backed themselves for a victory by 12-and-under. (The fact I had a 13+ wager on the boil was unrelated to my sarcastic snipe). Their lead was under threat 15 minutes into the second stanza when a cross-field kick by Brisbane pivot Corey Norman sailed over his chasing three-quarters and landed in the arms of Knights winger James McManus. The flying Scotsman, a former NSW Origin winger, raced 100 metres to dot down and again slice the margin to two points. But Newcastle's meagre resistance wilted in the 64th minute – a textbook backline movement involving Brisbane halfback Peter Wallace, Norman and Reed allowed winger Gerard Beale to step inside Knights fullback Darius Boyd (a former premiership-winner with the Broncos and Dragons under Bennett) and score for 16-10.

Brisbane skipper Sam Thaiday capped his 150-game milestone with a powerful charge four minutes later. On the ensuing play, interchange X-factor Matt Gillett ran a superb line off a short ball from hooker Andrew McCullough and scored under the posts. A Wallace penalty goal with six minutes on the clock extended the scoreline to 24-10, eliminating any possibility of a Newcastle comeback and ultimately rendering my meagre TAB ticket a winner.

It's hard to imagine a match further removed from the clubs' 1996 and 2006 regular season masterpieces – the contest lacked intensity, and was permeated by early-season rustiness and a glut of errors. The positives were drawn almost exclusively by the victors: Corey Norman's steady transition into Darren Lockyer's five-eighth spot; Ben Hannant's powerful performance up front; and Matt Gillett's burgeoning reputation as a game-breaking specialist. The 'reign of Wayne' hadn't brought the immediate superpower status some Knights supporters may have been expecting, while the 14-point loss represented the master coach's sixth defeat in eight games against his former club.

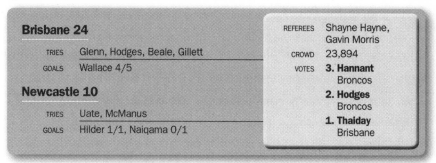

Brisbane 24		REFEREES	Shayne Hayne, Gavin Morris
TRIES	Glenn, Hodges, Beale, Gillett	CROWD	23,894
GOALS	Wallace 4/5	VOTES	**3. Hannant** Broncos
Newcastle 10			**2. Hodges** Broncos
TRIES	Uate, McManus		**1. Thaiday** Brisbane
GOALS	Hilder 1/1, Naiqama 0/1		

A perfect Storm ... or remember the Titans?

Gold Coast Titans *versus* Melbourne Storm
4.30pm, Saturday, 17 March
Skilled Park, Gold Coast

PAUL DALLIGAN

THEY SAY THAT NOTHING IN THIS WORLD IS FREE. Well nothing worthwhile anyway – but in the case of ticket holders to the Titans and Storm matchup on the Gold Coast, before the contest even started they were pretty much guaranteed exactly that.

As a result of the brainchild (per GOLDCOAST.COM.AU) of a local sponsor (who will not be named for legal reasons), all attendees of the game were guaranteed a free ticket to the next Titans game in the event that the Titans lost to the Melbourne Storm.

Yes, the Melbourne Storm. Not some band of weary travellers who would be lambs to the slaughter, but the Melbourne Storm, who had come off two very impressive wins over the Raiders and the Rabbitohs. Suddenly the promotion seemed less of a brainchild and more the worst idea emanating from the Gold Coast since Warwick Capper decided to run for the local seat of Beaudesert.

In the early stages of the game, thankfully the match did resemble the struggle all NRL fans were hoping for except, perhaps, fans of the Melbourne Storm.

Sadly, however, for Titans fans, lovers of a close game and also the doomed club sponsor, it didn't take long for the Storm warning to arrive. And wow, did it ever arrive ... I don't think the twister in the Bill Paxton movie of the same name arrived with as much force as the NRL version visited upon the Gold Coast, tearing through the Titans with a majesty the likes of which may not be seen again this NRL season.

The final *coup de grace* was a try by Billy Slater that had to be seen to be believed – and even though I saw it I still can't believe it. Judging by the sheer explosion on Twitter after the try, even other football codes stood up and saluted with the reigning Brownlow medallist Dane Swan one of the first to sing Billy the Kid's praises.

During the course of the magical 20 minutes of the Perfect Storm, Cooper Cronk and Cameron Smith exhibited their traditional precision and flair, ensuring that the Titans fans could at least look forward to their free tickets next week.

As a Melbourne resident, my heart went out to Beau Champion, who should still be in Storm colours but instead departed for the Titans last season. Beau's reason was as simple as it was honourable. After only one season in Melbourne he could no longer stand the shortage of pubs showing NRL games. Our man simply wanted to be able to enjoy a pot and parma in peace while he watched the NRL at a reasonable hour.

Sadly, Beau, in these parts it would be like wishing for a winter without scarves or a 96 tram without Collingwood fans.

During the heart of the Storm attack, the complete lack of any adequate response by the Titans makes one wonder whether John Cartwright was wearing a balaclava when he recently negotiated a monster coaching deal with the Titans. This from a coach who has had the luxury of a team boasting players of the calibre of Preston Campbell, Mat Rogers, Scott Prince and Greg Bird and yet has produced about as much of substance as the local Meter Maids.

With club sponsors throwing money away on ludicrous promotions that make Greek bonds seem a wise investment, sadly it's no wonder that only this week rumours have been circulating that there is a shortage of money on the Gold Coast and the NRL may even abandon the Titans.

The signing this week of yet another high profile player, Dave Taylor of South Sydney, is an indication that the club is heading in the right direction regarding player talent. Sadly, however, even with their star-studded line-up this season it seems that the Titans will get about as close to finals football as Warwick Capper would get to knocking out Wendell Sailor in a rematch.

It remains to be seen whether the current incarnation of the Gold Coast NRL team will survive, or whether it will be a case of remember the Titans...

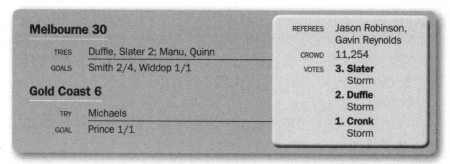

Melbourne 30		REFEREES	Jason Robinson, Gavin Reynolds
TRIES	Duffie, Slater 2; Manu, Quinn	CROWD	11,254
GOALS	Smith 2/4, Widdop 1/1	VOTES	**3. Slater** Storm
Gold Coast 6			**2. Duffie** Storm
TRY	Michaels		**1. Cronk** Storm
GOAL	Prince 1/1		

The luck of the Irish

North Queensland Cowboys *versus* **Parramatta Eels**
6.30pm, Saturday, 17 March
Dairy Farmers Stadium, Townsville
DOUG ROWETH

MY HEAD IS IN MY HANDS. It's all a blur. Green things litter my house. What on Earth happened? When I agreed to watch the North Queensland / Parramatta match down at the pub with my old mate Flanagan, it sounded innocent enough. Personally I thought it shaped as an intriguing match. Neither Parramatta nor North Queensland had begun the year in particularly sparkling fashion.

For the Cowboys, Matt Bowen had burgled their solitary win this year with a last-minute try, while Parramatta had lost both of their first two, with early murmurs of an off-field implosion and general panic.

So the match held plenty of interest for me wandering towards the pub. About a block away though, I saw the Irish bar we were meeting at. Or more accurately, I felt it. Packed wall to wall, patrons spilled out onto the footpath. My heart sank, as I realised it was St Patrick's Day. And the name Flanagan is about as Irish as they get.

Shamrocks hang from every rafter when I walk in and the whole place seems to glow in various shades of green. It's seven or eight deep at the bar, yet Flanagan is somehow sitting at the table right beneath the TV. Luck of the Irish, I guess.

A Guinness or two later, I inevitably yield to the Irish spirit as the talk turns to the upcoming clash. Fuifui Moimoi's late withdrawal hurts the Eels. Already without Jarryd Hayne, they will be up against it. Emboldened by a few pints, I throw some cash on North Queensland covering the 8.5. I'm riding the luck of the Irish.

We kick off and conditions are awful, almost monsoonal. Ball-handling is atrocious. Fifteen minutes in, Matt Scott burrows his way over after some smart work from Aaron Payne. This is the turning point. The floodgates open. Only a few minutes later, Ashley Graham is carrying three across the line to score and the Cowboys lead 10-0.

Five minutes later it's worse. Three quick tries and the scoreboard reflects the mayhem. Matthew Bowen lands a 40/20 before Jason Taumalolo tears holes in Parramatta, first scoring a try and having the final hand in another. Bowen scores himself.

Suddenly in the shadows of halftime, it's 26-0 and this match is over. Which could be for the best. I've lost count of how many pints of green Guinness we've had and things are getting rowdy. Another chorus of Wild Rover breaks out, a green-bearded bald man claiming to be a leprechaun is chuffed when Flanagan mentions to him that there's Jamesons on the way...

Which brings us back to the morning after.

With a head like a car accident, I curse the Irish, swear in Flanagan's general direction and blearily gulp down Panadol, certain my liver and kidneys have actually died. Coughing up shamrocks and pouring my second coffee, I feel almost ready to rejoin the human race. I flick the pre-recorded second half of the match on.

It flashes back to me pretty quickly. My bet won. The Cowboys were handy. The Eels imploded. Parramatta don't look any better in the light of day. So many missed tackles; a lack of direction and structure; poor ball control. Ben Roberts was more of a turnstile than a saviour.

While North Queensland will take a lot of confidence from the 42-6 win, Parramatta are in trouble. The Eels have used their proverbial pot of gold from the end of the rainbow, but value for money is yet to be realised. At 0-3 the vultures are circling.

After this loss I'm sure there are a few sore heads down at Parramatta looking for excuses as to what went wrong. I know the feeling. But at least I can blame my own troubles on drinking with a Flanagan on St Patrick's Day.

North Queensland 42		
TRIES	Graham 3; Taumalolo, Bowen, Linnett, Cooper, Scott	
GOALS	Thurston 5/8	
Parramatta 6		
TRY	O'Hanlon	
GOAL	Sandow 1/1	

REFEREES	Adam Devcich, Chris James
CROWD	8,239
VOTES	**3. Graham** Cowboys
	2. Taumalolo Cowboys
	1. Bowen Cowboys

You have to hand it to Benny Barba

New Zealand Warriors *versus* Canterbury Bulldogs
2pm, Sunday, 18 March
Mt Smart Stadium, Auckland

JACK MUIR

WATCHED THE GAME IN MY BED ON MY LAPTOP, LIVENRLTV dogging me again as the game just wouldn't stream. I watched the first half off an illegal feed as the legal means was not working. I managed to watch the second half in better quality. The service is really disappointing considering my $US100 annual subscription.

From Hong Kong, it looked like a good day for Rugby League in Auckland. The Warriors continued their run of poor form at the beginning of their matches this season, letting the Bulldogs run up an early 16-0 lead after only 16 minutes. The Bulldogs were able to capitalise on some lackadaisical effort in the Warriors defence with some good sleight of hand and the whole team keen and backing up the ball-carrier.

This definitely demonstrates the positive effect Des Hasler has brought to Belmore. The three early tries were scored by Ben Barba, Steve Turner and Jonathon Wright. The unexpected return to the Warriors of Jerome Ropati in the centres seemed to help the Bulldogs' early start as he looked to still be suffering from his injury.

The Warriors fought their way back into the game at the back end of the first half, firstly with James Maloney scoring off some beautiful ball work from Feleti Mateo.

The Maloney-Mateo combination developed well over 2011 and will be one of the Warriors' main attacking weapons in 2012. The second try of the Warriors fightback came again from Feleti Mateo as he gave a beautiful pass to rampaging Sione Lousi to crash over for his maiden first grade try.

The teams went to halftime with the Bulldogs leading 16-12 in an entertaining game of football. I went back to the legal feed and finally had the good quality stream coming through. The second half began and so did the good football. Hard running and strong tackling. The Warriors completed their fightback with Mateo showing and going to score in the left-hand corner in the 50th minute. Mateo's introduction into the match in the 20th minute inspired the Warriors' comeback. Parramatta would love to have him on their roster these days.

The Warriors were controlling the game and looked like they could have run away with it but the Bulldogs hit back with Sam Kasiano bustling his way over from ten metres out under duress from three Warriors defenders. It was a power try that changed the game. Sam Kasiano can be destructive. The Bulldogs regained the lead but the Warriors seemed to have the momentum: Kasiano's try was against the run of play.

The game-changing play came with about ten minutes left. Feleti Mateo put Kevin Locke over the line for what seemed like a certain try. The Warriors' reaction was positive, which suggested there was no doubt the try had been scored. However the referee went upstairs. Replays showed Ben Barba had managed to do enough to get his arm under the ball initially. I believe Locke's arm slid off Barba's onto terra firma. However, the video ref thought differently and no try was awarded.

Credit has to be given to Barba for being there to send the decision upstairs.

The Warriors still looked as though they could wrap the game up with their plethora of attacking arsenal. Alas, Shaun Johnson put a speculative grubber into the in-goal only for Ben Barba to pounce and get out of his in-goal and run 80 metres downfield before being run down by Kevin Locke. From the ensuing play the ball the Bulldogs spread left and managed to get Jonathon Wright in space to cruise over the line and effectively wrap the match up. Joel Romelo scored another try to blow the score out for the Bulldogs while the Warriors were all-out attacking.

This was a thoroughly enjoyable match from two teams who have the potential to be in the top six come September. Todd Greenberg and Bulldogs fans will be happy with what Des Hasler has been able to do in the first three rounds and things look positive for them. The Warriors looked untouchable in patches but they have been slow out of the blocks in each of the first three rounds. Superstar in waiting Glen Fisiiahi scored six tries in the NSW Cup on Saturday and is pushing very hard for inclusion in the first grade side for the Warriors. Dare I say it, the consistent Bill Tupou or destructive but flaky Manu Vatuvei may have to give way.

This match will be remembered for the turning point when Ben Barba miraculously stopped his opposite number from giving the Warriors a late lead. I will not say controversial, although I saw it that way.

Let's hope I can witness the rest of the Warriors turning points this season without streaming issues on LIVENRLTV.

Canterbury 32

TRIES	Wright 2; Barba, Turner, Kasiano, Romelo
GOALS	Turner 4/6

New Zealand 18

TRIES	Maloney, Sione Lousi, Mateo
GOALS	Maloney 3/3

REFEREES	Matt Cecchin, Ashley Klein
CROWD	17,067
VOTES	**3. Morris** Bulldogs
	2. Reynolds Bulldogs
	1. Matulino Warriors

A clash of cultures

Sydney Roosters *versus* **Canberra Raiders**
2pm, Sunday, 18 March
Allianz Stadium, Sydney

MICHAEL PEARSON

THE ROOSTERS AND RAIDERS don't have much in common. Bondi is a long way from Belconnen. Fyshwick is not quite Kings Cross. In footy terms the Roosters are poachers and plunderers, chequebook Charlies. The Raiders promote and progress from within. Every year the roster is an invention test. Gourmet meals expected from corner store pasta and a jar of Leggos.

Roosters play like they are dressed in dinner suits. Anasta and Pearce are prototype halves and exude a confidence they have a standing reservation at Tetsuya's after footy training each night. The Raiders are bread and dripping. McCrone is a talent but doesn't believe he deserves a seat at the head table. Campese is an enigma. A superstar waiting for the spotlight if only the lights would turn on.

And then there are the coaches. Brian Smith is an underperformer yet offers a prodigiousness that is unmatched by most. The wick on Furner's career is shortening with each loss. He is not yet an underperformer but his coaching talent struggles to find the light.

Raiders start well and play mistake-free footy to lead 8-0. The Roosters are not getting the calls and are not helping themselves, playing like they are on the lawns at Randwick sipping champagne. However as the game moves on and the Raiders run short of troops through injuries to Dugan and Fensom, the Roosters look the more threatening team. Anasta scores off a Beetsonesque offload from Leilua and then has the audacity to slot one from the sidelines into a breeze. Off three steps! The halftime score is 8-6 and Roosters look more likely.

The Raiders fans have sweaty palms. They have retreated to a basic plan to run one out and use their size to storm through the Roosters pack. Shillington and Learoyd-Lahrs are brave but the game-plan lacks creativity and leadership, if not heart. Josh Papalii has all the hallmarks of a wide running backrower but his weaponry is diminished by the need to act as a battering ram. Unfortunately, without Dugan, and with Campese still finding his rhythm after injury, the Raiders are impotent.

The athletic and enthusiastic Roosters forwards are up for the contest and have a sting to their defence. There is inevitability about the outcome and the Roosters, after blowing numerous chances, eventually score through Mortimer.

To their credit the Raiders persist in attack but the burden of only one interchange for the second half diminishes their effectiveness and no-one steps up to lay on a winning play. This, combined with the Roosters toughness in defence, means the Raiders and the Roosters will each be 1-2 for the year. Both have shown glimpses of promise but neither was considered a real contender pre-season and sadly for supporters, nothing has changed.

As a future guide to performance, the match has about as much relevance as a Moe maiden to a stakes race at Flemington during Carnival week. It does, however, provide an entrée as to how each team will be expressing themselves on the footy field during 2012.

The Roosters are gamblers with a predilection for low-percentage plays. They are entertaining to watch if and when it all clicks. The Raiders need a charisma injection. Steamrolling opposition forward packs alone does not win a premiership.

Despite the differences in style, coach Smith and coach Furner have one thing in common and that is that they have not extracted the best from their respective charges.

Sydney Roosters 14		REFEREES	Steve Lyons, Alan Shortall
TRIES	Anasta, Mortimer	CROWD	10,343
GOALS	Anasta 3/3	VOTES	**3. Friend** Roosters
Canberra 8			**2. Shillington** Raiders
TRIES	Berrigan, Croker		**1. Leilua** Roosters
GOALS	Croker 0/2		

Inglis is back! Are the Bunnies?

Penrith Panthers *versus* **South Sydney Rabbitohs**
3pm, Sunday, 18 March
Centrebet Stadium, Penrith

MARTY SPENCER

SOUTH SYDNEY RABBITOH GREG INGLIS gave a stunning performance in his first game at fullback in almost five years. It was highlighted by a sensational try just after halftime. The game commenced in frantic fashion. When Penrith five-eighth Travis Burns turned the ball over from the kickoff, the Bunnies went for the throat like The White Rabbit of Caerbannog in *Monty Python and the Holy Grail*. First cab off the rank, and on the receiving end of a deft flick pass from Matt King, was debutant winger Andrew Everingham, who scored after just two minutes.

Souths' big men got in on the act when first Roy Asotasi handled twice in a 50-metre movement to score next to the posts, then big Dave Taylor displayed the skills that every forward will tell you they possess. He grubbered ahead to re-gather and score. It was a wonderful try that would have made Billy Slater envious. Adam Reynolds converted all three tries and after 14 minutes, Souths led 18-0.

Then it was the Panthers' turn and Kevin Kingston (23rd minute) and Travis Burns (32nd minute) exposed some defensive weakness in the Rabbitohs' centerfield to register four-pointers, which were both converted by Luke Walsh. At halftime and with the score looking more respectable, Penrith fans might have expected the Panthers to come out in the second half and show why the Bunnies hadn't beaten them at Penrith since Round 17 in 2002. Halftime 22-12.

Most of the punters hadn't even returned to their seats when Inglis took a lovely short ball from John Sutton to move into space. As the Penrith cover moved across Inglis saw he had no option other than to go straight over the top of Penrith fullback Lachlan Coote. And he did. Straight over the top. It was wonderful to see an injury-free Greg Inglis again. He is fit, fast, confident and strong and I think his performance might see Nathan Merritt relegated to the wing on his return from injury.

When Chris McQueen waltzed through some mediocre defence from dummy-half to score in the 52nd minute the game was almost out of reach for Penrith and although Travis Burns scored in the 60th minute to briefly raise their supporters' hopes, Dave Taylor put the issue beyond doubt with a further affirmation of his skills. The big man took a high pass and on landing displayed a big step off the right foot to slice through and make it a double. Adam Reynolds made it 8/8 with the conversion and despite a consolation try to Nathan Smith in the 71st minute, Souths ran out clear winners 40-24.

Questions will be raised about the level of both skill and commitment displayed by the Panthers. Despite comparatively even possession and completion rates, Souths dominated the match and were clearly out there to play. They did everything at pace and this was reflected upon in the post-match press conference. Penrith coach Ivan Cleary suggested they were outplayed in every facet and pointed to poor starts in both halves of the game while captain Luke Lewis encapsulated it beautifully:

We were shit, they were good... everything they done was faster than us.

Conversely, Souths were buoyant after the match, confident that a late injury-scare to Greg Inglis would not be a concern. Coach Michael Maguire suggested that that type of form had "been coming for a while" and intimated that he might persist with Inglis at fullback even after Merritt's return.

"It allows Greg to roam so he can attack on both sides of the field – when he's locked in at centre it leaves him out there," Maguire said

Both teams now have the short back-up for Friday night with Souths going into their match against Brisbane as the quietly confident underdog. If Souths can maintain their intensity and tighten up some defensive weakness exposed on Sunday then they might just be back.

South Sydney 40			REFEREES	Gavin Badger, Gerard Sutton
TRIES	Taylor 2; Everingham, Asotasi, Inglis, McQueen		CROWD	13,876
			VOTES	**3. Inglis** Rabbitohs
GOALS	Reynolds 8/8			
Penrith 24				**2. Taylor** Rabbitohs
TRIES	Burns 2; Kingston, Smith			**1. Sutton** Rabbitohs
GOALS	Walsh 4/4			

One for the true believers

Cronulla Sharks *versus* **Manly Sea Eagles**
7pm, Monday, 19 March
Toyota Stadium, Sydney

MARK NICHOLS

TWO ROUNDS IN FOR A LONG SUFFERING SHARKS SUPPORTER and it seemed that season 2012 was going to be business as usual. As I sat on my mate's couch in Melbourne after the Knights debacle, my head cradled in my hands, I tried to find solace from somewhere.

"Who do we have next week?" I thought to myself.

I certainly didn't feel any better when I realised we had the premiers, whom we hadn't beaten in our last six attempts. And they had started the season on fire.

However, as it rolled around to Monday night I blocked out all the doom and gloom and could only see positives. I was certain that *Up Up Cronulla* would be belted out at full time. As we took our customary seats at the Durham Arms for MNF and two-for-one rib-eyes I started my losing battle of convincing the boys why it was the Sharks' night. "Don't you remember sitting in these exact seats in Round 2 last year on a Monday night, same ground, playing the premiers, no one gave us a chance and we smashed the Dragons?"

In response I got the same shakes of the head and scornful laughs I get from the boys whenever I talk up the Sharks. But at least I convinced myself. Well nearly.

As the pre-game began I was thrilled to see rain pouring and that captain courageous Paul Gallen had been moved to his best position, up front, with Wade Graham slotting in at lock.

The first ten minutes were typical Sharks – tough, physical, applying pressure to the opposition goalline but ultimately keeping the scoreboard attendant on his stool. After T-Rex Williams was penalised for doing a Chuck Liddell impersonation on Isaac De Gois, the ball went out to Sharks sensation Jayson Bukuya. With nothing on, he beat five Manly defenders and slammed the ball down for the first points of the night, which had Durham locals hoping he was a New South Welshman.

The Sharks remained on top for the next 10, the Sea Eagles continuing with an uncharacteristically ill-disciplined performance, conceding penalties and dropping plenty of pill. A great offload from Gallen was scooped up brilliantly by De Gois, who flicked it to Gardener, who dived under the posts, narrowly avoiding a ruptured spleen as T-Rex closed in on both him and the left upright. I was starting to dream of victory as Carney lined up the conversion and when Orange ticket B23 was called out and we scored a meat tray I was convinced it was the Sharks' night.

Shortly after, Michael Oldfield tore down the left flank but a botched pass inside to Brett Stewart allowed my heart rate to return to normal. A kick-chase by Tupou pinned Brett Stewart in-goal and in the ensuing six Pomeroy was in after some lead up work by Bukuya which had the locals insisting he would be a walk up start for the Anzac Test. A drop goal after the siren allowed the Sharks to head to the sheds with a 17-0 lead.

Second-half highlights were scarce. Manly fans enjoyed the brilliant one-handed put down from Brett Stewart in the 75th minute to get the Eagles within striking distance, but I didn't. Oldfield's second in the 77th minute to get them to 17-14 horrified me. A couple of dropped balls by the Sharks in the last three minutes convinced me the Eagles would get us after the siren like last year but two return mistakes had me drafting Christmas cards to Mr Lyon and Lussick at the fulltime siren.

First win of the season and my mind is firmly on September. That's exactly how we Sharks react.

Cronulla 17			REFEREES	Ben Cummins, Gerard Sutton
TRIES	Bukuya, Gardner, Pomeroy		CROWD	8,652
GOALS	Carney 2/3		VOTES	**3. Gallen** Sharks
FIELD GOAL	Carney 1			**2. Bukuya** Sharks
Manly 14				**1. B. Stewart** Sea Eagles
TRIES	Oldfield 2; B. Stewart			
GOAL	Lyon 1/3			

Round 4

How the west was lost

Parramatta Eels *versus* **Penrith Panthers**

7.30pm, Friday, 23 March

Parramatta Stadium, Sydney

EDWIN SMITH

AFTER ROUND 3, 2012		
1	Bulldogs	3-0
2	Storm	3-0
3	Broncos	2-1
4	Cowboys	2-1
5	Sea Eagles	2-1
6	Dragons	2-1
7	Roosters	2-1
8	Raiders	1-2
9	Rabbitohs	1-2
10	Knights	1-2
11	Warriors	1-2
12	Panthers	1-2
13	Sharks	1-2
14	Titans	1-2
15	Tigers	1-2
16	Eels	0-3

I T WAS BILLED AS "THE BATTLE OF THE WEST". Friday night footy, two Western Sydney teams facing off in a blockbuster match to prove rugby league was still Sydney's football code as the new AFL team, the Giants, played their first match for premiership points in a Sydney derby.

However, it seemed only one team really came to the match intent on battling and that was the Panthers. Both were coming off embarrassing losses in Round 3, the Panthers to the Bunnies and the Eels to the Cowboys. Pre-game, Eels fans had been told superstar Jarryd Hayne was an outside chance of playing but this wasn't to be the case, and you got the feeling that was the beginning of the end.

The final score ended at 39-6, with ex-Parramatta winger Etu Uaisele scoring a hat-trick of tries to further rub salt into the wounds of Eels fans.

Uaisele and centre Michael Jennings terrorised the Eels' right-hand defence all night, and this result means the Eels have now won just two of their last 18 games.

Jennings scored a try and set up two more, while Lachlan Coote, Brad Tighe and Travis Burns all crossed for the Panthers. Luke Walsh kicked five conversions while Burns kicked a field goal on the halftime siren to complete the rout.

After the game, prop Tim Mannah summed up the performance bluntly saying:

We are embarrassed. It's disappointing because we could do better for these coaches ... we are the ones on the field who are missing the tackles and dropping the balls.

And if Mannah and the rest of his teammates weren't already feeling bad enough, 50 cent coins were thrown onto the pitch on the hour mark as the Eels conceded another try.

Coach Stephen Kearney said that he was lost for words after the match.

It's a real low point for the footy club at the moment and there's only a group of men in the sheds and myself who've got the capability of working our way out of it.

Kearney also had to deal with calls for his resignation but, as Nathan Hindmarsh had put it after the loss of the previous weekend, the coach can only do so much. Once the players are on the paddock, it's up to them to put in the hard yards and that's something the Eels just aren't doing at the moment.

It's not panic stations just yet for diehard Eels fans, but if they come out on the weekend against arch-enemies Manly and put in another insipid performance, then some serious change needs to happen.

You get the feeling that once Hayne comes back and starts to gel with halfback Chris Sandow the Eels could cause some damage in this competition. It has been frustrating and difficult for Parramatta, having spent the entire pre-season training with Hayne as fullback, working on combinations with Sandow and Roberts, to lose Hayne for the better part of the first four games.

Let's not completely write the Eels off just yet, as some attention-seeking bookmakers have. They've already paid out on Parramatta winning the wooden spoon at the end of the year.

It was never going to be an easy start to the year with two brand new halves, and injury to your top player would hurt any team. If Hayne comes back for a few weeks and the Eels keep losing, then it will really be time to panic.

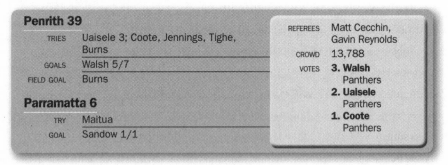

Penrith 39			REFEREES	Matt Cecchin, Gavin Reynolds
TRIES	Uaisele 3; Coote, Jennings, Tighe, Burns		CROWD	13,788
GOALS	Walsh 5/7		VOTES	3. **Walsh** Panthers
FIELD GOAL	Burns			2. **Uaisele** Panthers
Parramatta 6				1. **Coote** Panthers
TRY	Maitua			
GOAL	Sandow 1/1			

Unconvincing

South Sydney Rabbitohs *versus* Brisbane Broncos

6pm, Friday, 23 March
NIB Stadium, Perth

LIAM HAUSER

I TIPPED THE BRONCOS TO BEAT THE RABBITOHS IN THIS FIXTURE. But I wasn't overly confident. I considered the Broncos rather unconvincing in their two wins from three matches heading into the encounter with Souths, while the Queenslander in me was very wary of Greg Inglis and former Bronco Dave Taylor. He had been very impressive five days earlier as Souths beat Penrith. Inglis, meanwhile, was fit to contest the Broncos after battling an injury, while Scott Geddes was out with a hammy.

The Broncos had an early scoring chance but Jharal Yow Yeh propelled a bomb forward, and Inglis quickly made a break following an offside penalty. Switch on Broncos! Please! Souths centre Shaune Corrigan fumbled an up and under with the tryline beckoning before Hodges was penalised for a high tackle. With Jack Reed's defence ineffective on this occasion, Inglis made the sort of break I like to see from him in Origin football, and he set up a try for Andrew Everingham at the posts. Souths 6-0.

Reed made a try-saving tackle and then seemed to make a second effort. He was banished to the sin bin although replays suggested this punishment was harsh. The Rabbitohs, surprisingly, took the gift two points. A fumble from Josh Hoffman soon enabled Souths to attack and a knock on from Issac Luke let Brisbane off the hook before Andrew McCullough fumbled as the Broncos raided.

A controversial penalty went to Souths for obstruction during a high kick and then Inglis surged at the line and fumbled backwards. Everingham forced the ball over the tryline but it bobbled and the video referee gave Souths the benefit of the doubt. A missed conversion meant 12-0 felt more attainable than 14-0, but the rub of the green was with Souths.

The Broncos received their first penalty but then McCullough was held up over the line. Reed returned, then disaster struck after Wallace kicked high. Yow Yeh collided with an opponent before falling badly and suffering a compound fracture to the ankle. He was off on a stretcher and sure to miss Origin.

The Broncos had some attacking chances but couldn't seem to get their plays right, then Reed was held up after catching a cross-field kick. Matt Gillett inflicted a couple of bone-crunching tackles before a fumble from Souths led to a much-needed try for Brisbane before half-time. Dylan Farrell spilled Wallace's kick before Gillett crossed in the right corner. Souths led 12-4 at the break.

The Broncos received a penalty almost straight after play resumed but Gillett went too far across field and was taken into touch by great cover defence. After Brisbane's next penalty, Scott Anderson committed a simple knock on in a play-the-ball.

After a break from Sam Burgess, Souths almost scored from a grubber kick. Soon there was a 12-point turnaround as the Broncos produced some splendid offloads. Petero Civoniceva, Ben Hunt and Wallace combined before Hoffman busted a tackle and scored. Souths 12-10.

Just as I got my hopes up, the Broncos lost possession from the kick-off. Souths forced two goalline dropouts before a forward pass was pulled up. The Broncos were still mistake-prone and Souths looked to land the decisive blow. However the Rabbitohs fumbled with an overlap beckoning before Adam Reynolds made a threatening break until prop Ben Hannant chased him down, to the amazement of all, himself (probably) included.

Taylor charged for the line but fumbled with just 13 minutes left.

Suddenly the Broncos went from hanging on by a thread to looking threatening thanks to two half-breaks. Wallace was taken out after kicking but the Broncos were on the attack. Quick hands to the right sent Gerard Beale over in the corner and Brisbane led 14-12 with a few tantalising minutes to play after Wallace's kick hit the upright.

The Broncos maintained the momentum and forced a repeat set, then used the out-ball and in-ball before Hoffman linked with Hodges who sent Beale squeezing over in the corner. I was relieved as Brisbane had an eight-point lead with five minutes on the clock but then the Broncos erred from the kick-off and allowed Souths to gain possession. The Rabbitohs threatened but their chances disappeared as Luke fumbled late in the tackle count while Wallace clung to him desperately.

An unpredictable game ended with the Broncos in front, and a record Perth crowd of 15,599 suggested rugby league could well have a decent following there.

Brisbane 20		REFEREES	Ashley Klein, Chris James
TRIES	Beale 2; Gillett, Hoffman	CROWD	15,599
GOALS	Wallace 2/4	VOTES	**3. Hoffman** Broncos
South Sydney 12			**2. Beale** Broncos
TRIES	Everingham 2		**1. Inglis** Rabbitohs
GOALS	Reynolds 2/3		

Tough to gauge

New Zealand Warriors *versus* Gold Coast Titans
7.30pm, Saturday, 24 March
Mt Smart Stadium, Auckland

SAMSON McDOUGALL

THE WARRIORS SURPRISED MANY IN RUGBY LEAGUE when they made the Grand Final last year. No doubt the semi-final win over the Storm was well-deserved, but you have to question whether they were the second-best team of 2011. But that effort has helped them win a reputation and despite their poor 1-3 record in 2012, they went into this match hot favourites.

In Melbourne, Round 4 is pretty much the last time NRL fans get to watch their team from a pub as the AFL-crazed seize back every public wall-mounted TV for the duration of the season. Even today it's bloody hard to find an inner-northern watering hole that's prepared to show the game but we settle at the Great Northern, about a three-iron from Princes Park in Carlton.

The opening exchanges are, somewhat typically for the Warriors, marred by poor handling.

The first raids come via the Warriors but Manu Vatuvei and Jerome Ropati, in separate attacking movements, fail to cross. A lazy offside penalty releases the pressure on the Titans and they respond with a raid of their own, which is countered by a fabulous Kevin Locke pick-up from a probing kick.

The Titans are penalised and the Warriors enter Titans territory once again. A tidy set is followed up by a hanger of a bomb from Shaun Johnson, which the Titans let bounce, and a bobbling loose ball is snapped up by Elijah Taylor who weaves across the line for the first try of the match. James Maloney slots the conversion. 6-0 Warriors.

The restart is a shocker and the ball goes dead on the fly for a Warriors penalty from which Johnson almost scores. Manu Vatuvei crosses shortly afterwards but, despite replays showing a simultaneous grounding of the ball as his elbow goes into touch, the try is disallowed, much to the disgust of the vocal Warriors supporters. The subsequent 20 minutes are a bit of an arm wrestle. Both sides struggle to string meaningful sets together and despite a possession advantage, the Titans' predictable and sloppy attack fails to cause too many problems.

The Warriors defence holds firm for a while before a Johnson kick gets them out of trouble and deep into Titans territory. It doesn't take long for the home side to capitalise on their territorial advantage and Manu Vatuvei again crosses, this time from a suspicious looking pass. The try is allowed. Warriors 10-0.

New Zealand has a new energy during the final minutes of the half and punishes a lacklustre and tired looking Titans side with another try, capitalising on a botched Scott Prince attacking play. Through Ropati, Vatuvei and Johnson they run the length of the park to score. Warriors 14-0.

An early second-half Simon Mannering try (in his 150th match and 50th as captain) exposes a Titans side in trouble and, despite some gallant defence, the Warriors make the half and, consequently the match, their own. Shaun Johnson's 67th minute intercept try further cements the win and a last-ditch Luke O'Dwyer consolation will do little to lift the spirits of a side in turmoil on and off the field.

What's difficult to say is whether the Warriors' second-favourite-for-the-premiership status is deserved after a 2-2 start to the season and bungling performances against the quality of the Bulldogs and the reigning premiers Manly.

This was a much-improved defensive effort from the home side and they finally managed to withstand sustained periods of pressure. What's in question is whether a better side should have dealt further humiliation to the fumbling and predictable Titans attack.

Though Vatuvei again touched down, he was never tested in defence and he botched two try attempts. Nathan Friend's defensive effort was impressive and Warriors fans can rest easy now that a solid hooker has finally landed.

But with injuries mounting and Locke limping from the field late in the match, one wonders whether the Warriors are within striking distance of a finals campaign.

New Zealand 26			REFEREES	Jared Maxwell, Gavin Morris

New Zealand 26

TRIES	Johnson 2; Taylor, Vatuvei, Mannering
GOALS	Maloney 3/5

Gold Coast 6

TRY	O'Dwyer
GOAL	Prince 1/1

REFEREES	Jared Maxwell, Gavin Morris
CROWD	12,915
votes	3. **Friend** Warriors
	2. **Johnson** Warriors
	1. **Mannering** Warriors

Everyone's feeling alright

St George Illawarra Dragons *versus* Manly Sea Eagles
7.30pm, Saturday, 24 March
WIN Jubilee Oval, Sydney

NIALL CONNOLLY

IT'S A PERFECT EVENING TO WATCH A GAME OF RUGBY LEAGUE. I am three rows back from the southern fence between the goalposts and the right corner post (which wobbles theatrically in the gentle evening breeze like those inflatable air dancers you sometimes see outside car dealerships). To my left and behind me the sun is slowly receding. I'm glad I've brought my sunglasses and I tilt the brim of my hat a little rakishly against the warm glare. The grass on the field is thick, crisply cut and washes a vibrant green in the twilight.

It is a delight to take the weight off my feet and feel the refreshment delivered by my cup of beer. I am a pilgrim today and have taken it upon myself to walk to the cathedral from Leichhardt, over the Cooks River and down the Princes Highway to the reassuring vista of the ground's light towers.

On the field the Manly Toyota Cup boys make a good fist of losing an entertaining game, finally going down 26-24 while the floodlights on their corner pedestals slowly flare, like theatre footlights, to eclipse the waning sun. I feel an enthralling, liberating immediacy being so close to the action. TV broadcasts seem carefully choreographed and sterile by comparison.

Manly skip to an encouraging early lead.

One of the Dragons boys fires up his teammates as they wait in a cluster for the conversion attempt. "No one drop your head," he says with a galvanising urgency. No one drops their head. No one does. When the NRL players come out to warm up my immediate impression is that these are professional athletes. Brett Morris seems to float in the air forever as he leaps to catch a ball.

I am sitting in the away-supporters bay. I was here many years ago, before the impressive renovations, with my brother Paul (who is a Dragons Roundhead to my Manly Cavalier). Our family war has been civil in the positive sense (at least on the surface). We have a very much no-sir-after-you approach to game day. I have 1996. Paul has nearly everything else. Manly haven't won away against the Dragons since 2003. So no bragging rights.

I left my home in a chaotic mess as I ransacked my drawers for something maroon, finding an old (and slightly musty it must be said) polo shirt that fitted the bill. I hope that my long lost tribe, many of whom are kitted out in authentic and expensive corporate gear, are happy to acknowledge me. If you go to a game as a supporter of one of the combatants, you want to be swallowed up by the occasion. You want to be both cast member and audience at the same time. Like me, you can come by yourself and not feel out of place. It's not the awkwardness of dining for one. Like Billy Joel's regular crowd in *Piano Man*, we all come to forget about life for a while. We sit at the bar, put bread in their jar and say "Man, what are you doing here?"

Behind me a concrete path winds in front of a broad sweep of grassy hill holding up a tightly packed congregation and choir. Clowns make squeaking balloon animals for children and there is a Big Red V man loping about on stilts. The St George Dragon makes an appearance on a scooter, shaking his fist with a mock aggression very much at odds with his affable and cartoonish mien. I resist the urge to give him a hug.

The game has speed and an absorbing intensity. In the end, four minutes from time and with Manly chasing six points, Jason Nightingale puts the result beyond doubt when he falls on a neat Ben Hornby kick into the in-goal to score in the corner.

Everybody leaves feeling alright. It's that sort of game.

St George Illawarra 17		REFEREES	Shayne Hayne, Adam Devcich
TRIES	Nightingale 2; Weyman	CROWD	7,893
GOALS	Soward 2/3	VOTES	**3. Soward** Dragons
FIELD GOAL	Soward		**2. Weyman** Dragons
Manly 6			**1. Cherry-Evans** Sea Eagles
TRY	D. Williams		
GOAL	Lyon 1/1		

Beware the Shark in Northern Waters

North Queensland Cowboys *versus* **Cronulla Sharks**
8.30pm, Saturday, 24 March
Dairy Farmers Stadium, Townsville

PETER HULTHEN

OTH TEAMS PREPARED FOR THIS MATCH COMING OFF GOOD WINS setting the game up to be a terrific contest. Unfortunately the weather was not kind on the night: the players had to contend with intermittent showers. This caused a few fans to stay away. It was only a few days after the tornado which ripped through the Townsville suburb of Vincent. Sad part of this was the destruction of the Centrals Tigers Rugby League clubhouse.

The difference between these two teams on the night was Paul Gallen. Once again he put in a sterling effort and can only be admired by those north of the border. After the game Johnathan Thurston even said that he regarded him as one of the world's best. During his 80-minute effort he made 248 metres in 25 runs with 11 tackle breaks and 35 tackles. Every coach would want one of him. He did all this while playing with a stomach bug and was vomiting at halftime.

Matty Bowen remarked after the game that anyone that good deserves a couple of spews. Usually playing at lock, Gallen moved into the front row and followed up a try-saving tackle on Cowboys halfback Ray Thompson with a try late in the game to break the 14-all deadlock.

Thurston was off the mark with his kicking, missing three attempts, which was quite upsetting for Cowboys fans while, at the other end, Todd Carney couldn't miss, landing four from four including an early penalty.

Matt Bowen was again spot on with a bomb putting Gavin Cooper over for a try in the sixteenth minute. The try was converted giving the Cowboys a 6-2 lead.

Scott and Tamou gained some good ground for the Cowboys but Scott had some trouble keeping hold of the ball. Bowen preferred the grubber when close to the line. Ash Graham dived on one resulting in a try which put the Cowboys ahead 10-2.

Bowen was placed on report for an alleged late hit on Shark Nathan Gardner.

Gardner later left the field with concussion after colliding with Brent Tate's knee.

The Sharks were down by eight points in the final minutes of the first half but scored two quick tries to stun the parochial crowd. Halfback Jeff Robson's grubber deflected off the goal post padding outwitting Thurston to allow Andrew Fifita to score.

At the 39th minute, Paul Gallen had three possessions in one set. Carney headed for the sideline and pushed the ball back inside for Pomeroy to score. The Sharks chose to run the ball a number of times, a ploy which proved successful, as the Cowboys always set for the anticipated kick down field.

The try by Gallen really set the Cowboys back. Cronulla stood up in defence and locked the Cowboys out until the final hooter.

A frustrated Neil Henry said his side didn't deserve the win after spurning so many opportunities. The Cowboys had 52 per cent of possession and made fewer errors than the Sharks, but could not convert this into a much-needed win to stay in the top four.

Coach Flanagan was elated with the defensive effort of the Sharks, especially in the last 10 minutes of the game as the Cowboys launched a number of attacks on their line and looked set to level the scores.

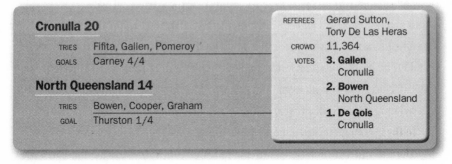

Cronulla 20		REFEREES	Gerard Sutton, Tony De Las Heras
TRIES	Fifita, Gallen, Pomeroy	CROWD	11,364
GOALS	Carney 4/4	VOTES	**3. Gallen** Cronulla
North Queensland 14			**2. Bowen** North Queensland
TRIES	Bowen, Cooper, Graham		**1. De Gois** Cronulla
GOAL	Thurston 1/4		

Slater(ed) for Immortality

Melbourne Storm *versus* **Sydney Roosters**
2pm, Sunday, 25 March
AAMI Stadium, Melbourne

MICHAEL GROSVENOR

THE WRITING WAS ON THE WALL FROM THE START. Once Billy Slater, Cameron Smith and Cooper Cronk safely negotiated the exit from the AAMI Park dressing rooms there was a feeling that the day was going to be a long and sorry one for Roosters fans. The Storm got off to a flyer, even by their lofty standards, thanks to the first of

Shaun Kenny-Dowall's many misreads in defence. Cut-out ball to Dane Nielsen, gaping hole left by SKD, try. Oh boy, a long day ahead alright.

Surprisingly, however, the game began to swing away from what looked to be a fairly predictable script. The Roosters started to climb back into the match: they had a perfect completion rate and started to dominate territory.

"Ah, steady on there," bellowed the men in pink. "We have some tip sheets that refs Bill and Stuart wrote for us some time ago ... you Chooks are an undisciplined rabble and you are not supposed to be playing with this much control so we'll have to start penalising you."

So, midway through the first half, the start of the dubious refereeing decisions began. They stymied any hope the Roosters had of getting back into the match.

Firstly, a great break down the left by Mitch Aubusson saw Boyd Cordner fall short of the line. The ensuing fifth tackle play broke down. Reason? The Storm were miles offside. Play on. The Storm ploughed up the other end where Kevin Proctor crashed over. But only after Todd Lowrie crashed into Boyd Cordner in a textbook case of obstruction. Not surprisingly, the video referee saw things differently. Storm 10, Roosters 0.

Given more of the possession, Melbourne were never going to be stopped. Or should I say Slater would not be stopped. Black Caviar – I mean Billy Slater - steamed onto an inside pass and sprinted away from Braith Anasta who looked like he'd already entered retirement. Storm 16-0.

In the lead-up to halftime, the Roosters tried desperately to score and looked to have done so through Sam Perrett after a brilliant passage of back-up play where Brad Takairangi showed superb vision. On closer inspection it appeared Perrett might have fumbled the ball after diving before the line. The vision wasn't clear and it seemed he should receive the benefit of the doubt. Of course, he didn't and it was halftime. Storm still 16-0.

Now I'd like to change the momentum of this article. Just like Brian Smith apparently did in the Roosters' dressing room at halftime. From the first set, it looked like the Roosters had sent on their SG Ball team as they were unrecognisable from the committed team that played the first half. Quickfire tries to Ryan Hoffman, Billy Slater (the first player in history to open the season with four straight doubles), Cooper Cronk and Will Chambers meant that a 50-plus scoreline was on the cards.

The Roosters were able to stem the tide briefly through Boyd Cordner's first-ever

NRL try, but then normal programming resumed with a final try to Cooper Cronk.

The Melbourne Storm looked thoroughly professional in support of their leading actor Billy Slater. They made almost no mistakes. It is hard to see them being beaten in this type of form.

And if Slater keeps this standard up, not only will he be considered the best fullback of all time, but one of the greats of the game ... dare I say an Immortal!

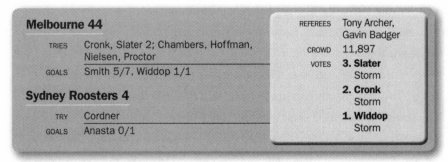

Melbourne 44		REFEREES	Tony Archer, Gavin Badger
TRIES	Cronk, Slater 2; Chambers, Hoffman, Nielsen, Proctor	CROWD	11,897
GOALS	Smith 5/7, Widdop 1/1	VOTES	**3. Slater** Storm
Sydney Roosters 4			**2. Cronk** Storm
TRY	Cordner		**1. Widdop** Storm
GOALS	Anasta 0/1		

Role reversal

Canterbury Bulldogs *versus* Newcastle Knights
3pm, Sunday, 25 March
ANZ Stadium, Sydney

DANIEL DWYER

THIS MATCH WAS EXPECTED TO FEATURE A NUMBER OF THINGS. One team that had struggled for consistency, made too many errors and failed to build pressure on their opposition, and the other, a team that could get into the grind, play field position and be patient in attack. This week, however, their roles were reversed.

The Bulldogs had been patchy in their wins over the Panthers and the Warriors but they had still managed enough moments of brilliance to get across the line. In their win over the Dragons they were clinical across the board. Against the Knights it was a new low with the only hint of a sparkle coming in the 78th minute when the game was truly over.

This was an important game for the Knights and Wayne Bennett. The work-in-progress explanation only satisfies if each week the fans can see some signs of improvement and, fortunately for Knights fans, this match had the hallmarks of a Wayne Bennett game plan. Minimise errors, minimise offloads, control field position and be patient.

From their first set of six, it was obvious that the Knights were prepared to get into a grind until opportunities arose, and it took just seven minutes before Richie Fa'aoso crashed over for the first four-pointer of the game. Five minutes later Trent Hodkinson went off with a knee injury and the Bulldogs never seemed to recover from that.

It would have been easy to blame the Bulldogs performance on the loss of Hodkinson but their real problem was their lack of respect for the ball. Cheap turnovers gave the Knights field position on too many occasions.

At the 18-minute mark, from close to the line, Jarrod Mullen chanced his hand and ran the ball, slicing past Dene Halatau and Ben Barba to extend the Knights' lead. Bennett moved Mullen to five-eighth to accommodate the early return of Kurt Gidley at halfback and it appeared to be a master stroke as the Knights dictated terms throughout the entire game. A lot of that could also be attributed to veteran Danny Buderus who, having returned from Leeds, looks every bit as influential as the game's best in Cameron Smith. He is, after all, 34. The combination of Gidley, Mullen and Buderus will only get stronger in the coming weeks and, based on Sunday's performance, wouldn't be a bad option for NSW.

The grind continued throughout the second half with the Knights kicking long and the Bulldogs hoping that something would happen. With 20 minutes to go the Bulldogs were awarded a penalty when Gidley crunched Michael Ennis well after he'd passed the ball and you got the feeling that if the Dogs were to mount a comeback, this was the time. The kick for touch saw the Dogs start their attack 30 metres out from the Knights' line but after the tap, Corey Payne dropped the ball before he'd reached the defensive line. Disaster. For me, that completely summed up the day for the Bulldogs. They had opportunities but every time they presented themselves they were gone just as quickly with a poor pass or a dropped ball. Just too many errors.

The Knights scored again in the 72nd minute through Alex McKinnon after what looked to be a forward pass from Gidley. That wrapped up the game. The chance to keep a second team scoreless remained but a late charge from the Dogs finally netted them a try to Joel Romelo. Steve Turner converted.

As a Knights fan I was really happy with the way we kept coming up in defence for the whole 80 minutes. Over the last couple of years we've definitely been found out through the middle of the field with the big forwards getting tired and leaving holes.

After watching this performance, I'm persuaded that Wayne has a plan and, if the team can stick to it, a top eight position beckons.

Newcastle 20			REFEREES	Ben Cummins, Phil Haines
TRIES	Fa'aoso, Mullen, McKinnon		CROWD	21,701
GOALS	Gidley 4/4		VOTES	**3. Buderus** Knights
Canterbury 6				**2. Mullen** Knights
TRY	Romelo			**1. Gidley** Knights
GOAL	Turner 1/1			

Tweeting the night away

Wests Tigers *versus* **Canberra Raiders**
7pm, Monday, 26 March
Campbelltown Sports Stadium, Sydney

STU WARREN

IT'S A SAD STATE OF AFFAIRS WHEN THE CLOSEST YOU CAN GET to televised rugby league on a Monday night is an *A Current Affair* beat-up on former Sharks star Andrew Ettingshausen. But this is Tasmania and even Channel Nine's five-minute character assassination of ET represents massive overexposure of the 13-man code in these parts.

If Victoria is Mexico to league lovers, the island state is something akin to Surinam, rarely visited and notably obscure.

So, just 30 minutes before kick-off at Campbelltown, I sat wondering how best to run an eye over the Tigers-Raiders contest. No Foxtel and no patience for a patchy internet stream of the radio broadcast equates to no live rugby league. Not fair!

And, then, with my best Gen-Y head firmly engaged and thanks to ten wonderful characters, all the updates and opinion I could ever hope for.

#NRLwstcan

Thank you, Twitter, for suddenly becoming the most helpful form of social media I've ever encountered. But, by God, don't people talk some shit online! Picking through the avalanche of pre-match tweets from twits across the country was no picnic.

@GhostofSirJoh harked back to days of yore with the memory of Mark the Magpie and had me thinking of Viktor the Viking and my own trips to Bruce Stadium during university days.

@Azsportza bemoaned the local mobile broadband coverage and promised his whinge would be his last for the night.

@TattsBet spruiked the Tigers as $1.42 favourites just before kick-off and, from there, it was time for the action.

Minutes after kick-off, and with the Raiders reportedly looking more like the Bulldogs than the Green Machine in an alternative strip, Wests were definitely having the better of things in the Twittersphere through weight of numbers alone.

And depending on whose tweet I trusted, the Raiders were robbed of an almost instant lead through a Beau Ryan trysaver and/or a spurned chance on their dangerous left edge.

But just minutes later, Josh McCrone went in for the visitors to deny @TrentKyle a winning first try-scorer ticket on Jack Wighton. Gareth Ellis hit a beautifully delayed ball to barge over and made it 6-6 after 13 minutes to leave both sets of fans happy with the opening exchanges.

And just when it seemed like a night of pure league was on the cards, the whistleblowers stepped in to award the Tigers a controversial four-pointer that prompted even self-confessed Wests fan @Russos1991 to label it a *#questionablecall*.

There was nothing questionable about the next scoring play, Jarrod Croker's 75-metre sprint to the line capping a length-of-the-field movement that saw the Tigers again coughing up points in the shadow of the break.

As a rule, not much happens during the halftime break of a regular season fixture. But on Twitter, that's clearly not the case.

The keyboard is the kettle of the 21st century, or so it seemed as 100+ tweets landed on my screen within moments of the half-time whistle.

Almost as quickly after the resumption, the Raiders were out to a six-point lead that grew like Jack's mythical beanstalk to a gargantuan 20 points as the half rolled on.

The Tigers snuck back with a converted score of their own as the contest petered out, but by then the proverbial bird had flown the coop and the ghost of the old Viking Viktor must have been high-fiving Odin way off in some far-flung Valhalla.

The Raiders are flying and the Tigers look pitiably toothless.

And doesn't the Twittersphere know it!

@TIMBOSS101   *The worst performance all year by the #Tigers so far.*

@tiger_claire   *Oh god, sympathy interviews now. SHUT UP.*

@GjoreJ   *Let's be honest, Tigers should be 0-4 right now. Favourites are they?*

@TheTrophyBox   *Missed Tackles. Raiders: 14 Tigers: 48*

@SoulRanch   *If I want to take a positive out if tonight, its 2 mins to get home from the pub as opposed to 1hr from c'town*

@C_Scotty   *Add the Tigers to the list of teams Parramatta wants to play*

And a final word from @AussieDudley to sum up the feelings of every Raiders diehard out there:

Woohoo! @RaidersCanberra Great Game!!!

Honey, we're getting drivethru and doing it twice!!!

#letsgoraiders #top8

Canberra 30		
TRIES	Croker 2; Campese, McCrone, Mataora	
GOALS	Croker 5/6	
Wests Tigers 16		
TRIES	Moltzen, Miller, Ellis	
GOALS	Marshall 2/3	

REFEREES	Jason Robinson, Brett Suttor
CROWD	14,388
VOTES	**3. Campese** Raiders
	2. Croker Raiders
	1. Robinson Raiders

Round 5

The roaring south

Melbourne Storm *versus*
Newcastle Knights
7.30pm, Friday, 30 March
AAMI Park, Melbourne

NATHAN BOSS

BEING A MEMBER OF THE RUGBY LEAGUE FRATERNITY IN MELBOURNE is as close as I will ever come to experiencing life as a bootlegger during prohibition. Forget your speakeasies and other artificial attempts to recreate this era, just spend a bit of time at the Imperial, the Limerick or any of the other rugby league affiliated public bars and you'll be lost in a secret world of nods, winks and underground rooms. The only difference being that the sweet elixir that we're consuming is the brilliance of Benji Marshall, the attitude of Paul Gallen and the dulcet tones of Darren Lockyer.

At these underground events I was fortunate enough to meet a collection of other rugby league addicts desperately struggling to deal with the demons created by lack of rugby league coverage in Melbourne. Some had taken to randomly tackling passers-by to get their fix. Others had begun taking to their faces with a staple gun in a bid to emulate great moments of Origins gone by. These fixes were nothing more than temporary, however, and by the weekend the league-starved junkies were salivating at the thought of the weekend's combat.

As such, I headed out to AAMI Park with a few other junkies to take in the exploits of the Storm and the Knights. Given the majority of my companions were Novocastrians, I gathered they already knew a thing or two about addiction.

The Storm were at their absolute best. I must admit that prior to this season I was well and truly on the *I-Hate-Melbourne* bandwagon. And while I still struggle to avoid the temptation to punch Craig Bellamy in the face, it's hard not to appreciate the brilliance of Slater, Cronk and Smith. This truly was Cooper Cronk's night who, after re-signing for the Storm for a modest amount and a small squadron of yachts, dominated the contest from start to finish. The Melbourne crowd was greatly appreciative of his talents, although this appreciation – of course – paled in comparison to the massive roar accompanying any of the regulation shots at goal.

The Newcastle faithful remained solid to the bitter end, however, with chants such as ONYA NEWWWWWWWWY reverberating throughout the stadium, while doing their best to avoid spilling beer on unruly Storm supporters. In the end, the Storm finished comfortable winners despite a late Knights comeback.

Relieved after their league fix, the crew adjourned to a nearby establishment to wet their whistle, where they were involved in an in-depth discussion surrounding the stamina, so to speak, of first grade rugby league coaches. But that's a story for another day.

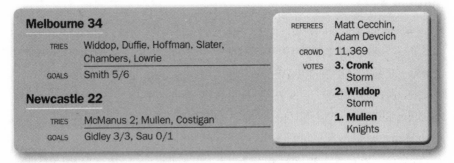

Melbourne 34				REFEREES	Matt Cecchin, Adam Devcich
	TRIES	Widdop, Duffie, Hoffman, Slater, Chambers, Lowrie		CROWD	11,369
				VOTES	**3. Cronk** Storm
	GOALS	Smith 5/6			**2. Widdop** Storm
Newcastle 22					**1. Mullen** Knights
	TRIES	McManus 2; Mullen, Costigan			
	GOALS	Gidley 3/3, Sau 0/1			

Where once was Wayne

Brisbane Broncos *versus* **St George Illawarra Dragons**
7.30pm, Friday, 30 March
Suncorp Stadium, Brisbane

MICK ADAMS

THANK GOD FOR ANDREW VOSS. That's not a statement I ever thought I would find myself typing, but after a month of ruined Friday nights courtesy of Ray Hadley's execrable commentary, it was a welcome relief to hear the dulcet tones of Vossy, everyone's 17th favourite sports-caller.

If, as has been suggested, Hadley is viewed as the long-term successor to Ray Warren, I will be starting up a fundraiser for Channel 10's TV rights bid. Donations welcome. I'll be putting in double if Darren Lockyer is also seen as a part of the future of Channel Nine's coverage. Wonderful player, great voice for print journalism.

To the game itself, and the dawn of a new era. Buried under the Cooper Cronk

non-event and the Robbie Farah/Matthew Johns beef this week was the observation
that this was to be the first Broncos-Dragons clash not involving Wayne Bennett.
A remarkable fact given the rich rivalry developed between the two teams in the last
quarter-century.

From "St George can't play" to the Gorden Tallis saga to the Broncos knocking the
Dragons out of the semi-finals in two of Bennett's three years at the Kogarah helm, this
was truly a fitting matchup for the NRL's Heritage Round.

It seems the Dragons' Michael Weyman also had an eye on history tonight. His
dropped ball and needless penalty in the opening 10 minutes suggested he was
applying for the "dumb front rower" position left vacant since Jason Ryles mercifully
departed. He made up for it a couple of minutes later, however, by flattening Matt
Gillett in a brutal hit-up. There's much of the old school in Weyman, and that was an
old school pole-axing. Brilliant stuff.

As it turns out, that proved the highlight of the first half for St George fans. The
Dragons were completely inept and clearly not up for the challenge presented by
the impressive Brisbane. If Melbourne's ominous form in the first month of the
competition suggests the 2012 premiership is theirs to lose, the time will surely come
for the young Broncos, who possess the best emerging talent in the competition. Not
that they had to do much – the Dragons were downright neighbourly in opening the
gates for the Broncos to run in four soft first-half tries, and when in possession, coughed
up more balls than Felix the Cat.

Come the second half, Dragons coach Steve Price made the wise decision to replace
the comedy troupe he sent out in the first half with a functioning NRL team. It was a
masterstroke which paid dividends 10 minutes in, Jason Nightingale acrobatically
crossing the line following some brilliant Jamie Soward play. The Dragons five-eighth is
always a threat when he takes the line on, and after going into his shell for much of last
season he appears to have regained his mojo.

Five minutes later the Dragons scored again, Ben Hornby's perfectly executed pass
allowing Kyle Stanley to slot through unopposed. In the lead up was a brilliant run
from Trent Merrin, who is bound for a Blue jersey based on what we've seen this year.

There will be a few of these Broncos being fitted up in Maroon too. At the top of
this list is Gillett, who was everywhere. After a spirited fightback from the Dragons,
who were superb in the second half, Gillett's try effectively ended the match as a contest
in the 70th minute. Dragons fans can take solace in the fact that it was the Kogarah-

bound Gerard Beale who conjured the try from nothing, chipping twice for the big lock forward to score in the corner.

And so an absorbing match ended with a 28-20 victory to the home team. On this evidence they will be thereabouts come September. The second half performance from the Dragons, however, suggests that, just as the Broncos have, they are ready to step out from the shadow of the man who – for the first time in 42 matches between these two great clubs – was not in attendance.

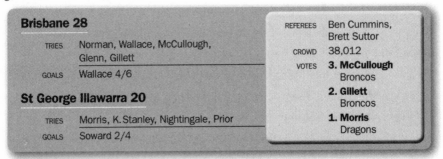

Brisbane 28

TRIES	Norman, Wallace, McCullough, Glenn, Gillett
GOALS	Wallace 4/6

St George Illawarra 20

TRIES	Morris, K. Stanley, Nightingale, Prior
GOALS	Soward 2/4

REFEREES	Ben Cummins, Brett Suttor
CROWD	38,012
VOTES	**3. McCullough** Broncos
	2. Gillett Broncos
	1. Morris Dragons

A lot to like on all sides

Penrith Panthers *versus* **Cronulla Sharks**
5.30pm, Saturday, 31 March
Centrebet Stadium, Sydney

PETER ABELA

WARM AND SUNNY CONDITIONS GREETED THE FAITHFUL. Penrith had lost five games at home on the trot. First set – the Sharks threw it wide on the fourth to get around the Panthers. From the ensuing bomb, they regathered and almost scored. Paul Gallen smashed Dayne Weston.

Travis Burns was penalised for being the third man in around the legs. Two or three tackles later, Jeremy Smith put his fellow second-rower Jayson Bukuya over for the opening try.

After 10 minutes, there were danger signs for Penrith with Cronulla making repeated inroads.

Another penalty in the 15th minute for a high shot on Carney.

The 18th minute, Cronulla's first error in their own half but Penrith themselves dropped it on the fifth.

The 20th minute, David Simmons caught a bomb and almost broke through. Penrith moved it quickly and advanced the ball almost 100 metres before Etu Uaisele was bundled into touch a couple of metres from Cronulla's line.

Scrum in the 24th minute, Lachlan Coote had the ball jarred loose inside his 20 on the first. Travis Burns went on with the tackle, giving up a penalty, which was converted by Todd Carney to extend the lead to 8-0.

The 29th minute, Lachlan Coote was unable to field a kick, knocking on 10 metres from his own line. It only took a few tackles for Wade Graham to cross against his former club, running off Paul Gallen to score the second try for the Sharks. Carney was unable to convert from the sideline, leaving the score at 12-0 after 32 minutes.

The 35th minute: Penrith went the length of the field for the second time but again failed to complete their set. David Simmons made a huge play to prevent a 40/20. Penrith made a break and were given a penalty when the back-pedalling Sharks lingered too long in the play-the-ball. The Panthers finally took advantage, Blake Austin sliding inside Ben Pomeroy off a well-weighted Travis Burns pass to score. Luke Walsh missed the conversion, leaving the halftime score at 12-4.

The 52nd minute: Penrith had dominated field position in the first part of the second half with nothing to show. Finally, Nathan Gardiner dropped a bomb with no-one near him right under his own goal posts. Penrith swung the ball first one way and then the other, a movement culminating in the fifth try of the season to Michael Jennings. Again Walsh was unable to convert from the corner, leaving the score at 12-8 after 54 minutes.

Some 60 minutes in, Kevin Kingston ran from dummy-half and split the Sharks defence. Lachlan Coote backed up to score under the posts, which was converted by Luke Walsh to put Penrith into the lead for the first time of the match.

Ben Pomeroy hit Sam McKendry in a big hit from the restart, knocking the ball free for a contentious knock on call.

For some reason, Penrith threw the ball around with gay abandon as they entered the final run. They dropped it, Cronulla scooped up a loose ball and from a lengthy play-the-ball, gave away a penalty to enable the Sharks to draw level at 14-14.

In the next set of six, the Sharks worked the ball forward before Carney kicked a 42-metre field goal from the blindside to enable the Sharks to regain the lead with only seven minutes remaining.

The 75th minute: Brad Tighe knocked on as Penrith looked to attack from their own half. Penrith had one last raid and when Jennings flashed down the sideline, a flicker of hope remained for the Panthers faithful. Burns had a shot at an equalising field goal, which went well wide. Simmons followed the kick through and attempted to force a try but the video ref correctly ruled him offside.

Luke Lewis made more than 50 tackles in his 200th game but it was to no avail.

Cronulla 15			REFEREES	Peter Kirby, Henry Perenara
TRIES	Bukuya, Fifita		CROWD	13,920
GOALS	Carney 3/4		VOTES	**3. Gallen** Sharks
FIELD GOAL	Carney			**2. Lewis** Panthers
Penrith 14				**1. Carney** Sharks
TRIES	Coote, Uaisele, Austin			
GOAL	Walsh 1/3			

Blue-and-Gold smiles ... at last!

Parramatta Eels *versus* **Manly Sea Eagles**
7.30pm, Saturday, 31 March
Parramatta Stadium, Sydney

ADAM MUYT

IT'D BE 35 OR 36 YEARS SINCE I LAST VENTURED to a Parra home game. That match, played at rickety old Cumberland at the height of the fierce Manly-Parra rivalry, remains vivid in my memory. Cumberland was chockers – most of the big crowd were Eels supporters naturally – and when Manly sealed a tight game with a try, I started blaring away on the brass bugle I carried with me to games back then.

That bugle hung around with me for a couple of seasons. My mates and I used to like sitting on the scoreboard hill at Brookie and once, innocently enough, I blew it close to halftime at an Under-23's match. The ref blew his whistle for halftime! A few minutes later a couple of ground attendants came up and told me not to do it again near the hooter or I'd be thrown out.

But I digress – back to Cumberland circa '76 or so. There I was, loudly displaying my Manly-ness, when a blue-and-gold draped teenager about my age whacked the front of the bugle with their open hand. Left me with bloodied lips and mouth. Yep, Parra girls back then didn't take kindly to noisy little pimply pricks from Manly.

I'm here tonight with Eddy, both at our first game since last year's Grand Final. I've told him about my last trip here – we laugh at the NO HORNS notice at the ticket booth.

"That's good news – she's no chance to get me again tonight."

Between the two of us we've travelled 1500 kilometres to link up for the match – he from Canberra, me from Hobart. Neither of us is cocky: Parra players may well lift in answer to all the criticism they've copped after their 0-4 start to the season. Plus Jarryd Hayne's back, and there's bound to be emotion floating about after Nathan Hindmarsh announced his retirement.

Manly's first month has been okay – some good play but without consistency. And some big names are missing. Looks good when we spot Steve Matai is back … then we notice Jamie Lyon missing. I try reassuring myself with thoughts of swings and roundabouts.

Parra get off to a flying start, literally, scoring a try from a high kick near the posts just five minutes in. And who else should it be taking to the air and plonking the ball down but their long-lost football weathervane, Jarryd Hayne himself.

Ten minutes later B. Stewart pulls the scoreboard back to evens after gathering a Matai kick and putting the ball down under the black dot. Phew.

Another try to Parra a few minutes later – Matt Keating strolls over from dummy-half far too easily.

And then Fuifui charges through but gets held up. The ball gets tossed wide quickly, finding young winger Jorge Taufua caught way too far infield. With a gimme overlap, Ken Sio scores in the corner. Chris Sandow's sideline conversion brings a huge roar from the Parra faithful, who are finally enjoying a decent display of footy by their boys.

Anthony Watmough goes over for a try a few minutes before oranges but Parra take a deserved 18-10 lead into the break. Ed and I take a deep sniff of changing footy winds, fickle as ever: we sense they can blow either way tonight.

Twenty minutes into the half and Manly are ahead 20-18 after tries to Taufua and Jamie Buhrer. The Parra fans around us are knotted – you sense them thinking: "Situation normal: Eels cause pain, yet again."

But then the game – and their mood – shifts gear completely. Hayne appears out of nowhere to score for the second time. And right under the posts. 24-20. Two minutes later Hindmarsh raises a figurative roof with a huge hit on Brett Stewart. Game on.

Tense footy follows but with Sandow adding two penalty goals and a field goal, Parra close out the match to win 29-20.

Ed and I head out of the ground and, as we near the Parra Leagues Club, pass an old gate piece from Cumberland, now a memorial. An image of 'She-with-the-Hand' pops into my head.

"Well if you're here tonight, go on, make a big racket. You lot deserve it."

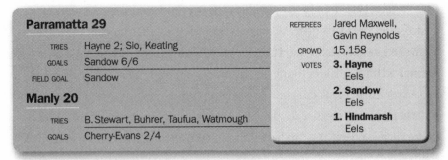

Parramatta 29			**REFEREES**	Jared Maxwell, Gavin Reynolds
TRIES	Hayne 2; Sio, Keating		CROWD	15,158
GOALS	Sandow 6/6		VOTES	**3. Hayne**
FIELD GOAL	Sandow			Eels
Manly 20				**2. Sandow**
				Eels
TRIES	B. Stewart, Buhrer, Taufua, Watmough			**1. Hindmarsh**
GOALS	Cherry-Evans 2/4			Eels

A local derby of sorts

Sydney Roosters *versus* New Zealand Warriors
7.30pm, Saturday, 31 March
Allianz Stadium, Sydney

CLIFF BINGHAM

IT IS DIGGING UP A WELL-WORN CLICHÉ TO SUGGEST THAT BONDI and its surrounds are littered with ex-pat Kiwis. This is despite the fact that, according to the 2006 Census, only 3.8 per cent of Bondi Beach residents were born in New Zealand. Perhaps they're all second-generation ex-pats these days. At any rate, urban folklore has it that the airport transfer lounges for flights from Auckland to Sydney are far busier than the return legs.

All of which brings me to James Maloney. Beginning his career at Wentworthville in 2008, he spent 2009 learning at the feet of Craig Bellamy in Melbourne before gaining a regular first grade gig with the Warriors in 2010. Auckland is rarely the first place that New South Wales selectors look for their five-eighths though and with the lure of the Bondi lifestyle and Roosters' chequebook too much to resist, Maloney will be sitting in that packed transfer lounge at season's end, a three-year deal with the Tricolours having been inked for 2013.

The position of Maloney made this the most intriguing Roosters versus Warriors match since their 2002 Grand Final encounter. That premiership decider was most famous for an accidental head clash (claim Warrior fans) or deliberate headbutt (in the eyes of Roosters fans) between Richard Villasanti and Brad Fittler. Adrian Morley shortened Villasanti up with a crunching tackle shortly thereafter and the Roosters reasserted their authority, going on to a convincing 30-8 victory.

My primary question that didn't involve the words 'James Maloney' went to who were the most likely suspects if this 2012 encounter was to get as fierce as its predecessor a decade earlier. Jared Waerea-Hargreaves was the prohibitive favourite to be involved for the home team; a Kiwi native plying his trade in Sydney these days. Funny that. For the visitors the market was more open, with Sione Lousi and Russell Packer topping the bookies' charts.

The game itself was one-way traffic in the end. The Roosters jumped out to 16-0 in the first half-hour with tries to Shaun Kenny-Dowall, Mitch Aubusson and Anthony Mitchell. Jerome Ropati scored in the 35th minute to get the Warriors on the board and when Glen Fisiiahi crossed with just over 20 minutes to go, the WARRIORS! WARRIORS! chant reverberated around the ground, affirming my view that Kiwis (ex-pat or otherwise) have a special bond with the east of Sydney.

That would be as close as the visitors got though, with Waerea-Hargreaves, Martin Kennedy and Frank-Paul Nuuausala (another Kiwi turning out for the red, white and blue) providing no shortage of punishing defence. A late try to Anthony Minichiello iced the cake, but the game had already been signed, sealed and delivered.

Warriors fans went home unhappy and concerned about their slow 2-3 start to the season; some had hours of travel across the Tasman Sea ahead of them, while others were already minutes away from their front door or, at the very least, the Coogee Bay Hotel.

What of James Maloney? Aside from setting up the try for Ropati, he had a quiet game. Roosters' fans may not have seen a glittering glimpse of their future in 2013 and beyond, yet you get the impression they went home completely satisfied nonetheless. They, better than anyone else, understand that Auckland and Bondi are much closer than you might think.

Sydney Roosters 26		REFEREES	Tony Archer, Tony De Las Heras
TRIES	Kenny-Dowall, Aubusson, Mitchell, Minichiello	CROWD	13,021
GOALS	Anasta 5/7	VOTES	**3. Kennedy** Roosters
New Zealand 8			**2. Waerea-Hargreaves** Roosters
TRIES	Ropati, Fisiiahi		**1. Minichiello** Roosters
GOALS	Maloney 0/2		

Worth every cent

Gold Coast Titans *versus* Canterbury Bulldogs
2pm, Sunday, 1 April
Skilled Stadium, Gold Coast

MATT O'HANLON

BLOODY NORA. IT HAD BEEN NORA'S 40-SOMETHINGTH birthday party the previous night. A long, hard night of fancy dress, karaoke, pina coladas for The Golden Girl, and Stella for me. Sunday morning and Gee Squared wasn't traveling well.

Looked like I was on my own at the footy.

I was a bit dusty myself.

I checked in with The Flame – Nora's other half – but he was in no state. I was buying tickets, anyway; I feel obliged to make a contribution to an ailing franchise.

Skilled Stadium is a great venue. But the meandering walk in the Gold Coast sunshine has its impact. I had a fair sweat up by the time I lobbed. Straight to the ticket office and $46 later I was solo in the western stand. Ready.

I learn Prince is in for Rankin, Idris still out. The ground looks a picture and the crowd is building in anticipation as the Titans have not lost to Canterbury at this venue. Coming off three losses and the week's crook financial news, however, the Titans have their concerns.

Canterbury-Bankstown had just had their paws trimmed by Newcastle who have taken to Bennett's methodical approach, and Hasler was sure to have his Dogs barking at shadows.

The Titans post an early try when Bird pecks the crumbs of a Prince bomb and, soon after, the player everyone loves to hate – Ennis – drops a ball cold and Lawrence cannot believe his luck, running 55m to score. 10-0 Titans. It is looking like another boilover in a round of boilovers.

My stomach tells me it's time for a pie. Good luck – quick service and a XXXX Gold (in a plastic cup). The pie and sauce is OK but the beer has bones in it. Canterbury play with width and a good ball from Keating to Pritchard then finds Barba on the inside. Rugby league poetry.

Prince delivers a magnificent kick-off, hitting the post, and his team regain the ball.

Tackle five sees a perfect Prince pass to Gordon. Try. The Prince conversion collects the upright. The Titans 14-6.

While Hasler is no doubt cranky with some aspects of Canterbury's play, their next try is again perfectly constructed. The enigmatic Pritchard drags his charges deep into the Titans right side before the ball is swung to the left. Crisp passing and a poor tackle have Reynolds back on his feet and in to score. There's contention in the crowd around me, but I enjoy the sweeping play. 14-10.

Again Prince collects the goal post on kick-off. A text from The Flame says that's a rare feat.

Then the play of the match. The brilliant Barba, using footwork, evasion, speed and guile engineers a 105-metre special ending with Morris scoring one for the highlight reel. 18-14.

At halftime I bump into an old mate, Rass Dancer, resplendent in his teal-coloured Cayman Islands Margaritaville T-shirt. He tells me how he spent a couple of hours in a Cayman bar giving a lesson to the locals on how we do it on the Coast. As an old Surfers Paradise Pirate, he is well proportioned for both comment and demonstration.

The second beer is better.

In the 53rd minute Myles scores a soft try to give hope to the Titans. However, an almost immediate and equally soft try to Pritchard gives Canterbury back the lead: 24-20.

A match-ending injury to Bird does not help the Titans cause, nor does the try with 13 minutes to go.

Slick passing to runners coming with good depth sees Turner score another excellent team try: 30-20.

The Titans' final chance to win is snuffed out by another Barba miracle, this time in defence. Bailey is set to score but is held up by the diminutive Barba, thus sealing the Titans' fate.

Canterbury, under Hasler's stewardship, will go a long way in this competition. The Titans were competitive but the absence of Idris is a worry. He is needed for both his skill and drawing power.

A pie, two beers and a try worth every bit of the entry fee made this a classic (hungover) Sunday arvo.

Canterbury 30			REFEREES	Gerard Sutton, Gavin Badger
TRIES	Barba, Reynolds, Morris, Pritchard, Turner		CROWD	14,344
GOALS	Turner 5/5		VOTES	**3. Barba** Bulldogs
Gold Coast 20				**2. Pritchard** Bulldogs
TRIES	Bird, Lawrence, Gordon, Myles			**1. Myles** Titans
GOALS	Prince 2/4			

Front-running Tigers felled by GI blues

Wests Tigers *versus* **South Sydney Rabbitohs**

3pm, Sunday, 1 April

Allianz Stadium, Sydney

JOHN CAMPBELL

IF THE LONG, LOW PASS FROM ISSAC LUKE AT DUMMY-HALF looked shonky, then Greg Inglis' drop-kick was as ugly as sin. But fickle fate's hand intervened at the death to feather the ball off the base of the left upright and over the crossbar to give South Sydney a pulsating 17-16 victory over Wests Tigers in extra-time.

Both sides arrived at Allianz Stadium on a balmy autumn arvo with only one win from their four starts. Another loss would see the 2012 campaign of one of the combatants drift further up that smelly creek without a paddle. By starting him on the interchange bench, coach Michael Maguire had publicly suggested that the Rabbitohs' man-mountain second rower Dave Taylor pull his finger out, while his counterpart Tim Sheens had opted for yet another halfback, Tom Humble, to play inside Benji Marshall, his champion five-eighth.

Wearing the spanking black-and-white of Western Suburbs, the largely forgotten half of the merger with Balmain, the Tigers struck in the second minute when, after a 40/20, Marshall made one of his typically mesmerising runs to put Tim Moltzen over untouched in the corner. The fullback's hubristic reaction to this gift suggested a cricket score looming, but there was no addition to the tally between then and halftime.

If anything, going to the sheds at 4-0 flattered the Bunnies. Like everybody else in the league world, they had come to the party believing that their opponent's forwards were soft and that it would be a simple case of running over the top of them. But the Tigers' pack, clearly stung by a week of criticism, dug their heels in and refused to follow the script. Souths, taking it up the guts without reward, showed that they had no Plan B.

Compounding the ineffectiveness of this approach, their tireless and always dangerous Pommy forward, Sam Burgess, was assisted from the field with a serious leg injury in the 24th minute. The Tigers, though playing the more adventurous footy, were nonetheless unable to build on their lead, relying too heavily on Marshall for inspiration.

With 'Coal Train' Taylor's presence, and perhaps sensing that they might profit by taking a wider route to the line, Souths began to work the edges of the ruck, but they did it as if they were doing unopposed training drills. Rattled by the swarming defence of Chris Lawrence and his fellow outside backs, Souths either put the ball on the deck under pressure or sold dumps to Inglis, Matt King and a butter-fingered Shaun Corrigan.

The second half proceeded with the same nerviness that had made the first 40 so tense. There was a game waiting to be unleashed, but the fear of losing was paramount in everyone's mind – including the mob in the outer, whose passion was a constant contributor to the unfolding drama.

It was the Rabbitohs who resumed the scoring and, not surprisingly, it was through a determined lunge from dummy-half Luke. The little bloke, so quick to assess a situation and act upon it, had been making ground every time he handled. Adam Reynolds' conversion attempt was unsuccessful, but if the Red-and-Green crew thought that the tide had turned, they were soon to be rocked by a brace of tries that put the home side ahead by 16-4 with the clock ticking down.

Marshall, drifting in and out of the action, asserted his visionary genius to send the space-making final pass (how does he make it look so easy and obvious?) to first a juggling Lote Tuqiri and then to interchange winger Blake Ayshford for converted tries and a 16-4 lead to the Tigers.

Game over, we all thought. Wrong.

With his socks around his ankles, the diminutive, irrepressible Luke took it upon himself to scamper over from dummy-half again. The extras from Reynolds made it 16-10, but Souths hadn't looked like winning all day, so who could possibly see them coming back with only two minutes left? The Coal Train, that's who.

Surging onto the ball in the south-west corner, he delicately chipped for his fleet-footed support. King and Andrew Everingham, one of the comp's genuine surprise packets, sprinted for the ball. Everingham got the bounce – fortune favours the willing

– and at 16-14 all we needed was for Reynolds to guide the conversion over from the sideline. He was never going to miss. It was 16-apiece and the unthinkable, the impossible, was about to happen.

In extra-time, Inglis' match-winning field goal showed us all – if we needed to be reminded – why we love the greatest game of all.

South Sydney 17		REFEREES	Shayne Hayne, Gavin Morris
TRIES	Luke 2; Everingham	CROWD	25,608
GOALS	Reynolds 2/3	VOTES	**3. Luke** Rabbitohs
FIELD GOAL	Inglis		**2. Taylor** Rabbitohs
Wests Tigers 16			**1. Asotasi** Rabbitohs
TRIES	Moltzen, Tuqiri, Ayshford		
GOALS	Marshall 2/3		

Mad Monday

Canberra Raiders *versus* North Queensland Cowboys
7pm, Monday, 2 April
Canberra Stadium, Canberra

MATT TEDESCHI

HAVE BEEN A CANBERRA RAIDERS FAN FOR AS LONG AS I CAN RECALL. I have some vague memories of cheering on Parramatta and their great halfback, Stu Galbraith, but it has always been Canberra. It may have started as a child when the Raiders were in a golden age. Then again, it may have been something as simple as liking the colour green. The reasoning is irrelevant. I am now, and will always be, a Canberra fan.

Life has never been easy following this team though. If you just so happen to be within earshot of me on game day, you'll realise that. You would almost have to be mad to follow such a team when they only make appearances in the finals every other year. And when we do, we inevitably suffer the heartache of witnessing the team eliminated through, say, a wayward Jarrod Croker penalty goal attempt from in front or a Jason Bulgarelli dropped ball over the tryline.

The disastrous 2011 provided only six victories and it was only a marginally superior points differential that kept us from winning the dreaded wooden spoon. This was a far cry from the extraordinary run of victories in 2010 that turned the Green

Machine into every rugby league fan's second team.

So now to Monday night. I was amidst Centrals' Mad Monday celebrations following a dominant 131-run victory in the ODCA 1st Grade Grand Final on Sunday. The Royal Hotel provided a great two days of celebrations but, as 7pm rolled around, the boys had either dispersed or reached a state of debilitating tiredness. It was still easy to muster up the excitement that always comes with watching my team run out each week.

The year had started like so many before, some great attacking prowess one week and the complete opposite the next. A 2-2 start to the year was very promising and, despite coming into Round 5 with a heavy injury toll, confidence was high. No Dugan, Shillington or Fensom lining up was concern enough but, after Reece Robinson's superb performance at the back against the Tigers and the return of Dane Tilse, we had some hope.

All that hope was quickly dashed when Johnathan Thurston discovered a major weakness in the Canberra defence, the left hand side. Once found out, he was relentless in targeting it. Local Orange boy Jack Wighton, Jarrod Croker and Bronson Harrison were the three responsible. One could be forgiven if you mistook them for Moe, Larry and Curly out there. But even The Stooges would have brought fewer laughs to a Cowboys supporter on Monday night than seeing these three clowns missing three tackles apiece. All four Cowboys tries came down their side.

I won't repeat the words I used about Wighton's performance, but he was likened to some of his predecessors, and not former heroes like Kenny Nagas, Noa Nadruku or Chicka Ferguson. His inept defensive reads and his obsession with trying to knock down the high ball instead of catching it were similar to the performance of a Daniel Vidot or Albert Fulivai. Hopefully he recovers from such a performance and plays as he did on debut. At the moment he is one injury away from a permanent first grade spot.

Eighty minutes later and I'm left to wonder how a team who played with such flair the week before could follow it up with this. Oh well, that is Rugby League, the game is over and there is always next week. What do we have to look forward to? Trying to avoid an 11th consecutive defeat in Sunday afternoon football.

North Queensland 22

TRIES	Graham 2; Tate, Thompson
GOALS	Thurston 3/4

Canberra 6

TRY	Mataora
GOAL	Croker 1/1

REFEREES	Steve Lyons, Chris James
CROWD	12,135
VOTES	**3. Thurston** Cowboys
	2. Linnett Cowboys
	1. Tamou Cowboys

Round 6

This time it's for real

South Sydney Rabbitohs
versus **Canterbury Bulldogs**

4pm, Friday, 6 April

ANZ Stadium, Sydney

LUKE CHARLTON

'LL TELL YOU RIGHT NOW THAT I'M A SOUTH SYDNEY SUPPORTER. I can't recall ever seeing another football team that has led its fans as astray the way Souths has these past few years. Since 2008 we have been privy to a charade. South Sydney haven't actually been a football team; they're just a bunch of dudes pretending to be one.

The only reason I can say this is because so far in 2012 we have seen behind the curtain. I think Friday's game against the Bulldogs was a perfect example. It was one of the best games of football I've watched all year. Maybe it was the perfect combination of sunshine mixed with public-holiday joy; fans were treated to a classic game of footy.

Both teams had a strategy: Souths kept the ball out of Ben Barba's hands; the Bulldogs played short and sharp down the middle. The difference was the Rabbitohs stuck to the game plan and the Bulldogs were brought unstuck by a 7-2 penalty count.

It was a total joy to see South Sydney competitive.

Logically speaking, Souths have been competing in the NRL since their return in 2002. The problem has been that their hearts have never really been in it. It has seemed like they were always at the dress rehearsal and not performing in the live act. As a spectator, now, it's such a boost to watch this year's team play the game from start to the end with what looks like a desire to compete for the whole 80 minutes.

Sure you could say that may not have happened in Round 1, but can you think of another occasion in 2012 where Souths weren't playing tough footy for the entire match? As a fan I honestly don't mind losing as long as my team seems hungry.

Can you honestly say you remember the last time that Souths were playing against a top four side (and potential Grand Final team) and they kept it close like they did against Canterbury-Bankstown?

I know this sounds like the ranting of some silly diehard Souths fan who will never see a Grand Final win in his lifetime. All I know is that this year, the only way Souths can be counted as a potential premiership threat is to stay competitive, no matter what the scoreline. It's called pride.

Friday's game was the start of good things at Redfern. You might have said that weeks ago but for me, grinding out a victory against a fantastic team like Canterbury is the end of the 10-year charade. The Rabbitohs have a few statements they need to make and they don't need words to say it. They need to win football games convincingly and they need to grind out wins against the teams who want that victory more than they do. Just like they did against the Tigers and exactly how they did it on Good Friday. Think about this hard South Sydney fans: I know you think you've seen this show before but this year Souths are performing at a different level.

Souths 20		REFEREES	Ben Cummins, Gavin Badger
TRIES	Everingham 2; King	CROWD	35,221
GOALS	Reynolds 4/4	VOTES	**3. Luke** Rabbitohs
Canterbury 10			**2. Reynolds** Rabbitohs
TRIES	Turner, Stagg		**1. Graham** Bulldogs
GOAL	Turner 1/2		

Bad Friday

Wests Tigers *versus* **Brisbane Broncos**
7.30pm, Friday, 6 April
Allianz Stadium, Sydney

NICK McGRATH

TIM MOLTZEN, MATT GROAT AND BEN TE'O. The Wests Tigers' 16-14 loss to the Brisbane Broncos on Friday night at Allianz Stadium, as a Tigers fan, was frustrating to say the least. But I'd hate to think what these three players took out of the clash. It's a game Moltzen would probably want to forget, a match Groat more than likely can't remember, and for Te'o, it's one that'll probably leave him scratching his head.

In the end, it was Brisbane who deserved to win the game. They took their chances and the Tigers didn't. And in rugby league, it's often as simple as that. But the Tigers never really gave themselves a chance. Poor execution, the feeble ruck defence Matt Johns labelled 'soft' earlier in the year, and Chris Heighington leaving the field with a broken hand after 20 minutes were all factors in this loss.

But the Black-and-Golds may as well have not had a fullback. Moltzen was non-existent. His communication with winger Beau Ryan in the bungled defusing of a Peter Wallace bomb was worse than Shane Watson's running between the wickets. Of course, letting the ball bounce led to Jack Reed's second try and a 10-0 lead for the visitors. At that stage of the contest, the Tigers were still in it, but Moltzen's night didn't get much better and neither did the Tigers'. The No.1 turfed another bomb and generally contributed nothing.

But it's fair to say Groat's night was even worse. The young front rower's head was lucky to still be on his shoulders following a shoulder charge gone wrong from Te'o. Te'o rocketed out of the defensive line and his shoulder hit Groat clean on the chin. Groat was out cold before he hit the ground.

I'm all for shoulder charges but when you get them wrong, you deserve to be banned. I've heard the shoulder charge called part of the game. Take it away and the game becomes soft. Please. Rugby league is a tough sport by definition. Players run hard and they tackle harder. It's the most gruelling collision sport in the world, and that's without big blokes throwing themselves around like uncontrollable missiles. Nowhere in rugby league is the shoulder charge needed. If anything, it lets your team down. How often do you see players attempt a shoulder charge only for the player with the ball to bounce off, gaining another 10 metres. Thank you, Matt Gillett and Chris Sandow.

Te'o's case at the judiciary has been called a test case for future shoulder charges that make contact with the head. If that is the case, then most others have little to worry about. The downgraded charge which netted the man they call 'The Terminator' just two weeks should see other hits escape with minor suspensions.

But neither Moltzen's bomb-defusing skills nor Groat leaving the field killed off the Tigers. What killed the Tigers was the if-you-score-30-points-we'll-score-32 mentality they have with the ball. Defence wins big games, and a match against the Broncos is a big game. Until the Tigers learn to hold their line and defend, a top eight berth is a long way off for the early season premiership favourites.

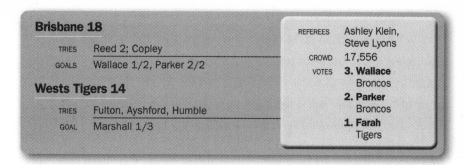

Brisbane 18

TRIES	Reed 2; Copley
GOALS	Wallace 1/2, Parker 2/2

Wests Tigers 14

TRIES	Fulton, Ayshford, Humble
GOAL	Marshall 1/3

REFEREES	Ashley Klein, Steve Lyons
CROWD	17,556
VOTES	**3. Wallace** Broncos
	2. Parker Broncos
	1. Farah Tigers

Another Titans loss

Gold Coast Titans *versus* **Sydney Roosters**

5.30pm, Saturday, 7 April

Skilled Park, Gold Coast

HUW FOWLES

'D BE LYING IF I SAID I WAS OVERLY ENTHUSIASTIC about starting my Saturday night off watching this game but I had promised a mate, a Gold Coast fan, who was away camping for the Easter long weekend that I'd send him regular match updates via text message and I stayed true.

07/04/12 17:28 Operation "Remember the Titans (are playing tonight and send me updates)" is ready for take-off, Johnno. Keep this channel open ...

What is it with the ongoing curse of sporting teams on the Gold Coast? Whether it's the short-lived existence of the local A-League team, the new AFL team struggling to get traction or a league team in serious debt and fast heading the way of the Giants, Seagulls and the Chargers before them, it's hard to fathom the sporting body blows this supposedly fast-growing region in Australia keeps taking. The Titans had lost $35 million and four straight games and were in dire need of an on-field win against a hit-and-miss Roosters outfit. A bold start was needed but Ash Harrison did his team a disservice early, dropping the ball in the opening set of six. And the Roosters soon made them pay.

07/04/12 17:44 Shaun and his brother Kenny Dowall have just scored. Roosters up 6-blot.

It was all too easy as Shaun Kenny-Dowall strolled through some lacklustre defence to put the first score on the board. But despite the apathetic start, the Titans began to improve and they started to string together some good hard sets of six.

07/04/12 17:52 Lovely try by David Mead. Titans back on even terms. 6 apiece.

Nate Myles pulled out all the stops against his old team. He was tireless in attack and defence. And he became playmaker in the 52nd minute throwing a wide bouncing forward's pass to Beau Champion, who found Luke O'Dwyer on the wrap around, who in turn put David Mead over untouched for the Titans' first points.

07/04/12 18:11 Halftime. Still 6-6. Tough but generally uninspiring footy.

07/04/12 18:25 HMAS Idris has just put one in the side of the Good Ship Anasta. Ouch!

Idris' inspiring pile-driver on Anasta in his own in-goal area along with an earlier smack down of Boyd Cordner set a positive tone early for the Titans in the second half. The Titans were making plenty of yards without troubling the scoreboard. Ashley Harrison's decision to use his teammate Steve Michaels as a deflector shield to put the ball down over the tryline proved to be an illegal manoeuvre. It relieved some pressure for the Chooks and they soon struck back hard.

07/04/12 18:32 Kenny-Dowall's done it again. Roosters 12-6.

Anasta (who had just bounced back from two serious creasings) combined well with Mitchell Pearce before putting through the grubber kick for the hyphenated Kiwi to swoop down on the ball and give the Roosters the lead again.

07/04/12 18:34 When it rains it pours. The Count is in under the black dot. Roosters 18-6.

Pearce, who looks to be keeping one eye on that No.7 jersey in the NSW Origin team, threw a cracking inside ball to Anthony Minichiello to score a second four-pointer in two minutes for the visitors. Gold Coast weren't helped by the fact that Idris was now in the sheds getting further treatment on that troublesome hammy of his.

07/04/12 18:50 Goldie not dead yet. Mead is in again. 18-12.

A lovely ball from William Zillman put Mead over in the corner for the second in his brace of tries but time was fast running out for the Queensland team.

07/04/12 18:59 The Count defuses the last Prince bomb of the game. All over my friend. Roosters win 18-12.

One last-ditch push to take the game to extra-time ended with Minichiello snaffling the last play of the game from Prince just a metre out from his own tryline. Job done for the Roosters. The Titans are consigned to their fifth straight loss and their worst ever start to a season.

To paraphrase the great darts commentator Sid Waddell, they might be showing *Australia's Funniest Home Videos* on Channel Nine but if you want real tragedy and comedy, on and off the field, tune in to watch the next chapter of the Gold Coast Titans saga.

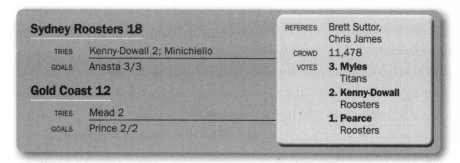

Sydney Roosters 18

TRIES	Kenny-Dowall 2; Minichiello
GOALS	Anasta 3/3

Gold Coast 12

TRIES	Mead 2
GOALS	Prince 2/2

REFEREES	Brett Suttor, Chris James
CROWD	11,478
VOTES	**3. Myles** Titans
	2. Kenny-Dowall Roosters
	1. Pearce Roosters

Shark season

Cronulla Sharks *versus* **St George Illawarra Dragons**
7.30pm, Saturday, 7 April
Toyota Stadium, Sydney
GLEN HUMPHRIES

MANY DRAGONS FANS CARRY AN INTENSE HATRED OF THE CRONULLA SHARKS. They refer to "little brother" as The Scum, their home ground as Scum Park and their fans as gap-toothed mouth-breathers. They mock the lack of premiership success with a chant that goes 45 YEARS AND WON FUCK-ALL.

But, as a Dragons fan, I don't get the intense hatred for the Sharks. I mean, what is there to hate beyond the fact the Sharks were brought into existence by carving a wedge out of St George territory back in 1967? That was 10 years before I started supporting the Dragons, so I'm hardly going to get my nose out of joint over that. Me, I prefer to invest my hatred in teams that have deprived me of something, like a Grand Final win. So I hate the Broncos, the Dogs, the Sea Eagles and (like apparently every decent footy fan) the Storm.

But the Sharks? What have they ever done to me? They're so seldom present at the pointy end of the season that it actually seems churlish to despise them. Yes, they do have a tendency to lift for local derbies at Endeavour Field but in the bigger picture the Sharks haven't really mattered much.

They've made an attempt to reverse that reality this season with a few wise purchases in the form of Tigers forwards Bryce Gibbs and Andrew Fifita and five-eighth and ticking time-bomb Todd Carney (and I'm still expecting Carney to implode at some stage this season).

On holidays down the South Coast with my brother and his family, we headed to the local club to watch this match. Things didn't start well when, in the seventh minute, Ben Hornby came in to make a two-man tackle but failed to shut down the offload. So, with an overlap, the Sharks flung a few quick passes and found themselves racing downfield, with John Morris capping things off with a try.

And that was the cue for a small but vocal crowd of Sharks fans at the club to let their presence be known.

Todd 'Tick, Tick' Carney slotted the conversion for a 6-0 lead. With their tails up, the Sharks began swarming in defence, at times overwhelming the Dragons. Defensively, they seemed very composed, repelling attacking raids easily. In fact, the only time we got over the line in the half was at the 20-minute mark, when Mitch Rein was held up.

Still, at the halftime break, I was full of confidence, reasoning that the Sharks would be disappointed they hadn't taken advantage of their domination.

The confidence levels dropped in the first tackle of the second half, when Michael Weyman knocked on at the play-the-ball. They went up five minutes later when Dean Young got over the line. Then they went down again when the ball was knocked loose. It went down a bit more when Fifita burst through and dropped even further 10 minutes later when Wade Graham pounced on a Jeff Robson grubber and steamed into a massive hole on our line to score.

There was a ray of hope when, in the 65th minute Jason Nightingale crossed in the corner. But that hope was dashed when video ref Russell 'Replay' Smith came up with the astonishing ruling that Nighty had put a foot into touch when no replay showed any such thing. At best it was a try – at worst a benefit-of-the-doubt call.

We get that try and ... well, we'd probably still have lost. The way the Sharks were defending, it would have been unlikely we'd have been able to find another try with just over 10 minutes on the clock.

My brother and I left the club to the vocal Sharks patrons singing the team victory song. Very loudly. Until they got to the fifth line when, realising they didn't know the words, started mumbling in tune until they reached the last line, which they did remember.

They might need to learn the words because they'll probably get a few more chances to sing it this year. At least until 'Tick, Tick' Carney implodes.

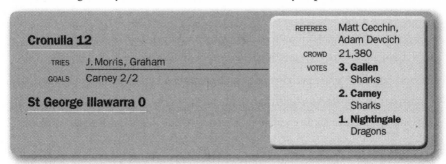

Cronulla 12	
TRIES	J. Morris, Graham
GOALS	Carney 2/2
St George Illawarra 0	

REFEREES Matt Cecchin, Adam Devcich
CROWD 21,380
VOTES **3. Gallen**
Sharks
2. Carney
Sharks
1. Nightingale
Dragons

Glory days

Canberra Raiders *versus* New Zealand Warriors
2pm, Sunday, 8 April
Canberra Stadium, Canberra

TIM NAPPER

"Who's taken it? It's loose. Picked up by Daley, Daley's given it on to Ferguson; Ferguson goes
for the line – a try! Oh can you believe this? Chicka Ferguson has scored alongside the posts."
Winfield Cup Grand Final, 1989, IAN MAURICE

THAT WAS THE MOMENT EVERY RAIDERS FAN IN AUSTRALIA ROARED. That was the moment the Raiders squared the Grand Final at 14-14. It was the moment – for the first time in rugby league history – that a non-Sydney team threatened to win the premiership.

And then, it happened: Steve Jackson scored his first try in first grade, breaking seven tackles (count them) and dragging three Balmain players over the line – in extra-time – for possibly the toughest try in Grand Final history. In the words of commentator Graeme Hughes:

I didn't think there was any way he was going to make it, but he did. What strength, what power, what a Grand Final, what a premiership! The Canberra Raiders have done the impossible. The Canberra Raiders have won the Winfield Cup.

It was the try that broke Balmain's heart. It was the day that cast a pall over the Sydney papers. WINFIELD CUP BROKEN lamented the headlines (admittedly, after Laurie Daley dropped the trophy off the back of a car): not a word of congratulations from the media in Sydney to the victors down south.

It was also the start of an era, of the glory days of the Canberra Raiders who became arguably the most dominant team in the competition for seven years, from 1989 to 1996. The Canberra Raiders won three premierships in that period and were runners-up another year. They made the finals every year except 1992. They had the most devastating halves combination (Stuart/Daley), the best lock (Bradley Clyde) and the most powerful centre in the game (Mal Meninga).

Those were the days I worked as a barman at the Raiders' Leagues Club, picking up ashtrays, pouring drinks, and watching my idols – Clyde, Meninga, Belcher – sinking beers late on a Sunday night in a club bursting at the seams with supporters and community spirit. Those were the days.

Which brings us to today.

Today I'm at the Raiders-Warriors game, Round 6. The Green Machine has been dominant, showing flashes of brilliance on the way to a 32-12 victory. David Shillington, (14 hit-ups, 150 metres gained), Tom Learoyd-Lahrs (10 hit-ups, 17 tackles) and Josh Papalii (nine hit-ups, 28 tackles) showed heart, while Reece Robinson (two tries) proved an able replacement for Josh Dugan at fullback. Jarrod Croker (2/7) needs to learn how to bloody kick.

But the flashes of brilliance were just that: mere flashes. And the win, while complete, was not convincing. The Warriors had opportunities but were too inept to take them.

The crowd was willing, but – on a warm autumn day (a rare event indeed in Canberra) – also disappointing. The 'Raiders Army', a group of supporters that has occupied Bay 72 since 2002, wasn't at the game. They disbanded last year. They quit because, while strongly supportive of the team, they'd become disillusioned with management.

The glory days for the Raiders are long gone, and the years since have witnessed a long, steady decline. A decay perhaps best summed up by Raiders Board Member John Mackay, who, after the club decided to extend David Furner's contract to 2014 said:

> If we had a choice between David and someone who was there to win games and nothing else, we'd have David every time. He'd have to lose another 30 games ... He has my support and the board's support, which runs deeper than a losing streak.

It'd be hard to think of a sentence that could show less respect for fans of the Raiders. Sure, all true fans should be prepared to stick by the Green Machine through good times and bad. But those fans are entitled to expect the club to place the team and its supporters at the centre of all decisions, not the connections of one individual.

I go back from time to time and watch replays of the 1989 Grand Final. I have to. It'll be a long time before I see my boys there again.

Canberra 32		REFEREES	Shayne Hayne, Alan Shortall
TRIES	Robinson, Croker 2; Ferguson, Wighton, Papalii	CROWD	10,800
GOALS	Croker 2/7	VOTES	**3. Robinson** Raiders
New Zealand 12			**2. Shillington** Raiders
TRIES	Henry, Maloney		**1. Learoyd-Lahrs** Raiders
GOALS	Maloney 2/2		

One forgettable Easter

Newcastle Knights *versus* **Parramatta Eels**
3pm, Sunday, 8 April
Hunter Stadium, Newcastle

MICHAEL KENNEDY

D O YOU REMEMBER WHERE YOU WERE ON THE NIGHT OF 30 SEPTEMBER 2001? I do. I was in a small hotel room in Lorne, as part of a road trip along the unforgiving Victorian coastline. It was also the date of the very first Grand Final played at night (an experiment as bizarre as renaming Vegemite 'iSnack 2.0', and nearly as bizarre as giving Kyle Sandilands his own TV show). The Knights ultimately defeated the Eels by six measly points, but had blown them away in the first half with a 24-point blitz. It was a dark day. Some eleven years later, I'm hoping the Eels can claim both victory and a vestige of vengeance.

With the Knights celebrating 25 years in the competition, setting up their own hall of fame (no mention of a round table), playing at home where a win was long overdue, and having a ref at Hunter named Archer, the odds (and evens) were against the Eels before they hit the field.

Like a couple of shy pillow-fighters, the teams sparred gently until the home team crossed over for the softest of tries. Three Eels defenders, having fallen asleep, forgot to wrap the ball up, allowing a simple pass to an unmarked Akuila Uate (whose name really does pay homage to the vowel). The try was converted and a subsequent penalty right in front stretched the lead to eight.

What followed was a 15-minute period in which the Eels had a wealth of possession squandered by a dearth of passion and purpose. Hayne was trying, but with a knee joint dodgier than a Sydney Casino deal, he struggled just to stay afloat. The Eels attack was directionless and, when Mannah failed to play the ball properly for the second time, I thought I was watching the reserve grade team. Just as I was about to suggest whips, wax, and water-boarding at Eels' training next week, Mannah redeemed himself by barging over close to the line and opening the Eels' tally in the 34th minute.

At 8-6 down at halftime, the Eels were, remarkably, still in the contest.

The Eels' plan (and I use the term 'plan' loosely) for the second half seemed to be to get through to the fifth tackle, chip the ball towards the goal posts and hope for the best. After a half-dozen cracks at this, surely it was time to cash in the chips and move on to another play. The lack of imagination and flair was obvious, although the Knights were not exactly at their jousting best either.

The Knights started slowly in the second half, but a telling 40/20 by Mullen aroused the Knights just enough for Uate to score his second. There was to be no miraculous resurrection for the Eels.

Sadly, from that point on there really was next to nothing to report, as the game was unadulterated awfulness. In fact, if humans were to showcase rugby league to a panel of visiting extra-terrestrials, one would certainly not be putting this one forward. It was uglier than a pugilistic pug. All tapes (or is it digital recordings now) of this game should be systematically and immediately erased.

The Knights did hold on to claim the two points but against any other team they would have been thrashed on the day. Bennett has his work cut out for him, while Kearney will be happy just to have work. Or maybe not – it's hard to see how any coach could salvage the Eels' season from here.

So, no victory today and if vengeance is sweet, it's probably lucky for me that I have a large chocolate egg to fill the void.

Newcastle 14		REFEREES	Tony Archer, Tony De Las Heras
TRIES	Uate 2	CROWD	24,158
GOALS	Roberts 3/3	VOTES	**3. Mullen** Knights
Parramatta 6			**2. Uate** Knights
TRY	Mannah		**1. Roberts** Eels
GOAL	Sandow 1/1		

Storming home

North Queensland Cowboys *versus* **Melbourne Storm**
7pm, Sunday, 8 April
Dairy Farmers Stadium, Townsville

DAVE FLETCHER

A BUMPER CROWD OF THE COWBOYS FAITHFUL TURNED OUT IN IDEAL CONDITIONS for their team's Easter Sunday matchup against the form side, the Melbourne Storm. It wouldn't require a painstaking study of the form guide to conclude that the home side would face a tough challenge against their southern counterparts. Melbourne, in scintillating touch, remained undefeated for the season with their bedrock of swarming, disciplined defence, and brilliant attack led by Smith, Slater and Cronk.

North Queensland, by comparison, has had an inconsistent start to its 2012 campaign. The heavily scrutinised switch to five-eighth of the game's best halfback has yielded signs of possibility and remains very much a work-in-progress. The main issue is in Thurston's defence. His tendency to pursue the ball at defensive pivot, positioning himself at the penultimate point in the line, often results in him being the man who attempts – and misses – the penultimate tackle.

Mat Rogers' taunt a few seasons back that Thurston was a 'turnstile' in defence has come back to us Cowboys fans in 2012.

But to be fair on the champion playmaker, Cowboys' line defence across the park has long been short of the premiership-winning standard, and particularly brittle out wide. If the Cowboys were to have any chance in this match, they needed to make an immediate impact with their brilliant attacking raids and hold out the inevitable Melbourne counter-attack with some committed defence.

The first try of the match suggested the Cowboys might do just that. Aaron Payne, in his 200th game for the club, executed a brilliant sleight-of-hand play to set up a try for fullback Matty Bowen. But again it was the Cowboys' defence out wide that resulted in a soft counter-attack try shortly after, with the Storm keeping the ball in hand on the left for winger Matt Duffie to stroll over virtually untouched by a staggered Cowboys line.

After this initial trading of body blows, the teams tested each other in the middle of the park. Some feverish attacking sets and impressive defensive displays from both sides suggested that the remainder of the match could be high-quality and, surprisingly, low-scoring – an arm-wrestle between two sides worthy of being in the top four on the table.

This impression, however, was short-lived. Melbourne's big three once again began to show why they are head and shoulders above any combination in the comp at the moment. The Cowboys' poor attempt to shut down a Slater kick return produced a line break that had the Cowboys back-pedalling. From this, the big men were not fast enough to regroup and the Smith/Cronk combination put rampaging forward Kevin Proctor in front of Thurston, isolated on the goalline. JT on his own was no match for Proctor.

Soon after, Cronk and Slater again combined to put Ryan Hinchcliffe over and take the score to 16-6 for the visitors.

After 25 minutes of matching it with the comp leaders, in a few moments things were beginning to look ominous for the home side. However, a determined Gavin Cooper raid just short of halftime took the Cowboys to 12 points and provided some hope going into the sheds. At least, it was enough hope for my mate to take the $2.70, a good price (he thought) with the margin at just four points.

Alas, the oddsmakers were (again) proven shrewd. Storm exploited some typical defensive lapses to pile on five tries to one after the break and run away with the match 42-18.

For Storm fans, the campaign north provided further affirmation that theirs is the team to beat for 2012. For the Cowboys faithful, it was another painful reminder that without a drastic improvement in their team's defence, they will once again be making up the numbers come finals time ... or worse, miss the playoffs altogether.

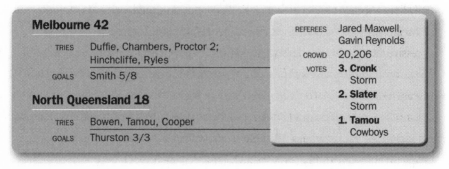

Melbourne 42

TRIES	Duffie, Chambers, Proctor 2; Hinchcliffe, Ryles
GOALS	Smith 5/8

North Queensland 18

TRIES	Bowen, Tamou, Cooper
GOALS	Thurston 3/3

REFEREES	Jared Maxwell, Gavin Reynolds
CROWD	20,206
VOTES	**3. Cronk** Storm
	2. Slater Storm
	1. Tamou Cowboys

Bad moon rising for sloppy Panthers

Manly Sea Eagles *versus* Penrith Panthers
7pm, Monday, 9 April
Brookvale Oval, Sydney

LINDSEY CUTHBERTSON

I HAVE A CONFESSION TO MAKE. I didn't watch this game live. I was given the opportunity to watch John Fogerty rock out at Bluesfest at the same time as Manly and Penrith were due to lock horns, and to be perfectly honest, who would turn down an offer such as that?

I refused to look at any social media until I had returned to where I was staying and watched the recording of the match (bless you, technology). That's a tough challenge in this day and age but, from the outset of this match, I'm glad I made the sacrifice.

After five games away from Brookvale Oval to start the season, the Sea Eagles are back to their spiritual home against a Panthers team still smarting from their one-point defeat to the Sharks last week. And the away team looks sharp early – the problem is that the Panthers keep making a meal of the tryscoring opportunities that come their way.

First, winger Etu Uaisele knocks an attacking kick on from halfback Luke Walsh, then fullback Lachlan Coote knocks on after a Michael Jennings break. Not long afterwards Penrith's other winger, David Simmons, drops a Walsh bomb over the Manly line. Their first-half performance is full of promise, but lacking in execution.

Meanwhile, Manly work their way towards controlling the match through an impressive kicking game and strong set completions. Five-eighth Liam Foran, filling in for little brother Kieran, has a left boot on him that manages to guide the ball towards the grass more often than not.

Once Manly manage to get in an attacking area, they demonstrate how important it is to take your opportunities when they're presented to you. From a standing start, Jamie Buhrer strolls through some weak defence to score beneath the posts.

With Manly leading 8-0 at halftime, it's still anyone's game, but the beginning of the second stanza is a precursor of things to come. In the 42nd minute, Sea Eagles winger David Williams scores in the right-hand corner after a Penrith error inside their own half.

After Jamie Lyon makes up for his missed conversion with a penalty goal from directly in front and stretches the lead out to 14, the rest of the match belongs to halfback Daly Cherry-Evans.

I'm beginning to wonder if there's anything this guy can't do. In the one set of six, DCE picks up a Luke Walsh grubber on his own goalline, takes a hit-up like a front rower and then kicks Manly out of danger. He sets up a try to Steve Matai with a well-weighted grubber, boots a 40/20, makes a break on the Panthers goalline before passing wide to set up Williams' second, and then chips ahead for himself before Anthony Watmough picks up the spoils and gives the match its 30-0 score line. The young half is the shining light in a team that doesn't appear to have many dim spots in their lineup during the evening.

As for the Panthers, they will be wondering how the game may have had a different outcome if they could have only made the most of their early opportunities. Their second half is one that they will happily forget, but they didn't play as badly as the scoreline suggests ... well, at least in the first half anyway.

On reflection, perhaps the three straight losses by Manly leading into this game are something that benefit the chemistry of the team further down the road. They are still missing key players (add to that the late withdrawals tonight), and while it may have taken the younger, more inexperienced Sea Eagles players some time to stand up on their own and claim a win, their performances – be it Dean Whare, Liam Foran or Jamie Buhrer – significantly contributed to this victory.

People may say that the Sea Eagles are back after this victory, but the truth is that they never really went away. They rocked tonight – but whether it was better entertainment than watching Fogerty belt out his outstanding back catalogue is a debate for another time.

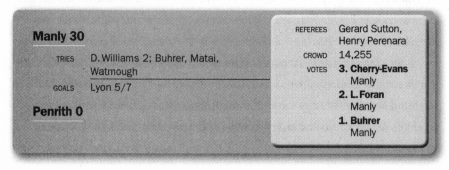

Manly 30

TRIES: D. Williams 2; Buhrer, Matai, Watmough
GOALS: Lyon 5/7

Penrith 0

REFEREES: Gerard Sutton, Henry Perenara
CROWD: 14,255
VOTES: 3. **Cherry-Evans** Manly
2. **L. Foran** Manly
1. **Buhrer** Manly

Round 7

Turncoat

St George Illawarra Dragons
versus **Newcastle Knights**
7.30pm, Friday, 13 April
WIN Jubilee Oval, Sydney

ARIANNA CANATO

Dear Wayne,

How's it going? You might remember me as one of your many (former) worshippers from the land of the big red V. The folks that used to cling to your every word and marvel at your legend and brilliance and all that it could bring us. A friendship that was exciting but, ultimately, short-lived.

You're gone now, but not without delivering all you promised, pissing off just in time for the fortress to start crumbling.

What have we been up to? Oh, you know, this and that. You might remember that in Round 1 we met briefly; us with a few minor changes but essentially still the same machine; you sporting new colours, a new army of believers and the look of a true sell-out.

I don't want to sound bitter (wait, yes I do) but let me be the first to tell you that the blue and red doesn't suit you one bit.

But we can't change what's happened. You wanted a new challenge, which is fair enough. Let me be the one to tell you that you're going to need all the luck in the world with the Knights if you're to maintain your esteemed record. They lack the depth, talent and mentality that was always present at the Dragons, something which you were able to develop and hone into what will be remembered as a stellar few seasons for the club and earned us that long-awaited premiership.

Of course I don't want to be too critical. Along the way you did help us out here and there. Yes, there's that premiership, you've taken a few players off our hands too, for which we can't thank you enough, and you've got us playing a style of football that can only be described as boring.

"It's not what I like to see, it's not what I like to coach but it's what's happening out there at the moment so there's not a lot players can do about it," you said.

So let me get this right. After three years of drilling the Dragons to play to their strengths with armour-like, match-winning defence, completing sets of six with a long and precise kicking game (plus occasionally using tactics such as kicking the ball dead to eliminate broken field running), you're denying your association with the style of play you've perfected and have outed yourself as a hypocrite? This is the stuff that wins you games. Since when did winning become boring, Wayne? Actually, hold that thought, because it's not something you'll have to get used to anytime soon.

You're right, in a way. The game started boringly enough. Your newest recruit Beau Scott dropped the ball cold (note: expect more of this once he receives his pay increase, like Chris Sandow and many before him), giving the Knights valuable possession, which they spread out wide with another of your signature plays, a sweeping move allowing Darius Boyd to put winger Akuila Uate in against feeble defence (please go back to Canberra, Daniel Vidot) once the clock entered double figures.

Shortly after, Scott made amends by spinning towards the tryline and planting the ball down, and in the very next set Jamie Soward produced one of the passes of the season to launch Brett Morris into space – a beautiful out-ball combining with Morris' acceleration and finishing with the best player in rugby league, Jason Nightingale, strolling over the line. It was beautiful to witness, almost too easy.

For the next 40 minutes the contest was dire. But with the scores so tight until the final siren and many opportunities created by both sides, it wasn't like the crowd were about to get in their cars and go home. Maybe you had something else on your mind, Wayne: a nap, or was it a tear in your eye as you remembered all that you've thrown away? It could've been great between us. But guess what, Wayne? We got the two points.

Sucked in,
ARIANNA CANATO

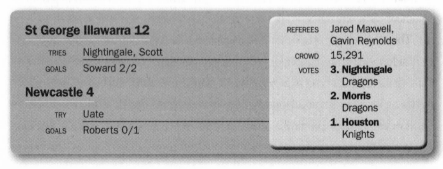

St George Illawarra 12		REFEREES	Jared Maxwell, Gavin Reynolds
TRIES	Nightingale, Scott	CROWD	15,291
GOALS	Soward 2/2	VOTES	**3. Nightingale** Dragons
Newcastle 4			**2. Morris** Dragons
TRY	Uate		**1. Houston** Knights
GOALS	Roberts 0/1		

Raiders at the Temple of Doom

Brisbane Broncos *versus* **Canberra Raiders**

7.30pm, Friday, 13 April

Suncorp Stadium, Brisbane

WILL EVANS

THE FIRST RUGBY LEAGUE MATCH I EVER SAW ON TELEVISION was a Lang Park clash between heavyweights Brisbane and Canberra in Round 14 of 1990. It was a classic and set me on a path to rugby league fanaticism. The Broncos surged to an 18-2 lead after 22 minutes on the back of the brilliance of Allan Langer, Kevin Walters and Gene Miles, but Mal Meninga and Ricky Stuart inspired a stirring fightback for the Raiders to lead 20-18 in the second half. A magnificent comeback victory for the defending premiers was foiled by a dazzling 50-metre try to Brisbane's mantis-man Paul Hauff, an emerging fullback. The home side – and my new heroes – got up 22-20.

The 2012 Broncos and Raiders don't have the superstars of the early '90s – pre-match focus is on the injury-enforced absence of Brisbane's linchpin, four-game NSW Origin halfback Peter Wallace, while injury-prone Canberra five-eighth and captain Terry Campese (who has represented the Blues in one Origin and Australia in one Test) has run into some form and holds the key to the visitors' chances. Tonight provides a valuable opportunity for the underrated Raiders to keep pace with the NRL's frontrunners.

It's a big night for my Canberra-born Kiwi mate Telly, too. A bunch of us bought him a Canberra jersey for his 30th birthday last year, but his wife Nic only lets him out of the house in the garish lime green for Raiders-related activities. One such occasion was the previous Sunday – we went to the pub and watched the rampant Raiders decimate the Warriors 32-12. Consequently, Telly fancies the Green Machine's chances at Suncorp Stadium.

There's typically a four-beer threshold before Telly starts reminiscing aloud about the Raiders' class of '94, and the chat about Daley, Mullins and Nagas arrived with the exact sip as the first tray of overpriced XXXX cups was polished off. An opportunity to duck off and collect tray No. 2 opened up when Brisbane fullback Josh Hoffman muffed a grubber from Canberra halfback Josh McCrone in the fifth minute. Second rower Joe Picker's effort to dive on the scraps earned a benefit-of-the-doubt try ruling and Telly fist-pumped his way to the bustling beer queue while Jarrod Croker lined up the conversion.

But the Broncos responded in the 17th minute when five-eighth Corey Norman combined with Wallace's replacement Ben Hunt, who sent skipper Sam Thaiday over for a four-pointer. Brisbane burst a tight first half wide open with three tries in the 12 minutes before the break – Ben Hannant and Matt Gillett forced their way over from close range, before interchange sensation Gillett produced a brilliant flick pass for Norman to dot down. Telly's annoyance at heading into halftime 20-6 down swiftly transformed into textbook anxiety as Campese – the Raiders' cursed skipper was carried off with a knee injury.

After the resumption, Raiders forward Joel Thompson was pinged for unleashing a swinging arm that connected only with teammate McCrone in one of the season's most bizarre penalties. Test centre Justin Hodges delivered the knockout blow for the Broncos a couple of minutes later, slicing through on halfway and finding Hunt backing up on the inside to score. The second half meandered along as the Broncos took the foot off the pedal and the Raiders were unable to muster any continuity in attack. Norman latched onto a kick from hooker Andrew McCullough to claim his second try and finish the scoring with 10 minutes on the clock.

Norman, the Broncos' much-talked-about replacement for the great Darren Lockyer, was a standout choice for man of the match. The 21-year-old has gradually asserted himself in the role with each start, while the young Broncos' fifth straight victory has the pundits entertaining thoughts of a seventh premiership for the club.

But the main talking point was the season-ending injury suffered by Campese and the nosedive the Raiders' 2012 prospects had just taken. Meanwhile, Telly could only take solace from the Friday-night beer buzz.

Pack that bright jersey away mate, maybe next year.

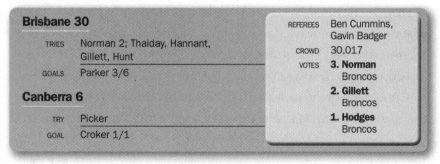

Brisbane 30		REFEREES	Ben Cummins, Gavin Badger
TRIES	Norman 2; Thaiday, Hannant, Gillett, Hunt	CROWD	30,017
GOALS	Parker 3/6	VOTES	**3. Norman** Broncos
Canberra 6			**2. Gillett** Broncos
TRY	Picker		**1. Hodges** Broncos
GOAL	Croker 1/1		

Old Opes

Melbourne Storm *versus* Canterbury Bulldogs
5.30pm, Saturday, 14 April
AAMI Park, Melbourne
NICK TEDESCHI

MISS CHRIS ANDERSON. Old Opes is my favourite rugby league figure.
When Canterbury and the Melbourne Storm do battle, it should be for the Chris Anderson Cup. Anderson is one of the great rugby league coaches, a champion of both clubs, whose old school approach brought premierships to each, making him one of only seven coaches in the long and storied history of the great game to win titles at two different clubs.

Other names on that list: Wayne Bennett, Jack Gibson, Phil Gould, Tim Sheens, Pony Halloway, Jimmy Craig.

Throw in a 22-3 Test ratio and Anderson has the record to rate as one of the top handful of coaches to ever have the reins in big time rugby league.

Wayne and Jack are the tops, no question. But on that level below – where the likes of Bellamy, Fulton, Gould and Sheens are often placed – should sit Chris Anderson.

Anderson was more than his exceptional record though. He was a coach with balls, an innovator and a hardhead who was fiercely loyal to his players and his principles.

His effort to guide Canterbury to the title in '95 was the finest coaching effort I have ever seen. The Bulldogs were mired mid-table for most of the season when the Four Traitors – Dean Pay, Jason Smith, Jim Dymock and Jarrod McCracken – turned their backs on the club and announced they were reneging on their contracts, taking Canterbury to court and joining the ARL and Parramatta.

I have never forgiven those bastards. Even though I came to like Jason Smith for his beer-swilling, cigarette-smoking ways and Jim Dymock did briefly coach the Dogs, I have never forgotten them for the treachery.

I did, luckily, get the pleasure of telling Dean Pay this. It was the opening of AAMI Park, the Test between Australia and New Zealand. I'd had plenty at the pre-game function and spotted Pay across the room. The poor bastard, cornered, offered me an apology, as I had demanded. He said he wasn't welcome back at the club. I took some joy in it. A certain bridge has been built – in my mind at least – with Pay.

It was a cathartic experience.

But I digress. Anderson. He pulled the team together for the most amazing finals run you could ever hope to see. He dropped McCracken, the Kiwi Test centre, believing he was dogging it, feigning an injury. He also saw him as the ring leader. Game over. McCracken never wore the blue and white again. The rest stayed but they were forced to do their penance.

Only a coach of Anderson's ability could get a team torn asunder together and get them to win four elimination finals games as massive outsiders in each.

His effort in 1999 with the Storm nearly matched that showing in '95. The Storm, in only their second season, shocked the rugby league world by going the distance. A stranger in a strange land, the boss in a rugby league outpost, Anderson pulled together a team of youngsters, cast-offs and aging stars to become the quickest team to win a title since the first year.

Anderson would have enjoyed the game on Saturday night between the two clubs where he built success. It was his style of football. Tough. Fierce. Smart. Uncompromising.

The Storm went into the match heavily favoured. Craig Bellamy called it though. He said it would be the Storm's stiffest test. It was. Des Hasler has Canterbury playing a tough brand of rugby league this year and the best indication of how far they have come in 2012 was how they managed to shut down Billy Slater, Cooper Cronk and Cameron Smith.

The Big Three had been killing it throughout 2012. They hardly got a look in against a gritty Bulldogs side who could have collected the points had they had a fit hooker or halfback. It was a gutsy showing.

This game was a grind, a test of strength, an old-fashioned slugfest where neither fighter would back down. This was Storm football. This was Bulldogs football. This was Chris Anderson football.

Melbourne 12

TRIES	Hinchcliffe, Hoffman
GOALS	Smith 2/2

Canterbury 6

TRY	Eastwood
GOAL	Turner 1/1

REFEREES Matt Cecchin, Adam Devcich
CROWD 14,192
VOTES **3. Hinchcliffe** Storm
2. Tolman Bulldogs
1. Morris Bulldogs

For King and country

Manly Sea Eagles *versus* Gold Coast Titans
7.30pm, Saturday, 14 April
Brookvale Oval, Sydney

LUKE JAMIESON

T HIS WAS MANLY'S ATTEMPT TO HONOUR JASON KING IN HIS 200TH GAME, being played at Fortress Brookvale, against the hapless Gold Coast Titans. They were also wearing Country Origin socks in a nod to grassroots rugby league.

The Silvertails were looking to equal an 11-in-a-row record at home. The Seagulls were on a five-game losing streak.

Not being a fan of either team, and in the case of Manly, like most normal fans, an often vocal opposer, I wasn't really expecting this game to get the juices flowing. What better way to generate some interest than by buying into the match with a punt?

The $1.36 on offer for Manly was money for jam, and thrown into a multi-bet for just that reason. The Friday night leg was already locked away. This game would be pleasurable for the simple fact that I would see my wallet get fatter before my very eyes.

Only a few minutes in it appears that it might not be all one-way traffic, as expected. 'Bull' Bailey taps and goes after a penalty on his own 40 in a bullocking run (seriously, that's the best adjective I could find here). Two plays later, he crashes over the Manly line, only to be held up. The early momentum is definitely going the way of the Chargers.

Ashley 'Handsome' Harrison flashes up on the screen for some unknown reason.

Down the other end there is a no try decision against Taufua. The decision is sent upstairs to former journeyman turned part-time DJ (probably) and video referee Paul Mellor, who promptly bats it back with the red light.

The Giants are making easy metres up the middle and the camera, panning to Glenn Stewart sitting solemnly in the stands, helps us join the dots as to why.

Pretty soon Aiden Sezer brushes past some weak DCE defence and plants down for his first meat pie in the top grade. Ben Ikin nearly pees his pants rattling off Toyota Cup stats trying to inform us that "I knew he was a prolific try scorer before anyone else did! Seriously, I picked him as a talent aaaaaages ago". *Shut up, Ben.*

The game grinds on and it becomes clearer that Manly are just not up for this.

"It's Kingy's 200th!" I can imagine none of them saying to each other.

"Let's do it for Kingy!" nobody screams.

The second half arrives. Scott Prince sets up more tries with kicks for his wingers. The luck is all with the Gold Coast. Manly are missing 'T-Rex' and 'Snake'. Why the hell did I bet on this game? Why didn't I know half of Manly's team were out? Shouldn't matter. The Titans are rubbish. This was money in the bank!

The match stats will show that Jamie Lyon, the pig hunter from Wee Waa, would score two tries and kick a few goals. What they won't show is that he comes up with a couple of simple errors towards the end of the game that put an end to any chance of Manly snatching what should have been victory.

I find myself amazed at the power that having a few dollars on a game has on me. How much energy I expend criticising every stupid play from Manly, every Paul Mellor decision from the video booth, every mistake from the pig hunter.

In the end though, the Titans just wanted it more and, in honour of Jason King, the Silvertails were just too slow, soft and lethargic. Harsh? Yep. Filthy? You bet.

Gold Coast 26			REFEREES	Jason Robinson, Tony De Las Heras
TRIES	Sezer, Idris, Gordon, Mead		CROWD	11,619
GOALS	Prince 5/6		VOTES	**3. Prince** Titans
Manly 14				**2 Bird** Titans
TRIES	Lyon 2			**1 Bailey** Titans
GOALS	Lyon 3/3			

Cowboys stampede

Sydney Roosters *versus* **North Queensland Cowboys**
7pm, Saturday, 14 April
TIO Stadium, Darwin

PAUL ROBERTSON

THE HIGHEST INDIVIDUAL HONOUR IN NORTHERN TERRITORY RUGBY LEAGUE is the Frank Johnson Medal and is awarded to the Best and Fairest player in the Darwin Rugby League.

Frank Johnson was a tireless servant of the game. Originally playing seniors for the Port Kembla Blacks in the Illawarra at the age of 16, he quickly established a reputation as one of the best young players on the South Coast. A wily rake, Johnson was peerless in the ancient art of ball-winning. Wearing his trademark headgear, he was never far from the ball in open play. In 1946 he was part of the first of the Southern Division teams to beat Great Britain.

Frank went on to play 23 games for St George, 118 for Newtown (whom he captained in his final years), five for NSW and toured with the Kangaroos in 1948. Coaching Newtown in 1953, he was persuaded to return from retirement in 1954, taking them to the Grand Final they lost to Souths, after which he finally retired for good.

Joining Wollongong Wests as coach in 1957, he took them to their maiden premiership in his first year. He was a founding member of the NSWRL coaching panel and became director of coaching in 1974. It was during this tenure with the panel that he answered the call for the development of league in the Territory and from 1970 to 1975 he coached the Darwin and Northern Territory teams.

With Frank at the helm, NT won matches against Western Australia in 1971, 1972 and 1974. He was honoured with life membership of the NSWRL and presented with an Order of Australia Medal. He passed away in 1993 and is rightly remembered as a man who fostered the great game in the Northern Territory, which receives its first game of top flight rugby league tonight in 17 years – the Roosters versus the Cowboys.

The previous venture into the Top End was 17 years ago when the Western Suburbs Magpies thrashed the Sydney Roosters 44-16. The Magpies team contained the likes of Andrew Leeds, Steve Georgallis, Cherry Mescia, Jim Serdaris and Paul Langmack and were coached by Tommy Raudonikis. The hapless Roosters included Luke Ricketson (at centre), Andrew Walker, Adrian Lam, Tony Iro and Nigel Gaffey and were coached by 'Gus' Gould.

In 2012, the Roosters' wins against Souths, Canberra and New Zealand were not convincing by any stretch, while the Cowboys also found themselves in Darwin with something to prove, despite holding off the otherwise undefeated Broncos in Round 2.

But this game belonged to two of Northern Australia's heroes: Johnathan Thurston and Matt Bowen.

In the 12th minute they combine in a standard backline movement to send Antonio Winterstein over in the corner for his second try of the match.

In the 19th, the Cowboys take advantage of a ricochet off a general play kick to gain 40 metres and a restart. Off the next tackle, with the Roosters still getting set defensively, Thurston performs an improv run-around with Matt Bowen and distributes to Faifai-Loa who, using the dexterity of a Romanian gymnast, manages to place the ball in the corner of the end zone while 99 per cent of his body hovers above the sideline. The Cowboys are ahead of the clock. The Roosters appear typically helpless when confronted with top-level skill.

In the 28th minute, Thurston banana kicks at 45 degrees to his running direction, to a surging Matt Bowen, who goes over untouched under the posts.

Still ahead of the clock.

After a halftime confrontation with Brian Smith, the Roosters mount a comeback which is ultimately stifled when, again, Thurston combines with Bowen to send Taumalolo over for another. The sliding defence of the Roosters is no match for the change of direction applied by the big Kiwi.

Thurston puts Big T through another gap and, looking like Dean Lukin running late for work, the big man strolls over.

Not satisfied with the work of the scorekeeper to date, Thurston swoops on a loose ball and finds his Townsville Glimmer Twin and Bowen is over. Not to be outdone, Bowen converts from the sideline.

Tonight the Cowboys served notice of their capability, albeit against a Roosters side which a red-headed PM might suggest had "lost its way".

Frank Johnson was cheering on Thurston and Matty Bowen in another kind of heaven.

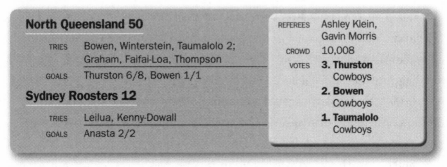

North Queensland 50

TRIES	Bowen, Winterstein, Taumalolo 2; Graham, Faifai-Loa, Thompson
GOALS	Thurston 6/8, Bowen 1/1

Sydney Roosters 12

TRIES	Leilua, Kenny-Dowall
GOALS	Anasta 2/2

REFEREES	Ashley Klein, Gavin Morris
CROWD	10,008
VOTES	**3. Thurston** Cowboys
	2. Bowen Cowboys
	1. Taumalolo Cowboys

Once were Warriors

New Zealand Warriors *versus* **South Sydney Rabbitohs**
2pm, Sunday, 15 April
Mt Smart Stadium, Auckland

PAUL DALLIGAN

WHILE WE ALL NO DOUBT FELT A STIRRING RESPECT AND ADMIRATION for Russell Crowe's character in *Gladiator*, surely Maximus had nothing on the sheer terror and brute force of Jake the Muss swinging that bar stool in *Once Were Warriors*.

It was a level of fear that Crowe and his Rabbitohs, and no doubt all other NRL teams, feel as they board a plane at Kingsford-Smith to head into battle against the Warriors in Auckland. I have it on good authority that NRL teams schedule an extra day off from training after matches against the Warriors, such is their size and power; and that some players don't leave their beds the next day, let alone take a freezing early morning swim at the beach in just their bathers (why do all football teams do that?).

There must surely be no tougher trip in Australian sport than having to board that plane to cross the Tasman. It was even tougher for the Rabbitohs given that the Warriors were coming home off losses to the Roosters and Raiders which were so bad that many were querying whether the 2011 Grand Finalists were already gone for 2012.

The match started brightly for the Rabbitohs, with Dave 'Man Mountain' Taylor crashing over after four minutes. But that try felt like merely landing a slap on the cheek of Jake the Muss as he held his bar stool. It was no time to rest on any laurels; rather it was time to make sure those laurels were safely fastened, as rugby league hellfire was about to be unleashed by the Warriors.

And my word, unleashed it was – four tries before halftime to Lewis Brown, Jerome Ropati, Bill Tupou and Simon Mannering put the result to bed and had the Rabbitohs, no doubt, wondering what misery would be in store in the second half.

But Season 2012 is all about the *New Rabbitohs*, with ex-Storm assistant and Craig Bellamy disciple Michael Maguire in charge. If Maguire has inherited even half of Craig Bellamy's volume and vitriol, they may have heard that halftime dressing-down in Redfern.

For a moment, it seemed to work. Dave Taylor barged over to narrow the gap to 20-16. However that stirred the Warriors into a wild retaliation, with tries to Simon

Mannering, Ben Henry, Ukama Ta'ai and Krisnan Inu. The outburst was broken only fleetingly by Souths' shining light of the season, Andrew Everingham, who crossed for his second try of the match.

Everingham's try sparked some hope for a miracle among the hardcore Rabbitoh fans, but when your team makes more mistakes than a certain taxi riding politician, the miracle was never going to eventuate.

The Warriors' win was even more impressive given that their superstar at the back, Kevin Locke, was missing the game through injury, Jerome Ropati having to slot into the custodian's role.

But the Warriors still had more sparks than a welding workshop, and Shaun Johnson was the brightest of them leading the Warriors to what was a comfortable 44-22 victory. It would be a brave man who suggests that the Warriors won't be challenging when the finals roll around.

The toughest road trip in the NRL looks like getting even tougher.

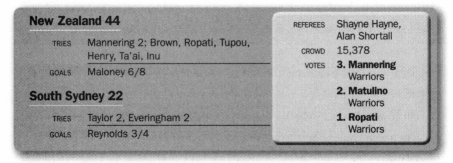

New Zealand 44

TRIES	Mannering 2; Brown, Ropati, Tupou, Henry, Ta'ai, Inu
GOALS	Maloney 6/8

South Sydney 22

TRIES	Taylor 2, Everingham 2
GOALS	Reynolds 3/4

REFEREES	Shayne Hayne, Alan Shortall
CROWD	15,378
VOTES	**3. Mannering** Warriors
	2. Matulino Warriors
	1. Ropati Warriors

Eels let it slip

Cronulla Sharks *versus* Parramatta Eels

3pm, Sunday, 15 March

Toyota Stadium, Sydney

MATT O'HANLON

THE CLASH OF THE EELS AND THE SHARKS at Endeavour Caltex Ronson Toyota Shark Park Field poses a real quandary for the Sharks – they are favourites for a game they should win, but it seems, after the Titans got the points at Brookie last night, no games are safe.

Ahh! That's better: XXXX Bitter to assist my lucidity after last night. The Golden Girl's sister and her Irishman were up from Sydney with their Rabbitoh friends, so off we went to Milan at Main Beach (I went the Bloody Mary Oysters and the Duck – spot on), preceded by Verve and Stella at Q1 Floor 46 and cocktails on the home deck til late. If the South Sydney friends were not dusty before the Rabbitohs' second half capitulation, they may well be feeling it now.

Game on. Try to Hayne. Six minutes in. Simple play. Weak defence from Cronulla. Maybe?

The Sharks reply quickly with a pinpoint Carney kick. 6-all. Oh no. Poor Eels defence on the left edge. Pomeroy scores a classic centre three-quarter's try, aided by an ordinary tackle. 12-6. For mine, Pomeroy has been one of the real improvers of 2012. With Robson (ex-Eel) proving the perfect foil for Carney, Best and Pomeroy look good.

When your luck is down, there is not much you can do. Buster Keaton could not have choreographed the next try to the Sharks. Pomeroy volley-balls a bomb back into an Eel hand, bouncing off Bukuya's head and over the tryline, Bukuya plants the hand – benefit-of-the-doubt, 18-6 in 23 minutes. The Eels are in trouble. Understatement?

The early expansive play the Eels have shown seems to have evaporated but that man Hayne throws a magic flick pass as Pomeroy rushes up. Blair in the corner. Sideline conversion by Sandow. 18-12.

With the introduction of Poore and Mannah, Parramatta seem to have increased their intensity and, as halftime approaches, Hayne levels the score when Sandow's bomb hits him perfectly. Halftime 18-all. Time to heat the Weber – to a temperature not dissimilar to Flanagan's halftime talk I would imagine.

G-squared feigns interest. "What's the score?"

I mumble my reply.

"That's good – *oh, what a tackle.*" Ah, that's better, Golden Girl. Good comment after a try-saver by McGuire.

Cronulla seem to be attacking the left edge. From a penalty, Carney sends a great pass to Mills. Try on the Eels' left flank. 22-18.

Parramatta must lift. Another Sharks penalty and Hindmarsh has said more words per minute to the ref than G-squared and the sister are throwing at each other in the kitchen. Penalty converted, 24-18.

The Eels are willing but lack options in attack. Cronulla hold their defence, always looking for Hayne. The Old Timer says Gallen has been quiet. I'm not sure. We have become used to Gallen being the sole Shark, so the performance today is testimony to a stronger team effort. His stats are still outstanding and he is the pick of their pack.

Parramatta build pressure. Blair is held up twice and the Eels are really searching. A Roberts knock on releases the valve. Further, Sandow has been replaced with 10 minutes to go and it is still game on.

"Is the Weber on?"

No answer to G-squared as the Eels look like scoring. *Noooooo!* Dummy-half pass, tackle two, straight to the Sharks. The Eels have botched it again. You must feel for Kearney. Coaches are not to blame for an error like that.

The Eels continue but yet another pushed pass turns the ball over with 90 seconds left. They may get one last chance.

They do. They have a couple of tackles to do something. One option. Find Hayne. Into touch. Sharks home 24-18.

With a 6-0 second half, the Sharks showed resolve in defence aided by some poor Parramatta options. The Eels are closer but must take their opportunities. Like the Eels coach, I'm ready for a drink with The Flame and crew before it's back to work on Monday.

Cronulla 24			REFEREES	Steve Lyons, Henry Perenara
TRIES	Wright, Pomeroy, Bukuya, Mills		CROWD	14,327
GOALS	Carney 4/5		VOTES	**3. Gallen** Sharks
Parramatta 18				**2. Hayne** Eels
TRIES	Hayne 2; Blair			**1. Wright** Sharks
GOALS	Sandow 3/3			

Tiger revival

Penrith Panthers *versus* **Wests Tigers**
3pm, Sunday, 15 April
Centrebet Stadium

GREG OBERSCHEIDT

T HERE WAS SO LITTLE HYPE SURROUNDING THIS GAME that you could have been forgiven for thinking the captains might agree to flip a coin for the points and all head off to hit the froth instead.

Penrith were not in a good place, devastated by their recent inability to cross the stripe. The Tigers were once again struggling with the favourites tag, having been poor at best and disgusting at worst.

The Panthers have struggled for consistency. Luke Lewis has been tireless but support has been thin. Lachlan Coote appears a shadow of the player who burst onto the scene a few years ago and as good as Luke Walsh's kicking game is, if you are kicking to Sandor Earl and Geoff Daniela, you are destined to fail.

Injuries and suspensions have played a role in the Tigers' poor form, in particular the loss of Keith Galloway who, in my opinion, is right up there with Marshall as the Tigers' most important player. He leads from the front and without him in the side, the pack really struggles to provide any go forward. He also sets the standard defensively, making ground with his tackles. The players taking the field needed to take a bit more responsibility in his absence, but they just haven't.

The clash kicked off in front of a modest crowd at Centrebet Stadium and to no one's surprise the first attacking opportunity came off the back of a Sandor Earl error. Three quick barrels up the middle, cue Benji, short ball to Blair, TRY TIME. It was a pretty innocuous raid towards the Panthers' line but the Mountain Men were powerless to stop it.

The Tigers could sense the tension in their opponents and, for the first time this year, they were able to maintain the ascendancy and convert their opportunities.

Tim Moltzen, desperately trying to make amends for his horrific start to the season, was creative and managed to score at the midpoint of the first half. Marshall again converted. Five minutes later, off the back of another Penrith error, the Tigers were in again.

This time Ray Cashmere was the beneficiary of some Marshall subtlety in a replay of the first try.

It was great to see big Ray get across the line. The journeyman giant hasn't played top flight footy for almost four years and, from the look of things, he wants to stay. It was 18-0 at halftime and the game was pretty much over.

Penrith, inspired by their skipper Lewis, came out firing in the second half but their inability to finish sets meant that they were unable to generate the field position required to make an impact on the scoreboard. The Tigers also blew a couple of chances before Tom Humble crashed over from close range to put the result beyond doubt.

The Panthers, down 24-0, then managed to do something I don't think I've ever seen before. The Chocolate Soldiers went into meltdown. They bombed tries in four of their ensuing five sets. They cut the Tigers' defensive line to pieces with scything runs and then managed to put the last pass down, throw it forward, get held up. It was mayhem.

While it probably wouldn't have been enough to get the job done, what it did do was allow the Tigers, for the first time in their 308 appearances as a joint venture, to keep their opposition scoreless, a feat that would please Mr Sheens no end.

The Tigers were able to throw together a bit of razzle dazzle at the end to ice the cake with Tim Moltzen, on the end of a 70-metre play that saw at least eight players involved, cross for his second of the afternoon. Marshall added the two and the Tigers ran away winners 30-0.

A pleasing result for suffering Tigers fans but there is still plenty to do to get back in contention in 2012.

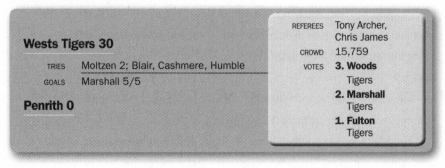

Wests Tigers 30		REFEREES	Tony Archer, Chris James
TRIES	Moltzen 2; Blair, Cashmere, Humble	CROWD	15,759
GOALS	Marshall 5/5	VOTES	**3. Woods** Tigers
Penrith 0			**2. Marshall** Tigers
			1. Fulton Tigers

2012 Anzac Test Match

Still world champions

New Zealand *versus* **Australia**
8.15pm, Friday, 20 April
Eden Park, Auckland

WILL EVANS

DURING THE MID-2000S, I GRAPPLED WITH A CONFLICT between my New Zealand heritage and my rabid support of the Brisbane Broncos. I found it tough to unreservedly back the Kiwi Test team against an Australian lineup boasting so many of my Broncos favourites – particularly after Darren Lockyer became Kangaroos captain in 2003. Trans-Tasman clashes were tinged with bittersweet emotions, whatever the result.

I was livid when New Zealand backrower Frank Pritchard knocked the Broncos' Kangaroo debutant fullback Karmichael Hunt unconscious in the 2006 Anzac Test, while the hollow disappointment of the Kiwis' golden point loss to Australia in the Tri-Nations final at the end of that season – one of the great Tests of the modern era – was tempered by Lockyer scoring the winning try to cap a year of extraordinary achievement.

Ironically, moving from Queenstown in New Zealand's South Island to Brisbane in 2008 set my parochial destiny on its rightful course. The predominantly good-humoured – but constantly simmering – trans-Tasman banter catapulted New Zealand v Australia Tests to the pinnacle of my rugby league calendar. The 2008 World Cup and 2010 Four Nations final triumphs at Suncorp Stadium consequently rank as glimmering highlights among two decades of obsession with the game.

I'm in the media box at Eden Park in my casual role with a Sydney-based rugby league magazine, but my desire to see another Kiwi upset firsthand is my chief motivation for flying across the Tasman. In saying that, I'm ecstatic with the butter chicken bonanza laid out for us – a step up from the party pies provided at Suncorp Stadium, which are inevitably snaffled by the hardened Aussie journos, while part-timers like me bashfully wait and miss out.

The atmosphere at the traditional home of rugby union in New Zealand is electric; the revamp for last year's Rugby World Cup has rendered Eden Park a first-rate venue. The haka has the neck-hairs standing to attention as usual, but disaster almost strikes for the Kiwis inside the first minute – Cooper Cronk's pinpoint cross-field kick finds Akuila Uate on the fly and New Zealand debutant Shaun Johnson appears to have injured his shoulder in an awkward attempted tackle on the powerhouse winger. But the Kiwis cover defence scrambles and halfback wunderkind Johnson eventually takes his place back in the line. The crowd's collective sigh of relief is damn-near audible.

The script soon veers in favour of the underdogs and much-maligned hooker Issac Luke. The Kiwi No.9 – pilloried after a slew of unsavoury incidents during the 2011 post-season Test schedule – throws an audacious dummy from acting half to plunge over under the posts in the 12th minute. But the lead is eradicated by a hot-stepping Johnathan Thurston eight minutes later, and slick backline play results in Greg Inglis surging to the corner to provide the Kangaroos with a 12-6 advantage.

Howls from the grandstand (and murmurs from the Kiwi contingent in the press box) for a penalty try are ignored when Billy Slater takes out Alex Glenn near Australia's line, but the superstar fullback gets 10 minutes in the bin for his misdemeanour. New Zealand fails to capitalise on the one-man advantage, however, and the Kangaroos head to the break eight in front after a Thurston penalty goal.

The deflated hush that permeated the crowd during halftime instantaneously becomes an ear-splitting roar when Johnson intercepts a Cronk pass and races 85 metres to score in the 46th minute. The remainder of the match balances on a knife's edge, with a sensational try-saving tackle by impressive Kiwi fullback debutant Josh Hoffman on Broncos teammate Justin Hodges rousing the partisan crowd and provoking less-than-diplomatic applause from the Kiwi pressmen and women, who are also bemoaning captain Benji Marshall's anonymous performance.

But the match reaches a familiar conclusion at the hands of an habitual gate-crasher. Kangaroos rake Cameron Smith – in his first Test as skipper in the post-Lockyer era – regathers a rebound from his own grubber and wrenches his way over for the sealer. Despite a 14th straight Anzac Test defeat, the crowd remains upbeat as they file out of Eden Park after New Zealand's wholehearted effort.

The Kiwis are still world champions for another 18 months, after all.

Big brother rules

IAN HAUSER

AUSTRALIA MAINTAINED ITS 14-YEAR DOMINATION of the annual Anzac Test against New Zealand in a willing but good-spirited contest at Eden Park, running out comfortable winners by 20-12. In the end, it was a case of the better team making the most of key moments in both defence and attack against a willing opponent who couldn't execute the right combination of skills when it counted most.

That's the official version.

Garbage!

We smacked them in every aspect of the game with better teamwork, by out-muscling them in defence, through monster runs by the forwards, finishing it off via the silky skills of our backs. We even gave them an extra man when Slater got 10 in the bin and still outscored them in that period! Even more humiliatingly, we only used sixteen men, keeping rookie Cherry-Evans on the bench throughout. And, yet again, we nullified Benji and made the so-called best player in the world look pretty ordinary. Going back to last October in Newcastle and then in November in Pommyland, that's three times in a row.

To be fair, the Kiwis were in it for the first 20 minutes as the forward packs tested each other out in some rough and ready exchanges before Issac Luke scored an opportunist try from dummy-half. Hannant came off the bench and lifted the Australians, the Kiwis gifted a couple of silly penalties and the pendulum swung to the visitors thereafter. Thurston soon levelled the scores with a touch of Fred Astaire footwork following a Hannant rush.

Then came the best passage of play in the whole game. After another forward surge to the quarter-line, a quick play-the-ball followed by an inch-perfect, split-second spread to the left via Cronk, Thurston and Slater gave Inglis a saloon passage to the line. Breathtaking in its simplicity and beautiful in its execution in the confined spaces available, this was true rugby league poetry!

From there onwards, the Kiwis lost their rhythm and structure, their handling deteriorated and silly penalties saw the Aussies go to the break with an eight-point lead. The Kiwis could have complained about Slater taking out Glenn when a try might have been on just before the break, but Watmough's vicinity to the ball created enough doubt to limit the incident to Slater being sin-binned and a penalty awarded to New Zealand. Then they coughed it up within a couple tackles with a huge overlap beckoning – it encapsulated their night.

New Zealand had a moment of hope not long after the break when Johnson scored an 85-metre intercept try, but it was against the run of play and proved a false dawn. The Aussies do grind better than everyone and their basic, mistake-free approach saw them in control, going close to scoring at least twice through Cronk and Uate. By contrast, the Kiwis were unstructured and ad-lib, making them easy meat for the Aussie defence. Smith racked up an incredible 51 tackles while that man Hannant made 34.

Eventually, pressure turned into points with Smith scoring the match-winner 10 minutes from time. From there, the Australian forwards rolled forward with a kick on the last forcing the New Zealanders to slog their way out from their own line. It was never going to happen and the match drew to its predictable close.

For the Australians, Lewis, Hannant, Thaiday and Gallen were strong up front; Thurston and Cronk fitted seamlessly into their new roles; Hodges was dangerous with the ball; Slater was a perpetual threat and Boyd was faultless at the back. For the Kiwis, Johnson and Hoffman on debut were a portent of things to come, Mannering was tireless, Luke was energetic (but isn't a good team player) and the forwards tried hard.

The biggest loser was Channel Nine with a hopelessly delayed telecast, shameless promotions which belittle their commentators and an irrelevant plug for a boy band!

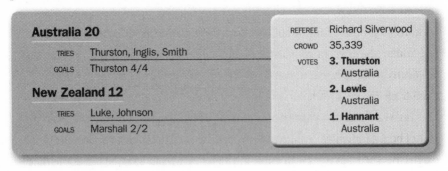

Australia 20

TRIES	Thurston, Inglis, Smith
GOALS	Thurston 4/4

New Zealand 12

TRIES	Luke, Johnson
GOALS	Marshall 2/2

REFEREE	Richard Silverwood
CROWD	35,339
VOTES	**3. Thurston** Australia
	2. Lewis Australia
	1. Hannant Australia

Round 8

The way it is

St George Illawarra Dragons
versus **Sydney Roosters**
4pm, Wednesday, 25 April
Allianz Stadium, Sydney

MICHAEL ADAMS

NOT LONG INTO OUR RELATIONSHIP, MY GIRLFRIEND ASKED what I would choose if I had to decide between music and sport. Not wanting to even consider a world without either, I had no answer for her at the time. Later, however, when in a more contemplative state of mind, I decided that it had to be music. The simple reason: there is nothing frivolous or silly about a passion for music, but not a day goes by that I don't realise how ridiculous it is to have my happiness dictated to me by the fortunes of 17 meathead football players.

Skipping my annual Anzac Day pilgrimage to the SFS in order to attend a music event earlier in the day seemed to bear this out, and yet the miraculous events that would occur in this glorious game left me wondering if I had made the right choice after all.

And so Moore Park was replaced by the Tempe Hotel. As the cameras pan to the two teams lining up, a bugler sounding *The Last Post*, Bruce Hornsby's *The Way It Is* blasts from the speakers. It is an oddly fitting juxtaposition. Terrible song though.

As the game begins we are in more familiar rugby league territory, with a double dose of bogan rock in AC/DC. We start with *Long Way to the Top*, as Benny Creagh coughs the ball up, making it an even longer way for the Dragons. Not long after, it's the Roosters with the first real chance. Minichiello has the ball with an open tryline in front of him before being brilliantly held up by Brett Morris. As the try is formally disallowed, the AC/DC double continues with *Dirty Deeds Done Dirt Cheap*, another perfect juxtaposition with the on-field action. We all know what Morris can do with the ball in his hands, but it has been his defensive work that has really stood out since taking on the fullback role at the Dragons.

Once again he shows he is not afraid of doing the dirty work.

However, it turns out I may have praised him too soon. He is dragged back in-goal by the Roosters defence, as The Eagles' *Heartache Tonight* sounds through the speakers. The heartache continues soon after as Mini plucks a bomb out of Morris' hands to score the second try for the Roosters, and so we go to the break with the Dragons two points in arrears at 12-10. The New Radicals' *You Get What You Give* adds a modern, if no less bland, touch to the classic rock playlist and, with the two teams effectively cancelling each other out in the opening 40, one gets the feeling it will be the team that gives the most who takes out this one.

So it proved, and what an absorbing second half it was. The Roosters had much the better of it and, when Jamie Soward was penalised in front of the goal posts in the 74th minute, it appeared the match was over. The penalty was duly slotted, giving the Roosters a seemingly insurmountable eight-point lead.

The Dragons recovered a short kick-off via Jason Nightingale, who not only regathered but also went on a run to send Matt Prior over in the corner. Still, with only a couple of minutes left, I was left to rue that penalty goal which looked like being the difference. As *Let It Be* sounded through the pub, I took comfort. You can't win them all, I guess. Let it be.

It turns out today there was an answer and his name was Michael Weyman. Moruya's finest capped off a sensational game by sending Ben Creagh over the line for the decisive last-minute try, following on from a miraculous Nightingale chip to force a Roosters dropout.

And so a thoroughly entertaining match comes to an end. I leave the pub to the opening strains of Tears For Fears' *Everybody Wants To Rule the World* on a day when both teams proved that they are well in the mix to rule the NRL world.

St George Illawarra 28		REFEREES	Matt Cecchin, Ben Cummins
TRIES	Creagh 2; Prior, Cooper, Weyman	CROWD	40,164
GOALS	Soward 3/4, Hornby 1/1	VOTES	**3. Weyman** Dragons
Sydney Roosters 24			**2. Rein** Dragons
TRIES	Minichiello, Anasta, Pearce, Guerra		**1. Pearce** Roosters
GOALS	Anasta 4/5		

Inu-believable

Melbourne Storm *versus* **New Zealand Warriors**
7pm, Wednesday, 25 April
AAMI Park, Melbourne
SAMSON McDOUGALL

S OMEBODY VERY CLOSE TO ME HAS THIS THEORY THAT Melbourne has only two seasons: summer and winter. She contends that summer begins at Cup week and ends at Easter. Adherent to this view, the weather turned the corner into winter a few days before Anzac Day and we busted out the woollies for the trip to AAMI Park.

A couple of pints at the Corner Hotel pre-match and we caught the last quarter of the oval-field game at the MCG (an uncharacteristic thriller whereby Collingwood snatched victory over a self-congratulatory Essendon, who fell victim to slapping themselves on the back oh too soon).

A short stroll to AAMI Park – which is far and away the premier NRL venue in the country – and we were seated with trays of beers in no time flat. The pre-match entertainment included Aboriginal dancing and a haka followed by *The Last Post* and *Dawn's Prayer* – moving stuff.

Molly Meldrum also made his return to AAMI following the Christmas fall that almost cost him his life.

The Warriors looked solid through the first few sets and applied early pressure resulting in first blood via quick hands to Bill Tupou's right wing. True to their terrible form thus far, the Warriors relinquished their advantage soon after, allowing Dane Nielsen a soft finish to open the Storm account for the night.

Will Chambers capitalised on some lacklustre defence and the Warriors trailed 10-6 despite the fact they applied a great deal of pressure through passages, only to relinquish control of the game through lazy penalties and lapses of discipline.

A greedy charge from Ben Henry cost the Warriors a realistic chance of scoring again before halftime as he was penalised on the second tackle for a blatant double movement.

The Warriors opened the second half scoring with a close range charge from a recently returned Lewis Brown, which was labelled as a benefit-of-the-doubt try though any reasonable idiot could see the grounding clearly on the replay. Justin O'Neill took advantage of the first of a string of Krisnan Inu mistakes, crossing in the corner.

Through a stroke of genius soon afterwards, Pita Godinet crafted a clever grubber into the Storm in-goal from dummy-half, which Tupou grounded millimetres from the dead-ball line for his double. Maloney posted the conversion attempt and the score remained 14-10. As the rain began to fall the see-saw soon swung back to the Storm through Will Chambers crossing for a well-formed try.

Inu's disintegration put the pressure squarely on the Warriors as he attempted to offload on the first tackle of a kick return – he couldn't have butchered the attempt better if he tried. The Storm stretched the far left of the Warriors defence once again and Chambers crossed for his third. With a magic kick from Cam Smith, they took their lead to 12 points, all but shutting the door on the Warriors for the night. A late Nielsen try sealed it for a comprehensive thrashing, 32-14.

The Warriors mixed it with the Storm in every aspect of the game apart from the brain explosions and loose play of one man: Inu's performance was inexcusable. It was almost as if with every touch he was trying to perform the brilliant, so as to expunge the memory of the previous sloppy carry. This is catch-up at its most destructive.

Not for the first time this season the Warriors will be questioning how badly they got it wrong. They successfully mixed it with an unbeaten Storm for 60 minutes but selfishness and stupidity proved costly.

Now just three from eight and sliding further down the competition ladder, it's hard to see this side replicating the heroics of 2011.

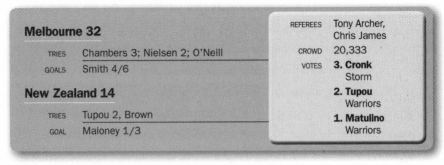

Melbourne 32

TRIES	Chambers 3; Nielsen 2; O'Neill
GOALS	Smith 4/6

New Zealand 14

TRIES	Tupou 2, Brown
GOAL	Maloney 1/3

REFEREES	Tony Archer, Chris James
CROWD	20,333
VOTES	**3. Cronk** Storm
	2. Tupou Warriors
	1. Matulino Warriors

War, minus the shooting

Canterbury Bulldogs *versus* **Manly Sea Eagles**

7.30pm, Friday, 27 April

ANZ Stadium, Sydney

PETA BRYANT

DIDN'T ACTUALLY WATCH THE GRUDGE MATCH BETWEEN the Canterbury Bulldogs and the Manly Sea Eagles on Friday night. I had just arrived home (to remote Cambodia) after a trip to Burma and I was too busy catching up on the local gossip and getting my fill of sour soup, after three weeks deprivation, to care much about Des Hasler's ego-crushing loss.

In retrospect though, as I watch the online footage (of Hasler's surly countenance as well as the actual game) and remember my recent travels through Burma, I can't help but recall George Orwell's writing. I had a copy of Orwell's *Burmese Days* with me as I travelled. It was useful for warding off book-selling touts ("I already have a copy, thanks!") if nothing else, but I brought it along because, even on re-reading, I find his dark playful language to be endlessly entertaining.

What Orwell does best is to rip out the most negative aspects of a place or situation and employ vivid imagery to create an indulgent, yet beguiling, rant. Some might call it a literary critique but I call it a rant. *Burmese Days* was a playfully yet passionately written rant against racism and imperialism. Somewhat less playful but no less impassioned, was Orwell's essay 'The Sporting Spirit'.

Here, Orwell claims that sport is an "unfailing cause of ill-will" because sport is competitive and, as such, "the game has little meaning unless you do your utmost to win". Orwell goes on further to say:

> Serious sport has nothing to do with fair play. It is bound up with hatred, jealousy, boastfulness, disregard of all rules and sadistic pleasure in witnessing violence: in other words it is war minus the shooting.

While I'm not sure that this week's match between Canterbury and Manly constituted war minus the shooting, I would concur that it represented an unresolved conflict bound up with jealousy and boastfulness. This game was a fine example of just how emotive competitive sport can be. Inherent to the match was the question of prestige for both coaches, Des Hasler and Geoff Toovey.

Hasler and Toovey have a long history together. They both played with Manly from the late 1980s to the mid-1990s and, from 2004, they constituted a dynamic coaching team that would take Manly to the finals every year between 2005 and 2011 and secure them two premiership titles.

After the 2011 premiership, Hasler announced that he had signed with Canterbury. Toovey was appointed head coach of Manly in his place. The merit of Hasler's decision was to be confirmed in the moment when his new charges beat his former team but, alas, Round 8 was not to deliver that moment.

Instead, it seems that the Sea Eagles continue to soar without the help of their pedantic former leader and are doing just fine under the guidance of Toovey.

The Bulldogs started the game well with Barba going over in the opening minutes, but they spent the rest of the match holding a strong line of defence, before scoring only once more in the closing minutes of the game.

The Sea Eagles, marginal favourites, showed themselves to be the stronger team, with a larger and more experienced forward line that monopolised ball possession. Brothers Glenn and Brett Stewart were stars for the Sea Eagles, with Brett scoring just after halftime. It was Steve Matai's try, however, that secured the match for Manly and subsequently sparked an uproar from thousands of supporters who still feel betrayed by Hasler's defection to Canterbury.

Although I am sorry that I didn't get to see Ben Barba's runaway try or watch Glenn Stewart's hit on Corey Payne, what I miss about watching live football is the feeling in the stands – the viscerally emotive energy of The Crowd.

Orwell describes football supporters with chagrin, saying how they:

> ... don't intervene physically [but] they try to influence the game by cheering their own side and rattling opposing players with boos and insults.

I'm sure that Hasler was subject to plenty of boos and insults throughout the game but I'm certain also that he has the broad shoulders to deal with it. I don't think that such impassioned support for football is tantamount to "sadistic pleasure in witnessing violence", but rather it is the product of team loyalty and community patriotism.

I agree with Orwell that sport has "little meaning unless you do your utmost to win" but I don't necessarily think that's a bad thing. In Des Hasler's case it just means that the Bulldogs did their utmost but it wasn't good enough.

Next time the Bulldogs go head to head with Manly, they will have to raise the bar on what constitutes their best game. They should maintain the strong defence exhibited on Friday night but use more strategic risk with the ball.

After one narrow loss to a team with whom they now share a bitter rivalry, the Bulldogs have little more to lose and a lot to gain from an offensive crack at the Sea Eagles the next time they meet.

Manly 12			REFEREES	Shayne Hayne, Brett Suttor
TRIES	Matai, B. Stewart		CROWD	24,743
GOALS	Lyon 2/3		VOTES	**3. B. Stewart** Sea Eagles
Canterbury 10				**2. Barba** Bulldogs
TRIES	Barba, Goodwin			**1. Rose** Sea Eagles
GOAL	Goodwin 1/1, Turner 0/1			

It was what it was

Brisbane Broncos *versus* **Gold Coast Titans**
7.30pm, Friday, 27 April
Suncorp Stadium, Brisbane

IAN HAUSER

A LOCAL DERBY HOLDS OUT THE PROMISE OF A GOOD STOUSH regardless of ladder places or form. Ladder positions have meant little in Broncos/Titans derbies over the years with the new boys choosing not to be overawed by big brother from up the M1. In this case, recent form suggested a real cracker with the Broncos on a five-game winning streak and the Titans solid last-round winners against Manly at Brookvale. Only light rain looked like putting a dampener on proceedings.

Unfortunately it was all over by halftime with the Broncos holding a 20-0 lead.

The Broncos weren't even that good in the first 40 minutes. Yes, they were safe, solid and confident in each other. Yes, they made only three errors for the half. Yes, it could have been 30-0 but for a disallowed try, a few other botched chances and a bit of an off night for Parker's goalkicking.

The Titans were just plain awful. Coach John Cartwright showed glimpses of frustration and dismay as the Coast lads fumbled and bumbled their way through an uncoordinated half of football hardly worthy of parkland teams.

They lacked spark, displayed no cohesion in attack and only got into the opposition quarter for six tackles with ball in hand.

To their credit, at times the Titans defended willingly against a glut of possession. Myles, in particular, put his body fairly and squarely in the line of fire, coming off the worse after his head copped a knee from Hodges. Eventually back on his feet, Myles played on to be the Titans' best on the night. But his efforts were undervalued and undermined by a pathetic defence that conceded soft tries to Glenn and McCullough.

The second half was more spirited. No doubt Cartwright had given his boys a good lashing during the break. Srama, Minichiello and Idris ran strong and straight, Prince brought players into the game and Brisbane were on the back foot briefly. After an exciting ad-lib set of tackles, a Prince dummy and sweetly delayed pass saw Peyroux score to give their fans hope. It was a false dawn. Brisbane reasserted themselves, through an excellent defensive line and a well-structured attack. Hoffman capped off another good night with a razzle-dazzle try, although the final pass was suspect, to say the least.

For the winners, Wallace and Norman continued to develop their combination, Glenn was a strong presence all night, Hannant continued his good form and McCullough picked his moments well. The Titans were best served by Myles, head and shoulders above anyone else, while Minichiello and Douglas were honest. Bailey attempted a goose-step at one stage and Idris needed to be more consistent.

The match officials had a mixed night with each side disallowed fair tries while Glenn's second try and Hoffman's late sealer both had dubious aspects in their execution. On the other hand, they probably got it right by denying Hodges in the final minute.

In the end, none of these calls affected the final score. Brisbane dominated or cut even for at least 70 minutes of the game and were deserved winners. That's what you'd expect when second plays 15th.

Channel Nine continued to plumb the depths of shameless commercial plugs and cross-promotion of their own programs. Who gives a stuff if they are bewitched by *The Voice*? What on earth has it got to do with the footy? And how long can Ray Hadley last in commentary?

Brisbane 26		REFEREES	Jared Maxwell, Adam Devcich
TRIES	Glenn 2; McCullough, Beale, Hoffmann	CROWD	30,083
GOALS	Parker 3/5	VOTES	**3. Wallace** Broncos
Gold Coast 6			**2. Glenn** Broncos
TRY	Peyroux		**1. Myles** Titans
GOAL	Prince 1/1		

The demons of Olympic Stadium

South Sydney Rabbitohs *versus* **North Queensland Cowboys**
7.30pm, Saturday, 28 April
ANZ Stadium, Sydney

DAVE FLETCHER

FOR SOME YEARS NOW IT'S BEEN A FOREBODING TREK to Olympic Stadium for the North Queensland Cowboys faithful. Save for that one glorious September day in 2004 when our unheralded side momentarily halted the march of that infamous Bulldogs pack to the premiership, the walk across the paved expanse from the stadium to the train station post-game has long been etched in our minds as the Boulevard of Broken Dreams.

I think I can safely say that Olympic Stadium (I refuse to call it whatever name the current corporate sponsor demands we call it) is a venue that – for all its sophistication and unrivalled ability to comfortably host the big games – has not been fondly embraced by rugby league supporters. Not even by the fans of clubs forced to call it their home ground.

The abundance of space surrounding and within the bowels of the behemoth structure, obviously designed for the much heavier traffic of the Sydney Olympics, now seems to mock the NRL faithful who bravely huddle in the few thousand 'good seats' for their regular-round fixtures. Leichhardt Oval this ain't. Pricey mid-strength Tooheys New served from bars that close just after halftime hardly reflects an effort to counteract the inhospitable atmosphere either, just quietly. Above all else though, for this Cowboys fan, the cavernous space, the sea of empty seats around the ground, and those towering white beams that arch above it, all loom as a monument to a painful truth: my team can't seem to win in Sydney.

Despite this apparent truth, or perhaps because of it, I muster up the courage (and whatever few mates are willing) to make the journey to this cold, sad place each time the lads play, hoping against hope that the first win in front of 8,000 hostile punters will be the catalyst for that sweetest-of-all victories in front of 80,000. Time and again, that hope is dashed upon the witnessing of sub-par team performances, Thurston's tantrums at referees and that grim sense of inevitability.

If the demons of Olympic Park are real for me, they must surely also lurk in the psyche of the Cowboys side. For the first half they played as if they were running scared from them. The Rabbitohs capitalised on dominant possession, woeful defence (brittle in the middle and non-existent on the line), and a lopsided penalty count to be 20-0 up after just 20 minutes, and held that lead going into the sheds at the break.

The few times the Cowboys did get the ball they looked sharp in attack. That is until the penultimate pass out wide ridiculously overestimated the considerable athletic prowess of Kalifa Faifai-Loa to go sailing into that space – and the paws of those demons – beyond the touchline.

After what must have been quite the rousing halftime serve by coach Neil Henry, the Cowboys' passes finally began to stick. Three unanswered tries later (including yet another double from in-form winger Ash Graham), and it seemed demons of a different kind may well rear their heads to torment the 'Burrow' once more. That notorious ability of the Rabbitohs to lunge elbow-deep down the throat of victory to salvage a defeat seemed to be on display once more, and the final 10 minutes of the game were alive with the score at 20-16. Some gutsy defence and a Cowboys attack suddenly hamstrung, perhaps by a sense of occasion (could we finally do it?), ultimately saw the Rabbitohs prevail with the scores unchanged at the siren.

As we forlornly trudged back down the Boulevard of Broken Dreams, the Olympic colossus darkly chuckling behind us, I couldn't shake the image of another colossus in the form of Greg Inglis. Seriously, seeing him in the flesh, the man is huge, and at fullback he is devastating with his kick returns and free-range lurking behind the attacking line. As a diehard Queensland fan, having now lived for a decade behind enemy lines, I took comfort in this image, knowing he will surely conjure more stadium-sized demons from this haunted place to torment the Blues once more.

Get over it New South Wales; he is ours!

South Sydney 20				REFEREES	Steve Lyons, Henry Perenara
TRIES	Inglis, Taylor, Luke			CROWD	12,213
GOALS	Reynolds 4/4			VOTES	**3. Taylor** Rabbitohs
North Queensland 16					**2. Inglis** Rabbitohs
TRIES	Graham 2; Segeyaro				**1. Graham** Cowboys
GOALS	Thurston 2/3				

Up, up, Todd Carney

Canberra Raiders *versus* **Cronulla Sharks**

2pm, Sunday, 29 April

Canberra Stadium, Canberra

CHRIS PARKINSON

A S I SIT BACK IN MY BAY 70 SEAT AT CANBERRA STADIUM taking in some Toyota Cup action, I find myself thinking back to a different time, a happier time. It was Round 5, 2008 when the Wests Tigers travelled to Canberra for a Sunday afternoon clash with the Green Machine. From the outset there was nothing remarkable about this game. At the halfway mark the Tigers lead 24-10, they had dominated the play, but not necessarily because they played well, more so because the Raiders persisted in making amateur-hour errors.

The second half was a different story. One Todd Carney took the game by the scruff of the neck and, along with the attacking brilliance of Adrian Purtell and stoic defence of Alan Tongue, turned what was an average encounter into one of the better Raiders comebacks I have witnessed. For want of a better cliché, Todd had the ball on a string.

The game finished 30-24 to the Raiders. For Todd's efforts the stats sheet recorded that he set up four tries and scored one himself in a dominant performance. I remember thinking at the time that Todd Carney had arrived. The superstar for whom the Raiders had been waiting (for what seemed an eternity) was finally here. Green-eyed fans dreamt of success again.

What happened next has been documented to death. A string of incidents many wayward teenagers have made unfortunately cut his career at the Raiders short. It was a sad day when the high and mighty powers that be in the Raiders head office ripped up his contract without much of an explanation to fans. We felt rather robbed by it all. I could probably write a quarterly essay on my thoughts on the likes of Furner and McIntyre but for now we will just leave it as it is.

I will be sad again today. He is now a Dally M Medal winner and, of course, he'll run out for the opposing team. My mind returns to the 20s' game in front of me, Malcolm Coongoo has crossed for his third try in about 10 minutes. Suffice to say the Raiders finished up the lesson against the Sharks under-20s not long after, winning 54-12.

And so it follows ... the Sharks' recent good form against the Raiders continues. The Paul Gallen and Todd Carney Show took care of a disappointing Green Machine. The strategy seemed pretty simple – run at the Canberra halves who, unfortunately, were found wanting in terms of their defensive effort – 13 missed tackles between Sam Williams and Josh McCrone is not good enough.

All credit to the Sharks though: the power up the middle, attacking flair on the edges and the finishing ability of the outside backs was complemented by a strong and consistent defensive line, which was the main point of difference between the two sides.

As the balmy Canberra weather cooled off for the evening, those Raiders fans left in the stands make their way for the gates. But before I make my way back over O'Connor Ridge to the car, I hang around to hear what has been an all too common occurrence in the past few years.

The faithful Sharkies fans shivering to the bone rejoicing in victory with their song *Up Up Cronulla*. Just to rub it in a little more I hear another rendition of this great song from a small section of fans: *Up Up Todd Carney*.

Unfortunately the Raiders board members in their climate-controlled boxes probably didn't hear that one.

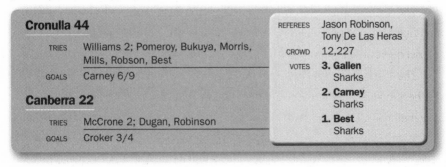

Cronulla 44		REFEREES	Jason Robinson, Tony De Las Heras
TRIES	Williams 2; Pomeroy, Bukuya, Morris, Mills, Robson, Best	CROWD	12,227
GOALS	Carney 6/9	VOTES	**3. Gallen** Sharks
Canberra 22			**2. Carney** Sharks
TRIES	McCrone 2; Dugan, Robinson		**1. Best** Sharks
GOALS	Croker 3/4		

Beef week

Parramatta Eels *versus* **Wests Tigers**
3pm, Sunday, 29 April
Parramatta Stadium, Sydney

MICHAEL HARRISON-FORD

I N A RECENT EMAIL FROM MY OLD MAN, HE MADE WHAT I THOUGHT was a pertinent insight into the team I inherited from him. "What worries me about the Tiges is what also excites me," he wrote. "While other teams seem able to construct a game, the Tiges work in surges. And surges followed by slumps. In fact they seem to lead whole seasons – not just games – that way."

Another way to put it might be is that they're hopelessly inconsistent and a constant frustration to supportors.

Season 2012 has been no different. Heading into today's game against the Eels, the Wests Tigers are 2-5 for the season and have shown little all year: marshmallow defence around the ruck, utter disorganisation in attack and a total inability to lock down games that were there to win.

Despite all this, I arrive at Melbourne's Imperial Hotel to watch the game filled with confidence. Their last round win against the Panthers was solid, the joint venture's first ever shutout, and the demeanour of the squad afterwards suggested an awareness of the hard work still to be done.

Their heads will be right today and they'll win by plenty. No question.

The curtain-raiser sees Canberra host the Sharks. My company is Bossy, a Cronulla and rugby league tragic who is loath to keep the company of anyone who doesn't meet a strict quota of watching at least four NRL games a week.

The Sharks make it six in a row in a truly impressive performance, marred only by the mind-boggling decision in the 72nd minute to take a shot at goal with the scoreboard reading 18-42.

Bossy thinks this is good, smart rugby league, and I can only assume this dour and defeatist attitude is the result of following a team that for so long was incapable of winning by more than a converted try, in those rare instances they got over the line at all.

But this is neither here nor there. For the main event we have the 13th-placed Tigers on the road against the last-placed Parramatta in what one blogger described as "the least interesting game of the round."

While Channel Nine has finally begun to broadcast the NRL direct into Melbourne, The Imperial is opting to show the game via their Imparja feed from the Northern Territory. This pleases me greatly – even if the game lives up to its billing, the regional ads and community service announcements never fail to entertain.

Everything unfolds pretty much in line with my expectations. Team lists are read out and Phil Gould is already rabbiting on about his love for Sunday arvo footy (surely that's a drinking game in the making ...).

It's 10 minutes into the match when Farah puts Lawrence through to open the scoring, and an ad that follows confidently proclaims: SEE YOU AT BEEF WEEK!

Fantastic efforts from Beau Ryan and Liam Fulton extend the lead further and, when Benji Marshall slots a field goal right before halftime, the 19-0 scoreline has me going into the break confident, relaxed and free to ponder the marketing nous of a company that would choose to target its natural remedies for menopause symptoms to the NRL-watching demographic.

My pre-game confidence was well-founded it seems. The Tigers are playing like a team with genuine resolve. Perhaps this is the game where they finally assert their claim to be considered among the competition's top teams.

Of course, that is complacency of the sort a blackjack player on a hot streak might demonstrate. Twenty minutes into the second half, scores unchanged, an old friend calls who is either oblivious to the delayed telecast or else has seized an opportunity to poke me with a stick for his own amusement. The jury's still out.

"How about that," he says, "crazy game!"

I scramble to avoid any further spoilers and pretend that maybe I misheard and, when Ben Murdoch-Masila crosses twice in quick succession, I can only assume I did.

It was 31-0, 15 on the clock. How close could the final result be? It's not long before I have my answer: one point.

In a flurry of attacking opportunism, the Eels put five unanswered tries past the Tigers' appallingly complacent defence, each softer than the last. It unfolds for me in a blur of despair. They got the two points, but a golden opportunity to assert a newly steeled attitude evaporated in the space of 15 minutes.

And it appears we can expect more of the same from the Tigers in 2012.

Wests Tigers 31			REFEREES	Ashley Klein, Gavin Morris
	TRIES	Murdoch-Masila 2; Ryan, Lawrence, Fulton	CROWD	19,654
	GOALS	Marshall 4/5, Moltzen 1/1	VOTES	**3. Woods** Tigers
	FIELD GOAL	Marshall		**2. Marshall** Tigers
Parramatta 30				**1. Galloway** Tigers
	TRIES	Hayne, Sio, Blair, W. Tonga, Ryan		
	GOALS	Burt 5/5		

A sickening clash

Newcastle Knights *versus* Penrith Panthers
7pm, Monday, 30 April
Hunter Stadium, Newcastle

DANIEL DWYER

IT WAS 2.15AM, MONDAY. I WAS WORKING THE NIGHT SHIFT. Pondering the changes I could make to my fantasy teams either through want or necessity. I felt an increase in core temperature and a gentle tingling at the back of my neck. Was this excitement or was I nervous about seeing big Willie Mason in Newcastle colours for the first time? I wandered to the restroom and, kneeling down next to the toilet, I realised that my anxiety was caused by a dodgy casserole ingested less than half an hour previously. With a mixture of toilet water, potatoes and celery splashing up into my face as I heaved, I prayed for Tuesday when this would all be over.

I made myself respectable and went back to my desk. I informed all that I had run into a spot of mischief and went home. On the way, I wondered whether it was a sign of how Monday Night Football was going to go down. Both Newcastle and the Panthers were renowned for playing other teams back into form so perhaps the events that transpired at 2.15am would be something of a highlight. I hoped not as I had earlier proclaimed that the Knights only needed to attend on Monday to get the win but I knew that they were more than capable of throwing up a disastrous performance.

For several hours later that day I remained huddled in a ball on the lounge, waiting for the nausea to cease or the football to start. Despite my feelings of woe for not only myself but also for the game, the start gave me hope. With both teams struggling, the focus was on completing sets and playing field position. Both were making a fair fist of it until an error by Penrith early in the count and some smart passing by the Knights put James McManus over in the corner right on six minutes.

Twelve minutes later a great pass by Timana Tahu put McManus away again down the left. He linked up with Danny Buderus on the inside who then put Jarrod Mullen away under the sticks. At that point I got the feeling that the Knights might be on song, but that feeling was crushed quickly.

On the last tackle, the Knights threw a cut-out pass from dummy-half that went straight past Kurt Gidley and into open space in the backfield. A keen Travis Burns chased hard and regained possession for the Panthers. A couple of tackles on and 204 minutes since the last time it happened, the Panthers had scored a try through Michael Jennings.

Not long after, big Willie Mason made his entrance onto the field with immediate impact. His first hit-up resulted in a Knights penalty. Newcastle shifted the ball quickly to the left before Tahu put Zeb Taia over for the Knights' third to make it 16-4 at halftime.

The second half never really got going. Constant errors from both teams frustrated the fans and nothing much happened until Tahu snapped up an intercept and ran 70 metres to score. Four minutes later, Matt Hilder broke the line from dummy-half and put Gidley away to wrap up the match. A late double to Clint Newton and a barge over by Neville Costigan rounded out the scoring.

The only significant things to come from the match were injuries, which could prove costly to NSW's Origin hopes. Gidley, Buderus, Luke Lewis and Jennings were forced from the field with problems. Gidley looks to be the worst of them after dislocating his shoulder again; he could be out for the remainder of the year.

After the game, I still felt nauseated – it was hard to work out whether it was the food poisoning or the second half. At the end of the day I had to be happy that the Knights had won. I hoped that I wouldn't feel so bad the next time we collected the points.

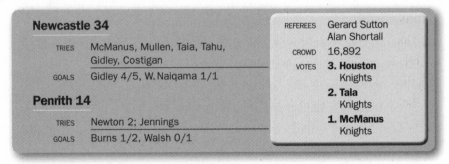

Newcastle 34		REFEREES	Gerard Sutton
			Alan Shortall
TRIES	McManus, Mullen, Taia, Tahu, Gidley, Costigan	CROWD	16,892
GOALS	Gidley 4/5, W. Naiqama 1/1	VOTES	**3. Houston** Knights
Penrith 14			**2. Taia** Knights
TRIES	Newton 2; Jennings		**1. McManus** Knights
GOALS	Burns 1/2, Walsh 0/1		

Round 9

Romping home

Parramatta Eels *versus*
Canterbury Bulldogs
7.30pm, Friday, 4 May
ANZ Stadium

JUSTIN McILVEEN

AFTER ROUND 8, 2012		
1	Storm	8-0
2	Broncos	7-1
3	Sharks	6-2
4	Dragons	5-3
5	Cowboys	4-4
6	Bulldogs	4-4
7	Knights	4-4
8	Sea Eagles	4-4
9	Rabbitohs	4-4
10	Roosters	4-4
11	Tigers	3-5
12	Warriors	3-5
13	Raiders	3-5
14	Panthers	2-6
15	Titans	2-6
16	Eels	1-7

FOR SOME UNKNOWN REASON I came into this game a little apprehensive. The Eels had stormed home against the Tigers the week before and that confidence, added with the extra spice this derby usually brings, had me treading cautiously.

For the opening half hour Parramatta looked like they may have turned the corner following last Sunday's remarkable comeback.

They actually led 12-4 midway through the first half after two quick tries from kicks to Ryan Morgan and Ken Sio had cancelled out Josh Morris' opener.

The Dogs attack hadn't exactly been setting the comp alight, so when a series of penalties came their way, it wasn't the silliest option to kick their way to victory. The tactic wasn't criticised from our corner of the ground.

But a five-minute spell of football, which could be better attributed to the Eels' inability to defend to an NRL standard rather than the brilliance of the Dogs' attack, turned the game on its head. In three consecutive sets the Dogs crossed through Morris, Lafai and Halatau. Two of these came from long range. Halatau's try, in particular, was one for the 2012 highlights reel.

Don't get me wrong, the Dogs were good in this flurry – Big Sam Kasiano caused the Eels all sorts of problems, Barba was a handful and Josh Morris continued the form that should win him a Blues guernsey in a few weeks' time.

But it was the Eels we had to thank.

The second half started with little fanfare and it wasn't until the 48th minute that the scoreboard ticked over again – once again in the Bulldogs' favour. Reynolds chipped from 15 metres out, the ball sat up nicely for him on the follow through and Hayne was too late. Way too late. He must have been dreaming about Sunday at

Hillsong. The Eels No.1 looks to be playing himself out of the rep season.

Further Dogs tries in the 50th minute to Morris (to round off his hat-trick) and 62nd minute to Jono Wright (yes, even he was scoring tries!) left this result well beyond doubt. In the middle of this Bulldogs romp, the Eels' mega-expensive recruit, Chris Sandow, joined the action. "Cheers for that, Steve", he must've been thinking.

A Dogs penalty goal and late try to Goodwin (which he also converted) brought proceedings to an end. Dogs 46, Eels 12. Job done. The pressure on Stephen Kearney is building. He looks in more strife than Peter Slipper.

Kasiano was man of the match but he was supported by Josh Reynolds, Morris and Barba. One notable mention goes to Kris Keating who had his finest match. He is starting to win over the knockers.

Ben Roberts produced a performance that in some small way paid back some of the efforts he produced when in the blue and white. Good on you, Ben.

All in all it was a very soft win, but we'll take the points however they are presented.

Canterbury 46		REFEREES	Tony Archer, Gavin Badger
TRIES	Morris 3; Wright, Lafai, Goodwin, Reynolds, Halatau	CROWD	15,006
GOALS	Goodwin 7/9	VOTES	**3. Morris** Bulldogs
Parramatta 12			**2. Keating** Bulldogs
TRIES	Morgan, W.Tonga		**1. Barba** Bulldogs
GOALS	Burt 2/2		

Forward strike

North Queensland Cowboys *versus* St George Illawarra Dragons
7.30pm, Friday, 4 May
Dairy Farmers Stadium
MARTY SPENCER

WITH INSUFFICIENT FREQUENT FLYER POINTS TO MAKE THE JOURNEY to Townsville, a serious degree of contemplation was required to determine the best venue to watch this Cowboys-Dragons match. The pub on a Friday night is enticing enough although distractions – welcome or otherwise – often make the appreciation of the game difficult.

I had come up with the perfect alternative. The temperature at Dairy Farmers was likely to be in the mid-20s at game time so the prospect of –3° in Canberra called for radical action. I threw on a pair of board shorts and a Bintang singlet, knocked the top off a Ned's Red ale and turned the ducted gas heating up to 25°! I was in Townsville ... sort of.

On paper the game looked tantalizing: fourth versus sixth on the ladder, Origin spots up for grabs and two sides looking for week-to-week consistency. It did not take long for the game to open up and when the Cowboys sent it through the hands in their first attacking set, the die was cast for the evening. Dragons prop Michael Weyman was caught wide in the defensive line and, with speed to burn, Johnathon Thurston, Brent Tate and Ray Thompson combined to score in the second minute. North Queensland had come to play and St George had no answer.

The Cowboys' diminutive triumvirate of Thurston, Thompson and Bowen dominated the attack out of their own 20 with clinical intensity, while the Dragons' defence lacked structure and commitment. With tries at 13 minutes (Bowen), 21 minutes (Linnett) and 33 minutes (Tate), the Cowboys were playing with a confidence that had deserted them in the previous week's loss to South Sydney. Even when the Dragons looked set to score under the posts, JT managed to knock the ball out of Jeremy Latimore's hands, denying them a much-needed lift. The return of Matt Scott had a massive impact. He had a hand in everything and the big mobile Cowboys pack made ground every time they touched the ball.

It was a dominant performance. The Cowboys had 60 per cent of possession, made four line breaks to one and led 22-0. Their completion rate was 88 per cent compared to just 54 per cent for the Dragons and my investment on the Red V +2.5 was looking a little green around the gills.

The Cowboys commenced the second half with the same intensity. The clockwork efficiency of the halves, the superiority of Thurston's kicking game, Matt Bowen back to his elusive best at fullback and a committed and dominant pack suggested that this might be a long night for the Dragons. It wasn't for Matt Prior. In the 55th minute he delivered a forearm jolt to the head of Thurston and was sent from the field. He faces a lengthy suspension after pleading guilty to striking.

Despite the brilliance of the backline, the big talking point from this game was the North Queensland pack. Tariq Sims looks to have completely recovered from his serious leg injury and James Tamou made 19 hit-ups and 25 tackles in his 60-minute stint. Despite the fact that Scott went off injured, his 31 minutes of game time produced moments of brilliance.

Queensland have so many talented forwards, a welcome headache for Mal Meninga in the lead-up to State of Origin I on May 23.

Where do we start with St George? Trent Merrin will come in to replace Prior but the real issue is consistency. The attitude cannot be brought out on game day alone – it must be an ingrained belief in yourself and your teammates – and that must start from next Monday night against Penrith.

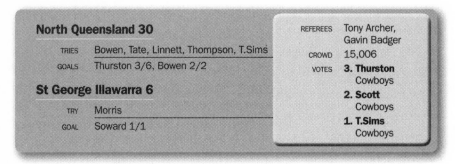

North Queensland 30

TRIES	Bowen, Tate, Linnett, Thompson, T.Sims
GOALS	Thurston 3/6, Bowen 2/2

St George Illawarra 6

TRY	Morris
GOAL	Soward 1/1

REFEREES	Tony Archer, Gavin Badger
CROWD	15,006
VOTES	**3. Thurston** Cowboys
	2. Scott Cowboys
	1. T.Sims Cowboys

A benchmark win

New Zealand Warriors *versus* Brisbane Broncos
7.30pm, Saturday, 5 May
Mt Smart Stadium

JACK MUIR

MY PERENNIAL DISLIKE OF THE BRONCOS is built out of boyhood jealousy more than anything else. It began in the early '90s when the Broncos, packed with state and international representatives, dominated. I couldn't stand Allan Langer – every time he played for the Kangaroos I would scream at the TV to try and get one of the Kiwi forwards to tackle him. They hardly ever did and I just couldn't understand why brutes like Terry Hermansson, Jarrod McCracken and John Lomax couldn't catch and destroy the little bogan from Ipswich.

Then the Warriors' inaugural season came about and I had more reason to hate the arrogant Broncos. They defeated the Warriors in the Kiwi team's first ever game in the big time. The DB Bitter Warriors had a perfect script written for them – there were huge flames around the tunnel they ran out of, and such was the interest that rugby league was mentioned by the principal at my school on the morning of the match. Rugby league? In a New Zealand school?

The Warriors were bringing rugby league to the New Zealand masses but those upstart Queenslanders ruined the script that Friday night in March nearly 20 years ago. Fast forward six months and the Warriors went to ANZ stadium in the final round of the regular season just needing a win to get into the finals in their first year. The Broncos shut the door on any hopes by rattling up 50 points to send us trudging back home for a long offseason. I was an impressionable 12-year-old and that set the scene for more dislike of the Broncos.

Notwithstanding my youthful dislike of the Broncos, as I have grown older and I hope a little more level-headed, I have actually really started to respect the Broncos. I wouldn't say I like them but I have definitely grown to admire their style of football, their toughness, their physicality and the conveyor belt of young talent they bring to our game. In the days of a tight salary cap, they must be doing something right, even if they have the advantage of being a one-town team.

So when I knocked off work on Saturday afternoon to get home to the couch in time to see my Warriors up against the Broncos on a dodgy stream over the internet, I expected the Broncos to give the Warriors a tough game of football. They did exactly that. However, the Warriors gave as good as they got.

This was a great game of football. The Warriors showed the ability that most punters thought they had but which has been hidden away for most of the season. I mean, we beat the Rabbitohs by plenty and, even though they are going alright, they are the Rabbitohs. They aren't a team to give you an indication of how you are really going. The Broncos are.

The Warriors' platform was laid by the forward pack running hard, but it was given back in kind by the Broncos. The quality of the game suggested the two teams will feature in September. So, at the conclusion of the match, there was a real sense of satisfaction. My team had defeated a team which I respect.

It made me feel good as a supporter and I'm sure all the Warriors from the boardroom to the front bar are similarly chuffed.

New Zealand 30		REFEREES	Ben Cummins, Jason Robinson
TRIES	Henry, Johnson, Taylor, Mateo, Lillyman	CROWD	19,012
GOALS	Maloney 5/5	VOTES	**3. Matulino** Warriors
Brisbane 20			**2. Hoffman** Broncos
TRIES	Reed, Glenn, Thaiday, Te'o		**1. Lillyman** Warriors
GOALS	Parker 2/4		

Out of the fire

Gold Coast Titans *versus* Wests Tigers
7.30pm, Saturday, 5 May
Skilled Park, Gold Coast

MATT FISK

THE WESTS TIGERS MADE IT THREE WINS ON THE TROT by defeating the Gold Coast Titans 15-14 in golden point extra-time. The 14,254-strong crowd at Robina was not treated to a great game of football but the gripping nature of the encounter ensured it will be remembered by both sets of fans for some time.

With Scott Prince pulling out of the clash early in the week, the Tigers were expected to march past the battling Titans without much trouble. Things didn't go to plan for the visitors, however, with reliable wingers Kevin Gordon and David Mead posting converted tries for the Gold Coast either side of an Aidan Sezer penalty goal. Had they taken a 14-0 lead into the break the Titans would have been set up for a win but Robbie Farah scored a clever try from dummy-half to make the score 14-6 at the halfway mark.

The game was very different in the second period, with much of the match played in the Wests Tigers' attacking end of the paddock. While they were winning the battle of the ruck, Wests still lacked confidence and structure in attack. Perhaps it had something to do with the late backline reshuffle which saw Chris Lawrence moved to five-eighth, Benji to halfback and Blake Ayshford brought into right centre. Lote Tuqiri had a tight video ref decision go against him but eventually the incessant pressure led to Ayshford stepping around a poor attempted tackle from Jamal Idris to score a try in the 56th minute. Benji made his second tricky conversion of the night and it looked just a matter of time before the Tigers would run away with things even though they still trailed 14-12.

They didn't. The game slowed to a walk and Wests struggled to build on their field position, even knocking back an easy penalty goal attempt with 15 minutes left on the clock, such was their self-assurance. Gold Coast's defence held solid but they did themselves no favours by consistently dropping the ball when coming out of trouble.

Their lack of match-management was exposed with four minutes left on the clock when, in a rare venture to the Tigers 20-metre zone, they attempted a low percentage pass infield on the last, only to see Ben Murdoch-Masila pluck it out of the air and run 85 metres to almost score. Murdoch-Masila combined well with Benji on the run upfield, only to see the video ref deny his try thanks to a David Mead and Phil Graham tackle.

That looked to be the match but, on the ensuing set, Jordan Rankin's clearing kick was charged down by Farah and the NSW Origin hooker was tackled off the ball by Graham five metres from the tryline. Graham was sent to the bin, Benji kicked the goal and the match headed to extra-time.

It seemed inevitable that the experienced Tigers outfit would get what they wanted in golden point time and, sure enough, Jordan Rankin dropped the ball in his own half on the first set of six. The Tigers methodically worked the ball towards the Gold Coast line and Marshall created enough room for Farah to pop over the winning field goal. After trailing all match, the Tigers were victorious.

Tim Sheens wouldn't have been happy with the way his side went about it but made a point of being proud of their commitment. The side has put together three away victories on the trot and now have the chance to work themselves back into the competition. The form of Aaron Woods, Keith Galloway, Beau Ryan and Liam Fulton is extremely encouraging while the likes of Marshall, Farah, Lawrence and Blair will certainly spark into action as the season heats up.

However there is no denying the fact the Tigers are carrying several players in the backline. Lote Tuqiri made five errors in this match and must be on his last legs while Tim Moltzen can be a liability at the back. There is plenty of improvement in this side but some tough decisions will have to be made on those two players and the overall backline structure in coming weeks.

The Titans keep on putting in despite their terrible off-field predicament. They stuck solid without their experienced playmaker and should be proud of Luke Bailey and Matt Srama in particular. Nate Myles, Ashley Harrison and Greg Bird are lifting their form now that they can smell an Origin jersey and Aidan Sezer is a star on the rise.

On the other hand, Phil Graham and Jordan Rankin will be lucky to play at this level again. This match won't be forgotten anytime soon.

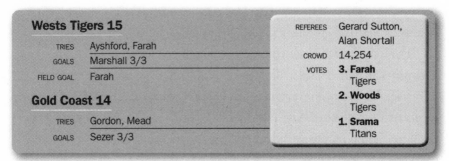

Wests Tigers 15		REFEREES	Gerard Sutton, Alan Shortall
TRIES	Ayshford, Farah	CROWD	14,254
GOALS	Marshall 3/3	VOTES	**3. Farah**
FIELD GOAL	Farah		Tigers
Gold Coast 14			**2. Woods**
			Tigers
TRIES	Gordon, Mead		**1. Srama**
GOALS	Sezer 3/3		Titans

Abandon hope, all ye Panthers supporters

Penrith Panthers *versus* **Melbourne Storm**
7.30pm, Saturday, 5 May
Centrebet Stadium, Sydney

GRANT VICKERS

OPE. AT THE START OF EVERY NRL SEASON, after the endless summer without league, every supporter is filled with hope. The reports are all positive with news of solid preseasons and players getting over their niggles, ready to hook in to Round 1. We haven't been disappointed yet. Even after a close loss to the Bulldogs in Round 1, it didn't seem that bad and that 2012 could be a good year for the Panthers. A shutout win against the Roosters the following week seemed to confirm this and things looked even more promising.

Fast forward to Saturday night in Round 9 and everything had changed. Four straight losses, two without scoring any points whatsoever, plagued by injuries, rumours of off-field indiscretions and injuries to star players, a 2-6 record and things did not look so bright. And now we face the unstoppable Melbourne Storm – undefeated with the big three of Cooper Cronk, Cameron Smith and Billy Slater shredding opposing teams every week. It didn't look like it was going to be a good night at the foot of the mountains. Almost all hope had faded and, as a long-time fan of the Panthers, I was considering not tuning in.

But there was still that little flicker; hope that Ivan Cleary's structure would suddenly click, that Michael Jennings and Luke Lewis could spark the Panthers, or that by some miracle the big three were contained. So I switched on, expecting the worst but hoping for the best.

Surprisingly, Penrith began the match well with the forwards winning at the advantage line and the outside backs making plenty of metres as well. Josh Mansour, in particular, was brilliant, consistently breaking tackles and muscling his way forward for extra yardage. However, despite all this, Melbourne scored first through Matt Duffie.

Then it looked like Penrith were getting it together, moving up the field well and scoring two tries through some excellent play by the newly promoted wingers, Etu Uiasele and Mansour. After 17 minutes, the Panthers led the invincible Storm outfit. Could this be it? Could Penrith actually have a shot at the biggest upset for the season?

Sadly, no.

Not knowing how to win from the front, Ivan Cleary's outfit slackened and the Storm capitalised, roaring back to their clinical best. Melbourne directed plenty of runners at Jennings and he began to show the inconsistency that has plagued him all season. The intensity in the Panthers hit-ups also disappeared, the tackling dropped off, the attack lacked direction, Lewis limped to the bench and Jennings' mystery 'stinger' shoulder injury reappeared.

By the end of the carnage, the Storm had scored seven straight tries to remain undefeated in 2012. Many of the tries came from Penrith errors and length-of-the-field runs, with the outside backs of the Storm completely dominating their opposing players.

Injuries to Penrith's two star players, Jennings and Lewis, who had been mooted as automatic selections in the Origin team, added to the already dire injury situation at Penrith.

At this point, it looks all too much and I've lost hope for the 2012 season. Although it was a loss to the competition front-runners, it highlighted what is wrong with the Panthers. Not enough application for 80 minutes and a lack of direction from the halves. With the injuries and disharmony in the club, I can't see how they will recover. I suspect worse is to come.

Melbourne 44		REFEREES	Steve Lyons, Henry Perenara
TRIES	O'Neill 3; Duffie, Chambers, Cronk, Hoffman, Hinchcliffe	CROWD	9,517
GOALS	Smith 5/7, Widdop 1/1	VOTES	**3. Slater** Storm
Penrith 10			**2. O'Neill** Storm
TRIES	Uaisele, Mansour		**1. Chambers** Storm
GOAL	Austin 1/2		

Starting again

Manly Sea Eagles *versus* **Canberra Raiders**
2pm, Sunday, 6 May
Brookvale Oval, Sydney

NIALL CONNOLLY

HAVE MOVED TO A NEW CITY. I've gone from sunrise over the ocean to sunset. Deepening, darkening crimsons and oranges on the horizon that say, almost a little sadly, "sleep now" as I skirt the water. I turn over the pedals of my new bicycle, my wheels squeaking, and peer into the space that my tepid headlight opens up on the bike path that twists and plunges a little.

I'm careful not to career into a negligent, somnolent local lying in space beneath the sweep of the tropical Milky Way that is beginning to reveal itself over East Point. In the sunshine here a turquoise sea laps clearly over the submerged littoral rocks at high tide. And you do feel, then, like you can see further and breathe more deeply when you watch it, reverently.

The true locals up here are the people of the Larrakia nation. My impression is of a proud people who seem almost ambivalent to intrusion. Not unaffected by it, obviously.

I listen to the musical unfamiliarity of their language on the bus and the naturally welcoming exuberance of their conversation when we talk. It's not all bad for them, or me. Some locals flit about me like ghosts. Momentarily there, like spectres, then receding.

Why am I here, 45, labouring towards a new bed in foreign darkness? Closer, almost, to where I was born just north of the equator, than to where I grew up and have lived? To home?

Including the Sydney suburb of Balgowlah, where my life changed once as a new arrival, and where I met my footy life-partner, who has presented me with eight lovely children. Eight! Yes, that's right, eight! As simple as a pleasing splash of colour and maybe a visit to Brookie with my Dad. "I like themuns, Dad".

Who knows? I'll never know now.

Dad played rugby for the Lansdowne Club in Dublin, himself an Ulster fish out of water, but he knew his footy. I miss his gentle remonstrations at my, sometimes, obscenity-laden gesticulations at a TV that had failed me.

"C'mon, Niall" was the limit of his severity.

My first clear recollection of a Grand Final was 1976 when I was nine. Pure joy. Only later would I learn how badly Parramatta had cocked up what could have been their first premiership.

Back to "Why"? There is a Hoodoo Gurus song *1000 Miles Away*:

Working for yourself ain't all that it's cracked up to be ...

All self-employed people who have been too generous with their time will know how hard it is to collect when you have worked towards the assurance of a promise. And if you're their plumber or sparky rather than their fool lawyer who might have, say, averted their bankruptcy with a clever argument, you're still likely to be paid more promptly, or at all.

I'm soft. Of heart. And I live in Darwin, which is wonderful. A nice place to be owed thousands and where many like me head to pick themselves up and start again.

Oh, the game. Right. Manly beat the Doggies in a grinding effort last week. They weren't with it for most of this one though. Theirs was a somnolent effort, like a slumbering body on a bike path at dusk but with enough presence of mind to roll away from the bicycle at the very last minute.

Manly 18		REFEREES	Jared Maxwell, Tony De Las Heras
TRIES	Whare 2; Lyon	CROWD	15,033
GOALS	Lyon 3/4	VOTES	**3. Lyon** Sea Eagles
Canberra 12			**2. Whare** Sea Eagles
TRIES	Dugan, Papalii		**1. Dugan** Raiders
GOALS	Croker 2/2		

The only points that count

Sydney Roosters *versus* **Newcastle Knights**

3pm, Sunday, 6 May

Allianz Stadium

BRETT OATEN

ERE'S WHAT THE LAST 11 DAYS HAVE TAUGHT ME: I will take a win in an ordinary game over a loss in a fantastic game, every day of the week.

Actually, I knew that already.

I loved everything about the Anzac Day game – the crowd, the atmosphere, the tension and the way the Roosters played (for 76 minutes) – but the last four minutes killed me. Looking back, I still thought it was their best performance of the year and it pointed to better days to come but, even so, it still killed me.

I hoped that today was going to be one of those better days and for 40 minutes it was, but those 40 minutes came after halftime and before that, we had to sit through an A-Grade snooze-fest.

The Knights announced their intention early by picking the nippy Neville Costigan at hooker and, for a guy who bitches about the NRL being boring, Wayne Bennett has sure learnt how to turn the boring stuff on this year. Yes, they were missing Gidley and Buderus, but does anyone other than Ricky Stuart actually think Buderus is going well? If you ask me, he's been playing like a guy who would take a holiday in Adelaide.

But I digress. The first half was tough but very dull. The Roosters had a ton of possession but couldn't do anything with it and the Knights succeeded in boring everyone including themselves. Jarrod Mullen opened the scoring with a neat dummy after getting a helping hand up the field from a refereeing howler. Then the Roosters hit back, Pearce grubbering for the busy Arona, and a subsequent penalty left it 8-6 to the Roosters at halftime. Nothing else of note happened.

The game came alive in the second half and, luckily for me, all of that life was in the Roosters' young team. Boyd Cordner provided the spark with two monster hits on Willie Mason which inspired his fellow players and warmed the hearts of those who sat through Mason's two superannuation years at Bondi. By all accounts, Mason is being paid next to nothing by the Knights and he looks set to deliver value for money. Cordner, still only 19, will be a star.

Off the back of a better forward effort, Friend and Pearce started to find space for Minichiello, Aubusson and the ever-reliable Perrett, with Takairangi's offloads a highlight as well. Uate was a constant danger for the Knights, being their toughest forward and their most dangerous back.

The rest of the Knights were pedestrian. Timanu Tahu was not looking enthusiastic, Darius Boyd continued his listless year and Kade Snowden was a passenger. Only Ben Roberts' and Chris Sandow's horror runs are keeping Snowden and Boyd out of 'year's worst buy' discussions, and both are internationals.

The Roosters may not have beaten anyone of note so far but the youngest team in the comp is still in the eight and improving.

The Knights are trending down and it's hard to see that changing. Wayne Bennett is generally considered a genius but I've often thought his genius involved always making sure he was in charge of a gun team. He isn't this year and so, it seems, genius is in shorter supply. No one will have this game in their top 50 list for the year but I loved it. Two points will make you feel that way.

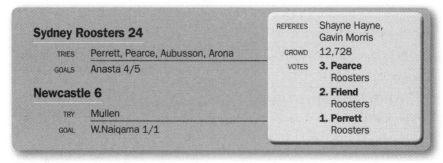

Sydney Roosters 24			REFEREES	Shayne Hayne, Gavin Morris
TRIES	Perrett, Pearce, Aubusson, Arona		CROWD	12,728
GOALS	Anasta 4/5		VOTES	**3. Pearce** Roosters
Newcastle 6				**2. Friend** Roosters
TRY	Mullen			**1. Perrett** Roosters
GOAL	W.Naiqama 1/1			

Is this the year?

South Sydney Rabbitohs *versus* Cronulla Sharks
7pm, Monday, 7 May
ANZ Stadium

RUSSEL HANSEN

MONDAY NIGHT FOOTBALL REQUIRES THE LONG WAIT. I feel well prepared for the occasion as over the weekend, as part of my long wait, I met a true Rabbitoh stalwart, Mick Coorey of The Spotted Cow Hotel in Toowoomba fame. I will be travelling back to that establishment during the season for a Souths game.

Mick's father was at Souths' first ever premiership game against North Sydney on that famous Easter Monday in April 1908.

Having scored the 1000th win for the club last start against the fast-finishing Cowboys, many experts, including *Grandstand*'s David Morrow, are once again talking up our chances.

I start to receive the usual array of text messages throughout the afternoon. Could this be the ideal weekend for a Souths' supporter based in Brisbane – a Broncos loss and a win for the famous cardinal and myrtle?

The Sharks are sitting in third place on the ladder after six straight wins. Our record against the Sharks is solid but this looks like being a stern test. Although we've won three of our last four, there are still concerns. We're yet to see a full 80-minute effort.

I am downstairs in the media room, flying solo for the game. My usual companion for MNF, brother Rob Bush, is in Sydney. He refers to the media room as "the home of Monday Night Football". Rob and I will speak on the phone often during the second half.

Sam Burgess is back for Souths, starting from the bench. Nathan Merritt is playing his second NRL match for the season. We have plenty of strike power.

The wait is soon over and the Greg Inglis show begins in the fourth minute with a try. After some slick passing, GI, revelling in his fullback role, fades to the left to finish a classy piece of attack.

The high-flying Sharks are always in the contest. Todd Carney plays as though he has spiders on his jersey. He crosses for the Sharks' first try virtually untouched. Carney is on song, displaying the form which has experts talking up his chances of Origin selection.

Inglis is on fire. A long run from a 20-metre tap having caught the Sharks' defence off-guard is all class (and poetry in motion!). Farrell is eventually brought down 30 from the Sharks' line. How the Sharks were onside in that frantic passage of play is beyond me.

Tries to Merritt – a vintage 50-metre run off a Gallen turnover – and Inglis give Souths a handy buffer. A try to Robson before halftime has me nervous as my Rabbitoh brother Rob and I spoke during the halftime break.

We are awarded a penalty when Sutton is hit after a kick and that makes the score 20-12. If Inglis isn't making huge yards in attack, he's saving tries in defence (this time holding up the Sharks attacker over the line) before Mills scores to bring it dangerously close at 20-16.

Gallen leaves the field in the 55th minute with a knee injury which immediately becomes a talking point in the lead up to Origin. Inglis continues his Herculean performance as he leaps high to score his third try. Souths lead 26-16 with 20 minutes left. Will tonight be the night of an 80-minute effort from the boys?

Inglis throws a magnificent pass to put Merritt over in the left corner for a 32-16 lead. Colin Best, who didn't live up to his family name during a couple of seasons with us, scores to keep me on edge, before Inglis saves another try as Williams loses the ball over the line. A late penalty goal to Reynolds, which gives him seven from seven for the night, pushes Souths out to a 34-22 lead.

Souths again lose concentration in defence as a Carney kick results in a try for Pomeroy in the final minute resulting in a 34-28 win.

All in all, a great win for Souths over a very solid Sharks team. Souths' season is building a quiet momentum. If quiet momentum is possible at Redfern Oval.

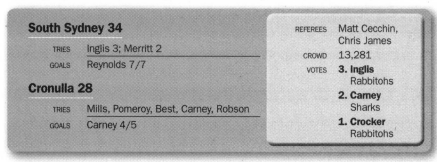

South Sydney 34

TRIES	Inglis 3; Merritt 2
GOALS	Reynolds 7/7

Cronulla 28

TRIES	Mills, Pomeroy, Best, Carney, Robson
GOALS	Carney 4/5

REFEREES	Matt Cecchin, Chris James
CROWD	13,281
VOTES	**3. Inglis** Rabbitohs
	2. Carney Sharks
	1. Crocker Rabbitohs

Round 10

Gone in 60 seconds

Brisbane Broncos *versus* **Manly Sea Eagles**

7pm, Friday, 11 May

Suncorp Stadium, Brisbane

LINDSEY CUTHBERTSON

FROM A YOUNG AGE I WAS TAUGHT THE VALUE OF TIME in rugby league; that the 60 seconds it takes to complete a set of six can provide a slew of opportunities for those willing to go the extra distance to reach them. It was also drummed into me that the pressure of a close contest can make those 60 seconds feel like an eternity or a moment that will slip past you in the blink of an eye.

Sitting up here high in the stands of Suncorp Stadium on a cool Brisbane night, with 41,000 spectators in this theatre of sporting battle, I wonder how much of an influence time and pressure is going to have on this contest. When these two teams play, it's always a tough, exciting encounter.

Manly couldn't have asked for a better start with a try to Jamie Lyon in the third minute. A penalty goal follows soon after and, with an 8-0 lead, it feels as if Manly can break away from the Broncos.

But they don't. A mixture of Sea Eagles errors and the Broncos finding their rhythm sees the momentum swing back to the home team. The Broncos set up camp in the Sea Eagles' half and proceed to punch holes in the Manly defence.

First, Corey Parker pops a ball out to Jack Reed, who goes through to score a fairly soft try in the 21st minute. Six minutes later, a Corey Norman cross-field kick finds its way onto Gerard Beale's chest for another try.

Unfortunately for the Broncos, Parker's kicking boot has lost its usually reliable radar as he fails to convert for the second time.

It doesn't seem to matter though because, when Alex Glenn bulldozes through Cherry-Evans' attempted tackle and plants the ball down in the left-hand corner three minutes later, the Broncos are up by four and are running high on confidence.

All except for Parker whose kicking confidence is shot: he sprays another conversion.

The Broncos blow the opportunity to really stamp their authority on the half when Manly is given a late attacking opportunity down their end of the field. And they take it, with a try to Steve Matai giving the Sea Eagles a 14-12 lead going into the break.

Manly seem to know the importance of hitting back before the break and it turns the pressure off themselves and onto the home side.

Once the second half starts, the Broncos take little time to respond with another Norman cross-field kick falling into the arms of Matt Gillett.

The scores remain close but even though a try to 'The Wolfman' 10 minutes later gives the Sea Eagles back their lead, it doesn't feel like enough. And it isn't because when Gillett scores another try in the 63rd minute – and Corey Norman successfully relieves Parker of the goalkicking duties – the lead changes hands again.

There's still time though, but the pressure's mounting on Manly as the seconds slip away. Only 10 minutes remain, then five, and still there is no change in the scores.

When Brett Stewart knocks on with 2:54 to play, inside I start to think that the pressure is affecting Manly - that it's too much to win from here and maybe the Broncos will manage to close out the match.

But three minutes is a heartbreakingly long time in rugby league. When Manly finally do get an opportunity down the left hand side through Steve Matai, they take it. He's tackled inside the Broncos half after a decisive break and, a few tackles later, the Sea Eagles spread it wide. Glenn Stewart finds his captain Lyon with some room to move and off he goes on the outside of Jack Reed with a two-on-one overlap on winger Dale Copley. Copley waits, then commits, Lyon feeds the ball to an unmarked 'Wolfman', and he scores right in the corner to claim the victory.

I proceed to do damage to my vocal chords. They will take some time to heal.

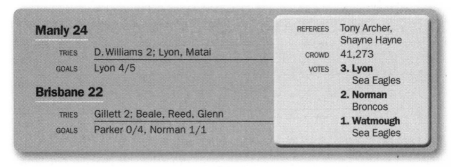

Manly 24		REFEREES	Tony Archer, Shayne Hayne
TRIES	D. Williams 2; Lyon, Matai	CROWD	41,273
GOALS	Lyon 4/5	VOTES	**3. Lyon** Sea Eagles
Brisbane 22			**2. Norman** Broncos
TRIES	Gillett 2; Beale, Reed, Glenn		**1. Watmough** Sea Eagles
GOALS	Parker 0/4, Norman 1/1		

Crippled by expectation

Canterbury Bulldogs *versus* **Gold Coast Titans**
8.45pm, Friday, 11 May
Suncorp Stadium, Brisbane

MARK SEYMOUR

THE MANTLE OF PRE-MATCH FAVOURITISM HAS ALWAYS BEEN A CONCERN TO ME. The experts were calling this game a gimme for Canterbury. I hate approaching a match as if we should win. For me, I revel in the feeling of being the underdog ... the team with no chance, for at no other time is victory sweeter, the celebration greater or the post-match analysis longer. So, with some apprehension, I noted that my Bulldogs were firm favourites for their Round 10 clash against the Titans. I think it's worse for me: favouritism infects any team I support with an inability to play to their true form.

When scrutinising this match in the lead-up, I convinced myself that, on paper, the Bulldogs did deserve to be the bookies' pick. The factors were clear. After trading Brookvale for Belmore the coach had settled in without as much as a hiccup, we were coming off a Round 5 victory against the Titans and the human highlight reel, Ben Barba, was in such great form that he surely had the No.1 jersey for Queensland and Australia in sight.

Perhaps the ultimate reason for my confidence was the prediction from noted NRL commentator Paul Dalligan that the Titans would be cellar dwellers this year.

So it was with quiet confidence that I sat down for what should have been an excellent Friday night's entertainment.

My only nagging worry was the thought of Canterbury playing a home game at, of all places, Suncorp Stadium. All of my pre-match confidence evaporated early as the Bulldogs played some pretty undisciplined football during the first half and I watched spellbound (like most of the Canterbury players) as Beau Champion seemed to have scored in the 22nd minute for the Titans. Fortunately, on review, replays showed a Titans player knocking forward during the preceding aerial contest.

I was reminded of the up and down of the rollercoaster ride when just over a minute later, after a clever exchange between Stagg and Halatau, Barba was on the end of a pass that saw him go in between the posts. Confidence is a wonderful thing that can be re-ignited with just such a play. Surely with the early lead, the Bulldogs would now press home the advantage like true favourites.

Little did I realise that this brief flurry was about the only shot Canterbury would fire for the rest of the evening. Spurred by a mountain of penalties against the Bulldogs (11 for the match), including two for giving it to the referee, the Titans managed to get back into the match just before the break with a try from Scott Prince. Worse was to come after halftime with the Titans going on a scoring spree with three tries in 15 minutes to Srama, Idris and Minichiello. Late tries to Barba and Morris failed to put a dent in the scoreline and the pre-match favourites went down by 11 points.

I have only one request of the oddsmakers between now and the end of the season. Please ignore Canterbury. That way I can enjoy watching the game without the very heavy burden of being expected to win.

Gold Coast 25		REFEREES	Jared Maxwell, Brett Suttor
TRIES	Idris, Prince, Srama, Minichiello	CROWD	41,273
GOALS	Sezer 2/3, Prince 2/3	VOTES	**3. Bird**
FIELD GOAL	Sezer		Gold Coast
Canterbury 14			**2. Srama**
			Gold Coast
TRIES	Barba 2; Morris		**1. Barba**
GOAL	Goodwin 1/3		Bulldogs

Just like old times

New Zealand Warriors *versus* Sydney Roosters
7.30pm, Saturday, 12 May
Mt Smart Stadium, Auckland

STEVE MASCORD

ONCE UPON A TIME, NEWSPAPER MATCH REPORTS had to have a newsy lead. If someone was sent off or hurt (er, sorry), the reporter would breathe a little easier knowing there was an issue to ask the coaches and players downstairs about and a straightforward story would emerge.

The thinking behind this was elementary: in Australia, most people interested enough to read your story were also interested enough to have watched the game on television and would, at the very least, know who won.

You had to tell them something new – and it sometimes involved staying in the sheds until the last player had left, piecing together the story of the winning field goal or the halftime talk or the "we did it for Joe Bloggs" angle.

Then, abruptly, newspapers waved the white flag in the face of the invading digital hoards of the internet. There was an all-pervading defeatism – we can no longer tell the readers anything new because they get that from turning on their laptops and iPhones.

We were left with what I call *It-Was-The...* journalism. Instead of "Julia Gillard spontaneously combusted in parliament yesterday", reporters started writing "it was the day that shocked a nation". These soft leads acknowledged the fact that you, the reader, already knew the basic facts of the story – we had been emasculated, reduced to the role of entertainers instead of informers.

And this meek approach infected rugby league match reports. How many do you read today that tell you something new in the first paragraph?

The worsening access to players exacerbated the problem. If you were determined to get the story behind the play of the day, it was harder to actually crack it for a chat with the players concerned before deadline.

So match reporting sunk into a navel-gazing abyss. Even though you already knew about the game and had no idea who the journalist was, you were going to get his opinion on events whether you wanted it or not.

I've never accepted this. Journalists are still more likely to find out something you don't know than a random Tweeter. I always try to get a line from the sheds and not settle for empty prose – mainly because it's just more fun to challenge yourself that way.

The Round 10 game between the Warriors and Sydney Roosters was the match of the year for colourful quotes. It's what covering rugby league used to be like.

I knew this would be an interesting night when Braith Anasta told referee Steve Lyons: "You referees have set a very dangerous precedent" after Boyd Cordner had been placed on report for clipping Jerome Ropati high – only for Ropati to go off with a knee injury that would subsequently end his season.

Just a word on SportsEars, the little green boxes that allow us to hear what the referees and players are saying. There are still people who believe we shouldn't be reporting what we hear on them, that what happens out there should stay there. Fine, stop selling SportsEars. If they are available to the public, then what is transmitted by them is in the public domain. And if it's in the public domain, it can be reported. This is black and white to me.

Anyway, Anasta and Brian Smith's post-match media conference was the best of the season:

> "I'm told it's not a pretty look when I'm angry and frustrated so I'll choose to be very proud instead … [of] … the complete resilience they showed to fight back after some diabolical decisions.
>
> The fans here are fantastic in support of their team but we shouldn't all get caught up in that. Coaches and players and referees and even video referees have got a job to do to stay balanced.
>
> We were playing for the game and the two referees looked to me like they couldn't wait to get off the field.

The good thing about interviewing the coaches for the ABC is that I can put things to them that the other coach and captain have said in the media conference. Often I will deliberately not ask a salient question in the press conference and save it for the ABC interview. I can then use the quote in my match report, too. After all, I have no responsibility to give stories to my opposition who are standing next to me at the media conference.

Warriors' coach Brian McClennan was not pleased with Smith and Anasta's account of the Ropati incident.

"The kid got whacked around the head," McClennan said, "and then he's come off with that, as well as the knee injury. What's their point?"

I remember Brian Smith himself hitting back at then Warriors coach Tony Kemp at the same ground, in the same circumstances, a few years ago. He pointed out that Kemp was rated the most likely coach to be sacked next – an incendiary comment by any measure.

Neither that match report, or this one, opened with the words "It was the …"

New Zealand 30			REFEREES	Steve Lyons, Henry Perenara
TRIES	Hurrell, Johnson 2; Vatuvei		CROWD	16,220
GOALS	Maloney 5/5		VOTES	3. **Hurrell** Warriors
Sydney Roosters 26				2. **Guerra** Roosters
TRIES	Minichiello, Moga, Leilua, Waerea-Hargraves, Guerra			1. **Johnson** Warriors
GOALS	Anasta 3/6			

The battle of the bulge

Newcastle Knights *versus* **North Queensland Cowboys**
7.30pm, Saturday, 12 May
Hunter Stadium, Newcastle

JOHN HARMS

LIKE FAT BLOKES. NOT JUST BIG BLOKES. FAT BLOKES. Blokes with tummies that look a bit soft and floppy. I like Mark Cosgrove. I like Jarrod Lyle. I liked Henri Leconte and Greg Ritchie.

I liked the old props who used to run out for Oakey in the Toowoomba comp when I was a kid, especially Sel Murphy, who was a big ranga from out west. Tara, I reckon. Or Warra. Sel's face would go bright red after about three minutes. He was gentle, but could fire up, and led the boys around the park on his day. He was definitely well-tummied.

There were others.

I remember Darren Lockyer telling me about an Origin match for which Queensland were real underdogs. It was the last-ever Origin match at the old Lang Park, played before a full house of charged Queenslanders.

"I was worried," he said. "How'll we get through this? We're gunna get a floggin' here."

As he was running out he caught a glimpse of John Buttigieg. "Look at the guts on that," he thought to himself. It confirmed his fears.

In the opening minutes of that match, Lote Tuqiri put Lockyer away for a brilliant length-of-the-field try and the Maroons went on to win the match easily, with Big Fat JB solid as a rock and even scoring a try. They took the series 2-1, at ANZ Stadium, when Alfie came back.

These days, I look out for the fat blokes. It's a brotherhood thing. And so as North Queensland run out at Newcastle, I notice Matt Scott. A white jumper is not flattering generally, but Matt Scott looks like he's got the spare tyre happening. And, for the Knights, Willie Mason is just a big middle-aged unit.

I am sure Scott will be looking for a strong performance as will many on the park. For as much as the points are at stake, Origin squads are being finalised. Scott's form has been fair, his body in better nick than last year. He should be there.

Newcastle at Newcastle is a tough gig, and the Knights open like it's their dung-hill. Uate is brilliant early with powerful kick-returns and a line break that should have resulted in a try. Mason is also forceful, in a chubby sort of way, but he blows up quickly, failing to last the first quarter-of-an-hour.

Weight of possession eventually tells and Darius Boyd puts Junior Sa'u into the clear and over. Newcastle 6 - 0.

The visitors string together some nice attack and Brent Tate looks like he'll score for sure when Roberts manages to drag him down. From the ensuing play-the-ball, Bowen finds Scott inside and the prop projects his bustling belly towards the line. He is brought down by Sa'u just short and reaches over for what is a try if you're watching in Townsville and a double movement in the Hunter. After a long deliberation, the refs side with those from Cessnock.

Then two classic attacks from North Queensland result in two tries. It's not often you see traditional, through-the-hands, width-of-the-field backline movements, but these are just that. Firstly to Ashley Graham, after a final pass from Tate. And secondly to Ray Thompson after Matt Bowen makes the extra man, who puts Tate away, and Tate having looked outside, comes back in with a pass to Thompson.

Momentum changes again and right on halftime Jarrod Mullen's short ball finds a rampaging Chris Houston who charges over. 12-12 at the break.

Both have plenty of tricks and the Knights played one after the resumption only to see Uate drop a dolly with the line wide open. The winger is having a mercurial game.

JT has been solid but he really takes control of the match in the way that fans of the game have come to appreciate. Having moved to halfback, his grubber kicks keep Newcastle deep in their own territory; his ability to read the moment leads to some brilliant attacks. It's all the Cowboys and eventually they break the deadlock with a try to Morgan, before pouring it on over the last 20 minutes to win comfortably.

Matt Bowen follows JT wherever he goes; Tate is mega-reliable, his ability to pick the right option so astute.

Matt Scott is interviewed at the end of the match. The camera-man has gone for a head shot.

It's his better angle.

North Queensland 32		REFEREES	Matt Cecchin, Gavin Morris
TRIES	Graham 2; Thompson, Cooper, Morgan	CROWD	18,191
GOALS	Thurston 6/6	VOTES	**3. Thurston** Cowboys
Newcastle 12			**2. Bowen** Cowboys
TRIES	Sa'u, Houston		**1. Tate** Cowboys
GOALS	Roberts 2/2		

A tough sell

Canberra Raiders *versus* **Parramatta Eels**
2pm, Sunday, 13 May
Canberra Stadium

MICK PEARSON

S O HERE'S THE MOTHER'S DAY PITCH. Sunday afternoon at Canberra Stadium wearing your best fluoro green outfit and Viking helmet. Chilli con carne in a noodle box with a plastic fork accompanied by a can of bourbon and Coke in a plastic cup, no ice required. Weather will be a little cool and windy, five degrees tops, but no rain. Two teams and coaches who are hungry and can't afford to taste defeat. The authenticity of the experience sells itself. Pure emotion assured. Lucky I live in Brisbane.

Any pitch including a footy match isn't going to fly in my world today, enticing or not. However, the alluring offer of spectating at a C-grade cricket match with a hamper on a blanket under sunny skies is another matter. Throw in a few chilled champers flutes and a bottle of good Aussie sparkling, the promise of relaxation under the cloudless 26° skies and the hook is in. Even if it is to pretend to watch a few older blokes trying to fill a day playing a 50-over match for the Brisbane Brothers Cricket Club. To be honest, the term '50-over, one-day' match is a tautology (and exaggeration) with the average innings rarely lasting beyond the second drinks session and change of innings doubling as morning tea. After-match beers need to be on the ice well before lunch to ensure the right level of frostiness when victory, or defeat, visits generally around 1pm or so.

Today, a seven-wicket victory is secured well before footy kick-off at 2pm. The champers has been the perfect entrée to an afternoon nap for The Bride and she is resting peacefully, as all should on Mother's Day. I am pinching myself it's not Father's Day.

I tune in. In the rooms, the Eels are moving through the sheds formally, shaking hands with each other as seems to be the pre-match custom these days. Sandow is conspicuous in his approach to Hindmarsh and they shake hands like they have never met or, maybe, wish they hadn't. In contrast, the Raiders are enthusiastic huggers, butting shoulders like some Viking tradition. They look like a team who might actually be enjoying each other's company.

Despite gloomy predictions, the teams put on a decent contest with some enterprising play. The Raiders are a team that can score points, especially at home on a dry and cold track. Dugan is the architect. He is back playing with genuine passion and desire, just as he showed when he earned representative honours a season or two ago.

His effort to strip Hayne within a millisecond of the Eels fullback taking a bomb on his own line is cutting-edge genius and it leads to a crucial try just before halftime. Ferguson shows glimpses of his best and, although it is never far from his worst, he is not under scrutiny today, unlike his left-side centre and winger counterparts, who have been impersonating a toll road in defence all season. Raiders lead 24-6 at the break.

It is a cheap shot to say the Eels are a bunch of non-trying, inconsistent milk-drinkers. Let's just say they look like the archetypal amalgam of talent but with nothing in common except the hope to win a footy match. This alone does not win footy matches. Meaningful achievements are earned through perseverance, belief and heart. As my old mum reminds me regularly, "patience and persistence will piss a hole in a stone". I only hope the Eels coach is dispensing the same motherly wisdom to his troops.

In the second half, the Eels mount a comeback and for a fleeting moment look as though they may blouse the nervous Raiders. Unfortunately for the Eels, the game requires they have to share possession of the football with the Raiders and having to tackle doesn't suit their current style of play.

With 20 minutes to play the Raiders skip away to a 36-18 lead and the result looks safe. Finally, the penny drops and the Eels commence to attack the Raiders' fragile left side defence and score three tries in six minutes, including some magic from Hayne and Sandow in the 77th minute to close the gap to two points.

Normality prevails and the Eels give up a try during the next Raiders possession from the worst attempted tackle of the year on Jack Wighton, who strolls 50 metres to seal the deal for the Raiders 40-34. The victory is a hollow one and the Raiders leave the field looking like they have just won a kiss from their sister.

The Eels depart to keep working on that hole in the stone.

Canberra 40			REFEREES	Gavin Badger, Adam Devcich
TRIES	Robinson, Thompson 2; Ferguson, Wighton, Papalii		CROWD	9,210
GOALS	Croker 6/7		VOTES	**3. Dugan** Raiders
Parramatta 34				**2. Ferguson** Raiders
TRIES	Morgan, Sio 2; Blair, Sandow			**1. Hindmarsh** Eels
GOALS	Burt 5/6			

Jeremy Smith, a Shark for the ages

Cronulla Sharks *versus* **Melbourne Storm**

3pm, Sunday, 13 May

Toyota Stadium, Sydney

MARK NICHOLS

DOES IT GET ANY BETTER THAN A SUNDAY AFTERNOON IN THE SUN at the Wrecking Yard (Shark Park to some people)? I'm here to tell you it doesn't. It just doesn't. As I took my seat on the tryline and looked straight into the eye of the sun, I almost cursed that I had left my 2012 Members cap at home.

That the hat is too small to fit a newborn, and that the sun would burn a hole straight through it, stifled any likely curse. Hopefully we are putting the money saved on our Members Pack into the salary package for a CEO one day.

So, to the game. The first 15 minutes are very willing, as you would expect from two physical packs, and Portugal's second favourite athlete (just behind Ronaldo and slightly in front of Nani), Isaac De Gois, is defending like a man possessed. Isaac Gordon decides he wants the scoreboard attendant to earn his pie and Coke and gets it ticking over. Cronk puts up a speculator, Gordon has an air swing after losing the ball in the sun and Nielsen falls on the ball for the easiest try he will score. The Storm drop the ball from the kick-off and, three tackles later, Gordon beats a few combatants and scores a great try to make it Isaac 6 Gordon 6 and it's all tied up.

Despite the Storm spending the majority of the half in the Sharks 20, they only score one more four-pointer and the Sharks head to the sheds to a standing ovation down 10-6.

The second half is a battle of attrition and Melbourne begin to gain the upper hand until Jeremy Smith rejoins the fray in the 65th minute. I haven't seen a forward change the momentum of a game with such single-minded determination since Tawera Nikau's second half performance in the '99 Grand Final.

Kamikaze-like in defence and making a mountain of metres with the ball, he often carries three or four Storm forwards to gain precious extra yards. His efforts seem in vain as the Sharks playmakers are unable to dent the defensive wall of the Storm until Smith takes matters into his own hands. In the 71st minute, he takes the ball from dummy-half on the last tackle and steamrolls his way over three defenders to score the winning try.

Has there been a better 15 minutes from a player this year? Has there been a better 15 minutes by a Shark ever? No, not this year, and I can't recall one in the last 24 years and I haven't missed many Sharks games since I spilt a few eight-year-old tears when we went down to the Tigers in the preliminary final in '88.

Where does Smith sit with the great Sharks players after only 25-odd games and where does he sit among the best Kiwis to grace the NRL? He is the best international player I have seen at the Sharks. Big call, I know, beating out international superstars Alan Bateman, Tiaan Strauss, Eion Crossan, Luke Covell and Bryson Goodwin and just pipping Nigel Vagana, Richie Barnett, the Sorensen brothers and that man Nikau.

As for the other two questions, it's hard to judge with him still in his prime and with a few good years left in him. If he can lead us to an improbable maiden premiership, he will be the first Kiwi and second man ever to win a Premiership at three different clubs and will prove he's the best Kiwi to have played in the NRL.

There is also no doubt that he will join Paul Gallen in the backrow for the greatest Sharks team of all time, relegating all but one of Greg Pierce, Gavin Miller, David Hatch and the Sorensens to fight it out for a spot on the bench.

Am I getting ahead of myself? Of course I am, I'm a Sharks fan and that's what we do.

Cronulla 12		REFEREES	Ben Cummins, Jason Robinson
TRIES	Gordon, Smith	CROWD	14,595
GOALS	Carney 2/2	VOTES	**3. Smith** Sharks
Melbourne 10			**2. Graham** Sharks
TRIES	Duffie, Nielsen		**1. Cronk** Storm
GOAL	Smith 1/2		

Football in the modern day

Penrith Panthers *versus* **St George Illawarra Dragons**
7pm, Monday, 14 May
Centrebet Stadium, Sydney

PETER ABELA

WHEN I WAS ASKED TO WRITE FOR THE FOOTY ALMANAC, the word 'impartial' was never mentioned. With Penrith performing so poorly, I've had precious little opportunity for gloating, although it hasn't stopped me writing Panther-specific reports. The tone has, understandably, been sombre. I'm expecting this report to be no exception.

It's Round 10, Penrith against the Dragons at CUA Stadium. Penrith have come off a wretched April where they didn't score a point until late on the 30th day of the month, a month that included two 30-0 floggings. The Panthers are yet to win a match at home this season and, at this stage of the competition, the only thing keeping Penrith away from the wooden spoon is a very ordinary Parramatta outfit.

Worse, the Panthers are going to have to do without their superstar centre and leading try-scorer for a few weeks - tonight because he is playing reserve grade and next week because he'll be playing State of Origin. Go figure!

The only thing favouring the Panthers is that the Dragons have been somewhat inconsistent this season – and were downright terrible in their last outing against the Cowboys. However, given they were bad last week, they are likely to be on fire tonight. Such is the logic of the despondent Panthers fan, devoid of hope and desiring nothing more than a hard-fought match.

It's Monday night and it's cold. A visit to the CUA Stadium is out of the question and access to Pay TV is also proving problematic. In this day and age, there's always a Plan B and, on this occasion, I'm hoping the NRL website with its video highlights will do the trick. All I need to do is stay away from the news for a couple of hours.

Alas none of my plans are working tonight. Hiding away in the study, I'm interrupted by my son, who charges in and shoves his laptop under my nose.

"Get that away," I growl. "I don't want to know the result just yet."

However, in that brief glimpse, I see something. If I'm not mistaken, the laptop shows the live score and it reads Penrith 12, Dragons 0.

"Sorry Dad," replies my crestfallen son. "I thought you'd want to know."

"Not yet – take it away from me."

The phone in my pocket beeps. A text message from Robbo. "Are you guys going to hang on?"

It must be true. I call out to my son. "How far into the match are they?"

"Fifty-fourth minute. Sorry that I showed you the score."

"That's alright."

Fifty-fourth minute. Can they hang on? We've been in front in other games this year only to be overtaken, most notably against the Bulldogs in Round 1. I reply to Robbo's text message: "Unlikely, although there's a first time for everything."

Now that the cat is out of the bag, I consider tracking the rest of the match. I waver but self-discipline wins out. I'll save myself for the replay. I put my head down and get back to my work.

Time flies and before I know it, my phone is beeping again.

"Nice work!" says Robbo. Pretty magnanimous, I think, given he's a Dragons fan.

"Good win Pete – they deserved that," my brother enthuses.

My plan is in tatters. Any thoughts of watching a suspense-filled match on the NRL website have flown right out the window. Truth be told, I don't care. They've won!

Now I might take a peek at the competition ladder to see how far out of the eight we are. Surely the finals aren't out of the question just yet?

POSTSCRIPT

I've just watched the highlights and I'm glad I wasn't watching that live. Up by 12 with 14 minutes to play before the Dragons scored converted tries in the 66th and 74th minutes to send the match into golden point extra-time. Penrith missed three field goals and St George one before Lachlan Coote finally hit the mark to give the Panthers a hard-fought 13-12 victory. Phew!

Penrith 13			REFEREES	Gerard Sutton, Tony De Las Heras
TRIES	Kingston, Simpkins		CROWD	10,367
GOALS	Austin 2/2		VOTES	**3. Kingston** Panthers
FIELD GOAL	Coote			**2. Coote** Panthers
St George Illawarra 12				**1. Merrin** Dragons
TRIES	Rein, Marketo			
GOALS	K.Stanley 2/2			

Round 11

This is our house

Wests Tigers *versus*
New Zealand Warriors
7.30pm, Friday, 18 May
Leichhardt Oval, Sydney

STU WARREN

JUST WHY JON BON JOVI USHERS IN FRIDAY NIGHT FOOTBALL HAS ME BEAT. The most plastic man in soft-rock could not be further from what rugby league is, surely. It's just so disappointing that designer denim and hairspray are used to introduce something that has so much going its way.

Bright lights in the suburbs – yes, the suburbs, the beating heart of all football codes (yet so roundly ignored by some football administrators) – live and free-to-air across the country, a meaningful contest between teams eager to stake a claim in the top half of the NRL ladder ... and a replay of one of the best contests in the 2011 finals series.

That time the Warriors got the cheese – this time it was the Tigers. But only just.

One thing that seems guaranteed when these two get together is glitz in the backs and it took only three minutes and a handful of tackles for the Kiwis to prove they'd come to Leichhardt Oval to play.

The ball zipped from left to right as if blown that way by exhaling fans on a packed hill and, through a clever decoy and delayed pass from the men inside him, Bill Tupou found an acre outside Lote Tuqiri and slid into the corner.

It was fodder for the snappers and their long lenses so close to the in-goal.

A mate of mine in England is a Getty photographer and once told me that, where sport is concerned, if you see the action through the viewfinder – your shutter open – you've missed the shot.

So whether the guy in Balmain saw Tuqiri's bulging thigh in the split-second before it thundered into his chin – the big winger stumbled having failed to get Tupou in cover – is worth knowing.

But it's sure as hell not worth waiting the best part of an hour for sideline expert Brad Fittler to get the scoop.

Not your best work, Fred.

Just as Benji Marshall's 22nd-minute blind flick inside with the Warriors line blown apart was not his best work.

The Kiwis duly punished Marshall's mistimed flair by scoring from the resulting turnover for a 10-0 lead, one they maintained until the break.

In the paraphrased words of Snorky: patience is a virtue and keep your powder dry for the second half, Benji.

As it happened, the powder was lit just eight minutes after the break, but it was a flashy foot – not hand – that did the job.

Marshall poked into the corner and Tuqiri managed to gather and ground (just), and when the makeshift halfback knocked over the conversion, the Tigers had hit the front.

Five minutes of defensive madness had seen the Warriors relinquish a comfortable halftime lead – first through Manu Vatuvei's arms being too short to collect a simple Beau Ryan grubber and then through Marshall's exploitation of a flat line and badly-positioned sweeper.

With the Kiwi maestro pulling the strings in the No.7 position – and getting a heap of the ball as a result of being played one closer to the ruck – the Tigers were suddenly in control.

Right up until the moment they weren't, that is.

A botched Tim Moltzen kick found its way to Konrad Hurrell who, in an act that seemed to defy logic, out-paced that man Marshall to the other end of the park and dived in for the Warriors' third try, giving them another lead and a real chance of victory.

When Marshall knocked over a sideline conversion to maximise Matt Utai's scoring play on 63 minutes, the Tigers had nosed back in front and memories of the grandstand finish to last season's semi-final came flooding back.

On that occasion the visitors had played the comeback role to perfection, but this time it wasn't to be.

The Tigers had moved eight points clear when Moltzen dashed over and Marshall converted and the last-ditch try the Warriors scored through Hurrell wasn't enough to overhaul the home side.

Benji and Beau had all but booted the Warriors off the park in the second stanza and the margin may well have been greater if they'd probed Vatuvei's wing more regularly with high balls or low – the hulking winger unable to deal with either at various times on Friday night, much to his team's detriment.

Wests Tigers 24		REFEREES	Tony Archer, Jason Robinson
TRIES	Ryan, Tuqiri, Utai, Moltzen	CROWD	16,406
GOALS	Marshall 4/4	VOTES	**3. Moltzen** Tigers
New Zealand 22			**2. Woods** Tigers
TRIES	Hurrell 2; Tupou, Henry		**1. Maloney** Warriors
GOALS	Maloney 3/4		

Break a leg

North Queensland Cowboys *versus* Penrith Panthers
7.30pm, Saturday, May 19
Dairy Farmers Stadium, Townsville

PETER HULTHEN

THE PENRITH PANTHERS CAME INTO THIS GAME with renewed confidence after a one-point victory over St George Illawarra the previous Monday night. They were without NSW players Luke Lewis and out-of-favour Jennings, but on paper still had a competitive outfit.

The Cowboys were missing Matthew Scott, Johnathan Thurston and Brent Tate to Queensland representative duties, as well as NSW debutant James Tamou.

Nevertheless, going into the match, the North Queenslanders expressed a strong resolve to continue their good form without their Origin players. Matt Bowen was captaining the team for the first time and, even though 'Mango' doesn't say much, he led by example on the field.

The Cowboys held out some early assaults by Penrith who were gaining the ascendency through a number of penalties, including one against Ashton Sims for trying to rake the ball back in the play-the-ball.

In the sixth minute, Luke Walsh's grubber kick was gathered by Clint Newton to record the first points of the game. Blake Austin converted to give the Panthers a six-point lead. After some strong lead-up work from Tariq Sims, Payne passed to Bowen, who put on a side-step to go over for a try. Bowen converted, levelling the score at 6-6.

After a good run from Glenn Hall, the ball went through the hands of Ray Thompson and Michael Morgan to Bowen, who delivered a cut-out pass to Ashley Graham, who set it down a metre from the corner. Bowen's conversion attempt was unsuccessful. Ivan Cleary would have been concerned about the number of missed tackles from his charges. Blake Austin then made a good break, passing to fullback Lachlan Coote, who scored under the uprights. Blake did the honours with the conversion. Penrith up 12-10 at the break.

A knock on from Chris Armit led to the Cowboys' first points after the break when a bomb by Matt Bowen found the waiting hands of Antonio Winterstein, who stretched out to score. Bowen converted to give North Queensland a 16-12 lead.

A grubber kick from Michael Morgan was dived on by Gavin Cooper centimetres from the dead-ball line. The try was converted by Matt Bowen. Cowboys up 22-12.

Failure to slide across in defence allowed Travis Burns to burst through a gap to score. Unfortunately Tariq Sims had tried to ankle-tap Burns and suffered a vicious broken leg as Ciraldo collided with him. Sims was taken off by the medicab to a waiting ambulance. He had broken the tibia and fibia again. He had only recently returned from the same injury sustained last year.

The try was converted by Blake Austin. Cowboys up 22-18. This was soon followed by a penalty to Matt Bowen which gave the locals a six-point buffer.

Brad Tighe went over for Penrith in the 65th minute after the Cowboys failed to rein in Lachlan Coote. Luke Walsh was also figuring in attack. Walsh added the extras, levelling the scores at 24-all.

An offload from McKendry saw winger Josh Mansour take a Travis Burns pass to score in the corner (whilst in mid-air). The conversion was unsuccessful. Penrith led.

The Cowboys were determined not to give it away and a fired-up Ashton Sims gathered a loose ball from Faifai-Loa to stretch out and score, levelling the scores. Bowen converted, giving the Cowboys a two-point lead.

The Penrith Panthers desperately tried to get back into the game but the Cowboys held out and the game finished with an Ashton Sims intercept from a last-ditch Panthers backline move. North Queensland rewarded their loyal fans with a 30-28 win, keeping them in the top four.

North Queensland 30		REFEREES	Steve Lyons, Chris James
TRIES	Bowen, Cooper, Graham, A. Sims, Winterstein	CROWD	11,648
GOALS	Bowen 5/7	VOTES	**3. Bowen** Cowboys
Penrith 28			**2. Walsh** Panthers
TRIES	Burns, Coote, Mansour, Newton, Tighe		**1. Coote** Panthers
GOALS	Austin 3/3, Walsh 1/2		

Dudded

Manly Sea Eagles *versus* Sydney Roosters
2pm, Sunday, 20 May
Brookvale Oval, Sydney

MICHAEL GROSVENOR

TO SAY MANLY HAVE HAD THE WOOD ON THE ROOSTERS in recent years is an understatement. There were three stats bandied around before this match that perfectly illustrated Manly's domination:

- The Roosters' 11 wins from 46 matches (23.9%) at Brookvale is their worst winning record at any permanent venue;
- In their past four matches at Brooky, the Roosters have been outscored 172 points to 26, the most points ever conceded by them in a four-game stretch at a single venue; and
- The Roosters have been held scoreless for at least an hour in three of their past four matches at Brookvale, and have been outscored 118-18 in the second half of these games.

So, even with six players missing through State of Origin commitments and injuries, and the Roosters only missing Pearce through State of Origin and Shaun Kenny-Dowall to a late injury, Manly went into this match as firm favourites.

The first tackle of the match showed that this young and improving Roosters team was not going to roll over as meekly as previous Roosters outfits might have. Anasta's kick-off went straight to Jason King who trundled forward only to be smashed to the turf by Jared Waerea-Hargreaves. This set the tone for the rest of the match – a ferocious and sapping battle between two desperate packs.

Manly's first foray in enemy territory produced a try out wide to Michael Oldfield after a beautiful cut-out ball by the in-form Daly Cherry-Evans. Yet the Roosters hit back straight away through a clever cross-field Anasta kick that saw Perrett leap high and score. The forwards then settled down to an intensive battle for field position before it appeared late in the half that the Roosters might be getting on top.

The highly promising BJ Leilua busted a tiring Manly defensive line before cleverly flicking the ball inside to Anasta, who then put the ever-present Daniel Mortimer under the posts. The defensive shackles had been broken but the breakthrough only served to energise Manly into action. With halftime looming, Manly's desperation saw them steamroll up the field before Liam Foran (deputising admirably for his injured brother Kieran) stabbed a hopeful kick towards the in-goal. It bounced straight back over four looming Roosters into the grateful arms of Steve Matai. With a bit of luck, Manly was able to square it up with 40 to play.

The Eagles started the second half like they finished the first with a soft try to newcomer Daniel Harrison. Manly had stepped it up a gear and the Roosters looked like they'd struggle to hang on.

Struggle they did, but this young Roosters team is made of sterner stuff than previous Brooky visitors. They continued to repel wave after wave of Manly attack to remain only six behind with about 20 minutes to go. It was at this point that Manly started running out of ideas. The Roosters got a sniff. They started to enjoy more possession. Brad Takaraingi looked particularly dangerous and it was no surprise to see him set up the next Roosters try ... or so everyone thought.

Takaraingi stood like a colossus in a three-man tackle before popping a beautiful ball out the back to that man Mortimer, who scooted past some tired Manly defence to score next to the posts. Just as the Roosters players and fans were jumping for joy, the referee inexplicably signalled to the video referee that he wanted to check something. No one quite knew what that something was. However, the replays showed a slightly raised but innocuous Takaraingi elbow in the tackle. That was enough for video ref Pat Reynolds to rule no try and award a penalty to Manly. And with it went all of the Roosters' momentum. Manly coasted to an 18-10 victory.

If you think this is a typical Rooster supporter blaming the ref for another loss, let me hand it over to Bill Harrigan to confirm what all Rooster fans thought at the time:

> "The video referee got this call wrong. It should have been ruled a try to the Roosters. The video referee believed that there was a raised elbow from the ball carrier in the lead-up to Daniel Mortimer crossing the line, but he got the decision wrong.

As Brian Smith said in the post-match conference, it is hard to know whether Easts would have gone on to win. The match was a see-sawing affair and Mortimer's try may have sprung Manly back to life just like Leilua's try seemed to do in the first half.

So all we are left with is the official scoreboard.

Manly 18			REFEREES	Ashley Klein, Jared Maxwell
TRIES	Oldfield, Matai, Harrison		CROWD	12,633
GOALS	Lyon 3/4		VOTES	**3. Watmough** Sea Eagles
Sydney Roosters 10				**2. Cordner** Roosters
TRIES	Perrett, Mortimer			**1. Galuvao** Sea Eagles
GOAL	Anasta 1/2			

It's not over until it's over

St George Illawarra Dragons *versus* **South Sydney Rabbitohs**
3pm, Sunday, 20 May
WIN Jubilee Oval, Sydney

JOHN CAMPBELL

ST GEORGE ILLAWARRA HAD THEIR HEARTS BROKEN BY A FIELD GOAL in golden point for the second time within a week in this Round 11 clash with South Sydney. For the Rabbitohs, who had not led at any stage of the game, it was an eleventh-hour victory that has entrenched them in the eight. Worryingly for the Dragons, it was their third loss on the trot and it sees them floundering on the NRL ladder.

Entering that time of the season when Origin, suspension and injury tolls are factors, the home side looked to be more under the pump for personnel. Creagh, Morris, Weyman, Scott, Merrin and Prior were all out, while the Bunnies, though losing Inglis and Taylor to rep duties, had been compensated by the returns of Merritt and Burgess.

On paper, the Red and Green looked like they would prevail, but no-names and young tyros have been known to rise to the occasion in the past.

That's on everyone's mind as they make that sacred walk from Carlton Station to Kogarah Jubilee Oval (okay, so it's not exactly the Camino de Santiago – but for league tragics, it is rich in memory, hope and portent).

Jubilee itself, even with its recent additions, still retains that grunge element from the days of unlimited tackle football. Along with venues like Leichhardt and Brookvale, it is at the centre of the debate that rages over the worthiness of small local grounds in today's media-driven business of professional rugby league.

Traditionalists argue that the code's history, folklore and grassroots connections would perish if the likes of Jubilee were abandoned in favour of all-seating concrete stadiums (with parking and public transport). Those who make that point most loudly are usually paid pundits doing so from the comfort of air-conditioned boxes. See how they feel after an afternoon of standing on the packed eastern hill at Kogarah, exposed to the miserable elements and with the cold damp of a wet arvo seeping through their boots. It's enough for any bloke to get narky about – especially if that any-bloke is a Souths supporter watching his team losing the on-field arm wrestle and falling behind 12-0.

Saints make a mess of Souths' right-side defence, only to see winger Daniel Vidot's try disallowed. Two tackles later they're over in the other corner when Jason Nightingale collects a perfectly-waited bomb from Jamie Soward.

The Dragons' second-string pack is taking it to their more experienced opposition and gaining the upper hand. Working shrewdly off their coat-tails, Soward is owning the game at the moment. Ben Hornby sends Brett Morris downfield and Soward supports his fullback to scoot away and notch a deserved try. Trailing 12-0, Souths look rattled and in need of the sort of magic usually provided by 'GI' or 'The Coal Train'.

But the modern game is rarely cut and dried so early in the piece.

The Bunnies start to get more possession. Dylan Farrell makes a scything run into the Saints 20 and 'Slammin' Sammy Burgess, with brute strength and determination, crosses next to the uprights.

After a speculative kick, Souths' Matt King bats a miracle ball to Adam Reynolds, who gallops away for his first four-pointer of the season. To everyone's surprise – and to the home supporters' angst – it is 12-all at the break.

On the resumption, Souths are more focused. Reynolds and Issac Luke are in everything and rookie winger Justin Hunt gathers a couple of scorching grubbers. But Saints have lifted, too. Vidot goes close after beautiful cross-field hands and Matt Cooper darts over on the blind side from dummy-half.

Soward's brilliant sideline conversion makes it 18-12 but, with half an hour to go, the result is a long way from decided.

As we all anticipated – it is one of those sorts of games – Andrew Everingham makes the most urgent chase for a Reynolds chip and it's 18-all.

Soward misses a penalty, Hunt is denied a try by the video ref and, in the surreal atmosphere created by the floodlights, both sides go into extra-time mode striving solely for a field goal. Five shots are taken in the last nail-biting 10 minutes, all unsuccessful, and the inevitable ensues.

Reynolds' teammates react ecstatically to his winning kick. Souths get out of jail. Saints might feel hard done by, but it's never over until it's over.

Did I say how much I love Jubilee Oval?

South Sydney 19			REFEREES	Shayne Hayne, Brett Suttor
TRIES	S. Burgess, Reynolds, Everingham		CROWD	14,894
GOALS	Reynolds 3/3		VOTES	**3. Reynolds** Rabbitohs
FIELD GOAL	Reynolds			**2. Luke** Rabbitohs
St George Illawarra 18				**1. Young** Dragons
TRIES	Nightingale, Soward, Cooper			
GOALS	Soward 3/4			

The curse of the Almanac

Canterbury Bulldogs *versus* **Cronulla Sharks**
7pm, Monday, 21 May
ANZ Stadium, Sydney

NATHAN BOSS

I AM ONE OF THE LEAST SUPERSTITIOUS PEOPLE GOING ROUND. Well, at least in relation to everything except rugby league. However, where the Cronulla Sharks are concerned, I become a vastly inferior OCD-suffering version of myself. Sort of like a reverse-Bupa. I truly believe that what I say, what I wear and how I behave will impact upon the team's performances.

Previous semi-final losses have been put down to wearing the wrong jersey or eating the wrong food for lunch. Back in my playing days, I used to wear the same pair of reggies every week in a winning streak. Nobody needed to know that, but there you go.

So it was with some trepidation that I agreed to write the match report for the Sharks-Bulldogs clash on Monday night. You see, the last match report I'd penned in relation to the Sharks was the Round 2 debacle against the Knights where the Sharks blew many chances. Since that time, the Sharks had gone on an unthinkable winning streak – albeit with a hiccup along the way – which culminated in a victory over the previously unbeaten Storm.

As I arrived at the Imperial Hotel last Saturday, I became aware of the magnitude of my offer. The Sharks, with no Carney and Gallen, coming off a Grand Final-like victory the week before, were in no condition to carry The Curse of the Almanac as well. I was getting flashbacks to 2001, of having to remove my Sharks jersey to access Canterbury Leagues Club and having young Bulldogs fans draping their flags in my face as the Sharks suffered another agonising defeat.

Sure enough, the match started as expected with the Dogs scoring two early tries through the flimsy Cronulla defence. Any hope that the Sharks could overcome these odds were well and truly extinguished in the few minutes that followed.

The Sharks had just made a break down the left. Canterbury were shot to pieces with Cronulla having what appeared to be a 20-on-one overlap. Jeff Robson, who up until this point had been one of the form halves of the comp, inexplicably decided that this would be an opportune time to dummy and take a hit-up. The Dogs ran up the other end of the field where the video referee made one of the worst calls of the season to give them an 18-0 lead.

At 24-0 at halftime, unable to handle any more of this humiliation, I staged a pub walkout. I have been known to go walkabout during difficult Sharks losses. Dad still talks to this day of my disappearance during the viewing of a Sharks-Tigers game at Dickson Tradies. He later found me walking listlessly through a wave of poker machines regaling random strangers with tales of woe.

I would like to say that my walkout provoked grave emotion from the pub faithful that night, but in reality the one other person was too busy engaging the bar staff in discussions on the price of chicken schnitzels, so my walkout did not have the impact that I might have expected.

In the end the Dogs were comfortable winners 26-6 and, after a promising start, the Sharks' season is looking particularly shaky.

Canterbury 26			REFEREES	Gerard Sutton, Gavin Badger
TRIES	Barba 2; Lafai, Wright		CROWD	12,012
GOALS	Goodwin 5/5		VOTES	**3. Barba** Bulldogs
Cronulla 6				**2. Graham** Bulldogs
TRY	Smith			**1. Kasiano** Bulldogs
GOAL	Williams 1/1			

State of Origin I

Not even once in a Blue moon ...

New South Wales *versus* **Queensland**

8pm, Wednesday, 23 May

Etihad Stadium, Melbourne

PAUL DALLIGAN

THE LAST TIME NSW WON A STATE OF ORIGIN SERIES AGAINST QUEENSLAND, I was a single man living in Sydney. That night, buoyed by the jubilance of the result, and perhaps fuelled by more than a few pints, I marched up to the woman who would later become my wife. Given my wife will readily tell you that I didn't exactly show Usain Bolt type speed in proposing, the fact that I am now married with a family and long settled in Melbourne shows how long it's been since the last Blue moon shone over the rugby league landscape.

Being a rugby league fanatic and living in Melbourne is like being Sting's *Englishman in New York*. But come State of Origin time, it is always easier to sell the greatest game of all to those in this AFL-obsessed city as there isn't much else in the way of quality live sport on a Wednesday night at prime time. And quality it is as many a hardened AFL fanatic will tune in to watch teams from Queensland and NSW belt the living suitcase out of each other.

I am always explaining to the locals - those who will listen anyway - that there really is nothing like this event in Australian rules football. The best of the best are on show, putting the Poms and Kiwis to one side for the sake of the argument. Sure, the AFL has their Grand Final, but Judd, Bartel, Swan, Franklin and Goodes won't all be on the field at once like they are in Origin.

The NRL, in its wisdom, decided to play the opening game of this 2012 series in Melbourne, much to the annoyance of the Sydney press which had been abuzz with a chorus of disapproval, led primarily by the NSW coach Ricky Stuart. Sticky wondered why NSW would sell themselves up the river (or down the Yarra in this case) and discard the treasured home ground advantage when it was so intent on stopping six years of Queensland dominance. The rumour that the Victorian Government is in discussions to obtain the neutral game each and every year at the MCG, thus ensuring a level playing field, did nothing to calm the baying masses in blue.

It was with a mixture of excitement, nervousness and anticipation that I ventured to Etihad Stadium, hoping the Maroons would crumble.

Ricky Stuart had decided to take a punt. His main gamble was the selection of Todd Carney, a man who at times in his life would make Brendan Fevola seem angelic. Stuart hoped that Carney would provide the spark that was needed to stop the brilliance of Inglis, Thurston, Smith and Slater.

It has always been hard to watch Greg Inglis star for the Maroons, given that he was born and raised in Bowraville, a town that won't appear on any map of Queensland. It is, after all, a fair drive south of the border. NSW fans couldn't say too much, though, given that James Tamou is about as Aussie as Jake the Muss.

NSW came out firing in the first half. Their neat set plays were more structured than a German kindergarten. It was a welcome change from previous Origin series, where systems went out the window as soon as Queensland applied the inevitable blowtorch and it was a matter of merely hanging on. But it seemed we were well-prepared, calm and ready to roar.

When the Fijian Flyer ("ahem" again to the Inglis-from-NSW argument) crashed over, it looked like NSW may be in for a good night. But as sure as bad news stories follow every Mad Monday, Queensland took the lead after a brawl which resulted in Michael Jennings being sent to the sin bin.

The final cruel nail was delivered when Greg Inglis (I won't start) crossed for the most controversial of tries. In my vicinity, even those in Maroon declared NSW had been robbed. But to the victors go the spoils. And I know of no other sporting team in Australia which has more tenacity, spirit and courage under fire than the Queensland Origin team. It has developed into the greatest in the history of rugby league.

But onwards and upwards we go with game two in Sydney where, somehow, NSW is the bookies' favourite. Sticky Stuart is still gambling with Todd Carney and I, more than any man, am hoping his ace in the pack will somehow trump the royal flush that has been the past six years of Queensland dominance. Even if it all ends with me seeing red, or Maroon in this case, I can handle pain. I am also a Rabbitohs fanatic after all.

In enemy territory

LIAM HAUSER

I FIND STATE OF ORIGIN GAMES THE PINNACLE OF ANY SPORT, not just rugby league. I've lived in the NSW town of Tumut for nearly four years, but I remain a passionate Queenslander after living most of my life in southeastern Queensland locations including Bethania, Redcliffe and Kingaroy.

The Maroons won their third straight series soon after I came to Tumut to work as a sports reporter at the *Tumut and Adelong Times* and *Gundagai Independent* newspapers. Then it was four. Five. Six. Now I want to see seven straight series wins. The Tumut Rugby League Club wears sky blue and is known as 'The Blues', but my Maroon allegiance is rock solid.

I started following sport in the early 1990s when NSW won three straight Origin series under Laurie Daley's captaincy. NSW also dominated interstate cricket, winning the Sheffield Shield for the 42nd time in 1994 while Queensland still hadn't tasted victory. So, with Queensland starved of success at that time, I developed an intense dislike of NSW in interstate sport. I've since been fortunate to see plenty of Queensland wins in the Sheffield Shield and State of Origin. That doesn't stop me wanting more.

I watch the opener of this year's Origin series in the lounge room in the unit I rent. I'm confident of Queensland success, but the Maroons look rusty early on. After a Matt Scott fumble puts the Blues on the attack, Darius Boyd spills a high kick to enable Akuila Uate to score. Todd Carney's first kick is poor. NSW 4-0.

The Blues make inroads as the Maroons are uncharacteristically brittle in the ruck. NSW has better field position as the Blues are quick around dummy-half while the Maroons do not move up well as a defensive line. After NSW gets the first penalty, Robbie Farah darts for the line but Billy Slater and Matt Scott hold him up. Blessed relief.

The turning point comes after a barney. Michael Jennings is sin binned for running a long way to jump into a brawling mob; his haymaker not well disguised. It's crucial for the Maroons to strike while the Blues are a player down. There's a near miss as Tate goes into the corner post. But then an intercept from Cameron Smith and a penalty against Glenn Stewart give Queensland another chance before Jennings returns. A great move to the left sees Slater scoop a quick pass to Boyd who scores.

Thurston's sideline goal puts Queensland in front.

The momentum has clearly changed. Carney doesn't find touch with a penalty kick: a cardinal sin. A penalty against Bird for a dangerous tackle gives Queensland a crucial chance two minutes from halftime. Thurston makes a darting run and sends Boyd in for another try. Another curling goalkick gives Queensland a crucial eight-point lead at the break.

Just a few minutes after play resumes Jarryd Hayne knocks back a high kick to send Jennings in for a converted try. Queensland 12-10. NSW soon threaten but Bird's speculative unload finds the sideline. I cringe as a defensive error from Cronk leads to Jennings making a half-break and kicking. Sam Thaiday just beats Brett Stewart to the ball behind the tryline.

With 20 minutes remaining, I sense there's at least one more try in this game. The Maroons appear to be struggling, so I'm nervous. Jennings makes a half-break with 10 minutes left before Scott gathers a loose ball. Then a pass is knocked down to give Queensland six more tackles. Come on Maroons, nail it! Slater knocks back Cronk's chip-kick and Greg Inglis eventually forces the ball. It's very confusing. Farah's boot has dislodged the ball before it inadvertently hits Inglis's arm, then Inglis forces it. It looks like a knock on and I'm surprised to see the try awarded. With an easy conversion, Queensland leads 18-10 with six minutes left. Farah slices an attempted 40/20 kick out on the full and the Maroons hold on.

I'm still perplexed by the Inglis try but I note that Sean Hampstead made the decision and that fellow New South Welshmen Bill Harrigan and Ricky Stuart supported it. It was certainly intriguing to hear the NSW coach say he thought it was a try. Regardless, it was a solid Origin match featuring many twists and turns, a brawl and plenty of talking points.

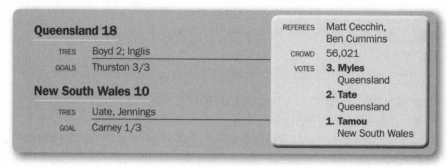

Queensland 18		
TRIES	Boyd 2; Inglis	
GOALS	Thurston 3/3	
New South Wales 10		
TRIES	Uate, Jennings	
GOAL	Carney 1/3	

REFEREES	Matt Cecchin, Ben Cummins
CROWD	56,021
VOTES	3. Myles Queensland
	2. Tate Queensland
	1. Tamou New South Wales

Round 12

Beaten fair and square

Melbourne Storm *versus* **Brisbane Broncos**

7.30pm, Friday, 25 May

AAMI Park, Melbourne

PAUL CONNOLLY

AFTER ROUND 11, 2012		
1	Storm	9-1
2	Broncos	7-3
3	Cowboys	7-4
4	Sea Eagles	7-4
5	Sharks	7-4
6	Rabbitohs	6-4
7	Bulldogs	6-5
8	Tigers	5-5
9	Warriors	5-6
10	Knights	4-6
11	Dragons	5-6
12	Raiders	4-6
13	Roosters	5-6
14	Titans	3-7
15	Panthers	3-8
16	Eels	1-9

GETTING THE KIDS TO BED CAN BE A CONTEST ANY NIGHT OF THE WEEK, not least Friday night, but I'd done everything short of wiping their noses with a hankie soaked in chloroform to get 'em down by kick-off.

So by the time the Storm and Broncos ran onto Melbourne's AAMI Park, the kids weren't quite asleep but they were in bed. To keep them honest, they'd also been read a harrowing tale containing overtones of paedophilia and bestiality otherwise known as Pinocchio. "Food for thought, right kids?"

Ah yes, not a bad effort, I thought as I slumped onto the couch, cracked a red and turned on the TV ... the three-step plan of modern parenting.

Giving my beloved a smug wink – she was sitting nearby with her laptop, earphones in, catching up on *The Good Wife*, having withdrawn her services on account of looking after the blighters all day – I sighed contentedly and took my first appreciative sip of wine. And here was the first hit-up: a canary-yellow Bronco running into a wall of purple before a disappointing crowd, scared off by a day so cold birds were dropping out of the sky encased in ice – avian hailstones if you will.

No doubt Origin I, played two nights earlier, had robbed the game of some of its appeal, what with players either backing up or absent, not least Broncos stars Sam Thaiday, Petero Civoniceva and Justin Hodges. Nevertheless, I was looking forward to this one. A possible Grand Final preview between two of the classiest, best drilled and, for a New South Welshman with a long memory, most disliked sides in the comp. The footy promised to be exciting. Unfortunately, there could only be one loser – or so I thought. Seven minutes in, the Storm opened the scoring. With marker Ben Hannant asleep (unlike my kids ... *was that one of them calling out?*), Cooper Cronk sent Jason Ryles through on the inside before Ryles passed back out to Todd Lowrie backing up. Too easy.

Gareth Widdop was lining up the conversion when my two-year old padded into the room oh so matter-of-factly. "S'up?" she might have said.

"Hey, you, it's bedtime."

"Why, Daddy?"

"'Cause it's nighttime. It's dark outside."

"Why, Daddy?"

"Because the sun has gone to sleep."

"Why, Daddy?"

"Because he's been illuminating the Earth all day and now he's knackered and all he wants to do is sit on the couch and watch football."

"Why, Daddy?"

An impasse. At this point I just had to pick her up and carry her back to bed. I was tucking her in when her older sister strolled in to ask me to come and give her another cuddle too. Not wanting her to have a future of paying psychologists to get to the root of her inferiority issues, I promised I would. A Victorian parent (*era*, not state) would no doubt have thrashed them both with a length of birch but what could I, a reconstituted 21st century male, do?

Having finally attended to both of them, I returned to the couch. I'd missed a Broncos try (Jack Reed Superman-diving in the corner) and conversion. Not to worry; I'd catch the full replay on NRL.COM and, besides, there was still an hour left.

I managed another 10 minutes when my youngest was heard bellowing. "Daddeeeeee ... I neeeeed you!"

"Are you trapped under a motor vehicle?" I shouted back, trying to determine the importance of her need.

"Daddy, change me!" she shouted back.

Sigh.

The dear thing had something in her nappy that made me weak at the knees and, like a coroner pouring over a ripe one, I could have done with a swish of Vicks under the nose. After an extensive clean up and a follow-up book to get her in the bedtime mood again, I made it back to the lounge room just in time to see Billy Slater going over under the posts (18-6 Storm, early second half) before my beloved, occupying my spot, changed the channel.

"You weren't watching anyway," she said.

As the Broncos discovered that night, sometimes it's not your day and you just have to admit you've been outplayed fair and square.

Melbourne 34			REFEREES	Tony Archer, Gerard Sutton
TRIES	Lowrie, Slater 2; Chambers, O'Neill		CROWD	13,200
GOALS	Widdop 5/6		VOTES	**3. Lowrie** Storm
Brisbane 10				**2. Cronk** Storm
TRIES	Reed, Te'o			**1. Gillett** Broncos
GOAL	Parker 1/2			

A GI-nius

South Sydney Rabbitohs *versus* Canberra Raiders
7.30pm, Friday, 25 May
ANZ Stadium, Sydney

DOUG ROWETH

A WEEK IS A LONG TIME IN FOOTBALL THEY SAY. Two nights earlier 56,000 Melbournians witnessed the first game of rugby league's showpiece State of Origin series – the game's best players clashing in a contest cracking with excitement, passion and atmosphere. The XXXX Maroons contentiously beat the VB Blues 18-10. Tonight a sparse and hardy crowd in a vast and cold stadium witness the Rabbitohs taking on a Raiders team minus two of their best players who had been banned by their club for getting on the piss.

Inappropriate intemperance changes aside, this was a definite danger game for the Bunnies who have a frequent and frustrating habit of suffering from *just-turn-up-itis* for games they are expected to win. With their pre-match TattsBet price resembling that of Black Caviar's, it was a nervous time up in the stands, not helped as the home side muffed its way through an opening punctuated with dropped balls, forced passes and trying to score off every tackle.

As is often the case in modern rugby league, a penalty was the catalyst for points.

Good field position bought about some calm and serenity as Souths executed a perfectly scripted set. Greg Inglis, with class and ease, chimed in from fullback, got himself between and behind two Raiders defenders, then offloaded to debutant Justin Hunt, the latest unheralded tryscoring winger the Bunnies have unearthed this season. The kick from out wide missed but not as badly as the kick-off by the Raiders, who sent the ball dead on the full by about five metres in what is surely the most unforgiveable faux pas in footy.

The resultant penalty saw Souths straight back on the attack and the track laid for 'The Coal Train' to take an express trip to the in-goal.

Then a great weaving dash from dummy-half by Issac Luke set the Raiders in reverse. A deft set play around the ruck saw John Sutton turn the ball back inside to a flying Inglis who, with pace and space to spare, evaded a futile tackling effort to score under the posts. 14-0 to the Rabbitohs.

It had been a near-faultless seven minutes of footy by the Bunnies and it looked like the score could be anything. The players were making a mental note of the positions of the TV cameras, and were considering elaborate high-five routines and how to avoid Issac jumping all over their backs at the next post-try celebration.

Inglis showed his fallibility by dropping a regulation pass, not before juggling it fancily three times mind you, and the faint resemblance of a buzz around the ground wilted, then became as muted as an elevator conversation as the Raiders went 70 metres for Jarrod Croker to score out wide thanks to some clever offloads. Canberra had had little ball and savoured some possession to sweep the Steeden gracefully up-field for Croker to score again from a grubber in-goal. With the help of the first penalty for feet across in the scrum since 1973, the Raiders forced their way over with 17 seconds left in the half to go in trailing 14-12.

The second half was eerily similar to the first in that, after another sluggish first 10, Souths unleashed another three-try burst in a matter of minutes on the back of some patient, well-drilled footy. An absolutely dire period of wasted opportunities followed which was only enlivened when Raiders skipper David Shillington wanted to bring his own piece of Origin to Sydney and ran right through Luke Burgess. Sam Burgess took umbrage at the treatment of his brother and was soon in Shillington's face. A loose arm was thrown and it was on.

Inglis showed some Origin-level class to beat four defenders and score to take the score to 36-12, and a short kick-off and soft consolation try to the Raiders left things at

36-18 at the bell. Souths had won four on the trot to claim fourth spot while the Raiders will rethink their second drink.

South Sydney 36		REFEREES	Ashley Klein, Chris James
TRIES	Taylor, Inglis 2; Hunt, Lowe, Farrell	CROWD	10,054
GOALS	Luke 3/4, Reynolds 1/3	VOTES	**3. Inglis** Rabbitohs
Canberra 18			**2. Taylor** Rabbitohs
TRIES	Croker 2; Thompson, Robinson		**1. Fensom** Raiders
GOAL	Croker 1/4		

A very special treat

Newcastle Knights *versus* **Gold Coast Titans**
5.30pm, Saturday, 26 May
Hunter Sports Stadium, Newcastle

MATT O'HANLON

AROUND SATURDAY LUNCHTIME, THE GOLDEN GIRL ADVISED ME that we had a special treat on that night. That really got the blood pumping. I asked what, trying to mask the anticipation that it would be a *Dirty Harry* double in Gold Class or possibly an evening at the Casino.

No. I was instructed that we were heading out to look after my baby sister's kids. My baby sister is in her early thirties, so the term may be a misnomer.

"What time?" I asked.

"6.30pm."

New problem. I was on *Almanac* duty.

"Have they got pay TV?"

Bad question, as the return glare told me. I quickly realised The Golden Girl and I were going to have a nice quiet child-minding experience with the little princess and her baby twin sisters. Three kids under three.

I baulked, offering to stay home and scrub the bathroom but the non-verbal communication put me in no doubt about any chance of that. That left ABC *Grandstand*.

So I have just turned the radio on. Prince is in, which is a plus for the Titans. So are their tough Origin forwards.

But I have a feeling the Knights will get the chocolates at home.

Before the game, Craig Hamilton and Matt Rodwell talk about Origin. *Sigh!* NSW supporters take note that when Inglis scored, Queensland already led 12-10. That's right. 12-10. A winning scoreline. Enough said.

We have to go.

We are cruising down the Pacific Highway when Uate scores a soft try down the left edge. Knights are away. 4-0. Hamilton, a noted Knights fan, is confident they are on-song. For the next 10 minutes, we are travelling easily and so are Newcastle. No road works for the babysitters. But Newcastle are slowed when, after a good break by Zillman, the diminutive hooker Srama scores. The commentary team feels it is against the run of play. After 20 minutes, the Titans lead 6-4.

From the ensuing kick-off, the Knights go from road works to road block. Idris makes a good break and offloads to Minichiello, no miracle pass but a quick play-the-ball follows. Newcastle have the numbers in defence but quick hands through Prince to Champion and onto Mead sees a try in the corner. The amber lights are flashing for Newcastle.

Three minutes before halftime Myles hits a flat Srama pass as I pull into baby sister's driveway. I have advised G-squared to get brother-in-law Putty to put the radio on as I listen to the halftime wrap. Titans 18, Knights 4.

Hamilton is very critical of Newcastle, especially after the Srama try. Listening to the call, the Titans sounded like they were on the ropes. This is reinforced by the commentators. The Knights have to lift.

New problem. Putty tells me that his radio is next to where the twins are sleeping. Play at my babysitting peril. *Solution.* He will stream the second-half broadcast on his computer. Will this will be a new experience – *iFooty* on the Apple?

Newcastle have lost all rhythm. Clearly the loss of Gidley is important and Coach Bennett is facing a major second-half challenge.

Bird – backing up from Origin and playing strongly – scores in the 53rd minute. 24-4. The internet call is good but drops out for a few seconds every couple of minutes. My niece – the little Princess – does not share my dedication to the *Almanac* nor to the mess I am making with the tandoori chicken. Her why-chromosome is strong.

A Newcastle try to Roberts with 12 to go sparks up the broadcasters. Hamilton says they don't deserve to win. The missed kick may be costly. Rodwell describes the Knights play as "lacking in enterprise ... lacking urgency ... [and] ... lacking football entertainment." Damning criticism of the preseason competition favourite.

McKinnon scores for the Knights to take the score to 24-14. Maybe?

Bailey's kick-chase late in the match sums it up for Hamilton. Newcastle show no enthusiasm to keep the game alive yet the veteran Bailey is chasing like a teenager, even with the result in the bag.

The Titans' Origin players are outstanding and could lead this outfit deep into the premiership. Sezer is a good foil for Prince and Idris has presence. For the Knights, Mason seems to be providing value and the commentators believe Boyd has to do a Lockyer and shift to five-eighth. For Wayne Bennett, the challenge is considerable, although there is no better equipped coach to scale the mountain.

The Golden Girl requires my assistance for the Wiggles dance with the little princess. *What a special treat!*

Gold Coast 24		REFEREES	Shayne Hayne, Alan Shortall
TRIES	Mead, Srama, Myles, Bird	CROWD	15,792
GOALS	Prince 4/4	VOTES	**3. Bird** Titans
Newcastle 14			**2. Myles** Titans
TRIES	Uate, Roberts, McKinnon		**1. Harrison** Titans
GOAL	Roberts 1/3		

Like two hobos fighting over a can of warm KB

St George Illawarra Dragons *versus* **Parramatta Eels**
7.30pm, Saturday, 26 May
WIN Jubilee Oval, Sydney

GLEN HUMPHRIES

AT ABOUT 4PM, I STARTED EYEING OFF THIS MATCH. The Eels had already shown that they were going to be awful for most of the season. I was sure that, when the Dragons met the Eels, we'd put a cricket score on them. We'd make the scoreboard attendant work so hard he'd get RSI. We'd beat the Eels like a red-headed stepchild who's just dropped a chocolate Paddle Pop on his new mum's white carpet.

I think you get the picture.

Then the last three weeks came along. It started with that last-gasp win against the Roosters, a win that papered over what was a below-par effort from the Dragons. What followed was two golden point losses (Oh Lord, how I loathe golden point) to Penrith and Souths, where the Dragons played like coach Steve Price hadn't thought to give them a game plan.

And so any thoughts of the Dragons handing out a flogging changed to fears that we might actually lose – to the team in last place on the ladder. A team with just one win. A team who, when they had the bye last week, probably had bookies accepting bets on whether they'd go home with the two points.

Those worries proved to be valid rather quickly. Just 30 seconds into the game, Dragons forward Jack De Belin coughed up the ball on the halfway. A few tackles later, the Eels were down our end and Sandow put up a kick. Ben Hornby muffed the catch and Eels five-eighth Casey McGuire caught the rebound and crashed through an ordinary tackle from Brett Morris to score. Luke Burt converted and the Eels went ahead 6-0. The game was only 90 seconds old and we were already losing to the worst team in the comp.

For the next 15 minutes, we had a wealth of possession in the Eels quarter and couldn't for the life of us find a way over the line. It wasn't until the 18th minute that the Dragons worked it out – Daniel Vidot tapped down a Jamie Soward kick for Kyle Stanley to score. With Soward's conversion going astray, the Eels still led 6-4. But I figured we'd just opened the floodgates and the Dragons try feast could begin.

Nope, a few minutes later Vidot coughed up the ball on the first tackle. Just a few tackles later Matthew Ryan ran straight through the Dragons defence to score. The conversion went over and the Eels were up 12-4 and actually looking like the better team. The score didn't change to halftime and neither did the Dragons' attacking efforts – dropped ball, losing their way inside the quarter, even throwing the ball over the sideline. The Dragons were doing just about everything they could to help the Eels to their second win of the season.

The second half had just two moments worthy of comment.

Five minutes after the break, Jason Nightingale got outside his opposite number, ran 40 metres downfield before finding Morris who hotfooted it to the tryline. Soward got the ball between the sticks (racking up his 900th NRL point in the process) and the score was 12-10 Eels.

The other moment happened less than three minutes from fulltime with the score unchanged. Inside the Eels quarter on the last tackle, Soward ran from one side of the field to the other and looked like he had no idea what to do. In the end he flung it out to Nightingale who got it onto Stanley for his second try. Soward missed the conversion for a final 14-12 scoreline.

The rest of that half was an awful mess – from both sides. Neither the Dragons nor the Eels had much clue about what to do in attack. It was a performance that was so poor that, had the Dragons lost, I fully expected to hear the Jubilee Oval faithful boo the team off the field. My brother, who was at the game, later sent me a text message describing the game as "like watching two hobos fight for a warm can of KB". Which pretty much sums things up.

For the first time in a long time, I was actually unhappy after a Dragons win.

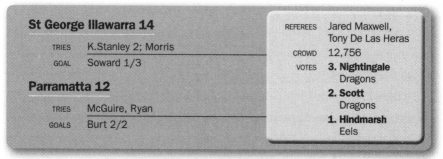

St George Illawarra 14			REFEREES	Jared Maxwell, Tony De Las Heras
TRIES	K.Stanley 2; Morris		CROWD	12,756
GOAL	Soward 1/3		VOTES	**3. Nightingale** Dragons
Parramatta 12				**2. Scott** Dragons
TRIES	McGuire, Ryan			**1. Hindmarsh** Eels
GOALS	Burt 2/2			

Meek Manly shocked

Penrith Panthers *versus* **Manly Sea Eagles**
2pm, Sunday, 27 May
Centrebet Stadium, Sydney

MIKE WILSON

IT'S SUNDAY AFTERNOON, ARGUABLY THE BEST TIME TO WATCH THE FOOTY, as I sink back into my recliner ready to watch my beloved Sea Eagles grace Centrebet Stadium for their match against the Panthers. As the game gets underway, I get my hot-dog lunch on the go and no sooner am I chewing it down when Panthers lock Luke Lewis is chewing on his opposing lock Glenn Stewart's arm thanks to a high shot right across his mouth. Six minutes in and the blood is flowing and I am feeling sadistically happy that Manly are already showing that they are prepared to play hard.

About 20 minutes later, Etu Uaisele makes a bust down the right flank and looks destined to flatten fullback Brett Stewart on his way to a four-pointer, but Stewart courageously throws his body on the line and prevents a certain try. Playing hard. I like what I see.

Then the moment I've been waiting for. I take to the air as Dean Whare dives over in the right corner for Manly and four points are imminent but for the pesky video ref deciding to deny it thanks to Whare's foot just glancing the sideline. Disappointed, I have a sip of beer to quell my frustrations and re-take my crumb-laden seat. I'm barely down when, contrary to early indications, disaster strikes in the form of Panthers halfback Luke Walsh. Walsh scythes his way through the Manly defence, setting up a play that dispatches Coote into the end-zone and puts Penrith ahead 6-0 after 32 minutes.

Thankfully, I only have to wait another four minutes before Whare is at it again. In the same corner of the field, Whare crosses in a carbon copy of his earlier no-try effort except that, this time, the video referee rules in our favour and gives us something to cheer about. Jamie Lyon misses the conversion and the boys from Brookvale head into the sheds trailing 6-4.

It takes 22 minutes before points are scored in the second half, so I fill the lull gorging on more food and drink. However, this does little to improve my mood as it's the Panthers who finally draw blood. Brad Tighe swoops on a Coote grubber and scores. Luke Walsh has no trouble converting and Penrith lead by eight.

Now I'm feeling worried. Manly are showing little respect for the lowly Panthers and it's biting them on the arse. My concerns become real just minutes later when Sea Eagles centre Steve Matai lands a swinging arm flush on the chin of Danny Galea, booking himself a date with the judiciary. Galea looks groggy and is forced to leave the field.

The Panthers capitalise on the resultant penalty and the team, once known as the 'Chocolate Soldiers', add another four points to their tally through a Geoff Daniela try. Once again Walsh converts and the Panthers are up 18-4 with less than 15 minutes to play. I am tearing my hair out. This is lackadaisical football.

Panthers stalwart Luke Lewis hammers the final nail in the Sea Eagles' coffin. He goes for a little dash of his own past Glenn Stewart who looks Origin-fatigued.

It's a big win for the battling Panthers who not only take down the reigning premiers but also take down my hopes of seeing the Sea Eagles finish the round in the top four.

At least the hot dogs and beer made me happy. Briefly.

Penrith 22		REFEREES	Matt Cecchin, Gavin Reynolds
TRIES	Lewis, Daniela, Coote, Tighe	CROWD	11,844
GOALS	Walsh 3/4	VOTES	3. Grant Panthers
Manly 4			2. **Mansour** Panthers
TRY	Whare		1. **Walsh** Panthers
GOALS	Lyon 0/1		

Carrying a seven-year grudge

Wests Tigers *versus* **North Queensland Cowboys**
3pm, Sunday, 27 May
Campbelltown Sports Stadium, Sydney

CLIFF BINGHAM

IT ALWAYS AMAZES ME HOW MUCH STOCK WE CAN PUT IN A SINGLE EVENT when assessing a person, a football team or even a life scenario. For example, my mate Parko still thinks that Geelong's Darren Milburn is essentially the reincarnation of Lucifer by virtue of a single shot he put on Carlton's Steven Silvagni a number of years ago. Ask Canterbury fans about someone like Jarrod McCracken and you'll immediately get a phrase like 'treacherous' (probably nestled within a more colourful arrangement of words). The name Steve Jackson will illicit great joy from Raiders fans for one bustling 1989 Grand Final try; the name Paul Carige groans of despair from Eels fans for a series of monumental errors in the losing 1998 preliminary final.

I carry a grudge towards the Wests Tigers because of just one game – they stood in the way of my beloved Cowboys and an inaugural premiership in 2005.

Admittedly, it was only the quirks of the McIntyre finals system that saw a team run fifth on the ladder, lose 50-6 (also to the Wests Tigers) in week one of the finals and somehow live to see the premiership decider. Still, when you support a team so starved of premiership success, you'll take whatever you can get (I can see you Sharks fans nodding in agreement).

Worse yet, our last three trips at Campbelltown had resulted in losses by 10, 24 and 12 points. Still, it could have been worse – two games at Leichhardt over the same period had resulted in losses by 44 and 20 points. Suffice to say, neither the Tigers, nor suburban Sydney footy generally, are the friend of anyone from up Townsville way.

The script was playing out as per historical precedent when a converted Moltzen try and a penalty goal had the home side leading within the first 10 minutes. My boys responded well though – stout in defence, and crisp and penetrating in attack.

The reward was a pair of tries and a deserved 12-8 lead going into *ha ... oh no .... why would you try to bat that rushed pass on Matty Bowen?* Why not just take the ball and prevent an intercept try to Tuqiri under the sticks? I know you have to take the good with the bad when it comes to the North Queensland custodian, but you don't have to be at all happy about such brain farts.

That try gave the Tigers a 14-12 lead at the main break – a lead they would never relinquish as the margin extended to eight, was cut back to two and then finally returned to eight in the final few minutes.

There was one clear shining light for the visitors though – the continuing upward spiral of one New Zealander (New South Welshman?), James Tamou.

While his hard-hitting defence and ability to bend the line with the ball in hand were important, two plays identified him as something out of the box. The first was a line break made by Benji Marshall in returning a kick. Benji looked set to go the distance, with No. 10 for the Cowboys his closest pursuant. Yet, while winger Ashley Graham could not make inroads, the big Kiwi Blues prop never shirked the task and forced Benji to slow down and look for support.

The second was a rampaging run which set the platform for Ashley Graham's try – he showed some fancy footwork to break the line, then speed rarely associated with a 113kg man. He is clearly a superstar in the making.

This may have been another road loss but this (long white) cloud definitely had a silver lining.

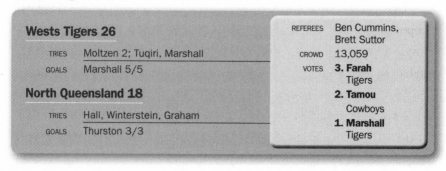

Wests Tigers 26		REFEREES	Ben Cummins, Brett Suttor
TRIES	Moltzen 2; Tuqiri, Marshall	CROWD	13,059
GOALS	Marshall 5/5	VOTES	**3. Farah** Tigers
North Queensland 18			**2. Tamou** Cowboys
TRIES	Hall, Winterstein, Graham		**1. Marshall** Tigers
GOALS	Thurston 3/3		

The great divide

Sydney Roosters *versus* **Canterbury Bulldogs**
7pm, Monday, 28 May
Allianz Stadium, Sydney

NICK TEDESCHI

M Y MUM IS A ROOSTERS FAN BUT I WAS LUCKY. I was born in the country where there is more choice about the premiership team you follow and clubs aren't inherited but selected on merit, mascot, players, style, colours and, of course, fate. I managed to avoid a life of self-loathing, undeserved entitlement, warranted misery and a total detachment from all that is good about rugby league.

I ran with Canterbury. The Roosters have always been grubs to my mind. When I was on the way up they were a hopeless mob. They made just one finals series between '83 and '95 as champions such as Brendan Hall, Wayne Portlock, Dennis Beecraft and Mark Protheroe regularly saw first grade action. It was a pleasant era.

And then came the Super League fiasco and the real nature of the Roosters came to the fore. Protected by big money and even bigger power, the Roosters used the war to reassert themselves as both an on-field and boardroom influence. They raped a broken Penrith, welcomed the upwardly mobile Phil Gould and then poached all-time great Brad Fittler and tryscoring champion Matt Sing.

This was all done on the coin of the ARL – money not afforded other loyal clubs like North Sydney, South Sydney and Western Suburbs. It was done on the pretence that a strong Sydney Roosters, one of the least supported clubs in premiership rugby league, was important for the game.

Logic didn't stand a chance against the overwhelming sense of entitlement that seeped out of Bondi. It soon came to pass. From 1996-2004, having ditched the name *Eastern Suburbs* for, first, *Sydney City* and then *Sydney* – a move so Roosters, so arrogant and so self-consumed – the Chooks made nine straight finals series, playing four Grand Finals and winning one premiership.

It was an era of tremendous disappointment. Just one title, one tainted and soiled premiership, that must eat up those few blowhards who call themselves Roosters fans; sleeping on their bed of money and smoking their privileged pipe must be very difficult.

That premiership came in 2002. The Roosters were not the best team that year.

That season Canterbury won 17 straight games before being unfairly booted out of the NRL. The Roosters were handed the title. Naturally, they lapped it up. But it was tainted and that showed over the next two seasons when the Ricky Stuart-coached teams choked as favourites in the decider, first to Penrith, then to Canterbury.

There have been few nights as joyous as that wonderful evening in October 2004 when Andrew Ryan ankle tapped Michael Crocker directly in front of me and secured the premiership. On one side, my old pal Kendall. On the other, Adam Perry's mum. We hugged with the unrestrained bliss that only a Grand Final win can bring.

That night would turn out to be an important crossroad for the Roosters. It was Brad Fittler's last game and it would not be long before the Roosters fell to last place and questions would be asked about Ricky Stuart. Some truths were affirmed – that entitlement does not equal success, that money does not ensure victory.

The Bulldogs-Roosters rivalry had become rather heated. It was part class warfare, part bitterness stemming from the early years of the decade, part antagonism that came about from the Roosters using their chequebook to buy Canterbury stars.

There was no love lost. I wondered how Roosters fans could look in the mirror and not feel a deep sense of shame. Mum always talked of Russell Fairfax, Arthur Beetson, Kevin Hastings and Jack Gibson. Perhaps they were a different club then.

Even on this wet and chilly Monday night, with the Roosters low on the ladder and the Bulldogs starting to find form, I found the burn to take a great deal of happiness from whipping the Chooks. The Roosters held a 12-4 advantage just five minutes before halftime but Canterbury scored two quick tries before the break and it was soon over when new recruit Krisnan Inu scored his second as former Bulldog Braith Anasta chucked a hissy fit.

When the Roosters faithful started banging on Brian Smith's coaching box and demanding Anasta's head, I thanked the Good Lord that I never liked red and I never liked the Roosters.

Canterbury 30		REFEREES	Jason Robinson, Adam Devcich
TRIES	Inu, Wright 2; Pritchard, Stagg	CROWD	11,343
GOALS	Inu 3/6	VOTES	**3. Inu** Bulldogs
Sydney Roosters 12			**2. Graham** Bulldogs
TRIES	Pearce, Minichiello		**1. Reynolds** Bulldogs
GOALS	Anasta 2/2		

Round 13

Civil peace

Manly Sea Eagles *versus*
St George Illawarra Dragons

7.30pm, Friday, 1 June

Brookvale Oval, Sydney

PAUL CONNOLLY

PING! An email from my brother. As anticipated.

"Here we go again," it begins. "Big game tonight. What's your prediction?"

Considering my mob, the Dragons, have won just 10 of their past 27 matches since 3 June, 2011 – in hindsight, the official end of a glorious, heady, two-and-a-half-year era, the best of my lifetime – my answer writes itself:

> Imagine Captain Mainwaring and co. from Dad's Army doing battle against a crack team of Navy Seals. I fear the Dragons could get slaughtered at Brookie tonight.

"You never know," my brother, a Manly man, replies. "I think it will be pretty close. Soward's getting back to some form and, as you know, Saints have had the wood on Manly lately. They're a real chance."

Bless him, my brother, my opponent, trying to keep my chin up, to give me hope instead of sticking the boot in. How times have changed. Not so long ago a Manly/St George encounter was, for us, a death match. It meant niggle, aggravation, accusation, merciless teasing and, yes, sometimes even physical violence. It was our own local derby.

But something remarkable has happened as we've aged. Sadly, this is underlined in the 18th minute of the match in question when Michael Oldfield scores the opening try off a deft Jamie Lyon grubber. Instead of a text telling me to "suck on that, shithead!" (something, possibly, Thomas Keneally might have been at that moment sending his Dragons-supporting mates), I get something much tamer:

> Nice try to Manly but still anyone's match. Saints looking much better than last week.

Clearly respect and mutual affection have come to outweigh our football allegiances which, nonetheless, remain strong. What's more, a sense that we should be above all the playground pettiness has come into play. We are not so much rival supporters these days as fellow sufferers in fandom.

He probably led the way in this transformation, being older and a fan of the more successful team (in our lifetimes at least), which allows for a more magnanimous mindset. It was probably sometime after the nadir of the 1999 Grand Final – which has given me a permanent twitch in the left eye and an aversion to the colour purple (not the Whoopi Goldberg movie) – that he came to sympathise with my plight and wish Saints well. Then, in 2010, he threw his support behind the Dragons in the decider knowing how I ached like a heroine in a romance novel for an end to 31 years of premiership drought.

I've replied in kind, more or less, and though it seems to go against all that is decent, I've come to hope Manly do well, for his sake. As we all know, this is enormously generous of me – and I tell him as much – considering Manly has on its roster Anthony Watmough and Steve Matai, two men still with one foot each in the primordial slime. It says something about fandom that he can somehow overlook their crimes against humanity as if they were simply misunderstood and not, in fact, cretins.

So here we are, 1 June, 2012, and he's sending me text messages – here comes another one after Manly's 44th-minute try that makes the score 10-2 – consoling me, suggesting hope, when his team is beating mine. It's a funny old world, isn't it?

Funnier still in the 54th minute when hope does in fact rear its head. After a long bust by Brett Morris and a second scamper by Nathan Fien, Daniel Vidot receives a ball from dummy-half (to his credit he catches it, something he often struggles with, given he has feet for hands) and barges through Manly's backpedalling goalline defence for a try. Soward converts. 10-8 to Manly.

"An interesting development," I text.

For the next 20 minutes, the Dragons have the better of it but they can't convert their momentum into further points. And it proves costly when, in the last five minutes, two late tries – the first a sweet, sweeping right-side play by Brett Stewart that puts Oldfield's hat-trick try on a silver platter – put the game to bed.

Manly win ("Closer than the score suggests," he consoles), Saints lose. But I'm happy for him. Really, I am.

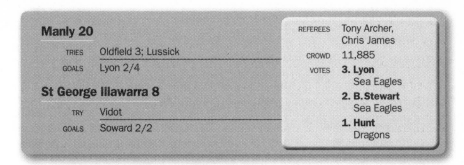

Manly 20			REFEREES	Tony Archer, Chris James
TRIES	Oldfield 3; Lussick		CROWD	11,885
GOALS	Lyon 2/4		VOTES	**3. Lyon** Sea Eagles
St George Illawarra 8				**2. B.Stewart** Sea Eagles
TRY	Vidot			**1. Hunt** Dragons
GOALS	Soward 2/2			

It's a simple game

Gold Coast Titans *versus* North Queensland Cowboys
7.30pm, Friday, 1 June
Skilled Stadium, Gold Coast

IAN HAUSER

A S A BRONCOS SUPPORTER, I TURNED THE TELEVISION ON struggling to know who to support. Both teams contain players I regard highly: Thurston, Tate, Johnson and Scott for the Cowboys; Harrison, Myles and Prince for the Titans. Maybe it was my Maroon blood and the Titans' three NSW men in Bird, Bailey and Idris that swayed me towards the Cowboys.

In the end, the winners deserved their victory because they stuck to the basic tenets of the game. There are some cardinal rules that make rugby league essentially a simple game. These include:

- Defence wins matches;
- Forwards win matches;
- Run straight and hard, not sideways;
- The opposition can't run without legs;
- Halfbacks need to attack the defensive line with the ball held in front in both hands;
- Take your chances;
- Good teams overcome setbacks to win.

And therein lies the story of this game. Starved of the ball for the first seven minutes of the match, forced to concede four successive line dropouts and called on to absorb 40-plus consecutive tackles, the Titans defended their line grimly to hold the Cowboys scoreless in the opening phase.

It was shades of NSW repelling Queensland at the start of Origin III, 2005 but, on this occasion, the Titans held out for an additional 10 tackles.

The scythe-like tackling of Srama and Bird demonstrated repeatedly that the opposition couldn't run without legs. Their teammates showed that a good team can overcome botched kick-offs and some glaring refereeing errors. For example, there was a blatant knock on and a clear forward pass by the Cowboys in the opening frenzy. And, too, the Titans lost their forward leader, Bailey, in the first ten minutes with serious rib problems but they fought back and earned their win in an emphatic fashion.

By contrast, the Cowboys had too many of the basics wrong. They were over-structured early in their attack with a predictability that made them too easy to read. They ran sideways too often and, consequently, were bundled into touch several times. They waited in defence, allowing their opponents to dictate terms. Their cause wasn't helped by the early loss of Segeyaro, the one player who looked creative enough to break the Titans' line.

Enter Scott Prince. On his day, he displays genuine royalty among halfbacks.

Just like Brent Tate, Prince deserves every credit for overcoming years of serious injuries and setbacks to deserve his standing in the top three halfbacks in the comp alongside Cronk and Cherry-Evans.

On the back of his go-forward, the up-the-guts big men (the uncomplicated Myles, Harrison, White *et al*), Prince ran at the line, ball in front of his body in two hands, causing defenders to retreat before unloading a lovely pass to the straight charging Bird, who made it look ever so easy. It really is simple stuff.

Thurston and Bowen tried all their tricks but were well read by the defenders every time.

Tate gave his usual 100 per cent but was caught running sideways too often, even if it was in the face of advancing defence. Johnson handled his usual 40-odd tackles. Scott and Tamou didn't do enough apart from one Scott run after the game had been decided.

Srama was the Energiser Bunny throughout the game. He organised the forwards *à la* Cameron Smith and familiarised himself with the bootlace knots of every opponent. He tackled low, hard and often.

Myles, Harrison and Bird were tough and strong in attack and defence. Sezer provided a good foil for Prince and Idris displayed his defensive qualities on Tate. Zillman was safe at the back and popped up in the right places in attack.

The Titans understood the basics. The Cowboys made everything difficult.

I started the night supporting the Cowboys; I ended up admiring the Titans.

Gold Coast 28		REFEREES	Shayne Hayne, Alan Shortall
TRIES	Champion 2; Gordon, Bird, Harrison	CROWD	12,092
GOALS	Prince 4/5	VOTES	**3. Srama** Titans
North Queensland 12			**2. Prince** Titans
TRIES	Paterson, Taumalolo		**1. Harrison** Titans
GOALS	Thurston 2/2		

The floodgates open

Canberra Raiders *versus* **Wests Tigers**
5.30pm, Saturday, 2 June
Canberra Stadium, Canberra

DOUG ROWETH

THERE'S SOMETHING ABOUT BEING IN CANBERRA IN JUNE that defies common sense. It's never warm and rarely pleasant, a point demonstrated as the rain begins to fall on the long walk up through the O'Connor Ridge in the national capital, where Canberra Stadium looms large through the drizzle.

In the ACT, it's cold, it's wet and it's altogether miserable. I'm not quite sure why I would expect anything else.

Through the turnstiles, there's a buzz at the ground with the anticipation of an exciting match to challenge the conditions. The Wests Tigers are in town on the back of five victories in a row and, central to the revival of course, is Benji Marshall. If Benji is on, the West Tigers are on. But taking our seats in the rain, there is hope among fans that perhaps Josh Dugan at five-eighth is the answer and that he can spark an upset.

The attendance is moderate at best. There can't be many more than a few thousand at the ground. Most Raiders enthusiasts have opted for the warmer, drier and infinitely more sensible alternative of watching on television. Spending two hours in these dreadful conditions requires a special kind of loyalty. Otherwise, why would you bother?

It's god-awful out here. (Am I getting the point across?) When the game kicks off, the weather gods have given us the finger and the rain has settled in for the evening. Unsurprisingly the match begins with plenty of dropped ball and ill-discipline, sending the first few sets of six to both ends of Canberra Stadium.

After 14 minutes of errors, Curtis Sironen, in his first full match for the club for whom his father Paul so famously donned the colours, shrugs off a few tackles to dive over for the Tigers.

As if there wasn't enough water teeming from the sky, this opens the floodgates on the field as well. A penalty goal, another try and the Tigers lead 14-0. The Raiders continue to flounder. In these conditions, it's almost over. Eight minutes later, a try to Ben Murdoch-Masila and it really is curtains.

Hitting the sheds, it's not just the scoreboard that has the local fans flummoxed. It's the lack of creativity in attack. Josh Dugan has done nothing to suggest he's a five-eighth and, worse still, this doesn't look like changing. Down by 20 points, it's wet and miserable sitting in the stands. Why would you bother?

Any flickering hope for the locals dissipates straight after halftime. Benji Marshall puts Beau Ryan in with a wonderfully shaped kick making it 26-0 and now it becomes a case of how many. Forget the conditions, this is vintage Benji – he's got the ball on a string, albeit in a disciplined way. The razzle-dazzle we associate with the Tigers has been conspicuously absent, instead replaced by a classic display of determined, disciplined wet weather footy.

In contrast, the Raiders are poorly prepared for the conditions and ill-disciplined. They are simply woeful and, when Matt Utai scores with 15 minutes to go, it gets beyond disappointing and enters embarrassing territory. Why would you bother?

I don't see the end. The siren sounds as I leave the ground, the 40-0 scoreline difficult to fathom. Records were broken, all for the wrong reasons. This is touted as the worst defeat at Canberra Stadium in the 30-year history of the club.

On the bus back into town, amidst the head-scratching and soul-searching, it is difficult to determine which was the most miserable: the fans, the weather, or the insipid performance of the Raiders.

Why would you bother?

Wests Tigers 40

TRIES	Sironen, Farah, Murdoch-Masila, Ryan, Lawrence, Utai, Fulton
GOALS	Marshall 6/8

Canberra 0

REFEREES	Gavin Badger, Phil Haines
CROWD	9,210
VOTES	**3. Marshall** Tigers
	2. Ryan Tigers
	1. Woods Tigers

Not like the old days

Canterbury Bulldogs *versus* **South Sydney Rabbitohs**
7.30pm, Saturday, 2 June
ANZ Stadium, Sydney
LUKE CHARLTON

A S I PASS THROUGH THE EXIT OF OLYMPIC PARK STATION, I'm overcome with a sense of déjà vu. All over again, to quote Yogi. Not just because a few weeks ago I was leaving this station to watch the Bulldogs play Souths but because, in my short life, I feel like I've watched loads of Souths-Bulldogs games. I seem to remember them. This matchup provides me with my own rivalry round.

I'm especially reminded of a Friday night almost 10 years ago walking towards the Sydney Football Stadium. I was a teenager and just starting to discover my passion for rugby league. I'd enjoyed the game as a kid but this night I really felt connected again; I really felt that this game was part of me and what mattered to me. This probably had to do with the fact that my team had just been reinstated after being thrown out of the competition. That Friday night the Doggies took on the Bunnies.

The problem with that particular matchup was that, in 2002, the Bulldogs were awesome and Souths were terrible (which remained that way for about five years from that night). I remember thinking after the game that nobody was going to stop the Bulldogs in 2002. Turns out that David Gallop was the only person who could, and he took away every point they earned that year and sent them straight to the basement of the NRL ladder.

That Friday night, two things happened: Nigel Vagana scored five tries and, from memory, equalled a club record set by Edgar Newham in 1942; and more significantly, Souths lost 32-6. I left that game being heckled by Bulldogs fans. That's no way to go through life.

Not unlike that night a decade back, the Bunnies lost this one as well. It was a different sort of loss, though, because most of the Bulldogs fans would be saying that they escaped with a victory. This was tight all night; it was just a matter of who took their opportunities and when.

Both teams are a long way from those 2002 incarnations. A decade on, both have young halfbacks, both have English imports, both have exciting fullbacks, speedy wingers and centres to boot. The fullbacks are worth travelling to see. Ben Barba is as slippery as an eel and clever to boot. He can grab a game by the collar and drag it his way. And Greg Ingls is Greg Inglis. For Souths fans he is adored. For the rest he is feared and respected. He combines skill and speed with brute strength and power and he attracts the eye even when he's standing around the back having a suck on a water bottle.

Souths and Canterbury are actually very closely matched this year. I wouldn't be surprised to see them in a major semi-final matchup.

That's a long way off. Now, as I hop on the train heading home, my déjà vu has disappeared and I'm only thinking about the loss. I play the 'what if' game, especially after Ben Barba's amazing tackle on Dylan Farrell. It saved what looked like a certain try.

Only moments prior, Krisnan Inu had snapped a field goal to put Canterbury up. To put the icing on the cake, wily veteran David Stagg scored in the corner.

As much as I love reminiscing on past Souths/Bulldogs matchups and, as much as I feel a sense of disappointment, as I get home I'm still feeling okay. I'm glad I can watch my team lose, yet appreciate that they have a very good chance to make the finals. They look good enough to be competitive.

We are a far cry from the side that let Nigel Vagana in for five tries. That being said, it does give you an idea of where these teams have come from since that sad year of 2002.

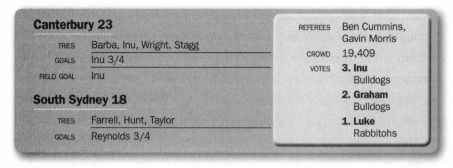

Canterbury 23

TRIES	Barba, Inu, Wright, Stagg
GOALS	Inu 3/4
FIELD GOAL	Inu

South Sydney 18

TRIES	Farrell, Hunt, Taylor
GOALS	Reynolds 3/4

REFEREES	Ben Cummins, Gavin Morris
CROWD	19,409
VOTES	3. Inu Bulldogs
	2. Graham Bulldogs
	1. Luke Rabbitohs

Life's a beach

New Zealand Warriors *versus* **Melbourne Storm**
4pm, Sunday, 3 June
Mt Smart Stadium, Auckland

JACK MUIR

T HE BETTER HALF HAD ORGANISED A DAY AT THE BEACH for Sunday afternoon. Foresight was completely absent from me when I answered in the affirmative. Once I realised my mistake, the negotiating started and I succeeded in moving the start of the beach excursion to the end of the game.

I settled down on the couch after a nice brunch knowing that the Warriors were capable of upsetting the Storm, as they have done many times before. In fact, the last time the two sides faced each other, the Warriors took it right up to the Storm only for Krisnan Inu to destroy the Warriors' chances of winning, guilty of two horrendous, heart attack-inducing mistakes.

Since then, the Warriors had offloaded Inu to the Bulldogs (good luck with that, by the way), so the confidence of grabbing the win was sitting just underneath the reality that it was the top team that had crossed the Tasman.

The game started and you could not wipe the smile off my face with the Warriors crossing twice to take a 12-0 lead. That was the best 15 minutes of football the Warriors had played all season: controlled and ruthless, the only blemish a single penalty. Konrad Hurrell showed why many believe he is rookie of the year material, latching onto a pass from his inside to crash over in the right hand corner. Big Manu Vatuvei also scored, hinting that his confidence has turned the corner.

The hope that the Warriors season had also turned the corner with this newfound consistency petered out pretty quickly, however, as the Storm rattled on two tries before halftime, England international Gareth Widdop showing some electric footwork to have the Warriors' defence grasping at the air.

Jaiman Lowe, arguably not in the top 300 players in the NRL, scored in the only possible way he could, by barging over employing the method of a fornicating rhino. You know you are watching a very good side if they can get Jaiman Lowe over the line and also make him look like a half-decent first grader.

The Warriors were hit with a couple of crucial injuries, one a season-ending tricep tear to big Sam Rapira, which is unfortunate as he had only just returned after time on the sideline. Glen Fisiiahi also went down after landing awkwardly on his knee but managed to return later in the second half. 'The Fish', as he is known, failed to have the fans add 'The Sword' to his name as he had in the NSW Cup, the NRL being a real step up.

The second half began with some good old-fashioned, rugby league attrition. The Storm gradually got on top. Will Chambers scored, blood clots in his legs and all, to put the Storm ahead with about 20 minutes to go. Try as they did, the Warriors could not get back into the game. Big Manu Vatuvei was more determined than anyone but he lacked pace. It was like a bad dream watching Big Manu; one of those ones where you're chased by a zombie, your legs are going flat out but you ain't goin' anywhere. Desperate flicks inside from Big Manu allowed Billy Slater to pounce and use his exhilarating speed to put Cameron Smith over the line. And that closed the door on the valiant Warriors. I could only marvel at the brilliance of Slater and his mate Smith.

I trudged off to the beach in the afternoon, disappointed but not gutted; the Warriors had tried hard but were undone by a couple of rugby league geniuses. Sometimes, as a rugby league fan, you just need to appreciate what you are witnessing despite the disappointment of watching your team go down.

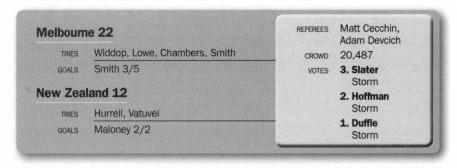

Melbourne 22		REFEREES	Matt Cecchin, Adam Devcich
TRIES	Widdop, Lowe, Chambers, Smith	CROWD	20,487
GOALS	Smith 3/5	VOTES	**3. Slater** Storm
New Zealand 12			**2. Hoffman** Storm
TRIES	Hurrell, Vatuvei		**1. Duffie** Storm
GOALS	Maloney 2/2		

They only come in fours

Brisbane Broncos *versus* **Newcastle Knights**
3pm, Sunday, 3 June
Suncorp Stadium, Brisbane

HUW FOWLES

ON FORM, THIS WASN'T THE MOST APPETISING OF FIXTURES. Neither team had won a game since April. But (Sir) Wayne Bennett was back visiting his old kingdom with 16 eager young Knights (plus Danny Buderus) looking for win 410 in the NRL. That was always going to add spice to this little battle.

Although I've never supported any club team he's coached, I've been a fan of Sir Wayne since his days of coaching the likes of Meninga, Jackson, Belcher and Lindner at Souths in Brisbane in the '80s. I don't think I can name another man who can be so simultaneously grumpy and engaging.

But I digress. It's time I start undigressing and turn my focus to the action on the box. Flick the eyes to the corner of the screen for a quick score check. 24-0 to the Horses after 22 minutes. I once heard a story where Bennett ... ahhh excuse me? What? Do mine eyes deceive me? 24-zip? At better than a point a minute? Extraordinary.

It seems the Knights have turned up for this little joust sans lances. Instead, they've built 13 flimsy ticket booths 10 metres out from their own tryline and they are attracting record numbers of visitors to the 'Newcastle In-goal Area Experience'. To the casual observer, it seems they're not even checking to see if the Broncos have appropriate photo identification. Beale, Hodges, Reed and Copley are all tall enough to get on any ride they want. It's a total free-for-all. The only thing missing from this carnival is fairy floss. Cue a Darius Boyd crying joke here.

Roy Masters once famously said of Bennett:

Wayne as a person can be very tough and very straight. I've seen people vomiting who look happier than Wayne.

At the 25-minute mark of this game, there's a fair chance Bennett no longer retains all of his brekkie. But before he has a chance to clean up the mess, his players take his mind off the troubles that ail him. The second of three halves begins. (Work that out!)

Buderus tunnels his way under the Broncos line (must be hard to do that at his age), and then Naiqama adds another. We've a proper joust on our hands, good sirs.

And rightly so. How could the Knights lose a joust? More to the point, how could the Knights lose a joust to a band of horses? Have you ever seen a horse on the back of another horse jousting? Nope, me neither. Don't get me wrong. I'd like to but it just seems imposs ... Darius Boyd makes a line break! I repeat. A line break. Andrew Voss reckons it's only his second for the year. While I'm wondering where the other one happened, Boyd tears straight up the guts of the Broncos defence. Old Man Buderus shuffles up in support and plants his second four-pointer under the posts at the Caxton Street end.

Just before the half, Mullen runs the length of the field only to be brought back on the advice of the third referee, with Mullen declared offside. Controversial alright. So the Knights could feasibly have gone into halftime all square! How? Parker slots the subsequent penalty and the Broncos lead 26-18 as they trudge off.

On the hour, Richard Fa'aoso's try narrows the gap to just two points. But that proves to be the end of the remarkable comeback.

In the third of the three halves, the Broncos upped the ante and put on another lazy four tries of their own. As you do. Because tries only come in fours these days. Thaiday, Hodges, McCullough and Hoffman seal the deal for the Clip Clops.

Farewell Sir Wayne and your knights of the oval-ball table. You were brave but alas your efforts were in vain. However your contribution to the 74 points for the match were greatly appreciated and made this a far more entertaining game than I expected.

May your passage back to the distant mystical lands of Novacastria be incident-free.

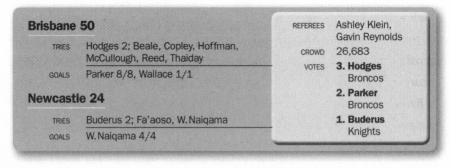

Brisbane 50

TRIES	Hodges 2; Beale, Copley, Hoffman, McCullough, Reed, Thaiday
GOALS	Parker 8/8, Wallace 1/1

Newcastle 24

TRIES	Buderus 2; Fa'aoso, W. Naiqama
GOALS	W. Naiqama 4/4

REFEREES	Ashley Klein, Gavin Reynolds
CROWD	26,683
VOTES	**3. Hodges** Broncos
	2. Parker Broncos
	1. Buderus Knights

Rob, Melanie and Jeff, known as Kenny

Parramatta Eels *versus* **Cronulla Sharks**
7pm, Monday, 4 June
Parramatta Stadium, Sydney
MICHAEL KENNEDY

O N THIS VERY DAY, I WAS BOUND FOR AOTEAROA, or the Land of the Long White Cloud. Perhaps the sporting gods thought this would go some way to assuaging my deepening despair about the cellar-dwelling Eels. As I flew across The Ditch at 30,000 feet, I also considered some of life's other imponderables: Why do we never hear of shark attacks in New Zealand? Why is the NRL not called the ANZRL? Will I get a square of chocolate with my meal?

I was staying in the heart of Auckland just off Queen Street and on a nippy night I set out around 8pm (NZ time) to try to locate a bar televising the game. You have to remember that most New Zealanders would prefer to watch their beloved rugby union, even if it happened to be a replay of the 1975 under-12s B-grade playoff for the wooden spoon, rather than a live rugby league game from Oz that doesn't involve the Warriors. Still, where there's electricity, there's hope.

As luck would have it, the first bar I found down near the harbour was showing the game live. Travelling solo surely has its blessings, but is there a more miserable image than that of an Australian Eels supporter in a Kiwi pub without a mate? I quickly ordered a soft drink (I was working) and perched myself on a barstool feeling much like a canary in a coal mine.

By the time the game started I had befriended a young, recently-married couple visiting from Melbourne (Rob and Melanie) and an older chap originally from Christchurch whose name was Jeff but who inexplicably preferred to be called Kenny. We were really the only people interested in the game, although Rob's allegiance lay with the Tigers and Jeff (sorry, Kenny) the Warriors. Melanie wasn't fussed. Unfortunately, I could hardly hear the broadcast and so watched the score on the screen slowly mount heavily in Cronulla's favour as halftime approached.

By this stage Rob was lubricated enough to start giving me stick about being an

Eels supporter. I thought about flirting with his wife but feared I wouldn't score there either. I started eating Kenny's chips.

As an intrepid roving reporter, I carried a notepad and pen (even if it was the hotel stationery). After scribbling 20-6 under some other indecipherable doodles, I turned over a new leaf for the second half ... just like the Eels, who were about to embark on a most remarkable comeback. Before I knew it, the Eels had scored two terrific tries to trail by a paltry two points. With Hayne running amok, Rob became noticeably more taciturn. The Eels looked like serious contenders. Melanie took up the slack in conversation and promised to become an Eels fan if they won.

With 10 minutes to go I was still anticipating an Eels loss, particularly when Colin Best nearly scored for the Sharks in the corner. But then Burt scored his second and I was on my feet. "Welcome aboard Melanie," I chirped. Rob made a comment about singing and fat ladies, while Kenny's comment is unprintable.

Hayne's final try was a ripper and, with an eight-point lead, I could actually contemplate victory. Sandow finished the scoring with a stabbing field goal and I was awash with smiles. Fittingly, the name of 'Kearney' originates from the Gaelic tongue meaning 'warlike' or 'victorious'. He must have channelled that and his inner haka to inspire the Eels tonight.

We hung around for another hour to debrief before I eventually called it a night.

I really do love New Zealand. Despite being a long way from Oz, I felt right at home. If it means I have to cross The Ditch just to see the Eels victorious, it would be a delightful sacrifice.

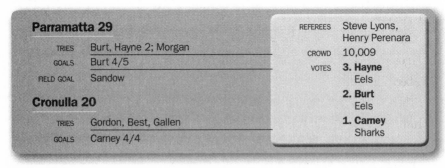

Parramatta 29		REFEREES	Steve Lyons, Henry Perenara
TRIES	Burt, Hayne 2; Morgan	CROWD	10,009
GOALS	Burt 4/5	VOTES	**3. Hayne** Eels
FIELD GOAL	Sandow		**2. Burt** Eels
Cronulla 20			
TRIES	Gordon, Best, Gallen		**1. Carney** Sharks
GOALS	Carney 4/4		

Round 14

Friday night feast

Melbourne Storm *versus* **Wests Tigers**
7.45pm, Friday, 8 June
AAMI Stadium, Melbourne

NICK McGRATH

AFTER ROUND 13, 2012		
1	Storm	11-1
2	Broncos	8-4
3	Bulldogs	8-5
4	Tigers	7-5
5	Sea Eagles	8-5
6	Sharks	7-5
7	Rabbitohs	7-5
8	Cowboys	7-6
9	Warriors	5-7
10	Titans	5-7
11	Dragons	6-7
12	Roosters	5-7
13	Knights	4-8
14	Panthers	4-8
15	Raiders	4-8
16	Eels	2-10

IT'S FRIDAY NIGHT AND ALL I WANT TO DO IS GET HOME FROM WORK and crack open a cold one while kicking back and watching the footy. Half the time I don't even care who is playing (although the Broncos' monopoly on Friday Night Football is becoming increasingly tedious). In this case, the fact it is the mighty Wests Tigers is a cracking bonus. Against Melbourne too: I should have called in sick to work for the week, such is my excitement about banking a certain two points.

But nine words from the better half ruined what was meant to be the night of the week: "You're coming to dinner with me and my friends."

At the time I thought there couldn't have been a worse phrase ever spoken. She may as well have said: "We're going to get matching flannelette pyjamas."

I could have set myself on fire then and there. Assured there would be other blokes there, I foolishly agreed to go.

Dinner is at the pub and at least they have the footy on at the pub, so it wasn't as if I was going to the local chew and spew (a fine establishment none the less) where I'd have been forced to play stick footy with chop sticks on my own.

There's roughly 30 minutes before kick-off when we arrive at the pub and I insist we rush, order, eat and find a telly – even though none of the other girls have arrived yet. That plan doesn't go down well. Still, worth a shot.

Everyone else arrives. But, to my surprise, not one other bloke. Fail.

So there I was. Sitting at the end of a table full of women. Dudded. Each one of them knew less than the other about the greatest game of all. It's taken me close to three years just to get my girlfriend to know what number Benji Marshall wears (of course then that changes – thanks for nothing, Sheens!) and I effectively have to start from scratch with six of her mates! I give up.

But I can't. It's Friday night. I'm determined to make a point. If I can't sit there and watch my beloved Tigers take on the Storm in Melbourne from the comfort of my own home, I'm sure as hell going to talk to everyone and anyone who'll listen about it.

I get as far as saying the 2005 Grand Final victory over the Cowboys was without question the greatest game since ...

Nothing.

They all start talking at once, each one louder, over the top of the other about *Fifty Shades of Sex and the City*. Or something like that. I'm gutted. Kick-off was five minutes ago and, for all I know, the Tigers could be up by 20 but more than likely down by 30. All I know is it would mean nothing if I can't see at least some of it.

After ordering ribs (I was trying to at least pretend I was at home watching the footy), I take a toilet break and catch a glimpse of the action. It's a wet game and both teams are without their State Of Origin players, so naturally I am expecting Benji to work his magic and get us home easily against a Storm side minus Slater, Cronk and Smith.

I manage to watch until just before halftime, at which point it was 2-all, with both sides struggling to handle the pill in the Melbourne damp.

I decide to go and see if the second half has begun and, sure enough, it has. I sit with one of the local bouncers for a bit and he asks who I'm going for. I don't need to use words. My incessant fist pumping after Lote Tuqiri scores makes it clear. Utai crosses shortly after and it's 10-2. If only Benji could kick a goal.

Understandably happy, I return to the table even happier. My ribs are waiting. My girlfriend asks how the Tigers are going, to which I reply (dismissing a 12-year Melbourne hoodoo, cockily), "Winning, of course – we always win in Melbourne."

Eating like a banshee, I devour the ribs and estimate there's probably 10 minutes remaining in the contest. Perfect! I again hint to my better half that my bladder is about to burst and run out to see if I was right. I am. There's 10 minutes to go and it's still 10-2. But just as I pull up a stool next to the pub's hard-working bouncer, in goes Dane Nielsen. Damn! Luckily the Storm have zero ability in the goalkicking department when Smith's not there and the score goes no further than 10-6.

It's a torturous final 10 minutes. To me, it feels like the Storm has the ball for the entire time. They go close but are rightly denied by the video referee. That is too close for comfort.

But the Tigers hang on, 10-6, to record their seventh straight victory. It's one of the gutsiest, un-Tigers-like wins I've seen (albeit only about 40 minutes of it).

So, despite being dragged to dinner and being forced to fake an inflamed prostate to rationalise my frequent bathroom visits throughout the night, we did it!

Ribs, beer and a Tigers victory: never in doubt. It was the Friday night I'd been hoping for.

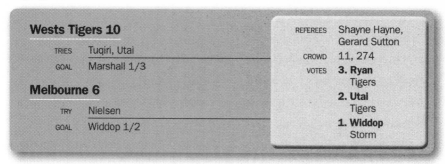

Wests Tigers 10		REFEREES	Shayne Hayne, Gerard Sutton
TRIES	Tuqiri, Utai	CROWD	11, 274
GOAL	Marshall 1/3	VOTES	**3. Ryan** Tigers
Melbourne 6			**2. Utai** Tigers
TRY	Nielsen		**1. Widdop** Storm
GOAL	Widdop 1/2		

The superstition of desperation

Newcastle Knights *versus* Canberra Raiders
7.30pm, Saturday, 9 June
Hunter Stadium, Newcastle

MATT TEDESCHI

DESPERATE TIMES CALL FOR DESPERATE MEASURES. With both teams winning just four of their opening 12 games and sitting on a measly 10 competition points, it does not get much more desperate than this. Canberra looks set to fight it out for the wooden spoon for the second straight season after yet another devastating injury to star playmaker Terry Campese, while preseason favourites Newcastle, with Wayne Bennett at the helm, are faring significantly worse than many expected.

The previous week saw the two teams concede a total of 90 points in abhorrent displays of defence. We could be in for some cricket scores here, but then again Canberra couldn't post a single point at home amidst the Tigers' seven tries. So this game could yield anything.

Although well within reach of the top eight, both sides would be crushed by a loss and it would require a Herculean effort in the second half of the year to make the finals.

Canberra is desperate, Newcastle is desperate, I'm desperate!

What do you look for when in such a state? Something that you think can make a difference, even if it is only in my mind alone. Some call it superstition. For me, it's all about location, location, location!

I convinced fellow league tragic Nick McGrath to venture into the dark side of Orange on a cold Saturday night. We were headed to The Ophir Tavern, likely to be ranked in the bottom two pubs in town and, for an outsider like Nicko, a place he'd feared.

The Raiders were 2-0 at the Ophir in 2012: a quality Easter Sunday victory over the Warriors and a scrappy win over the Eels a few weeks ago. The Royal has provided mixed success while my love for The Robin Hood has dwindled, having not tasted victory there since 2011. Throw in losses at home on a Friday night and at The Canobolas. That meant the only option available was to grab a mate and head to The Ophir.

It was the Raiders who jumped early with two tries inside the opening 10 minutes, makeshift five-eighth Josh Dugan instigating both tries. Despite a few handling errors and missed tackles, the more Dugan had his hands on the ball, the more dangerous the Raiders looked. Big Willie Mason barged over for Newcastle right on halftime to make it 20-12.

Travis Waddell tried his best to get the Knights back in the game, offering up a forward pass and penalty inside his own 20 in the space of 60 seconds. Newcastle scored and my heart rate spiked. Having sat comfortably in the lead for the entire match, that lead was reduced to four points and a textbook Raiders capitulation seemed possible.

But more handy work from Dugan resulted in Trevor Thurling crossing the line in his first game since he was injured in Round 3. The game was capped off with Edrick Lee flying 70 metres to score.

The Ophir delivered the goods once again: a 32-16 victory that reinvigorates my hope for a late-season surge.

Shaun Fensom was, once again, the backbone of the team with 46 tackles, 15 hit-ups and advancing the Raiders 98 metres.

It was promising to see second-gamer Matt McIlwrick finally breathe some life into the Raiders. At last Canberra have a dynamic dummy-half. Despite playing about half the minutes of starter Travis Waddell, who is better-suited to the NSW Cup, McIlwrick made as many tackles and looked far more competent and dangerous around the ruck. He managed two offloads and a tackle break in his time on the park while Waddell fumbled his way around, as usual.

Another youngster, Edrick Lee, provided two magnificent highlights during the game. None more so than that sprint down the left hand touchline. If I wasn't having flashbacks of Noa Nadruku streaking down the same wing in the '94 Grand Final, then I'll give it away.

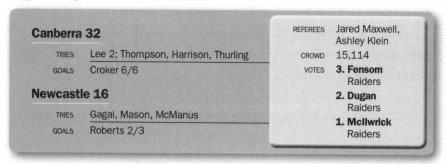

Canberra 32		REFEREES	Jared Maxwell, Ashley Klein
TRIES	Lee 2; Thompson, Harrison, Thurling	CROWD	15,114
GOALS	Croker 6/6	VOTES	**3. Fensom** Raiders
Newcastle 16			**2. Dugan** Raiders
TRIES	Gagai, Mason, McManus		**1. McIlwrick** Raiders
GOALS	Roberts 2/3		

Nearly sport

Cronulla Sharks *versus* **Gold Coast Titans**
2pm, Sunday, 10 June
Toyota Stadium, Sydney

DANIEL DWYER

FANTASY FOOTBALL CAN DO MANY THINGS TO A PERSON. It might be that one moment of pure elation as you pull off an unlikely win in the last minute of Monday Night Football or, at the opposite end of the spectrum, you might be so far behind after Friday's games that you don't bother watching the remainder of the matches for fear of falling into an even deeper depression.

Whatever the case, one thing is for sure: once the addiction of fantasy football has taken hold, you will never watch a game of football the same way again.

To get an understanding of how I view the game through my addiction, I first need to explain the game that I play. I've never been a big fan of the 'dream team' games as each team can have the same players and the scores can get quite ridiculous.

The game I play is called *Nearly Sport*. In this game you have to bid for your players at the start of the year but nobody else can see your bid. After the first 24-hour period the bids expire and whoever has the highest bid for each player gets them in their team and their team only. Bidding continues until you have a full squad up to a maximum of 25 players.

With the bidding complete, it's time to learn how the games are scored. You start by naming your top 17 each week. Once named, they are the only players who can score points for you that week, so you must choose wisely. If any of your listed 17 score a try you will receive four points (as in real life). You also have to name a goalkicker and for any goals they kick you receive two points. Pretty simple so far.

As forwards don't score as many tries as backs, they can receive a bonus try, which is referred to as a 'dominant forward', for achieving a specific workload in either attack or defence or both. This is also worth four points.

Then there is the 'dominant player'. This is worth four points and is awarded to the top three players of each NRL game as voted by the participants and administrators of the Nearly Sport website.

Now that we have that sorted, this is how the Round 14 match between Cronulla and the Gold Coast or, more importantly, the Drunken Slurries versus the Silent Assassins, looked to me.

In a game missing Paul Gallen, Todd Carney, Greg Bird, Nate Myles and Ashley Harrison, you'd be forgiven for thinking that interest in this match would be pretty low. For me, however, this was the most important game of the round as my goalkicker, Scott Prince, was playing and I had a chance to get some decent points.

Because it was a bye round, I was only able to name eight players but the one advantage I had over my opponent was that I actually had a proper goalkicker and he didn't. Go Titans, I hope it's a drubbing.

As the coverage started, I took note of the team lists. Scott Prince had been ruled out with a back injury, which meant Aiden Sezer would do the kicking and I only needed one guess to figure out who had Sezer named as their goalkicker! The Silent Assassins! Damn!

Instant emotional switch. Go Sharks, I know you can do it. That's exactly how this stuff works.

I stared on intently, watching only William Zillman, Aiden Sezer and Jeff Robson. Nothing else mattered now except those three. It's surprising how much you see of individual players when they command your focus. Every good read, you notice. Every bad read, you notice. Every second effort, you notice.

Every goal of Sezer's, I noticed! Those points were supposed to be mine!

As the game drew to a conclusion, I felt I had dodged a bullet. Zillman had dropped everything and struggled in attack and I had only conceded two goals to Sezer. The Sharks had won the day but, unfortunately, Robson claimed a dominant player as one of the best on ground, leaving me trailing 16-4 with two matches left to play.

Even though the best players may have been missing from the game, Nearly Sport had made that game just as exciting as any other and, despite my misfortune, my luck changed the very next day on the back of a couple of dominant players for the Warriors.

Go ye Drunken Slurries!

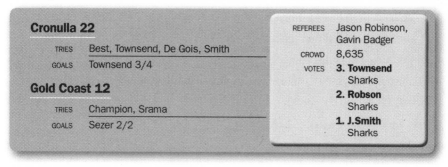

Cronulla 22

TRIES	Best, Townsend, De Gois, Smith
GOALS	Townsend 3/4

Gold Coast 12

TRIES	Champion, Srama
GOALS	Sezer 2/2

REFEREES	Jason Robinson, Gavin Badger
CROWD	8,635
VOTES	**3. Townsend** Sharks
	2. Robson Sharks
	1. J.Smith Sharks

Pavlov's Chook

Sydney Roosters *versus* **Brisbane Broncos**
3pm, Sunday, 10 June
Allianz Stadium, Sydney

BRETT OATEN

FRANKLY, I DID NOT WANT TO WRITE THIS REPORT. It was hard enough to experience Sunday's game once, much less live it a second time at the computer.

Each week of my rugby league life has been like a sine wave (or something) recently. It's the same pattern: depressed every game day, hard bitten and realistic the couple of days after that, cautiously optimistic by Thursday and Friday and rabidly enthusiastic by Saturday or Sunday. You see, I happen to think the Roosters are a very good team in the making, despite all evidence to the contrary. Mind you, I also thought that Trent Clayton and Ben Wellington were future internationals.

On Sunday, we were presented with a lot of evidence to the contrary. The Roosters were ill-disciplined, lacking strategy, useless in key positional play and generally brain-dead. The Broncos, by comparison, with six or seven out, were composed, well-drilled and organised, as they always are. Despite these two perspectives, the Roosters were still alive with five to go, much like they have been in every game for the past six weeks. They are stupid. I am stupid for failing to accept that they are stupid.

And it's killing me.

And did I mention that it pissed rain throughout? And that the referees were hopeless? And that I said, quite loudly, that I didn't understand why Tinarou Arona was in the Roosters team, only to discover that the giant man sitting in front of me was his brother? It was a top day out.

Let me say that I hate it when people blame referees for losses. Refs make errors, sure, very bad ones, but they make far fewer than players. The refs did not cost the Roosters this game by any stretch. Arguably, by awarding my great mate Arona a try, they kept the Roosters in it. But in this match, like so many others this year, they were hopeless. The Friend try, the Arona try, the Wallace try were all, at best, suspect and, at worst, demonstrably wrong. The Maranta play-the-ball decision is simply the most mystifying decision I've seen in years. The refs are struggling at the moment. I don't know why but they are. Just like the Roosters.

I will continue to believe that the Roosters are a good team here at Bondi but I'm not sure that Brian Smith is the man to extract the best out of them. I'm not a Smith-hater but his continued failure to get rid of Anasta, to support Jake Friend over Anthony Mitchell and to ignore Jack Bosden and, to a lesser extent, Brad Takairangi, sees our season slipping away very quickly. It's very disheartening and I'm not getting any younger.

Full credit to the Broncos (did I just write that?). They were excellent, knew what they needed to do and Griffin is clearly an organised and composed coach. Mind you, given that half the Australian schoolboys team shows up every November to report for duty, why wouldn't he be composed?

I didn't enjoy writing this report. Now, excuse me, but I'm off to see my psychiatrist. Go the Roosters!

Brisbane 40

TRIES	Maranta, Reed, Beale, Norman, Wallace, Glenn, Te'o
GOALS	Wallace 6/7

Sydney Roosters 22

TRIES	Leilua, Moga, Friend, Arona
GOALS	Anasta 3/4

REFEREES	Matt Cecchin, Adam Devcich
CROWD	9,738
VOTES	**3. McCullough** Broncos
	2. Glenn Broncos
	1. Tasi Roosters

A *dog day all round*

Penrith Panthers *versus* **New Zealand Warriors**
5.30pm, Monday, 11 June
Centrebet Stadium, Sydney

PETE ABELA

THE SECOND MONDAY IN JUNE IS ALWAYS ONE TO LOOK FORWARD TO – the Queen's Birthday long weekend. It's a strange holiday given the Queen's birthday was almost six weeks ago. There were, however, some royal activities of note this week with the Queen celebrating 60 years on the throne and Prince Phillip turning 91 overnight. The real joy for many Aussies though is the day off work.

That joy was short lived. Monday 11 June revealed itself to be an absolute dog of a day with the thermometer struggling to rise above 10 degrees and the rain bucketing down across Sydney.

So much for a day off. For your correspondent, there wasn't much to do besides lounge around, play a few board games with the kids and pay a visit to Grandad, who – like Prince Phillip – also turns 91 this year.

The main focus was trying to stay warm. Sunday had been similarly challenging on the weather front and, after two days, lethargy and cabin fever had set in. I could only hope the Panthers were feeling a little more enthused, although my confidence levels weren't high.

Despite being second last on the ladder, the Panthers were short three players on Origin duty. The Warriors – last year's Grand Finalists – were at full strength and they were sure to feel comfortable, given conditions at Penrith were rather Aucklandish.

As I feared, the Panthers began with no more energy than I had. Lachlan Coote dropped a bomb cold, giving Manu Vatuvei his first try and, when Shaun Johnson grubbered through a few minutes later, Vatuvei pounced to score again.

In a bid to dispel the icy chill that seemed to have come over me, I turned up the heater and huddled deeper into the blanket. It didn't seem to be working as the Warriors launched yet another raid. With three on one, a Warriors try seemed inevitable before Josh Mansour plucked the last pass out of mid-air, juggled it and sprinted 85 metres to score.

Finally something to get the blood pumping.

Over the next eight minutes, Kevin Kingston backed up Luke Walsh as he burst clear to register a converted try and then Geoff Daniela scored after Brad Tighe cut through. The Panthers ahead 16-12 at halftime.

Mildly enthused in the break, the most I could muster was a mug of hot chocolate.

The warmth it brought was only fleeting. In the 52nd minute the cold came back with a vengeance. Luke Walsh decided to run the ball on the last tackle and threw a loose pass. Konrad Hurrell became the second Warrior to scoop up a Panther's gift, running 30 metres through the Penrith backfield to score.

The wind howled and the din of the rain grew louder.

Meanwhile, at Penrith, James Maloney strolled through some limp Panthers defence to extend the lead to eight. With the clock winding down, prospects didn't look good.

I felt colder than the 5,778 hardy souls at Centrebet Stadium looked and so – in what may be termed a dereliction of a fan's duty – I snuck away to turn on the electric blanket. When I returned it was to see the tail end of some Warrior's razzle-dazzle play resulting in a try under the posts to Kevin Locke.

An 18-0 second half meant that it was the Panthers – and their hapless fans – who would bear the brunt of the cold-snap.

Meanwhile, half a world away in England, the Queen was waking to a day of 14° with rain. And they think that's summer. At least we call it winter.

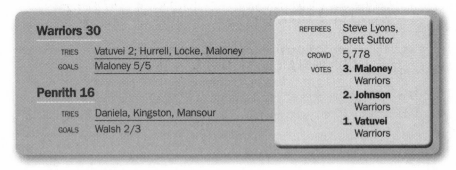

Warriors 30

TRIES	Vatuvei 2; Hurrell, Locke, Maloney
GOALS	Maloney 5/5

Penrith 16

TRIES	Daniela, Kingston, Mansour
GOALS	Walsh 2/3

REFEREES	Steve Lyons, Brett Suttor
CROWD	5,778
VOTES	**3. Maloney** Warriors
	2. Johnson Warriors
	1. Vatuvei Warriors

Ticket to pride

New South Wales *versus* **Queensland**
8pm, Wednesday, 13 June
ANZ Stadium, Sydney

NICK TEDESCHI

T RYING TO FLOG A TICKET TO A SOLD-OUT ORIGIN should be an easy experience. When doing so a day before the big game, it is not. Jesus, I couldn't give the bastard away. This is not to say that nobody was interested in going – just that every joker I knew either had his marker or had laid his commitments to some other rugby league function.

That probably says more about the company I keep than the popularity of the game itself. Sydney was at a standstill for Origin II, a buzz in the air. Newsagents wanted to chit-chat, sandwich-makers were asking questions, bakeries were decorated in blue. The passions had been stoked, old buttons pushed, the latent violence inside all rugby league fans channeled and focused.

But I could not palm off this ticket. I worked the phones like I was trying to sell mobile plans on a one per cent commission with the threat of castration if I didn't make my quota. Had I offered a bottle of Jack and a set of steak knives, it still wouldn't have mattered.

"Already going brother, you should have called a month ago ..."

"Locked in with my old man ..."

"Got a corporate function, bud ..."

Bloody Parko, the only man in the throes of a midlife crisis who goes and actually finds a job. He bails two days before the game. There wasn't a rugby league fan worth his brass who didn't have plans by then.

In the end, I dragged my girlfriend along. Louise comes from good rugby league stock, good Canterbury stock, dating right back to her grandfather who knocked about in the district when the Berries joined back in '35.

But she doesn't care much for The Greatest Game of All. Being a kindhearted soul she decided she could throw herself into rugby league for one night.

She witnessed one of the great Origin matches.

Of course, we always say that after Origin. Its continuing greatness has distorted all historical perspective. Every year we have "one of the great games", an "all-time classic", "one for the ages". Hyperbole is as much a part of Origin as Wally and Joey and the Grasshopper and Gordy and MG and Ben Ikin and 'Sparkles' McGaw and bad selections and disputed man of the match calls.

The second Origin of 2012 was no different. I had very much expected to see the Maroons seal their seventh straight series. I have been crippled by a sense of despair for four, maybe five years and I just felt this overwhelming sense of futility.

Yet the Blues jumped slight favourites in game two! I thought this was ridiculous and hence made numerous calls to bookmakers to back the Maroons.

Seated high on the halfway line, adorned in blue myself, I couldn't help but catch Origin fever. The sea of colour was astonishing, the noise nothing like I have heard in rugby league.

The first half was tense. From the opening tackle, when debutant Tim Grant sat retiring veteran Petero Civoniceva on his backside, the Blues held the upper hand. The forwards dominated Queensland's massive pack. The Maroons were making some uncharacteristic errors.

The Blues could not score. Again, they lacked punch. Mitchell Pearce will not fare well when blokes in pubs rank the Blues Origin halfbacks. He did not put a good kick in all night.

Brett Stewart eventually crossed in the corner for a 4-0 lead but the Blues had far more of the match than the score suggested.

When the Maroons made it 6-4 just on halftime thanks to a non-attempt by Akuila Uate to catch a Cooper Cronk bomb, the old cynic raised his head. It was all over now. The Blues couldn't win.

The game was still on a paper cut at 6-4 when the telling moment of the game came. Todd Carney, Cooper Cronk and Billy Slater converged on a loose ball in the Maroons' in-goal. Cronk held Carney off it. The decision was sent upstairs. No penalty try. But Cronk was in the bin.

While he was marching around the dressing sheds, the Blues scored twice – the second try to Josh Morris in dubious circumstances, a square-up for the Greg Inglis try in game one perhaps. It felt as if we were witnessing a miracle.

That sense of divine intervention became more apparent with 10 minutes to go and Queensland, having pulled the margin back to four with a Greg Inglis try only eight minutes earlier, looked certain to score. Brent Tate had collected a cross-field kick. He just had to ground the ball. As he went to fall, Michael Jennings, from nowhere, punched it clear, his only real contribution all night. It was an act of salvation.

Those last 10 minutes felt like an eternity.

When the siren blasted though, the Blues had hung on. We were going to Brisbane. We had a decider. We had renewed faith.

Origin in a foreign land
HUW FOWLES

WENT TO ORIGIN I IN MELBOURNE, WATCHING THE ENTIRE GAME from behind the glass at the EJ Whitten Bar, courtesy of my standing room only ticket. It was a last-minute decision to go to the game: I wanted to introduce a few Mexicans from work to their first ever game of rugby league. Origin footy was always going to make this a successful endeavour. But for Game II, I had to make do with a trip to the Rising Sun in Richmond.

It's a funny experience watching a State of Origin game at a pub outside rugby league country. If you pick up Melbourne and shake it hard enough, though, dozens of Cockies scuttle out from under fridges and congregate on the streets alongside numerous rugged up Cane Toads. The trick is to find a publican so desperate for patronage that he's prepared to challenge the status quo and put the game on the TV.

I get a beer, order the rissoles and grab a pew. Out comes Seal, replacing Fatty Vautin's daughter from Game I as the pre-match entertainment. He sings his only recognisable song wearing his Après ski gear.

Finally the 34 gladiators sent to entertain us march out. There's the maroon half, jerseys adorned with XXXX logos, the local Queensland beer – that started out in rural Victoria in 1857 and was later bought out by the Kiwis and is now owned by a Japanese company. The other half wears the blue jerseys proudly displaying their favourite local drop – Victoria Bitter, made by CUB, which is now owned by South Africans.

The QRL and NSWRL might think about a strict local-sponsors-only policy for their teams! How much better life would be if the announcer introduced the Queensland Brisbane Bitter Maroons and the NSW Reschs Blues? Come to think of it, I don't know if they make either beer in any great quantities any more if at all.

So maybe we could have the Queensland Point Lookout Civic Association Maroons and the NSW Dubbo Pottery Centre Blues? Maroons v Blues, Canetoads v Cockies, Pointers v Potters. Perfect.

The whistle blows.

Petero Fridge-Freezer tries to dish out the obligatory welcome to Origin footy to Potter debutant Tim Grant as he takes the first hit-up of the game but Grant fluffs his lines and rudely knocks Petero onto his backside. It's a sign of things to come as the Potters dominate the territory and the physical contests for the first 20 minutes. The NSW decision to pick genuine prop forwards to beef up the pack and match the size of the Pointers' forwards is a sage move. They leave dents and scuff marks in Queensland's maroon duco.

The Potters are rewarded with the first try to Brett Stewart after 25 minutes. But Todd Carney's kicking woes continue. 4-0.

How often do you see a team dominate a half of footy yet go to the break trailing? It happens again as Uate fails to defuse a Cronk bomb and Harrison puts Hannant into one of the posts. Pointers up 6-4 at the break. I can't bring myself to talk about Dave Taylor's first half of football.

The second half sees the Pointers come out a little spritelier. But this is soon quelled when Cooper Cronk brings down Carney illegally as he's about to score. It's 10 in the bin for him. Lucky not to be a penalty try. 6-6. Gus Gould praises the Cronk decision but the Potters pooh-pooh that thinking and put on two quick tries while the Pointers are down to 12 men. Carney cuts through a hole left by Cronk and put B. Stewart in for try two. 12-6. Then minutes later, the Hayne Plane takes evasive action to avoid the oncoming B-52 Inglis but Thursty strips Hayne of his payload. Fortunately, he toes it ahead before it hits the deck and Morris (the good looking twin) picks up the shrapnel and runs it in. 16-6.

This game has eerie shades of 1989 with Cane Toads dropping like flies or gallantly playing on one leg. Back then Queensland lost Vautin, Meninga and Langer early. This time Tate, Hodges and Slater all suffer first-half knocks and play on under obvious duress. Back then it was Bobby Lindner famously playing on with a broken leg. This time it's Parker with the horror leg injury, when he manages to insert one of his own boot tags in his shin while running up the ball. With his leg gashed to the bone, he is helped off the field. He asks the trainers if he's okay to go back on. Origin football proves yet again man's ability to throw all medical logic out the window when the competitive juices and adrenaline are flowing.

With Cronk back on deck, concerted defensive pressure and repeat sets of six, the Maroons finally capitalise courtesy of an Inglis try (a record 14th in Origin footy) which sets up another grandstand finish. 16-12. You can hear NSW supporters groaning around me. Surely these Toads won't do us over in the dying seconds again? Where's Mark 'Two Dollar' Coyne when you need him? Tate nearly adds the cruel icing to the comeback in the final minutes but a clever strip by Jennings denies him and the Potters hang on to tie up the series.

Luke Lewis (good Origin surname that) was ruthless from the bench; Bird, brilliant; Gallen, heroic despite his damaged knee. But it was Farah who was outstanding, each of his record-breaking 63 tackles inspired by his gravely ill mother watching from her hospital bed. Going in without a utility to give Farah some dummy-half relief was a risk for Stuart and the Blues, but one that paid off handsomely. I can't even bring myself to talk about Dave Taylor's second half of football.

John Harms was right when he suggested that Game I had only reached the heights of Mt Gravatt. This game was definitely more compelling. Perhaps a Mt Glorious. And despite one or two talking points, it was a fair result in the end. But as one NSW supporter surmised after the game, NSW had thrown the kitchen sink and a number of whitegoods at Queensland tonight and it was only just enough to take home the meat tray.

So Game III can't come quickly enough at the Cauldron. I'm hoping for an utter Mt Kosciusko.

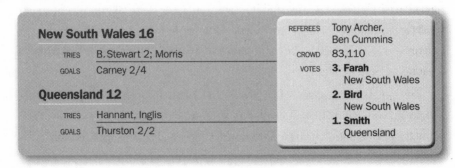

New South Wales 16

TRIES	B. Stewart 2; Morris
GOALS	Carney 2/4

Queensland 12

TRIES	Hannant, Inglis
GOALS	Thurston 2/2

REFEREES	Tony Archer, Ben Cummins
CROWD	83,110
VOTES	3. Farah New South Wales
	2. Bird New South Wales
	1. Smith Queensland

Round 15

That extra sting

St George Illawarra Dragons
versus **Canterbury Bulldogs**
7.30pm, Friday, 15 June
WIN Stadium, Sydney

MICHAEL ADAMS

SOME LOSSES HURT MORE THAN OTHERS. Ask a Souths fan, who can begrudgingly accept the old axiom 'you can't win 'em all' when denied by 16 points against the Titans, yet still be in pain weeks after going down to Easts. Same goes for a New York Jets fan after a loss to the Patriots; a Red Sox fan to the Yankees; Liverpool/Manchester United; Barcelona/Real Madrid; or Collingwood/every other team. It's the same story. It's never pleasant watching your team lose but losses to some teams just hurt more than others.

As a Dragons fan, I have always thought the Bulldogs are that team. I rejoice in their failure and despair at their success and, when those failures and successes are brought about by St George, those feelings are amplified a thousand times. In recent years I've been on the smiling side of that ledger more often than not, but this season the picture has altered considerably.

To put it bluntly, as it currently stands the Bulldogs are a far better side than the Dragons. They've reached the top of the pile sooner than expected following Des Hasler's celebrated arrival. With Ben Barba's rapid and exciting improvement, the emergence of Josh Reynolds and Sam Kasiano and the acquisition of James Graham, I fear my nemesis will go deep into the season this year. That hurts.

The Mighty Red V, on the other hand, are a team in sharp decline. Before March I thought that a top eight finish could be considered an unmitigated success. Halfway through the year I'm amending my position as a finals appearance would be enough to set the wheels in motion for the beatification of Steve Price.

It is with this gloomy mindset that I turned my attention to Wollongong in the hope that the tide could somehow be turned. It didn't take long for those hopes to be suffocated by some appalling play by the Dragons: dropped ball, penalties, kicking out on the full. It was the type of inept display that has become common for the Dragons this year and they were soon 18 points in arrears without looking like troubling the scoreboard attendant.

On the stroke of halftime the moment that dampened any thoughts of a comeback unfolded. Looking to close out the half with an innocuous hit-up, Dean Young, playing his 200th game, had the ball stripped by Josh Reynolds and the Bulldogs were in for their fourth try of the half. A manageable 18-6 deficit had become 22-6 and the game was all but over.

That incident summed up the position in which the 2012 Dragons find themselves. Young, like his captain Ben Hornby, is an admirable clubman who could never be accused of not putting in. Not once in 200 games. Yet effort alone is not enough anymore. There is a glaring lack of firepower in this outfit and, though they threatened to come back thanks to a better performance in the second half, in the end they just gave too much of a start.

And so, for the second time this year, I must carry the burden of a Bulldogs loss. It shouldn't still sting like this but it does. It no doubt dates back to my youth when I attended a high school dominated by Bulldogs fans. Dragons fans were the next biggest population by some distance which meant that, on the Monday following a meeting between the two teams, there was always carnage in the playground. Fronting up after a loss made those Monday mornings absolute torture.

Why now, fifteen years removed from that schoolyard gloating, does a loss to the Dogs still feel so humiliating? It's not like my quality of life is determined by how well the Bulldogs are going, why do I even care? I haven't worked out the answer yet. Unless something drastic occurs, it is a feeling I am doomed to experience for a while yet.

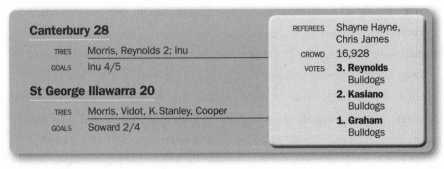

Canterbury 28

TRIES	Morris, Reynolds 2; Inu
GOALS	Inu 4/5

St George Illawarra 20

TRIES	Morris, Vidot, K.Stanley, Cooper
GOALS	Soward 2/4

REFEREES	Shayne Hayne, Chris James
CROWD	16,928
VOTES	**3. Reynolds** Bulldogs
	2. Kasiano Bulldogs
	1. Graham Bulldogs

Brave hearts

North Queensland Cowboys *versus* **Brisbane Broncos**

7.30pm, Friday, 15 June

Dairy Farmers Stadium, Townsville

DAVE FLETCHER

I T WAS WITH MUCH TREPIDATION THAT I TUNED IN TO WATCH the delayed telecast (in NSW) of this Friday night derby between the Brisbane Broncos and my beloved North Queensland Cowboys. Still reeling from the Maroons' narrow defeat to the Blues only two nights before, I predicted a tired and emotional outing from talisman Johnathan Thurston. I expected a night of lacklustre playmaking options, missed tackles and petulant tantrums to the refs when, try though he might, things would just not go his way.

While a lot of this certainly happened throughout the course of the game, there were also two sublime combinations with playmaking counterpart Matty Bowen that resulted in the only two tries of the match and the only two plays worth writing home about, from a game which was a turgid display of dogged defence in the face of uninspired attacking raids from both teams.

With the Broncos resting all but one of their Origin stars (Ben Hannant putting in a gut-busting effort to finish among the top in the metres-gained and tackles-made stats) the men from the southern capital were always going to lack that go-forward in attack and struggle defensively towards the end of the match. Indeed, it was telling that the first try of the game – coming after an hour of agonisingly unproductive footy – came when Thurston and Bowen exploited the tired and scrambling Broncos defensive line.

They made it look so easy ... that sublime inside ball to a lurking Matty B, who powered through the huge gap as if – like his vintage efforts of 2005 – a rugby league god watching the game on Foxtel decided to put him alone on fast forward for those crucial two seconds. He was too quick for the cover defence once that break had been made and found Cooper who had strolled in under the posts.

JT kept the pressure on the Broncos with a fine kicking game and eventually the Thurston-Bowen combination clicked again to set up yet another simple try, Kane Linnett waltzing over. The shattered Broncos just had no answer to the JT-Mango show, and the score was 12-0 when the siren sounded.

Notable mentions go to the other Origin players backing up on the night: Brent Tate, who ran and tackled like a man possessed following on from an outstanding performance in Origin II; James Tamou, who ran with energy and confidence after inspiring his Blues counterparts to their big win, and co-captain Matt Scott who, clearly tired, still managed to win many metres for his team.

So while this will be a game most remembered for less than a minute of inspired playmaking from the Cowboys' little men, it also was a game in which the Cowboys stood up defensively across the paddock to deny one of the form sides of the competition a single point.

A crucial victory for North Queensland over their traditionally more-fancied southern city cousins!

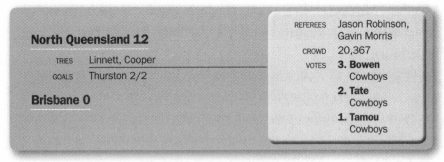

North Queensland 12

TRIES	Linnett, Cooper
GOALS	Thurston 2/2

Brisbane 0

REFEREES	Jason Robinson, Gavin Morris
CROWD	20,367
VOTES	**3. Bowen** Cowboys
	2. Tate Cowboys
	1. Tamou Cowboys

Where once were puddles

Cronulla Sharks *versus* New Zealand Warriors
5.30pm, Saturday, 16 June
Toyota Stadium, Sydney

JOHN HARMS

W HEN I LOOK BACK TO THOSE GLORIOUS DAYS OF FOOTBALL IN MY CHILDHOOD (all codes) one of the things that I remember is rain, and mud.

The one win we Oakey Bears had in four seasons (from Under-12s on), a victory against Allora-Clifton (home of the Platzes and Rohan Hancock), came during a downpour that left ankle-deep water on the un-flat surface. Our prop Mudguts Hudson lost a boot but we found it at the bottom of a puddle after a while. That was unusual for Queensland, where winters are frosty and dry.

But in those days mud was a key part of the NSWRL and the VFL. That was the

'70s. Then the drought came. For a decade conditions were good for football. Groundsmen became far more professional as well. Gone were the days when they'd surface at smoko-time on Tuesday (after a big Sunday night in the social club). They'd wander out to the middle hitching up their King Gee workers, Ardath hanging from the bottom lip, to admire the stop marks. They'd replace a few divots and make a mental note to order a truckload of sand for October.

It's been wet this winter in south-east Australia – and cold. So mud was on the cards at Shark Park for this match against the visiting Kiwis. I was glad to be in front of my Melbourne fire (after a week visiting the very wintery Warrnambool).

At Cronulla, umbrellas dotted the outer, there were ponchos galore and face-painting was for the brave and ghoulish only. Hardly anyone sat on the hill, although one group had set up a two-man tent from which they peered gingerly.

All credit to the new breed of groundsmen, though, the well-grassed surface held up. No observable mud and the players enjoyed reasonable footing. Indeed, despite some excusable errors, it was an entertaining match, even if it was played in the shadow of the cracking State of Origin fixture midweek.

The Warriors (were they really Grand Finalists last year?) desperately needed to revive their ailing season and the Sharks wanted to consolidate their improvement. Paul Gallen didn't come up, which helped the Warriors cause, but Todd Carney did.

Cronulla opened the scoring capitalising on sloppy handling from the visitors. They went wide allowing Ben Pomeroy to step past the cover and get over.

The Warriors finally settled and started to control the match, their strong forwards helping them to set up camp in Sharks' territory. They put together a couple of tries from kicks – the first to Kevin Locke from what initially looked to be an innocuous grubber and the second from James Maloney's bomb which, having been allowed to bounce, finished in Shaun Johnson's hands for New Zealand to lead 12-6.

Near halftime Maloney put boot to ball again; this time a field goal from outside 30. A handy point. Although the Sharks responded immediately, taking the option of a penalty despite the derisive cries from the experts outside the fence. At halftime it was 13-8 and anyone's game.

Warriors centre Konrad Hurrell had looked threatening from limited opportunities all evening and finally went over with strength (and a bulky pirouette that would have made Nureyev proud). 19-8 and the locals were in strife.

Enter the Sharks halves. Carney took hold of the game and brought the sodden crowd to life. He attacked the line and offloaded (like he was channelling Artie) to Jeremy Smith who burst clear and linked with Jeff Robson who slid over in the covering tackle. 19-14 and a few minutes left.

The Warriors defence held its ground but Carney went one better with a huge roost for a 40/20. With time getting away Robson dinked, dummied, and dinked again, stepping through tired Warriors defenders to score out wide. Carney needed to nail the conversion for an unlikely victory.

He did, with a powerful place kick. The boy is a talent, as we all know.

The Sharks banked the points and the fans drifted away in the mizzle knowing that this is the sort of win which makes a difference when those last places in the eight are being decided.

The crowd drifted off feeling rewarded. The groundsmen, pleased with their work, went looking for beer.

Cronulla 20			
TRIES	Robson 2; Pomeroy	REFEREES	Ashley Klein, Steve Lyons
GOALS	Carney 4/4	CROWD	9,271
New Zealand 19		VOTES	**3. Carney** Sharks
TRIES	Locke, Hurrell, Johnson		**2. Robson** Sharks
GOALS	Maloney 3/4		**1. Hurrell** Warriors
FIELD GOAL	Maloney		

Bleeding red and green

Parramatta Eels *versus* **South Sydney Rabbitohs**
7.30pm, Saturday, 16 June
ANZ Stadium, Sydney

ANDREW RYAN

NOT LONG AFTER I WAS BORN, my family moved from the Rabbitoh heartland of Mascot, where as a kid Dad donned the famous two-blue jumper, to reside in Carlingford, a suburb on the edge of the urban sprawl. It was Eels heartland.

My schooling began just as Parramatta embarked on their era of glory in the early '80s. In year three the teacher subjected every student to the indignity of having to enter a Parramatta poster competition. I drew a poorly scaled picture of a Roman-nosed Ray

Price with a feebly small Balmain defender hanging off him. In the background I drew a crowd made up of a few dozen badly drawn circles. To my complete surprise it was enough to impress the judges. I scored a leather Steeden and an Eels cap. An article about my win, with photo, appeared on page seven of the *Parramatta Advertiser*. My insincere smile beneath the demeaning yellow and blue piece of millinery and the fact I wrote my name, age and address in alternating red and green texta letters on the back of the poster was at least a silent protest if not an act of subversion.

In year five at a 'dress in your supporter gear' day, I spied a girl wearing the subtlest and skinniest red and green ribbons in her hair – the only other hint of red and green in a sea of yellow and blue. I had my first crush. Recently I saw a photo of her wearing an ostentatiously phallic band in her hair, up on stage with some rockers at the Orient Hotel. She was on her hen's night. Crush over.

The only other person to ever wear the red and green at my school is still my good friend to this day. In year eight, I went along with his whole family to watch an opening game of the season between the Eels and the Bunnies, I was so annoyed at another hope-dousing loss and the jibes of every local idiot I encountered that I broke my flag on the way home. I still get teased about it.

The tide has turned in recent years.

My Bunnies, sitting pretty in the top half of the table, were expected to win this fixture and win well. The Eels had lost eight of their past 10 coming into this clash, a record I found rather pleasing. Their spiralling footy fortunes had seen them sign Chris Sandow, a player who polarised opinion while playing at Souths. Sandow hadn't started the season well and had been sent off to the Wentworthville Wombats to get his form back.

Sandow's replacement in the famous cardinal and myrtle number 7 was Adam Reynolds, an unassuming kid who grew up 300 metres from Redfern Oval and only ever dreamed of having a Rabbit insignia on his chest.

He orchestrated the opening points with a deft chip kick for Nathan Merritt. Then he completed a second glorious sideline conversion after Greg Inglis ran right through Sandow – making a quite satisfying 'slap' sound on the replay – and offloaded for Justin Hunt. Souths led 12-0 at halftime.

Two minutes into the second half and Inglis, nursing a hyper-extended elbow and general Origin soreness, again took on the line and this time set up Dylan Farrell.

The Eels got the score back to 18-6 when Reni Maitua crossed out wide.

A Souths try from a bomb was mystifyingly disallowed and then there was the moment that defined the game. It also typified the fortunes of the two teams in 2012. Sandow intercepted with Souths deep in attack and took off. He looked like going the length of the field until his opposite number came steaming across from the far side of the ground and bundled him into touch two metres from the line. Reynolds leapt to his feet and proudly thumped the Rabbitoh logo on his chest before being embraced by his teammates. The crowd went beserk while Sandow was left splayed against an advertising hoarding wondering what could have been.

His wound was further salted a few minutes later when Rabbitohs captain Michael Crocker ran right through a tackle to seal a comprehensive 24-6 win.

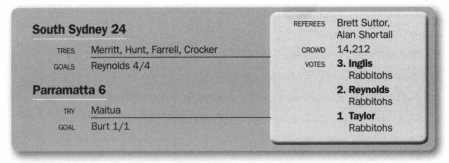

South Sydney 24			REFEREES	Brett Suttor, Alan Shortall
TRIES	Merritt, Hunt, Farrell, Crocker		CROWD	14,212
GOALS	Reynolds 4/4		VOTES	**3. Inglis** Rabbitohs
Parramatta 6				**2. Reynolds** Rabbitohs
TRY	Maitua			**1 Taylor** Rabbitohs
GOAL	Burt 1/1			

Show no mercy

Gold Coast Titans *versus* Penrith Panthers
2pm, Sunday, 17 June
Skilled Park, Gold Coast

ALEX MADGE

WITH THE ORIGIN SERIES HANGING IN THE BALANCE after a cracking second contest, this game between last year's wooden spooners and one of this year's spoon favourites was not exactly making waves in the rugby league world. For a Titans fan though, every game is a chance for the team to atone for the heartbreak of 2011. With three players returning from Origin duty, fans could be forgiven for not expecting an all-out effort especially against the lowly Panthers.

What a shock then to see Aiden Sezer – already filling a much-needed gap in the Titans side in 2012 – strolling over the line untouched with less than 12 minutes gone. The Gold Coast have typically scored their points out wide using their twin speed machines David Mead and Kevin Gordon to test defences on the flanks. The 'Miracle Mead Try' of 2011 is one such play that inevitably puts pressure on Scott Prince to get full value from the try.

Sezer was well aware of this and used the sleepy kick defence to improve the position of the ball to give the Titans six points in the early stages of the game. Things only improved for Prince after this with the next two tries coming under the posts and allowing the home side to head into the sheds up 18-0 at halftime.

Mead and Steve Michaels put their tokens in the turnstile taking advantage of attacking errors to put a further 12 points on the board. Prince couldn't have hoped for three easier kicks, nor the team an easier start, in what was becoming a real flogging.

The second half started the same as the first; Sezer straightened off a Prince ball and scored under the posts without being touched. What a godsend to Titans fans, a genuine five-eighth, not to mention one with an NRL double!

To make sure it wasn't just the backs having all the fun, big man Brenton Lawrence amplified the Panthers' embarrassment showing fans how forwards play in South Australian park footy. With footwork that would make Ben Barba proud, Lawrence made it five-blot for the Titans with yet another gift to Prince to send them 30 points up.

It was here the Titans needed a quick lesson in NRL finals history. For and against was always going to be critical to determining the last teams in the top eight and, with a piss-poor start to the year, this is where the Gold Coast needed to be aiming. With their foot on the Panthers' throat and a chance to secure a great differential on the ladder, some lazy in-goal defence let the Panthers in for a try and a shot at respectability.

Luke O'Dwyer didn't get the memo about scoring under the posts and gave Prince his first challenge of the day. That said, it still wasn't a difficult kick and the Titans extended the lead to 30 points.

Then came the inevitable release of pressure. Even when they've been in the top four, the Titans have rarely put teams to the sword. Up 30 points with 10 minutes to go, they should have been eyeing off a 40-point win. Instead they allowed the Panthers a few late consolation tries and left fans wondering how much starch their season comeback might contain.

The Titans are a side that can ill-afford to lose three keys players for Origin. With their three stars returning, it was a good chance to put an understrength Penrith side away. While they came away with an 18-point win, all the stats suggest it should have been more.

Gold Coast 36			REFEREES	Gerard Sutton, Phil Haines
TRIES	Sezer 2; Mead, Michaels, Lawrence, O'Dwyer		CROWD	11,591
GOALS	Prince 6/6		VOTES	**3. Prince** Titans
Penrith 18				**2. Sezer** Titans
TRIES	Taumata, Ciraldo, Simpkins			**1. Myles** Titans
GOALS	Walsh 3/3			

The West Wyalong twizzle

Wests Tigers *versus* **Sydney Roosters**
3pm, Sunday, 17 June
Leichhardt Oval, Sydney

GREG OBERSCHEIDT

HINGS DON'T CHANGE A GREAT DEAL at the West Wyalong Services and Citizen Club. Sunday arvo froth and a casual punt leading into the footy is the norm for many of the local luminaries. A nod, a wave and "it's your shout!" greets the late-comers. A handful of peanuts to complement the brew so long as 'Gruesome' hasn't doused the snacks with half a bottle of tabasco in his own sadistic attempt at humour.

'Soup Bones' has had a few since social golf and, after a number of assertions from 'Jacko' that he should invest in a calculator, tempers get frayed and threats of pending doom begin. Given that Soupy is seven stone dripping wet and his form shows the signs of his childhood battle with polio, he doesn't cut the most intimidating figure so his threats are treated in the usual manner: with good-natured scorn.

'Jumbo' has confused another new starter behind the bar with his demands for screwtop long necks to the knowing grins of the 'Knights of the Round Table'.

As the afternoon wears on, the froth flows and the winners are sparse. Except, of course, for 'Lucky' Hill who is kissed by a fairy when it comes to the ponies. Jack Lowe, a 90-year-old retired shearer, has just made his last ride down for the day to pick up two more tall bottles and check his Keno. Everyone says a silent prayer as he leaves that he doesn't stack it on the mile-long ride home again.

"Flick the Chooks on, Gruesome," chortles 'Kezza', who's been going beer for beer with 'Irish' again and is pretty close to singing on his table. He doesn't have a bad voice but his recall for lyrics is lacking.

'Block-Buster' is a mad Dragons man. Disinterested in proceedings, he purposefully moves beneath the television screen and sits, facing the crowd, stiff armed, eyeballing the throng and ready to hurl abuse when the opportunity arises. No-one pays him any mind. The footy's about to start.

News filters through the crowd that Farah is a late scratching due to the tragic passing of his mother. Greg Miles is the only voice that can be heard during the moment's silence. Neville forgot to mute the races.

The game starts hot and, within the blink of an eye, Utai is over in the corner after a neat kick from Marshall found Minichiello flirting with the sideline and subsequently misjudging the bounce.

The next 50 minutes of play belong to the Roosters. Some solid play from the halves create opportunities for Guerra and Waerea-Hargreaves to score after running some nice outside-in lines.

Back-to-back tries to Cordner and Anasta in the shadows of halftime stretch the lead out to 20 points and the Roosters faithful are crowing. Kezza is in full voice now, joined by 'Parkesy' and 'Swarn', who have snuck out of the shed to pick up a case for the evening.

Seemingly the sting has left the match with the Roosters well in control. More points follow early in the second half. 'Lucky' and 'Bonzo' have had a gutful of proceedings and take their leave to the jeers of 'Kezza' and 'Irish'.

The Roosters lead 36-10 and the game is all but over.

Beau Ryan scores a long-range try to ease the suffering. Marshall converts. The next set the Tigers go 100 metres and Moltzen crosses. Surely not. When Lawrence scores moments later, the chins begin to drop among the Roosters. Everyone knows how well the Tigers can finish and it is 28-36 with nine minutes to go.

The Tigers have their chances, the air is full of profanity as the Roosters supporters sense a last-minute defeat.

It was not to be. Kennedy crossed to tumultuous applause to end the issue.

'Kezza' and co are on top of the world. "Never in doubt!"

"Hey Gruey! When's the next courtesy bus?"

Sydney Roosters 42			REFEREES	Ben Cummins, Gavin Badger
TRIES	Anasta, Pearce, Waerea-Hargreaves, Kennedy, Guerra, Cordner, Tasi		CROWD	20,327
GOALS	Anasta 7/7		VOTES	**3. Woods** Tigers
Wests Tigers 28				**2. Friend** Roosters
TRIES	Utai, Galloway, Ryan, Moltzen, Lawrence			**1. Pearce** Roosters
GOALS	Marshall 4/5			

Hardly spineless

Manly Sea Eagles *versus* Melbourne Storm

7pm, Monday, 18 June

Brookvale Oval, Sydney

MARK SHANNON

FORTRESS BROOKVALE: ANDY RAYMOND TELLS US THAT THE PREMIERS have only lost one of their last 15 matches here but the Storm are leading the competition and are Monday night specialists. This one should be a classic. The Battle of Brookvale part two, the press are calling it. Laurie Daley tips the Eagles. His eyes appear to be trying to convince each other that he has made the right decision. The bookies and the experts agree, the loss of Slater will prove too much. It is too hard to win when you're missing a third of your spine. Brandy bucks the trend and tips the Storm.

I feel for the Storm. My partner Karla is away on a camp for three days and I'm chief cook and bottle washer for the three boys. That is the entire spine out of our team. It's a bit like replacing Billy Slater with Scott Minto. I throw a couple of dodgy frozen pizzas in the oven and check on the troops. Dan has fashioned a homemade crossbow that fires rubber bands with deadly accuracy and speed. His younger brothers are paying the price for his craftsmanship. A bit of harmless fun, I decide. Play on.

The game itself is of the highest quality. The Storm bounces out 12-0, full of running. Todd Lowrie finishes off an 80-metre move accepting an inside ball from Justin O'Neill to start the scoring. Moments later, Smith beats Watmough with embarrassing ease. Manly get some possession and penalties (Ryles, of course) and hit back to lead 18-12 at oranges. Great football, great tries, great defence and another shocking video ref blunder. Billy Harrigan, not Billy Slater, might be in the headlines tomorrow.

Pizzas have been served. They are nearly as thin on top as King Wally but everyone seems happy enough. Somewhere, something is beeping; I think it's the microwave. No, it must be the dishwasher. No, it's the washing machine. I empty it and throw another load on. I head back for the second half.

Glenn Stewart's knee injury seems serious. He'll miss Origin III by the looks of it. Speaking of Origin, Norrie does what Dave Taylor could not and scoops up a loose ball near the line and scores. Smith makes it 18-18 with his conversion.

Duffie leaps high and grabs a Cronk bomb. Another brilliant try. The Storm are back in front and will be hard to run down from here. The two remaining spine members are in terrific form; Billy has hardly been missed. Widdop has done a great job at the back. Smith sends the score out to 26-18 with a penalty goal. He is easily the man of the match after another flawless performance. Manly score a breathtaking try on the bell to close the final margin to four. It is too little, too late. The boys from the old graveyard have beaten the team from the fortress, 26-22.

Coach Toovey laments the Melbourne wrestling tactics in the play-the-ball.

"We can't seem to get to push the boundaries as much as they do and they're good at it," he says.

What a surprise. Geoff spent his entire career at hooker doing the Mexican wave at dummy-half. Manly have not had a quick play-the-ball in the last 20 years, according to Toovey.

The Storm have defied the odds and succeeded without their superstar. They are impressive. At home, we have overcome the loss of our star as well, though it hasn't been easy. Somewhere outside, something is beeping again. It is the washing machine? I turn the telly off and head for the laundry.

Melbourne 26			REFEREES	Tony Archer, Jared Maxwell
TRIES	Lowrie, Smith, Norrie, Duffie		CROWD	12,106
GOALS	Smith 5/5		VOTES	**3. Smith** Storm
Manly 22				**2. Cronk** Storm
TRIES	Taufua, B. Stewart, Cherry-Evans, Whare			**1. Lyon** Sea Eagles
GOALS	Lyon 3/4			

Round 16

Domestic hiss

Brisbane Broncos *versus* **South Sydney Rabbitohs**

7.30pm, Friday, 22 June

Suncorp Stadium, Brisbane

DOUG ROWETH

AFTER ROUND 15, 2012		
1	Storm	12-2
2	Bulldogs	9-5
3	Broncos	9-5
4	Rabbitohs	8-5
5	Sharks	9-5
6	Cowboys	8-6
7	Tigers	8-6
8	Sea Eagles	8-6
9	Warriors	6-8
10	Titans	6-8
11	Dragons	6-8
12	Raiders	5-8
13	Roosters	6-8
14	Knights	4-9
15	Panthers	4-10
16	Eels	2-11

WE ALL HAVE THOSE FRIENDS. YOU KNOW THE ONES. They live and breathe their rugby league teams. They love their footy and we love them for it. Personally, my friends are Craig, a lifelong Rabbits fan who has stood by the cardinal and myrtle throughout all their adversity, and his wife, Monica who bleeds Queensland maroon and is amusingly prone to four-letter words while watching her beloved Broncos play. Which means at Suncorp this evening, this is their household's annual grudge match, fittingly during Women in League round, with the Broncos decked out in pink in a poignant nod to the ladies behind the NRL.

But there's more at stake; something that goes beyond household bragging rights and even Women in League. Tonight is about Petero Civoniceva. A true gentleman of the game, he has earned universal admiration. After 14 seasons and 32 Origin appearances, he is playing game 300 and, as we kick-off, *it goes out on the full*.

The first expletive takes just seconds. The language gets more and more colourful as mistakes flow early on. It's clear these household bragging rights are important.

It takes 20 minutes before there is a score. Peter Wallace spots room on the right, when attacking the South Sydney line, as Justin Hodges takes advantage of a Rabbits error. Then the Rabbitohs dig in.

While Brisbane are camped down the South Sydney end of the park for the rest of the half, the Rabbits make almost 50 more tackles and their extraordinary defensive effort keeps the deficit to just four.

Then suddenly it's not even a deficit. Chris McQueen finds space and loads up a big step around the fullback to score. Unbelievable. The Broncos have had all the possession yet South Sydney somehow lead 6-4 at halftime. Craig suggests Souths deserve their lead on the back of their defence. Mon disagrees. She's furious. Fortunately the television doesn't disappear through the window and the second half begins.

Two minutes later Brisbane, attacking the South Sydney line on the last tackle, have the ball stripped. Or is it a failed offload? South Sydney are unluckily penalised and Craig is incredulous. Moreso when Wallace puts in a kick for Alex Glenn to score two minutes later. Brisbane back in front 10-6.

This Rabbits defence is consistently tested. Brisbane push forward through the hands to Norman who floats it wide. But look out! Nathan Merritt comes off his wing, intercepts and runs 90 metres up the other end to score. Again, inexplicably, the Bunnies are back in front 12-10 with just 30 minutes remaining.

The Suncorp crowd is as furious as Mon has been most of the night. She's muttering something about losing Petero's 300th. At least that's what's discernible amid the swearing.

Brisbane keep pressing. How long can Souths hold them out?

On the hour we find out. Another attacking set from Brisbane and Wallace spreads it wide to Corey Norman – who floats a pass to Jack Reed. Wow. That was at least two metres forward. Craig is on his feet swearing at his wife, who argues vehemently the pass was flat. It's a try, converted from the sideline. Ouch. Craig apologises but Brisbane lead 16-12. It's slipping from the Rabbits.

Then it disappears completely. Andrew McCullough chips over the top for himself and gets boot to ball again. It deflects off Greg Inglis into the waiting hands of Corey Norman who scoots away for a try. Pure fortune. Mon suggests they practised that at training but you can't script that stuff. Craig looks shattered.

As fulltime sounds, the Broncos score a final try and give the conversion attempt to Civoniceva. He kicks it like a front rower but it doesn't matter. Even Craig concedes it's fitting that such a humble star celebrates his 300th match with a win.

And a well deserved win at that. Souths have been admirable in defeat but the Broncos pressed all night and controlled the game.

And as for those friends, well, Craig doesn't have to sleep on the couch and Monica holds bragging rights for a year.

Unless, of course, they meet in September.

Brisbane 26		REFEREES	Tony Archer, Chris James
TRIES	Hodges, Glenn, Copley, Norman, Te'o	CROWD	33,602
GOALS	Parker 3/4, Civoniceva 0/1	VOTES	**3. McGuire** Broncos
South Sydney 12			**2. Parker** Broncos
TRIES	McQueen, Merritt		**1. Merritt** Rabbitohs
GOALS	Reynolds 2/2		

Too far from anywhere

St George Illawarra Dragons *versus* **Gold Coast Titans**
7.30pm, Friday, 22 June
WIN Stadium, Sydney

PAUL ROBERTSON

FREMANTLE. IT'S A PLEASANT ENOUGH PLACE to sit and watch the rest of the world spin, but it is barely a city. For all of its industrial attachments, Fremantle's charms are quite easily found in numerous other port cities. Everything that happens here from the marketplace to the bus timetable seems to be going through the motions of a metropolis without actually being one and that presents me with a feeling more vacuous than I had-imagined.

Empty city circle buses glide by me as I sit staring through a restaurant window that could be any restaurant, apart from the chicken Tikka Masala settling in my stomach. The dessert menu will be reviewed but will go untried yet again. I search the seats of a series of these buses to determine if yet again it would be full of the inevitable emptiness but, without fail, there is a solitary person on it which means it's one too many.

Freo emerges from its slumber on a Sunday arvo where it seems to become home to every second Perth hipster looking for a pile of coffee and a Sunday sesh, all of which is seemingly found within a 500m radius of the main street and barely anywhere else. The rest of its suburbs are sleepy; deathly quiet again save for a couple of hamburger shops and general stores. Legend has it that AC/DC wrote Highway to Hell somewhere between Melbourne and Perth and there is no need to guess which direction they were driving.

I've watched the first two marvellous games of Origin from this vantage, for the want of a more appropriate word, on two-hour delay. While it doesn't lose any lustre from such distance, the two-hour delay drives you stir crazy. Lock down Facebook and wait!

Today is the shortest day of the year. I've spent the best part of the last two weeks here – a town almost completely devoid of reference to rugby league and almost anything else interesting. If it wasn't for the New Edition bookshop on High Street this week, I would have probably passed out from boredom.

As I walk around browsing the shelves of New Edition with a copy of *Rugby League Week* under my arm, I contemplate tomorrow's matchup between the increasingly rudderless Dragons and the increasingly buoyant Gold Coast Titans. I decide to pick up a copy of *Granta 118 Exit Strategies* – which appears to be an appropriate choice in the circumstances.

As far as slumps go, St George Illawarra is in a particular boring one. Suffering the worst attacking record in the game, Steve Price is getting deeper in the mire with every match. It appears that Ben Hornby has stayed a year too long and Jamie Soward is not taking the common sense, percentage approach to his footy that seemed to come so naturally to him under Wayne Bennett.

And this game against the Titans is no different – numerous offensive opportunities missed. Hornby drops the ball cold in the eighth minute deep in Titans territory. In the 11th minute, Jamie Soward gives the ball away at the end of a promising movement. In the 36th minute, Trent Merrin carpets a sitter 10 yards out from the try line. Numerous line breaks are not completed by quality finishing, typically ending with poor pass options or from a lack of enthusiastic support play. Empty, boring football.

But the Dragons somehow escape. Nate Myles gives away two avoidable penalties near the Titans goal posts and the completely uninspiring rabble from Wollongong sneak home.

The talking heads suggest that the Titans were just as uninspiring and that the Dragons defence did enough. However, this footy is a far cry from the tradesman-like performances of 2010. We're a shadow of our former selves. We are now the rugby league equivalent of Fremantle. We know we are entitled to be better but we're just going through the motions. The excitement is somewhere else.

This is not the way home.

St George Illawarra 8		REFEREE	Gavin Morris, Jason Robinson
TRY	Vidot	CROWD	10,194
GOALS	Soward 2/3	VOTES	**3. Hunt** Dragons
Gold Coast 6			**2. Srama** Titans
TRY	Prince		**1. Morris** Dragons
GOAL	Prince 1/1		

Happy bloody birthday!

North Queensland Cowboys *versus* **Canberra Raiders**
5.30pm, Saturday, 23 June
Dairy Farmers Stadium, Townsville

MICHAEL PEARSON

F RANKLY, I WAS NO CHANCE TO WATCH THIS FOOTY GAME. Birthday party preparations, babysitters and a preoccupation with Black Caviar's tilt at Royal Ascot glory conspired against any meaningful enjoyment or analysis of this fixture. It's a pity because, as a Queenslander, I am a fan of the Cowboys; I like the way they play. Of course, the Raiders are always of interest in my house. They were the first Queensland team in the Sydney competition, back when coach Wayne Bennett had in his squad the likes of Meninga, Belcher, Jackson, Walters, Backo et al. Queensland legends.

Every TV and radio portal throughout the house is tuned to my local ABC and Fox as the family scurries about getting ready for its Saturday evening social event. Wrapping of presents, pressing of floral blouses, coloured jeans and my trusty Ben Sherman Saturday night special need to be demonstrated as priorities to the main show.

There is an art to being focussed on a footy match while seemingly preoccupied with the domestic duties. Say no more. Mind you, ear pieces tuned to radio dripping out of a shirt collar can be problematic, especially when those around can't seem to attract your attention.

The Cowboys are deserved favourites. The Raiders have been at their inconsistent worst and are experimenting with Dugan at five-eighth, a clear sign of enforced desperation.

The Raiders score first and I'm careful to exude a muffled cheer while standing half-naked in the lounge room among the pandemonium of hair dryers, curling wands and the unrelenting and frustratingly dextrous challenge of denim button zippers!

Things are looking good for an upset and I can feel the vibe. A good night looms. Tonight's 21st birthday is the commencement of a second-generation wave of family functions that will cascade over the next decade. I am particularly fond of the 21st party. They are peculiar gatherings of family and guests who are either youthfully ambitious friends of the key holder or friends of parents who are looking for an excuse for temporary obliteration and escape.

Without doubt there is always a best on ground. Generally from the younger team, but sometimes from the older guests themselves. I recall attending the 21st party of a colleague who, at his own party, reappeared from the density of a large garden hedge smothered with lipstick, ruffled clothes and disturbed spectacles (not unlike Rick Moranis in Ghostbusters) after a brief drunken dalliance with a busty ex-girlfriend at the exact moment his parents and girlfriend were preparing to present him with best wishes, gifts and a microphone! Priceless.

By the time we arrive, the teams are in the sheds for halftime and the game is over. The Cowboys are up 30-6. The ABC radio commentators reckon that Thurston is laying on a master class. The sous chefs are Bowen and Tate. A completion rate of 40 per cent is killing the Raiders; it's a familiar story. They simply can't apply their raw talent to the battle which is an issue that surely must keep Coach Furner up late at night watching re-runs of *Colombo* seeking inspiration.

I give the game away and later hear that the Cowboys are further ahead and ultimately win 40-18. Focus turns to the party, which turns out to be a cracker, highlighted by a guest appearance by a nephew who arrives garbed as Reg Reagan (for no reason at all) and is the life of the party. He is BOG.

A midnight departure coincides with the ABC radio match summary on the car radio. The newsreader's trailing tone in describing the Raiders result is just salt in the wound and I just want to get home and see Black Caviar win by a space in front of the Queen so I can wake up on Sunday happy! Well for a moment, about 50 metres from the winning post, it looks like Luke Nolen is wearing a lime jersey and I am the Jenny Craig loser of the week! Thankfully the mare sticks her neck out and wins.

Faith is restored and I feel hopeful again when I remember that next week the Raiders play the Dragons!

North Queensland 40		REFEREES	Brett Suttor, Alan Shortall
TRIES	Hall 2; Graham, Winterstein, Thompson, Linnett, Bolton	CROWD	14,344
GOALS	Thurston 5/6, Bowen 1/1	VOTES	**3. Thurston** Cowboys
			2. Bowen Cowboys
Canberra 18			**1. Tate** Cowboys
TRIES	Croker, Dugan, Ferguson		
GOALS	Croker 3/3		

A bitter-tweet night

Penrith Panthers *versus* Parramatta Eels

7.30pm, Saturday, 23 June

Centrebet Stadium, Sydney

PETER ABELA

MY MATE MICHAEL (@IMANVERU) IS AN EELS FAN. I'm a Panthers fan. We started our Twitter-jousting (I'm @PeteAbela) early in the week. I had a couple of digs about the Eels' lack of recent success:

PETE   Welcome to the 21st century. Eels have no Sterling, no Kenny, no Price, no Cronin, no hope.

MICHAEL   Premierships (Eels 4/Pan 2); Panasonic Cups (Eels 2/Pan 0); Head to head (Eels 51/Pan 32); 23/06/12 (Eels 28/Pan 10)

PETE   Did you reply? I had my relevance filter enabled and I can't see anything from you.

MICHAEL   The Parramatta name is relevant and universal, even in the Apple Isle.

The last tweet was accompanied by a photo of a road-sign in Tasmania pointing to Parramatta Creek. It didn't take me long to respond:

PETE   Up the creek is exactly where Parramatta will be on Saturday night. The paddle will be nowhere to be found.

MICHAEL   Look to the rear brown boys! The Chocolate Soldiers will be extracting the paddle's splinters for weeks to come.

Not wanting to encourage the vaguely proctological tone of Michael's latest comment, I broke off the engagement for a day or two in order to let the dust settle, although I started niggling him (again via Twitter) on match day:

PETE   I note the Eels have picked Sandow. The odds are lengthening all the time.

MICHAEL   The longer the odds, the richer I'll be.

PETE   If you put money on the Eels, it'll be the bookies who get richer.

MICHAEL   They'll only be richer in the knowledge that they have been bettered.
          Latest tip: Eels 24, Panthers 10.

Once the match started, I couldn't help but point out a few early indicators of
Penrith success:

PETE   After only five minutes I note the Eels have missed two tackles (Panthers 0), made 70 metres
          (Panthers 111) & 0 line breaks (Panthers 1).

PETE   The floodgates are open. 6-0 after 15 minutes. It's going to be a long night for you in the
          monkey suit.

MICHAEL   Don't start peeling your bananas just yet. You'll slip up.

Michael's reply, which came late in the first half, was followed shortly after by a
blistering solo try to Ryan Morgan. I held my fire for a while but, with Penrith holding a
12-point lead and only 15 minutes remaining, I sailed back into the breech.

PETE   It's a long road back from here.

A couple of minutes later, Parramatta scored their second try of the evening
bringing the score to 18-12 with 10 minutes of regulation time still remaining. I was
starting to feel vaguely uneasy and decided I shouldn't tempt fate any longer.

PETE   Every time I open my mouth the Eels score. I'm going to stay quiet for the last 10 minutes.

Alas, Nathan Hindmarsh engineered another try and, after 75 minutes, the scores
were locked at 18-18. Both teams had numerous unsuccessful shots at field goal in
normal time and during golden point extra-time. Just when it appeared neither side
would claim the points, Chris Sandow popped one over in the 90th minute to create a
19-18 win for the Eels. Michael had been quiet for quite some time but it didn't take
him long to spring back into life.

MICHAEL   Even long roads have an end. However, I'm going to go back now and pick up Pete
          after his slip ups.

MICHAEL   Gold! Absolute gold!

MICHAEL   [replaying one of my tweets from earlier in the day] "I note the Eels have picked Sandow.
          The odds are lengthening all the time". Noted.

My experiment with reporting on rugby league matches via Twitter is now over.
I consider it an unmitigated failure. I closed off with one final, sorry tweet:

PETE   I hope Ivan and Gus have a good long-term plan because the short-term one isn't working. I'm
          withdrawing now, red-faced.

Parramatta have now drawn level with Penrith in equal-last place, both teams on
10 points. Only Penrith's superior for and against is keeping them from the wooden-
spoon position. That fact provides little comfort.

Parramatta 19			REFEREES	Jared Maxwell, Adam Devcich
TRIES	Burt, Hayne, Morgan		CROWD	15,275
GOALS	Burt 3/3		VOTES	**3. Hindmarsh**
FIELD GOAL	Sandow			Eels
				2. Sandow
Penrith 18				Eels
TRIES	Lewis, Simmons, Uaisele			**1. Lewis**
GOALS	Austin 2/2, Walsh 1/1			Panthers

Couched in dog wonder

Canterbury Bulldogs *versus* **Melbourne Storm**
2pm, Sunday, 24 June
Virgin Australia Stadium, Mackay

JUSTIN McILVEEN

SUNDAY AFTERNOONS ON THE COUCH. MY COUCH. My beautiful couch. It's my fave time of the week. I like to lie there with paper in hand, couch to myself, Al Bundy style. Hasn't happened very often this winter though. Often on Sunday afternoons that Grand Old Girl, the Coogee Bay Hotel, has welcomed my patronage for a few beers after footy (I play reserve grade, sometimes off the bench reserve grade). Quality.

However, this Sunday I managed to get home. This is a game that could provide the watershed moment that propels Boy Wonder, Ben Barba, into Dally M contention.

Now I don't want to talk down the performance of the Dogs this day. It was scintillating. Spectacular. Wow-ish. Barba was on another planet.

But it was nothing compared to the show the Coogee Dolphins 'Blue' reserve grade team put on earlier that same afternoon against the Alexandria Rovers. Talk about Showtime. Talk about the Harlem Globetrotters.

As we slugged it out on a muddy field and were about to form what felt like the 80th scrum of the afternoon, I was well aware my beloved Dogs were about to kick-off in Mackay against the competition leaders – I'm sure I wasn't the only one wishing I was somewhere else.

That couch was in my thoughts. I loved that couch. I say loved because that couch is gone. It was recently sold against my wishes for a piece of furniture that has been deemed more aesthetically pleasing – why, oh why? Quantum physics is far easier to understand than the mind of a woman. Game over. Time to head.

As I walked in the door and turned on the TV, I realised I hadn't missed a beat. This was in fact about the only time in my life I was grateful for Channel Nine's advertisement-riddled, delayed telecast.

And even though I suffered from my usual bout of FOMO (Fear of Missing Out), I happily watched this game on the new couch while the rest of our team worked hard celebrating another loss at the boozer.

The Dogs' performance was not only enjoyable but borderline inspiring. I certainly worked harder getting off the couch to celebrate Morris' miraculous try than I did at Erskineville Oval that day.

It was a real celebration of rugby league all round as the Dogs won 20-4, Barba scoring one, setting up two and walking away with the man of the match while I walked around the house stiff, sore and pining for my old couch.

Canterbury 20			REFEREES	Ben Cummins, Gavin Badger
TRIES	Inu 2; Barba, Morris		CROWD	11,876
GOALS	Inu 2/4		VOTES	**3. Barba** Bulldogs
Melbourne 4				**2. Tolman** Bulldogs
TRY	Quinn			**1. Inu** Bulldogs
GOALS	Smith 0/1			

Then and now

Sydney Roosters *versus* Manly Sea Eagles
3pm, Sunday, 24 June
Allianz Stadium, Sydney

MICHAEL GROSVENOR

B EING AN AVID ROOSTERS FAN, I WAS AS EXCITED ABOUT THIS MATCH as I'd been all year. Manly is one of the better teams in the comp and has had the wood on Easts in recent years. Yet we were coming off an excellent attacking performance against the Tigers (granted they were missing Robbie Farah) and it looked like our confidence might be back after several weeks of so-near-yet-so far-performances.

Like most delusional fans after a good win, I envisaged another impressive performance against a premiership heavyweight which would continue our unbeaten run to Grand Final glory. Oh yeah!

Oh yeah? Just 10 minutes after I sit down it is Manly 12, Roosters 0. After 20 it is Manly 18, Chooks 0. Come 30 in and it's Manly 24, Feather Dusters 0.

I've gone from a Grand Final win to a meeting with my fellow Rooster comrades that resolved (let me check the minutes of the meeting) to hook Sam Perrett and give him a cabcharge voucher as a parting gift to get him to Belmore ASAP; ask the taxi to come back and take Braith to Campbelltown or Leichhardt or Ashfield or wherever the hell the puzzled Tigers think they are based; thank Brian Smith for his efforts in 2010 but show him the door; tell Mitchell Pearce to organise that meeting with Peter Doust and sort out a transfer to Wollongong before the end of the year; and send Tautau Moga back to Jersey Flegg with his P-plates still on.

How depressing. So depressing that my mind started wandering in all directions. I was day dreaming about nothing, which was a whole lot better; having empty thoughts and contemplating the oxymoron that is an empty thought, which at least required thinking; wishing I could fill the emptiness with something substantial, something tangible, like a structured Roosters attack.

When I came out of my dream, the Roosters had clawed back to 24-14 with 24 minutes to go. The emotional rollercoaster that is rugby league had seen Coach Smith, Pearce and Anasta orchestrate a stunning comeback and Tautau Moga go from dodgem car driver to Formula One swashbuckler in 20 awe-inspiring minutes. Geniuses the lot of them! Future Hall of Famers!

Now 20 minutes to go and I am alive, alert and in the moment. Mose Masoe takes the kick-off and steamrolls up the middle leaving defenders in his wake. He reaches the halfway line. This is amazing. This is fantastic. We'll score again on this set. Oh ... he drops the ball. I sit back down. Normal depressed thoughts come flooding back. Manly 34-14 after 60. Manly 40-14 after 70. Fulltime, Manly 52-14.

I trudge home resigned to the fact that 2012 is as good as gone. I do the maths ... if 30 points gets you into the finals then Easts would need to win seven out of their last nine matches to have a shot. Not impossible but the realist in me knows it is unlikely.

I also think about how good Manly were today. Tony Williams, in his first game back from State of Origin and injury, was sensational. Easts simply couldn't handle him. Ditto Anthony Watmough. Manly has to have one of the best backrows any club has offered: Glenn Stewart (who didn't play today), Anthony Watmough and Tony

Williams. Brett Stewart: just about back to his best. Kieran Foran's defence: unbelievable. I think Brian Smith might have got it right in the post-match conference: "Execution-wise they were almost faultless ... they were right on the money for everything that came to them and created plenty."

What's the bet we see two Des Hasler teams fight it out at the end of the year? The team he built, Manly, playing the team he is building, Canterbury. All day I have been thinking about how well Des Hasler has gone and is going. Today he is the No. 1 coach in the game. By a country mile.

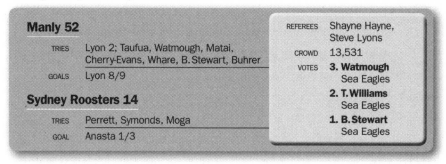

Manly 52			REFEREES	Shayne Hayne, Steve Lyons
TRIES	Lyon 2; Taufua, Watmough, Matai, Cherry-Evans, Whare, B. Stewart, Buhrer		CROWD	13,531
GOALS	Lyon 8/9		VOTES	**3. Watmough** Sea Eagles
Sydney Roosters 14				**2. T. Williams** Sea Eagles
TRIES	Perrett, Symonds, Moga			**1. B. Stewart** Sea Eagles
GOAL	Anasta 1/3			

Good Knight

Newcastle Knights *versus* Wests Tigers
7pm, Monday, 25 June
Hunter Stadium, Newcastle

LUKE JAMIESON

TALK BEFORE THE GAME IS ABOUT AKUILA UATE, fresh on the back of being dropped from the NSW State of Origin squad. He's sure to have a blinder.

"He's bouncing around in the rooms," Kurt Gidley beams.

No one except Gidley gives the Knights a chance. I certainly don't. Our punters club has thrown the kitchen sink at the Tigers.

Uate's acrobatics and skill are on display early as is Robbie Farah's exciting running from dummy-half which leads to the Tigers' first try. Sixth minute, Farah slices through some poor defence from Chris Houston to put Chris Lawrence away under the sticks.

As I think about Lawrence and his previous injury woes with a dislocated hip, I cannot help but shudder as I recall another dislocated hip story. At an Under-15s game, a young lad is felled in a tackle and dislocates his hip. The boy is in obvious agony and the concerned onlookers cast around for some medical expertise. One father steps forward and identifies himself as having a medical background of some description which allays the concern of all and sundry. Murmurs of reassurance ripple through the crowd.

Dr Dad assesses the situation and makes the decision to operate. "We'll just pop that hip back in!" he states confidently. So, with the help of some parents who hold the boy's torso, he gives a solid tug on the leg to stretch out the muscles and allow the ball of the femur back into the hip socket. The socket pops together and, as Dr Dad is no doubt expecting to be lauded with praise, the young lad lets out a hideous blood-curdling scream and passes out.

Dr Dad has unwittingly performed a semi-castration, au naturale.

The grisly lesson here is that if you're ever getting your dislocated hip put back in, make sure you hold your tackle up out of the hip socket lest you find yourself singing soprano like our young hero.

Anyway, back to the game.

Tenth minute, Marshall pokes one in behind the line and Uate is beaten to the ball by Lote for the Tigers' second meatie in the space of two sets. Wok makes note of what could well be the key to Uate's fall from grace, the removal of his beard. Samson Uate.

Tim Moltzen leaves the field with an injury. This is a blessing for the Tigers and a blow for the Knights.

Tigers penalty goal. 14-0.

Aku is awarded a try after video analysis. 14-4.

This stripping rule? Newcastle get six more tackles because Aku can't hold onto the ball. Suddenly Tahu steams onto a tip on from Darius at a squillion miles an hour and it's 14-10.

Lortay gets belted. Boyd to Tahu. Knights take the lead 16-14. Jesus wept. I feel a little bit ill in the lower stomach region. Not sure if it's the punters club bet or the lingering thought of undisolocating a hip and removing a plum at the same time.

Ray Cashmere is lazy.

Halftime arrives and surely Tim Sheens will hit the reset button and this match will get back to the script.

Farah gets an early penalty working out of dummy-half. The Tigers are sure to be sparked into action now!

Nope. Boyd gets outside Marshall and Tahu goes past Joel Reddy for a hat-trick. Timana Tahu! I'm definitely ill now.

Marshall has donned a fluoro vest, pink of course in support of Women in League round, and is directing all Knights attack directly to the tryline.

The TV goes off. I leave the house for some dinner. I'll come back to this later in the desperate hope that I've missed 30 minutes of the Tigers' best football of the year and everything is okay.

Nope. The Tigers, former flag favourites no less, have been royally stuffed by a previously uninterested and disjointed Knights outfit. I watch the last 20 minutes on fast forward. The final score is something like 320-4.

The one positive out of this is that Mick Sullivan's kids will be getting new X-Box games and remote control helicopters for their birthdays.

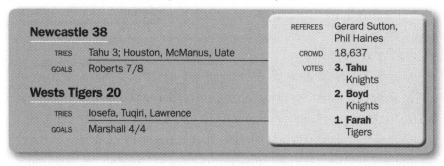

Newcastle 38

TRIES	Tahu 3; Houston, McManus, Uate
GOALS	Roberts 7/8

Wests Tigers 20

TRIES	Iosefa, Tuqiri, Lawrence
GOALS	Marshall 4/4

REFEREES	Gerard Sutton, Phil Haines
CROWD	18,637
VOTES	**3. Tahu** Knights
	2. Boyd Knights
	1. Farah Tigers

Round 17

Where everybody knows your team

Brisbane Broncos
versus **Cronulla Sharks**

7.30pm, Friday, 29 June
Suncorp Stadium, Brisbane

MARK NICHOLS

A S I TOOK OFF DOWN THE MONARO HIGHWAY, I couldn't decide what I was more pumped about: the Sharks' first Friday night game of the year or that I was returning to the local in my home town to watch a game for the first time in years.

Coffeys Hotel, situated in God's country, Cooma, was built by Michael Coffey in 1880 and was originally called the Railway Hotel. I couldn't begin to guess how many Friday night games I've watched at this grand old girl over the years. The lure of the coldest beer in the world, yes the world, would leave us with no time to change after Friday night training with the mighty Cooma Stallions.

This often led to us devouring schooners at the bar in our footy gear, best laid plans to head home and change after two quick ones soon brushed aside. This led to inevitable late-night shenanigans at the Aussie Hotel where you would see a group of burly gentleman cutting the rug on the dance floor in an assortment of footy jumpers, shorts and torpedoes (or, in later years, skins) and walking crab-like towards the bar so as to not slide arse over in their footy boots.

Although it's quite a few years since I'd been to Coffeys on a Friday night, I was confident I'd know at least a dozen old characters and where they'd be sitting, standing or leaning against the bar. In fact, I reckon I could predict exactly where Roy Hankinson would be sitting and that he would have his early-'80s Roosters jumper on. If only TattsBet ran a book on such things.

As I walked in the corner door with Mum, Dad and my three uncles, straight into the heart of the bar, I quickly took in the familiar surroundings. Pat and Darrell left bottom corner (*tick*), the Blewett brothers mid-bar (*tick*), Ganny holding up the top corner bar (*tick*), Mattner mid-left table (*tick*), Moony, Bobby and Dennis midright bar (*tick*), Robbie Salvestro bottom right (*tick*), Mic Mac floating around the top left of the bar (lucky this game is live, Mick has a habit of waltzing in when a game is on delay and saying to no one in particular and the whole bar at the same time "how 'bout those Rabbits getting up?", a hanging offence in any country pub) (*tick*) and, finally, old Roy talking to Broom, resplendent in the aforementioned Roosters' jumper (a big *tick*). I wish sports betting was this easy.

Coffeys reminds me of *Cheers* – everyone knows your name and, more importantly, knows your team. As I shook hands with many I haven't seen in quite a while, the greetings were all Sharks-related: "Geez you blokes are going alright"; "I think the baby Broncs will be too good for youse tonight" and "No Gallen and Carney, no chance."

As we settled in, it felt like I had never left, the beer was still teeth cracking, meat raffle, 100 club, all the talk about the Stallions' last-gasp upset win over the Eden Tigers last Sunday and the same club stalwarts selling mini-lotto tickets for the Colts junior league club. Just before kick-off I notice Jenny is here as well, ensuring I am not the only Sharks supporter in the pub and that, along with Mum, this is the first time two females have been this side of the bar since the Sharks won the Amco Cup in '79.

The crowd is very quiet and they leave me alone as the Sharks run in three tries in the first 16 minutes. However, the crowd love to turn and see my reaction as the Broncs run in two of their own to make it 16-12.

"They're gone, Boof; you can't even beat a team with seven Origin players out," is all I can hear as the Broncos look set to hit the lead. But, with a two-man overlap, Nathan Stapleton intercepts and runs 95 metres to make it 22-12. Another try and the siren sounds on a 26-12 victory. I help the stalwarts count the money from the mini lotto.

It's a shame there isn't a second game so Mick can spoil the replay.

Cronulla 26				
TRIES	Best 2; Pomeroy, Stapleton, Graham		REFEREES	Jason Robinson, Gavin Badger
GOALS	Townsend 3/5		CROWD	26,268
Brisbane 12			votes	**3. Graham** Sharks
				2. Townsend Sharks
TRIES	Glenn, Whitchurch			**1. Gibbs** Sharks
GOALS	Wallace 2/2			

Word play... or should that be a wary plod?

Parramatta Eels *versus* **Newcastle Knights**
7.30pm, Saturday, 30 June
Parramatta Stadium, Sydney

MICHAEL KENNEDY

ONIGHT'S REPORT IS AN AUDACIOUS ATTEMPT TO UNLEASH AND HARNESS the force of words with the help of the humble anagram – God's gift to the word nut. For those of you unfamiliar with this word-twisting magic, take a look at some of these timeless classics: George Bush – HE BUGS GORE; Astronomer – MOON-STARER; Schoolmaster – THE CLASSROOM. You get the gist!

Tonight, the Parramatta Eels, A PEARL STAR TEAM, face the Newcastle Knights, otherwise known as TACKLING STEW HENS. Led by the mercurial Nathan Hindmarsh, or HAND IN THRASH MAN, the Eels are sadly without Jarrod Hayne's RARE JOY HAND. However, the ever-reliable Luke Burt, or TRUE BULK, will fill in at fullback. Danny Buderus, being a SUNDAY BURDEN, obviously favours playing on a Saturday night and will therefore have to be marked closely. Much has been made of Willie Mason's recent resurgence, but it's hard to imagine WOMAN LILIES will be much of a threat.

Chris Sandow, AH! CROSSWIND, kicked off but it was the Knights, courtesy of McManus, or MUM'S CAN, that opened the scoring in the fifth minute. The conversion attempt from the touchline sailed through the goal posts, O' SLOTS GAP, and the Knights led 6-0.

The 13th minute saw a high tackle by not one, but two of the Knights and this isn't surprising when you learn that the Newcastle Knights TANGLE WITH NECKS! From the ensuing play Sandow showed his class and set up Matthew Keating to TAME A WET KNIGHT and score adjacent to the posts. Sandow converted and it was all tied up.

From this point, the confidence of the Eels was evident and they came close to scoring several times. Timana Tahu, A HUMAN AT IT, was bundled into touch at one stage with the help of Cheyse Blair who, given his susceptibility to AIRY BELCHES, is probably on the wing for reasons other than his turn of pace.

At halftime it was 6-6 and I was hoping Willie Tonga, ALLOWING TIE, would be replaced in order for a result either way. That was until the Knights scored early in the second half courtesy of Jarrod Mullen who lived up to his other name JAM UNDER ROLL, and jammed through the tackle before rolling over the line. Then, against the run of play, Naiqama, who will remain Naiqama, ran the length of the field, somehow evading True Bulk to score a scintillating try.

Dane Gagai AGED AGAIN and went down with an injury but somehow got himself into a position a few moments later to throw a neat pass to Akuila Uate (unanagrammable!) who scored in the corner. Suddenly it was 20-6 and the ailing Eels' prognosis showed POOR SIGNS. Kade Snowden, with a KNEE DOWN – SAD, then went off with his injury but Chris Houston, contrary to his off-field name, SHORT CUSHION, compensated by becoming the Knights' tackling machine. With 10 minutes to go, Ken Sio, as if on ONE SKI, ran along the dead-ball line and scored one-handed. Did I hear Matthew Ryan shout "WHAT A TRY MEN!"? Could this signal yet another frenzied comeback? Sandow, NOW SAD, tried in desperation, NOT REPS IDEA, with a couple of chip kicks but it was to no avail.

The fulltime siren, which NULLIFIES TERM, sounded with the Eels now a splinter away from grasping the wooden spoon – OOPS! DOWN ONE. For Bennett, an honorary Novocastrian, ICON OR SAVANT, it was a happy night but he'll need a miracle to claim the premiership or the PRIME SPHERE HIT. Stephen Kearney will seriously have to consider if there are ANY KEEPERS THEN for the next match against the Sea Eagles even if they are just GEESE, ALAS! He will also have to KEEP HAYNE STERN!

Despite the result, this wasn't a bad game, but no doubt this week's deciding State of Origin, where GIANT FOES RIOT, will justly relegate this game to the far margins of history. Nevertheless, I hope that this report leaves you with an appreciation of word and name power. Perhaps, for the next report, I will use The Morse Code, or HERE COME DOTS!

Newcastle 20		REFEREES	Matt Cecchin, Phil Haines
TRIES	McManus, Mullen, K. Naiqama, Uate	CROWD	12,022
GOALS	Roberts 2/4	VOTES	**3. Mullen** Knights
Parramatta 12			**2. Sandow** Eels
TRIES	Keating, Sio		**1. K. Naiqama** Knights
GOALS	Burt 2/2		

Sweet relief

South Sydney Rabbitohs *versus* Penrith Panthers
3pm, Sunday, 1 July
ANZ Stadium, Sydney

JOHN CAMPBELL

IT'S A TOSS-UP TO DECIDE THE LESSER OF TWO EVILS: your side is either confronted with an opposition that is at full-strength and smashing all before it, or you're the odds-on favourite to beat an outfit that's underperforming, missing its best players and therefore, according to a logic that is endemic among diehard footy partisans, even more threatening.

For the tragic whose psyche booms or busts according to each round's results, there is no such thing as the middle ground. We dread the easy game, the one that we are expected to win.

South Sydney's lowly adversary today, the Penrith Panthers, might be fighting the good fight against the two hours of knock ons that snake-oil salesmen from the AFL are attempting to flog in western Sydney, but on the field they have been duds. There's no other word for it. Penrith: duds.

Can you imagine, as one who was cherry-picked for the job, how their coach, Ivan Cleary, must feel with the lugubrious Gus Gould on his case? When he's not on the stump insisting that it's every Australian pensioner's right to feed their meagre savings into a club's pokies, Gus is blathering away like Toad of Toad Hall about anything and everything, from scrum feeds to who was the best Cartwright in *Bonanza* (Hoss, he has pontificated), Cleary must be inwardly seething.

With Luke Lewis, Michael Jennings and Tim Grant in Brisbane on Ricky Stuart's quest for the Holy Grail of Origin triumph, his boys are also minus their regular halfback, Luke Walsh, for the clash with the Rabbits and, would you believe, Nigel Plum is listed as one of their starting props!

Thursday's news that Dave Taylor has been dumped from the Canetoads' bench and will turn out for the cardinal and myrtle has made us look even more like dead-set certs, but will he come back in a sulk or with murder in his heart? Adding to my stress, the pundits in Friday's sports pages have unanimously forecast a Bunnies victory. Jeez, I hate that. It is the cruellest cut of all ... and breaking news says that Slammin' Sammy

Burgess is a late inclusion. There's no way we can lose – is there?

Souths have been going okay but the eight or, to paraphrase Benny Elias, that carrot at the end of the rainbow is as far away as ever. We need this win, big time.

I've packed up the market stall early so that I can get from Byron back to Goonengerry in time for the four o'clock TV kick-off. As far as sales go, it's been an abysmal day and things go from bad to worse when I get in the car. The battery is as dead as a doornail. *Aaaaarghhh!* I can't even listen to David 'Thirsty' Morrow and Warren 'Wok' Ryan call the game on ABC *Grandstand* ... but wait! The laptop! There's enough charge left in it for me to go online.

The NRMA's on its way and I've found the footy streaming. Even better, Souths are away to a flyer. They lead 12-0 ... and Sammy has just put it over the line. *You beauty!* Hang on ... the try is disallowed and (I could feel this coming in my bones) Penrith fight back. In no time, it's 12-all and there's still no sign of the NRMA.

I'm having a meltdown by the time he arrives.

"What's the score?"

I tell him.

"Jeez, I thought Souths'd shit it in."

I fang it out of town. Climbing up the hill to Coorabell, tension eases as Andrew Everingham crosses, then Chris McQueen gets the greatest try of all time, only for the ref to call the last pass forward. Thirsty and Wok go ballistic!

"The worst decision of the year." I'm livid. Off the highway and into the hills, aglow in the setting sun. The world is a warmer, cosier place as the Bunnies pile on the points.

Home at last, on the lounge with the dog and a Guinness, in front of the flat-screen. Gould has a whinge about play being stopped for Shaun Corrigan, who's been decked and is with Huey, Dewy and Louie in Disneyland. Suck it up, Gus.

38-12. What a relief.

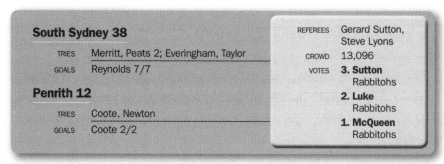

South Sydney 38		REFEREES	Gerard Sutton, Steve Lyons
TRIES	Merritt, Peats 2; Everingham, Taylor	CROWD	13,096
GOALS	Reynolds 7/7	VOTES	**3. Sutton** Rabbitohs
Penrith 12			**2. Luke** Rabbitohs
TRIES	Coote, Newton		**1. McQueen** Rabbitohs
GOALS	Coote 2/2		

The only constant is inconsistency

New Zealand Warriors *versus* **North Queensland Cowboys**
4pm, Sunday, 1 July
Mt Smart Stadium, Auckland

ANDREW SMITH

S UNDAY AFTERNOON IN AUCKLAND IN THE MIDDLE OF WINTER usually means two things. The Warriors are on at Mt Smart and the weather is miserable. Today we are in luck and the sun is shining even though it is bitterly cold. Ah well, can't win them all. At least there is league to watch.

Up until this year my support of the Warriors has consisted of Sundays at home on the couch, usually nursing a wicked hangover, and listening to Jason Costigan babble on about rubbish. This year, though, I have moved to the big smoke and taken my support to the next level with a season ticket.

Watching the Warriors live had never bought much success for me. In my first eight games, I only witnessed one victory and that was in Christchurch in what was technically a Roosters' home game in 2010. On that day, the temperature didn't get over three degrees and we only won due to a committed Kevin Locke pole-axing himself against the uprights in the process of scoring the winning try.

At Mt Smart, their official home, they had failed me time and time again and I was beginning to think I was bad luck. Things turned though in the third home game this year against the Titans and now the boys have not looked back (at home that is, don't get me started on away form).

When it comes to the Warriors, I certainly wear my heart on my sleeve. When we are winning, there is no better feeling. On the other hand, when things are going bad, I feel like the weight of the world sits squarely on my shoulders and it is my fault. Frustration is part and parcel of being a Warriors fan. Since their inception in 1995, perhaps the only consistent part of their game has been their inconsistency.

However, it's the joy that comes from witnessing moments like the Locke try that keeps me coming back. No one else in the competition is able to play like the Warriors do on their day. The only problem is that these occasions don't occur as frequently as I would like.

This week sees the Origin-depleted Cowboys come to town. This is great news for my team who, as usual, are struggling with this consistency thing.

Our season is on a knife edge, any more losses and we will slip further away from the top eight. The team though seem to like a challenge. Last season we were in the same position as we are now. What followed was a magnificent run to the Grand Final. I think we will do the same again this year. The boys are just toying with us fans and will sort it out during the run to September.

This game is no different. A brilliant start sees us streak out to a big lead. I want to sit back and relax, safe in the knowledge we have it in the bag. However experience ensures I am not lulled into a false sense of security.

Then, as if on cue, it begins. From 22-6, it becomes 22-12. Then it becomes 22-18.

I have seen enough of the team this season to guess where things are going. It looks ominous, another game squandered and the season going down the drain.

Had we been in Australia, this is how it would have played out. However at Mt Smart, it proves to be a different story. Home advantage is a wonderful thing. Two more tries and a classic field goal seal the victory for the Warriors. On the scoreboard it looks comfortable but we all know better.

Two more points to the total and we are close to the magical mark that is the top eight. I think the run to the finals has begun. The relief is immense and it will keep me happy for another week.

Bring on the Titans.

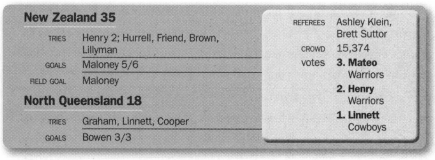

New Zealand 35		REFEREES	Ashley Klein, Brett Suttor
TRIES	Henry 2; Hurrell, Friend, Brown, Lillyman	CROWD	15,374
GOALS	Maloney 5/6	votes	**3. Mateo** Warriors
FIELD GOAL	Maloney		**2. Henry** Warriors
North Queensland 18			**1. Linnett** Cowboys
TRIES	Graham, Linnett, Cooper		
GOALS	Bowen 3/3		

Dangerously cold

Canberra Raiders *versus* St George Illawarra Dragons
7pm, Monday, 2 July
Canberra Stadium, Canberra

TIM NAPPER

THE WIND BLOWS ACROSS THE SNOWS OF THE BRINDABELLAS sending its icy currents deep into the heart of Canberra, biting into the lungs and leaving numb the extremities of hardened Raiders fans. Here they sit, the faithful, shivers running down their spines as stoically they watch the boys in green march out onto the field to do battle.

Which is why I am at a mate's place watching the Raiders-St George game on the huge plasma screen he has sitting in his living room. I mean, I love the boys in green but, good lord, sitting there at Bruce Stadium for two hours on a Monday night, it's just not worth the risk to your family lineage.

Don't get me wrong, I'm willing to make sacrifices for the Raiders but until they make that one, important sacrifice for the fans – sacking the well-connected but lamentably bad David Furner – I'm sticking with free beers and a giant plasma screen in the civilised warmth of a north Belconnen abode.

St George don't handle the cold either. They haven't won at Bruce in 12 years. It makes you wonder how many points the horrid conditions at Bruce Stadium have given the Raiders over the years. Seriously, I'd love to see a stats nerd conjure an algorithm to give us that little factoid.

Anyway, here we are two-thirds of the way through another season of disappointment and underachievement for the once-mighty Raiders. I'm watching Jamie Soward getting ready to convert another try. Preparing for a conversion like a strutting bantam cock searching for a piece of corn. Ready to kick the Dragons to an 18-16 lead late in the second half. And I'm thinking: damn you Furner; damn you for coaching this team to nail-biting mediocrity yet again.

There are so many frustrations these days.

Take Jarrod Croker's kicking. I have never seen a player who can make a kick look as ugly as it leaves the boot as Croker. They wobble, they tumble end-on-end and off-centre. They hook to the left,yet sometimes manage a remarkable reverse-swing to the right. They jag low at the crossbar one time, then the next soar inexplicably, the next skying off at random angles into the stands.

It reminds you of the glorious Mal Meninga toe-kicking days when even the simplest of conversions had the Canberra fan holding their breath waiting for Mal to choke. Big Mal was so worried about his kicking that, at one point, he even started seeing a voodoo hypnotist (or sports psychologist, take your pick) to improve his focus.

I remember him lining up conversions, standing there looking up at the uprights and mouthing "black dot black dot black dot black dot" over and over. I think every Raiders supporter in those days chanted along with the skipper, willing his conversions through.

Of course, horrible kicking is one of the very few comparisons the Raiders of today have with the mighty Green Machine of the late '80s and early '90s. The Raiders were true contenders back then. Today they are a faded bottle-green to the once-pungent lime-green of yore. We had a real coach in those days as well, not this weird situation today with Furner who apparently has a billion-year contract.

Watching Reece Robinson score a last-gasp try to give himself a hat-trick – and the Raiders the game – reminded me how much more the Green Machine can be. Even an injury-ravaged Raiders showed they have enough players with talent and heart to make the finals – like Reece Robinson (3 tries, 28 runs for 279m) or Dane Tilse (27 tackles, 23 runs for 164m). And let's not forget half the team were wearing bloodied face-slings after a world record number of broken noses during the game. Now that smarts on the chilliest of nights.

So come on Raiders, reprise the (non-kicking) glory of Mal and you'll bring the fans back into the cold.

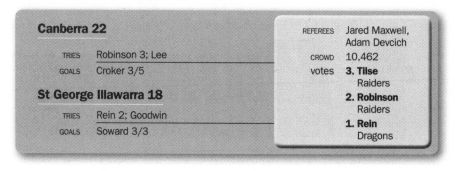

Canberra 22

TRIES	Robinson 3; Lee	REFEREES	Jared Maxwell, Adam Devcich
GOALS	Croker 3/5	CROWD	10,462
		VOTES	**3. Tilse** Raiders

St George Illawarra 18

TRIES	Rein 2; Goodwin		**2. Robinson** Raiders
GOALS	Soward 3/3		**1. Rein** Dragons

State of Origin III

A *three-syllable chant*

Queensland *versus* **New South Wales**
8pm, Wednesday, 4 July
Suncorp Stadium, Brisbane

CLIFF BINGHAM

THE NAMING RIGHTS MAY SEE IT OFFICIALLY REFERRED TO AS SUNCORP STADIUM, but in my heart of hearts it will always be Lang Park – The Cauldron. I was walking in there for the first time ever: soaking up the atmosphere, thinking back to all of the great Queensland victories at this venue I had watched on television as a kid, and crossing my fingers that there was enough juice left in the lemon for one more series victory. We had taken far too many years to cross paths; I couldn't stomach the thought of Lang Park letting me down in any way.

In its current construction, Lang Park is without peer as a venue for watching rugby league. The action is so close ... especially when your 'restricted viewing' seat is eight rows back from the fence and directly adjacent to the visitors' tunnel, thus making it easier to pass on handy hints and constructive criticism to the Blues bench. For example, after a punishing 20-minute opening half stint on the exercise bike, I pointed out to Luke Lewis that the Tour de France breakaways rarely happen until after midnight our time, so he'd best stick with the peloton in the shorter term. His road crew down on the sideline seemed to agree as, 30 seconds later, he was off the bike entirely.

For the greater part though, there is no time for helpful hints or set pieces of constructive criticism. Most vocal resources are devoted to three syllables, repeated ad nauseum... QUEENS-LAND-AH! QUEENS-LAND-AH!

Granted, it's a simple chant. But as Laurie Daley once said, rugby league is a simple game played by simple people. Moreover, in moments of high tension, the tendency is to revert to what is natural – in our case this constituted yelling for anything in maroon and yelling at anything in sky blue. The difference is subtle, yet important.

High tension was the order of the day. After wresting back the momentum before halftime and heading for the sheds with a 16-8 lead, I started to get nervous.

This series had already provided so many ebbs and flows; more were all but certain over the ensuing 40 minutes. Apologies in advance to the future mother of my children but, based on last night's distinct lack of second half composure, something like imminent fatherhood is unlikely to be handled with calm and aplomb in the delivery room.

Thankfully, more composure was being displayed on the field than off it. *Cometh the hour, cometh the man.* The Thurston-Cronk combination hadn't set the world on fire in the first two games but their ensemble came together beautifully when it mattered most. Thurston was a deserving man of the match, controlling so much of the Maroons' attack and crossing the stripe himself. Cronk played the role of late-game assassin: he joined Allan Langer circa 1992 in providing the killer punch to get the boys home.

Just as importantly, Petero Civoniceva was able to walk off into the representative football sunset a victor. When Cameron Smith called him up onto the dais and gave him the shield to hold aloft, the crowd rose as one. More hugs and high fives with complete strangers were dished out, more chanting, more joy. This was one more fantastic night for one fantastic side. The Blues' time will come.

The live Origin experience at The Cauldron was everything I'd ever hoped for and then some – even if it left me sounding like Darth Vader after he'd chain-smoked Camel 16s for a day. Above everything else though, the sound of tens of thousands of people belting out the same three-syllable chant in unison over and over resonated with me the most.

I can still hear them. I will always hear them ... QUEENSLANDER! QUEENSLANDER!

Inspiration, courage, attitude and belief

LINDSEY CUTHBERTSON

I N THE LEAD-UP TO THIS DECIDING STATE OF ORIGIN CLASH, we heard a lot about how the world was back in 2005, the last time New South Wales won an Origin series. Facebook wasn't in Australia. Twitter wasn't invented. I was still in high school.

But here's the most telling one for me: I have never experienced a Blues series victory while living in Queensland.

It's a life of hard knocks being a NSW fan behind enemy lines but you do these things for love. I grew up in the Northern Rivers of New South but I have managed to fall in love with a Queenslander. It's the Capulets and Montagues in our house.

And when I'm out and about it's no easier. Not only are you subjected to the smug taunts of Maroons fans once they realise that you come from south of the border, but you are also exposed to the kind of propaganda that only an experienced and astute political machine knows how to execute. The New South Wales media has nothing on the shock and awe tactics of its Queensland counterparts during Origin season as they whip the hordes of Maroons fans into a frenzy.

It doesn't help that Queensland keep winning either and, for a while, there they were doing it comfortably. 2010 was a dark year for many NSW fans as the Maroons waltzed to a whitewash. We'd hit rock bottom. Enter Ricky Stuart as coach and Paul Gallen as captain and, for the last two years, the Blues fought tooth and nail against this Queensland juggernaut.

The Queenslanders' grip is loosening. In 2009 and 2010 the Maroons only failed to get to 20 points once. In the past two years – including the 2012 decider – they have only done so twice. The gap between the two sides is closing and, if anyone needed proof of this, this decider was a perfect example, an unforgettable spectacle of everything that made us fall in love with Origin in the first place.

It's never just about winning and losing. What really stays with us are the inspirational qualities displayed in such an event – courage, belief in yourself and those around you, and never giving in, even when all hope seems lost.

I saw those qualities in the New South Wales side tonight. Perhaps it is why their

21-20 loss was so hard to take. The Blues pushed one of the greatest Origin teams ever assembled to its very limits.

They were there to be seen in the Blues' first try when Brett Morris used all his power to push through the Queensland goalline defence and draw first blood.

They were there when Robbie Farah was knocked cold in a head clash with Nate Myles but refused to leave the field.

They were there in the Blues' second try minutes after halftime when Brett Stewart latched onto a Farah grubber to score less than a metre away from the dead-ball line.

They were there in Josh Morris' try-saving tackle on Greg Inglis, pulling him down like a lion does a wildebeest.

They were there in Luke Lewis who made up for an errant forward pass by making three influential tackles in a row as the Blues sought to pin the Maroons deep in their own half.

They were there when Josh Morris scored with 10 minutes to go, catching a Farah cross-field kick over the top of Darius Boyd and riding his opponent to the turf to plant the ball down in the corner.

They were there in Todd Carney's sideline conversion to level the scores.

Those qualities were there until the very end, even when Mitchell Pearce's field goal attempt went wide and the siren sounded with the finality of a gallows-crash.

So close. So very close. But, once again, Queensland was too good.

I could complain about the result and bring up several contentious decisions but tonight I saw skill and toughness that defied belief. The question now is no longer how the Blues will beat Queensland but when. The fall of the Maroon Empire is coming.

And when it does come tumbling down, I will be celebrating with my Blues jersey on among its smoking ruins. But not yet. I will be living in the victorious state of Queensland for another year and they deserve every ounce of praise they get.

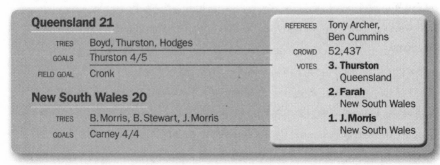

Queensland 21		REFEREES	Tony Archer, Ben Cummins
TRIES	Boyd, Thurston, Hodges	CROWD	52,437
GOALS	Thurston 4/5	VOTES	**3. Thurston** Queensland
FIELD GOAL	Cronk		**2. Farah** New South Wales
New South Wales 20			**1. J. Morris** New South Wales
TRIES	B. Morris, B. Stewart, J. Morris		
GOALS	Carney 4/4		

Round 18

Obstruction?
Obstruction overruled!

Wests Tigers *versus* **Canterbury Bulldogs**

7.45pm, Friday, 6 July

Allianz Stadium, Sydney

MICHAEL HARRISON-FORD

WITH CHANNEL NINE FINALLY DELIVERING MELBOURNIANS some decent rugby league coverage, an unanticipated consequence has been that, with fans now able to stay home to watch the games, regular haunts for league fans are less reliable. So to avoid disappointment tonight I'm travelling to the outer reaches of Melbourne to watch the game with Bossy, a fellow NSW ex-pat whose passion for the greatest game of all is matched only by his love of professional wrestling and keen interest in the history of the Third Reich.

Tonight's match is taking place in the aftermath of one of the most thrilling Origin contests I expect I'll ever see. The result didn't go my way but, days later, I'm still abuzz from the spectacle. Strangely though, that hasn't translated into enthusiasm for tonight's match. I don't feel good about it. When Wests were winning seven on the trot after an awful start to the season, I let myself get excited. A loss to the Roosters to end the streak could be explained away by sad circumstances. The next game, though, where they shot off to a 14-0 lead against Newcastle only to concede the next 38 points ... that was when my faith evaporated.

It's always a topsy-turvy ride following the Tigers; even their best seasons are beset by inconsistency, but there's been some intangible element evident in the years they've made finals runs. This year though, as good as they've been in patches, the times they've been exposed have felt telling. Against the Dogs, a team that is starting to develop a real aura about them, I'm not confident.

When I get to Bossy's I see that, right alongside his DVD box set of Hitler's Henchmen, there's a printout of the NRL's obstruction rule. In his estimation,

Hodges' try for Queensland two days earlier was an atrocity unparalleled in human history and, when I take a closer look at the printout, I see that it is covered with scrawled notes that plainly reveal the indignant fury that drove him to jot them down.

The page resembles evidence the prosecution might introduce into a grizzly murder trial and, if Bossy and Steve Clark ever cross paths, then one day maybe it will. An unsolicited lecture about the theory and historical application of the obstruction rule dominates the pre-game discussion and, as kick-off approaches, I have no choice but to submit to his point of view without reservation.

When the game gets underway, the Tigers are more competitive than I expect. The squad is somewhat diminished. Farah doesn't back up from Origin; Matt Utai is a late withdrawal and, within 10 minutes, Tuqiri is taken from the field with what is later revealed to be a clean snap to his humerus.

Nevertheless they plug away, withstanding some early pressure to score first when three Dogs players who each yell "yours!" in response to a Marshall bomb and Reddy scores uncontested. The try is somewhat emblematic of a half that, while hard-fought, isn't of the highest standard.

Some time after the Reddy try, Josh Morris barges over to even the ledger. My instinct is to despairingly question the efforts of the four defenders he crashes through, but the sheer strength and tenacity he showed is truly impressive.

Somewhat surprisingly the Tigers snatch back the lead just before halftime, again off a kick, this one a freakish effort from Marshall who somehow manages to land a no-look effort off the side of his boot right on the spot, setting up Beau Ryan under the sticks. It's exciting stuff but still, even with a 10-4 lead, there's a sense it's the Dogs who are about to unleash.

And so it is. A minute into the second half, Barba slices through from long range to set up Reynolds. Five minutes later he's put Morris over in the corner and Wests won't hit the lead again.

The 32-20 fulltime scoreline feels about right. Not a demoralising loss by a long stretch. They fought hard against the odds and were in the game on the scoreboard at least right until the dying stages.

But they're simply not up to pace with top-level teams such as the Dogs.

Canterbury 32		REFEREES	Jason Robinson, Gavin Morris
TRIES	Morris, Reynolds 2; Barba, Inu	CROWD	19,034
GOALS	Inu 4/6	VOTES	**3. Barba**
			Bulldogs
Wests Tigers 20			**2. Ryan**
			Tigers
TRIES	Ryan, Reddy, Lawrence, Iosefa		**1. Morris**
GOALS	Marshall 2/4		Bulldogs

Sins of the past

Melbourne Storm *versus* Canberra Raiders

5.30pm, Saturday, 7 July

AAMI Park, Melbourne

CHRIS PARKINSON

THE BACK TO THE FUTURE TRILOGY AND, TO A LESSER EXTENT, *Bill and Ted's Excellent Adventure* and *Bogus Journey* opened my mind to time travel as I meandered my way through my teenage years. Although I wasn't the sci-fi aficionado that many of my peers would have admitted to being, I was quite taken with the endless possibilities of time travel. It would not be an uncommon occurrence to lie awake at night pondering what it would be like if things had been done differently.

It was never really about going back in time to change the course of history. The good of humanity is a tiny blip on the radar of a self-obsessed teenager; it was more about exploiting it for personal gain and limiting those embarrassing moments that a teenager worries so much about.

Now in my mid-30s I still dream of the same things, but with the difference that these days I might like to give a little more importance to helping humanity. For instance, if I had access to time travel I might like to go back to the late '80s and do everything within my power to preserve the contested scrum. The art-form that was the 12-man scrum was ordained by the rugby league gods; it's how they intended play to be restarted. I might also go back to 1998 to explain to Paul Carige the circumstances in which you can take a ball dead from the field of play ... but I digress.

I sometimes wonder if the powers that be at the Melbourne Storm might like to have their time over again and maybe not do what they've done to rugby league and its fans.

Anyway, the time travel concept hit me again throughout the Green Machine's demolition of the Storm. My mind started to wander as a relatively average Raiders outfit seemed to be doing it pretty easily against a top side. It makes me angry that the Storm won all those games by deception, but what would their side have looked like if Greg Inglis had not had such a love of the open water?

There is no doubt they would have still been a great side with a pretty good coach, but there would have been differences. Namely with consistency, a direct result of going over the salary cap is to have at your disposal more quality players than other clubs.

Anyway, we now move on with our lives. The injury-riddled Raiders dominated from start to finish. Eight tries to two gave an inconsistent Green Machine one of the upsets of the season.

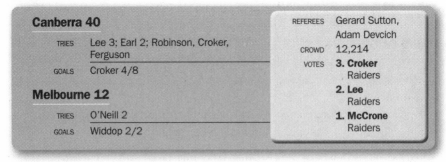

Canberra 40		
TRIES	Lee 3; Earl 2; Robinson, Croker, Ferguson	
GOALS	Croker 4/8	
Melbourne 12		
TRIES	O'Neill 2	
GOALS	Widdop 2/2	

REFEREES	Gerard Sutton, Adam Devcich
CROWD	12,214
VOTES	**3. Croker** Raiders
	2. Lee Raiders
	1. McCrone Raiders

League at its purest

Gold Coast Titans *versus* New Zealand Warriors
7.30pm, Saturday, 7 July
Skilled Park, Gold Coast

MATT O'HANLON

LOVE SCHOOLBOY RUGBY LEAGUE AS IT REALLY IS – in my humble opinion – the purest form of the game. Without question the ASSRL 18-years championships is the cream; the best young men from Queensland and NSW baring their all for a coveted Australian Schoolboys' jersey.

I am in the beautiful city of Port Macquarie for the Under-18 Championships and the pre-championship meeting starts at 7.30pm at the bowls club. Our Queensland Schoolboys' team is in good shape and well prepared by former Queensland Cup legend (in his own lunchbox) Don Saunders and his crew. I position myself well so I can see a TV as the godfather of the QSSRL – the indomitable Phil Hall – reminds us that these Blue blokes are still sulking from their Origin loss. Hang on.Warriors 4, Titans 0. Strong try, Hurrell, in the second minute.

If championships convenor Dave Whittock is not the best publicist for the region of Hastings then I am not here. He and his sidekick, Peter Walsh (maker of the best fishcakes in the Hastings), speak of the virtues of the area. They love the place and with good reason. It is a sensational vista. In 2006 when they last hosted the championships, Taylor, Sandow, Folau, Williams, Pettybourne, Lawrence, Foran and Pearce were some of the names who played. What an advertisement!

ARL salary cap auditor Ian Schubert is from the area and is a former Aussie Schoolboy. He will be here during the week. Whittock, a passionate supporter of school sport – Titans try ... Champion off Sezer – lets us know that the council has embraced not only rugby league but sport generally for the area. That's a positive message and the local paper and TV are promoting the championships.

Idris somehow gets the ball and Gordon scores. Titans 10-4.

Doyen of the QSSRL Phil Hall says that Queensland Schoolboys' sponsors, Struddy's Sports, have had car trouble with their horsefloat full of sportsgear to sell to the punters at Port. Ross and Grub have spent half a day trying to get to Port but Ross the Boss has had a rest on the side of the motorway while Grub has gone back for a new vehicle. We were planning to have a few but that's now under threat.

As is the Warriors' line with a magnificent try by Mead. Watch that on the highlights. 14-4.

This game is crucial to both sides. The Warriors were in this position last year and made the Grand Final. I don't think the Titans can afford to lose, although the Tigers loss last night gives some hope. Hurrell has scored again and the Warriors have gone past the Titans. Halftime, 16-14. I have missed something.

I text The Golden Girl to get her to send me some notes via text. I thought it was a good idea. She's at home, tucked up with a busted ankle.

"Are you nuts?"she replies.

Maybe she doesn't watch the footy when I'm not home. I'll ask her about that later.

Schoolboy footy is fast and open. The speakers remind us of the many great players who have competed at the championships. Without the wrestle that plagues the NRL, the game allows sides to spread the ball and showcase their skills.

The wily old doyen of the QSSRL still reckons that Manly's Ashley Alberts was the best schoolboy he saw in his career that started in 1970. Alberts played in the NRL for just 13 games.

The meeting finishes and there's 10 to go. The Warriors lead 26-14. I speak to a veteran at the bar who calls me "son" and says the Kiwi kid built like a brick outhouse has scored three. As we talk, Locke crosses in the 78th minute. It is 32-14 at fulltime. "Listen son," the veteran says, "the Titans' ball control was ******* terrible."

Their season is on life support. The Warriors, however, have a young backline who could be stars of the future. They are an enigmatic side but the finals surely beckon.

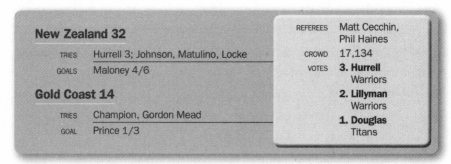

New Zealand 32		REFEREES	Matt Cecchin, Phil Haines
TRIES	Hurrell 3; Johnson, Matulino, Locke	CROWD	17,134
GOALS	Maloney 4/6	VOTES	**3. Hurrell** Warriors
Gold Coast 14			**2. Lillyman** Warriors
TRIES	Champion, Gordon Mead		**1. Douglas** Titans
GOAL	Prince 1/3		

Versing?

South Sydney Rabbitohs *versus* Newcastle Knights
2pm, Sunday, 8 July
ANZ Stadium, Sydney

MARTY SPENCER

THE MATCH BETWEEN SOUTH SYDNEY RABBITOHS AND NEWCASTLE KNIGHTS was eagerly anticipated, as much for the battle between the coaches as anything. Michael Maguire has instilled a new belief in the Bunnies that has their fans coming out of the woodwork and the team looking a genuine finals threat for the first time this century. Conversely, legendary coach Wayne Bennett's team has struggled for much of the season with star recruit Darius Boyd failing to register a meat pie for his new club to date.

As I sat down in front of the magnificent Fox HD coverage to see if the old bull could conjure up something to counteract the enthusiasm of the Rabbitohs, my nephew came through the front door.

"G'Day Marty, what are you watching?"

"The Bunnies match, mate".

"Oh, okay – who are they versing?"

I felt a couple of blood vessels pop close to my temple on hearing my most hated misuse of a word *ever*.

"Versing?" I spluttered, spraying a mixture of Jatz, smoked oyster and Crown lager into the air. "Versing? *Versing*?"

He sat there looking at me incredulously and said, "Yeah – who are they versing?"

I tried to explain to him that the match in question was Souths *versus* Knights. Versing was the art or science of making verse – *you know* – poetry. If there was any versing involved it would be something like this, using William Blake as an example:

Blake sets the scene:

> And now the raging armies rush'd
> Like warring mighty seas;
> The heav'ns are shook with roaring war,
> The dust ascends the skies.

Kyle O'Donnell, on debut for Newcastle, takes it up:

> The shepherd leaves his mellow pipe,
> And sounds the trumpet shrill;
> The workman throws his hammer down
> To heave the bloody bill.

Dave Taylor comes up with a huge hit on O'Donnell, leaving him Led Zeppelined:

> The King is seen raging afar,
> With all his men of might;
> Like blazing comets scattering death
> Thro' the red fev'rous night.
>
> Beneath his arm like sheep they die,
> And groan upon the plain;
> The battle faints, and bloody men
> Fight upon hills of slain.

Boom! O'Donnell has no answer aside from some Lewis Carroll gibberish:

> Twas brillig, and the slithy toves.
> Did gyre and gimble in the wabe:
> All mimsy were the borogoves,
> And the mome raths outgrabe.

"So do you follow my explanation of why I hate the use of the word *versing*, mate? Hear endeth the lesson."

Distractedly he calls to his brother, "Hey Tom, want to verse me on PlayStation?" "Sure."

Now that was a tangent! I believe some observations of the match are in order.

Dave Taylor has played out of his skin since being dropped for Origin III, ably supported by the monstrous Burgess brothers. Will there be a fourth brother at Redfern soon? Nineteen-year-old Tom Burgess is reported to be the biggest of the four of them and has one year to go on his contract with Bradford Bulls and seems made to fill the gap left by Taylor's impending departure for the Gold Coast.

Every time I see John Sutton play I see in him a player about to fulfil his potential. With GI running the angles off Sutton, Souths look like world-beaters and I look forward to seeing their potent style come finals time.

When Jarrod Mullen fires, Newcastle look a different outfit. He got the backline moving forward only intermittently during Sunday's loss and, given space, Uate will always be a handful for the defence – he needs to see more ball.

Newcastle's backline defence is not operating at the required standard, Timana Tahu alone missing seven tackles. Bennett's coaching style is reliant on discipline and defence and this will undoubtedly be addressed by the supercoach this week.

Now I am 50 years old and I do have a tattoo and I understand that getting inked is *de rigueur* among young people but I have heard that the Souths players have so much ink on their bodies that it's almost impossible to buy a biro anywhere near Redfern.

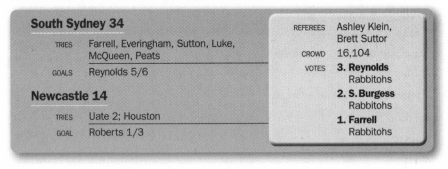

South Sydney 34			REFEREES	Ashley Klein, Brett Suttor
TRIES	Farrell, Everingham, Sutton, Luke, McQueen, Peats		CROWD	16,104
GOALS	Reynolds 5/6		VOTES	**3. Reynolds** Rabbitohs
Newcastle 14				**2. S. Burgess** Rabbitohs
TRIES	Uate 2; Houston			**1. Farrell** Rabbitohs
GOAL	Roberts 1/3			

A Turvey afternoon

Manly Sea Eagles *versus* **Parramatta Eels**
3pm, Sunday, 8 July
Brookvale Oval, Sydney

ANDREW BOMM

I F THERE IS ONE THING THAT I'VE LEARNT IN LIFE, it's that time spent in a drinking establishment with the word 'tavern' in its title can carry certain risks. In my first experience, as a 16-year-old in the 'Tav' opposite Spencer Street Station prior to catching the train home from Melbourne, the risk was that female junkies would walk out on trestle tables and take their underwear off. Mistakenly walking into the Page Tavern in Canberra during university, the risk was more closely related to personal safety. Growing up, the Turvey Tavern in Wagga Wagga was a place that also carried that tavernly mood of angry underemployed men with a predilection for picking fights with smarty pants middle class types.

So with a sense of trepidation I embark on my first visit to the Turvey Tavern to watch Manly v Parra from Brookvale on a sunny Sunday afternoon. I would like to say I'd come here to challenge pre-existing prejudices but, in fact, it's the closest pub to my house. I have to be able to walk back in quick time to look after the kids so the wife can go to the pictures.

It's packed for a Sunday afternoon and they're all on the gas, but the vibe is all "please" and "thank you" and "beg pardon, guvnor". Alright.

Mercifully, the Channel Nine commentary is not audible in the Turv, so I muse wistfully on why league players now wear jumpers so tight that they need assistance to get them on. Absurd. Furthermore, what is the continuing drama that is Phil Gould's hair? Streaks of colour appear to have returned, which seems to defy my Barbara Bush theory.

I have to barrack for the Eels in this one. I had a Western Suburbs player from the Fibros versus Silvertails era at my wedding and my wife's grandfather used to sell hot dogs at Cumberland Oval in the `40s. But all this can't get me to cheer with any heart for the Eels. The game threatens to be a bloodbath. The rot starts early with a Burt error and one of those boring kick to corner, tap back, force down tries.

Living right on the Barassi Line, I grew up thinking that rugby league could learn a lot about ball skills from Australian Rules. Especially kicking. A number of years ago

I had a conversation with a Knowledgeable Rugby League Man where I suggested that tryscoring would be facilitated by playmakers being able to kick accurately to wingers leading to a spot in the in-goal area. The bomb or the grubber was the preferred attacking kick of choice at the time. He told me to stop talking nonsense.

This is a rare occasion when I wish I was wrong. The ability of rugby league halves to actually direct an accurate kick to the corner has become a boring, predictable blight on the game, letting sides without an ability to get through their opponent's defence off the hook. League is about going through, not across and over, and the game is worse for its belated willingness to learn from another code.

But I digress. This tactic is not again required as the Parramatta defence turns to pus over the ensuing 40 minutes. The lowlight for the Eels is Sandow laying a stupid shoulder charge that leads to Manly's fourth try. No player acquisition better encapsulates the madness that seems to have engulfed Parramatta.

"This could be a cricket score," mutters my fellow adventurer Glen, the large and intimidating mental health worker from Queanbeyan. Not that his sizey presence is required in the Turvey Tavern this Sunday. Friendliness and tranquility prevail. This place has changed, and not just with the addition of corrugated iron and an odd internal verandah over the bar to give the place that 'authentic' outback feel.

Halftime comes and it's 34-0. I'm not unhappy that Her Indoors has given me a return home time prior to the conclusion of the match. Parra scores off the back of the worst penalty decision ever, and I'm off. Manly: easily.

It's just nice to know I can go to my local without fear of violent confrontation. Hurrah! Next stop, the Ashmont Inn.

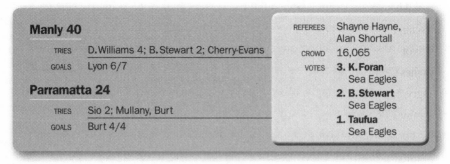

Manly 40		REFEREES	Shayne Hayne, Alan Shortall
TRIES	D. Williams 4; B. Stewart 2; Cherry-Evans	CROWD	16,065
GOALS	Lyon 6/7	VOTES	**3. K. Foran**
			Sea Eagles
Parramatta 24			**2. B. Stewart**
			Sea Eagles
TRIES	Sio 2; Mullany, Burt		**1. Taufua**
GOALS	Burt 4/4		Sea Eagles

When worlds collide

Cronulla Sharks *versus* Sydney Roosters

7pm, Monday, 9 July

Toyota Stadium, Sydney

DANIEL KEARY

I HATE WATCHING ROOSTERS GAMES AT HOME ON TV. The Roosters invariably lose, but that's not entirely why. Nor is it that I need to experience the atmosphere and excitement of the game first hand to truly enjoy it.

In fact, when the typical Roosters home crowd rarely tops 9,000 and the halftime entertainment gets no better than a few fat blokes spilling some up and unders, I can confidently say that there's more atmosphere in my living room than there is at the SFS.

No, I hate watching Roosters games from home because when I do, my footy world collides – head on - with my home world. And, as George Costanza once saliently observed, worlds should not collide.

Being there, at the game, gives a rare and liberating latitude to act like a jerk for 80 minutes. Make that 90 if you include halftime.

Only at the footy can you carry on all you like, unencumbered by the normal mores of shame or embarrassment. And it's great fun.

But at home? Scream and jump around I might, but then I've just gone and scared the kids and annoyed my wife. Yell at the TV, but it isn't the TV's fault we've dropped the ball on the first tackle or had a try inexplicably disallowed by the video ref. My TV's still sulking from the spray it copped when Daniel Mortimer was ridiculously denied a try against Manly in Round 11.

Not to mention the endless distractions which require sudden and frequent switches between footy world and home world. Fixing a snack for the kids when they're hungry, or tending to their toilet emergencies, or dealing with another tantrum (theirs, not mine), or helping them with a drawing, or answering my wife's question about what I'd like for dinner.

Important issues, I know, but nevertheless issues that I can't and surely shouldn't be expected to deal with while I'm trying to watch the Roosters. I pace, I fidget, I try to act cool and hopelessly pretend that I'm not a nervous wreck, and I hate every moment of it.

And so it was that I sat down with enormous trepidation to watch the Sharks and the Roosters on TV. Although there was an early nerve-settler in the form of a neat Shaun Kenny-Dowall try, the game soon reverted to type and, sure enough, worlds collided. After reluctantly agreeing to piggyback one of my daughters around the lounge room, I witnessed – in quick succession – two tries to the Sharks, a cruel forward pass call against the Roosters that denied them a try, a string of Roosters dropped balls and the Sharks being helped by a 5-0 penalty count. The Roosters dropped their bundle. I did well not to drop my daughter.

Halftime offered little respite. It was bedtime for the girls. Somehow I managed to put aside my complete agitation at this point and helped with the teeth brushing, tuck-ins and songs. But my mind was elsewhere – replaying every painful moment from the first 40 and dreading every painful moment from the next.

I'd underestimated the impending pain. Because the Roosters, despite being completely hopeless for the next 30 or so minutes, rallied with two late tries to level the scores and take the game to golden point. Terrific. A bonus 10 minutes of hell.

Come fulltime, with the scores still at 14-all, I was just glad it was all over. Glad that the Roosters were at least one point further away from the wooden spoon. Glad that I'd made it through. And glad that I'd kind of kept it together – after all I'd remained seated on the lounge, I hadn't thrown a slipper at the TV and I'd miraculously limited my abuse of Mitchell Pearce to an innocuous "idiot" when he butchered a couple of regulation field goal opportunities.

Most of all, I am glad that next week's game against the in-form Souths is at the SFS where, although I'll hate the likely loss as much as I hate Souths themselves, I'll still be able to enjoy the game. And, best of all, if it goes to golden point and Pearce screws up again, I'll be able to tell him what I really think of him.

Cronulla 14		REFEREE	Jared Maxwell, Chris James
TRIES	Leutele, Pomeroy	CROWD	13,139
GOALS	Carney 3/5	VOTES	**3. Graham** Sharks
Sydney Roosters 14			**2. Gibbs** Sharks
TRIES	Guerra, Kenny-Dowall, Leilua		**1. Pomeroy** Sharks
GOAL	Mortimer 1/3		

Round 19

End of the line

Canterbury Bulldogs *versus* **Parramatta**

7.30pm, Friday, 13 July

ANZ Stadium, Sydney

NICK TEDESCHI

I OFTEN THINK ABOUT PAUL CARIGE. I nearly always think about him when the Bulldogs are set to take on Parramatta. There isn't a year goes by when I don't have at least one conversation about this player who, on one fateful September day in 1998, saw his career come to an end. He set a new benchmark for horrid individual performances on a rugby league field.

Now, to give Carige's performance context, it is important to understand the simmering hatred between Canterbury and Parramatta at the time. The Bulldogs and Eels were wild rivals in the 1980s but that was an enmity built out of style and the pursuit of superiority rather than any underlying natural disposition of dislike between the two outfits. These days, the rivalry remains strong but it is a very one-sided deal with little respect given to the Eels by the Bulldogs faithful.

But, in the 1990s, the feud was hot – the hottest feud in the game. As with most rivalries of the era, it was born out of the Super League War. Canterbury had become a dominant force in the mid-'90s, winning minor premierships in 1993-94 and the title in 1995. They were heading to Super League. Parramatta, at the time, was a joke. It was the middle of the '95 season, the Eels were heading for their ninth straight year sans finals football when, with the backing of the ARL bankroll, they raided the Bulldogs, poaching four of Canterbury's best.

It resulted in a Bulldogs premiership, a protracted court case, an additional chapter to Terry Lamb's fairytale finish and a lifetime of bitterness. Dean Pay, Jarrod McCracken and Jason Smith have never been forgiven. I'm not entirely sure why Jim Dymock got off scot-free.

So when the two competitions were reunited in 1998, Canterbury and Parramatta were in a state of outright war. Like a Shakespearean drama, the Bulldogs and Eels were drawn for one great showdown, one final battle, one ultimate confrontation.

The scene was the preliminary final. The Four Traitors were lined up for an Eels team that had finished fourth in the regular season. Canterbury had barely stumbled into the finals, finishing ninth and winning their way into the top 10 only on the final Sunday when a Craig Polla-Mounter field goal gave the Bulldogs a 25-24 win over Illawarra.

For the faithful in the blue and white, evil seemed to have triumphed with 11 minutes to go. The Eels led 18-2. A miracle was required.

And then it happened. God did exist. The Bulldogs piled on 16 points and Daryl Halligan slotted a conversion from the sideline to level the scores. As the fulltime siren blared, Polla-Mounter stepped back and punched a field goal from halfway. It fell millimetres short.

By extra-time though, history had been written. The Bulldogs were destined to win. And Paul Carige's career was over.

Carige had debuted three years earlier for Illawarra and was in his 61st top grade match. It would be the scene of one of the great mental implosions. It was a showing that surpassed Steve Mavin's for mammoth ineptitude on a mammoth stage. Carige caught the ball over the sideline, continually dropped the pill when it was in the field of play, chipped from his own in-goal and stepped dead when undefended.

Calamity does not begin to describe the carnage Carige's catastrophes caused.

Carige was soon being widely mocked by the Canterbury faithful and abused by the Parramatta lot. So brutal were the Eels fans, Carige was forced to flee to the North Coast. Parramatta cut Carige. He played in England for a season but his career had been defined by a devastating collapse.

Rugby league can be a cruel mistress. Nobody knows that more than Paul Carige who, in 14 years, has never publicly spoken about the game. As Craig Polla-Mounter said in 2007: "He disappeared off the face of the planet after that."

I have had my fun with Carige. I still look back on that game with a great deal of fondness. But I do wonder what happened to Carige. I wonder not what he is doing or where he is living but how he dealt with having his life – at least his life as a professional sportsman – defined by such a public implosion.

And I still wonder if he watches Canterbury-Parramatta matches – like this one where the Bulldogs ran away from the Eels 32-12 on the back of Ben Barba's brilliance

– and if he enjoys the greatest game of all. I wonder if the memories are still too raw, the game still too traumatising.

I doubt we will ever know. One thing is certain though – both Canterbury and Parramatta fans will never forget Paul Carige, no matter how much Carige wants to be forgotten.

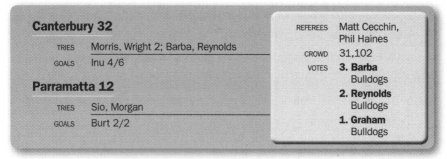

Canterbury 32		
TRIES	Morris, Wright 2; Barba, Reynolds	
GOALS	Inu 4/6	
Parramatta 12		
TRIES	Sio, Morgan	
GOALS	Burt 2/2	

REFEREES	Matt Cecchin, Phil Haines
CROWD	31,102
VOTES	**3. Barba** Bulldogs
	2. Reynolds Bulldogs
	1. Graham Bulldogs

Crossing the ditch

Brisbane Broncos *versus* **New Zealand Warriors**
7.30pm, Friday, 13 July
Suncorp Stadium, Brisbane

WILL EVANS

AFTER PLENTY OF SOUL-SEARCHING AND SLEEPLESS NIGHTS, I made the patriotic decision late in 2011 to switch my first-team allegiances from the Broncos – my beloved club of 22 seasons – to the Warriors. Rugby league supporter sacrilege, you say? Perhaps, but the heart wants what it wants.

I revelled in Brisbane's dominance over Auckland during the Warriors' early seasons as a teenager living in New Zealand. And despite the Warriors being my fervently-supported second team, they were the club I hated losing to the most after the balance of power in the rivalry began to shift in the early 2000s – undoubtedly due in part to the merciless ribbing I copped from my flatmates, friends and my dad when the Warriors upset the star-studded Broncos.

The 30-20 victory over Brisbane in Round 9 was a real highlight – albeit a rare one, as the season panned out – of my first year as a Warriors supporter. No regrets so far, and my national pride (buoyed by a few pre-game pints) superseded the tinges of guilt as I made my way through the Suncorp Stadium turnstiles in a black jersey instead of a maroon and gold one for the first time.

The massive Warriors contingent in the crowd – an ever-growing phenomenon at games in Brisbane and on the Gold Coast – also made me feel more at home. Fittingly, the drizzly weather and cooler temperatures resembled Auckland on a wintry Friday night.

Among our seven-strong crew at the game was my workmate Esse. A Togo national who played semi-professional soccer in Hong Kong before moving to Brisbane a couple of years ago, Esse has an unusual pedigree for a rugby league nut, but his love for the code has been accelerated by a father-in-law with a disturbing obsession with the Melbourne Storm. The best of Esse's epic father-in-law tales involve the Billy Slater figurine that never leaves his side. He even takes it to work, and was reprimanded for going berserk when his colleagues hid it from him.

Esse's unbridled enthusiasm for his first Suncorp Stadium outing was matched only by my dad's at the corresponding clash last season. A Warriors diehard since 1995, Dad had never been to an NRL game before. His live rugby league experience to that point consisted of the 1988 World Cup final at Eden Park and a Warriors v Cowboys trial match in Invercargill during the 1997 preseason. Both were dismal experiences – in the first instance because the highly-touted Kiwis were thumped 25-12 by a Wally Lewis-inspired Australian side and, in the second, because, well, it was in Invercargill and we were surrounded by Southland bogans heckling the Warriors' former All Black Marc Ellis.

But his Suncorp debut made up for those disappointments in spades – despite the Warriors' 21-20 loss in a thriller, Dad said it was one of the best experiences of his life.

The Warriors started this 2012 clash sluggishly, falling behind 8-0 early after a try to Brisbane pivot Corey Norman and a penalty goal to Corey Parker. But a determined four-pointer to Kevin Locke put the visitors on the board in the 15th minute before they pegged back to level via a Manu Vatuvei try featuring two run-arounds by hooker Nathan Friend – a movement sure to warm the cockles of Peter Sterling, rugby league's No. 1 proponent of the run-around.

The Warriors' fightback was much to the chagrin of Esse, our work tipping comp's version of the Parramatta Eels, but he was pretty chuffed after we stared down the barrel of James Maloney's inexplicable penalty goal miss from in front at the Caxton Street end. Parker's 56th-minute penalty goal nudged the Broncos in front and was to be the only score of a frenetic second half. The Warriors launched a last-second attacking raid, with a Shaun Johnson kick finding Bill Tupou on the fly. The winger flung the ball in-field as the Warriors' fans rose in anticipation of a miracle finish but Maloney's kick to the opposite corner was cleaned up by Gerard Beale.

As Dad reminded me during our weekly post-match phone debrief, I'd better get used to losses like this supporting the enigmatic Warriors – a sentiment I became painfully familiar with in the weeks that followed.

Brisbane 10			REFEREES	Ben Cummins, Chris James
TRY	Norman		CROWD	32,148
GOALS	Parker 3/3		VOTES	**3. Parker** Broncos
New Zealand 8				**2. Matulino** Warriors
TRIES	Locke, Vatuvei			**1. Hoffman** Broncos
GOALS	Maloney 0/3			

A name game

Melbourne Storm *versus* North Queensland Cowboys
5.30pm, Saturday, 14 July
AAMI Park, Melbourne

LUKE JAMIESON

A S I WAS SHOWERING RECENTLY I STARTED TO THINK, which isn't to suggest that I shower or think only occasionally, but my thinking was this: where do team names come from? What is it that at the inception of a football club causes the founding members to choose one moniker over another? I did some more thinking and a negligible amount of research and this is what I uncovered.

Some football team names are literal and obvious like the Maitland Pumpkin Pickers or the Young Cherry Pickers. They are obviously teams consisting of backpackers who are doing some cash-in-hand labouring work while on their two-year tourist visas and having a break from living 10 to a room in Bondi.

Some are steeped in history like the Parkes Spacemen, homage to the Spacemen family who were the first family to farm olives in the Parkes region and donors of the inaugural Moonbeam Cup.

Other names like the Coonabarabran Unicorns or University Scholars are names that were adopted purely to strike fear into the opposition because, as we all know, football is 50 per cent mental, 40 per cent skill and 10 per cent luck. You win the mental battle and that's 90 per cent of the challenge.

Some clubs choose to abide by the 'alliterate or die' mentality. It's no coincidence that Australia's greatest team playing on UK soil, bar none, is the Hammersmith Hills Hoists. And no one can argue with the success of the now defunct Bredbo Barbarians (1995-96) whose sponsor wall in the local pub was adorned with a giant 'Bredbo Babarians' sign, typo included.

The Jacksonville Axemen is close enough to a rhyme to count and ticks the all-important multi-syllabic requirements for chanting: "Let's go Axe-men, let's go!"

A little known fact is that the Toowoomba Clydesdales were formed by two formerly opposing teams one lunchtime at Toowoomba Central Primary School. The respective teams, captained by none other than Clyde Jeffreys and Dale Perkins respectively, joined forces for a huge game of British Bulldogs against their more fancied East Toowoomba Public School rivals. Ultimately beaten, the bond forged in the heat of battle gave birth to the famous Galloping Clydesdales.

At the national competition level, there are some interesting cases of namology. The Newcastle Knights were formerly known as the Boogie Nights. The Gold Coast Seagulls were founded by a one legged bloke with white hair whose favourite pastime was squawking at all the players. They exited the comp after a nasty alka-seltzer incident, possibly at the hands of some mischievous teenagers.

The Melbourne Storm. The records concerning the origins of their name were either missing, deliberately misleading or entirely false. My best guess is that they were initially going to, and should, be called the Melbourne Drizzles.

This game probably deserved a better write up given that North Queensland gave the Melbourne Drizzle an unexpected stuffing in Melbourne. A rare event indeed, but the Drizzles' run of five straight losses takes a bit of the sheen off the huge effort from Thursty and the 'Boys'.

North Queensland 20		REFEREES	Tony Archer, Gavin Morris
TRIES	Linnett 2; Tate	CROWD	10,688
GOALS	Thurston 4/4	VOTES	**3. Thurston** Cowboys
Melbourne 16			**2. Tate** Cowboys
TRIES	Duffie, Quinn, Widdop		**1. Linnett** Cowboys
GOALS	Smith 2/3		

The price of passion

Newcastle Knights *versus* Manly Sea Eagles
5.30pm, Saturday, 14 July
Hunter Stadium, Newcastle

LINDSEY CUTHBERTSON

THE RIVALRY BETWEEN MANLY AND NEWCASTLE holds a lot of meaning for me. I wasn't alive to experience the Sea Eagles' rivalry with Parramatta in the 1970s and '80s, and I now know the fierce contests between Melbourne and, to a more recent extent, the Bulldogs. But the rivalry that sprung up from Newcastle's miraculous victory in the 1997 Grand Final is the most special because it is where I truly discovered my passion for the Sea Eagles.

In the week leading up to that epic match I found it hard to sleep. I watched and read the news like a crazed fan for any mention of either my side or the Knights. Come Sunday I woke up at an ungodly hour, the time you wake up on Christmas morning. I won't run over what happened but I remember how painful those final few seconds were after the fulltime siren went.

Seeing Manly come down from two big wins on the trot to lose 32-6 to the Knights is certainly not as painful, but it's deflating. What makes it worse is the fact that my plans to view the game fell through and I was left to consult the commentary of Twitter and an app on my phone to determine what was happening.

To then discover that Manly made three times as many offloads in the first half yet found themselves 10-0 down at the break was even more frustrating. The Knights defended strongly but also took their chances when they were presented.

The Sea Eagles' attack has been stifled by injuries and a lack of cohesion all year: they've scored 30 points or more in only three matches, and two of those instances have occurred in the last two weeks. That statistic has given fans a sense that Manly fires when it's most important. But this game proved otherwise.

Not only did it show that Manly still hasn't overcome its inconsistent form, but it also highlighted our leaky defence without the Stewart brothers and Steve Matai. Tyrone Roberts just strolled through for the Knights' second try before halftime and the tries continued to flow after the break as well.

When I got home I did the only thing that a person without pay TV could do.

I hopped online and scrutinised the match reports and statistics more closely and discovered that while Manly was well behind on the scoreboard, there was not much separating the two sides in completion rates, tackles made and errors.

If this proves anything, it's that the intangibles in rugby league are far more important than anything you can record on a piece of paper. Except the score. Newcastle's victory demonstrated that when it comes to taking on your rivals, fans can't be the only ones with their emotions invested in the contest. And it seems that I'm not the only one with that point of view.

"It was a big game for them out there tonight because of the rivalry between the two clubs," Knights coach Wayne Bennett said after the game when describing his side's performance. "They knew that they had to aim up and they did show what wonderful spirit they do have."

I guess they were right when they said that you can't put a price on passion.

Newcastle 32		REFEREES	Jason Robinson, Tony De Las Herras
TRIES	McManus, Uate 2; Gagai, Roberts	CROWD	20,154
GOALS	Roberts 4/6	VOTES	**3. Buderus** Knights
Manly 6			**2. Roberts** Knights
TRY	Kite		**1. Uate** Knights
GOAL	Lyon 1/1		

The story of The Betrayal

Wests Tigers *versus* **Penrith Panthers**
7.30pm, Saturday, 14 July
Campbelltown Sports Stadium, Sydney

GREG OBERSCHEIDT

AT THE FOOT OF THE MOUNTAINS THERE WAS A FOOTBALL FIELD called Centrebet Stadium. Lewis often went to this place. Outside he left eight of his fans, saying to them: "Sit here while I go inside and train."

He took with him the three chosen ones, Lachlan, Travis and Kevin and went inside. Lewis knew that in a little while Gus would be there with a band of men to seize him; that in a few hours he would be led out to die. The thought of finishing his career with Parramatta came upon him and filled his soul with grief. He said to Lachlan, Travis and Kevin:

"My soul is filled with sorrow, a sorrow that almost kills me. Stay here and watch while I am training."

He went a little further among the trees, flung himself down upon the ground and cried out: "O Ivan, if this cup cannot pass away, and I must drink it, then thy will be done."

He was now ready for the fate that was soon to come, and his heart was strong and already the Son of Penrith was given by the traitor into the hands of Parramatta.

They heard the noise of a crowd and saw the flashing of iPhones and the gleaming of VB cans. In the throng they saw Gus standing and they knew now that he was the traitor of whom Lewis had spoken the night before. Gus came rushing forward and kissed Lewis as though he were glad to see him.

"Gus, do you betray the Son of Penrith with a kiss?"

Then he turned to the media and said: "Whom do you seek?"

They answered: "Lewis of Penrith."

Lewis said: "I am he."

Then he spoke to the media: "Do you come out against me with salary cap issues as though I were Michael Jennings? I was with you every day of 2003 and you did lift the trophy with me."

Lachlan, Travis and Kevin, whom Lewis loved, had followed after the crowd of those who carried Lewis away and they came to the door of Ivan's house. Lachlan knew Ivan and went in but Travis at first stayed outside. Lachlan went out and brought him in. He came in but did not dare to go into the room where Lewis stood before Gus. In the courtyard of the house, they had made a fire of charcoal and Kevin stood among those who were warming themselves at the fire.

While Gus and his cronies were showing their hate toward Lewis, who stood alone among his enemies, Kevin was in the courtyard warming himself at the fire. Benji looked at Kevin sharply and finally said to him: "You were one of those men with this Lewis of Penrith!"

Kevin was afraid to tell the truth and he answered him: "Benji, I do not know the man and I do not know what you are talking about."

And to get away from him, he went into the house. There, Chris Heighington saw him and said: "This man was one of those with Lewis!"

And Kevin swore with an oath that he did not know Lewis at all. Soon a man came by, he looked at Kevin and heard him speak, and said: "Beau knows you are the one who took this man's captaincy!"

Then Kevin began again to curse and to swear, declaring that he did not know the man.

Just at that moment the loud, shrill crowing of Robbie Farah startled Kevin and at the same time he saw Lewis, who was being dragged through the hall from Ivan's to the council-room of Gus, and Lewis turned as he was passing and looked at Kevin.

Then there flashed into Kevin's mind what Lewis had said on the evening before!

"Before the sun sets on my career, you bloody Judas, I'm going to stick it right up you blokes. Even if I am playing for Parra!"

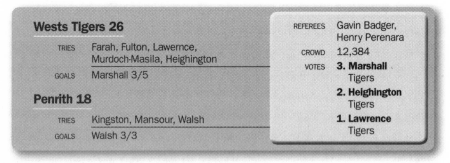

Wests Tigers 26		REFEREES	Gavin Badger, Henry Perenara
TRIES	Farah, Fulton, Lawernce, Murdoch-Masila, Heighington	CROWD	12,384
GOALS	Marshall 3/5	VOTES	**3. Marshall** Tigers
Penrith 18			**2. Heighington** Tigers
TRIES	Kingston, Mansour, Walsh		**1. Lawrence** Tigers
GOALS	Walsh 3/3		

A Lego hat of commitment

Canberra Raiders *versus* **Gold Coast Titans**
2pm, Sunday, 15 July
Canberra Stadium, Canberra

TIM NAPPER

AHH, THE SOUTHERN CROSS CLUB OF WODEN, CANBERRA. When you go to the Cross Club, you can't help but wonder if the management searched for a moment in time – 1989 perhaps – and decided that the club would never change from that day on. The carpet, the menu, the mopes sitting at the bar, the enduring aroma of stale beer and chicken parma – it's all there, every day of the week, every month of the year, for eternity. And that's fine by me. As long as Cold Chisel is on the jukebox, Old is on tap and the Raiders are playing, I wouldn't want them to change a thing.

Except for the massive plasma screen in the main bar, that is new. One of the few additions since 1989 and one of the few extras I would agree with. Good to see all that poker machine revenue isn't going to waste. There is also a sign next to the big screen in the Cross Club that says: THIS SCREEN IS FOR RUGBY LEAGUE. I like that. There's also a much smaller screen a little way down the wall that says THIS SCREEN IS FOR AFL. I like that too. These are people who understand their sporting priorities.

So the game began and the start was promising. A Titans player put one foot out receiving the kick-off and Canberra scored at the two-minute mark. Snap. I was feeling upbeat. The boys in green had smashed the Storm at home the previous week and I was ready to kick back and watch them demolish the hapless Titans.

Unfortunately, everything from that point on sank the Raiders supporters in the room into a miasma of despair.

Jamal Idris was given too much latitude. Yes, he is an overrated creampuff but that doesn't mean you don't put anyone on him in defence. I believe he was unmarked the entire game. He was just walking around, strolling through gaps in the defence. Passing the ball, of course, after 20 metres when he became exhausted from all the jogging he was forced to do. Unfortunately, whoever it was running off his shoulder – usually William Zillman or Steve Michaels – was also running into space.

The atmosphere was getting tense in the Cross Club. At one point a supporter behind me yelled in fury after a suspicious-looking Titans score: "If that's a try, *I'm a try*." Well, I tell you something, reader: I have no idea what that means. I really don't. But I agree entirely.

While the game unfolded I flicked through a nearby *Canberra Times*, trying to distract myself from the depressing shellacking the Raiders were receiving. Inside there was an article about a Lego exhibition taking place in Canberra. The story told of a 36-year-old Melbournian who travelled up to Canberra just for the event. The dude even wore a hat made of Lego to the exhibition. Yes, you read that right.

The paper reported the plastic-crowned gentleman as saying:

> I've spent [hundreds of] hours creating models and spent one hour building a hat and yet it's the most popular thing I've ever made ... I get home from work, have dinner and sit down with a tray of Lego and think: "What will I build tonight?"

All I could think was that maybe I should wander down and check out this Lego exhibition because it'd be a helluva lot better than this crap I was watching on the big screen. Hell, a Lego hat? That rates better than the average Raiders game all by itself.

So what if the guy wearing it is a Lego tragic? At least the man is passionate about something, at least he sets a goal and doesn't stop until it is completed. Unlike the insipid pack of the Canberra Raiders.

Come on boys. Build that Lego hat of commitment to the game, and don't stop until it is done.

Terrible game. Shocker.

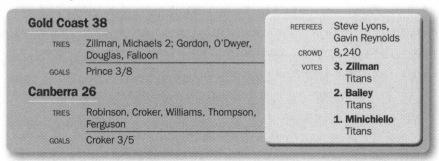

Gold Coast 38		REFEREES	Steve Lyons, Gavin Reynolds
TRIES	Zillman, Michaels 2; Gordon, O'Dwyer, Douglas, Falloon	CROWD	8,240
GOALS	Prince 3/8	VOTES	**3. Zillman** Titans
Canberra 26			**2. Bailey** Titans
TRIES	Robinson, Croker, Williams, Thompson, Ferguson		**1. Minichiello** Titans
GOALS	Croker 3/5		

Daylight derby

St George Illawarra Dragons *versus* Cronulla Sharks
3pm, Sunday, 15 July
WIN Stadium, Sydney

GLEN HUMPHRIES

BEING IN MY 40S, I HAVE SEEN A LOT OF FOOTY OVER THE YEARS. I've seen a lot of things go by the wayside. Things that I miss. In no particular order they include: black and white cardboard corner posts; blokes smearing black goo under their eyes for night footy games; players sporting beards and moustaches; wingers wearing shoulder pads; guests on rugby league shows being given a tray of meat and bottle of orange juice for coming on; goals kicked on mounds of sand; teams running through crepe-paper banners; nightly news reports crossing live to players at training; midweek competitions and seeing three grades play at the same ground on the same day.

Another thing I miss is footy being played in the afternoon. Sure, it happens on Sundays but the rest of the games each round kicks off as darkness falls (which makes me wonder why no players today smear that black substance under their eyes. Did it not actually do anything?).

Back in my day all the games were played in daylight hours. And it was wonderful. There was one ground where it was especially wonderful. Which is why, if I'm ever made NRL CEO (note to all: this will never happen), one of my first edicts would be that every game played at WIN Stadium has to be during daylight hours.

With the ocean right behind the hill, it's the most picturesque ground in the league – and it looks fantastic in the afternoon light.

And a game during daylight also means that you don't have to worry when there's a power blackout. Which happened shortly after kick-off in this local derby, when a substation installed as part of the western grandstand work malfunctioned.

For the Dragons, it had been a disappointing season up to this point with the team never really making me think: "Hey, we could win this season" (and I'm the sort of fan who is stupidly optimistic on that score). It was a different story for Cronulla who had been playing some good footy – and not just against the Dragons (which is how things usually go over in The Shire).

So a win didn't look likely for the Red V. Especially when No. 6 Jamie Soward was injured pre-match. Even more so when his replacement Kyle Stanley was injured five minutes in. That meant that we faced a better opponent and had to do it with a third-choice playmaker in Nathan Fien.

So who'd have thought that the Dragons would take the lead in just the seventh minute – courtesy of a stepping and weaving try to big improver Mitch Rein – and never relinquish it for the remaining 73 minutes. And who'd have thought the team with the worst attacking record in the League would come out and throw the ball around so much?

The Sharks closed the gap to 6-4 through a Wade Graham try and that looked like being the halftime score until Todd Carney threw a pass into the ground with a minute to go and Brett Morris swooped. B-Moz ran the length of the field to make the halftime score 12-4.

The second half saw the Sharks edge closer again with Graham crossing over for a 12-10 scoreline. But the Dragons' defence blocked the Sharks out for the rest of the match (the Red V would make 355 tackles to the Sharks' 274) and closed it out with a try to Trent Merrin in the last quarter of the match.

It was a win that put the Dragons back into the top eight picture. And that caused coach Steve Price to engage in a bizarre post-match rant against those in the media who had written the Dragons off.

Ahh, Pricey. Best leave those sort of comments for a time when we've won more than one game in a row.

St George Illawarra 18			REFEREES	Ashley Klein, Adam Devcich
TRIES	Morris, Rein, Merrin		CROWD	18,282
GOALS	C. Stanley 3/3		VOTES	**3. Nightingale** Dragons
Cronulla 10				**2. Rein** Dragons
TRIES	Graham 2			**1. Graham** Sharks
GOAL	Carney 1/2			

Love to hate

Sydney Roosters *versus* **South Sydney Rabbitohs**
7pm, Monday, 16 July
Allianz Stadium, Sydney

DANIEL KEARY

"LOVE TO HATE." All week, the Roosters' marketing department has been bombarding me and other Roosters members with emails imploring us to do so. We're playing Souths after all.

But I'm over hate. I'm trying to give it up. Lately I've been hating way too much, not least the Roosters' form this year. And their woeful completion rates. And the cruel refereeing decisions that always seem to go against us. And the reported terms of SBW's deal with the Roosters. And the sight of Sam Perrett running around in a Bulldogs jersey.

It's hate overload and it isn't healthy. I did some soul-searching this week. Do I really hate hate Souths? Or have the cunning marketers simply manipulated me into believing so? I compile a list of reasons why I should like Souths:

- A foundation club. which has won the most premierships.
- A host of legendary players, including several impossible to dislike legends such as Clive Churchill, John Sattler and Ron Coote (although he's really ours just as much as theirs).
- Michael McGuire seems okay.
- Souths' captain Michael Crocker is apparently still a good mate of Anthony Minichiello.

I realise that if this list is going to get any longer, it's also going to get even more piss-weak. Truth is, I'm struggling to find reasons to like Souths which begs the question, why should I dislike them? So I write another list:

- They stole half of Easts' junior area back in 1937. It's true – it's in the history books.
- The myth clung to by Souths' fans that Easts steal all their players. Okay, we got Ron Coote. Forty

or so years ago. Since then, it's been pretty much one-way traffic – Royce Ayliffe, Craig Salvatori, Mark Minichiello, Bryan Fletcher, Stuart Webb, Peter Cusack, Shane Rigon, Shannon Hegarty, even Craig Wing (yeah, yeah, but remember he was CLUBLESS when Easts picked him up).

- They hate us. In 1999, I donned my Easts jersey and, in a show of pro-ARL/anti-Murdoch solidarity, marched with thousands of others to protest Souths' exclusion from the comp. What did I get in return? A few hours of spiteful abuse from the Souths faithful. Hindsight's a wonderful thing – perhaps Murdoch was right after all.
- The Pride of the League. Forever in Our Shadow. Moronic, meaningless phrases.
- Russell Crowe – almost a list within the list: his hypocritical "chequebook rugby league" swipe at the Roosters. *The Book of Feuds*. That hilarious DEAN WIDDERS – I LOVE YOU speech in that ABC doco from a few years back. The Gladiator posturing from the stands at the games. Enough said.

Off I go to the match at the SFS, telling myself that I'm looking forward to a good game and one that confirms my newfound feeling of, well, neutrality towards Souths.

But, Souths being Souths, they quickly do their best to challenge my new outlook. Just 20 minutes in and Shaun Kenny-Dowall is sickeningly spear tackled by Issac Luke. Not long after, Souths score and Sam Burgess gives Braith Anasta a gobful.

Meanwhile, the Souths fans on the other side of the ground are booing everything and everyone not in a Souths jersey, generally going feral and generally annoying the crap out of me.

Then the heartbreaking last couple of moments when Souths do an us on them and snatch the game with two miracle tries in the last two minutes.

It's a bitter loss alright but I'm surprisingly philosophical about it. Easts played their guts out. They were the better side for most of the game and there wasn't a bad player for them out there. As for Souths, they ended up showing why they're in the top four.

But then, on the drive home, I can't help but think back to Luke's tackle and Burgess' spray, and the abuse I copped when I marched in '99, and how many players they've pinched off us over the years, and Crowe's chequebook rugby league comment and ... ah bugger it, it's the natural order of things. Easts and Souths. Love to hate.

South Sydney 24

TRIES	Merritt 2; Everingham, Reynolds
GOALS	Reynolds 4/4

Sydney Roosters 22

TRIES	Cordner, Leilua, Moga, Pearce
GOALS	Anasta 3/4

REFEREES Shayne Hayne, Alan Shortall
CROWD 19,934
VOTES **3. Guerra** Roosters
2. Reynolds Rabbitohs
1. Minichiello Roosters

Round 20

Ramblings with Ron

Manly Sea Eagles
versus **Canterbury Bulldogs**

7.30pm, Friday, 20 July
Brookvale Oval, Sydney

HUW FOWLES

AFTER ROUND 19, 2012		
1	Storm	12-5
2	Bulldogs	12-5
3	Broncos	11-6
4	Rabbitohs	11-6
5	Sharks	10-6-1
6	Cowboys	10-7
7	Sea Eagles	10-7
8	Tigers	9-8
9	Warriors	8-9
10	Dragons	8-9
11	Titans	7-10
12	Knights	7-10
13	Raiders	7-10
14	Roosters	6-10-1
15	Panthers	4-13
16	Eels	3-14

HAVE BEEN A MANLY SUPPORTER FOR OVER 30 YEARS BUT UNTIL THIS GAME I'd never seen a match at Brookvale. I'd driven exactly 888km from Carlton to Brookie on the day of the game.

Maybe it was the No Doz I'd been popping like a truckie on the drive up from Melbourne or perhaps it was the effects of the free guarana-laden energy drink given to me by the promo girls outside the ground, but I was buzzing by the time I took my seat in the Ken Arthurson Stand.

I'd forgotten how brilliant big games at suburban footy grounds can be. It made for a pleasant change from watching a game at a generic concrete and steel behemoth, festooned with corporate logos and, sadly, so often three-quarters empty.

The 17,000 rabid Sea Eagles supporters and a handful of diehard Doggies jammed into this tiny ground were making a lot of noise. I was pumped.

Minutes into the game, my mate Wrucky turns to me and says: "It's amazing how being at the game makes the players more real."

Hard to argue with that statement.

Perhaps the greatest statement of blinding obviousness since renowned English football manager and commentator Ron Atkinson famously uttered:

They've got to go for it now as they have nothing to lose but the match.

When I lived in London in the late '90s, I fell in love with Big Ron for four reasons – his Donald Trump-esque hairstyle, his unintentionally comical commentary and his counting ability.

Ron, how did you see the game at Brookie tonight?

I'm most interested in watching three excitement machines in the flesh for the first time this season – Sam Kasiano and Manly. But they all got soundly hammered tonight.

A very handy start was made by Canterbury, with tries to Barba and Perrett ...

Indeed, Huw. For me Canterbury's biggest threat was when they got into the attacking part of the field.

Where were the Silvertails going wrong, Ron?

Huw, it's all about the two Ms. Movement and positioning. You can see the ball go past them, or the man, but you'll never see both man and ball go past at the same time. So if the ball goes past, the man won't, or if the man goes past, they'll take the ball."

Manly down by 12-0 at halftime. What would Tooves have been most concerned about?

If Geoff Toovey said one word to his team at halftime, it was concentration and focus. Someone in the Manly team had to come out and grab the ball by the horns.

The disallowed try to Josh Morris late in the match. Good call or bad call?

Indeed, Huw, my son. Stagg was treading on dangerous water there when he charged into Whare. Morris would have scored, but his try was too perfect.

Pardon the pun Ron, but Manly were dogged in the last half hour but just couldn't quite do enough to get back on level terms could they?

Manly picked their heads up off the ground, but they then had a lot to carry on their shoulders. I tell you what, if the Manly lads had managed to get a try back at that point in the game, they were literally gonna catch on fire.

Did we see any possible premiership contenders playing out there tonight?

The Canterbury players are tried and trusted. Well, I'm not sure they can be trusted. But they are my new flag favourites. It looks like they've got a couple more gears left in the locker.

Toovey had some very harsh words for the refs after the game. Were they justified, Ron?

I never comment on referees and I'm not going to break the habit of a lifetime for those prats.

Who were the standout players this evening?

I wouldn't say Ben Barba is the best fullback in the NRL, but there are none better. And with the loss of Kasiano to the fractured cheekbone early, Tolman and Graham had to stand up. I thought they could have done a lot more there, but full marks to the lads.

Thanks for the sage words, Ron.

At least I'd popped my Brookvale cherry. And I know what you mean, Wrucky. Nothing beats seeing these blokes plying their trade in the flesh. I wasn't happy with the result but I'm sure it won't be another 35 years before I'm back at Brookie again.

Canterbury 20			REFEREES	Ben Cummins, Brett Suttor
TRIES	Barba 2; Perrett		CROWD	16,820
GOALS	Inu 4/4		VOTES	**3. Barba** Bulldogs
Manly 12				**2. Graham** Bulldogs
TRIES	Lyon, King			**1. Tolman** Bulldogs
GOALS	Lyon 2/2			

The short straw

Gold Coast Titans *versus* Brisbane Broncos
7.30pm, Friday, 20 July
Skilled Stadium, Gold Coast

IAN HAUSER

THERE WAS A CRACKER OF A GAME AT BROOKIE TONIGHT as the Dogs and the Sea Eagles tore into each other as if there was no tomorrow. Apart from the Origin games this year, this one would be hard to go past for tough, brutal, old fashioned footy.

Dessie returned to his old stomping ground for the first time since his defection to the west and, as you'd expect, copped it from the Manly faithful. From the word go, the forwards belted the billy goats out of each other and the backs weren't too kind either. This was possibly the best club game of the year so far, at least of those I've seen.

The baying Manly hordes, surely the least likeable of all fans (and that's saying something when you consider the proclivities of Dogs fans), couldn't get the locals home. James Graham was a colossus for the Dogs while Ben Barba was at his wizard-best although his performance was punctuated by a howler that allowed Lyon to score.

The good news of the night was that Manly lost; the bad news was that I also got to follow the Titans/Broncos game. The contrast couldn't have been greater. This was a very ordinary match for any game, more so for a derby between one team trying to stay in finals contention and the other, supposedly, among the frontrunners. Opposition teams won't lose much sleep over the prospect of playing against either in September.

Neither team showed much system, ball handling was poor, last play options lacked vision and, with over an hour gone, it was a dull game likely to be decided by a mistake rather than some creative play.

And so it turned out – just on the hour, with the scores level, a penalty for a lazy Te'o hit to Bailey's head changed the flow and, within a minute, the very same 'Bull' Bailey scored. He copped another one on the snoz for his troubles and an eight-point try settled the issue.

There were a few highlights. The Titans' first try came from a clever Prince retrieval of a kick through. Running towards his own line, Prince instantly flicked the ball to Zillman on the fly and his swerving run put Mead away. Prince also featured in a light-hearted moment that helped us remember that it's really only a game. Hoffman looked sure to score before being swooped on by Prince from behind. As they lay in the tackle, they exchanged what might have been Hoffman saying: "How the hell did an old bugger like you ever catch me?" to which Prince may have replied: "Experience, son. It's all between the ears." They both smiled.

Zillman was best afield, always dangerous with the ball in hand, bobbing up in the right places in attack and defence. Bailey rolled back the years to lead from the front in the absence of Harrison and Bird. Nate Myles reinforced his hard-man reputation, carrying a sternum injury all night but never shying away from the heavy stuff. Prince is a schemer who plays with greater subtlety in his later years.

The Broncos were awful, even when they seemed to be in control through the middle half of the game. Gillett tried hard and Te'o had his moments but Wallace was well covered and the forwards lacked penetration. Two reports and several injuries will test the Brisbane lads in coming weeks.

Several weeks ago when the Titans beat the Cowboys, I was impressed by the underdog Titans. Tonight they got the job done again, this time without two top players (Harrison and Bird) and with Myles far from fully fit.

Maybe I'm too hard on them; maybe, just maybe, they might throw a spanner in the works.

Gold Coast 14			REFEREES	Jared Maxwell, Alan Shortall
TRIES	Mead, Bailey		CROWD	20,067
GOALS	Prince 3/3		VOTES	**3. Zillman** Titans
Brisbane 10				**2. Bailey** Titans
TRIES	Norman, Te'o			**1. Myles** Titans
GOALS	Parker 1/1, Wallace 0/1			

Ripped off

New Zealand Warriors *versus* Newcastle Knights

7.30pm, Saturday, 21 July

Mt Smart Stadium, Auckland

JACK MUIR

I HAVE A THEORY ABOUT THE WARRIORS. When you expect them to do well in a season they invariably disappoint. When you have no hopes or expectation for a season, they seem to grow another leg and really turn it on, giving fans on both sides of the Tasman some really entertaining football to enjoy.

So it comes to this Round 20 game against the Knights. This seems like another must-win game. It is must-win because the Warriors must start showing their fans that they are a decent football side that can compete in the finals. And they must secure a spot.

I finish work just after lunch on the Saturday and take a leisurely taxi trip home to my Hong Kong apartment. I settle down on the couch full of expectation at 3.30pm Hong Kong time. This could be the match when the Warriors machine clicks into motion. I lounge on the couch supremely confident.

Being a rugby league fan in Hong Kong isn't as difficult as people may think. Sure there isn't a lot of live rugby league action, and when you are at the local pub and you try and spark up a conversation about the great game you are slagged off generally by some Aussie or Pommy banker who says it's a thug's sport.

A few years ago I would have stirred the pot and returned to the private schooler later on to continue the discussion. However you mellow with age. You start to have more confidence in your own skin, and I have started to have more confidence in my game as well. The reason being a leaguie in Hong Kong these days is fine is that there is so much coverage via the internet: you can stream any game you want with some of the world's best internet speeds, pay TV shows about five games a week and, when your team is getting flogged, you don't have to be reminded about it by mates and sundry others.

The Warriors start off with a hiss and a roar. For the first 20 minutes they really look like a team that can push for the premiership from the backend of the eight but, as has happened so often this season, nothing goes right and things start to fall apart. The Warriors go into the halftime break 19-10 up, having led at one stage 18-0. To rub salt into the wound, Kevin Naiqama scores for the Knights right on halftime. Tries scored in that fashion (off the back of an horrendous cough up from Jacob Lillyman) and at that time of the match are effectively worth double when their mental and emotional effect is taken into account. As the players trudge off, in my heart of hearts I'm thinking that we're just not going to win.

The second half is so difficult to watch. It's like when you're out clubbing and you are trying to attract the fairer sex – the harder you try, the worse it gets. You've just got to relax and let the girls come to you.

I did watch it though. Like one of those rubbish Sundance movies you get recommended, you hang in there expecting a big payoff but it fizzles out and you feel like you have been ripped off.

The Warriors are ripping me off this season.

The Warriors are up against the toughest team in the NRL, Manly, next week in Perth. I'll be in Vegas. I hope to be blissfully unaware of the Warriors' next capitulation.

Newcastle 24			REFEREES	Gerard Sutton, Adam Devcich
TRIES	Uate, K. Naiqama, Tahu, Gagai		CROWD	15,112
GOALS	Roberts 4/5		VOTES	**3. Boyd** Knights
New Zealand 19				**2. Gagai** Knights
TRIES	Friend, Matulino, Johnson			**1. Taia** Knights
GOALS	Maloney 3/3			
FIELD GOAL	Maloney			

A welcome distraction

South Sydney Rabbitohs *versus* **St George Illawarra Dragons**
7.30pm, Saturday, 21 July
ANZ Stadium, Sydney
GLEN HUMPHRIES

THE LAST COUPLE OF MONTHS HAVEN'T BEEN ENJOYABLE FOR ME. I have spent my time worrying whether or not I still had a job. I was a sub-editor for a newspaper and two months ago it was decided that the sub-editing would be sent offshore to New Zealand. What followed was strikes, talks with the union and nervous hopes that everything would, somehow, be okay. But it wasn't – they decided to go ahead with the New Zealand solution.

I was on edge and nervy throughout the entire process. It's a deeply unpleasant feeling to face the possibility of being made redundant from a workplace you've been at for nearly 20 years. The worry about my family's future was something I carried around with me from the moment I woke in the morning until night-time, when sleep offered salvation and silenced the fear in my head.

It was especially hard to look at my four-year-old daughter. I kept wondering how all of this was going to affect her. Would I still have a job? Would I be able to find another one? Would it be far enough away that I'd have to leave home before she woke up and not get back until after she'd gone to bed – meaning I'd only see her on the weekend? How would she cope going from seeing Dad every day to just two days a week?

In the end I was one of the lucky ones, being moved into a vacant news reporting role. That relieved much of the worry.

Aside from sleep, there was really only one other instance where that inner dread would leave me alone for a while, and that was when the Dragons were playing. I'd stop well short of saying "my team saved me" or some such grandiose statement – because they didn't really.

But they did provide me with a very valuable distraction, a way of losing myself for two hours. And perhaps even venting a bit of frustration at the refs, the opposition and, yes, even my own players (and sadly, the 2012 season has presented too many moments where the Dragons have frustrated me).

It didn't matter that the Dragons weren't very successful during this dark few months for me – they only won one game against the Titans. Nor did it matter that one of those losses was to Canberra in Canberra – a game I desperately, desperately want us to win each year. Their value wasn't in cheering me up (which was just as well) but simply in giving me something else to think about for a few hours. The Dragons matches were a way of checking out for a little while.

Last weekend's win over the Sharks made me start to wonder if the Dragons, too, had just emerged from their recent funk. This game against the Rabbitohs confirmed that they had. They didn't do a lot of scoring but looked more likely to this Saturday than at pretty much any other time this season. It's like they just decided last week to work on their attack while the rest of the comp started doing that before Round 1.

And the Bunnies looked like a team that had spent the year working everything out. The Bunnies are definitely not the joke of the league any more. They won't win the premiership but they'll give the finals a shake.

Finally, the biggest talking point of this match was Greg Inglis' sickening shoulder charge to the head of Dean Young. There is no doubt he should have been marched. He wasn't trying to tackle Young, just put a vicious hit on him. If you're going to use a shoulder charge, you have to take the full consequences when it goes wrong. But rather than send Inglis off, the referees resorted to the cop-out of placing him on report.

Really, putting someone on report is a way of appearing to make a decision while not actually making any decision at all. All it does is pass the buck to the match review committee to actually make a ruling.

And if they suspend Inglis – as they bloody well should – that provides absolutely no benefit to the Dragons, the team against which he committed the offence.

A send off would have.

South Sydney 36

TRIES	Merritt 3; Inglis, King, Everingham, Sutton
GOALS	Reynolds 4/7

St George Illawarra 14

TRIES	Morris 2; Creagh
GOAL	Soward 1/3

REFEREES	Tony Archer, Gavin Morris
CROWD	21,071
VOTES	**3. Reynolds** Rabbitohs
	2. Merritt Rabbitohs
	1. C. Stanley Dragons

The horror

Parramatta Eels *versus* **Melbourne Storm**
7.30pm, Saturday, 21 July
Parramatta Stadium, Sydney

BRETT HUTCHINS

THE ROUND 20 MATCH BETWEEN PARRAMATTA AND MELBOURNE showed all the signs of a sport going slowly insane as it chased its own managerial tail. Over 15 years of mindless corporate management-speak, action plans, free-wheeling ownership structures and internal performance reviews produced the following: the worst run club in rugby league taking on the News Limited moneymen from the most unlikely league city in the western world. The marketers had their work cut out for them: cellar-dwelling incompetence versus an artificially manufactured franchise with a proud history of rorting the salary cap.

Adding idiocy to intrigue, the Eels had just sacked and possibly wrecked the career of yet another coach, Stephen Kearney, just two days earlier. He would be the fifth coach to leave the club in six years, representing an excellent case study in turnstile economics. Ironically, Kearney was signed from the Storm where he had worked for four years as an assistant to Craig Bellamy. Harking back to an age of conscripted military service, discipline was Kearney's credo. His approach did not gel with a club culture more suited to Luna Park than Puckapunyal.

Sitting in the visitor's box, Bellamy was in charge of a team that had lost four of its last five matches, placing a severe dent in his 2012 KPIs. Over the course of several seasons, Bellamy had also managed to 'revolutionise' the code by perfecting techniques of boring violence – wrestling and choke holds – that proved more effective than the entertaining violence that once defined the sport. Close-range observation of the Storm reveals a team with the football ethics of a death adder, especially as player safety is definitely not the No.1 concern when they chase the all-important win.

It was also a cold night at Parramatta Stadium, which summed up my feelings towards the whole wretched event. The last two seasons had been a misery for an Eels supporter who had attended Peter Sterling's alma mater and played junior football (very poorly) in the district junior leagues during the 1980s. Sitting down to voluntarily watch the rightful 2009 premiers capitulate to the Storm summed up the irrationality of football fandom – self-inflicted misery parading as leisure time.

Thankfully, events failed to unfold as predicted. In a radical departure from past tactics, the Eels tackled their opponents for much of the first half and looked almost competent in attack. The fact they led 10-0 after 20 minutes, with tries to Ken Sio and Ben Smith, was simultaneously heartening and dispiriting. It was cause for hope that they were a chance to win only their 10th game out of the last 42. The disappointment was for Stephen Kearney who now knew that the key to motivating the team was for him to leave. A 39th minute Storm try to Rory Kostjasyn at least held out the promise that Kearney's consistent record would be protected.

Yet, the same pattern repeated itself in the second half. Parramatta protected their tryline against set after set of Melbourne attack. Cameron Smith looked frustrated, which is always fun to watch. I even let out a rare yell when Nathan Hindmarsh scored for the Eels with 10 minutes to go, reminded of how much he deserves a premiership that will never arrive. A sense of foreboding emerged when Jarryd Hayne suffered a season-ending knee injury and left the field on a medicab. Melbourne then scored late.

But Parramatta held on for a 16-10 upset.

Normal programming resumed when word filtered through from the Fox Sports commentators that Ricky Stuart was set to take over as Eels coach in 2013. His task is to somehow restore confidence in the Eels brand, with the term brand encapsulating everything that is wrong with the modern game. The prospect of watching Stuart on the sideline screaming forlornly into the abyss is a frightening prospect. My guess is that after a promising first season in charge, the famously intense coach will slowly but surely become league's equivalent of Colonel Kurtz.

"The horror ... the horror" will be the line spoken during group-therapy sessions passed off as Parramatta press conferences.

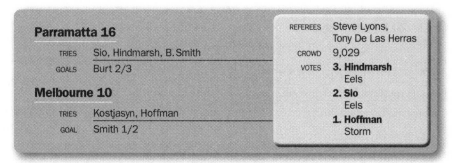

Parramatta 16		REFEREES	Steve Lyons, Tony De Las Herras
TRIES	Sio, Hindmarsh, B. Smith	CROWD	9,029
GOALS	Burt 2/3	VOTES	**3. Hindmarsh** Eels
Melbourne 10			**2. Sio** Eels
TRIES	Kostjasyn, Hoffman		**1. Hoffman** Storm
GOAL	Smith 1/2		

The Sharkies drive in '95

Cronulla Sharks *versus* **Canberra Raiders**
2pm, Sunday 22 July
Toyota Stadium, Sydney

NATHAN BOSS

QUITE LIKE TO WRITE BUT I AM FINDING THAT MY RECENT EFFORTS have been pessimistic and depressing. I need a shot of positivity, so it's best I delve back in time to when I was an optimistic young whippersnapper from the Central West of NSW.

The year was 1995. Urkell was a television icon and Greg Inglis was just a young New South Welshman dreaming of one day representing his beloved Blues. For some reason I devoted myself to the boys from the Sutherland Shire, having no idea at the time the lifetime of pain and suffering that this would cause.

Growing up in country NSW, I didn't get too many chances to see my beloved Sharks in action. So when I looked at the Group 10 draw and saw that an away trip to

Oberon coincided with the Sharks hosting the defending premiers, the Canberra Raiders, at Shark Park, I embarked on a CAN WE GO? campaign that even Lisa and Bart Simpson would be proud of. After constant nagging, I eventually wore down my dad, Peter Boss, Australian hearing and Orange CYMS legend (or 'Divot Head' to those who know him well), and a weekend of adventure awaited.

As we took off, we attempted to disguise our fears that the old white Ford Falcon, affectionately termed *The Boss Mobile* by some, would fail to make it over the Blue Mountains by listening to the recently released Twelfth Man cassette, *The Wired World of Sports*. This was during the time when Billy Birmingham was Australian sporting comedy royalty rather than a *Back Page* panellist. After giving our nostrils a thorough workout in our attempts to blow out the *Wide World of Sport* theme music, we arrived in the backwater that is Oberon.

Everyone hated playing in Oberon. It always rained. The players gave the appearance that they had just spent the past 12 years of their life in Chernobyl. One of their brethren literally had six fingers. Most were blood nuts. They would bite, scratch, pull your hair and rub your face in the mud, which made up 90 per cent of the playing surface. There were no grandstands, no shelter and cold, runny pies. In short, it was very much like the Underworld depicted in the recent *Batman* movie.

We managed to escape with the two points (and, more importantly, all of our limbs) and were off to the Big Smoke to watch the mighty Sharkies. The Cronulla club was seen as an innovator at that time, with Saturday night football proving a massive hit for The Shire faithful. From all reports, it was the place to be as a teenager in the mid-90s, the area behind the hot dog stand being the go-to venue for any extra-curricular activities.

When we arrived at the stadium, I had never seen such a crowd in my life. I surmised that there must have been around 100,000 people in attendance. It was a fantastic night. Hot dogs were eaten. Abuse was hurled. And the Sharks achieved a famous victory, absolutely demoralising the premiers. Little known Sharks Craig Greenhill and Paul Donaghy were my heroes that night, with the latter scoring what was, in my mind, one of the greatest individual tries in the history of rugby league.

But that was then. Today, as expected, we got flogged. The Raiders were dominant, the Sharks listless.

But that takes nothing from my memory of that night in 1995.

Canberra 36		REFEREES	Shayne Hayne, Henry Perenara
TRIES	Croker 2; Williams, Papalii, Ferguson, Dugan	CROWD	12,139
GOALS	Croker 6/6	VOTES	**3. Croker** Raiders
Cronulla 4			**2. Papalii** Raiders
TRY	Taufua		**1. Robinson** Raiders
GOALS	Carney 0/1		

Panthers iron out

Penrith Panthers *versus* **Sydney Roosters**
3pm, Sunday, 22 July
Centrebet Stadium, Sydney

PETER ABELA

I HAVE FOUR KIDS, ALL OF WHOM HAD SOME INFLUENCE ON THE WAY I watched the Panthers match against the Roosters. Two of the kids are babies – under the age of three. They have their dinner and bath early, so watching the Channel Nine coverage at 4pm was out of the question. I hit the record button and kept well away from the television and internet as I went about the business of feeding and watering the tribe. The other two kids are much older and one of them, Ryan, is an ardent Roosters, Dream Team and NRL fan, in that order. He too stayed away from the television so that we could watch the game together.

Ryan has Luke Lewis in his Dream Team, so his ideal outcome would be for the Roosters to flog the Panthers but have Lewis make 50 tackles, score a try or two and make no mistakes. Alas, Lewis suffered a neck injury and was not able to take part in the match, so the first part of Ryan's preferred scenario fell over before it started.

At 7.20pm, all was in readiness. The littlies were in bed and quiet and I was set up in the lounge room with the television, a remote control, Ryan and a week's worth of ironing. Doing the ironing on a Sunday evening earns me enough brownie points that I can watch the football without getting into trouble.

During a tense first 15 minutes, I made little progress with the ironing and Ryan sat pensively on the lounge. Neither of us was confident given the Panthers had lost five on the trot and the Roosters eight of their last nine. I had been telling Ryan all week that the Roosters had no chance, but that was all bluster.

I nearly burned myself on the iron when Brad Tighe just missed scoring off a Luke Walsh kick, but my anguish quickly turned to joy a minute later when Tighe crossed. The Roosters fought back through the middle and latter stages of the first half, being denied a try in the 32nd minute from a very bad forward pass call (and that's the view of a Panthers fan) and then scoring in the 37th minute through Shaun Kenny-Dowall.

By this stage, Ryan was leaning forward in his seat and espousing many of the virtues of the Roosters attack to me. To Ryan's chagrin, they conceded a late penalty, and Lachlan Coote – the experimental five-eighth – made them pay on the stroke of halftime, scything through and putting Matt Robinson over for his first try in the top grade and giving Penrith a 10-6 lead at the break.

Penrith made a very good start to the second half with Michael Jennings continuing his rich vein of post-Origin form. He set up a try for Brad Tighe in the 49th minute and scored a long-range try of his own in the 56th.

After my experience in the Penrith v Parramatta match of calling the result too early, I didn't want to get too confident and downplayed Penrith's chances to a gloomy Ryan. He was having none of it and complained about the Roosters' lack of discipline as he put his freshly ironed school shirt away.

Boyd Cordner managed to cross and narrow the gap, which awakened a few more butterflies in my stomach, but when Brad Tighe crossed in the 69th minute, I thought only a dreadful calamity could bring the Panthers undone.

Travis Burns – the feisty interchange player – did his best to keep Roosters interested, smashing Martin Kennedy across the nose in the 71st minute. This followed a 'chicken-wing' tackle in the first half and resulted in him being sent off, leaving the Panthers with only 12 players for the final proceedings.

When Minichiello scored in the 74th minute, the lead was down to two converted tries and my nerves were really jangling. The Roosters have been involved in two matches so far this season where two tries were scored in the last couple of minutes, and the Panthers have lost numerous games from this position. I must have ironed up and down on the same spot for some time but, fortunately for my wardrobe, Penrith was able to hold on for a well-deserved 28-16 win.

Penrith 28			REFEREES	Ashley Klein, Gavin Reynolds
TRIES	Tighe 2; M. Robinson, Simmons, Jennings		CROWD	9,646
GOALS	Walsh 4/5		VOTES	**3. Walsh** Panthers
				2. Tighe Panthers
Sydney Roosters 16				**1. Jennings** Panthers
TRIES	Kenny-Dowall, Cordner, Minichiello			
GOALS	Anasta 2/3			

On the road to premiership glory

North Queensland Cowboys *versus* **Wests Tigers**
7pm, Monday, 23 July
Dairy Farmers Stadium, Townsville

CLIFF BINGHAM

WE WATCH RUGBY LEAGUE THROUGH MANY PRISMS. At a base level comes that of the footy fan, complete with an appreciation of good quality play, a mockery of cowardice and stupidity and an unyielding hope that your side will see premiership glory. Occasionally, wallets will enter the fray and a multitude of possible financial outcomes arising from the match add a further layer to the viewing experience. Dollar signs, however, are not the only sets of numbers that may be whizzing through the mind of a league fan in 80-minute intervals.

The prospect of reading an NRL Supercoach/ Dream Team-based article may send many eyes rolling into the back of heads at an alarming rate. The good news is that this column will be about neither. The bad news is that, by the end, you may wish that it had been.

Unsatisfied with the notion of having an online salary cap and watching everyone draft Corey Parker, 10 of us embarked on our own fantasy football journey in early March, 2006. The first (and undoubtedly most important) rule – a player can only be contracted to one team at a time. We allow a core group of players to be kept by each club from one year to the next – Greg Inglis may not be a one-club man in the NRL, but I'll be damned if he's ever going to line up against my Tuncurry T-Rexs. Nathan Hindmarsh will retire at the end of 2012 having played for only one club in both the NRL (Parramatta Eels) and the FFL (Otford Orangemen). And so it goes.

After six seasons of limited success (one losing Grand Final appearance being the highlight), the minor premiership fell my way in 2012. As a result, this match didn't just act as the finale to Round 20 of the NRL – it also brought down the curtain on our FFL's major semi-final. The winner would advance to our Grand Final in a fortnight while the loser would get another bite at the cherry in the following week's preliminary final.

As a consequence, I was no longer merely a Cowboys fan for the evening. I was overbearing tennis-father coach, aware of the exploits of Matthew Scott and Aaron Woods, of Kane Linnett and Dallas Johnson. Much like the anchor leg of a 4 x 100 metre relay team, it was left to these four to bring home the bacon. With the fantasy match delicately poised heading into Monday night, the outcome was placed in their hands.

Ordinarily, this would be the place to discuss the glorified game of touch football that was the first half, the dominance of Matthew Bowen and the physical toll the opening stanza inflicted, resulting in the tank registering empty for many players in the final 20 minutes. But that would betray the statistical penchant of this yarn. Instead, I can happily report that the engine room of Woods and Scott was fantastic, while Dallas Johnson almost reached the half-century mark in defence. The upshot of all this was a hard-fought and narrow victory, complete with a pass to the Grand Final and a spot on the precipice of premiership glory.

The combatants, along with footy fans of all persuasions, will have to wait for the last Sunday in September to find out who will reach the pinnacle. By contrast, I am only one week of favourable numbers away from premiership glory.

Such is the benefit of watching rugby league through many prisms.

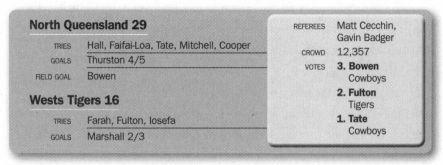

North Queensland 29			REFEREES	Matt Cecchin, Gavin Badger
TRIES	Hall, Faifai-Loa, Tate, Mitchell, Cooper		CROWD	12,357
GOALS	Thurston 4/5		VOTES	**3. Bowen**
FIELD GOAL	Bowen			Cowboys
				2. Fulton
Wests Tigers 16				Tigers
TRIES	Farah, Fulton, Iosefa			**1. Tate**
GOALS	Marshall 2/3			Cowboys

EDITOR'S NOTE *Cliff Bingham and his Tuncurry T-Rexs did indeed go on to premiership glory.*

Round 21

Pay up

St George Illawarra Dragons
versus **Melbourne Storm**
7.30pm, Friday, 27 July
WIN Stadium, Sydney

JOSH SMITH

AM SITTING IN THE GOLD SEATING AT WIN STADIUM watching the Dragons and Storm battle it out. Both teams have a lot to play for, with a loss for the Dragons likely to see them out of finals contention. The Storm started the season with 11 wins from their first 12 matches. They are now staring down the barrel of five straight losses.

As a young kid Dad would take me to the Sharks' home games – back in the day when games were on Saturday or Sunday afternoons. *Big League* in hand, we would arrive at halftime in the reserve grade. This tradition continued for many years until I graduated to attending games with my mates, which seemed to coincide with the Sharks moving to a schedule dominated by Saturday night fixtures.

In my high school years I was one of the few Cronulla supporters. Most were St George fans and there was always ongoing banter between us. Cronulla made the finals in 1995, the Dragons made Grand Finals in the 1990s. Thankfully, they kept losing, but the rebuttal was always: "How many premierships have you won? Where do you keep that Amco Cup?"

Enter the year 2000 and I was offered a job with the Sharks, working as the accountant for the football and leagues clubs. My first season in 2001 saw the Sharks make it to the preliminary final only to lose to the Knights 18-10, a game in which Ben Kennedy dominated as the Sharks attempted to hide Preston Campbell on the wing.

My tenure at the Sharks ended during that offseason and, on parting company, we had a slight disagreement about some funds owing to me. I was never paid this cash and vowed not to support the team I loved from a boy over an acrimonious parting (the sum seems trivial now). I moved on to the Bulldogs and my first season saw the

Bulldogs rattle off 17 straight victories. Then it all crashed around me in August 2002 when the Bulldogs were found to be exceeding the salary cap. Having come out the other side, I left at the end of 2003 for a job out of league.

I had found a soft spot for the Bulldogs (they were paying the bills). Still bitter from the Sharks split and painting myself into a corner, I needed a team. I was living in the St George area, I attended the University of Wollongong and I had fallen into the company of several St George Illawarra fans who were keen to drag me along to games with them. It wasn't long and I found myself here, cheering on the Dragons, albeit still with a soft spot for the Bulldogs and the Sharks.

My involvement in rugby league is back this year with a podcast, *NRL Today*.

That brings me back to my seat at the game. The Dragons are without Jamie Soward, although that means they're a chance to throw the ball around more than they have for the last three years. The Storm have rested five-eighth Gareth Widdop, who has been playing fullback during the Origin period and when Billy Slater is out.

The Dragons get off to a flying start with three tries in the first 25 minutes. The Storm hit back with two tries before the end of the half to lead 18-12 before the break.

St George need to score first in the second half but start poorly and are under pressure when a loose pass is scooped up by Morris who runs the length of the field again for his second try of the match. Five minutes later he's over again and the Dragons look certain winners.

The Dragons put the cue in the rack and the Storm come back strongly. Jason Nightingale is the star in the final quarter, thwarting numerous attacking raids from Smith and Cronk.

They hold on and live to fight another day. Melbourne are reeling.

St George Illawarra 26		REFEREES	Ben Cummins, Chris James
TRIES	Morris 3; Scott, Merrin	CROWD	11,477
GOALS	C. Stanley 3/5	VOTES	**3. Morris** Dragons
Melbourne 18			**2. Young** Dragons
TRIES	Chambers, Hinchcliffe, Proctor		**1. Nightingale** Dragons
GOALS	Smith 3/3		

Empty house

Sydney Roosters *versus* Gold Coast Titans
7.30pm, Friday, 27 July
Allianz Stadium, Sydney

MICHAEL GROSVENOR

'M NOT SURE WHAT IT IS LIKE IN OTHER CODES, but with many Sydneysiders who throw their spare time into matters rugby league, where you grow up doesn't necessarily mean you'll follow the local team. I lived in the Canterbury-Bankstown district until my uni days were complete but my family are lifelong St George supporters and I am a lifelong (well, since I was eight years old) Eastern Suburbs Roosters supporter. That probably says more about me and my family's contrary ways but that's the way it is, has been and will be.

I always had a vision growing up, however, of walking to my local ground to catch the Roosters play every sunny Sunday just like many Bulldogs supporters seemed to do at Belmore Sports Ground or Saints supporters did at Kogarah Jubilee Oval. I got to know a bit about the passion of these loony groups of fans while growing up and begrudgingly admired them for it (please don't tell anyone).

I've now been walking to my local, the Sydney Football Stadium, for well over 10 years. Every second weekend I catch the mighty Roosters. The more exciting the match in prospect, the quicker I walk. I can always tell how many Easts fans are going to be turning up by the number of red, white and blue fans chewing the fat over a schooner or three at the many pubs I pass on the way to the ground. I get a more exact feel for the type of crowd figure we are going to get when I hit the grass of the Moore Park car park. If it's close to full by the time I walk through, I know we are in for a bumper crowd. Or, it could be like it was tonight ... where the pubs and car park were literally empty and I started to question whether I'd mixed up the kick-off time, or even the day?

I get to the ground and, yes, the game is on ... but I feel like I am just about the first one there. The earlier Toyota Cup game has already finished. I arrive at my seat, have the obligatory discussion about our chances with the few season ticket-holder mates (the ones who bothered turning up) and sit back to wait for the players' arrival on the ground. It dawns on me this has to be the quietest, most morbid atmosphere I can ever remember at the SFS. I went to a funeral a few months ago that had a more exciting atmosphere.

I start wondering whether this might affect the Roosters players in getting up for the game. I mean, I am still recovering from the devastating loss to the Rabids a couple of weeks ago, and the players showed last week against Penrith that the cruel loss had hit them hard. My pessimism has well and truly set in for the night. By the time Braith Anasta kicks off, I estimate that they would be lucky to post a crowd of 4,000 (they eventually posted a crowd of 8,000, so obviously they decided to count legs instead of bodies this week).

The match starts well. The Roosters dominate territory because the much-improved kicking game of Pearce and Anasta results in repeat sets. This is the type of Roosters side I've witnessed several times during the year and why I have been so forgiving of them in light of their lowly position on the table. I mean, they had totally outplayed the premiership second-favourites for 38 minutes of the second half only two weeks earlier. Anyway, they race out to a 10-point lead and I am thinking how well they are doing given recent events and the lack of crowd support. This domination actually lasts 30 minutes. But this is a young team that clearly doesn't handle adversity well.

Against the run of play, the Gold Coast field a Pearce bomb and with the help of David Mead's pace travel the length of the field to score a try (to the reborn Scott Prince). Unfortunately for the few Roosters fans who are there to give a damn, this changes the course of the match.

For the next 50 minutes, a combination of growing Titans optimism and Rooster resignation lead to the Titans posting another 30 of the easiest points they'll ever rack up. For the Roosters, it is the type of capitulation that characterised their 2009 wooden spoon performance. After so many close and, at times, very unlucky performances this year, this was the first match in which I sense they actually give up.

But as I trudged back home the way I came, I couldn't help feel that the Roosters players might have found it acceptable to give up because, put simply, the fans had shown them that they also had given up. It was so easy for them to capitulate because when they looked up at the crowd after the first Gold Coast try, they saw, and got, nothing. It made me think ... do the Bulldogs and Dragons fans, when times get tough, just fail to turn up to their beloved local grounds? Maybe, but surely not in the numbers Roosters fans did tonight.

Gold Coast 36			REFEREES	Jason Robinson, Phil Haines
TRIES	Zillman 2; Prince, Idris, Falloon, Srama		CROWD	8,134
GOALS	Prince 6/7		VOTES	**3. Prince** Titans
Sydney Roosters 16				**2. Mead** Titans
TRIES	Arona, Pearce, Aubusson			**1. Bailey** Titans
GOALS	Anasta 2/3			

Superstar

Canterbury Bulldogs *versus* North Queensland Cowboys
5.30pm, Saturday, 28 July
ANZ Stadium, Sydney

JOHN HARMS

HAVE LIVED IN RUGBY LEAGUE COUNTRY AND I HAVE LIVED IN AFL COUNTRY. Even though these days Australians are more ecumenical about football, in some places one code dominates. That ain't rocket science.

After living in Melbourne for six years, where you cannot escape the saturation coverage of AFL footy, we moved to Canberra. I was surprised, at first, at the degree to which rugby league returned to my consciousness. I worked out why. I call it the *Ruled Out Factor*. I have listened to the ABC all my life and, in their news bulletin, they will often have a brief sports item which goes:

> And, finally, in the NRL, Brisbane's Steve Renouf has been ruled out of this weekend's match against Manly with a hamstring injury.

Any sporting news titbit north of The Barassi Line is rugby league. That is not insignificant. It reflects the culture and it entrenches the culture. Living in Melbourne again now, I only know when Brent Renouf has been ruled out.

So, here in the Deep South, I managed to miss the enormity of the Ben Barba phenomenon. I had seen him play and I'd seen him in the many highlights packages, but I now realise that all the May-debate about whether the lad from Mackay should have been selected in the Queensland Origin side was fair dinkum.

I had just assumed that, with Billy Slater around and Mango Bowen the SCG MacGill of rugby league, that the argument was just puff. How could anyone come near Slater?

Watching this game while up in Queensland, I had my eyes opened. I know I'm not telling you anything new, but let me say it anyway: Ben Barba is a sensation. He has pace, evasive skills, a slippery sort of strength and the most remarkable sense of timing.

This was a terrific match between the Bulldogs on a roll and the Cowboys, desperate to hang on to a top four spot and to test themselves against the premiership favourites away from home. It was also a classic example of fullback on fullback.

Although the Queen jumping out of an aeroplane with James Bond captured the world's gaze, the Olympics' opening ceremony was never going to command the focus of true rugby league fans. This match had so much to offer.

It started quietly, two boxers pawing away and then throwing a few jabs. But once it got going, it was on. Not your classic in-the-trenches scrap. More a showcase of crafted attack: fine ball skills and brilliant running.

After 10 minutes, Josh Reynolds probed and sliced through. There was plenty of cover from the forwards dropping back and the wingers edging in and, besides, Matty Bowen was perfectly positioned to deal with the threat. As Reynolds took Bowen's tackle, Barba came from nowhere at top pace. Reynolds popped the Steeden up, Barba burst onto it, swerved between two defenders and ran 40 metres to score. Exhilarating.

The Cowboys fought back. Bowen's grubber bobbled and, on the third bounce, sat up. The Bulldogs defenders were on their heels and Kane Linnett swooped. 6-6.

Both teams looked enterprising when they had the ball; the defences were stretched. Josh Jackson found himself in space and looked around for his fullback. Bang! Again, on the fly, Barba swerved between defenders and sprinted away for another signature try.

The Bulldogs scored again when Krisnan Inu tussled for possession with Cowboys defenders after a bomb: 18-6 at the break.

It was going to take something from North Queensland to get back into the game. James Tamou, who'd had a solid first half, lifted, giving his side good go-forward. Johnathan Thurston started organising his troops and the pressure was on. Barba slipped and was beaten to a kick by Antonio Winterstein, who touched down. Shortly after, Thurston, who had fed his runners all night, threw a dummy, stepped one, stepped another and went in close to the posts. Scores were level.

Inu landed a penalty but, with 10 minutes to go, it was still anyone's game. The Bulldogs established good field position and threatened.

Reynolds' well-weighted up-and-under wound up in the hands of Sam Perrett who lurched over and the Dogs were home.

Barba added another try at the death when he backed up Jackson from close range. That should have been his fourth try. When the game was there to be won, Josh Morris pinned his ears back and charged 60 metres to the corner, only to be brought down by a superb Bowen tackle. Barba was free on his inside.

The Dogs were just that little bit better, made so by a brilliant fullback who can make the most of the hint of an opportunity.

I now get it: Ben Barba is a superstar.

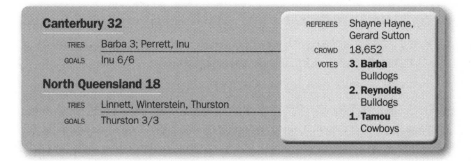

Canterbury 32

TRIES   Barba 3; Perrett, Inu

GOALS   Inu 6/6

North Queensland 18

TRIES   Linnett, Winterstein, Thurston

GOALS   Thurston 3/3

REFEREES   Shayne Hayne, Gerard Sutton

CROWD   18,652

VOTES   **3. Barba** Bulldogs

2. Reynolds Bulldogs

1. Tamou Cowboys

Another cheap surrender

Manly Sea Eagles *versus* New Zealand Warriors
5.30pm, Saturday, 28 July
Patersons Stadium, Subiaco

SAMSON McDOUGALL

GIVEN THERE ARE BUGGER ALL VENUES TO CATCH THE NRL in Melbourne in the grips of AFL season, I'm forced to hit up my Foxtel buddy for a spot on his couch.

The Warriors have been in touch with every team this season, but their tendency to go to sleep in the latter periods of both halves has cost them at least six matches that should've been in the bag, and has them losing touch with the top eight with only a few rounds left. There's a running gag among Warriors fans at this time of year that "every game's a Grand Final". A loss tonight and their finals' aspirations become mathematical.

I find my buddy with a room full of youngsters strewn over the floor, smashing tumblers of goon and playing bad music. My mate rolls his eyes and introduces me to the teenagers. One's apparently his cousin and the others have travelled down from Shepparton to catch a gig in the city this weekend. Much to their disgust (it was like they owned the joint) we flick on the telly and catch the end of the Cowboys-Bulldogs match, which further cements my feeling the Bulldogs will go all the way this year. Despite a gallant effort from the Cowboys, the Bulldogs prove too strong at the death and Ben Barba nabs himself a hat-trick.

We settle. The Warriors start well, as usual, and set up three beautiful tries before the Eagles even know what's hit them. Manu Vatuvei is acting captain due to the absence of Warriors' skip Simon Mannering and I have to say he steps up quickly, gets involved and, through the early stages at least, handles the football more than competently. He inspires some great passages of play – even putting Lewis Brown away for the Warriors' third try via an AFL-style leap and quick pass back to a storming Brown.

Kevin Locke comes in for a mention with a cracking opening score (something he won't be repeating in the near future after going off injured thanks to Anthony Watmough's shoulder wrench which should see the Sea Eagles wild man banned for at least a month). It is Shaun Johnson who picked up the second try with a trademark turn of pace from dummy-half. And then ... the Warriors go to sleep.

As per usual this season, after building a decent lead by halftime, the Warriors succumb to fatigue and a brilliant Sea Eagles kick out of their own quarter. The visitors leak a try right on the halftime buzzer.

Things look up immediately after the break as Manu Vatuvei crosses for a try of his own, blowing the score out to 22-6. Surely there won't be another devastating comeback like last week when the Knights got going?

Again ... the Warriors go to sleep. I'm not even going to describe what happened.

As much hype as there is surrounding Warriors centre Konrad Hurrell's attacking prowess at the moment, there's been little mention of his defensive lapses, of which there have been many – not that he's solely to blame for the Eagles' stunning comeback to win this one.

There is an inherent laziness in this Warriors side that is making them a team of heartbreakers. Sure, the forwards are big and the backs are young, but to squander 18-point leads two weeks in a row, only a few rounds out from finals time, suggests that this team simply doesn't have the intestinal fortitude to make it this year.

What's upsetting is that next year they're losing some marquee players (most notably, utility player Lewis Brown). This was always the year to do it, coming off a losing Grand Final campaign and with a plenty of young talent starting to shine.

But they haven't wanted it enough and once again they prove they can't commit to 80 minutes.

Manly 24			REFEREES	Jared Maxwell, Alan Shortall
TRIES	Cherry-Evans 2; Taufua, D. Williams, K. Foran		CROWD	20,095
GOALS	Lyon 2/5		CROWD	**3. Brown** Warriors
New Zealand 22				**2. Vatuvei** Warriors
TRIES	Locke, Brown, Vatuvei, Johnson			**1. Johnson** Warriors
GOALS	Maloney 3/4			

Culture club

Cronulla Sharks *versus* Penrith Panthers
7.30pm, Saturday, 28 July
Toyota Stadium, Sydney
GRANT VICKERS

I N THE CONTEXT OF THE SEASON, THE LEAD UP TO THIS MATCH between the Sharks and Panthers represented a low point for the Panthers. Luke Lewis, a favourite son of Penrith, had announced he would be leaving the club and would be going to the Sharks. His hand had been forced. Travis Burns had had a couple of brain snaps, copped a lengthy suspension, and looked as though he would never play for the Panthers again. Lachlan Coote, having earlier forced Michael Gordon to make a decision about his future, moved to the halves to replace Burns.

Ivan Cleary and Phil Gould have had a big year. They have done most of their cleaning out of the club and signed a few players for the coming season.

But, in the process, the heart has been ripped out of the side.

Now, only playing to avoid the wooden spoon, it doesn't look like much can go right for the Panthers. Similarly, the Sharks were in their own slump following the Origin series and this hitout against the hapless Panthers seemed just the ticket to get their season back on track.

Fortunately for Panthers fans, the game turned out to be a lot better than expected. Matters were helped when Todd Carney and Paul Gallen were unavailable for the

Sharks. And the Panthers looked like they'd come to play.

A strong performance from the Panthers' forwards helped set up a good platform, and Lachlan Coote was a key factor with two tries.

The exciting match went to extra-time. Luke Walsh, who combined well with Coote all night, slotted the field goal to give Penrith a terrific (and unlikely) victory. There was finally light at the end of a dark tunnel.

However, sitting on my own (a Panthers/Sharks clash on a Saturday night is a hard-sell to all bar the desperate), contemplating the game and Penrith's future hopes, I wondered what could have been. Gould and Cleary (more the former than the latter) have spent the season instilling their own brand of 'culture change' to the club, attempting to turn the fortunes of the Panthers around. Through their handling of some disciplinary issues surrounding Michael Jennings, they managed to alienate some players at the heart and soul of the club. Now Luke Lewis is gone. This is no mean feat, with Lewis having spent his entire career playing for the Panthers, even winning a premiership back in 2003 as a winger. It's the equivalent of Stephen Kearney driving Nathan Hindmarsh from the Eels or Anthony Griffin pushing Darren Lockyer out the door.

This, combined with their handling of the battle between Coote and Gordon for the fullback spot, saw two of the better players in the squad being sent off to the Sharks. After seeing how well Coote performed at five-eighth, it was clear that there was a way to keep Gordon and Coote in the same team and have them both contribute strongly.

Unfortunately, this was not to be and the Sharks will be the beneficiaries of the club's poor decisions next season. Additionally, it seems as though Jennings will be at another club next season (if Gould can find a club willing to pay the big price for his jet boots).

Hopefully Gould doesn't consider losing three Origin and Test representatives through ill-feeling a successful year. Not many fans do.

Still, the win over the Sharks does show that all is not lost and that perhaps the club can rebuild without its star players. Ideally, the noble goal of avoiding the wooden spoon is achievable and once the preseason starts anew, the hopes of a better year will lift the spirits again. With new signings, a very different lineup and the long-awaited culture change, the Panthers can hopefully move up the ladder and even challenge for a spot in the eight. Perhaps this win over the Sharks is the start of the long climb back.

Penrith 21			REFEREES	Gavin Badger, Steve Lyons
TRIES	Coote 2; Jennings, M.Robinson		CROWD	7,848
GOALS	Walsh 2/4		VOTES	**3. Coote** Panthers
FIELD GOAL	Walsh			**2. Walsh** Panthers
Cronulla 20				
TRIES	Leutele 2; Robson, Frizell			**1. Smith** Sharks
GOALS	Townsend 2/4			

The danger seat

Canberra Raiders *versus* **Newcastle Knights**
2pm, Sunday, 29 July
Canberra Stadium, Canberra

BRENDAN PEARSON

ACCORDING TO LEGEND, KING ARTHUR'S KNIGHTS always left one seat vacant at the Round Table. It was known as the 'Siege Perilous' or 'danger seat'. During his two Origin appearances in 2012, Knights winger Akuila Uate was also prone to leaving the danger seat vacant when it came to defusing bombs.

In the first moments of this critical clash against the Knights at Canberra Stadium, the Raiders sent Uate an invitation to the danger seat. Blinded by a shard of sunlight on a cold crisp day, Uate was unconvincing insofar as bomb disposal is concerned. But the error went unpunished.

That was the first and only glimpse of sunshine that the Raiders saw as the clouds closed in Canberra. Within two minutes of his error, Uate had outmuscled Raider winger Reece Robinson to take a terrific mark close to the Canberra tryline and place it over the white chalk. The problem was that the white line was the touchline.

With the aid of regular penalties, enthusiastic running and lethargic defence, the Knights were establishing dominance. After six minutes, a sweeping backline movement and a long cut-out pass found rookie winger Kevin Naiqama over in the left corner. Newcastle was winning the forward battle with Willie Mason unlocking the Raiders' defence with clever offloads. Newcastle was denied again but only after great scrambling defence by Joel Thompson. The trend of the forward battle was not going unnoticed in the coach's box –ineffective Canberra giant Tom Learoyd-Lahrs was replaced by Dane Tilse after only 15 minutes.

After half an hour, Canberra had missed 12 tackles, conceded four line breaks and created none. Canberra's left-side defence was as leaky as a bad government on its last legs. Traffic was running through the Raiders' edges as smoothly as a Canberra morning rush hour. During a rare visit to the Knights' red zone, a deftly judged kick had Uate cornered behind his own tryline. But a shimmy, a jiggle and 11 seconds later he was 98 metres downfield, a metre short of the goalline, a certain try only prevented by Sandor Earl's professional foul. Earl was promptly dispatched to the sin bin.

With halftime approaching, the Knights had been dominant everywhere except the scoreboard. Then impressive young halfback, Tyrone Roberts, tested the Raiders' right edge with a Thurstonian dummy, slicing between McCrone and Papalii, before outrunning Dugan to the corner.

The Raiders' only hope was a rousing halftime address, a strong start and to score first. But in the first ruck, Tom Learoyd-Lahrs' hamstring unravelled and with it Canberra's chances. He was still hobbling from the field when the Raiders turned the ball over. With only 11 functioning opponents on the field, the Knights spun the ball wide to winger Naiqama, whose ears were soon pinned back further than a Beverly Hills matron. Any prospect of a Raiders recovery disappeared and Knights tries followed at regular intervals.

The Canberra crowd that had booed every decision to penalise the Raiders and the failure to discipline the Knights began to focus on the 17 men in lime rather than the two men in pink.

Traditionally, the Raiders have been good at home and terrible away. This can be tolerated – the Canberra faithful relish being part of a forbidding, bitingly cold, green fortress. On the other hand, there is nothing more galling to Raiders supporters than a team that wins well away but then plays badly at home. The Raiders faithful don't appreciate being complicit in an easybeat arrangement. There aren't many natural rewards for spectators on cold, wintry afternoons or evenings at Bruce, but sending more fancied opponents home with a chill and a beating is one of them.

A consolation try which came with 15 minutes to go raised a cheer but no one expected a withering finish and none were disappointed. A 36-6 win gave the Knights the edge in the battle for the final eight. By the game's end, man of the match Akuila Uate had been welcomed back to the Round Table of the NRL's most exciting players.

Canberra coach David Furner was preparing to take his place in the 'siege perilous'.

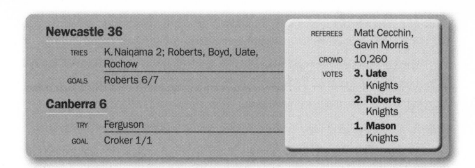

Newcastle 36			REFEREES	Matt Cecchin, Gavin Morris
TRIES	K.Naiqama 2; Roberts, Boyd, Uate, Rochow		CROWD	10,260
GOALS	Roberts 6/7		VOTES	**3. Uate** Knights
Canberra 6				**2. Roberts** Knights
TRY	Ferguson			**1. Mason** Knights
GOAL	Croker 1/1			

An afternoon with Gentleman John

South Sydney Rabbitohs *versus* Wests Tigers
3pm, Sunday, 29 July
ANZ Stadium, Sydney

MARK SHANNON

RUNAWAY BAY SPORTS CLUB IS A GOOD SPOT. A bistro, a pub TAB, a few pokies. But not that nice that you'd drive 25 minutes to get there.

My mate, Steve Wilson, and I have driven past some nicer clubs to get here. The Parkwood Tavern and the palatial Southport Sharks, to name just two. Why?

The man behind the bar, three days beyond his 70th birthday, is none other than the great John Sattler. Four-time premiership captain with South Sydney, four Tests for Australia, three as skipper. His place in rugby league folklore is assured. He played most of the 1970 Grand Final with a broken jaw after being king hit by John Bucknell. He is the personification of courage in rugby league. Every time an injured player leaves the field, his courage is measured against the Sattler yardstick.

An almost perfect career. There is only one piece missing from the puzzle. The 1969 Grand Final, when the Tigers beat Souths in one of the all-time great upsets.

Today's game bears some resemblance to the '69 Grand Final. Souths are on a roll, seemingly unstoppable. The Tigers have limped in with a heavy injury toll and poor form. John says the Tigers limped into the Grand Final in '69. Souths are almost unbackable favourites today, despite the absence of Inglis and Luke.

The result should be a formality. Like '69. Sitting in the grandstand with 'Satts', looking down at the JJ Giltinan Shield, the late, great John O'Neill said: "Why do we even have to play these cats, it is embarrassing, they should just give us the shield now".

When the Tigers hit the front in the last minutes, an incredulous O'Neill turned to Sattler and said: "Satts, these cats are going to beat us."

Today's game is different. Souths score a couple of tries through their hooker, Peats (in for Luke), and Merritt (in for Inglis). Souths have depth as well as ability. They go on with the job in the second half and win easily. The much-maligned John Sutton has a blinder; Crocker, Burgess and Taylor are terrific. Young Reynolds is a revelation.

Sattler is a man from a bygone but not forgotten era. A time when you could go out and water your lawn and leave the lights on inside without having to take out a personal loan to pay the bill. A time when a bottle of beer cost more than a bottle of water. A time when rugby league was a great and brutal game.

John is not a great fan of the modern game. It is too sanitised these days, too many refs. "I can only watch about 15 minutes of a game these days," he says. He still goes down to Souths, talks to the coach and the players. He likes Maguire, Burgess and Inglis. Souths are a good side but he is not sure they can win the comp. He thinks Taylor has ability but he is not a big fan. With that, he is off. "I better go and do a bit, boys."

He does his rounds of the club, talking to the regulars, a smile on his face. Fellow Almanacker Matt O'Hanlon joins us, a bit the worse for wear after a big weekend. He coached Dave Taylor and Tom Humble in their younger days in Blackwater, along with Ben Hunt and his own son, Patrick, now with Parramatta.

He ruefully recounts the day that he managed to get that team beaten by Springsure, courtesy of some ill-timed replacements. He has thousands of footy stories. His dad was a tough backrower for Ipswich in the Bulimba Cup's halcyon days of the 1960s and his grandfather played on the wing for Australia in the 'Battle of Brisbane' back in 1932 before going on to star for Wigan.

They say everyone knows him as 'Satts' and 'Gentleman John'. On this occasion, I reckon they're spot on.

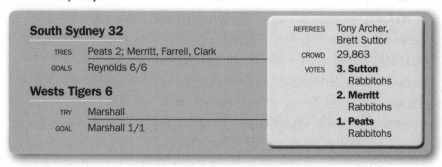

South Sydney 32		REFEREES	Tony Archer, Brett Suttor
TRIES	Peats 2; Merritt, Farrell, Clark	CROWD	29,863
GOALS	Reynolds 6/6	VOTES	**3. Sutton** Rabbitohs
Wests Tigers 6			**2. Merritt** Rabbitohs
TRY	Marshall		**1. Peats** Rabbitohs
GOAL	Marshall 1/1		

The Games we play

Brisbane Broncos *versus* **Parramatta Eels**

7pm, Monday, 30 July

Suncorp Stadium, Brisbane

MICHAEL KENNEDY

I T'S MONDAY NIGHT AND I'M SO STRETCHED I RECKON I'M SEE-THROUGH. Not only am I keeping an eye on this game while staying in touch with the Games of the XXX Olympiad, it also happens to be my weekly tennis comp night. Clearly, I can't watch this game or the Olympics live but, through the wonders of the digital age, I will attempt to check in on live updates from both Brisbane and London.

Tonight I draw on the iconic and inspirational Lord Sebastian Coe, who succinctly stated during the opening ceremony: "You have to love sport to compete at it."

For tonight at least, his words have encouraged me to tackle as much sport as the gods can throw at me because one fact I'm sure of is that I do love sport.

My tennis team is called *Highly Strung*. Tonight the name seems more apt than usual. It's a mixed team and my two fellow players are not fellows at all, with one of the fillies being my delightful sister-in-law. We're up against *The Hornets* and, as luck would have it, they're the No. 1 team. Perfect!

Conditions for tennis are less than ideal. Blizzard-like squalls sweep across the court making us question, yet again, the wisdom of playing winter competitions. Between games we huddle in the cabana discussing the psychology of nemeses and bunnies, the scoop shot and the best way to marinade and barbecue pork. Half-listening, I badger my smart phone for the latest from Brisbane and London. So much for technology – not a pixel, byte or bar in sight!

With little or no reception, all I can manage is a short desperate text message to a mate in Adelaide who replies with a halftime score of 30-6 to the Eels. I can only assume he is kidding and throw the phone down in a frosty fug of frustration.

Back on the court, I'm now set for my singles matchup. Despite being reasonably competitive, our team is down 3-0. Not feeling in the best form of my career, I need to fire up! Lacking in many ball-skill facets, I usually counteract by finding and exploiting my opponent's Achilles heel. This time it's his fitness (or lack of) so I do what I can to make him run. It's keeping me in the game and at 4-4, I have the edge. Unfortunately, a crucial break of serve results in a 6-4 loss.

It's now after 9.30pm and my message mate informs me that the Eels, the Golden Eels, have beaten the Broncos 42-22. Astonishing! The last time the Eels scored that many points, Sterlo had hair and Twitter was something birds did. Suddenly my loss in the tennis seems as relevant as a parliamentarian's promise. My sister-in-law, obviously inspired by the Blue and Gold, has gone on to win her singles in a nail-biting tie-breaker, so we at least finish the night with a small victory.

The greater victory is learning the details of the Eels' night. It's the first brace of wins for the season and all against a tumultuous background of coach-chopping and spoon-stirring. It's as if the HSC is done with a couple of weeks of school to see out – the pressure is off, so let's just have a bit of fun.

As for tennis, *Highly Strung* will return next Monday night to pursue our dream of winning the comp. In the meantime, it will be a sleepless week watching the elite athletes of the world putting everything on the line. For hackers such as myself, I'm reminded that perhaps holding that medal or trophy is not as important as holding onto the dream of it.

Parramatta 42		REFEREES	Ashley Klein, Tony De Las Herras
TRIES	Sandow 2; Burt, Moimoi, Poore, Sio, N. Smith	CROWD	22,626
GOALS	Burt 7/7	VOTES	**3. Maitua** Eels
Brisbane 22			**2. Sandow** Eels
TRIES	Capewell, Maranta, McCullough, Norman		**1. Burt** Eels
GOALS	Wallace 3/3, Norman 0/1		

Round 22

Two years is a long time in football

Sydney Roosters *versus*
St George Illawarra Dragons
7.30pm, Friday, 3 August
Allianz Stadium, Sydney

MARTY SPENCER

AFTER ROUND 21, 2012		
1	Bulldogs	14-5
2	Rabbitohs	13-6
3	Storm	12 7
4	Cowboys	11 8
5	Broncos	11 8
6	Sea Eagles	11 8
7	Sharks	10-8-1
8	Titans	9-10
9	Knights	9-10
10	Tigers	9-10
11	Dragons	9-10
12	Warriors	8-11
13	Raiders	8-11
14	Roosters	6-12-1
15	Panthers	6-13
16	Eels	5-14

THE MEDIA FOCUS PRIOR TO THE DRAGONS-ROOSTERS CLASH was on the exclusion of Dragon five-eighth Jamie Soward. He had suffered from back spasms prior to last week's match against the Storm, which allowed Nathan Fien to star in that role and helped secure a timely victory for the Dragons.

Steve Price's decision to omit him from the NRL team to play the Roosters forced Soward's hand. He insisted he be allowed to play with the Dragons' feeder team, the Illawarra Cutters. Price was then forced to defend his working relationship with Soward. All of this was an unwelcome distraction for the Dragons who were seeking to keep their ailing finals hopes alive.

Players are dropped every week yet the media tends to focus on the internal workings of a club, particularly underperforming clubs where the coach's security of tenure is under scrutiny. As a long-time Dragons supporter, I would prefer to see analysis of the performance of the club and of individuals within the club rather than speculation about the 'internal ructions' which the media and the ever-burgeoning blogspert brigade trot out.

Much of the criticism of Soward's game relates to his cross-field running and poor defence yet Nathan Fien, despite playing well at five-eighth, shares those attributes with him. The real cause for concern is the Dragons' inability to convert scoring pressure into tries. A lack of imagination in attack and failure to execute at crucial times cost the Dragons on a number of occasions. The only time the attack assumed any potency was in the 10-minute period when the Roosters were reduced to 12 men after a professional foul by Joseph Leilua. The Dragons ran in two tries to get themselves back into the game. Crucially, the last play of the first half and the first play of the second half were the difference between the teams.

When a Dragons decision to run the ball out from their own quarter in the 40th minute went awry, the Chooks scored under the posts. The Dragons went from going in at halftime down 0-6 to being down 0-12. Compounding this, Nathan Fien knocked on from the kick-off and from the ensuing set of six the Dragons conceded a penalty in front, and the score was 14-0.

Both teams were willing but at times were going through the motions of set after set. Merrin and Hunt worked hard but need to add the offload to their respective repertoires. Josh Miller was knocked out in the 42nd minute after a fearless yet clumsy tackle on Kennedy and, despite looking like Zab Judah after a Kostya Tszyu left-right combination, was initially given the all clear by training staff to remain afield. This decision was even more remarkable given that he subsequently failed a cognitive assessment and has been ruled out of this week's match against the Tigers.

It is hard to imagine that these two teams competed in the 2010 NRL Grand Final, with the Roosters no longer in contention and the Dragons now forced into sudden death every week. For the Chooks, maligned halfback Mitchell Pearce, despite scoring three tries, must strive to be more creative if he is to retain the NSW No. 7 jersey.

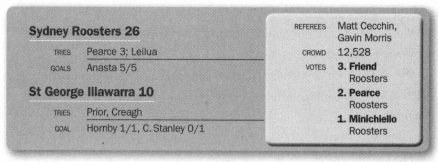

Sydney Roosters 26		REFEREES	Matt Cecchin, Gavin Morris
TRIES	Pearce 3; Leilua	CROWD	12,528
GOALS	Anasta 5/5	VOTES	**3. Friend** Roosters
St George Illawarra 10			**2. Pearce** Roosters
TRIES	Prior, Creagh		**1. Minichiello** Roosters
GOAL	Hornby 1/1, C. Stanley 0/1		

Love of the game

Melbourne Storm *versus* Penrith Panthers
3.30pm, Saturday, 4 August
AAMI Park, Melbourne

MICHAEL ADAMS

AVING SPENT THE MAJORITY OF MY WORKING LIFE in the alcohol-selling racket, missing out on watching sporting events has become a regular misfortune. This year, the final year of my Masters degree (to hopefully free me of this burden), it has been even harder to get my weekly sporting fix. Though my passion hasn't waned at all, it has become increasingly rare that I am able to just sit in front of the TV to watch some footy, let alone get out to games. It's been tough.

And so it is I find myself behind the bottle shop counter on a sunny Sydney Saturday, tuning into Grandstand for a rare Saturday afternoon match. Sending my underling up to the storeroom to complete some thankless busywork, which should keep him out of my hair for a couple of hours, I settle in for a lazy arvo of footy on the radio.

At least that was the plan. Visualising how my day would go, I had neglected to factor in the single most frustrating element of my job: customers. I am quickly jolted back into reality, however, when, just before kick-off, a local deadshit enters the shop. A frequent visitor, her faded arm tats and drawl suggest she would be more at home cheering on the Panthers than arguing with me about the price of Woodstock & Cola cans.

She's having none of it though and we spend the next several minutes engaged in a highly intellectual debate. There is some commotion in the background as the radio commentators ramp up the intensity and it appears that Melbourne has scored barely two minutes in. I finally shake off this thirsty woman just as Melbourne score again. It appears the poor Panthers are in for a long day.

So am I, it turns out. I have some lovely regulars who come into the shop to discuss music or sport and generally make life more pleasant. They seem to have deserted me today, however, while the confederacy of idiots who do their best to ruin every shift seem to have organised to arrive at the same time.

We're right on halftime now and, unfortunately, I have no idea of the score. I have heard the words "Cooper Cronk" mentioned on the radio a thousand times already though, which suggests Melbourne is doing well. My suspicions prove accurate and

Melbourne goes to halftime well ahead. During the break I experience the greatest joy I get from my job: arguing with elderly Greek men about the price of VB. Due to the changing prices we are charged for it, we were forced recently to raise the price of a case by a dollar, and the ensuing pandemonium has been most entertaining. So when a grey-haired man with a Vincent Price moustache enters the shop, I brace myself.

"How much for the VB small bottles?"

"Thirty-four dollars."

"Why?"

He forces this last word out with a bitter fury in his eyes, as if I raised the price as an insult to him, his family and everything he stands for. After four years on the job, however, I know that Newtonian principles apply and I must return serve with equal force. I won't budge, not for a cent and, after a brief Mexican standoff, he relents.

"Give me one box."

I take his money, fetch the beer from the coolroom and take it out to the old man's car. The scowl on his face has been replaced with a wry smile and he thanks me warmly. I have a feeling he enjoys the game just as much as I do.

Back to the footy, and Melbourne is in again. It must be about a billion to nil by this stage, but I've given up trying to keep up. The poor old Panthers finally cross for a consolation try and the Panthers are done. Three more hours and I will be, too.

Melbourne 46		REFEREES	Ashley Klein, Adam Devcich
TRIES	Waqa, O'Neill, Cronk 2; Bromwich, Manu	CROWD	9,223
GOALS	Smith 7/8	VOTES	**3. Cronk** Storm
Penrith 6			**2. Waqa** Storm
TRY	M.Robinson		**1. Smith** Storm
GOAL	Walsh 1/1		

The Knights of the lower table

Newcastle Knights *versus* **Canterbury Bulldogs**

5.30pm, Saturday, 4 August

Hunter Stadium, Newcastle

ADAM DONNELLY

I N A TOWN FULL OF BEAUTY, THE FOOTBALL STADIUM may be the most beautiful thing in Newcastle. How great a stadium it is dawned on me as I took my seat in the newly constructed stand for this game on a crisp, cool Saturday night. It was the most elevated I'd been for a league game, looking down on the corner post with a great perspective. With an hour before the first whistle, at both ends of the paddock the two hills were filling quickly, generous patches of blue and white among the blue and red.

Six days previously, I'd been at ANZ Stadium. The sheer enormity of that stadium dwarfed me, while the Tigers' game made me want to hide under the seat. Sitting in the Hunter Stadium with my box of chips, Coke and Mars bar, I could smell the woodfires burning in New Lambton, saddled next to the stadium. I wasn't just there as an unaligned observer, I had an agenda of my own. I wanted to see the Knights get smashed.

My general ambivalence towards the Knights had turned into an open dislike over the course of the season. The appointment of Wayne Bennett had caused a swelling of heads in the town, many fairweather Knights fans I knew acting like the 2012 premiership was guaranteed. The dislike turned into open *schadenfreude* as the season failed to fire and began to falter. I didn't mind saying: "Tinkler has tried to buy a trophy and ended up with a spoon instead." The Knights' losing streak had sat many a local on their backside but, when the Knights bashed my Tigers in Round 13 as I sat dejectedly on the hill, some of my mates acted like the Knights had won the Grand Final.

While it is hard to rise above the belligerence of tribal identification in rugby league, I'm a fan of Des' Dogs simply because I'm a fan of rugby league. In particular, I've loved Josh Reynolds' season. Although lacking others' freakish talent, he comes across as a player who has made his own luck. I respect his competitive attitude.

The first 20 minutes of this game was a blitzkrieg and, for my money, almost perfect rugby league from the Bulldogs. Romelo and Wright crossed and I enjoyed the Reynolds pizzling of Darius Boyd when he got his meat pie through some fairy-floss defence. Among the blue and white faithful around me there was excited chatter that if the Dogs kept it up, it'd be a 40-0 trouncing, maybe 50-0.

Any hope the Knights would be embarrassed in their own kingdom was put to bed when Akuila Uate scored. It's a special thing in the Hunter Stadium when Uate touches the ball. The sheer roar of excitement when he gets in the clear and opens the throttle is scintillating and, even though Aku wore the dunce's cap in State of Origin, he is Newcastle's favourite son.

After halftime, it appeared the Knights had drunk their Staminade. The Dogs were denied ball, Uate posted his second and Mason made several barnstorming runs with every Knights fan urging him on. Four line dropouts kept the pressure on, but the Dogs were simply too well-drilled, too strong. The Dogs made it 10 in a row and I felt quite content as I left the game for a big feed of Mexican at the packed Wests Lambton Leagues club as Bulldogs guernsey sat next to Knights guernsey at the pokies in a strange peace.

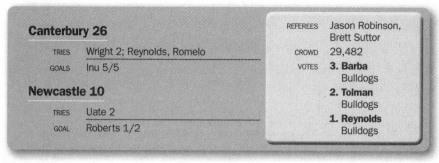

Canterbury 26		REFEREES	Jason Robinson, Brett Suttor
TRIES	Wright 2; Reynolds, Romelo	CROWD	29,482
GOALS	Inu 5/5	VOTES	**3. Barba** Bulldogs
Newcastle 10			**2. Tolman** Bulldogs
TRIES	Uate 2		**1. Reynolds** Bulldogs
GOAL	Roberts 1/2		

Tate sets a standard

North Queensland Cowboys *versus* Manly Sea Eagles
7.30pm, Saturday, 4 August
Dairy Farmers Stadium, Townsville

IAN HAUSER

NORTH QUEENSLAND AND MANLY ARE TWO TEAMS THAT CAN TURN IT ON and are likely to feature in September. Both can be entertaining. Both can play it tough. Up here in Queensland, one is much-loved, the other you can hardy hear a civil word about. This match showed me these things:

- There are few more competitive players in the NRL than Brent Tate;
- It really is easy to dislike Manly;

- Grind and free-flowing play can exist in the same game;
- The very good teams find a way to win in the end;
- Did I mention that I can't stand Manly? Although I will make exception for Cherry-Evans, Ballin and, possibly, George Rose.

At halftime, the commentators suggested that this had been an ugly 40 minutes of footy. *What crap!* Yes, the forwards engaged in a bash-a-thon, but it was hard, up-the-middle, straight running to make good metres. Both sides used their go-forward to set their backs loose with Cherry-Evans and Thurston providing Lyon and Tate with space for pace. Gains of 50 metres or more per set plus kick were the norm. *Ugly?* Utter rubbish. It may have been only 6-0 at the break but Manly had one try that was correctly disallowed for obstruction and saved a couple at the other end through crunching defence. It could easily have been about 16-10.

Part two was not dissimilar. Both sides looked for the holes to open but kept finding them closed on arrival. The Cowboys scored through a defensive lapse after a bomb; Manly counter-attacked but couldn't breech the wall. The Cowboys conceded a silly penalty on the fifth tackle (a coach's worst nightmare) followed by another for an unlucky offside which gave Manly two points and enough to win the game. The Cowboys' late surges were brought undone by poor options and a desperate defence.

Why is Manly unlovable? Think Matai, Watmough, Stewart (multiplied by two), Kite, Williams (T), Lussick, *et al*. This team has so much pure talent that they don't need to bother with the bully-boy tactics to which they often resort. They didn't intimidate the Cowboys or run over the top of the boys from the north. Instead, they conceded stupid penalties and easy metres.

Why don't they let their mobile forwards run and allow Cherry-Evans and Foran to spread the ball more to unleash the talents of Stewart (B), Lyon, Williams (D), Taufua and Matai? In full flight, they'd be irresistible.

Brent Tate set the standard in both attack and defence. His one-on-one defence against Matai was worth the ticket, a delightful sub-plot in proceedings. Matai dishes it out but he would have been a sore boy after Tate's job on him in this game. In attack, Tate ran just as aggressively and made huge yardage. He allowed his talent to speak for itself. Maybe there's the lesson for the Manly glamour boys to take to heart. We wonder up here whether they have that sort of self-knowledge.

In the end, Manly defended well enough to protect their narrow margin. Good teams do that, but it doesn't make them any more likeable!

Manly 8			REFEREES	Shayne Hayne, Gerard Sutton
TRY	K. Foran		CROWD	14,401
GOALS	Lyon 2/2		VOTES	**3. Tate**
				Cowboys
North Queensland 6				**2. Thurston**
				Cowboys
TRY	Linnett			**1. Cherry-Evans**
GOAL	Thurston 1/1			Sea Eagles

Testing the faith

New Zealand Warriors *versus* Cronulla Sharks
2pm, Sunday, 5 August
Mt Smart Stadium, Auckland

ANDREW SMITH

I WAS FORTUNATE ENOUGH TO HEAD ALONG TO THE FINAL WARRIORS team training on Saturday, the day before the Sharks game. The club put on a barbie and we sat in the stand at Mt Smart as 'Bluey' put the boys through their paces.

We had the privilege of listening to Kiwi legend Ruben Wiki say a few words along with Captain Mannering and, finally, Coach McClennan. He explained what the training had been about and how they were focussing on countering the Sharks.

Well, what a waste of time that turned out to be.

I'm not sure if it was the fact it was a final training session the day before game day or they were distracted by the fans watching, but their intensity at training matched the horror show that was to be Sunday's game.

I hope that all team trainings aren't as shambolic as what I witnessed. If so, then the finger can squarely be pointed at McClennan. I'm surprised that Big Rubes stands for it in his role as trainer, being such a talismanic figure in the team. It beggars belief.

On a positive note, the team hung around after training to meet the fans. It was great to rub shoulders with them and the commitment they showed taking photos and signing autographs was top notch. It's a pity this doesn't translate to performances on the field.

Leaving the training session, I was stoked after meeting the boys who make up the team I support with the passion of a religious zealot.

I was confident that the recent run of poor form would be turned around and that we would start our late-season charge to the finals. A mate of mine thinks that the Warriors only perform once they are in a must-win scenario. Maybe he is onto something as, after this Sharks shocker, we are now well and truly in the mire.

What transpired on a nice Sunday afternoon at Mt Smart was a massacre, the second worst loss at home in Warriors history.

I have never left a game prior to fulltime. Until today. With 14 minutes remaining, I had endured enough punishment. I tossed in the towel. I wasn't the only one. For many years, the Warriors' catchphrase has been "keep the faith". I have this faith by the bucket load but a man has his limits.

It was not the fact that the boys lost. As a Warriors supporter, I am well and truly used to that. It was the way that we lost. We were pathetic. We didn't just give up, we were never up to begin with.

I felt like they had personally let me down. After being there to help them prepare and wish them all the best the day before, my bond to the team had become so much stronger. So I took this loss hard.

There are still two home games to go this season and I will be there for them. However, after the rollercoaster ride of the past few weeks, it takes a special fan to keep coming back for more.

I hope for the sake of the many young and inexperienced players in the side that this game is the lowest of lows for the team. The potential they have is significant but, now they know how it feels to hit rock bottom, I hope they make a promise to themselves to do everything in their power to never experience it again.

As for me, there is always the chance that my mate's must-win thesis plays out. I will probably convince myself that it will happen. Most people would call me crazy and I cop a lot for my support of the Warriors, but there is nothing like it and anyone with the faith will tell you the same thing.

Cronulla 45		REFEREES	Tony Archer, Alan Shortall
TRIES	Williams, Carney, Fifita 2; Robson	CROWD	13,812
GOALS	Carney 8/8	VOTES	**3. Carney** Sharks
FIELD GOAL	Carney		**2. Fifita** Sharks
New Zealand 4			**1. Gallen** Sharks
TRY	Tupou		
GOALS	Henry 0/1		

Notes from the Wagga RSL

Canberra Raiders *versus* Brisbane Broncos
2pm, Sunday, 5 August
Canberra Stadium, Canberra

ANDREW BOMM

HHH, THE GOOD OL' WAGGA RSL. SO MANY MEMORIES. It probably started with the Wagga Wagga High School Year 10 formal. Oh Cassy, how I loved you. Then, unusually, it was the focus of a Year 11 geography assignment.

I never got what geography was really about and nothing exemplified the fact better than my geography assignment on the changing faces of the Wagga RSL. The summer after I finished Year 12, I used to go down and win beer tickets playing sports trivia. The old regulars hated it, but if they don't know who we played Test cricket against for the first time in 1956, then stiff cheddar to them. On a return visit while at uni, there were cigars, good times and stories best kept to myself.

But on this particular Sunday afternoon, it's the Raiders versus the Broncos from tropical Bruce Stadium in Canberra. When I lived in Canberra, I loved going to Bruce on a midwinter's Saturday night and seeing an ordinary Raiders outfit defeat better credentialed teams in -2° in front of 6,000 hardy souls. The official attendance would always be listed at 9,000, no matter how wildly misleading that assessment was. Then the club apparently complained about the poor gate-takings and Saturday nights became a rarity. Shame.

Anyway, the RSL sport-on-TV precinct is really jumping this afternoon. Some 12 of the 13 are primed for league, while there is a lone gentleman glued to the riveting Gold Coast Suns versus Melbourne AFL yawn. They appear to be lawn bowlers from the tournament going on outside, dragged away from the play and the beguiling alternative of pokies to sit around and banter about rugby league.

As the game is about to start, a young Chinese couple begin playing pool adjacent to us, speaking loudly in what is presumably Mandarin. We're in a country RSL full of ageing men and nobody bats an eye. Times have changed for the better in Australia.

Enough of that and onto the game which is being covered by Fox. The Raiders on pay TV? The volume is down so I satisfy myself pondering the dreadfulness of the Broncos' caramel strip and wondering how to pronounce the name of the Raiders'

Chinese sponsor. Perhaps I should ask the couple playing pool, but I'm no Kevin Rudd on the Mandarin. Boy, the Raiders have had some strange sponsors. I remember when the CFMEU was sponsoring them and the crowd at a home game against Easts had to endure a Work Choices demonstration as halftime entertainment. That letter of complaint was one of my best ever.

The contest starts slowly, punctuated by a couple of Gavin Badger howlers that facilitate the Broncos' first try. Then a soft try from Waddell evens things up. Wait, the conversion from point blank hits the post! 6-4.

"Ordinary game of football," says one of the lawn bowlers wearing a purple and white shirt. He's right, although I can't help thinking that lawn bowls has gone all World Series Cricket on us.

To my right, one of the lawn bowlers starts nodding off. He's momentarily startled by the RSL's 'Calamity Key' promotion for those upstairs sitting on the pokies. But come the 35-minute mark and he's off again. The ribbing starts from his mates.

"Haven't you blokes been to sleep in front of the TV before?" he retorts.

[NOTE TO SELF: *you don't get kicked out of the Wagga RSL for going to sleep on the drink.*]

Still 6-4 at halftime and the game is not living up to even my modest expectations.

After the break there's a little action. Croker scores off a high ball that Hoffman misses because of a lack of intensity. At the 51-minute mark, Dugan finds the sideline with a dropout from a wicked off-break. Compounding the malaise from the Broncos, they fail to find touch from a penalty and a try to the Raiders ensues on 56 minutes.

Glenn gets an easy one and Brisbane gets back into it but then it's all Raiders. An appalling forward pass call from Badger costs the Raiders a try at 70 minutes but then Dugan gets over and that's it. Dugan crosses again and it's the Raiders easily.

I cast my eye across the *World Series bowling*.

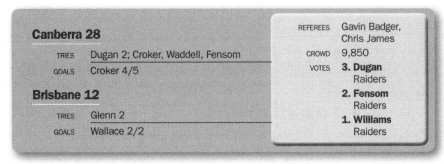

Canberra 28

TRIES	Dugan 2; Croker, Waddell, Fensom
GOALS	Croker 4/5

Brisbane 12

TRIES	Glenn 2
GOALS	Wallace 2/2

REFEREES	Gavin Badger, Chris James
CROWD	9,850
VOTES	**3. Dugan** Raiders
	2. Fensom Raiders
	1. Williams Raiders

Closing the gap

Gold Coast Titans *versus* South Sydney Rabbitohs
3pm, Sunday, 5 August
Skilled Park, Gold Coast

PAUL DALLIGAN

HERE WE ARE, ROUND 22 AND THE PRIDE OF THE LEAGUE. My battlers from Struggle Street arrive on the Gold Coast riding high on the back of a five-game winning streak. Round 22 was declared by the NRL to be CLOSE THE GAP ROUND in order to highlight indigenous heritage and also to bring attention to the difference in life expectancy between Indigenous and non-Indigenous Australians. Sadly, it stands at more than a decade.

The CLOSE THE GAP slogan was more than appropriate for the Rabbitohs as their season had been ignited when new coach Michael Maguire made the bold decision (at that time) to move their own indigenous star Greg Inglis from his usual position in the centres (where he had great success with the Storm) to the custodial role at fullback. It seems, in hindsight, that the gap between the perennial strugglers in red and green and the class teams of the league was significantly narrowed from that point forward.

Inglis would prove throughout this fine season of NRL to be such a revelation for the Bunnies that amazingly some were saying that Billy Slater's iron-like grip over the Queensland and Australian No. 1 jerseys may have been in danger. Sadly, Inglis wasn't playing in this vital matchup due to suspension. His replacement, Nathan Merritt, is also of Indigenous heritage and grew up in the shadows of Redfern Oval.

But it wouldn't be all smooth sailing for the Rabbitohs on the Gold Coast. The land known for nightclubs and skimpily-clad meter maids is also now the home of one fine football team which boasts flying wingers, proven hard men, classy halves and exciting rookies. In Scott Prince, Greg Bird, Nate Myles, Luke Bailey, Jamal Idris and wonder-kid Aidan Sezer, there was more than enough talent on show to stop the Bunnies' resurgence in its tracks.

The Titans also got a glimpse of Souths' Dave Taylor, the Titans' big signing for 2013 and a player who would prove to have a big 135kg impact on this game. There surely would never have been a scarier sight for the Titans wingers and centres than the big man lurking on the fringes and charging like someone had just pushed through the doors to the all you can eat buffet at Jupiters.

The first half was a tough encounter right from the kick-off with Souths' best forward Sam Burgess collecting the Titans flyer William Zillman with a high shot in the second minute. Big Sam arrived in fine form and had been swallowing up the metres. Thankfully for the Bunnies faithful, he stayed on the field after the high shot.

The Titans scored first and Scott Prince landed the conversion from so far wide of the posts that he may as well have been kicking it from his waterfront mansion.

But the Rabbitohs surged back through unanswered tries to Dylan Farrell, Andrew Everingham and Justin Hunt (two) to set up a 16-point lead with 20 minutes to go. The locals were, however, in no mood to lie down like a dancer from the nearby nightclubs and a crowd of over 20,000 sensed a comeback of, dare I say it, Titanic proportions.

In the 72nd minute the man many say is the next Brad Fittler, the Titans five-eighth Aidan Sezer, combined with his seasoned partner Scott Prince to create a try under the posts. For a man who many say is too big to be a fine half, he sure looked nimble enough to me.

It was at this point this Rabbitohs fanatic of 30 years became mega-nervous. This was the type of unloseable game the Bunnies have managed to lose on many occasions over the years. But maybe this 2012 team is different, and maybe all of that hard luck and tragedy is behind us with more than a healthy dose of a winning culture instilled by Coach Maguire.

And just maybe the gap between mere hope and actual success isn't that far away. While the Titans crossed for another try in the closing minutes, the Rabbitohs defended like their lives depended on it and held off the spirited Titans to win 22-18.

While the biggest Rabbitoh, Dave Taylor, will be in Titans colours in 2013, before he departs he may be able to share in the moment we at Redfern have been waiting for for 40 years.

South Sydney 22		REFEREES	Ben Cummins, Phil Haines
TRIES	Hunt 2; Farrell, Everingham	CROWD	20,187
GOALS	Reynolds 3/4	VOTES	**3. Taylor** Rabbitohs
Gold Coast 18			**2. S. Burgess** Rabbitohs
TRIES	Gordon, Michaels, Sezer		**1. Prince** Titans
GOALS	Prince 3/3		

Superstitious

Wests Tigers *versus* **Parramatta Eels**
7pm, Monday, 6 August
Campbelltown Sports Stadium

DANIEL BOSS

THE BIGGEST QUESTION FACING ME THIS MORNING was whether I should again wear my Tigers jersey over my shirt and tie to work. I had done this for the previous three Tigers games on Monday night. They all ended in disaster. I decided against wearing the jersey as I felt that it was cursed. Mind you, I'm not some superstitious supporter like my brother Nathan, who truly believes that if he wears the majority of his Sharks jerseys while they play, then the Sharks will lose.

I put the jersey on as soon as I got home.

For the majority of 2012, I have been apathetic in supporting the Tigers. This is because we've been crap and heartbreaking finals exits over the past two seasons haven't helped either. However, for this game I was the most excited I've been for weeks.

This was a big game for both teams as the Tigers were looking to keep their finals hopes alive and Parramatta were looking to get off the bottom of the ladder. I was hoping that Parramatta would avoid the wooden spoon as Nathan Hindmarsh and Luke Burt deserve better. But not at the expense of the Tigers. Surely not.

On the way home from work, it was fitting that Bon Jovi came on as they do sing the theme song for the NRL and Wests' season really was living on a prayer. While I was fairly confident, there were a few nerves as the Tigers were without star centre Chris Lawrence and young gun Curtis Sironen. The selection of Liam Fulton at five-eighth was a good move as he possesses underrated ball skills and helps solidify the defence. As for Parramatta, they had back-to-back wins against teams in the top eight. They were playing carefree football and were looking to impress incoming coach Ricky Stuart. I was very wary of them. Still, they were without Jarryd Hayne. Surely the Tigers could not lose to a Parramatta team without Jarryd Hayne.

The Tigers got off to a flying start through an early try to Adam Blair. However, a 40/20 from Chris Sandow helped give the Eels the momentum and they poured on four tries in 15 minutes. In a sickening sight for Tigers supporters, young gun Jake

Mullany (who might have stayed at the Tigers if he were given a go) scored two of those tries. Parramatta was completely on top, showing the form that had won them their previous two.

The Tigers bounced back to score two tries prior to halftime to get the margin back to four points. While the attack in the first half was of a high standard, the defence was simply appalling.

According to Andy Raymond, the focus of the halftime talks from both coaches was on defence. Tim Sheens would have barely reached his seat when Taulima Tautai crossed for the Eels. What was even more surprising was that the Tigers went for two short kick-offs back-to-back at the start of the second half. Is this why they signed Braith Anasta? It looked like Parramatta would score again from a chip and chase from Sandow but, five metres out from the line, second-game winger Marika Koroibete came up with a Darrell Eastlake *huuuuuuuuuuuge* tackle to force a mistake. That was the turning point in the game as Wests scored six unanswered tries to win 51-26, which included four to Koroibete.

In summary, this was two points for the Tigers. A bit stressful for supporters (nothing new for Tigers fans) but they showed that if (and that's a big if) their defence improves, they have the potential to make some noise in September. As for Parra, they have the attack to trouble some teams in the final four weeks.

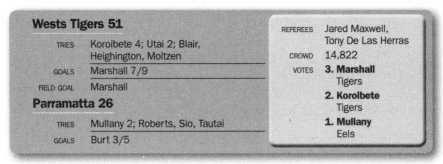

Wests Tigers 51			REFEREES	Jared Maxwell, Tony De Las Herras
TRIES	Koroibete 4; Utai 2; Blair, Heighington, Moltzen		CROWD	14,822
GOALS	Marshall 7/9		VOTES	**3. Marshall** Tigers
FIELD GOAL	Marshall			**2. Koroibete** Tigers
Parramatta 26				**1. Mullany** Eels
TRIES	Mullany 2; Roberts, Sio, Tautai			
GOALS	Burt 3/5			

Round 23

AFTER ROUND 22, 2012		
1	Bulldogs	15-5
2	Rabbitohs	14-6
3	Storm	13-7
4	Sea Eagles	12-8
5	Sharks	11-8-1
6	Cowboys	11-9
7	Broncos	11-9
8	Tigers	10-10
9	Titans	9-11
10	Knights	9-11
11	Raiders	9-11
12	Dragons	9-11
13	Warriors	8-12
14	Roosters	7-12-1
15	Panthers	6-14
16	Eels	5-15

Blown to kingdom come

South Sydney Rabbitohs
versus **Manly Sea Eagles**
7.30pm, Friday, 10 August
Bluetongue Stadium, Gosford

JOHN CAMPBELL

SOME OF US SAW IT COMING, BUT THE PAPERS WOULD NOT LET US COUNTENANCE IT. The media had been all over Souths. It was a rugby league love-in. Gus Gould himself wrote that the boys were headed for the Grand Final. Coming from His Eminence, that sort of appraisal carries more gravitas than a papal bull. Even so…

The blinding praise – of the side's new found resolve, of coach Madge Maguire, of halfback, rookie of the year and next year's Origin No. 7 Adam Reynolds – was beginning to weigh heavily on the true believers. We've spent too long in the role of competition shit-kicker to ever forget that pride cometh before a fall and I, for one, was discomfited by the portents. Just five days ago (the short turnaround itself is a handicap), the Bunnies were ever-so nearly run down by the Titans, an honest but hardly scintillating outfit, while the Sea Eagles (remember when they were simply Seagulls?) earned a tenacious 8-6 victory over the full-strength Cowboys in Townsville.

No, things weren't as rosy as those who had recently boarded the cardinal and myrtle gravy train wanted to believe. But what the hell, when the team that you've loved since the year dot has shot into second place on the ladder, not even the perverted dominance of the Brits over Oz at the Olympics can throw you off your stride.

In any case, after six fabulous wins on the trot, including a glorious last-gasp victory over the repulsive Roosters, a stumble against the reigning premiers will not be of seismic relevance … like hell it won't!

It's blowing a gale outside as I sit down on the lounge with my notebook and the dog. I sense that I am going to need every drop of the comforting shiraz that stands within easy reach.

But we're away to a bright start. Maybe I've let my entrenched pessimism get the better of me. Sammy Burgess gets an arsy try, 'Reyno' converts and it's 6-0. Easy as.

Manly strikes back immediately and it looked alarmingly simple.

NOTEBOOK: *Manly sharper, smarter, better in every way ...*

It was stating the bleedin' obvious. The Rabbits appear out of sorts and outclassed. By contrast, the Eagles are eating up the metres in centre-field and dissecting Souths on the edges with callous precision.

NOTEBOOK: *wtf!*

Barely 20 minutes of play has elapsed and I'm giving the shiraz a nudge big time. There is the stench of horrible inevitability about the game.

NOTEBOOK: *Sammy in everything.*

We've taken the lad from Dewsbury to our hearts. That Souths have signed the fourth Burgess brother, young Thomas, seems a Corleone-like way of ensuring that we hang on to the Pommy champion but Sam has unexpectedly emerged as the Hero of Redfern. Compare his unstinting effort with that of the great galoot Dave Taylor. The Coal Train might yet contribute a freakish, match-winning turn, but at present he's having a bludge – hang on, he's just taken it up ... and dropped the ball cold.

Manly's lead at the break is a narrow 9-6 but Souths aren't in it. I'll need to decant some more of the De Bortoli.

The second 40 starts where the first left off – only worse. Manly is killing us.

NOTEBOOK: *George C. Scott's Patton, repelling Rommel's tanks, yells: "I read your book, you bastard!"*

It's a scene from the great movie about the American WWII general. As the previously invincible German tanks make their advance, Patton's forces hammer them in a preconceived counter attack. The Eagles know exactly what Souths are going to do and Souths are incapable of adapting to the premiers' preparedness. Manly, on the other hand, continue to exploit deficiencies that they have exposed on the flanks. They are putting the challengers in their place. Ruthlessly.

NOTEBOOK: *Pettybourne would rather run into a defender than a gap. Why? The Tigers can have him.*

I'm getting narky now as defeat looms ugly and large. Manly rubs salt into the wound when Matt Ballin strolls in for the softest of tries. The drubbing is complete.

"Is the pain of losing more telling than the joy of winning?" Ian Fleming put the unanswerable question into James Bond's head one night at the baccarat table in Monte Carlo. It's still blowing like buggery outside and, as it always does, the footy has taken me to an extreme of my psychic realm.

NOTEBOOK: *Game dispiriting. Result evident from long way out.*

Manly 23		REFEREES	Ben Cummins, Phil Haines
TRIES	Taufua 2; Whare, D Williams, Ballin	CROWD	17,947
GOAL	Lyon 1/5	VOTES	**3. Cherry-Evans** Sea Eagles
FIELD GOAL	Cherry-Evans		**2. Lyon** Sea Eagles
South Sydney 6			**1. S. Burgess** Rabbitohs
TRY	S. Burgess		
GOAL	Reynolds 1/1		

When men were men

Melbourne Storm *versus* **Gold Coast Titans**
7.30pm, Friday, 10 August
AAMI Park, Melbourne

LUKE JAMIESON

WENT TO SEVERAL GAMES AT AAMI PARK THIS YEAR, barracking vocally each time for the team that happened to be playing against the Storm. The beauty of AAMI Park is the proximity to the field and, by default, the players. They are regularly within earshot if you're sitting in the front rows, which I make a point of doing. After a particularly vocal match, where the Cowboys turned over the Storm, I was left thinking about how bland the Storm were as a team to sledge. There is a complete lack of imagination when it comes to nicknames among the playing group.

Quinny, Coops, Billy, Cam Smith, Sika, Hoff, Widdop. In fact, the only notables at the whole club are Craig 'Bellyache' Bellamy and 'The Proctologist'. Sisa Waqa is the only other name worth mentioning, but that's the bloke's actual name!

Being the deep thinker that I am, I took the next logical step and asked myself, what are some of the great nicknames in the NRL?

Some of the characters of the game were known by their nicknames, many instantly recognisable for their contribution to rugby league, good bad or otherwise.

- 'Brandy' Alexander – his nickname is better than his commentary;
- Barry Gomersall, 'The Grasshopper' – even refs have got nicknames!
- 'Florence' Nightingale;
- 'Cement' Gillespie;
- 'Beaver' Menzies – rangy 87 year old backrower with 912 games under his belt;
- 'Bobcat' Ryan;
- 'Waltzing' Matt Hilder – the bloke everyone wants to play with;
- Trevor 'The Axe' Gillmeister;
- 'Crusher' Cleal;
- 'Slippery' Morris – father to the good J-Moz and B-Moz;
- 'Chief' Harragon – nicest man in rugby league;
- 'Spud' Carroll;
- 'Changa' Langlands – white boots;
- 'Pig' Riddell – owner of this fantastic yarn:

   > It was early in my career at St George Illawarra and Loz, then the assistant coach, wasn't impressed after I rocked up to preseason training after a particularly festive Christmas. It didn't take long to work out that the amount I was drinking – rather than eating – was the cause of the problem. I can still remember Loz's reaction when I told him that I regularly put away 20 or so schooners in an average week. I could see the concern written all over his face, but I thought he took the news pretty well.
   >
   > "Well, Piggy," he said. "At least you're being honest."
   >
   > We danced around the issue for a bit and, just as I was about to walk out the door, I decided to come clean.
   >
   > "Well, if we're being totally honest," I mumbled before scurrying away, "I probably put away about 20 or 30 bourbon-and-Cokes as well."

- 'The Germ';
- 'Whatsapacketa' Sigsworth – clubhouse leader for mine;
- 'Chicka' Ferguson;
- 'Chook' Herron;
- 'Chook' Raper;
- 'Rocket' Rod Reddy;
- 'The Zip Zip Man';
- 'The Special Needs Penguin';
- 'General' Patten; and
- 'Buster' Warburton.

Then there are some well-known Roy and HG specials:

- 'Three Knees' Hancock;
- 'The Poo in the Shoe';
- 'Two Dollar Coyne';
- 'The Unmade Bed'; and
- 'Dish-head' Dowling.

And some current players:

- 'The Pig Hunter';
- 'The Gift' and 'Snake' Stewart;
- 'Petrol 70 cents a litre';
- 'Big Keefy' Galloway;
- 'Bull' Bailey;
- 'The Hornbag'; and
- 'Hotdogs' Williams.

Now read this bit in that really annoying *Sex and The City* inner monologue voice that the horsey character does:

Has the nickname gone the way of striking for the ball from marker? Has imagination and rhyming slang become as rare as genuine footballers as we move towards a game of talented athletes? Are we becoming boring?

I don't really have anything to tie this up with except to say that I love the game and the spectacle but I sometimes long for yesteryear, when men were men and their nicknames were bloody great.

Oh, and Melbourne won.

Melbourne 24			REFEREES	Shayne Hayne, Alan Shortall
TRIES	Slater, Widdop, Cronk, Hoffman		CROWD	9,108
GOALS	Smith 4/4		VOTES	**3. Smith** Storm
Gold Coast 16				**2. Myles** Titans
TRIES	Mead, Michaels, Ridge			**1. Hoffman** Storm
GOALS	Prince 2/3			

Roll on 2013, please!

Parramatta Eels *versus* **Sydney Roosters**
5.30pm, Saturday, 11 August
Parramatta Stadium, Sydney

DAN KEARY

'VE BEEN OUT TO A FAMILY DINNER. I KNOW THE SCORE. I know the Roosters lost and I know that Chris bloody Sandow scored the final two tries to give the Eels victory – which, in itself, makes the bitter pill of defeat even harder to swallow.

I also know that it was yet another hopeless performance by the Roosters. The email I received not long ago from a fellow Roosters fan that concluded with THE TEAM IS STUFFED was spot-on.

And, despite a great win over the Dragons last week that delivered me some brief rugby league happiness, I know the spectre of the wooden spoon still looms large.

I've recorded the Roosters v Eels game but the Olympic 50 kilometre walk is on TV. What to watch?

I opt for the Olympic walking – despite it being the most ludicrous sport of all – because I know I'll come out the other end of watching the Roosters game even madder and more distraught than I already am just being aware of the score.

That's how dire it's become this year – choosing a sport that's comparable to watching a bunch of blokes walking out of the hospital after a colonoscopy over watching my team fumble and bumble its way to another humiliating loss.

How it can all change so quickly in rugby league. Only two years ago the corresponding match between these two sides was hyped to the hilt. Parra were on a roll, largely as a result of the brilliant form of Jarryd Hayne from back when he was still a train ... or plane, or automobile, or whatever it was that week.

The Roosters, meanwhile, had won their last four, including a few epic come-from-behind wins. The team was looking better by the week and, after the fiasco of the 2009 wooden spoon season, we Roosters fans were digging every moment of it.

It was enough for me to make the long drive out to Parra Stadium to watch the game with my (then) six-year-old son.

And wasn't it worth it? The Roosters were on fire and blew the Eels away 48-12.

My son and I still talk about it today (okay, I admit, I'm the one who usually brings it up and he just nods along.)

Two short years later, the Roosters-Eels match has been reduced to a battle to avoid the wooden spoon. Sure, the Eels found a touch of form following the departure of Stephen Kearney, but their flogging by the Tigers last week appeared to signal that normal transmission had resumed.

As for the Roosters, I've learned over a lifetime of supporting them never to be fooled by the mirage of one good performance. Like night follows day, bad usually follows good in Rooster-world.

And so it was tonight, apparently: 36-22 says it all. That's some vapid defence right there. I'd also guess the usual dose of directionless attack, dropped balls and another lost penalty count.

I don't need to watch to know what went down. I've been experiencing it for years.

I can only hope that the Roosters' much heralded youth policy starts to reap some benefits next year. It's true that there are some fine young footballers playing for the Roosters this year. It's also true that they are part of a very poor football team.

Hopefully that changes next year. James Maloney should make a difference. While Braith Anasta has been a solid player and fine leader, his best footy is now behind him.

Maloney, on the other hand, is young, fast and tough. Perhaps he'll also be the tonic needed to get Mitchell Pearce playing some decent footy again. Pearce has shown glimpses of good form this year – such as last week's game against St George – but, overall, has been disappointing. Whether it's a new halves partner, a new coach or some other wake-up call, he needs something to get his mojo back.

Sonny Bill Williams will be a hero or villain. I hope the former. I fear the latter. I'm not bold enough to predict either. I'll leave it to him to prove.

Back to the now, the Olympic walking is over. I'm not remotely tempted to watch the Roosters-Eels game.

Roll on 2013. And please be nothing like 2012.

Parramatta 36			REFEREES	Jared Maxwell, David Munro
TRIES	Morgan, Sandow 2; Blair, Hindmarsh		CROWD	12,193
GOALS	Burt 6/7		VOTES	3. Hindmarsh Eels
Sydney Roosters 22				2. Sandow Eels
TRIES	Anasta, Friend, Henry, Takairangi			1. Mannah Eels
GOALS	Anasta 3/4			

Magic in the mud

Wests Tigers *versus* St George Illawarra Dragons
7.30pm, Saturday, 11 August
Allianz Stadium, Sydney

ADAM DONNELLY

HOW SATISFYING IT IS THAT THE DRAGONS' 2012 CAMPAIGN was shut down by their public enemy No. 1 Tim Moltzen. When Moltzen reneged on a contract to play in the Red V, every Dragons fan took it personally, and I think Moltzen served as a suitable scapegoat for a support base whose team was disappointing and whose players were walking out one by one.

If you know rugby league, and if you have a foot in either camp, you know there is no love lost between the Dragons and the Tigers. They hate us and we hate them. On *The Gameplan* last week, Dean Young could barely conceal his disgust when the seven-year-old junior he was interviewing told him his goal was to one day play for the Tigers.

I missed the first game between Dragons and Tigers this season and Moltzen's first gauntlet run against the team he rejected, due to being in unenlightened, backwards Melbourne at the time. Despite finding a pub with a pirated Imparja feed and sitting through Brisbane-Newcastle to watch the Dragons and Tigers on delay, some techie buggered up and showed the Dragons players backslapping and hugging in victory at the 80th minute before jumping to the start of the delayed game.

I left in disgust and avoided replays but, from what I saw, it was a shellacking. The last few weeks, as they tend to, the Tigers had spluttered along, bold and attacking one week, limp and uninvolved the next. However, slightly buoyed by a second-half resurgence last week against the Eels and the sheer might and speed of the Fijian Marika Koroibete, I found myself with a nervous anticipation for the rematch against the Dragons. I needed a win.

The venue for the evening was the Gallipoli Club in Hamilton on a horrid Saturday night, wind and rain threatening to pick up Newcastle and blow it up the Hunter. The club is a sad old RSL haunted by a few cranky old grey ghosts and, I suspect, the last resort for drinkers banned from other establishments on Beaumont St. It's the closest venue with pay TV to me and, sitting with a few half-asleep geriatrics and with the pokies tinkling behind me, I settled in with that ball of nerves, half-excitement and half-dread that you know well if you're a Tigers fan. If you were there at Allianz Stadium, it looked like you were at risk of drowning.

Early tries to Morris and Rein had me in the doldrums and I was doing my best to telepathically will the Tigers to do something, anything. Moltzen scored his first of the night running over Jamie Soward. Soward was simply horrible on the night and was probably feeling as miserable as the weather. 8-4 at halftime, a scoreline I knew the Tigers could work with.

After the resumption, Moltzen got his second try off a skidding kick from Farah and Benji set up Liam Fulton for a try. I love Fulton, not for being a well of freakish talent or a world-beater, but for being an honest servant for my club. It's always of special satisfaction for me to see him find the line.

Morris got his second and brought my nerves to the surface again. I wasn't in the mood for heartbreak but Moltzen got his third and shut the game down off a no-look pass from Benji. It's moments like that pass that I crave. It was sheer magic, a combination of sleight of hand and a stony poker-face. His body turned one way, the ball floated out in the opposite direction. Watch the replay, it fooled the Dragons,

fooled the cameraman and glided into Moltzen's hands like a penny from heaven.
I felt like channeling half Laurie Nichols, half The Angels and giving the Gallipoli Club
a display of shadow boxing.

Bloody hell, the Tigers can do some great stuff when they want to.

Wests Tigers 22		REFEREES	Gerard Sutton, Adam Devcich
TRIES	Moltzen 3; Fulton	CROWD	10,546
GOALS	Marshall 3/4	VOTES	**3. Farah** Tigers
St George Illawarra 12			**2. Marshall** Tigers
TRIES	Morris 2; Rein		**1. Moltzen** Tigers
GOALS	C. Stanley 0/2, Soward 0/1		

A sad state

North Queensland Cowboys *versus* New Zealand Warriors
7.30pm, Saturday, 11 August
Dairy Farmers Stadium, Townsville

STEVE MASCORD

ABOUT TWO HOURS BEFORE SITTING DOWN TO WRITE THIS PIECE, I had contrived a rather
self-righteous – even pious – theme about how the match in question
exemplified the impact of declining newspaper budgets on what rugby league
information reaches your eyes and ears – and more importantly on what doesn't.

But 24 hours ago, I received a text from Michael Coorey, the former Brisbane
Broncos utility who I got to know on a couple of overseas trips with the Lebanon
Cedars. Michael had also played for North Queensland and the August 11 game
against the Warriors had been Old Boys Day.

I had expected to see Mick there.

Mick is also a personal trainer and the previous week he had taken on the
imposing task of trying to whip this pudgy hack into shape. His suburban Brisbane
gym is a going concern and he employs several Broncos under-20s players on a
part-time basis.

Now, I recalled that a Brisbane Toyota Cup player was recently left in a coma
following a car crash. In responding to the text, I asked if he knew the poor fellow.

"Yep, Matty worked for me. He helped train you last time you were up. Very sad."

Shit.

Matt Berwick was involved in a collision on August 9 – just two days before this match – driving home from training. At last report he was still in a coma at Royal Brisbane and Women's Hospital, with his family by his side. It's no surprise that Coorey – who had suggested a few beers in Townsville after the match – was nowhere to be seen.

And so when it comes to the significance of the North Queensland-Warriors match, nothing will match someone I didn't see – and the reasons I didn't know for a month or more. Matt, from Dalby, had turned 19 just the week before the accident. I hope by the time you have read this, he's recovered.

I'll now go over the point I was going to make, involving matters of far less gravitas.

You will be aware that newspapers are cutting staff and budgets but you may not be aware of how that impacts on your weekend NRL match coverage. Basically, reporters no longer travel. Generally speaking, your match report about the Wests Tigers' game in Melbourne is written by someone who works for a paper in Melbourne, as paying for travel costs is not considered worth it in the current climate.

That reporter's principal loyalty is to the boss he sees every day – so he will lead on the home team, whether they won or not. In Sydney (or wherever), the story will be rewritten in the office, but you will not find out much about your team because a press conference quote from the bottom of the story will be moved to the top – as opposed to the travelling reporter going into the dressing rooms and trying to get the best yarn he can on (in my example) the Wests Tigers.

There were no reporters from New Zealand at this game. Aside from me, they were all from Queensland and all had to lead on the Cowboys. So, when Warriors coach Brian McClennan said that after the 52-12 defeat he expected to be sacked, it was largely unreported.

This is what McClennan said: "I'm big enough and ugly enough to cop it. I'm the bloke steering the ship, steering the bus. The pressure comes on me. I accept that."

Asked what form he expected that pressure to take, McClennan answered: "I'm not sure as yet. That will unfold I guess. All I can say is I'm doing the best I can do, I'm doing what I know and what's worked for us in the past."

Of course, a couple of weeks later, he was sacked. And New Zealand readers, for a start, had been cut off from this information by the savage budget cuts in the newspaper industry. This scenario – though not as dramatic – is repeated every weekend and it will become more dramatic to you as time passed.

But don't take that away from reading this yarn. Take away the name Matt Berwick. I personally don't believe prayer does any good at all – but there's nothing wrong with a bit of hope, is there?

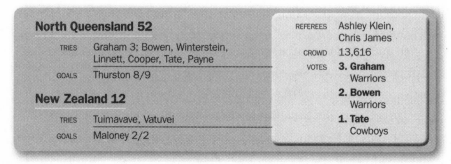

North Queensland 52			REFEREES	Ashley Klein, Chris James
TRIES	Graham 3; Bowen, Winterstein, Linnett, Cooper, Tate, Payne		CROWD	13,616
GOALS	Thurston 8/9		VOTES	**3. Graham** Warriors
New Zealand 12				**2. Bowen** Warriors
TRIES	Tuimavave, Vatuvei			**1. Tate** Cowboys
GOALS	Maloney 2/2			

All dark on the western front

Penrith Panthers *versus* **Canberra Raiders**

2pm, Sunday, 12 August

Centrebet Stadium, Sydney

STU WARREN

D RIVING THROUGH RURAL AUSTRALIA AT NIGHT IS AN EXERCISE in keeping your eyes open. Save for the aid of a full moon, it's near impossible to see beyond the range of your headlights – while there's nothing but inky blackness in rear-view mirrors – and, other than the occasional flash of cars passing at high speed from the other direction, there's really very little stimulation for the driver.

It can be a lonely place, perhaps made lonelier when you consider the potential for a mechanical mishap to leave you marooned by the roadside for a long, cold night.

But it can hardly be considered as lonely a place as the foot of the NRL table, and that looks to be just about where the Penrith Panthers will see out the 2012 season.

It's the right time for Phil 'Gus' Gould to roll up his sleeves, pop the bonnet and get busy with a socket set and a can of WD40 down at Centrebet Stadium.

For a man who knows as much as he knows about rugby league – and don't we all know it, too – Gus hasn't exactly restored his Panthers' machine into the purring model of two seasons back.

And on the strength of this home capitulation to the hit-and-miss Canberra Raiders, it could be argued that Gus needs to reacquaint himself with the owner's manual – because any restoration he has achieved this year is no more than cosmetic.

In fact, the whole Penrith organisation is staring straight ahead at what could turn out to be their darkest drive during the last few weeks of the 2012 premiership season. Such was the bleak nature of their second half submission to the Raiders, the wooden spoon is a real possibility.

There were bobbling balls bouncing to hand for the Canberra outfit – and at least one questionable call for a try to the visitors. Even still, that the Panthers leaked 20 points in the second half, and scored just four of their own, is telling.

They've got real work to do to keep their nose in front of Parramatta. Unless they reverse the trend that saw them make 11 errors and give the Raiders 10 penalties, they may just find themselves in an embarrassing situation as Parra sneak ahead. And I bet Gus doesn't want that to happen on his watch. It's just not a good look for a general manager to drive his steed further into the ground than where it was when he arrived.

Even if the club doesn't hit rock bottom, Gus still has questions to answer.

Luke Lewis and Petero Civoniceva head a list of quality players gone from the Panthers since last season – and the haemorrhaging may not have finished just yet.

Rugby league writer Phil Rothfield laments Gould's unwillingness to admit there are problems at Penrith.

He also claims the club's fan base is growing dissatisfied with the lack of information forthcoming from the organisation. He's right: we are!

It can't be much fun following a club that appears to be travelling towards a huge wreck – and all the while sitting in the backseat wondering why the guy behind the steering wheel doesn't have his lights on.

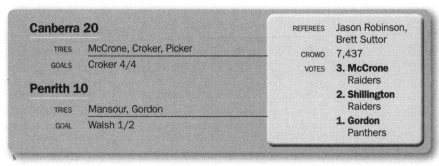

Canberra 20

TRIES	McCrone, Croker, Picker	REFEREES	Jason Robinson, Brett Suttor
GOALS	Croker 4/4	CROWD	7,437
		VOTES	**3. McCrone** Raiders

Penrith 10

TRIES	Mansour, Gordon		**2. Shillington** Raiders
GOAL	Walsh 1/2		**1. Gordon** Panthers

Afternoon delight

Canterbury Bulldogs *versus* **Brisbane Broncos**
3pm, Sunday, 12 August
ANZ Stadium, Sydney

NICK TEDESCHI

I F YOU WANT THE BEST VIETNAMESE FOOD THIS SIDE OF SAIGON, there is only one place to eat: Bau Truong, in Cabramatta. It was before the Canterbury-Brisbane game that I made the trek west from the *Making The Nut* offices in Erskineville. Joining me was my girlfriend and a hunger that would only be sated by the delicious prawn and pork rice paper rolls, the finest crispy skin chicken I've ever tasted, the amazing goat curry, the spit-inducing lemongrass venison.

It had been a late start to the day after a late end to the previous night. Something about free cocktails, Mexican hats and Jimmy Buffett tunes. We were sans breakfast and the grumble was on. There was also the little matter of that afternoon's prime activity: Canterbury and Brisbane, two top eight teams, two stern rivals, squaring off at ANZ.

There was a lot of Sydney to be covered, not much time to cover it and even less will of the body to try it. Hangovers aren't pretty these days, particularly when they entail tequila and near-dawn finishes. But, hell, the lure of Vietnamese food got us out of Erskineville by 11.30. By the time we lobbed, close to an hour later, I would have slashed Tony Soprano across the face for just a bite of that crispy skin chicken.

"Hello, hello ... please wait ... names please ... five or 10 minutes," the friendly host said.

As she turned away, in unison Louise and I fired off our best Seinfeld: "Five, 10 minutes".

Twenty minutes later, we were down for the nosh. I was wild with hunger. Louise wasn't far behind. The food was all you can imagine and more. Holy moly, when I had my seat, Bulldogs jersey on, I thought that this was better than a Bulldogs win. And it was close.

But there's nothing better than a Bulldogs win, particularly on a Sunday afternoon against a big-name rival while riding a 10-game winning streak.

By the time we finished up in Cabramatta, time was very much of the essence. There was a stadium that was impossible to get to. And I was heading in, not out. But the sun was shining, there were blue and white scarves aplenty and the Bulldogs were premiership favourites. Life was, as they say, good.

That chirpy mood turned sour very quickly, however, on arrival at ANZ.

I received two text messages within two minutes from the two bastards I was supposed to go with – both late scratchings. It was disappointing all round.

And before you could say "get some bottle, you weak pricks", the Bulldogs were down. This Broncos team that had lost three in a row, all to teams below them on the ladder, had the Bullies on the ropes.

I sat there – one out mind you – and saw Ben Te'o crash over after two minutes, followed by Corey Norman four minutes later. A penalty goal and the Bulldogs were down 14-0 after 10 minutes.

Horrible thoughts raced through my head. This team was nothing more than a myth, blown up but without substance. Ever the weekend pessimist, my midweek peacocking seemed ridiculous.

The wrestle had evened up though midway through the first and, when Josh Jackson crashed over on halftime, the Bulldogs had the momentum but not the lead.

The second half was one-way traffic. The temperature dropped. So too did the heart rate. The Bulldogs cruised home on the back of one man: Ben Barba. He has risen to superstardom under Des Hasler and he was at his best against Brisbane, scoring a magnificent try off a kick and then ran an angle that put him over for the match-winner.

The Bulldogs didn't cover the 10-point start but they had made it 11 straight. With some pork and prawn rice paper rolls waiting at home, this had been one hell of a day.

Canterbury 22		REFEREES	Tony Archer, Gavin Badger
TRIES	Barba 2; Taupau, Jackson	CROWD	19,870
GOALS	Inu 3/4	VOTES	**3. Barba** Bulldogs
Brisbane 14			**2. Tolman** Bulldogs
TRIES	Norman, Te'o		**1. Reynolds** Bulldogs
GOALS	Wallace 3/3		

Team talk

Newcastle Knights *versus* Cronulla Sharks
7pm, Monday, 13 August
Hunter Stadium, Newcastle

MARK NICHOLS

T HE PATH BETWEEN SHARK PARK and the Newcastle International Sports Centre is well worn with 16 players donning both the blue, black and white of Cronulla and the red and blue of Newcastle since the Knights entered the premiership 25 years ago. Since Dean Carney, a long-forgotten 71-game Shark veteran who joined Newcastle for a two-game stint in 1989, many players have called both The Shire and The Hunter home.

There are the bit-players. Those like Dustin Cooper and Terrence Seuseu, those who never quite made it. There are the journeymen veterans, those tough and robust warriors who just kept going like the Energizer bunny.

Tim Maddison played 11 seasons in the top grade at five different clubs, starting and finishing with Newcastle with a spell at the Sharks in the middle. Maddison is most remembered for a nasty incident against Justin Holbrook while a Cowboy.

Wily utility John Morris is verging on 300 games, having started his career at Newcastle and racking up 68 for the Sharks.

Russell Richardson, the Cronulla centre who went on to play for Australia but is certainly best remembered for his debut performance where he went 100 metres before spilling the ball over the line mid-swan dive, spent his farewell season in red and blue.

Brett Kimmorley, a premiership winner of 307 games – 140 with Cronulla – who was a rep staple for over a decade, started out at Newcastle but was stuck behind future Immortal Andrew Johns.

Wayne Bennett's arrival in the Hunter has certainly seen the pipeline between the two teams open up. Bustling prop Mark Taufua was not required by Bennett. Crafty hooker Isaac De Gois was another not wanted by The Master. He returned to the Sharks where he is having an excellent 2012. Smart with the ball in hand, De Gois is dreadfully underrated but a key part of everything the Sharks do.

The toughest pound-for-pound player in the premiership is arguably Matt Hilder. Barely six-foot in the old money and no more than 90 kegs, the Cronulla junior is the only man to have played 80 games for each club. He would tackle the XPT if he could.

A favourite of Bennett, Adam Cuthbertson followed his mentor at the Dragons to the Hunter. Bennett's greatest reclamation project is arguably the burly forward who spent most of his one-year stint at Shark Park in Ricky Stuart's bad books. He hasn't performed much better at Newcastle, though he was very good at St George Illawarra.

Local Kade Snowden left Newcastle in the Brian Smith cleanout and rose to international status at Cronulla before controversially leaving the Sharks to return home on a big-money deal. Few fans believe he's been value for the big money since being back. There was no Blue or Green and Gold in his closet this year.

The two players who perhaps looked most out of place wearing blue, black and white were Newcastle legends Matthew Johns and Darren Albert. After 176 games with the Knights, Johns guided the Sharks to the 2002 preliminary final while '97 Grand Final hero Albert returned to Australia for one season with the Sharks in 2006. Very odd indeed.

On this Monday night at Hunter Stadium, five players who had represented both clubs lined up: Snowden and Cuthbertson for the Knights and De Gois, Morris and Taufua for the Sharks.

It was the Newcastle duo who came out on top, the Knights winning 26-4 in a match that wasn't a rout although the Knights always held the picture cards.

Cuthbertson had his finest game for the year, making 114 metres on the back of some strong running. There was no poor handling to be seen.

Snowden, as he has been all year, was quiet. Jarrod Mullen laid on three tries while Akuila Uate continued his run of form. Despite standing on the winning side of the ledger, Chris Houston managed 62 tackles in a gladiatorial effort.

The former Knights at Cronulla couldn't quite get it together, barely noticeable in one of the Sharks' poorer showings in 2012.

To be fair though, there weren't many for the road team who did. The Knights were good but the Sharks drowned in a sea of mediocrity.

Newcastle 26		REFEREES	Matt Cecchin, Gavin Morris
TRIES	Boyd, K. Naiqama, Gagai, Uate, Mullen	CROWD	15,394
GOALS	Roberts 3/5	VOTES	**3. Mullen** Knights
Cronulla 4			**2. Gagai** Knights
TRY	Williams		**1. Boyd** Knights
GOALS	Carney 0/1		

Round 24

AFTER ROUND 23, 2012		
1	Bulldogs	16-5
2	Storm	14-7
3	Rabbitohs	14-7
4	Sea Eagles	13-8
5	Cowboys	12-9
6	Sharks	11-9-1
7	Broncos	11-10
8	Tigers	11-10
9	Knights	10-11
10	Raiders	10-11
11	Titans	9-12
12	Dragons	9-12
13	Warriors	8-13
14	Roosters	7-13-1
15	Panthers	6-15
16	Eels	6-15

Robbed

Brisbane Broncos
versus **Melbourne Storm**
7.30pm, Friday, 17 August
Suncorp Stadium, Brisbane

IAN HAUSER

THE OMENS WEREN'T GOOD FOR THIS GAME. As soon as I tuned in, I heard the voice of Ray Hadley. *Shit!* I'd hoped that this traditionally hard-fought clash might attract the (so-called) A-team of Channel Nine commentators but, no, we had Ray Hadley. Not a good start. I should have turned the sound down and tuned into the ABC.

But wait – a momentary reprieve as Jaimee Rogers appeared and did her thing for TAB Sportsbet. There was national approval; people from Broome to Bruny Island were pleased that it's not Munsie as Jaimee gave us the latest odds and options. When will Channel Nine twig to the potential of *Being Jaimee Rogers,* not as just some internet joke but for real? But Jaimee disappeared all too soon and we're stuck with Ray.

Hasn't Darren Lockyer added something via his sideline expert comments? You could sense his brain working out the options one or two plays ahead, sussing out a weakness on the left, spying a defender a yard or two too close in to defend a quick spread to the right. Locky knows that less is more when it comes to commentary and is all the better for it. Funny how the newbie has it all over the supposedly vastly experienced callers.

I remember going to see the Broncos play the Storm at Lang Park a few weeks from the finals in 2006. The Storm were riding high while the Broncos were borderline finalists. There was a tissue paper between them – two missed tackles cost the Broncos a win that day but suggested that a friendly rub of the green might see the result reversed. Cue forward several weeks and the Grand Final went to the northerners after they made their tackles and had a couple of good bounces.

No Broncos fan will forget Locky's agony after Greg Inglis scored in the last minute in the Grand Final qualifier a few years ago. It's always like that with games between these two. Who will have the odd slice of luck tonight?

And the answer is ... *the Storm! Twice!* Once in each half. First, it was Waqa's try just before the break when even the usually anti-Broncos commentators unanimously called for the red button after the video showed a clear loss of the ball on the way down and, therefore, a blatant knock on. Maybe Channel Nine hates the Storm even more than the Broncos. Six points gone and, in a one-point game, *we wuz robbed!* Then, early in the second half, Cronk's grubber hit the bloody goal post and ricocheted nicely into his hands as he followed through – another six points gone west.

Look at the match stats – every single one of them favoured the Broncos except the final score – and even that was just a single point. The Storm 19-18 could just as easily have been Broncos 18-6. Where's the justice? When you're down (and a fifth loss on the trot is about as down as you can get at this stage of the season), the breaks just don't seem to go your way. And to add further salt into the wounds, why wasn't Norrie sent off for the raised elbow to Thaiday's head? There had been a precedent for that earlier in the season – just ask JT. *Fair dinkum!*

Only three things saved the night from total depression – the Tigers lost too although they had reason to cry foul on a dubious obstruction decision. The Broncos might hold on to a spot in the eight and, lastly, we had Jaimee.

If ever so briefly.

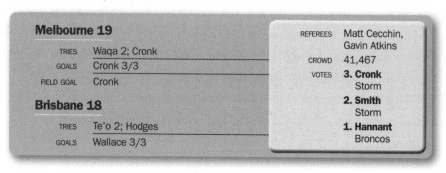

Melbourne 19		REFEREES	Matt Cecchin, Gavin Atkins
TRIES	Waqa 2; Cronk	CROWD	41,467
GOALS	Cronk 3/3	VOTES	**3. Cronk** Storm
FIELD GOAL	Cronk		**2. Smith** Storm
Brisbane 18			**1. Hannant** Broncos
TRIES	Te'o 2; Hodges		
GOALS	Wallace 3/3		

Dirty dozen

Canterbury Bulldogs *versus* Wests Tigers

7.30pm, Friday, 17 August

ANZ Stadium, Sydney

MATT FISK

S EARCHING FOR THEIR TWELFTH WIN ON THE TROT, Canterbury Bankstown was always going to test the inconsistent Wests Tigers. However, the Tigers themselves had found a bit of form and were quietly confident of surprising the competition leaders. It was potentially one of the games of the season and the best part of 30,000 fans were on hand to witness it.

Mindful of the possibilities, I headed to the Olympic Stadium with my family, my son's footy coach, an old mate from school, his son and the one and only 'Uncle Punt', Nick Tedeschi. I thought when I managed to get this rag tag bunch through the stadium's corporate box security with only three genuine tickets that it was going to be my night. However, luck can only take you so far. Especially when Tim Moltzen is involved.

I got the young fellas sorted on the iPads, organised a drink for my wife, pinched a *Big League* from the TAB's Matt Jenkins and sat myself down. I needed to get my thoughts together. Despite my reliance on player ratings, situational analysis and enough sports metrics to give Billy Beane a headache, I decided to turn back the clock. I conducted my foolproof schoolboy method of going through the *Big League* and working out how many better players we had than the Dogs, and how many of their players had our measure. In a nutshell, there was little between the teams.

The props and backrow cancelled each other out, Wests had the clear edge at halfback and hooker while the Dogs three-quarter line (excluding the error-prone Jonathan Wright) was vastly superior. But this is where the system runs into trouble. How can one accurately predict the unsettling effect a player like Tim Moltzen can have on an NRL side? How do I begin to document his recent record? He has limited respect for possession, has poor positional play, struggles with the very idea of anticipation, has little concept of the game and can create a highlight reel with missed tackles and weak last ditch attempts. He's had better seasons.

Moltzen, you may recall, was the subject of much criticism over his dealings with the Dragons. St George-Illawarra is only just beginning to comprehend the blessing that has fallen their way.

Wests trailed for much of the match but typically stellar performances from Liam Fulton, Robbie Farah and Aaron Woods kept the Tigers within striking distance. The star trio have papered over the cracks of what is an increasingly dysfunctional Tigers outfit. Many experts are calling for the head of Tim Sheens and the way he has stuck with Moltzen makes fans ask questions about his judgment. But even Sheens had had enough late in the match and Moltzen was dragged for a knock on from a kick-off.

The top six teams in this year's premiership all possess star custodians. Ben Barba, Billy Slater, Greg Inglis, Brett Stewart, Matt Bowen and Josh Dugan are true stars of the game. To have them all playing in one era is a gift for all league fans. Fullbacks have clearly overtaken halves as the most important players in the game. Whether this has occurred simply as a result of the immense talent of these particular individuals, whether we are in a cycle of pedestrian halves, or because the structure of the game has changed is the subject of debate. However, one thing is certain: a team without a good fullback simply does not stand a chance.

And one with a fullback as troubled as Moltzen is sentenced to as much success as the Washington Generals.

On reflection, the Wests Tigers stood little hope of defeating a premiership heavyweight with all of their baggage. A broken hand to Farah followed by an Inu drop goal in golden point time were mere formalities.

The Bulldogs wouldn't have been happy with their performance but they won a thoroughly enjoyable match. They deserved to; they were the marginally better side on the night.

Canterbury 23

TRIES	Barba, Wright, Reynolds, Tolman
GOALS	Inu 3/4
FIELD GOAL	Inu

Wests Tigers 22

TRIES	Koroibete 2; Marshall, Woods
GOALS	Marshall 3/4

REFEREES	Ben Cummins, Jared Maxwell
CROWD	29,194
VOTES	**3. Farah** Tigers
	2. Tolman Bulldogs
	1. Inu Bulldogs

Clothesline in the capital

Canberra Raiders *versus* **Sydney Roosters**

5.30pm, Saturday, 18 August

Canberra Stadium, Canberra

MICHAEL PEARSON

CATO FONG WAS A CHARACTER IN THE PINK PANTHER SERIES OF MOVIES in the '60s and '70s. He was Inspector Clouseau's manservant and a martial arts expert with the express instruction to attack his master unexpectedly in order to keep his combat skills and vigilance sharp. This usually consisted of him dropping from the ceiling or swinging from a chandelier with snap kicks or karate chops aimed directly toward Clouseau's head!

Of course, Clouseau would always survive such attacks despite the seemingly treacherous intent of Cato to kill or hurt him. This was due to the pure luck of Clouseau's ineptitude, or by Cato being required to quickly resume the role of servant when a doorbell or telephone rang just as he was ready to strike a fatal blow.

As Josh Dugan was streaming toward the tryline in the 75th minute of tonight's game, he could have been impersonating Peter Sellers' bumbling Inspector. Anthony 'Cato' Minichiello launched a crazy assault on the Canberra custodian. In one of the more remarkable and spectacular tackles of the season, Minichiello's flying leap was reminiscent of a *Matrix*-style martial arts manoeuvre perfected by Bruce Lee, Jackie Chan or Cato himself.

The unsuspecting Dugan was a sitting target and couldn't do much but brace and accept the human missile, leaving him momentarily dazed. Not yet sunk or held and showing the tenacity of a Clouseau investigation, Dugan quickly dusted himself off for another tilt at the line. But this time the flying Rooster performed the knockout punch that Cato built a career on perfecting, springing to his feet to launch his whole body, arms and legs, at Dugan's body and head. This time the collision brought Dugan to his knees. It certainly grabbed the attention of the law enforcers who quickly dispatched "Mini" to take an early shower for the first time ever in his 249-game NRL career.

The impact of the assault was significant. The Raiders were awarded a penalty in front of the posts and took an eight-point lead that would ensure them a crucial win and a sniff at an unlikely final eight spot on the ladder. The Roosters, already out of finals contention, felt the pain for 'Mini' who, with a suspension, could miss the fairytale opportunity to celebrate his 250th game against the Wests Tigers next week or, even worse, have to wait until next season!

The incident is likely to stir some passionate debate about how an impeccable record such as Minichiello's should be considered against a reckless (at worst) and clumsy (at best) tackle. Apparently Minichiello was an excellent gymnast at school before taking up football. It is not difficult to imagine him hanging upside down on the rings before looping into a triple backward somersault with twist only to land on his toes in the upright stance ... *ta da!*

To be frank though, 'Mini' would need to be a contortionist to escape culpability and suspension for the manoeuvre he put on Dugan. The Wally Lewis Medal winner for player of the Origin series in 2005 – the last won by NSW – has established a reputation as one the most likeable, honest, loyal, talented and athletic fullbacks of the game. That doesn't deserve to be blighted completely by a moment of near-lunacy.

Fortunately Dugan's injuries are superficial and he will recover. Whether he'll forget the incident and move on remains to be seen. The Raiders and the Roosters don't have much in common other than a mutual dislike for each other. Indeed, the Roosters have done some fishing in the Raiders' talent pool and have set a bait for Dugan himself. These are not easily forgotten by Raiders officials and it is unlikely that Dugan will be giving evidence for the defence as 'Mini' faces the judiciary during the week.

POSTSCRIPT   Minichiello was subsequently cleared of a striking charge to the head of Josh Dugan and went on to play his 250th game against the Wests Tigers. In a Clouseauian decision, the judiciary determined that it could not be satisfied that Minichiello's actions were deliberate or even reckless and found him not guilty of the striking charge.

Canberra 24		
TRIES	Thompson, Papalii, Ferguson, Robinson	
GOALS	Croker 4/6	

Sydney Roosters 20		
TRIES	Kenny-Dowall, Nu'uausala, Bosden, Moga	
GOALS	Anasta 2/4	

REFEREES	Shayne Hayne, Alan Shortall
CROWD	8,860
VOTES	**3. Fensom** Raiders
	2. Shillington Raiders
	1. Ferguson Raiders

Cold and beaten at Shark Park

Cronulla Sharks *versus* **South Sydney Rabbitohs**

7.30pm, Saturday, 18 August

Toyota Stadium, Sydney

MARK COURTNEY

CAN'T SAY THAT I'VE EVER REALLY LIKED GOING TO TOYOTA PARK. It's a cold, windswept, unwelcoming joint. Always has been, even when it was called Endeavour Field back in the 1960s. And Souths have always had trouble there, even when we were the champs and the Sharks had just entered the comp. It's just never been a happy hunting ground.

I met Greg on the Redfern Hill one day in 1977 (against Cronulla, actually – and we bloody well lost that day too) and have sat with him pretty much every week since. For both of us, though, the lead up to this game could hardly have been worse. I'm having a hellishly tough period at work, while Greg lost a really good mate this week to a massive stroke. Aged 46. 46! I knew him too, but not as well as Greg did. Neither of us really felt like going to Shark Park but we went anyway. We always do.

We took our seats about half an hour before kick-off. Despite the fact Souths struggle at the venue, I do kind of like Cronulla fans. They've always been reasonably hospitable. Maybe it comes from never having won a comp, I don't know. What did Jack Gibson say after coaching there:

> Waiting for Cronulla to win a competition is like leaving the porch light on for Harold Holt.

Or something like that. Anyway, they're a hardy lot and I reckon it'll be a mighty huge night in The Shire if they ever do win it.

It was cold last night. Windy and cold. I went to the shop for some tucker and the pies were cold. Footy food ... honestly. I got a warm sausage roll instead, went to put the sauce on, pushed the lever down on the huge container and squirted the red stuff all over my hand. The night really wasn't going well.

Oh, and then there was the game. As Cronulla prepared to kick-off, Greg and I reflected on the start of last year's match here. After a superb away win against the Broncos in Perth, we turned up expecting big things. Cronulla kicked off and, just as our winger caught it a metre from the sideline, John Sutton ran into him by mistake and pushed him out. Sharks feed, 20 metres out. And it only got worse from there. But that was last year.

This year, Cronulla kicked off and the wind caught the footy. It was going out on the full by about three metres right in front of us when big Dave Taylor stuck his big hand up and tried to knock it infield. Ended up conceding a line dropout. To start the bloody game! Greg just looked at me. "I thought it was impossible," he said, "but that was worse than last year."

As the game developed into an arm wrestle and Souths showed nothing of the spark we'd come to expect during the recent six-game winning streak, we both did what we always do at the footy. We got consumed by the game. We forgot – for a couple of hours – all the crap going on in our lives just at the moment. I guess that's what was truly remarkable about last night. That's the wonder of being a true footy fan.

Anyway, down 6-0 at halftime, Sam Burgess charged onto a Sutton pass, pirouetted out of a tackle and crashed over. 6-6. And when Adam Reynolds jagged a 39-metre field goal for a 7-6 lead with 13 to go, we thought we had them.

Ah, but it wasn't to be. Not this week.

Souths gave away field position via a ridiculous stripping penalty, conceded a converted try, then a penalty goal, and then, with the last play of the game, another converted try. 20-7. It wasn't the end of the world. Not even the end of the season. We're still in the top four, after all. But it was the end of the night and it kind of fitted in with the rest of the week.

Greg stood up. "Let's get the hell out of this God-forsaken place."

And off we trudged to the car.

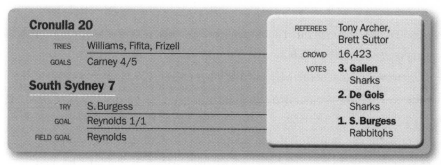

Cronulla 20		REFEREES	Tony Archer, Brett Suttor
TRIES	Williams, Fifita, Frizell	CROWD	16,423
GOALS	Carney 4/5	VOTES	**3. Gallen** Sharks
South Sydney 7			**2. De Gois** Sharks
TRY	S. Burgess		**1. S. Burgess** Rabbitohs
GOAL	Reynolds 1/1		
FIELD GOAL	Reynolds		

The hair up there

Gold Coast Titans *versus* Parramatta Eels
2pm, Sunday, 19 August
Skilled Park, Gold Coast

ALEX MADGE

WOW, WHAT A CRACKING WAY TO SPEND A SUNDAY ARVO, watching a replay of 2011's battle for the wooden spoon. What then, to keep a rugby league fan in the game with a desperate yearning for finals footy really kicking in?

Some of the most marvellous heads of hair in the NRL of course!

Some teams grow a finals beard – the Warriors of 2011 were a particularly splendid bunch. Viewers could really appreciate the peach fuzz of some players developing into a genuine mane of man-fur that would make Grizzly Adams proud.

The Bulldogs haven't had full participation, but this year's effort from big men Frank Pritchard and Sam Kasiano make you proud to be a rugby league fan. The evidence of the last two years seems to be – grow a finals beard, make the Grand Final

Without finals aspirations, the Eels and Titans have very little to offer in facial hair. Greg Bird's 1970's porno mo is disgraceful at best and the retirement of Brad 'Big Red' Meyers has left the Titans lacking in this department.

Despite the lack of whiskers, the Eels and Titans lineups have plenty of hairy heads. Some of the greatest manes in rugby league took to the field for this end of season clash.

Eels stalwart Nathan Hindmarsh has really embraced an unkempt look; his apparent lack of concern with his appearance really suits his laconic style and befits a man prepared to quote Ron Burgundy of *Anchorman* fame in his retirement announcement. It's a model that should be followed by more of the tattooed pretty boys that seem to flood our sports fields these days.

At the other end of the scale, Titans advertising blimp Jamal Idris should care more about what people think of his appearance. His ridiculous haircut screams "look at me", but his on-field performance and offseason weight gain invited nought but laughter. Young, hard-working rake Matt Srama, despite far less in the scalp department, provokes far less criticism on and off the park. Idris would do well to follow this example.

Ben Ridge gets his curly locks out for the punters and is certainly a sight when he gets hit hard in full flight. To add to that, backrow partner Ryan James gets back to our caveman roots with a wild haircut. He was lucky to escape suspension for a similarly wild hit when turning out for Tweed Heads in the Queensland Cup. Unluckily for viewers, he didn't get a run in this game.

For the Eels, Fuifui Moimoi has tried to mix up the hairstyles over the years and doesn't mind the long braids, corn rows or a shaggy do.

All in all, it's a great look for the sport. There's nothing like a big hit between two big blokes, with hair and limbs flying all over the place. There wasn't a lot on the line in this game given the Eels had locked in the spoon and the Titans had all but extinguished their finals hopes with some poor form early in the season. However, with a few players taking the time to grow a full head of hair, there is still plenty for those viewers who are trying to squeeze the last drops out of the regular season's footy watching.

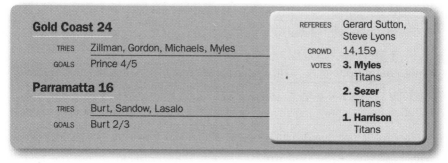

Gold Coast 24		REFEREES	Gerard Sutton, Steve Lyons
TRIES	Zillman, Gordon, Michaels, Myles	CROWD	14,159
GOALS	Prince 4/5	VOTES	**3. Myles** Titans
Parramatta 16			**2. Sezer** Titans
TRIES	Burt, Sandow, Lasalo		**1. Harrison** Titans
GOALS	Burt 2/3		

The times they are a-changin'

New Zealand Warriors *versus* **Penrith Panthers**
2pm, Sunday, 19 August
Mt Smart Stadium, Auckland

JOSH SMITH

AM AT SYDNEY INTERNATIONAL AIRPORT, IT'S 19 AUGUST, 2012 and the ability to keep track, watch, read and interact during games has changed dramatically in recent years as a result of unprecedented technological advances. Sometimes the game itself can seem incidental in the experience.

Technology has changed the way we consume our rugby league. Television and radio coverage of the game are old hat now.

Remembering back to my early days, it was all about free-to-air TV coverage (three games per weekend): Friday night footy, the 3pm game on Saturday and a Sunday afternoon match. If you were not at the game, you had AM radio with around the grounds to update you on the scores. Towards the end of the season you might have two callers at different grounds if it had some finals bearing. Reading about the game meant waiting for the paper the next day or reading *Big League* the following week to check out the stats and information about the game.

All of this still exists today but Facebook, Twitter and blogs have increased our diet and our consumption and we now have the capacity to share it all quickly.

In today's game it's information overload. Twitter and Facebook have proven fertile grounds for players, commentators, bloggers, punters clubs and podcasters to react to happenings in a game in real time on a medium effectively free of charge and not bound by the stricture of editorial review. The Twitter revolution is particularly interesting. The concept of 140 characters to convey one's thoughts has proven to be a vital part of NRL interactions, especially during the 2012 season.

Today's match pits the New Zealand Warriors up against the Penrith Panthers. I digested this game from 36,000 feet up on inflight wireless (another recent advance) only, from Twitter, Facebook and blogs, shunning the traditional media to gauge my thoughts on the match ... and this is what I learnt.

This match was tipped to be a game of touch football. Shaun Johnson was expected to dominate and the Warriors would account for the Panthers easily as the boys from Penrith would not be able to keep up with the scoring prowess of this ad lib Warriors lineup.

The match started exactly that way. My Twitter feed fired up with a try to the Warriors. First on line was the Vodafone Warriors feed with a try within the first five minutes. In recent weeks, with their season on the line, the Warriors had performed poorly and, with their finals hopes dashed, they were expected to play loose ... another try in the 23rd minute to the Warriors and the floodgates looked like they were about to open. The Panthers, though, hit back just before the break with a try and headed into the sheds 10-6 down ... maybe the second half was going to open up?

The Warriors scored early in the second half and it seemed like they might be ready to crack the game open. But again, like the last three weeks, the Warriors couldn't go on with it and let the Panthers back into the match. The Panthers stuck with it and kept themselves close enough to force a win. When Travis Robinson went over in the 76th minute, scores were level. To make matters worse, the defenders allowed him to come around and make the conversion simpler. The Panthers held on and won the match 18-16.

The prospect of the wooden spoon is clearly a good motivator.

Penrith 18		REFEREES	Gavin Badger, David Munro
TRIES	Coote, Kingston, T.Robinson	CROWD	11,000
GOALS	Walsh 3/3	VOTES	**3. Coote** Panthers
New Zealand 16			**2. Mateo** Warriors
TRIES	Henry 2, Johnson		**1. McKendry** Panthers
GOALS	Maloney 2/3		

Brilliance at Brookie

Manly Sea Eagles *versus* **Newcastle Knights**
3pm, Sunday, 19 August
Brookvale Oval, Sydney

ADAM MUYT

I
T'S A PICTURE PERFECT DAY IN SYDNEY FOR THIS SUNDAY ARVO CLASH AT BROOKIE. And the
weather isn't too bad down here in Tasmania, either. I settle in to watch the Sunday
telecast with Sterlo, Freddy, Gus and Vossy. Good on Channel Nine/GEM who,
this year, finally gave league-lovers in Melbourne and Tassie (and elsewhere in AFL-
land) regular broadcasting of games.

This looks to be an intriguing match: both teams have been playing well in recent
weeks with Newcastle needing to win to have any chance of a finals spot and Manly
looking to cement a top four spot. Throw in the 'Wayne Bennett factor' – no team he's
coached has missed the finals since 1991 – and the 'Manly-at-full-strength-at-last factor'
and who knows how it'll unravel.

It unravels quickly – at least for the Knights. From the kick-off, Roberts boots the
ball out on the full. Gus captures the moment perfectly, as only he can: "I kin
unnerstan' someone missin' a dart board but how do ya miss 60 metres of field?"

A penalty to Manly puts pressure on Newcastle straight away. Three minutes in,
Lyon goes over on the right. Conversion. A few minutes later, Glenn Stewart crashes
over, carrying a couple of Knights players with him. Lyon converts: 12-0 after six
minutes.

Taufua gets the chance to make it three tries in 10 minutes but lets the ball fly
through his fingers and over the sideline. Things are looking ominous for the Knights.

"It's men against boys at the moment," comments Voss but, three minutes later, in their first foray up the other end of the ground, the Knights fling the ball wide on the right to Uate who juggles the pill before grounding it. 12-4.

Just as Newcastle look to be finding their feet, the monster that is Tony Williams collects the ball in the backline, offers the don't argue to Mullen and strolls over for a try. To their credit, Newcastle, don't drop their bundle – they take Manly on, only to have a try disallowed for a double movement.

And then Manly go into overdrive: Foran's over at the 22-minute mark, T-Rex gets another after 27 and Brett Stewart grabs two in the last 10 minutes of the half. The siren sounds: 38-4. Nothing but plain ugly for the Knights – just about perfect for the defending premiers.

Manly put in a similar first-half display against Parra a few weeks earlier and then went to sleep. I'm a little wary they'll do it again; they need to keep scoreboard pressure going, if only to build a better for and against in this tight competition. But it doesn't happen – not because of any slackening off though. Rather, the injury toll mounts. King and Ballin went off early in the first half – now David Williams and Buhrer are gone too. With 30 minutes still on the clock, there's no-one left on the interchange bench.

Toovey makes the best of a bad situation with some player adjustments but Newcastle smell the positional awkwardness and grab three tries in 12 minutes. It's 38-20 with 17 minutes left on the clock. Enough time to steal a win; the tension rises in one Hobart lounge room.

And then Daly Cherry-Evans shows us pure genius. Newcastle has a line dropout coming their way – the Knights players move out beyond the 20 to regain the kick. DCE fools them with a short kick that goes just beyond the required 10 metres and straight into Foran's arms, who then takes the ball 60 metres downfield. A rough finish on him ends with a penalty to Manly. Pressure relieved – a game changer.

The match finishes with Taufua scoring in the final minutes to give Manly a 42-20 win. Wayne Bennett's fine run of coaching teams to finals appearances ends.

Manly have been very good today but with all the injuries – Watmough ended up injured, too – I'm a little worried. How many of the wounded will be back in time for the big Broncos game in just five days?

Manly 42		REFEREES	Jason Robinson, Phil Haines
TRIES	B. Stewart, T. Williams 2; G. Stewart, Lyon, K. Foran, Taufua	CROWD	14,191
GOALS	Lyon 5/8	VOTES	**3. Cherry-Evans** Sea Eagles
Newcastle 20			**2. B. Stewart** Sea Eagles
TRIES	K. Naiqama 2; Mullen, Uate		**1. K. Foran** Sea Eagles
GOALS	Roberts 2/4		

Sitting out September

St George Illawarra Dragons *versus* **North Queensland Cowboys**
7pm, Monday, 20 August
WIN Stadium, Sydney

MICHAEL ADAMS

AT A DINNER A FEW WEEKS AGO, I SAID TO MY STEP-SISTER: "We've got to sit this one out." Perhaps the maddest in a family of mad Dragons fans, Adriana has nonetheless not had to carry the lifetime of frustration and disappointment the experience of being a Dragons fan has been for me, having only been converted in the last decade or so. Sure, she was there on that terrible night at the SFS in 2005. And yes, like me, she bought her GF tickets in June back in 2009. Unlike me, she had the balls to front up to Homebush regardless for that memorably Dragons-less match. Anyone who can make it through the trauma that was routine for a Dragons fan of the early 21st century doesn't need to prove their worth to me. That glorious October night in 2010 is hers as much as mine.

Seeing a premiership after only 10 years of unwavering support gives you a sunny perspective and optimistic outlook that a jaded old fool like me just can't share. As we sat at dinner bemoaning the state of our club this year, she got out her metaphorical calculator to talk mathematical chances. "But we could still make the finals if..."

"No," I said, cutting her off. "Some years you've just got to sit it out. "

In the weeks that followed, I disregarded my own words. A home victory against the Storm came when most other teams in the mediocrity pool, stretching from sixth to thirteenth on the premiership ladder, had dropped their respective bundles. "We could be in the eight after we beat the Roosters next week", I caught myself thinking.

Of course, that win never came and now here we are back in Wollongong. Victory over the Cowboys would still not be enough. Defeat would snuff out the flame for good. It's a wretched situation to be in and, as much as I believe in that philosophical pearl of wisdom I dropped to Adriana that night at dinner, it is no less bitter a pill to swallow for the fact. How great must it feel to not care about football?

The game is underway and misery is piled upon misery. The Dragons are listless and have no idea how to get across the tryline. Johnathan Thurston is everywhere and the Cowboys are up by 12. Ben Creagh scores for the Dragons, only to drop the ball cold after the ensuing Cowboys kick-off. The Cowboys are in again and I'm in agony. Not for the first time in my life I silently curse my father for lumbering me with this joke of a team. Would it have been too much to ask to bring me up a Bulldogs supporter? Or a Broncos one? They know how to win. For Christ's sake, even as a Panthers fan I would have seen more premierships than this mob has been able to produce in my lifetime.

But wait! Hang on Dad, all is forgiven. By halftime we are only behind by two. Shortly after the break we take the lead. "Screw sitting this one out," I think as I get my calculator out. Sweet, this one's in the bag. We should be able to give the Warriors a towelling in the 'Gong next Saturday. Then we just need to overcome the emotion of Hindy's last match at Parra Stadium and flog the Eels – no dramas there. The Tigers are rubbish; the Broncos will struggle to win another game. We're going to the finals!

No sooner have I begun plotting our miraculous route from eighth spot to the premiership when the Cowboys jolt me back to reality with a try. Another soon follows and it is all over – the game, the season, my chances of a peaceful sleep tonight. I guess I should thank the Cowboys for putting me out of my misery. We just haven't been good enough. We've just got to sit this one out.

North Queensland 32		REFEREES	Ashley Klein, Adam Devcich
TRIES	Linnett 2; Bowen, Graham, Thurston	CROWD	9,245
GOALS	Thurston 6/6	VOTES	**3. Thurston** Cowboys
St George Illawarra 22			**2. Bowen** Cowboys
TRIES	Vidot, Hunt, Rein, Creagh		**1. Johnson** Cowboys
GOALS	Soward 3/4		

Round 25

Riding the coattails of the Silvertails

Manly Sea Eagles *versus*
Brisbane Broncos
7.30pm, Friday, 24 August
Brookvale Oval, Sydney

HUW FOWLES

AFTER ROUND 24, 2012		
1	Bulldogs	17-5
2	Storm	15-7
3	Rabbitohs	14-8
4	Sea Eagles	14-8
5	Cowboys	13-9
6	Sharks	12-9-1
7	Broncos	11-11
8	Tigers	11-11
9	Raiders	11-11
10	Titans	10-12
11	Knights	10-12
12	Dragons	9-13
13	Warriors	8-14
14	Roosters	7-14-1
15	Panthers	7-15
16	Eels	6-16

THIS IS ALWAYS ONE OF MY FAVOURITE FIXTURES OF THE YEAR. I have an unusual soft spot for both teams. Despite being a Brisbane boy, I grew up in a Bronco-less era and adopted Manly as my team at the age of six, having mistaken Manly's maroon jerseys for traditional cane toad colours. I just thought these guys were from that bayside suburb of South East Brisbane that had a harbour and views of Moreton Bay and that Wynnum-Manly (where greats like Lewis, Miles and Dowling played in the mid-'80s) was the name of another Brisbane suburb altogether.

By the time I'd learnt the error of my ways, it was too late. I'd fallen in love with the likes of 'Crusher' Cleal and Ronny Gibbs and I believed that Bobby Fulton could walk on water. I'd even arranged that when I turned my Queensland State of Origin baseball cap inside out it had MANLY shabbily emblazoned across the front in the same shade of beige as my brother's newly painted bedroom. Hey, don't knock it. It got the message across and that's all that matters. The fact that the paint flecks looked like dandruff was the price I chose to pay. Anyway, everyone knows there's only one true cause of dandruff – black t-shirts. So now that we've cleared that up, let's move on. To 1988.

The year 1988 was an interesting time in Brisbane's history. Until then Brisbane was still a big country town at heart that had been ruled for decades by Sir Johannes Bjelke-Petersen, the Deen brothers' renovations and brown paper bags of cash. Bris-Vegas announced its arrival on the world stage with the Fitzgerald Inquiry (my soap opera of choice as a teenager), World Expo 88, Stefan's Skyneedle and the formation of the Brisbane Broncos.

Thanks to Barry Maranta and 'Porky' Morgan, the Brisbane Broncos entered the NSWRL with much fanfare and they played their first game at Lang Park against the reigning premiers – the Manly-Warringah Sea Eagles. The Broncos, coincidentally led by former Wynnum-Manly greats Lewis, Miles and Dowling, smashed the Sea Eagles 44-10 in front of a respectable crowd of 17,000. In doing so, they had also taken only 80 minutes to firmly quash the view of some Mexicans that the Queenslanders would struggle to hold their own in the big boys' competition.

So here these teams were again, nearly a quarter of a century later, in front of a similarly sized crowd but at a very different venue. Unlike that first game at The Cauldron, this game was set in the smaller Brookvale *bain-marie*.

The home side won.

Highlights were thin on the ground. It was a 10-minute burst in the middle of the first half that did the job with Brett Stewart, Daly Cherry-Evans and Jamie Lyon doing most of the damage. 16-0 at the half. Game over.

The second half reached no great heights. The score remained unchanged for the entire 40 minutes with the Broncos not opening their account until after the final siren.

Like their canary yellow away strips, the Broncos' performance was putrid from head to toe. If they scrape into the eight, no one is going to be quaking in their boots at the prospect of facing them in the first week of the finals. Most teams will relish the scenario.

Manly, on the other hand, never needed to get out of second gear. They are peaking at the right time of the year and have all their guns fit and firing. At this rate, I may enjoy another fruitful September riding on the back of the Silvertails' coattails.

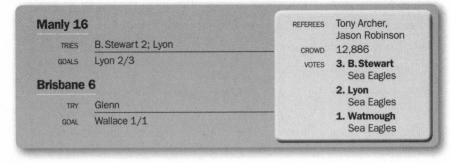

Manly 16				REFEREES	Tony Archer, Jason Robinson
TRIES	B. Stewart 2; Lyon			CROWD	12,886
GOALS	Lyon 2/3			VOTES	**3. B. Stewart** Sea Eagles
Brisbane 6					**2. Lyon** Sea Eagles
TRY	Glenn				**1. Watmough** Sea Eagles
GOAL	Wallace 1/1				

Radio silence

Canberra Raiders *versus* **Canterbury Bulldogs**
7.30pm, Friday, 24 August
Canberra Stadium, Canberra

MATT TEDESCHI

A S A RUGBY LEAGUE FAN LIVING IN REGIONAL NSW, unable to get to many football grounds a year, television coverage is critical. In this Round 25 match, for only the second time in 2012, Canberra has snared a free-to-air game on Channel Nine. The only downside to this is that we have been shafted into the delayed 9.30pm graveyard timeslot.

In my experience, there is nothing worse than knowing the result before watching the game. *Nothing!* It is a pain I have felt too often in the past and I wouldn't allow it to ruin this game. The only solution I could come up with was complete radio silence. The house was in lockdown from 7.30pm to 11.30pm. No phones, no internet, no visitors, no radio and no changing the channel. Nothing was going to stop me enjoying the season-defining game against the top of the table Canterbury Bulldogs in the comfort of my own home.

As enjoyable as watching Manly beat Brisbane in the live game was, it was simultaneously two hours of torture. I was sitting on the couch with Rob McInnes, another Canberra tragic. I was biting fingernails, fidgeting, doing everything to make time go faster. It didn't work. The first game lasted an eternity and it only heightened my nerves. I desperately wanted to check the phone to ease my suffering but I knew if I did, the night would be ruined.

All my confidence in the team, a confidence that never waivers despite not having won a premiership since 1994, could not have prepared me for the following 80 minutes. We were hosting a team that hadn't lost in over three months, but we were on a winning streak of three.

The rugby league gods were indeed on Canberra's side. Temperatures were somewhere below freezing which was perfect for the home team but less so for the Channel Nine sideline commentators.

I am a fairly stubborn person. It is rare that an opinion that I have held on a player ever changes. Gareth Southgate is a classic example. He will never be forgiven, after missing his penalty against Germany in the Euro '96 semi-final. Jason Bulgarelli was always on thin ice, but dropping the ball over the line in the final minute of the 2003 finals while trailing 17-16 permanently secured him a spot in my most hated list. Brett Finch joined that list when he foolishly kicked the ball out on the full from a 20-metre restart, giving Newcastle a two-point win from the ensuing after-the-siren penalty goal. Raiders players who show general incompetence can quickly fall on my bad side too. More recently these have included Daniel Vidot, Justin Carney and Travis Waddell.

This is a story of redemption though. Josh McCrone had spent a good couple of seasons in the company of the aforementioned players. After yet another abhorrent display in 2010, he became subject to a verballing from yours truly as he walked off the SFS: "Crone! You'll never play NRL again!"

Josh McCrone, I am sorry. I rarely admit it, but I am happy to say that I was wrong. 'Crone' has had to step up in the absence of Terry Campese. Not only has he done that, he has developed into a leader and the heart and soul of the Raiders team. He cemented that on Friday night by putting on another dominant display which included three try assists, two line break assists and a line break of his own.

Canberra showed class and tactical genius to highlight the few weaknesses in the Bulldogs team and the result was a 34-6 upset.

Welcome to the team, Sandor Earl. A hat-trick of tries and, if not for Russell 'Replay' Smith, he would have had an unbelievable fourth. The only feature of the game that might have outshone his performance was seeing young prop Mark Nicholls get over the line for the first try of his career. The joy on his face was priceless.

The lockdown is now over. The Raiders are back! And I couldn't be more excited. Bring on the finals.

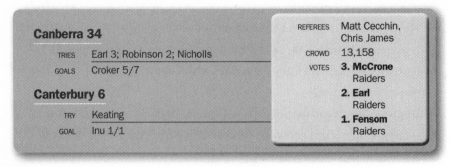

Canberra 34		REFEREES	Matt Cecchin, Chris James
TRIES	Earl 3; Robinson 2; Nicholls	CROWD	13,158
GOALS	Croker 5/7	VOTES	**3. McCrone** Raiders
Canterbury 6			**2. Earl** Raiders
TRY	Keating		**1. Fensom** Raiders
GOAL	Inu 1/1		

Hot tips

Penrith Panthers *versus* **Gold Coast Titans**
3.30pm, Saturday, 25 August
Centrebet Stadium, Sydney

MARK SHANNON

I HAVE AN SMS INBOX FULL OF HOT RACING TIPS. My mate assures me that these tips are the real deal. He has sent them to me late, just as I am about to head down to South-port Sharks to watch the Penrith-Titans clash. A quick internet check shows that three of the first four tips have already saluted. Matt is right. These tips are the real deal.

Like all good race tips, their origin seems to be unknown. Matt gets them off a bloke at work, who gets them off a mate, who gets them off a mate, who gets them from a bloke in Sydney. The whole tipping game seems to work a bit like a drug cartel where Mr Big remains anonymous and a long way from the street action.

The next tip is due to go soon. I bustle past a few pensioners on walking frames, past the glass tanks with the real sharks and past the bored reception staff and manage to get on just before they jump. $30 a win. You beauty. I'm on. I check the tote. It is paying $15 and I'm straight out. It races like it has been trained by Ricky Stuart, and finishes well back.

I grab a schooner and look for the footy. There is one small monitor showing the NRL but no sound. Thankfully it's close to the TAB. Scott Prince is running back after converting a Mead try. The Titans have too much to play for. They'll belt the hapless Panthers. I better get back to the TAB. Tip No. 6 is getting ready to jump.

The guy on SKY channel says my horse will be very hard to beat.

He is spot on. My horse is very hard to beat but one just manages to beat it. An unlucky second. Things aren't looking too good. I glance back now and then to the footy. Brad Tighe and Michael Jennings seem to be featuring heavily. The crowd is very small. I reckon Gus Gould might be in the TAB as well.

Another SMS tells me to back Southern Speed in Adelaide. It's a certainty, says my mate Colin. I load $50 on it. It bolts in like a good thing should. It wins by so far that the second horse wouldn't protest, even if it was ridden by Paul Gallen.

The footy looks like it is heading for a close finish. There are only two points in it with 20 minutes to go. The Titans will surely turn it on now and put paid to the Penrith boys.

Next thing Jennings and Mansour combine for a brilliant try and the Titans are in trouble.

The last tip is a $4 chance in the last in Sydney called Dystopia. This animal will determine my financial destiny for the day. He strides to the front in the straight and appears headed for an easy victory until it gets a stitch with 50 to go. A horse is flying home along the inside rail. They hit the line. It is desperately close.

"The outside just hung on," I say to the assembled punters with confidence I do not feel. The slow motion replay is excruciating. Heads up, heads down. I don't know. And the winner is ... Dystopia. You beauty. The tips have saved the day.

No-one has saved the Titans. The Panthers have pulled away for a comfortable win. It ends the season for the Titans; they can no longer make the semis. Brad Tighe has had a real day out. The gallops are finishing up and the 'cheats on seats' fire up. The needy and the greedy are in the TAB to plot their way through this minefield. I join them and donate back $50 of my winnings. As Gus would say: "No, no, no, no,no ..."

I can't believe my stupidity. I head for the exit. Just like the Titans.

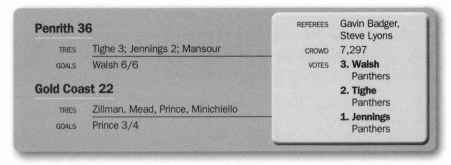

Penrith 36		REFEREES	Gavin Badger, Steve Lyons
TRIES	Tighe 3; Jennings 2; Mansour	CROWD	7,297
GOALS	Walsh 6/6	VOTES	**3. Walsh** Panthers
Gold Coast 22			**2. Tighe** Panthers
TRIES	Zillman, Mead, Prince, Minichiello		**1. Jennings** Panthers
GOALS	Prince 3/4		

At the footy with Margaret and David

St George Illawarra Dragons *versus* New Zealand Warriors
5.30pm, Saturday, 25 August
WIN Stadium, Sydney

PAUL CONNOLLY

MARGARET   Set against the backdrop of a once-thriving industrial city – one now searching for a new raison d'etre – *Dragon Warriors* tells the story of two struggling rugby league teams, each carrying emotional and physical scars from a season of profound disappointment. Coached by young newcomer Steve Price, a man struggling to decide whether to follow in the footsteps of his legendary predecessor or to forge his own path, the Dragons are a shadow of the team they once were. The Warriors, meanwhile, have just sacked their coach having endured what could only be called a disastrous year, going from preseason heavyweights to easybeats. On the eve of the big game, the sacked coach's assistant, Tony Iro, comes in to help the star-studded side salvage something from the wreckage. Amid this over-arching narrative is the touching story of two men, Dragons Dean Young and Ben Hornby, playing their final home game after years of service to the club they love and looking to go out on a high.

Dragon Warriors is the latest film in the long-running 2012 NRL series and while, for me, it lacked some of the excitement and suspense of the earlier installments, its undercurrent of sadness gives the film real meaning and offers an insight into both the human condition and the roller-coaster life of the professional athlete. The direction is adequate, the camera work clean and crisp and the script mostly believable but, for me, the performances make the film worth watching. Young and Hornby play the ageing stars quite wonderfully while Price steals the show with his turn as the put-upon rookie coach. He really does look as if the weight of history is sitting squarely on his shoulders. *David?*

DAVID   I was irritated by this film.

MARGARET   *Oh, David!*

DAVID   I just found it unbelievable. We're told the Dragons are a team bereft of spark and ideas and yet they come out and play with the kind of razzle-dazzle we haven't seen since Baz Luhrmann's *Strictly Ballroom*. The Warriors, meanwhile, are a team supposedly packed with stars yet what they serve up would not be out of place within the oeuvre of George A. Romero.

MARGARET   *Yes, but ...*

DAVID   We're also meant to buy that a football club, the Dragons, with a supposedly proud and successful history, would have a gormless rookie in the top job. It beggars belief.

MARGARET   *Gormless?* That's harsh, David. For me, Price reminded me of Bogart in *Casablanca*, his mournful visage hinting at a whirling internal life. I found him an intriguing character.

DAVID   Not me, Margaret. For me, he brought to mind Bernie from *Weekend at Bernie's*, though Bernie had more personality.

MARGARET	*Oh, David!* [LAUGHS]
DAVID	But there were some nice moments.
MARGARET	There were.
DAVID	When that red-headed character, Ben Creagh, flicks a ball behind his back setting up a try for his teammate. That was a nice touch.
MARGARET	Yes, I loved that scene too, David. Matt Cooper it was. Leading man looks, don't you think, David?
DAVID	If you say so, Margaret.
MARGARET	Surely you also enjoyed the scene where that warhorse Josh Miller scored his first try of the year, thus saving himself the indignity of a Mad Monday nudie run — another narrative thread that hangs tantalisingly over the main storyline.
DAVID	*Implausible.*
MARGARET	That grown men would indulge in a ritual like the nudie run?
DAVID	No, that anyone with the profound footballing limitations of Josh Miller would make an NRL side.
MARGARET	*Oh, David.* It's the movies. You have to suspend disbelief.
DAVID	Yes, but not throw it out the window altogether. One star from me.
MARGARET	Three from me.

St George Illawarra 38

TRIES	Nightingale 2; Cooper, C. Stanley, Creagh, Matthews, Miller
GOALS	Soward 5/6, Hornby 0/1

New Zealand 6

TRY	Johnson
GOAL	Maloney 1/1

REFEREES	Jared Maxwell, Adam Gee
CROWD	11,261
VOTES	**3. Merrin** Dragons
	2. Nightingale Dragons
	1. Creagh Dragons

Many colours

North Queensland Cowboys *versus* Newcastle Knights
7.30pm, Saturday, 25 August
Dairy Farmers Stadium, Townsville

JOHN HARMS

'M NOT SURE IF I BARRACK FOR A TEAM IN THE NRL. I mean really barrack. When we first moved to the Darling Downs in 1972 and got caught up in rugby league, the team I felt most strongly about was the Oakey Bears, our home-town team. They meant a lot to me. I went to all the home games and listened when they were involved in the broadcast match on 4WK.

In the BRL, I followed Wynnum-Manly because they were the bottom team (that's the sort of kid I was). In the NSWRL I chose Western Suburbs because they wore Oakey colours – black with a white V. I was a genuine barracker for a while. No posters on the wall though. A couple years later when I was into wearing footy jumpers (Geelong, West Ham) the only Sydney jumper the local sports shop had was Cronulla (with those innovative three-quarter sleeves), which I bought with lawn-mowing money. So, for a while I had a soft spot for the Sharks.

I liked Newtown when they were the under-est of dogs, and then Parramatta in the early '80s because I admired their lightweight backline which could match other sides with sheer pace and skill (although Eric Grothe was a gorilla). When the Broncos were formed, I didn't much like them even though I lived in Brisbane. They really knocked the suburban comp about and that loss was never going to be retrieved. I liked some of the characters who played for the Broncos: Alfie and Kevvy and Pearl.

Then Super League came along and I thought that rugby league had lost its way completely – because it had. Writing a book about Steve Renouf helped me connect with the game again and I developed a soft spot for the Broncos, which may also have been thanks to a few wagers here and there.

Most recently I've kept an eye on two teams – the Cowboys, because I love Townsville and the Deep North, and Melbourne, because I have lived here. I think Cameron Smith is one of the best leaders in Australian sport. And Billy Slater is Billy Slater.

Nowadays, I am motivated by a childish dislike of Manly and a love of the game. Often it takes a few minutes of a game before I know where my heart is and which team

I'm supporting. I am always a barracker in the AFL (Geelong mean a lot to me); I'm an observer in the NRL. I'm a barracker when State of Origin comes around.

When the Cowboys come up against Newcastle in Townsville I am hoping the home team does well. I am keen for them to finish in the top four. I don't really care if Newcastle miss out on the top eight. They have a mathematical chance but it is highly unlikely unless a whole series of results go their way.

Things start well for the northerners but, when the Knights attack, Timana Tahu strolls over after a cross-field bomb. The crowd is not thrilled with this start and they call for Johnathan Thurston to lift his team. Well-fed by Anthony Mitchell, a late replacement for Michael Morgan, the champion five-eighth controls the attack and waltzes through a hole to go in near the posts. The Knights defensive woes continue with Bowen slicing through to score. I am barracking for rugby league but this is not a stellar example of a contest.

At least there's plenty of tries. The Cowboys register their third in quick time when Bowen steps through on his own line and races clear. Tate positions himself perfectly on the inside and streaks away. A typical length-of-the-field Cowboys try.

Newcastle fight back with another try to Tahu and Dane Gagai penetrates the line to make it 14-18 at halftime.

The second half is surprisingly dour. Both sides tighten their defences, probably on the back of lemon-time sprays. Matt Scott leads the Cowboys with a powerful display. Thurston's kicking game keeps them safe and wins them enough field position for the skipper to land a couple of penalties.

It's a sound win, 22-14, but not a head-turning win. The Cowboys show enough to make me think they can do some damage in the finals.

I wonder how the Oakey Bears are faring this season.

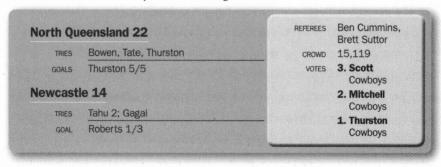

North Queensland 22		REFEREES	Ben Cummins, Brett Suttor
TRIES	Bowen, Tate, Thurston	CROWD	15,119
GOALS	Thurston 5/5	VOTES	**3. Scott** Cowboys
Newcastle 14			**2. Mitchell** Cowboys
TRIES	Tahu 2; Gagai		**1. Thurston** Cowboys
GOAL	Roberts 1/3		

Toothless Tigers

Sydney Roosters *versus* **Wests Tigers**
2pm, Sunday, 26 August
Allianz Stadium, Sydney

DARA LAWLOR

WAS KNACKERED BY THE TIME I ARRIVED IN AUCKLAND. I hadn't realised the inbound journey from Bangkok was only 10 minutes shorter than the trip to Bangkok from London. I was down to see my country play in that four-yearly sports jamboree that you all despise – sometimes with good reason. I'd planned the trip to coincide with the 2011 NRL Grand Final and travelled with the hope that the Wests Tigers – the team I fell for in 2005 during the visit to Australia for my brother's wedding – would be there.

Deirdre, an old mate from my university days in Dublin, picked me up at the airport and her husband Rik handed me a bottle of Speights as I arrived in the door and collapsed on the couch. He flicked on the telly in time to show a bearded Tim Sheens ripping off his headset and throwing it down in disgust. The replay showed Krisnan Inu scoring the winning try for the Warriors and the Tigers were out. Bugger!

I didn't quite cry myself to sleep that night – I hadn't the energy after a 32-hour trip from Dublin and was crucified with jetlag – but I was livid. Ireland smashing the Wallabies the following evening at Eden Park along with Dublin winning their first All-Ireland football final in 16 years that weekend went a long way towards tempering my disappointment but I had a nagging and lingering irritation over the following weeks and the Grand Final wasn't as enjoyable as it might have been.

The Tigers did it to me again yesterday morning. I woke at 4am to discover that their Round 25 match against the Roosters was actually taking place an hour later. "Balls," I muttered and reset the alarm for 10 minutes to five.

Watching NRL matches on internet streaming sites can be an amusing experience, especially when there are recurring ads in the background for curing "your constipation" soundtracked by funky music. Neither I, nor the Roosters, were suffering from constipation yesterday. A week after succumbing to the high-flying Bulldogs in golden point extra time, the Tigers walked on to the pitch without Robbie Farah. They squatted down, took aim and never fired a shot.

Pitch dark outside my window, I watched in horror as the Tigers, after a promising first 10 minutes, rolled over and conceded a nightmare five tries in the first half. Great games build tension and like classic novels and films, they always ebb and flow. There was absolutely no drama when practically every Braith Anasta kick to the in-goal came down in a Rooster player's arms, no surprise when Tim Moltzen's restart went dead on the 20-minute mark and no shock when Gareth Ellis conceded another penalty two minutes later.

When Frank Paul Nu'uausala and Daniel Tupou scored in the first 20, I had a feeling that the game was up. Tupou is a great find for the Roosters, deserved his hat-trick, and his take for the Roosters' second try was Folau-esque. Tries from Shaun Kenny-Dowall, Tautau Moga and a second from Tupou saw the Roosters lead by 26-0 at halftime. This increased to 32-0 once Mitchell Pearce went over and Anasta converted within three minutes of the restart and any hopes the Tigers had of a resurgence once Marika Koroibete and Blake Ayshford scored in the 48th and 51st minutes respectively were extinguished as soon as Tupou scored his third two minutes later.

It's hard to know what to make of this performance. Were the Roosters fantastic or the Tigers bloody awful? I'd say the arrow on the gauge is pointing more towards the Tigers not having the stomach for the fight and being flat after running the Bulldogs so close last weekend. A flick through the Tigers' roster shows a squad with more than its share of stars and a pack with which Craig Bellamy could win a Grand Final. There's one glaring omission though. They don't have a halfback that binds the team together. I said to a Manly fan in the jacks at halftime during last year's Grand Final that I reckoned Benji Marshall needed a strong and disciplined player inside him. He hasn't had one since Scott Prince moved on in 2005. The Tigers won't win a Premiership as long as Marshall is filling this role.

And for the Roosters? They have a lot to look forward to with the emergence of some fine young backs, a fantastic prop with a serious rep future in Martin Kennedy and the arrival of Sonny Bill Williams. What happens once Williams rubs their noses in it and returns to the All Blacks to prepare for the 2015 Rugby World Cup is anyone's guess, but next year could be their year.

Marshall was placed on report for a hit on Jared Waerea-Hargreaves towards the end of the game. He's confident he'll be cleared to play the Storm next weekend, but I don't think his presence will make any difference. I'm pretty sure that 2012's title dreams have now well and truly withered and died.

Sydney Roosters 44

TRIES	Tupou 3; Minichiello, Moga, Kenny-Dowall, Pearce, Nu'uausala
GOALS	Anasta 6/8

Wests Tigers 20

TRIES	Ayshford, Koroibete, Heighington, Murdoch-Masila
GOALS	Marshall 2/4

REFEREES	Ashley Klein, Adam Devcich
CROWD	15,736
VOTES	**3. Cordner** Roosters
	2. Kennedy Roosters
	1. Tupou Roosters

Surreal

South Sydney Rabbitohs *versus* Parramatta Eels
3pm, Sunday, 26 August
ANZ Stadium, Sydney
DOUG ROWETH

I T'S SUCH A WEIRD FEELING. INDESCRIBABLE, LIKE NOTHING I'VE EVER EXPERIENCED. But it's something that just about every other rugby league fan already knows. Many are well accustomed to it: what it feels like when your club plays finals football.

But it's not that they've missed out before. In recent times, the South Sydney Rabbitohs, a club with arguably more history (and success) than any other in the NRL, haven't even gone close. Since 1989, the Rabbitohs have been conspicuously missing every September (bar one). The Pride of the League have been to hell and back in that time, with four wooden spoons and even eviction from the competition for two seasons.

But now, curiously, the Rabbits take on Parramatta knowing that a win today will propel them into third place and a peek behind the curtain of finals football. What a remarkable proposition! Old-school Bunnies fans have waited a generation for this: to be at the pointy end of the competition at the pointy end of the season. For the rest of us, these are uncharted waters. It's all a little surreal.

By contrast, the bottom-placed Eels haven't much to play for, other than their remote chance to avoid the wooden spoon and salvage a vague sense of dignity for spiritual leader Nathan Hindmarsh and veteran Luke Burt, whose image adorns the Parramatta jersey in recognition of his efforts.

But minutes after kick-off, it all looks unlikely when a pinpoint Adam Reynolds kick finds Matt King and South Sydney are in. When Moimoi hits Reynolds with a shot that has him placed on report, the Souths halfback adds two points . The Rabbits lead 8-0.

More ill-discipline costs Parramatta field position, forcing the Eels to hold out a rampaging Greg Inglis from point blank range, unsurprisingly unsuccessfully. South Sydney is firmly in control at 14-0. We're only 19 minutes in and this certainly looks like a top four side against a cellar-dweller.

But before halftime, the Eels come to life. Parramatta revelation Joseph Paulo turns a ball inside, putting fullback Jake Mullaney in space, who then finds farewell hero Luke Burt and the Eels run 60 metres from nothing to score beneath the posts. Parramatta isn't out of this now at 14-6, a message Michael Maguire will be undoubtedly drumming into South Sydney as they hit the sheds at halftime.

The Rabbitohs know how critical the next 40 minutes is. A few minutes into the second half, Greg Inglis defuses a Chris Sandow kick on his own goalline, returning it 20 metres or so, brutally bumping off attempted defenders in his wake, and then two sets later at the other end of the field, he comes up into the line and throws a perfect cut-out pass to Nathan Merritt. The Rabbits lead 18-6 and the green and red faithful laud the value of Greg Inglis. They salivate thinking of what he may produce in the finals.

By the time an hour is gone, this match is wrapped up. Adam Reynolds creates the overlap for Dylan Farrell to make amends for an earlier bombed try. And then Greg Inglis strolls over for his second of the afternoon and the score becomes 30-6.

When the siren sounds, after two more late tries, the Rabbitohs leave the field in third place having clinically disposed of Parramatta 38-6 yet, curiously, have not been inspiring. There is still a lot of work to do as they head into September.

Finals football is not just a dream anymore, it's not just something that happens to someone else. In two weeks, South Sydney are playing in September. That's when the real test begins, the one that fascinates the entire NRL. The one Rabbitohs fans have waited 23 long years for now: a realistic shot in the finals. What a surreal thing to be writing.

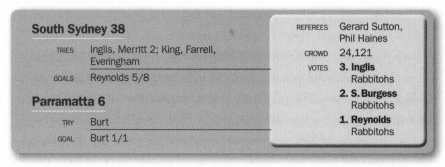

South Sydney 38		REFEREES	Gerard Sutton, Phil Haines
TRIES	Inglis, Merritt 2; King, Farrell, Everingham	CROWD	24,121
GOALS	Reynolds 5/8	VOTES	**3. Inglis** Rabbitohs
Parramatta 6			**2. S. Burgess** Rabbitohs
TRY	Burt		**1. Reynolds** Rabbitohs
GOAL	Burt 1/1		

Spooky

Melbourne Storm *versus* Cronulla Sharks
7pm, Monday, 27 August
AAMI Park, Melbourne

NATHAN BOSS

'VE MENTIONED BEFORE THAT I AM SOMEWHAT SUPERSTITIOUS. Many people find this
amusing. Some even go to some lengths to ridicule my beliefs. To those people I
put forward the following evidence of the existence of *The Curse of the Almanac*
(quite the catchy title, isn't it?). For those of you unfamiliar with the results of the
Cronulla games I have covered so far, I would highly recommend flipping through
the *Almanac* manuscript to discover some insightful pieces of modern literature.
Here is a quick snapshot:

- The Round 2 fumbling, bumbling display against the Knights;
- The Round 11 listless effort against the Bulldogs; and
- The Round 20 decimation at the hands of the Raiders.

In all, the combined total of Sharks-related *Almanac* games that I worked stood at
80-16 in favour of the bad guys. As such, you could imagine my enthusiasm when I was
assigned the Sharks' crucial Round 25 clash against the Storm. Add to that the Sharks'
abhorrent record on Monday nights and the night did not bode well for the Sutherland
Shire superstars.

The night started on a bright note at one of the many Chinese restaurants in Little
Bourke Street. My refusal to use chopsticks provided a constant source of amusement
to the group. I replied that they must be looking forward to hailing down a horse drawn
carriage to take them home so they could listen to the wireless.

We became so caught up in the general ambience of the restaurant that we were
forced to make a mad dash for the ground. Taxis were impossible to find, the traffic
insane. Mik's attempts at lightening the mood with witty insights were not well
received. Finally we made it to the ground to find a fellow Cronulla supporter fuming,
having missed the start of the game. Just a general warning to others: years of
dejection, disenchantment and depression have turned Cronulla supporters slightly
nuts. Disruptions, delays and other chaos, especially on game days, have been known
to turn the average Cronulla fan crazy.

Despite this, the action at AAMI Park actually had a calming effect on the Sharks supporters on the ground, in stark contrast to almost every other Sharks game in history. Studies have shown that blood pressure and heart-related diseases have risen dramatically in the shire since Cronulla's inclusion in the competition in 1967.

After 77 minutes of the contest, I felt I had conquered my demons. The idea of any curse was laughable. The Sharks had arrived at one of the most daunting rugby league venues in the country and proceeded to smash the Storm. They were in complete control of the contest. And then it happened …

With three minutes to go, Ryan Hoffman strolled through some brittle defence to score next to the posts. The heart palpitations began. Watching the next set unfold, I felt like I was enduring some form of out-of-body experience. I could see *The Curse of the Almanac* laughing at me as the Storm stretched the Sharks from sideline to sideline. Sure enough, the curse enveloped the body of John 'Hotdogs' Williams, who decided to leave a gaping hole down the right touchline and the Sharks yet again had snatched defeat from the jaws of victory.

Melbourne 20		REFEREES	Shayne Hayne, Alan Shortall
TRIES	Hoffman 2; Waqa, Chambers	CROWD	12,847
GOALS	Smith 2/4	VOTES	**3. Hoffman** Storm
Cronulla 18			**2. Gallen** Sharks
TRIES	Gordon, Stapleton, Tagataese		**1. Waqa** Storm
GOALS	Carney 3/4		

Round 26

Past players' day

Newcastle Knights *versus*
South Sydney Rabbitohs
7.30pm, Friday, 31 August
Hunter Stadium, Newcastle

LUKE JAMIESON

A S EVERY LEAGUE FAN WORTH HIS SALT KNOWS, the last home game of the season proper for the Newcastle Knights is normally past players' day. For omen punters, the Novacastrians are usually a solid bet as they're fuelled by the prospect of lavish praise in victory from half-cut club legends, or scathing analysis in defeat by half-cut club legends.

This season the Knights had a loose official club reunion organised by 'The Chief'. Having recently attended a past players day for a 10-year premiership reunion, I was well aware of the tall tales, bravado, rose-coloured glasses and general thirst-quenching that an event like this entails. I was lucky enough to tag along as a guest of past Newcastle player Jason 'Haircut' Moodie.

We arrive at Sydney airport mid-morning Friday. No one is carrying luggage. Chief is waiting with a mini bus for the interstate travellers. An esky of beer is parked in the aisle of the bus. Chief, being the conscientious bloke he is, has also packed a couple of garbage bags and, on each seat, there's a handmade salad roll and a bottle of water. Chief reminds the boys that there is some fresh fruit up front next to him and that it's not a sprint.

Ten or twelve salad rolls go out the window before we've hit the Pacific Highway.

Matt Parsons has had quite a few by the time we hit the F3.

The boys are starting to get a bit merry as we roll into town and pull up at the Mary Ellen Hotel. A host of other Knights past players are already scattered throughout the pub. Actually, 98 per cent of them are in the TAB with schooners in hand.

A few hours of steady schooners, war stories, comparing notes on the latest players' biographies (*Adam Cuthbertson – Coaches Pet* is due on shelves soon) and it's time to start heading to the match. Once at the Stadium there are a few vigorous handshakes thrown around from Matt Gidley and The Tinkler. Chatter is about the club being in a rebuilding phase. The Under-20s are playing. None of the ex-players are watching.

The players from the '97 and '01 premierships gather around for a photo. 'Haircut' storms out for a durry muttering something about Parramatta. The game starts and holds the past players' interest for as long as it takes to drink a schooner. Robbie O and Matty Parsons are the only players who see the lone Knights try. Robbie O is pumped. By the time Reynolds is lining up to convert John Sutton's 60th minute try, Billy Peden is honking the horn on the mini bus yelling out for Chief: "Hurry up and get us to The Brewery!"

The players are greeted like superstars at The Brewery and then again when we wander next door to Fannys. There is a section roped off for the Knights, literally with blue and yellow Telstra rope. Watered down vodka and cokes till stumps. Groupies galore. Glory days.

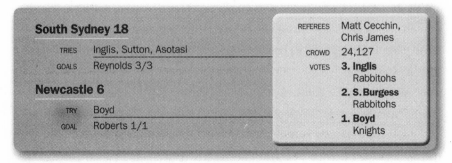

South Sydney 18		REFEREES	Matt Cecchin, Chris James
TRIES	Inglis, Sutton, Asotasi	CROWD	24,127
GOALS	Reynolds 3/3	VOTES	**3. Inglis** Rabbitohs
Newcastle 6			**2. S. Burgess** Rabbitohs
TRY	Boyd		**1. Boyd** Knights
GOAL	Roberts 1/1		

Powerless in Cambodia

Brisbane Broncos *versus* **Penrith Panthers**
7.30pm, Friday, 31 August
Suncorp Stadium, Brisbane

PETA BRYANT

FRIDAY NIGHT WAS ONE OF THE BEST I'VE SPENT IN RURAL CAMBODIA. I wish I could say that the Broncos-Panthers game was a highlight but really it was all about karaoke, darts and kitchenware.

The evening began with a friendly dinner and a sojourn to the local amusement park. At dinner, the culinary delights included fish head soup, dog curry and egg with duck foetus. After a year in Banlung I should be used to this kind of surf 'n' turf but the thought of canine curry and infant poultry still turns my stomach. The post-dinner visit to a local amusement park made up for unappetising food and provided the platform for a bit of competitive punting.

I put money on my Khmer friend to out-skill her husband in a game of balloon darts while everyone else placed bets on the neighbouring game of fighting rhino beetles. Balloon darts is one of the more competitive games in Banlung. I thought it was just for the kudos of winning but Cambodians play to win highly coveted household prizes including can openers, vegetable peelers and plastic strainers.

Forget giant stuffed toys and sample bags. In Banlung, it's all about sophisticated western kitchenware! After my friend had robbed her husband of the bullseye a few times and secured herself a hamper big enough to rival Victoria's Basement, there was talk of heading to our favourite karaoke joint to dance the night away. I excused myself from the party and headed home to set up my computer in preparation for the evening's 2GB broadcast.

I was excited, not because I dislike karaoke, but because it's been almost a year since I've seen a proper game of football and, more importantly, the internet has only been fast enough in the last few weeks to stream 2GB in Banlung. Even Ray Hadley, whose voice usually irritates the crap out of me, was a welcome sound as I settled in on my balcony and waited for the game to start.

Unfortunately my joy was short-lived. After 20 minutes in, even old mate Ray agreed that the game wasn't scaling any great heights. I had expected Brisbane to take the field with some force in their bid to make the finals but, despite Penrith defending their own line a number of times, the Broncos failed to cross for a try.

At the 30-minute mark, I'd given up on someone scoring in the first half but Michael Gordon made a break and quick hands delivered the ball to Josh Mansour for the evening's first try and Luke Walsh converted. 6-0 at halftime, in Penrith's favour.

During the break, sheets of lightning began to roll into Banlung. That's not unusual during the monsoon season and, often, the lightning is accompanied by blackouts. As I listened to Hadley and Steve Roach's halftime filler, I worried about the imminent threat of a power outage. To most computer owners, a short electrical schism is no cause for alarm because the average computer battery has a decent lifespan. With my antiquated laptop, however, a power outage meant:

NO COMPUTER = NO INTERNET = NO FOOTBALL COMMENTARY

[Insert gasp of horror here.]

In the second half, I rested a little easier as the storm quietened and the power remained on. Five minutes later, I was bouncing around on my balcony as Peter Wallace crossed the line and Corey Norman made a successful conversion for the Broncos. That only put the Broncos on par with Penrith but, still, I took it as a sign that they weren't prepared to sing Petero Civoniceva's swansong just yet. My excitement was fleeting though as, only a few minutes later (and probably right before Ben Te'o strolled across the line for the Bronco's second try), the power went out and, with it, the sound of the only football game I'd been able to enjoy in over a year.

I would like to report that I took the loss of power with grace and dignity but, in truth, I threw a tantrum that would have rivalled Gordon Ramsay's vitriol and turned the air blue for anyone who cared to listen. It's a good thing that my neighbours don't speak English or I might have offended somebody.

After about 20 minutes of waiting for the power to return, I finally conceded defeat and decided that there was no point mourning this game alone in the dark. Despite how expensive diesel generators are in Cambodia, every karaoke bar in Banlung has one. (You can live without power and water in this town but God forbid you should live without pop music.)

As a result, my friends were still dancing the night away as I sat morosely on my darkened balcony. I ended up joining them for a night of crucifying Lady Gaga in Khmer and shaking my booty to Beyonce. It was only the following day, with a heavy head from too much rice wine and a sore throat from too much singing, that I found out about the nail-biting finish that Panther Lachlan Coote created. Coote scored in the 70th minute but the Broncos recovered as winners, thanks to a runaway try from Alex Glenn and a field goal from Peter Wallace in the 78th minute.

Despite the Broncos having broken their six-game losing streak, I remain dubious about whether they will place well in the finals. In Khmer, you would say the Broncos need more *Gum-Laing*, which means 'energy or the will to play'.

I'd send them a vegetable peeler (my friend now has a few to spare from her darting victories) but something tells me that the Broncos need more than Western kitchenware to inspire a win.

Whatever triggers their *Gum-Laing*, I hope the Broncos find it before next Saturday's game against the Cowboys.

Brisbane 19			REFEREES	Shayne Hayne, Alan Shortall
TRIES	Wallace, Glenn, Te'o		CROWD	35,178
GOALS	Wallace 2/2, Norman 1/1		VOTES	**3. Gordon** Panthers
FIELD GOAL	Wallace			**2. Hannant** Broncos
Penrith 12				**1. Hodges** Broncos
TRIES	Mansour, Coote			
GOALS	Walsh 2/2			

Damn, I wish I was your lover

Gold Coast Titans *versus* Manly Sea Eagles

5.30pm, Saturday, 1 September

Skilled Park, Gold Coast

STU WARREN

N THE HEADY DAYS OF 1992, I HAD TWO LONG-HAIRED LOTHARIOS to thank for the most prominent tracks on my favourite mix-tape. Bearing in mind my first iPod was some 15 years away – and that CD technology wasn't exactly portable at this point in time – it was just me with my trusty Casio Walkman, Axl Rose and Nuno Bettencourt bringing the pick of the tunes.

Dubbed from local AM radio courtesy of the trusty 'play+record' method, Rose's melancholy piano masterpiece, *November Rain*, is an epic rock ballad that has just never grown old – not even to this day – while Bettencourt's soulful and sing-along-friendly Extreme classic, *To Be With You*, still transports me to nights spent revising for Year 8 maths and listening on loop.

As years in pop music go, '92 was a beaut.

Sir Mix-A-Lot preached about 'thick soul sisters', Tom Cochrane taught me that *Life is a Highway*, Shakespear's Sister begged me to *Stay*, James Blundell and James Reyne headed *Way Out West*, while Charles and Eddie asked that eternal question, *Would I Lie to You?*

But, generally, it was Axl and Nuno that I really wanted to see on *Rage*.

And, truth be told, I'm sure I wanted to see them staring back when I looked in the mirror but, at its longest, my hair never even made it to shoulder length and I looked awful in stretch denim.

Then, one fateful day, a young lady by the name of Sophie B. Hawkins happened into my life and things changed. I had a new favourite song to obsess about and things just kept getting better when my folks announced plans for a family trip during the September school holidays.

It was to be no football weekend in Melbourne, no Taronga Zoo pilgrimage to Sydney, no week away in St Helens, the jewel of Tasmania's east coast. This was the big one. It was the destination teens across the Apple Isle longed for. The Gold Coast.

Tall hotels with heated swimming pools, sun and acres of sandy beach, *Ripley's Believe It or Not*, theme parks, Currumbin bird sanctuary. Sizzler! These were all beautiful things. Not as beautiful as Sophie B. Hawkins, but beautiful nonetheless.

And I would get to make the most of them for the best part of a fortnight and it would be wonderful. Just as long as I had Sophie B. with me.

But once we jetted off from Launceston Airport, things soon changed. Just days into the trip, tragedy struck. Not real tragedy, mind you, but I still had reason to mourn a terrible loss. There was to be no more Sophie B. for me - not until I got home again, at least. She and my Walkman – as well as various other items belonging to my mother, father and brother – had been stolen by callous burglars who had struck our hotel suite while we were out to dinner.

Imagine, if you will, the horror of returning to a ransacked room to find that my small reserve of cash had been looted from my suitcase and my personal stereo had been swiped to boot, favourite mix-tape and all. Talk about the perfect way to spoil a kid's first Sizzler experience.

Like the stomach cramps I was suffering after over-extending myself at the dessert bar weren't enough, these low-life opportunistic pricks had topped a meal I was already struggling to digest with a bitter garnish.

All of 20 years on, it's amazing how much of my first trip to the Gold Coast I can recall. It's probably testament to the power of music in helping store memories.

And while I wouldn't have a clue what was playing in the dressing rooms before Manly defeated the Titans by 24-16 at Skilled Park, I genuinely doubt whether, in two decades, many players from either side will recall with any clarity what was a fairly unremarkable game of rugby league.

Manly 24		REFEREES	Gerard Sutton, Phil Haines
TRIES	B. Stewart, Taufua, K. Foran, Ballin	CROWD	14,927
GOALS	Lyon 4/4	VOTES	**3. K. Foran** Sea Eagles
Gold Coast 16			**2. Ballin** Sea Eagles
TRIES	Gordon 2, Failoon		**1. Myles** Titans
GOALS	Prince 2/3		

Trouble in Tiger-town

Wests Tigers *versus* **Melbourne Storm**

7.30pm, Saturday, 1 September

Leichhardt Oval, Sydney

MICHAEL HARRISON-FORD

I CAN'T HELP BUT FEEL THAT SUPPORTING THE TIGERS since Tim Sheens came to the helm has been something like raising a child you thought had the world at its fingertips, but never amounted to anything. There was so much precocious talent on display when, out of nowhere, they won it all in 2005. We beamed with pride that year! Telling anyone who'd listen that this team of ours was something special. Sure, they backed up with a disappointing season or two (maybe it was four), but we never doubted their flair or ability. Put it down to simple growing pains. With experience would come maturity, and success was sure to follow. Just a matter of time.

Seven years later, though, and it's hard to maintain the delusion: this team never did come of age. Rather than committing itself to the pursuit of greatness, they instead spent their formative years sitting on the couch playing Xbox, eating Pringles and drinking Passiona.

So forgive me if I'm not enthused about tonight's encounter. After being smashed by the second-to-last placed Roosters, if the Tigers are to scrape into the eight they need to win this game against the Storm and hope for the hapless Warriors to beat Canberra and to make up a 14-point for-and-against differential in the process. I'd love to see it! Don't get me wrong. But even if it does happen, would we really make an impact in the finals? True contenders don't need to sweat on results in the final round.

So, whatever it says about my status as a true fan, I'm not glued to a screen somewhere watching with other Tigers fans. Rather, I'm at Crown Casino watching the game on the one small screen that's not tuned to an equally trivial AFL match. I'm fostering the new delusion that I'm a winning poker player.

It turns out I don't need to distract myself from the cards for too long. From the opening stages, it's one-way traffic for the Storm. Almost all of the action takes place in the Tigers' half of the field and, while Melbourne take 15 minutes to cross the line, they're not at all troubled defensively before they do.

The blunder leading to that first try is emblematic of the Tigers this season. With their first real attacking opportunity close to Melbourne's line, a decoy play goes wrong when Benji Marshall passes the ball a full metre behind the intended receiver. It's a simple task for Sisa Waqa to pounce on the ball and race downfield, stopped only through a remarkable effort from Marika Koroibete, who has been a revelation this year. The damage is done though and, clinically, the Storm follow the play through to score on the other side of the field.

Another try to the Storm follows soon after and, although Benji Marshall crosses for a flashy four-pointer shortly before halftime, they're never really in it. The Storm cross three more times in the second half and keep the Tigers to nix.

It's an even money bet at worst that, at some point in the second half, one of the commentators would remark that the Storm had better be careful because the Tigers were capable of scoring from anywhere on the park. But that hasn't actually been the case in 2012 where something went badly wrong with the Tigers' cohesion in attack. They doggedly stuck with a lateral approach but came to look quite silly doing it as they rarely troubled anyone. It was no different in this game, where time and time again they spread the ball wide only to run out of space and be forced into error.

In the end, while Melbourne weren't at their best, they had no trouble putting a full-stop on the Tigers' season and claimed second spot for themselves in the process.

Fans leaving Leichhardt were spared a nervous wait for the Canberra game. Instead they headed off to ponder whether their boys were ever any good.

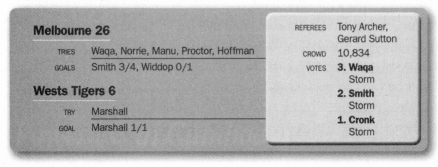

Melbourne 26

TRIES	Waqa, Norrie, Manu, Proctor, Hoffman
GOALS	Smith 3/4, Widdop 0/1

Wests Tigers 6

TRY	Marshall
GOAL	Marshall 1/1

REFEREES	Tony Archer, Gerard Sutton
CROWD	10,834
VOTES	**3. Waqa** Storm
	2. Smith Storm
	1. Cronk Storm

Chooks hooked

Canterbury Bulldogs *versus* Sydney Roosters
7.30pm, Saturday, 1 September
ANZ Stadium

MICHAEL GROSVENOR

IT'S THE LAST GAME OF THE YEAR – AT LEAST FOR SYDNEY ROOSTERS players, coaches and fans. I've been thinking all week that the Roosters may have started their Mad Monday a week early given the emotion around last Sunday's successful home game against the Tigers. As such, I was expecting an announcement during the week that the Roosters had forfeited their season-ending match against the high-flying Bulldogs. That they did turn up and stayed competitive for at least half the match was a good sign against the impressive Hasler-dogs. But more on this later.

This has been a week of reflection for Rooster fans. It was a mixed bag of a year: a few good wins, many more awful losses (including several unlucky ones), some great new stars emerged and some old ones continued to frustrate. I can count at least six games where we were in winning position with 20 minutes to go only for poor decision-making – some by us, some by Bill Harrigan's lot – to cruel our chances.

Let me see: we got off to a pretty good start with four wins and two losses from the first six matches. Then two weeks of carnage that scarred our season – the debacle of the 50-12 "home ground" loss to the Cowboys in Darwin (someone should be sacked for selling our home game off to the hottest place in Australia where we played a team from the second hottest place in Australia) and then, the following week, somehow recovering to get up for the biggest club game of the year against St George on Anzac Day, playing magnificently for 76 minutes of the match to lead 24-16, only to get bloused by a Saints team that suddenly worked out how to attack after three years of Bennett's dummy-half football.

The scars of those losses affected our confidence. We had a run of gut-wrenching matches where we lacked self-belief and some disgraceful refereeing decisions killed us. I think I am right in saying that quite a few video refs spent time in Coventry for their misdemeanours. In these matches, the results were in the balance well into the second half but all ended in frustrating losses. The season then deteriorated from there.

Unfortunately, fans of Brian Smith-coached sides have to endure such rollercoaster seasons because the style of play he encourages these days is based on individual creativity and confidence and the momentum that generates. If everyone gets on the same page, this can be wonderful to witness with 2010 still being one of the greatest rugby league rides I've experienced. But when confidence is dissolved and key individuals have off days (I'm looking at you, Mitchell Pearce), things can go pear-shaped very quickly. Such an approach also doesn't work well with the current refereeing system – these refs struggle with unstructured play.

Yet, last week's win against the Tigers showed that there are some positives to come out of the year. Some of the youngsters are outstanding prospects. They finished the year as established first graders – Roger Tuivasa-Sheck, Tautau Moga, Daniel Tupou and Nafe Seluini. Some of those who were introduced a few years ago have grown into potential leaders, especially Martin Kennedy, Boyd Cordner and Jared Waerea-Hargreaves. At least James Maloney will add much needed direction to the team next year.

This brings me on to the Bulldogs who are the epitome of the structured approach. Des Hasler now has to be considered in the Jack Gibson class of innovators. He has honed a structure perfectly suited to the attributes of his squad and the team carry it out to mind-blowing effect.

The most important thing in Des' system is a sweeper who has the ability to play off this shape and create something from nothing. At Manly, he had Brett Stewart. At the Bulldogs, he has Ben Barba who will win the Dally M Medal by the length of the straight. Des has landed the club a minor premiership with much the same players who finished ninth in 2011.

On Saturday night, the Roosters surprisingly turned up to play. They had one last dig for the departing Braith Anasta. But the Bulldogs did more: they took their season to another level, producing one of the most dominant forward displays of the year.

Sam Kasiano and Frank Pritchard look like giants and play as such. Their smaller backrowers take on the role of ball distributors behind what appears to be dozens of decoy runners running in all different directions.

I can't see anything but a Des Hasler Grand Final coming up and we will get a preview next weekend in the first final.

Canterbury 42			REFEREES	Jared Maxwell, Gavin Badger
TRIES	Jackson 3; Barba, Morris, Keating, Pritchard		CROWD	23,391
GOALS	Inu 7/7		VOTES	**3. Kasiano** Bulldogs
Sydney Roosters 10				**2. Jackson** Bulldogs
TRIES	Minichiello, Moga			**1. Pritchard** Bulldogs
GOAL	Anasta 1/2			

Time to gamble

New Zealand Warriors *versus* Canberra Raiders
4pm, Sunday, 2 September
Mt Smart Stadium, Auckland

TIM NAPPER

HOLLYWOOD LOOKS AT ME over the rim of his beer glass.

"The problem is that you don't have any gamble," he said.

Coming just a couple of hours after I busted from a $5,000-entry poker tournament, I find the statement pretty absurd.

I snort a reply: "Your definition of someone with gamble is someone who is broke. Like you."

Hollywood is a professional poker player who is struggling at the moment. He's getting backed by another professional to play cash games at Crown Casino.

Hollywood got his name after auditioning as an extra three times for *Home and Away*. He was rejected three times. He told me afterwards that the casting director told him he looked "too much like a homeless person" to even get a bit-part on the soap opera. He's been doing it tough, trying to grind his way out of a vicious downswing that won't seem to let go.

But three jugs of beer later, Hollywood's accusation still stings.

In poker circles, there's nothing worse than being known as someone without any gamble. By gamble we don't mean someone who truly gambles – that is, who doesn't apply skill, but rather just mindlessly rides their luck to work up a big score.

We're not talking about the pokies here. Not at all. In poker, those who rely only on luck end up broke.

When poker players talk about *gamble*, they're really talking about a quality that is true of all the best players in the game. They are talking about *heart*. When poker players have heart, they forget about the money. They play with an instinct that has been fine-tuned by experience and a study of the game. Within this nexus of skill, discipline, fearlessness and heart, a good poker player becomes a great player.

The paradox is that a lack of regard for the money is the one true way to make the real money from the game. So do I lack *gamble*? I don't think that's the problem. I reckon I've got enough gamble, when it counts. I can put it all on the line. As an amateur playing in my spare time, I built a bankroll big enough to play in the World Series in Vegas (and blew it at the World Series in Vegas). When I'm in a tournament, I rarely think about the money. Sure, I'll glance at the first prize and allow myself to savour what a score that big will feel like, but that tends not to determine my actions.

The problem I had in the $5k event was a bit more commonplace than lacking gamble. It was the old standard of poker players and sportspeople, indeed of anyone who has ever engaged in a competitive pursuit: self-doubt. My problem was not trusting reads and experience, and forgetting lessons learned a thousand times over.

I wander by to chat to Hollywood later in the poker room. He is slouched in a chair playing at stakes far lower than he is used to. He is sitting there with dishevelled hair, wearing a worn jacket that looked like a blanket you'd bury a dead dog in and with an unlit hand-rolled cigarette dangling from his mouth. I watch him four-bet a wild Asian player pre-flop and take the pot down with an all-in bet on the turn. He looks like a bum but the man can play.

I ask him: "How did the Raiders do?"

Hollywood replies: "They were down early but came back and scored shitloads. 42-22."

"Ahh, that's good."

I wonder briefly if the Raiders have the heart to make it through to the Grand Final. Probably not, but you never know. Five weeks ago, a finals berth looked close to impossible for the Raiders and yet, this weekend, here they are hosting a final at Bruce Stadium against the Sharks.

An announcement in the poker room breaks my reverie:

Contestants in the $250 tournament, please take your seats, the game will begin in 60 seconds.

It's not $5k, but it's still action. I make my way over to my table. Time to gamble.

Canberra 42			REFEREES	Jason Robinson, Adam Devcich
TRIES	Ferguson, Robinson 2; Berrigan, Papalii, Fensom		CROWD	11,455
GOALS	Croker 7/8		VOTES	**3. Robinson** Raiders
New Zealand 22				**2. McCrone** Raiders
TRIES	Vatuvei 2; Godinet, Matulino			**1. Ferguson** Raiders
GOALS	Henry 2/3, Maloney 1/1			

In the money

Cronulla Sharks *versus* **North Queensland Cowboys**
3pm, Sunday, 2 September
Toyota Stadium, Sydney

CLIFF BINGHAM

MAKING ENDS MEET CAN BE DIFFICULT AT TIMES. Perhaps you're a university student with little income. Perhaps the arrival of a little bundle of joy puts the squeeze on mortgage payments and the family budget. Or perhaps you have a business venture that is barely treading water, desperately searching for that one big deal that will put you on a secure financial footing. Like it or not, even those who are exceptional at compartmentalising parts of their lives can find such issues pervading their subconscious and affecting other aspects of their life, if only indirectly.

Anyone who has experienced such testing times and comes out the other side probably remembers the feeling when the storm clouds lifted. When a part-time job or scholarship provided enough income to keep things ticking over; when a promotion and pay rise made the impending bills much easier to handle; or maybe when a long-debated $300 million land development was approved and gave your 45-year-old rugby league club a leg-up.

Within a week, Cronulla had secured a place in the finals and its financial viability. Over the past decade and a half, Cronulla stuck it out alone as other clubs successfully merged (St George/Illawarra, Balmain/Western Suburbs), unsuccessfully merged (Manly/North Sydney) or have been lost and come back again (South Sydney). Neither glory nor security found their way to The Shire. If the Sharks were a university student, two-minute noodles had been their staple diet for many years.

The announcements of the previous days brought a happy optimism – but after years of dealing with adversity, how would Cronulla deal with this prosperity?

The Cowboys fan in me hoped they would take at least one weekend to figure it out. The Canberra resident in me held the same view, with the prospect of driving for a mere handful of minutes to attend a finals match at Canberra Stadium next weekend certainly worthy of my support.

The opening 20 minutes were scrappy, while the remainder of the first half was not for defensive purists, with tries traded. The visitors led 18-12 at halftime. After Paul Gallen crossed early in the second half, minutes 45 to 60 were dominated by the Townsville boys as they posted three tries to break the game apart and skip out to a 34-16 lead. The Cowboys will need to tighten up if they're to be competitive in the first week of the finals.

As for the Sharks, they will make the trip to Canberra to take on the Raiders in what should be a very tight match. At least they won't have too many other worries.

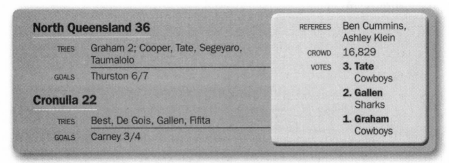

North Queensland 36		REFEREES	Ben Cummins, Ashley Klein
TRIES	Graham 2; Cooper, Tate, Segeyaro, Taumalolo	CROWD	16,829
GOALS	Thurston 6/7	VOTES	**3. Tate** Cowboys
Cronulla 22			**2. Gallen** Sharks
TRIES	Best, De Gois, Gallen, Fifita		**1. Graham** Cowboys
GOALS	Carney 3/4		

Full time

Parramatta Eels *versus* St George Illawarra Dragons
6.30pm, Sunday, 2 September
ANZ Stadium, Sydney
MICHAEL KENNEDY

THE LAST HURRAH! THE SWAN SONG! THE FINAL GOODBYE! Call it what you will but tonight is both a commiseration and celebration of The End. Not only is the stage set for the final match of the regular season that will draw the curtain on the playing careers of some of the game's stalwarts – Hindmarsh, Burt, Hornby and Young – but it also marks the end of yet another year of my life as today happens to be my birthday. As I was born in the Mother Country, today really is the last day of another year. Birthdays are a grey area for me. One half relishes the refreshing of my life and setting a new goal or two, while the other prefers to watch others score goals. The jury is still out as to which will rule my destiny for the next year, but maybe tonight's game will have some bearing.

I'm lodged squarely at the wrong end of the depression scale as the Eels have inherited the wooden spoon for the first time in 40 years. Offsetting this melancholy is the birthday largesse which includes a memory foam toilet mat (don't knock it until you've tried it), a gold movie pass and drinking cocoa so dark a theobromine overdose is assured.

A family barbecue in the backyard was the day's focal point. I was the only one present who knew how the Weber ticked. After sparking her off with a zephyr of warm gas, silky oil and a sizzling smoky grill, I cooked the snags until they sang. In this wattle-scented air on a perfect spring day, surely the Eels could finish with a win.

From the start the teams played according to their ladder positions. An Eels win was looking unlikely but sometimes one has to look beyond the scoreline. It's a changing of the guard tonight. Pocket-rocket wingers like Burt have been replaced by behemoth battle-tanks and the old school one-club warriors will become rarer than a Toovey smile. In truth, this game was really about the four warriors and, in particular, the tribute to them as characters both on and off the field, which is why so many fans turned up.

No moment epitomized this more when, following a penalty in the final minute of the game, Tim Mannah sprinted faster than he has all year from the opposite side of the field to ensure that the Eels opted for a shot at goal rather than taking a quick tap. Fittingly, Hindmarsh lined up to take the kick. Burt's advice was limited to a wry grin. Using an old-fashioned mound of sand, Hindmarsh finished his illustrious playing career with a speculator. Even the Dragons applauded his effort as the ball sailed over. It will be remembered.

The Eels will return next year. Hindmarsh, Burt, Hornby and Young will embark on new enterprises and I'll set off on another journey around the sun.

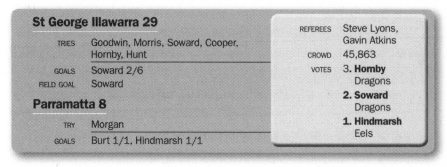

St George Illawarra 29		REFEREES	Steve Lyons, Gavin Atkins
TRIES	Goodwin, Morris, Soward, Cooper, Hornby, Hunt	CROWD	45,863
GOALS	Soward 2/6	VOTES	**3. Hornby** Dragons
FIELD GOAL	Soward		**2. Soward** Dragons
Parramatta 8			**1. Hindmarsh** Eels
TRY	Morgan		
GOALS	Burt 1/1, Hindmarsh 1/1		

The Qualifying Finals

League letters

Canterbury Bulldogs *versus* **Manly Sea Eagles**
7.45pm, Friday, 7 September
ANZ Stadium, Sydney

NICK TEDESCHI AND HUW FOWLES

Canterbury diehard **NICK TEDESCHI** *and Manly lover* **HUW FOWLES**
reflect on the first qualifying final between the Bulldogs and the Sea Eagles.

NT   Huwge! Have you recovered from that Old Son? Sitting in the grandstand, I feel about as bruised and as battered as Sam Perrett after your thug Steve Matai cleaned him up, such was the intensity and brutality of the match. I had to go home and get a rub down from Louise, ice up the neck and replace those electrolytes. And never mind the heart after the referees did their best to stitch us up during those first five minutes ... I was sure Ashley Klein had pulled a Darcy Lawler and loaded up on your mob ...

HF   Speaking of stitch ups, Punter, you get known as the *Canterbury diehard* while I'm referred to as the *Manly lover* in the intro! Never mind Lawler, Barry Gomersall would be proud of that one (though, just quietly, I am adding this title to my CV under the 'Skills' heading). Brutal game of finals footy though. Isn't there some unwritten rule in the NRL that if you switch clubs halfway through, a la Perrett, you're fair game for the odd high shot? If not, then I suspect Mr Matai will be warming the pine for a week or two. Come to think of it, I don't think there were many Sea Eagles who weren't either injured or reported. I'm pretty bloody sick of the length-of-the-field Bulldogs tries though...

NT   I have always considered you a Manly lover ... tender but strong, sweet with a touch of authority ... but I digress, Huwge. There's no doubt the Bulldogs can score a try from a distance. It helps having Ben Barba back there and when he combines with Josh Morris, it is what they call in the sportswriting business "poetry in motion". And, to be fair, I've never felt the same way about Yeats or Wordsworth or Sylvia Plath as I do about those two boys. I was sitting in the grandstand where Barba finished off that magical play and I still don't know how J-Moz stayed in. It helped that Jamie Lyon was in the showers trying to shake off a calf injury. That was a stroke of luck seeing him go off. How important is he to you guys? You're a shadow of the team without him. How close to throwing up your steak tartar did you come when you saw him on the hobble?

HF About as close as you were to choking on your Chiko Roll when Ennis was in the rooms. Only problem was, he came back on. I thought that might spell trouble. We desperately missed Lyon but, on the flipside, it's the best game I've seen from Taufua. He kept us afloat in that first half after J-Moz, the ugly twin, put Wright over. We were fortunate to have that halftime lead but, with the way the Seagles had been playing their second halves of late, I wasn't overflowing with confidence heading into chapter two. You just knew Dally Barba (and his 16 thieves) was going to pull some magic out of his little bottle at some point. Can't wait to see him playing in maroon next year. Who else did you like the look of in blue and white tonight, Punt?

NT I'll tell you what I did enjoy seeing, Big Cat – Jonathan Wright's breaking of Adam Dykes' crabbing record, breaking the all-time mark for cross-field metres! Good luck with that next year, Sharkies! Seriously, it was the big boppers up front that impressed me. Jimmy Graham has had me fired up all year with his toughness, workrate, ball playing and love of Vaseline. Aiden Tolman has had an underrated year and should be closing in on a rep jersey soon. And big Sam Kasiano may not be able to fire off a sentence but the boy has plenty of skill and plenty of beef. Did you see his effort at the Dally Ms, Huwge? Better or worse than Uate's?

HF I like men who are short on the gab and big on the action. They make up for the likes of us banging on incessantly about rugby league, and so forth and so on. It seems to be the year of the big forward packs and, as my grandad used to say, big blokes don't get any smaller in September. So Graham, Tolman and Big Sam will do a lot more damage before the season is out. Can't wait to see Kasiano playing in maroon next year.

NT It wouldn't surprise me at all to see you poachers from north of the border pinch Big Sam. You've been doing it for 20 years – since Adrian Lam became PNG captain and Queensland halfback – but we Blues have lost the high moral ground since claiming James Tamou. Now it is just a free-for-all, like a *Fritz the Cat* comic strip. But back to matters at hand. Do you see these two meeting again down the road? Do we have a replay of the '95 Grand Final ahead? If we do, hopefully we can get Eddie Ward out of retirement.

HF A '95 rematch would be superb. A chance for sweet, sweet revenge. I remember the Sydney Bulldogs coming from the clouds to win the whole shebang that year. I was dirty that we'd been rolled in just the three games all year and then got pumped by a team that was totally lost in the wilderness midseason, had to ask for directions and somehow stumbled into the finals. Bloody Jim Dymock. And never ever mention Eddie 'Emergency' Ward in my presence again, Punter. Did you hear about that NFL ref that was sacked from a New Orleans Saints game last week when it was discovered he was a fan of the team? That's what should have happened to Eddie. Arko should have sacked him. I guarantee if you look in his kit bag, you'll find a Bulldogs membership there. The fundamental idea of league is to throw the ball backwards, Eddie! Call a forward pass for once in your life, man. Come to think of it, the NFL should get him on their payroll. He's a real expert at ruling on balls that get thrown forward.

NT What was Arko thinking? Arko ran the ARL just for the pleasure of Manly. How they only won two premierships during Arko's reign is an indictment on a club that claims to be a powerhouse. Luckily, we had the Bullfrog and if Arko had his match in the rugby league politics realm, it was Bullfrog. He even bred to maintain his grip, God rest his soul. And leave Eddie alone. He called it straight in '95. Forward pass? Line ball at worst! Just quality rugby league! So Huwge, it is about time to wrap this bad boy up, I reckon. Let's finish this with the man in the middle – Des Hasler. Your thoughts on him before this year and your thoughts on him now? I'm sure we'll be on the same page!

HF Hasler ... the man in the middle ... now there's an idea. Let's just let Hasler ref the GF if the Dogs and Seagles make it. Good luck for the rest of the season, Punter.

NT Dessie is already being deified out Belmore way ... he takes us to a premiership and Haslerism may quickly become the religion of choice west of Marrickville. Good luck to you too, Huwge – may you enjoy getting knocked off by the Bullies in the GF.

Canterbury 16

TRIES Barba, Keating, Wright

GOALS Inu 2/3

Manly 10

TRIES B. Stewart, Taufua

GOAL Cherry-Evans 1/2

REFEREES Ben Cummins, Ashley Klein • CROWD 36,420

Purple rain

Melbourne Storm *versus* **South Sydney Rabbitohs**
5.45pm, Saturday, 8 September
AAMI Park, Melbourne

PAUL DALLIGAN

A LOT HAS HAPPENED IN THE WORLD SINCE 1989 with the Soviet Union having long gone the way of Super League, the internet having impacted upon all our lives and a man named Nelson Mandela finally being freed after nearly 30 years in prison. While I am not intending to compare the suffering of my fellow South Sydney tragics with that endured by the great man, our own form of suffering of a sporting kind has now extended over 40 years since that magical day back in 1971 when the Rabbitohs last reigned supreme.

After a fine 2012 season, in which Struggle Street was close to again becoming The Pride of the League, an army of expectant Souths fans descended on AAMI Park in Melbourne to take on the Storm in the first week of finals action. They seemed beatable.

Souths had last made a final in 2007 and that night I flew up from my new home city of Melbourne to Brookvale Oval (proudly wearing my 1988-era Smiths Crisps jersey) to take my place in the main grandstand. Sadly, one of the worst nights of my sporting life followed as the Rabbitohs were no match for a rampant Sea Eagles outfit.

But, on a September night some five years later, I didn't have to fly anywhere to get to AAMI Park as all I needed was the No.70 tram from the city. Again I was wearing my green and red armoury, however this time I was not surrounded by the maroon of enemy supporters, but instead more purple than seen on a 1984-era Prince video clip.

The rock tragics amongst us would know that the title track to *Purple Rain* opens with the immortal lines:

I never meant to cause you any sorrow,
I never meant to cause you any pain,
I only wanted to see you laughing in the Purple Rain ...

I am not sure if the Storm boys are big fans of the pint-sized genius, but the words were more than fitting. On the night there was plenty of sorrow and pain delivered by the ruthlessly efficient trio of Cronk, Slater and Smith, and the only laughing in the purple rain was certainly not happening in the away-supporter bays.

All that was needed at fulltime was a drive-by from the Storm coach Craig 'Bellyache' Bellamy on a purple motorbike and the howls from The Burrow may have eclipsed the epic banshee wail that closes *Purple Rain*. In that haunting finale, the sorrow that emanates from Prince is his final realisation that the love of his life has forever slipped from his grasp. As a Rabbitohs tragic, it was hard not to leave AAMI Park with a sense that the Rabbitohs may have let their best chance at winning that elusive premiership slip past as well.

The game had a sense of the *Karate Kid*'s Master and Grasshopper about it with Craig Bellamy having mentored Souths' revolutionary new coach Michael Maguire during many successful years at the Storm. Souths' fullback sensation Greg Inglis was also facing one of the best ever in the position in Billy Slater.

But despite all the subplots, I was feeling that I would have had more chance of catching a fly with a pair of chopsticks than Souths stopping the Storm on the night.

After only 20 minutes, the Storm had crossed twice through a barging effort from Ryan Hoffman and then a typically classy effort from Slater. While no one would ever compare one of the fieriest characters in Australian sport, Craig Bellamy, to the patient and serene Mr Miyagi, on the night the red and green Grasshopper was put back in its box and the Master reigned supreme.

Given that the Storm were missing hard men Jason Ryles and Sika Manu, and also their seasoned back Anthony Quinn, the full-strength Rabbitohs were expected to pose much more of a threat.

The only threat on the night, however, was this long suffering fanatic being drenched in the Purple Rain, left wondering if Prince himself had scripted the proceedings.

Warm fires, pure footy

JOHN HARMS

SATURDAY IN MELBOURNE. Antarctica is in the process of relocating to Richmond. Which is unfortunate for me, because it's where I am. The rain stings as it whips into my face and there's more coming. As I get off the train, I have no choice but to run. This isn't in the game plan.

The game plan is to have a few quiet ones at the All Nations; then head to AAMI to catch the NRL live; then cross the road to the MCG to see Geelong take care of Freo. As I crash through the front doors, I have the feeling I've just walked into a pub in Yorkshire. It's all scarves and overcoats and people rubbing their hands together in front of the fire.

The joint is warm and buzzing football; the beer is sensational. Some Storm fans head out into the elements and are farewelled like members of the Royal Geographical Society. I have had the best intentions but I'm going nowhere.

Weiner schnitzel and red wine. Plenty of footy talk.

Scarf-spotters have detected a rare species: a limited edition first season Dockers. They also comment that it's not often you see two sets of purple colours at a sporting fixture.

I've had a little nibble at the Storm at various stages during the season and again now. They're very good but I'm still unsure what that losing patch means. Was it just the absence of Billy?

Some in the pub watch the opening minutes while others face away from the TV and talk about Sydney's demolition of Adelaide.

However, they respond to the cheer as Slater dashes away. In an instant everyone is watching as he approaches the halfway line, stepping off his right, and off his right again, steering a passage clear of the cover and then, when corralled, throwing a long ball outside to Nielsen. The centre sprints for the corner, turns and pops a soft pass which seems to hang in space. Mahe Fonua, the local kid in for Quinn, reads the moment perfectly, snaps the motionless ball from mid-air and crashes for the line. The sheer sporting brilliance of the pass earns cheers from the whole pub. But Fonua is held up by Farrell whose tackle defies gravity.

Melbourne pepper the line. Souths look stretched and Cameron Smith sniffs it. He times a beaut short pass to Ryan Hoffman who crashes over.

Minutes later, after a successful penalty attempt has put Melbourne 8-0 up, Smith launches Hoffman with another neat pass. The backrower forces a warren of defenders to come to him, gets one arm free and finds Slater on the fly. The pub goes up again. Try.

The Storm are playing very disciplined, clean, entertaining football; taking good options and making no mistakes in the ordinary conditions. By contrast, the scoreline puts pressure on Souths who have moments when they look threatening and moments when they are in the headlights.

Merritt knocks on and, from the scrum, Slater exploits the open side. In a panic, the Souths defenders go to him, leaving Widdop to receive the offload with space to burn and he puts Fonua away. Too easy. And probably game over.

Melburnians feel a pang at watching their own team. They are supporters for the moment.

More red wine. This is a celebration. Steam-breathed footy fans arrive and look at the TV screen. And smile.

The first try after halftime is crucial. It goes to the Storm. Again Slater draws the defenders, times his pass to Widdop whose steady hands find Sisa Waqa on an angled run and the winger darts to the corner.

It is over now.

The score sits on 24-0 for half an hour and the bar crowds' interest is peripheral again. Souths don't waste any energy seeking the outrageous comeback. They decide to leave it for next week. They do register a consolation try in the last few minutes.

By then, those heading to the MCG for the Geelong game were buttoning overcoats and saying their prayers as they prepared to take on the elements.

It was about 6° and blowing, with the rain still about, as the pub bus crunched through the gears, across Hoddle Street and through East Melbourne.

Those wild conditions had been good for the Storm whose convincing win put them into a preliminary final.

They seemed good for Geelong, too, at the time.

How wrong we were.

Melbourne 24

TRIES Hoffman, Slater, Fonua, Waqa
GOALS Smith 4/5

South Sydney 6

TRY Pettybourne
GOAL Reynolds 1/1

REFEREES Shayne Hayne, Jason Robinson • CROWD 19,750

Heartache tonight

North Queensland Cowboys *versus* **Brisbane Broncos**
7.45pm, Saturday, 8 September
Dairy Farmers Stadium, Townsville

WILL EVANS

FEW EXPERIENCES IN THE LIFE OF A RUGBY LEAGUE DIEHARD rival the hollow disappointment of your team's season being extinguished, that feeling somewhere in between a death in the family and high school heartbreak. Whether it be the moment it becomes mathematically impossible for your boys to make the finals or when they lose a sudden-death match in September, it's a numb sensation. Fortunately, I guess, in two decades supporting Brisbane the vast majority of seasons have fallen into the latter category. But Broncos fans have endured their fair share of finals heartache.

I can't recall feeling less confident of the Broncos winning a finals match than this one – thanks to their dire late-season form, as opposed to North Queensland's current hot streak. This acceptance of impending doom has tempered the anxiety that usually accompanies the prospect of a premiership dream dying. But seeing the Broncos run out at Dairy Farmers Stadium provokes a sickly *déjà vu* of my side's 10-0 upset loss to the Cowboys in a pulsating 2004 semi-final, bringing the curtain down on Gorden Tallis's marvellous career. My pride suffered a double-blow that night, my hand came off second-best when I took my frustrations out on a soap dispenser in the Dunedin pub at which I watched the game.

After mulling over Tallis's tearful farewell, my mind wanders back to finals exits that have signalled the end of the careers of champion Broncos clubmen: the injury-ravaged Broncos' gallant 24-16 loss to minor premiers Parramatta in the 2001 preliminary final, with Wendell Sailor inspirational in his last game before switching to union; a 36-year-old Allan Langer throwing a loose pass in his final game to give the Roosters what turned out to be the match-winning try in a gut-wrenching 16-12 preliminary final defeat; and the biggest lump-in-the-throat finals exit of them all – last year's preliminary final loss to Manly that robbed my sidelined hero Darren Lockyer of a Grand Final farewell from the NRL.

Then there was the most soul-destroying loss of the lot – Melbourne's last-minute 16-14 escape act through a Greg Inglis try on the back of that dropped ball by Ashton Sims, ending Wayne Bennett's tenure in Brisbane. Locky's anguished screaming after the siren is the most poignant rugby league image I can remember. I was at Suncorp that night and I masochistically watched a replay of it for the first time recently in a 'Classic Finals' timeslot on Fox Sports. Harrowing.

Josh Hoffman's muffing of a bomb to allow Cowboys halfback Michael Morgan to score was a doppelganger for North Sydney fullback Matt Seers' howler to give Wendell Sailor a first half try in the 1994 minor semi – before the Bears bounced the Broncos out of the finals race 15-14 courtesy of Jason Taylor's late field goal, reducing my fragile 13-year-old self (who had celebrated the Broncos' premierships in the preceding two years and couldn't accept anything less) to tears.

After Morgan bags his second to make it 18-0, my mind trails off to some of our heavier season-ending defeats – Cronulla's 42-20 thrashing of the Broncos, who had climbed off the canvas just to scrape into the eight, in 1999; Wests Tigers' comprehensive 34-6 semi-final win on their way to the 2005 title; and twin 40-point drubbings at the hands of Melbourne in 2007 (qualifying final) and 2009 (preliminary final).

At this stage, I'm just hoping for a bit of fight in the second half, like the eighth-placed Broncos' stoic 28-18 defeat to minor premiers Penrith in 2003. It comes courtesy of a brilliant 40-metre solo try to Corey Norman.

The Cowboys push out to 26-6, but back-to-back Brisbane tries raise hopes of a miracle comeback – 2012 has been inundated with them, and there's five survivors of the 2006 preliminary final comeback triumph over the Bulldogs in tonight's Broncos side (plus Brent Tate in the Cowboys' line-up). But Morgan completes his hat-trick to seal Brisbane's fate.

It hurts but the Broncos' underdog status has dulled the pain to a degree – unlike semi-final capitulations to the Bulldogs in '95 and Cronulla in '96 after starting red-hot favourites. It's the ache of defeats such as these that make the glorious victories – such as the '06 preliminary final and six Grand Final wins – all the more sweet.

The wonder years
CLIFF BINGHAM

I LOVED *THE WONDER YEARS* GROWING UP. For whatever reason, other kids making the simple things in life seem quite difficult resonated strongly. Kevin Arnold was neither especially cool nor especially outcast by the social set - after all, anyone who could date Winnie Cooper was doing alright for himself. His regular sidekick Paul Pfeiffer was a different story though. Paul was the nerd of nerds. He struggled with popularity, with women, with sports ... frankly, it would be easier to list those things in life which weren't a trial for poor old Paul.

In season four, one episode featured their high school basketball tryouts. Amazingly, Paul made the team. Kevin, being Kevin, could not comprehend this and tried to prove to Paul that he was not good enough to gain a spot on Coach Cutlip's team. One-on-one home games of hoops were always Kevin's domain, racking up 790 straight wins against his bespectacled best friend. But with his ire sufficiently drawn out, Paul broke the duck and put one over his once dominant opponent. Kevin finally acknowledged that his friend may have some talent and switched to the role of ardent supporter. Everyone learned a life lesson, as would appear to be required by law for all episodes of TV shows aimed at children.

The first 16 games between the Cowboys and Broncos failed to yield a single victory for the Townsville faithful. They were becoming the Paul to Brisbane's Kevin. Four wins in the next six encounters started to balance the ledger before the Broncos bounced back and won eight of the next nine. Entering 2012, the overall head to head record stood at Brisbane 24, North Queensland 5, drawn 2. Only the defunct Bears (no wins in five games) and Reds (no wins in four games) had troubled the Cowboys more. Even after 17 seasons in the competition, 'big brother' continued to dictate terms.

In 2012 though, the Pfeiffer-esque Cowboys looked a premiership contender, just missing out on a coveted top four position and beating Brisbane twice along the way. The Broncos stumbled into eighth, winning only one of their final seven games. For once, the Broncos looked beatable to the point where I didn't hesitate to lay the 6.5 points start for my boys.·

They didn't disappoint, making all of the early running and racing out to an 18-0 lead at the main break. Josh Hoffman made some costly mistakes at the back and the home side made them pay as good sides do. The Broncos threatened to make a charge in the second half, closing the score to 18-6 before a penalty goal and try seemed to put the match beyond doubt at 26-6. Brisbane refused to go quietly and banged on two quick tries of their own to put my little flutter in jeopardy at 26-16 but the third and final try to Mick Morgan snuffed out any hope for both the visitors and my friendly bookie.

The final siren also ushered in the retirement of Petero Civoniceva. Such a fine stalwart of the front row engine room for club, state and country over many years deserved a better curtain call, but very few are lucky enough to conclude their career with a victory lap on Grand Final day.

Defeating Manly in Sydney next weekend may be a far more challenging proposition but, irrespective of that outcome, I'll always look back on 2012 as a season where 'Kevin' had little choice but to dip his lid and concede that he was beaten fair and square on the day.

North Queensland 33

TRIES Morgan 3; Bowen, Tate
GOALS Thurston 6/7 • FIELD GOAL Bowen)

Brisbane 16

TRIES Norman, Thaiday, Copley
GOALS Wallace 2/3

REFEREES Matt Cecchin, Gerard Sutton • CROWD 21,307

Field of dreams

Canberra Raiders *versus* **Cronulla Sharks**
4pm, Sunday, 9 September
Canberra Stadium, Canberra

ANDREW BOMM

S UNDAY ARVO. HAD I STILL BEEN LIVING IN CANBERRA, I would have been at this match. But these days I live in Wagga where parental responsibilities and the tyranny of distance means I just can't get there. So the tour of Wagga's finest licensed establishments continues and today it's The Sportman's Hotel.

First, I've got to get some Sunday afternoon KFC, the perfect antidote to a session of Tooheys Old at the Home Tavern blues festival last night. The delay on the tower burger hash brown puts me in danger of missing the kick-off, space filled somewhat unsatisfactorily by 1927 and Billy Idol music videos on the in-store TV.

This less-than-flattering scene concludes with a hastily scoffed burger inhaled in the smokers' area out the front of The Sportsman's Hotel watching the passing Kincaid St traffic. Not all moments in life can be in the top league.

The Sportsman's is visible from the front bedrooms of my childhood home. It's a suburban pub opposite the racecourse and Wagga Cricket Ground. In those days it was another of Wagga's no-go zones. It's not exactly been gentrified these days. It still has the purple, orange and green swirly carpet that indicates working men are always welcome, but it's no longer a smoke-filled mire.

The game starts as I arrive and, amid a rash of errors and some dreadful refereeing, the Sharks get out to an early lead. The Raiders respond with some razzle dazzle and hit the lead.

The fellow at the bar, wearing a Transport Workers Union polo shirt and draining schooners, rises to reveal a most unpleasant case of gout as he shuffles to the gents. Sportsman's Hotel indeed. Stay off the salami, man!

After the break, a horrible forward pass miss gives the Sharks a try to stay in the match and I'm starting to realise that my facade of being above primitive club parochialism has crumbled.

I care about the Raiders and start yahooing at the television to help the boys over the line. It clearly works as the Raiders romp home and live to fight another day.

I don't know when they last won a finals match, but I was certainly younger and thinner then. *Come on Raiders!*

The Age of Aquarius
MARK NICHOLS

WITH THE WOUNDS STILL FRESH FROM THE SHARKS' EXIT, I could not bring myself to put pen to paper. Enter my ghost-writer 'Whippet' and his take on what I would have written if I could.

With their rich history of finals football and as a diehard fan, I was as excited as a kid in a lolly shop to be at Bruce Stadium to see the Sharkies take on the Faiders in the second elimination final. However, my optimism dissipated quickly as it appeared thoughts were already turning to 2013 – seeing Flanno's head buried in the Wests Tigers player catalogue minutes before kick-off evidence of that. It was a Raiders field day and, for this reason, I won't be focussing on the rubbish I witnessed that day. This is all about a hugely promising 2013.

Here are the reasons why the Sharks will win the NRL in 2013:

FINALS EXPERIENCE I'm not sure why the Sharks have a reputation as big game players but it is one that sits very, very comfortably with me. I suspect, however, it has something to do with our Amco Cup success in the 1970s and '80s – I was always proud how our commitment to that thing never wavered. Unlike other clubs who would spend all the time and effort chasing a competition that runs the whole winter, we would concentrate on the shorter competition – a trophy is a trophy, as they say. Plus, celebrating Mad Monday in June meant we had a big offseason to prepare for it again. To put into perspective our dominance, of the 16 times it was played, the Sharks won one and contested (and lost) another three finals. Only Balmain, Manly, St George, Easts, Parramatta, Combined Brisbane and Western Division boast better records. You cannot buy that experience.

THE PACK Never has a Shark pack looked so intimidating. The difference with the 2013 edition is they combine skill and smarts with the grit. Gibbs is a good example: if anyone can be considered a halfback trapped in a front rower's body it's him. Gallen, say no more. And Fifita, one of three in the club who can count without the aid of his fingers. Out-smart, out-play, win.

TODD CARNAGE While some may see Todd Carnage's injury in the capital as a potential problem, I don't. Knowing Toddy, and him knowing the game was out of reach, he clearly feigned an injury, was taken off and in Mooseheads before fulltime. I'm sure he'll be back to his damaging best for next season.

Here are the reasons why the Sharks may not win in 2013:

RECRUITMENT The Sharks' recruitment has always proven to be central to success. Acquiring players on the verge of 'breaking-out' and not paying overs for established performers seems to be a strategy that paid handsome dividends.

THE REST The administration's capacity to think outside the box has suffered since former CEO Tony Zappia left. The tough current ecomomic climate, competition for the fans' dollar, the carbon tax – all conspire to make it very, very difficult for clubs to get ahead and compete with the NRL big-boppers. Now we rely on solid property investments and fan memberships. I'll give it to 2015.

See you at Homebush on the October long weekend in 2013.

Canberra 34

TRIES Earl, Ferguson 2; Papalii, Buttriss
GOALS Croker 3/4, Dugan 0/3, Ferguson 0/1

Cronulla 16

TRIES Leutele, Graham, Stapleton
GOALS Carney 1/1, Stapleton 1/2

REFEREES Tony Archer, Chris James • CROWD 24,450

The Semi-finals

The eyes do have it

Manly Sea Eagles *versus* **North Queensland Cowboys**
7.45pm, Friday, 14 September
Allianz Stadium, Sydney

MARTY SPENCER

AS I WRITE THIS REPORT, THE WORLD IS IN TURMOIL OVER A RUGBY LEAGUE VIDEO. That video clearly shows Manly's Kieran Foran knocking the football on yet, despite that empirical evidence, the two video referees, Steve Clark and Paul Simpkins, opted to give Manly the benefit of the doubt and award them a crucial try.

That incomprehensible decision capped off a stellar 20 minutes in the second half for the video referees during which they ignored an Ash Graham hand in the play-the-ball which resulted in a scrum feed for the Cowboys, who scored a try in the ensuing set; then allowed a dubious benefit-of-the-doubt try to Jorge Taufua; then made the mystifying Foran decision.

This game is being talked about for all the wrong reasons. I would love to describe the raw-boned intensity of the battle, the controlled aggression of both packs and the brilliant hands of both backlines. But alas.

The *Foran Hand* reminds me of the Four in Hand Hotel in Paddington, a pub which used to serve the best bangers and mash for Saturday lunch prior to a big game at the SFS. Ah ... I miss you, Saturday arvo footy ... but I digress.

The use of technology in rugby league has caused more controversy than its introduction sought to dispel and it may be enlightening to examine other spheres where technology is used to good effect only to be let down by the humans who use it.

I know video refereeing is not rocket science but there is an historic parallel. In 1999, Lockheed Martin was forced to blow up the Titan 4 Centaur rocket carrying the Milstar 2 satellite over Cape Canaveral after a software programming error of one decimal point caused it to malfunction, costing US taxpayers in excess of $1 billion.

Now the cost of refereeing decisions does not stretch into double figures but the ramifications are far-reaching. It can result in momentum swings within games and it can affect seasons. In this instance, it may have ended the season for the Cowboys. Having said that, Manly was the better side on the day, although the game was upset by the clanger.

On the same weekend in England, Everton was robbed of a win against Newcastle when a goal, which clearly crossed the chalk, was disallowed by a linesman. No video decisions are made in the English Premier League and many fans are screaming for its introduction.

Ironically, many here are screaming for it to be scrapped or, at the very least, modified. The American Football system of appeal would not be ideally suited to the fast pace of rugby league and the bottom line of any review system by referees is human fallibility. Referees have been getting it wrong since competitive sport began, but what must be done in the NRL to maximise the benefits associated with the use of technology?

For a start, the contentious "benefit-of-the-doubt" decision should be reviewed. Why should an attacking team arbitrarily receive a benefit? If doubt is evident, then surely the try itself is doubtful and should not be awarded! Am I being too simplistic? Referees are only human – well most of them – and by removing "benefit of the doubt" we indeed remove that possibility from their psyche, allowing them to make informed decisions based on conclusive evidence.

For the rest of the finals series, Manly needs to tighten up its ruck defence if it is to have any chance against Melbourne – the Cowboys made easy yards up the guts on a number of occasions with the hard working props, Scott and Tamou, between them making 34 runs for 410 metres. They also made 56 tackles. Not bad considering they were both on for just under 60 minutes.

Canberra-born Manly winger Jorge Taufua was absolutely electric for the Sea Eagles. On that form, he might well be looking at a sky blue jumper as early as next year.

Mixed feelings

LINDSEY CUTHBERTSON

Y OU KNOW SOMETHING ISN'T RIGHT when you react to a favourable decision with sheer and utter confusion rather than celebration.

All the talk from this final was of a refereeing decision which no doubt had an impact on the game, the mood of the game. It was like someone let the air out of the whole shebang with the sense of deflation permeating the ground and every lounge room in the rugby league nation. Even some on the northern beaches.

With the match in the balance, Kieran Foran appeared to knock the the ball on during a play that resulted in Michael Oldfield's second try, which eventually proved to be the difference.

It looked obvious in real time. In slow motion, it looked even worse. But after a couple of reviews, the video referee moved on and appeared to focus on what happened afterwards. I began to feel like Manly had not only dodged a bullet but were about to receive an early Christmas present. Unfortunately, I was right.

But let's back it up for a moment. I'm talking about the last try of the match and there were six in total. You need only compare my reactions to all of them to understand how much something was amiss.

The first was created by a piece of Jamie Lyon brilliance with the Manly co-captain batting a cross-field bomb back to Glenn Stewart, whose quick hands saw Oldfield score in the corner. Sitting cross-legged on my lounge room floor, I responded with a loud and enthusiastic clap.

Manly's second came off a Jorge Taufua line break down the left wing, somehow managing to catch an errant pass behind him one-handed, clutch it to the small of his back and slowly work it around to his chest while sprinting at full-speed down the touchline before drawing Matt Bowen and passing to Brett Stewart. By the time Stewart planted the ball down between the posts, I was up on my feet and cheering at the television.

This was a big game for Manly. They only lost by six the week before against the Bulldogs but, by the way some skewed the result, it appeared that the Sea Eagles were ready to be de-feathered by a rampant Cowboys side buoyed by a 33-16 demolition of the Broncos. But the Sea Eagles won the first quarter of the match.

The Cowboys came back in the 10 minutes each side of halftime and their resurgence was driven by substitute hooker Anthony Mitchell, who made the most of props James Tamou and Matt Scott's powerful runs up the middle by continually forcing the Manly defence backwards.

The Cowboys' first try was a case of something coming out of nothing, thanks to some great footwork by Tamou and some lazy Manly defence. I didn't applaud this piece of footballing skill but I certainly paid it the respect it deserved by staying silent.

The Cowboys' second was the exclamation mark on the period they dominated. Winger Antonio Winterstein crossed on the left side and my heart rate quickly rose. It was a simple overlap play but it spoke volumes of the gradual momentum shift. And I may have thrown a couple of naughty words at the TV for good measure.

I cheered when the Sea Eagles hit the lead once more through Taufua's dubious try and didn't doubt that it should have been awarded. But Oldfield's second try was something different. Natural justice was not served.

This controversial decision left a sour taste.

Yet there was some relief as well and a renewed sense that Manly could hold on to win. That they managed to repel a desperate Cowboys side in the last 10 minutes is evidence that, while the media and quite a few emotional people on the internet will bemoan the contentious decision to give the Sea Eagles their last try, the argument that it cost the Cowboys the game just doesn't hold up.

More than anything, this match proved two things: Manly is far from dead in this competition and even when their game is a little off, they can still graft out a victory; but most importantly, officiating in the NRL has hit an alarming low. I can handle a big call overshadowing a result – but only when they get it right. I only have to consult my gut feelings to know what I thought of the Oldfield try – and coming from the mouth of a Sea Eagles fan, that's saying a lot.

Manly 22

TRIES Oldfield 2; B. Stewart, Taufua
GOALS Lyon 3/5

North Queensland 12

TRIES Tamou, Winterstein
GOALS Thurston 2/2
REFEREES Shayne Hayne, Ben Cummins • CROWD 16,678

Death to the Bunnies

South Sydney Rabbitohs *versus* **Canberra Raiders**
7.45pm, Saturday, 15 September
ANZ Stadium, Sydney

TIM NAPPER

O N ANY GIVEN DAY, I QUITE LIKE THE RABBITOHS. Indeed, they are my second favourite team. I like that they are one of only two remaining foundation clubs in the game. I like that they have a working class history and they are the perennial underdogs. The Rabbitohs have tradition behind them – a weight of history that says every time they play it's a game for the ages.

But this isn't any given day. This is a final and I'm watching South Sydney play my beloved Raiders. It's been a long time between Grand Final drinks for the men in Green and I am filled with venomous fury against any team that would stand in their way.

Oh – and the whole *South Sydney hasn't won a finals game in 25 years* thing? Don't give a rat's. Happy to see it become 26, you bastards. *Haven't won a premiership since 1971?* Hmm, that's a long time to suck at footy. The last time you won the minor premiership was 1989? Yeah, I recall that was the year you were smashed by the rampaging Raiders on the way to *their* first premiership.

The way this matchup between the Raiders and South Sydney unfolded wasn't an inspiring one. There were too many handling errors early on. Souths did play some good passages of footy, I guess. Some say that the Bunnies have flashes of brilliance and moments of disaster but the same could be said of the Raiders. And it was the Raiders who were furthest from their best in this match.

If we want to be objective, we can say this about the game: the Raiders were robbed. I was furious watching the match. The Rabbitohs were lying all over the Raiders in tackles and getting away with it whereas the Raiders were penalised for minor infractions. Half the tries from the Bunnies came from shepherds, forward passes or blatantly offside players. And the penalty try awarded to that lumbering loaf Inglis was an outrage. It was nothing less than a diabolical smashing of both the scales of justice and the bell of liberty.

In the last 10 minutes, when it became clear that the Raiders could not win the match, I switched to wishing for what I always wish for when the Raiders are getting beaten badly: for the other team to suffer serious injuries. The only red and green I wanted to see was blood on the grass.

But that didn't happen. Souths, injury-free, walk into the finals while I weep the bitter tears of defeat known only too well to a Raiders supporter.

The remainder of the finals look bleak. Three teams I loathe remain.

So, as Ray Warren gave his eulogy for the Canberra season ("came well at the end of the season," and "have a lot of good young players from country NSW" and so on and so forth), I come to the only conclusion I may at this time: I want the Bunnies to take down the premiership. I want that great club of battlers, steeped in league tradition, to rise to grand final glory.

Up with the Bunnies!

— ◆◆◆ —

Footsteps ...

DOUG ROWETH

I WANDER THROUGH THE GATES IN THE FOOTSTEPS OF THE MANY MORE who have made the journey before me. I shiver as I breathe in the atmosphere and walk through the history. This is the first time I've ever been to a South Sydney home final, opportunity denying me all my adult life. Until now.

I look around. ANZ Stadium didn't exist the last time South Sydney won a final. Back then Bob Hawke was PM and there were corner stores everywhere. In Homebush tonight, Flash is my sole kindred spirit, here head to toe in red and green. Flanners and Parko have come along, decked out in Raiders gear. Vested interests all round.

Inside the stadium, Flash is a picture of anxiety. Nerves are good I remind him, they keep us on edge. He doesn't listen. Part of him just wants this to be over. He bleeds cardinal and myrtle. His entire supporting life has built to this moment. And, more importantly, just what is at stake should tonight's match not follow the script.

Turns out Parko has purchased space smack bang in the middle of the Raiders' faithful. Worse still, I'm left alone as others source beers and food. I'm feeling engulfed by lime green. It's only as I'm trapped by the sheer weight of numbers around me that I get a sense of the occasion. What a moment.

At kick-off, I have beer in hand. The Burrow is in full voice, attempting to monopolise the noise inside the stadium. We understand what's at stake.

This one is for keeps. We are all afraid. Afraid of losing. Afraid of dreaming.

But after 25 minutes, when Andrew Everingham scores, South Sydney lead 14-0. Issac Luke's injection into the run-on side is genius. Canberra's one-on-one defence is woeful. The Rabbits look much more composed in the finals this time around. Over on the concourse South Sydney fans are singing but around us is silence. And swearing. Mostly from Parko. Raiders fans are all a bit stunned. I smile. Perhaps these seats aren't so bad after all. I begin to believe.

Too soon. The Rabbits relax and the Raiders score twice in three minutes. Around us, the Canberra crowd finds its voice. Flash and I cop plenty. Led by Parko. It's not fun. We suffer in silence. 14-10; the game is back in the balance. Sweet merciful crap. I knew it was too good to be true. I resume shitting myself.

Then, in the shadows of halftime, English import Sam Burgess receives a ball from a high-flying Chris McQueen on the Canberra line and he strolls in almost untouched. Parko cringes. Flash exhales. That was huge.

A 10-point lead at halftime is enormous for South Sydney fans. Flash is still so very nervous. Parko shows signs of hope. Flanners sucks down a cigarette. We all know this match isn't over. Anything could happen from here.

It pretty much does. A couple of minutes in, the Raiders put a stray pass in touch. Then a Josh Dugan error allows Dylan Farrell to pounce for South Sydney. Shut the gate. Flash almost smiles. He is slowly relaxing. It's South Sydney 26 Canberra 10. The drought is breaking.

The Rabbits maintain their composure. It's almost eerie for South Sydney fans. They belong in this match, they belong in the finals. It's real. An awkward penalty try to Greg Inglis seals it. The Canberra faithful disagree with the decision. But they are lucky Blake Ferguson isn't sin binned. Not just for impeding Inglis. For sheer incompetence. Souths are home.

I look around. Flash has disappeared off into the Rabbitohs members. He was five years old the last time South Sydney won a final, yet his loyalty has never waivered. So proud. Parko and Flanners seem resigned to the result. The minutes count down. The realisation washes over me as to what has just happened. Souths have won. This is what the finals are all about. I get it now.

Michael Maguire has taken this team much deeper than any in a generation. Not since the days of corner stores and Hawkey has there been so much to be excited about down at Redfern. They will talk about this for a long time.

Flash is speechless, the elation breaks through. We return next week now. Will South Sydney beat the Bulldogs? Perhaps. If they don't tune out for those dopey patches and settle early, then who knows?

Either way, the journey continues. We make history at every turn. And leave behind more footsteps.

South Sydney 38

TRIES Everingham 2; Inglis, Farrell, Reynolds, S. Burgess

GOALS Reynolds 7/8

Canberra 16

TRIES Earl, Ferguson, Williams

GOALS Dugan 2/3

REFEREES Matt Cecchin, Tony Archer • CROWD 35,874

The Preliminaries

Parallel universes

Melbourne Storm *versus* **Manly Sea Eagles**
7.45pm, Friday, 21 September
AAMI Park, Melbourne

STU WARREN

I N THE END, IT WAS MONEY THAT STOPPED ME. Travelling interstate to watch the boys battle out their prelim had looked the goods ... but this dream was eventually dashed by harsh fiscal reality. Between airfares, cabs, tickets and hotel room to crash in – not to mention beer money – I figured on being out of pocket at least a grand over the course of 48 hours.

And, to be honest, it looked a hefty price to pay, especially considering I didn't like my chances of coming away from the stadium with a smile on my face.

The preliminary final is a strange beast. It's one step from the ultimate match of the season and can be enough to convince fans and scrutineers alike that the year has been worthwhile. But it's not the 'granny'. There's no lasting glory to be derived from a winning prelim.

In most cases, losing in the penultimate week isn't a fantastic look either.

It smacks of hastily spruiked intangibles like guts and determination, passion and spirit, but can equally see the loser marked as a dud or, worse, a choker.

In the days leading up to the 2012 preliminary finals, I was close to being a nervous wreck. Consternation coursed around my body.

I spent far too many daylight hours (as well as valuable nocturnal time) thinking deeply on every last permutation that could impact the outcome.

Would it fall my way? Who knew? Definitely not the TV pundits. Maybe the bookmakers?

But even then, their analysis deals with fixtures in the cold, callous manner you might expect from a market analyst ... they don't consider the potential for romance or fairytales in sport.

I do, but normally that fairytale aspect takes on the same look. My team wins.

Sometimes I imagine they'll win in the last minute. Sometimes I convince myself they'll win by the length of the straight. Sometimes I get it right ...

Just not this time.

But it's not like it was going to be an easily done thing, anyway.

Compound the ravages of two previous finals hit-outs, an interstate road trip and the unquantifiable impact of players carrying injuries into a big match and the odds were pretty heavily stacked against.

Does that sound defeatist?

How about the fact my side was packing a first year coach and had lost our previous flag-winning boss to a cross-town rival?

What about the clowns in charge of the video referral system?

If they hadn't shanked us in the liver with their bullshit and buffoonery it might have been a whole different ball game!

It might have been. But it wasn't.

And for all of those reasons, my decision to stay home on prelim weekend was prudent.

The Swans were preened and purring whereas my Collingwood boys didn't really move beyond fourth gear and were never going to worry the hosts who now face Hawthorn in the decider.

And there were you thinking I was talking about Manly the whole time!

That the contest was one-sided is just one of the similarities between the AFL match in Sydney pitting the Swans against the Pies and the NRL equivalent played in Melbourne between the Storm and Sea Eagles.

On the surface there were numerous parallels. They shared the same free-to-air television slot – allowing me to look away from time to time as it became increasingly obvious the Pies were done for the year.

Going in favourites, the Storm (and Swans) spent large chunks of the year flying high, wobbling somewhat towards the backend of the home-and-away season before surging through the finals with barely a care in the world.

They went in to the Grand Final qualifier as heavy favourites having won the right to host their prelim after success in the first week of September action.

Manly (and Collingwood), however, had battled throughout the regular season, sometimes playing well but often relying on recall to get them over the line.

They are both recent champions after all and, on occasions, it is little more than that ingrained grit and know-how that chalks up the 'W'.

The Swans veritably leapt from the blocks, leading to my first channel change of the evening after only 20 minutes of play.

Happily, I found that the Magpies weren't alone in their struggles.

The Storm had taken to Manly in no uncertain terms and could have been out by further at the half had Cameron Smith not duffed a trio of conversions.

Manly, for their part, played horrible football during the first half hour.

If I had been told they'd done away with using resin on their hands to grip the ball, replacing it, unthinkingly, with lubricant, I could have believed it.

Tony 'T-Rex' Williams couldn't catch cold, more through sloppiness and inattention than having tiny and immobile arms (like his namesake), while Jorge Taufua looked absolutely nothing like a professional footballer as he set about racking up four errors for the night, including a brace of early howlers.

The Storm, meanwhile, strung together a number of impressive passages and now look capable of bringing another (legit) premiership to Melbourne.

But as a contest, this one wasn't long-lived.

Manly were in it – on the scoreboard, at least – until the early stages of the second half, but they never truly threatened.

The Sea Eagles fell further behind as the night unfolded.

And so did the Magpies.

Whose turn tonight?
ADAM MUYT

TONIGHT'S MATCH ENTICES, AN ALL-OR-NOTHING ENCOUNTER pitting the reigning premiers against one of this year's form sides. Melbourne has to be considered favourite on the back of good recent form, home-ground advantage and a week's rest after easily disposing of the Bunnies a fortnight ago. But Manly is a battle-hardened side with plenty of big match experience.

Of course, these sides have a bit of history built up between them over recent seasons, the spoils – and bruises – shared just about evenly. Neither team likes the other, a point emphasised and then heightened by the infamous *Battle of Brookvale* match of last season. All week I've been looking forward to this game – bring it on!

Within 20 minutes I'm feeling shell-shocked, rattled. It's three tries to zip the Storm's way. Manly hasn't looked like worrying Melbourne and mistakes are plentiful, beginning right from the first set of six. Phil Gould sums matters up: "Manly look like they're playing with a brick. It's mind boggling!" The only thing keeping us in it at this stage is the length of time remaining and Cameron Smith's wayward kicking, reducing what could be an 18-0 lead to two converted tries instead.

The next five or so minutes sees Manly continue with the fumbling morass, as first Glenn Stewart loses the ball about 25 metres out from the Storm's tryline followed by Galuvao knocking on about the same distance out. What is happening? A little bit of luck goes Manly's way: Melbourne has a try disallowed after Fonua puts his foot into touch when passing in-field to Nielsen. But the luck dissolves as quickly as it arrives: Ballin does a hamstring and is gone for the night.

And then, with a couple of minutes left before halftime, Lyon scores a try off a kick and then converts. It's 12-6. It feels very, very odd being so close, a complete contradiction to the true rhythm of the game. As one of the Nine commentators puts it: "It feels like it should be 100 to six!" I can't argue with that. But now we're right back in it with a half to go.

Four minutes into the second-half and the hope and optimism I'm feeling evaporate after Cronk scores his second try of the night off the back of a 60-metre run from Will Chambers. Impressive stuff. A penalty goal to Smith takes the score to 20-6 with less than 30 minutes remaining. Ominously, Manly don't look like they're capable of scoring. And then out of nothing – actually a dropped ball from Widdop – Lyon dashes 60 metres to score under the posts for his second try of the night. The conversion makes it 20-12. Somehow Manly is still in it.

And then the Manly clangers return. First, a Daly Cherry-Evans line drop-out fails to go the required 10 metres giving Melbourne a penalty 10 metres out. The ball goes out to Bromwich who knocks on. Manly gets the scrum feed, wins the ball but Glenn Stewart knocks it on at the base of the pack. So it's another scrum. Out it goes to Bromwich who makes up for his earlier mistake by going over for a try. Conversion and it's 26-12. Just about game over.

Two more tries follow for Melbourne in the last 15 minutes. Kite knocks on for Manly in the final minute, encapsulating what's been a horror night for them. Thankfully the siren sounds: Melbourne thoroughly deserve their victory.

As for Manly, it's been the worst performance in a big game since the Storm belting in the 2007 Grand Final. I try consoling myself with the thought that these two sides keep swapping beltings, which means it's our turn to wallop them next time we meet. But, of course, that's now a long way off.

Melbourne 40

TRIES Slater, Cronk 2; Chambers, Bromwich, Proctor

GOALS Smith 5/8, Widdop 1/1

Manly 12

TRIES Lyon 2

GOALS Lyon 2/2

REFEREES Matt Cecchin, Tony Archer • CROWD 25,543

Fate

Canterbury Bulldogs *versus* South Sydney Rabbitohs
7.45pm, Saturday, 22 September
ANZ Stadium, Sydney

JOHN CAMPBELL

SHORTLY AFTER SOUTH SYDNEY DEMOLISHED ST GEORGE ILLAWARRA in Round 20, I had a rush of blood to the head. I rang my old mate and fellow Bunnies tragic, 'Rapid Eye Movement', and suggested we get tickets for the Grand Final.

"How much'll they cost?"

"About a hundred bucks, I suppose."

"Bugger me dead! What if Souths don't make it that far?"

"Love is in the air, iMoo. We're dead-set morals."

Twenty-six minutes into the preliminary final against Canterbury, the Bunnies' halfback Adam Reynolds hobbled from the field and our dreams were as irreparably torn as the little bloke's hammy.

We sat in front of the flatscreen stunned. The Rabbitohs were ahead 8-4 and putting it all over the Dogs, but a suffocating gloom descended on the loungeroom. Neither of us wanted to think it but, in the dark corner of our hearts, we feared the worst.

The new finals system had, to this point, proceeded with unforgiving logic. Teams seven and eight (Cronulla, Brisbane) departed without a whimper in the opening prelims – it seems like an age ago. Five and six (North Queensland, Canberra) followed as per design. Third-placed Manly were flogged by Melbourne the previous night, dumping the horrible onus on Souths to buck the system.

As the red-and-greens do their warm-up drills, they appear to be composed, unfazed by the history that they carry with them. The cameras seek out Ben Barba and Greg Inglis, the pundits' pre-ordained match-winners. Nothing more could possibly have been written about either man in the lead up to the game – iMoo and I have devoured every word. Both are focused. There is no sign of stage fright among the players.

"The boys look calm, mate."

"Wish I felt same way."

I've drained my first beer and the suits still haven't wound up their gabfest.

We kick off. The Dogs start at a million miles an hour. They know that if you've got any idea of how to create an overlap, you'll do it against Souths' outside defence – left and right side. In the blink of an eye they are at our throats, pressing the line.

"They're gonna score here."

No sooner does iMoo say it than Krisnan Inu goes over in the corner. Des Hasler's mid-season, bargain basement buy from the Warriors bungs on that affected smile as he lines up the conversion of his own try.

"Poser."

He misses, Souths steady and five minutes into the game they at last get the ball.

Canterbury's frenetic opening has been awesome but coach Madge Maguire has instilled a steely resolve in his charges. The Bunnies fight back and, with Issac Luke running amok from dummy-half, they wrestle the ascendency from the Dogs.

Luke exploits a yawning gap to put us on the board.

"Shit iMoo, even I coulda got through there."

"In your dreams, mate."

Two goals from Reynolds and Souths are in command. But the tattooed rookie has no idea of the disaster that awaits him. That's the merciless thing about fate ... it always happens.

Ever the optimists – ever the dreamers, more like – we agree that if the boys can hang on and go to the break at 8-4, then Madge will come up with a plan.

Ben Barba soon scotches that idea, creating tries for Sam Perrett and Jonathan Wright. The ref rubs salt into our wounds when he penalises Sammy Burgess for accidentally collecting Perrett's scone in attempting to stop the winger.

"What utter bullshit," iMoo howls. He's ropeable. So am I.

I trudge to the kitchen and get a couple more stubbies. Rapid Eye Movement opens his as if he's wringing a chook's neck.

"Wha'dya reckon?"

He takes a deep draft.

"Souths are gonna hafta play the best half of football that they've played all year just to stay in it."

There's a shot of Reynolds in the sheds in his dressing gown. He's gone for the duration.

"We're fucked, aren't we?"

That we were.

The Dogs pile it on in the second stanza. They weren't minor premiers for nothing. Souths don't turn it up but they are a rudderless ship.

32-8 at fulltime. A harsh judgment. We are two hollow footy fans.

"Will we still go to the Grand Final?"

"Might as well. There's a coupla boys from the Mullumbimby Giants in the Tigers' under-20s."

"Cool. Who we goin' for in first grade?"

I don't need to think about it too long.

"It's not that I'm a bad loser or nothin', iMoo ... "

"Carn the Storm?"

"Totally!"

Just one more hurdle

MARK SEYMOUR

PRELIMINARY FINALS ... THE LAST HURDLE TO CLEAR before being able to play in the season's ultimate game. Having done almost everything right in season 2012, the Bulldogs needed to get by the surging Rabbitohs in order to make it.

I was worried about the fervent South Sydney supporters and the emotion of playing in a preliminary final for the first time in nearly 40 years. I was also concerned about the in-form Greg Inglis and the Bunnies' forward pack, although the Melbourne Storm had shown two weeks earlier that it was possible to overcome Inglis and co.

Canterbury's path to the game had been almost faultless, completing 14 wins from 15 games including a narrow Round 13 win over the Rabbitohs at the same venue. The qualifying final win over the old enemy, Manly, was full of merit and it appeared that the Bulldogs had momentum at the right time of the season. Having an experienced finals coach in Des Hasler at the helm (three Grand Final appearances in the last five years) was a definite bonus and it looked like things were set for a Canterbury victory.

No doubt Bulldogs fans thought a Grand Final appearance was almost a foregone conclusion when Sam Kasiano laid a ball on to Krisnan Inu, who crossed the tryline only three minutes after the start of the game. That try, though, seemed to stir the South Sydney players and for the next 25 minutes the Rabbitohs looked like the team that had finished on top of the NRL ladder with the match being controlled by the team in red and green. Instrumental in shaping an 8-4 lead was halfback Adam Reynolds, with a deft kicking game that had the Bulldogs players on their heels.

As with any successful season, there is always a fair amount of good luck required and Canterbury got their fair share in this match when just on the half hour, Reynolds pulled a hamstring while orchestrating another attack on the Bulldogs line. The despair from the Rabbitohs supporters was palpable when Reynolds fell clutching at his leg. He was to disappear up the tunnel, his night and season over.

As crucial moments in a game go, this was the turning point with South Sydney not troubling the scorers thereafter. Canterbury, on the other hand, found another gear with Perrett and Wright scoring before halftime and Perrett, Pritchard and Eastwood scoring after the break. Although the margin of victory was large, one wonders just how the match would have evolved without the injury to Reynolds.

Certainly full credit to the Bulldogs props who provided a great base for the victory and to coach Des Hasler, who has developed an exciting brand of football for the Blue and White Army to watch. Now only one win from the ultimate prize!

Canterbury 32

TRIES Perrett 2; Inu, Wright, Pritchard, Eastwood

GOALS Inu 4/7

South Sydney 8

TRY Luke

GOALS Reynolds 2/2

REFEREES Shayne Hayne, Ben Cummins • CROWD 70,354

The Grand Final

Celebration time

Canterbury Bulldogs *versus* **Melbourne Storm**
5.15pm, Sunday, 30 September
ANZ Stadium, Sydney

IAN HAUSER

NRL GRAND FINAL DAY IS ONE OF THOSE SACRED DAYS ON THE SPORTING CALENDAR. Everything else on that day is arranged to fit around the two hours which will decide the season's premiers. After seven months, we've arrived at the competition's climax – a one-day carnival that celebrates the game of rugby league. Admittedly, it's great if you support the winning side and hellishly deflating if you're with the losers. But nothing ventured, nothing gained. You can't win it if you're not in it. It's all or nothing.

My Grand Final day unfolds in stages so that, come kick-off, I'm ready, waiting and in the moment. I start early in the day by taking my wife to the airport for her flight to Hong Kong to spend a few days with her sister.

Later I go down the street to have a few drinks with Dave the landscaper who is hosting a *Goodbye to Rock Street* get-together. I end up cooking a late barbecue lunch for about a dozen. There's talk of watching the Grand Final when it comes on but I'm skeptical that this will happen. Most of this crowd aren't footy types. I quietly take my leave. Besides, I'm particular about the company I'm with for the big games like Origin, Tests and the finals. Today I'm comfortable to watch by myself as my three preferred companions for such matches (Liam, Michael and Peeter) are all interstate. They appreciate the subtleties of the game.

This is all about no distractions and no interruptions. Earlier in the year, the good wife, no lover of our great game, made the mistake of sitting down to watch Origin II with Michael and me. Okay, so I get tense as I watch and I have a tendency to squirm around in my chair, physically urging the ball in the direction I want it to travel. But it's another thing completely to have my intense focus disrupted with a serious and well-meaning: "Ian, I've never seen you so wound up." *Aaarrrggghhh!* This is no time for a philosophical dissertation on the male psyche and sport. This is Origin and the Maroons are under pressure. Just let me watch the bloody game! I restrain myself to a gently spoken: "Well, you don't have to sit there and watch me." It works, she moves off and I'm back to the task at hand.

As a Broncos supporter, I'm a comparatively impartial observer of today's game. I admire what the Dogs have achieved this year under Hasler. It's hard not to be dazzled by Ben Barba and the Dog forwards are not pretty in any sense. Still, they are a mob of goers and the mid-season reincarnations of Perrett and Inu have been admirable.

The Storm has Cam, Cooper and Billy – Queenslanders – and they've made something out of a set of Neville Nobodies accumulated from various clubs. A late season stutter has morphed into ominous finals form and then there's Bellamy.

I don't buy into all the hype about "an opportunity for redemption for the Storm", or "can Des do it in consecutive years with different clubs?" Both clubs have had their share of unpleasantness in the past and have rebuilt on and off the field. Let's give them the credit they deserve to have reached this moment.

This is an ideal grand final. It's first versus second. These two teams deserve to be in this ultimate stoush for season supremacy.

Teams practise set plays squillions of times in training even if they only bring some of them out occasionally during games. The big question is always whether or not a team can execute its training plays at the key moments in a match. Well-drilled teams such as the Dogs and the Storm can make them look easy.

Three key attacking moments in the first half and two desperate defensive saves in the second half, all by the Storm, are pivotal to Melbourne's win. And Smith, Cronk and Slater are at the heart of these five moments.

Cooper Cronk is the puppet master in three scoring plays. Early on, he orchestrates one of Melbourne's more common set pieces – the left-side spread to a rampaging Hoffman running the angle a couple passes wide of the ruck. Opposition teams have seen this play often during the year and many of them have their own variations of it. But Hoffman has scored from it several times. You'd think the defence would be ready and waiting to defuse it. But such is the timing and finesse of the passe, together with the angle and the force of the Hoffman run, that Dogs defenders can't get across in sufficient numbers or strength to hold him out. *Absolute precision!*

Later in the half, deep in attack following a glut of possession, Cronk goes left while keeping an eye on the defensive line. This time he chooses a no-look, double-pump pass. The first pump sends the defenders one step wider creating a gap immediately to Cronk's left. The second pump is hardly a pass, more a gentle upwards promotion of the ball so that it hangs in the air as if it is waiting for a runner to come through the gap created by the first pump. On cue, Slater presents himself and it's try time again. This was a thing of beauty. It was subtle and sublime.

With only a minute or two until the halftime break, Cronk is at it again. This time, it's a kick towards the corner for the winger to get outside the up-and-in defence. The key is in the pinpoint accuracy of the kick – height, angle, speed and distance from the tryline so that the attacking winger catches the ball at pace with momentum to carry him over the stripe against an outwitted defence. Cronk plays his part to perfection; O'Neill obliges and Barba is helpless to prevent the try. In cricket, they say that some bowlers can land it on a sixpence. On this occasion, Cronk would have hit a threepence. In its construction, rhythm and completion, it's a piece of poetry.

These are three set plays, three different methodologies, three tries and each clinically dissects the defence with surgical precision. On the biggest stage of the year, the Storm plays an almost perfect half of football to lead 14-4 at the break. It's been almost artistic, inviting the audience to admire its resolution.

The second half is, by way of contrast, a classic, scoreless slog as the Dogs try every trick in their repertoire to get back into the game. They have a better share of possession and field position but can't find the last play to score. They have two great chances but the other two members of the big three extinguish them.

About 10 minutes into the half, Dogs captain and crafty dummy-half Ennis attempts to barge over from close to the line. He gets well over the chalk but is held up by his opposite number Cameron Smith who envelopes Ennis and manages to get his whole body between the ball and the ground. A Canterbury score at this stage throws the game wide open. But no cigar. Complementing the sparkling attack in the first half, Smith's desperate effort in defence sets a standard that becomes the hallmark of Melbourne's second half performance.

With less than ten minutes on the clock, Barba makes a break down the left side. He's corralled by the defence but kicks infield for a rampaging Morris. The Storm defence is spreadeagled but the ball doesn't sit for Morris. He toes ahead and only has to regather and he's under the posts. But the oblong ball has a mind of its own and it props and bounces high forcing Morris to wait for its descent. This creates enough time for the chasing Slater to get back, leap above Morris and fist the ball dead. Six points saved, Dog's hopes dashed and the Storm regroup and grind out the final minutes.

Two key plays, no tries – each incident snuffed out by desperate defence that simply would not yield. The Dogs couldn't take a trick. The Storm have what it takes in both attack and defence.

The game deserves to be celebrated for these five moments alone. They encapsulated the skills and athleticism of rugby league at its best. They just happened to be all completed by the one team. The Storm won, the Dogs were not disgraced.

There were many other facets of the game to appreciate. For the Storm, Widdop was the perfect foil for Cronk and made a claim to expand the big three to the big four; the unfancied and underrated centres Chambers and Nielsen defended vigorously; unheralded retreads such as Norrie, Hinchcliffe and Lowe provided old fashioned grunt in the engine room. This was a complete team performance. For the Dogs, Morris gave all he had and looked the most likely to create something; Ennis led from the front and tackled himself into the ground; Eastwood, a most unlikely looking footballer, made some uncanny bursts; Barba showed flashes of his talent but seldom had space to move. The Dogs were honest but just not up to it on the day.

Yesterday the AFL put on a Grand Final for the ages on one of sport's greatest stages, the MCG. Today the NRL provided a compelling piece of theatre at the Olympic Stadium that showcased all that's great about rugby league: scintillating team play, brilliant individual skills, big hits, near misses, passion and drama in front of a huge crowd. What's not to like about it?

I sit alone but I celebrate a great game with the community of rugby league across the country.

You've just got to love it!

Not so innocents abroad

MATT O'HANLON

HAVE ALWAYS CALLED IT THE SYDNEY GRAND FINAL. I just can't get my head around these modern-day acronyms. They have no soul. No, bugger it: it's the Sydney Grand Final. To a Queenslander, anyway.

In February, four mates and I decided we'd start a punters club to get us down there. Big thing for Queenslanders: crossing the Tweed. But we're brave and so we talked all year of heading to the Sydney Grand Final; not the Brisbane Grand Final or the Rocky Grand Final or the Mackay Grand Final, as was the way for country kids in the '60s and '70s. These competitions were always important to Queenslanders of my generation. That was our rugby league. And still is.

But we kept an eye on Sydney and what was happening down there. It was the Queensland imports who made the comp what it was. This winter we banked the winnings and made our plans. The Golden Girl thought it was a great idea provided the other blokes eventually went home and we followed it up with a nice quiet week around her favourite NSW town of Berry. I was prepared to make this sacrifice.

Sydney. The boys' weekend started at lunchtime Friday with a pub crawl designed by the Irish brother-in-law. First stops were the Old Fitzroy and The Bell (home of Jimmy Carruthers in the '50s) in Woolloomooloo. The Bird could not join us until Saturday night but Mr Perpetual Motion, The Stooge, Tommy and myself started a 50-hour discussion on rugby league, racing and a range of other boys-own topics, interspersed with a little sleep. Work talk, or even the hint of it, yielded a $5 fine.

The Irish brother-in-law's pubs-of-Sydney tour placed us at Baxter's Inn (1920s style Chicago speakeasy) where we held centre stage. So we stayed for a good while. The chat flowed. When my son (a Queensland country kid who has now been Sydneyfied) joined us, he was embarrassed. He thought we were a posse of pen-pushers who'd turned into a bunch of blue-collar yobs. (I regarded this as a compliment.)

After Martini's, Negroni's and a few more stops, we somehow ended up at the Wenty Park dogs. The serenity was magnificent and we fitted in a treat. I think I saw Darryl Kerrigan in his dress thongs. Needless to say, we lost the shirts off our backs.

The punters' lament was soothed by a Harry's pie, served sometime after midnight.

Our accommodation at the Woolloomooloo Waters was strategic; it was ideal for genuine pie eaters. Ongoing discussion over a pie had us tipping Melbourne (at this point).

On Saturday, we headed to the Rosehill races where the syndicate punted reasonably well. MPM was the star because he was following my tips. Tommy advised MPM and The Stooge that following my tips would lead to a life sleeping on park benches with nothing more than the classifieds to keep warm. We were still tipping Melbourne

We met up with Borker and his family from Mackay in Chinatown and he was in fine fettle as his horse had run a good second earlier in the day at Kembla. Dinner led to a brush with the Triads when we felt entitled to dispute our bill. We paid for all our drinks (considerable) but unders for the banquet because it was well and truly unders. A fair percentage of the courses didn't lob and those that did weren't flash, one re-located from a table nearby when we'd gone without for a while. At one stage, I was arguing with six of the employees including a ten-year-old-kid who had the best command of English of any of the staff and, if the truth be known, better than any of us blokes on tour. He really dished it up to me. So we skedaddled.

Bird arrived after dinner with fresh legs and pushed for the Casino. I didn't take much pushing. Melbourne were still the tip although Bork warned us to be wary of Ben Barba – a Mackay local whom Bork had watched through his career. Bird's son was playing for Balmain in the NSW Cup Grand Final, so their clash with the Bluebags also got a run. We were up plenty but decided that we wouldn't be much good owning the joint. By 4.15am, we had enough left for a cab to Woolloomooloo and another pie at Harry's and that was all.

The tip was still Melbourne.

The big day started with a couple of Olds at the Fresno before we got a Nigerian cabbie to take us to the ground. We told the driver we needed an emergency trip from Central to Homebush because Bird had to see his lad kick off for Balmain. He took us literally and made the trip in 21 minutes. Phenomenal, and a highlight of the weekend. He broke at least 50 road rules and became actively engaged in five bouts of road rage. We dubbed him "the Idi Amin of Sydney cabbies" because that's the sort of knowledge of African politics we have.

Bird's young bloke got injured early and, as a key playmaker, he was missed by Balmain. His disappointment was soothed when another club approached him for a contract in 2013. Just before kick-off, Kenny Barba (KB) – Ben's dad - and a mate texted me to catch up inside the ground as if we were at Brothers in Mackay. We know KB and family very well from our Mackay days. His son Marmin (better than Ben?) and my bloke played with each other from age ten and are good mates. KB said we should back Wright as first try scorer as he could feel it in his bones that Benny would create a space on the right edge for him. With the season Ben had had, we got set and started to warm to the Dogs.

Melbourne, however, strangled the Dogs out of it. We were sitting bang in front of where Graham got into Slater and I said to the boys: "Hey, he F@#KEN bit him." Since their days at Brisbane Norths (or Norffs as we like to call them) Smith, Slater and Cronk have been special. During this game they showed why Melbourne and Queensland have been so strong and why Melbourne have received so much support north of the Tweed. Barba was exceptional as well. His second half was outstanding. He tried everything but his magical season fell ten points short. KB would have been proud. We thoroughly enjoyed the match except that we had to drink mid-strength beer.

After the match, they were giving away free Baked Bean sausage rolls from SPC. We got stuck into them and made our way to the Cross on Sydney's finest rattler. Next morning I picked the Golden Girl up at the airport. She asked how my weekend was.

"Quiet," I said

"That is FU@#EN BULLSH!T," she replied.

Great girl, G Squared. We headed for Berry.

I was in the house when the house burnt down

NICK TEDESCHI

I HAVE NEVER TAKEN FOOTBALL DISAPPOINTMENT WELL. When Canterbury lost the 1994 Grand Final to Canberra, a decisive and thorough beatdown from the moment Martin Bella made a complete mess of the kick-off, I came down with a violent case of sinusitis. It hit midway through the second half and, by the time of the final bell sounded, I was not in a good state. I was in bed for the better part of a fortnight.

Those at school fancied I'd been floored by the result. They were probably right.

The night after we were whipped by a star-studded Brisbane team in '98, I brushed a party to lie in bed for three days. It was a time of devastation.

Mum rang this year to wish Louise well if the Bulldogs were to get rolled.

Thoughts of defeat, however, had not crossed my mind in the week leading up to the big game. I could not bear the consideration. I was also strangely confident about Canterbury's chances. We did feel like we had the rugby league gods on our side.

It wasn't hubris, although perhaps that's how it came across. NRL touch judge Daniel Eastwood claims that the moment I expressed such confidence on *Fire Up* that Friday all was lost for the Bulldogs. It would be nice to know I have that pull. At least those who wave the flag pay good attention.

Really, you can't contemplate defeat in Grand Final week. It would kill you. You get to enjoy the last week of the season so rarely that you can't let miserable thoughts ruin it.

When Sunday morning rolled around, Sydney was bathed in sunlight and I was bathed in the spillage from the session that went until close at the Erskineville Hotel the night before. The hangover was rough and I was due back at The Erko at 11 for the traditional Grand Final breakfast.

It was morning beers, first and last try-scorer sweeps, Churchill Medal auctions, nerve-calming cigarettes and ball-busting that would have shamed Tony Soprano. It was Grand Final morning, the buzz was already on and my boys were right in it.

We watch the NSW Cup while knocking down kransky rolls, chicken fingers and chicken burgers that don't look like chicken before making a quick dash out to ANZ. The trains are already full and packed with blue and white. Even those who claim to loathe all that is blue and white are cheering on the Bullies, now a matter of pride for Sydney. The hatred for Melbourne seems to supersede that cross-town spite.

We get to the ground and everywhere it is blue and white and hope. The occasional Storm fan cops a scowl and is politely told on which side of the Murray they belong.

The first order of business is to purchase buttons. I bought David Stagg, James Graham and Aiden Tolman, arguably the palest purchase of buttons ever made.

The Toyota Cup is something to endure. Our multi is ruined by an insipid Raiders team hammered by the Tigers. The only highlight comes at the final siren when a potential Raiders try goes to the video. Cliffo has set a total points line of 55.5 just 15 minutes earlier. A try will send it over. Great line. It sure looks a try. But the punting gods sent Sting into a fury.

A little joy comes our way. We say goodbye to Hindy, Pet and Hornbag and the rest. It's time to play football.

Eventually, after an unbearable wait, the game starts. It is at this stage the Storm put the foot to the throat and they never let up. The Storm are relentless, playing a near-perfect game. Experience is telling. They play an up-and-in defence with tremendous aggression and kept Canterbury on the back foot by kicking to the corners.

Ryan Hoffman is first to cross after the Storm have about a dozen straight sets at the line. The Dogs hold firm at the line and score next through Sam Perrett. It would be a costly try with the skirmish afterwards seeing Pommy prop James Graham take a nibble at Billy Slater's ear. He would get 12 weeks.

The last 10 before the break are crucial. Slater scores a dubious try before Justin O'Neill crosses right on the break. At 14-4, it is only Cameron Smith's woeful goalkicking that is keeping the Bulldogs alive.

But 10 points down against an experienced Storm was not really alive. There isn't a point scored in the second stanza. When the siren went, I was already out the back with a Marlboro in the mouth.

I had scored in the sweep but I had lost a premiership. Canterbury were never in it. The Storm played the most complete game of football I have ever seen in a decider. Canterbury built zero momentum. They weren't allowed to.

The Storm are deserving premiers. But you never know when you will be back at the dance. And sitting at home is a lonely experience.

A brilliant victory

JOHN HARMS

SUNDAY MORNING. MELBOURNE. I am a little shabby. I have celebrated solidly at the Cricketers' Bar at the Windsor with some visiting Sydney Swans supporters after a cracking AFL Grand Final.

No doubt Sydney town is on fire already but the city of Melbourne is coming to life slowly. People wake to ABC TV's *Offsiders*. Roy Masters and John Stanley are doing a live cross from a Grand Final brekkie in the harbour city. The penny drops for some Melbournians: "Oh, that's right, it's the NRL Grand Final today."

Others need no reminding whatsoever.

There are plenty of serious Storm fans, and rugby league fans, in this city and a growing number of general sportslovers who feel some sort of connection with the team of their town. They are in for a big day.

"Storm will win by 10 points," Roy claims, with confidence.

"Churchill Medalist?" he ponders. "Cooper Cronk."

He says Melbourne have been the best team for most of the year and they're the better team now. He has a lot of time for coach Craig Bellamy and the way he has the players patiently in control of their own game. He knows Melbourne are blessed with brilliant on-field leadership as well.

I am persuaded. Although I don't need much persuading. Cameron Smith is one of the finest leaders in Australian sport. I think back to that Round 25 match when, trailing by two tries with three minutes to go against Cronulla, he calmly orchestrated the attack. Storm scored. They went back to receive the kick-off. Smith led them up the park again. And they scored a second time to win. Ridiculously brilliant. There was not a hint of panic in the hooker. I was clapping like a seal.

As a Queenslander living in Melbourne, today the Storm are mine. Not only do I enjoy their commitment to performing the skills of the game at an optimum level, I like that as a club they did not drop their bundle and fall away after the salary-cap controversy. The Storm tend to be relatively popular in Queensland thanks to the Queensland connection.

But, my goodness, they are absolutely despised in Sydney. The level of vitriol spat at them is remarkable. Many fans just cannot let go of their anger regarding the Storm. They just can't seem to acknowledge that Melbourne have copped their whack, have re-built and are now deserved Grand Finalists.

I spend the day with the family. Meanwhile, in Brisbane, a group of our friends has gathered for the match, as they always do for the Grand Final – and State of Origin battles. A barbecue and maybe the first swim of the Spring. My old mates, all Dads now, preparing themselves with an ale. Finding a spot in the TV room.

We have watched many a Grand Final together. I remember some great days in Toole's shed (he played first grade for Easts in Brisbane) at Lettuce Land (as we called his small crops farm) watching the Broncos get up. And an absolute classic on the back deck at Bardon where it was such a beautiful day and lunch had been so relaxing, we didn't go back inside. Instead I got the old 14" portable Sharp out and we set it up at the end of the table. It was 1997, one of the great Grand Finals, and you could hear the cheers coming from similar gatherings along the ridges and down in the hollows of the neighbourhood. It was clear people were barracking for the Knights. The hootin' and hollerin' as Andrew Johns put Darren Albert over at the death went on for a long time and was reprised with each replay that followed.

The teams run out. It's a terrific moment.

I am reminded of my childhood on the Darling Downs: of those days when Sydney was a world away, a place where I'd never even been. When images were beamed in from the SCG to our black and white TV. When you sensed the occasion even from 1000 kilometres away. My Dad liked Easts back then because of Arthur Beetson.

They were terrific moments and now, nearly 40 years later, I have a far better sense of their significance: the collective effort it takes to get to a Grand Final; the willingness to commit to the common cause; the opportunity you have to impose your will on the chaos of the game.

It's all very stirring. Alive. And I am alive to it as well.

I am interested in the Cam Smith-Michael Ennis battle. I am interested in the Billy Slater-Ben Barba battle. I wonder how these big Canterbury runners will go.

In the opening moments the players look a little nervous. Slater retrieves and throws a risky pass. It is almost intercepted. What is Billy doing? Is his knee still troubling him?

Ennis looks out for Smith. The play-the-ball is going to be crucial and hence the refs will play their part in this. What an inexact science!

Bryan Norrie belts the ball up. Canterbury hold. It's a tight battle.

Gradually the Storm get on top. They control possession, sweating on Bulldog errors. The blue and white absorb the pressure. But set after set proves too much and the probing attack of Melbourne eventually finds an opening.

The first try is based on the fear that emerges out of reputation. Just as Melbourne is looking out for Barba, so the Dogs are conscious of the great mover, Slater. He runs a decoy line and a short pass finds Ryan Hoffman who charges over. The defence has misread the situation and Storm have exploited it. Smith misses the conversion. He has not kicked well in recent times. Will this be a factor?

Again Melbourne camp in Canterbury's half. The defence holds to the point where Smith feels Melbourne need some reward and takes a simple penalty shot. He misses again. This is getting serious.

When Canterbury do take possession after Gareth Widdop loses the ball, they knock on in the first tackle. However they eventually make some territory and Sam Perrett heads for the line. Slater looks like he's going to try to toe-poke the ball from Perrett's hands as he dives over but, late to the contest, he pulls out and his knees go over and into the winger's back. It's harmless enough, but not to the Canterbury players or their rabid fans who go nuts. A scuffle breaks out which teeters on the edge of a barney, with players coming in. There is anger in the moment and the Merrie-Melodies fuse is alight. She goes off with James Graham not covering himself in glory in his attack on Billy Slater.

The game is stopped for various committee meetings, trials and judgments, where witnesses are called and processes followed and Billy Slater is asked if he wants to make a complaint.

"Bloody oath I do," says Slater.

More importantly the score is 4-4 and I am wondering how Storm will respond.

They are not flustered. They take complete control of the game. Their system is working; every player understands what is to happen and what his role is in making it happen. Their skills – basic passing, for example – are pure.

But it will take more than a system to penetrate this defence. It will take brilliance, and it comes in the form of a set play from 10 metres out: a short pass from Cronk which hangs in a gap as Slater bursts onto it. Barba has read it but he is powerless to stop his opposite number and Slater goes over in the tackle. A classic.

Now Melbourne is really on top and look threatening. Cronk kicks for Jason O'Neill who flies down the left, eyes on the ball. Barba sprints across. He is half a step from the contest and O'Neill snaffles the ball to score. Precision. And it's that matter of centimetres which is the difference in top sport. 14-4.

Melbourne could easily be further in front.

The signs are not good for Canterbury. The Storm's attack is hyper-organised, the Dogs lack structure. Their big forwards lack depth in their running. The defence looks tired.

Des Hasler has been lauded as the top coach going around. He will need to find his best words in the sheds. They need to rid themselves of this malaise; find a way to overcome the dispiritedness.

The Dogs return with energy. But they are faced with a wall. The Melbourne defence is ordered and aggressive. Canterbury throw everything at their opponents but hardly have an opportunity. They don't have any luck either.

When Ennis skips out of dummy half, his opposite number, who understands body movement like Wally Lewis did, finds a way of getting between the ball and the turf. They lie there nose-to-nose in an exhausted tangle of arms and legs.

Ennis looks like he needs a cigarette.

Barba is everywhere in the second half, trying to create a spark. But he is contained. If he's not mopping up grubbers, he's shooting them through although the bounce of the ball just won't go his side's way. When running the football, he is forever herded back inside although once, just once, he gets to the outside and nearly scoots away down the right. It's a difficult evening for him and he's observably frustrated. He expresses his disappointment. His side will learn a lot.

Many big matches have a celebratory moment and, although this one ultimately doesn't count, it brings a smile to Melbourne fans. Slater flies for Cronk's up-and-under and knocks it back. Norrie trails like a good rover, grabs the ball and is over. The boys love it. But it's disallowed.

With just minutes to go Barba is still trying his heart out but Melbourne remain solid until the end.

When the siren sounds there is a sense of jubilation, and probably of relief.

Roy Masters is spot on: 10 points and Cooper Cronk. The old fox!

The Melbourne fans are in raptures. They will celebrate long and hard.

Many of them will stay the night before heading back down the Hume Highway in the morning. They might even sit in a service station at Tarcutta or Holbrook and chew the fat with a Sydney family going the other way.

It is a new footy world we live in: Melbourne are the kings of rugby league, Sydney Swans the toast of the AFL.

I sit back after a huge season, a little sad that it's all over.

Melbourne 14

TRIES Hoffman, Slater, O'Neill

GOAL Smith 1/4

Canterbury 4

TRY Perrett

GOALS Inu 0/1

REFEREES Tony Archer, Ben Cummins • CROWD 82,976

THE PLAYERS

Brisbane

	AGE	STARTS	BENCH	TRIES	GOALS	F–GOALS	POINTS
ANDERSON, Scott	26	1	3	–	–	–	–
BAPTISTE, Kurt	21	–	1	–	–	–	–
BEALE, Gerard	22	25	–	8	–	–	32
CAPEWELL, Luke	23	1	4	1	–	–	4
CIVONICEVA, Petero	36	17	3	–	–	–	–
COPLEY, Dale	21	15	–	4	–	–	16
DODDS, Mitchell	23	2	8	–	–	–	–
GIBB, Brendon	23	1	2	–	–	–	–
GILLETT, Matt	24	9	14	6	–	–	24
GLENN, Alex	24	23	–	13	–	–	52
HALA, David	22	–	1	–	–	–	–
HANNANT, Ben	27	20	2	2	–	–	8
HODGES, Justin	30	18	–	5	–	–	20
HOFFMAN, Josh	24	23	–	3	–	–	12
HUNT, Ben	22	6	19	1	–	–	4
LUI, Dunamis	22	3	6	–	–	–	–
McCULLOUGH, Andrew	22	25	–	4	–	–	16
McGUIRE, Josh	22	7	17	1	–	–	4
MARANTA, Lachlan	20	7	–	2	–	–	8
NORMAN, Corey	21	24	1	10	2	–	44
PARKER, Corey	30	16	1	–	34	–	68
REED, Jack	24	22	–	7	–	–	28
SLYNEY, Nick	23	–	3	–	–	–	–
TE'O, Ben	25	12	9	10	–	–	40
THAIDAY, Sam	27	21	–	4	–	–	16
WALLACE, Jarrod	21	–	2	–	–	–	–
WALLACE, Peter	26	23	–	4	36	1	89
WHITCHURCH, Aaron	20	–	2	1	–	–	4
YOW YEH, Jharal	22	4	–	2	–	–	8

COACH Anthony Griffin
CAPTAINS Sam Thaiday (21), Alex Glenn (3), Corey Parker (1)

Canberra

	AGE	STARTS	BENCH	TRIES	GOALS	F-GOALS	POINTS
BERRIGAN, Shaun	33	9	14	2	–	–	8
BUTTRISS, Glen	27	10	3	2	–	–	8
CAMPESE, Terry	28	7	–	1	–	–	4
CROKER, Jarrod	22	25	–	16	81	–	226
DUGAN, Josh	22	17	–	6	2	1	29
EARL, Sandor	22	12	–	8	–	–	32
FENSOM, Shaun	23	22	–	3	–	–	12
FERGUSON, Blake	22	25	–	13	–	–	52
HARRISON, Bronson	26	8	2	1	–	–	4
KENNEDY, Jarrad	23	–	2	–	–	–	–
LEAROYD–LAHRS, Tom	27	15	7	–	–	–	–
LEE, Edrick	19	7	–	6	–	–	24
McCRONE, Josh	25	26	–	5	–	–	20
McILWRICK, Matt	21	–	4	–	–	–	–
MATAORA, Sam	21	1	15	2	–	–	8
NICHOLLS, Mark	22	–	12	1	–	–	4
PAPALII, Josh	20	26	–	7	–	–	28
PELO, Dimitri	27	5	–	–	–	–	–
PICKER, Joe	24	3	18	2	–	–	8
ROBINSON, Reece	25	24	–	17	–	–	68
SHILLINGTON, David	29	23	–	–	–	–	–
THOMPSON, Joel	24	20	5	7	–	–	28
THURLING, Trevor	28	–	4	1	–	–	4
TILSE, Dane	27	9	12	–	–	–	–
WADDELL, Travis	23	16	5	1	–	–	4
WHITE, Brett	30	4	1	–	–	–	–
WIGHTON, Jack	19	9	–	2	–	–	8
WILLIAMS, Sam	21	15	–	4	–	–	16

COACH David Furner
CAPTAINS David Shillington (16), Terry Campese (7),
Josh McCrone (3), Tom Learoyd–Lahrs (3)

Canterbury

	AGE	STARTS	BENCH	TRIES	GOALS	F-GOALS	POINTS
BARBA, Ben	23	27	–	22	–	–	88
EASTWOOD, Greg	25	19	5	3	–	–	12
ENNIS, Michael	28	26	–	–	–	–	–
FINUCANE, Dale	21	–	14	–	–	–	–
GAVET, James	22	–	1	–	–	–	–
GOODWIN, Bryson	26	11	–	4	14	–	44
GRAHAM, James	27	2	24	–	–	–	–
HALATAU, Dene	29	17	–	1	–	–	4
HODKINSON, Trent	24	4	2	–	–	–	–
INU, Krisnan	25	16	–	9	55	2	148
JACKSON, Josh	21	10	2	4	–	–	16
KASIANO, Sam	22	24	–	1	–	–	4
KEATING, Kris	23	21	–	3	–	–	12
LAFAI, Timoteo	21	5	–	2	–	–	8
LANE, Brett	24	1	–	–	–	–	–
MacDOUGALL, Luke	30	2	–	–	–	–	–
MORRIS, Josh	26	26	–	17	–	–	68
PAYNE, Corey	28	–	27	–	–	–	–
PERRETT, Sam	27	12	–	5	–	–	20
PRITCHARD, Frank	28	26	–	4	–	–	16
REYNOLDS, Josh	23	27	–	10	–	–	40
ROMELO, Joel	23	3	10	3	–	–	12
STAGG, David	28	9	18	3	–	–	12
TAUPAU, Martin	22	3	3	1	–	–	4
TOLMAN, Aiden	23	25	2	1	–	–	4
TURNER, Steve	27	8	–	3	20	–	52
WRIGHT, Jonathan	25	27	–	14	–	–	56

COACH Des Hasler
CAPTAINS Michael Ennis (26), Frank Pritchard (1)

Cronulla

	AGE	STARTS	BENCH	TRIES	GOALS	F-GOALS	POINTS
BEST, Colin	33	24	–	8	–	–	32
BUKUYA, Jason	23	18	6	4	–	–	16
CARNEY, Todd	26	21	–	4	61	3	141
DE GOIS, Isaac	27	23	–	3	–	–	12
FIFITA, Andrew	23	2	20	5	–	–	20
FRIZELL, Tyson	20	2	8	2	–	–	8
GALLEN, Paul	31	16	–	3	–	–	12
GARDNER, Nathan	22	6	–	1	–	–	4
GIBBS, Bryce	28	19	1	–	–	–	–
GORDON, Isaac	25	10	–	3	–	–	12
GRAHAM, Wade	21	11	8	6	–	–	24
GREEN, Jon	27	–	6	–	–	–	–
LEUTELE, Ricky	22	7	–	4	–	–	16
MILLS, Stewart	20	6	–	3	–	–	12
MORRIS, John	32	2	23	2	–	–	8
POMEROY, Ben	28	19	–	9	–	–	36
ROBSON, Jeff	30	23	–	6	–	–	24
ROSS, Ben	32	22	–	–	–	–	–
SMITH, Jeremy	32	22	–	3	–	–	12
STAPLETON, Nathan	22	13	–	3	1	–	14
TAGATAESE, Sam	25	2	11	1	–	–	4
TAUFUA, Mark	30	6	13	1	–	–	4
TOWNSEND, Chad	21	3	–	1	8	–	20
TUPOU, Anthony	29	8	4	–	–	–	–
WILLIAMS, John	27	19	–	6	1	–	26
WRIGHT, Matthew	21	21	–	1	–	–	–

COACH Shane Flanagan
CAPTAINS Paul Gallen (16), Jeremy Smith (6), Wade Graham (3)

Gold Coast

	AGE	STARTS	BENCH	TRIES	GOALS	F-GOALS	POINTS
BAILEY, Luke	32	17	–	1	–	–	4
BIRD, Greg	28	17	–	3	–	–	12
CHAMPION, Beau	25	9	–	4	–	–	16
DOUGLAS, Luke	26	16	8	1	–	–	4
DOWLING, Jamie	21	1	–	–	–	–	–
FALLOON, Beau	25	1	7	3	–	–	12
GORDON, Kevin	22	21	–	10	–	–	40
GRAHAM, Phil	31	2	–	–	–	–	–
HARRISON, Ashley	31	17	–	1	–	–	4
HENDERSON, Michael	28	1	6	–	–	–	–
IDRIS, Jamal	22	19	1	5	–	–	20
JAMES, Ryan	21	–	3	–	–	–	–
LAWRENCE, Brenton	27	1	8	2	–	–	8
LAWTON, Kayne	23	2	2	–	–	–	–
MEAD, David	23	20	–	10	–	–	40
MICHAELS, Steve	25	16	1	8	–	–	32
MINICHIELLO, Mark	30	18	5	2	–	–	8
MYLES, Nate	27	20	2	3	–	–	12
O'DWYER, Luke	29	9	12	3	–	–	12
PEYROUX, Dominique	25	8	4	2	–	–	8
PRINCE, Scott	32	22	–	4	61	–	138
RANKIN, Jordan	20	5	1	1	–	–	4
RIDGE, Ben	22	5	12	1	–	–	4
SEZER, Aidan	21	18	–	4	7	1	31
SRAMA, Matt	21	21	2	4	–	–	16
THOMPSON, Bodene	24	2	5	–	–	–	–
WHITE, Matthew	28	3	16	–	–	–	–
ZILLMAN, William	26	21	–	6	–	–	24

COACH John Cartwright
CAPTAINS Scott Prince (22), Luke Bailey (17), William Zillman (1)

Manly

	AGE	STARTS	BENCH	TRIES	GOALS	F-GOALS	POINTS
BALLIN, Matt	28	27	–	2	–	–	8
BUHRER, Jamie	22	5	21	3	–	–	12
CHERRY–EVANS, Daly	23	27	–	7	3	1	35
FORAN, Kieran	22	21	–	4	–	–	16
FORAN, Liam	24	6	1	–	–	–	–
GALUVAO, Joe	34	2	20	–	–	–	–
HARRISON, Daniel	24	14	2	1	–	–	4
KING, Jason	31	22	–	2	–	–	8
KITE, Brent	31	27	–	1	–	–	4
LUSSICK, Darcy	23	2	22	1	–	–	4
LYON, Jamie	30	26	–	11	73	–	190
MATAI, Steve	28	18	–	6	–	–	24
MAURO, Vic	25	3	16	–	–	–	–
OLDFIELD, Michael	21	9	–	8	–	–	32
ROBINSON, Tim	24	–	5	–	–	–	–
ROSE, George	29	1	16	–	–	–	–
SKINNER, Nick	24	–	4	–	–	–	–
STEWART, Brett	27	21	–	14	–	–	56
STEWART, Glenn	28	17	–	2	–	–	8
TAUFUA, Jorge	20	23	–	10	–	–	40
WATMOUGH, Anthony	29	27	–	3	–	–	12
WHARE, Dean	22	21	–	6	–	–	24
WILLIAMS, David	26	16	–	12	–	–	48
WILLIAMS, Tony	23	16	–	4	–	–	16

COACH Geoff Toovey
CAPTAINS Jamie Lyon (26), Jason King (7)

Melbourne

	AGE	STARTS	BENCH	TRIES	GOALS	F-GOALS	POINTS
BLAIR, Maurice	27	4	–	–	–	–	–
BROMWICH, Jesse	23	22	5	2	–	–	8
CHAMBERS, Will	24	18	–	13	–	–	52
CRONK, Cooper	28	26	–	10	–	1	41
DUFFIE, Matthew	22	17	–	10	–	–	40
FA'AOSO, Richard	28	–	6	–	–	–	–
FONUA, Mahe	19	5	–	1	–	–	4
GREENFIELD, Michael	27	–	1	–	–	–	–
HINCHCLIFFE, Ryan	27	11	16	4	–	–	16
HOFFMAN, Ryan	28	25	2	11	–	–	44
KELLY, Luke	21	–	1	–	–	–	–
KOSTJASYN, Rory	25	6	8	1	–	–	4
LOWE, Jaiman	29	–	15	1	–	–	4
LOWRIE, Todd	29	21	2	4	–	–	16
MANU, Sika	25	13	6	3	–	–	12
NIELSEN, Dane	27	22	–	7	–	–	28
NORRIE, Bryan	28	18	7	2	–	–	8
O'NEILL, Justin	21	21	–	11	–	–	44
PROCTOR, Kevin	23	12	11	6	–	–	24
QUINN, Anthony	29	14	6	3	–	–	12
RYLES, Jason	33	15	7	1	–	–	4
SLATER, Billy	29	21	–	16	–	–	64
SMITH, Cameron	29	24	1	2	78	–	164
VAVE, Siosaia	23	–	14	–	–	–	–
WAQA, Sisi	26	10	–	7	–	–	28
WIDDOP, Gareth	23	26	–	4	12	–	40

COACH Craig Bellamy
CAPTAINS Cameron Smith (23), Ryan Hoffman (4)

Newcastle

	AGE	STARTS	BENCH	TRIES	GOALS	F-GOALS	POINTS
ADAMS, Chris	26	–	3	–	–	–	–
BOYD, Darius	25	22	–	3	–	–	12
BUDERUS, Danny	34	22	–	2	–	–	8
COSTIGAN, Neville	27	17	6	2	–	–	8
CUTHBERTSON, Adam	27	4	18	–	–	–	–
EDWARDS, Joel	24	11	8	–	–	–	–
FA'AOSO, Richard	28	4	4	2	–	–	8
FILIPO, Marvin	25	–	2	–	–	–	–
GAGAI, Dane	21	12	–	5	–	–	20
GIDLEY, Kurt	30	5	–	1	14	–	32
HILDER, Matt	30	2	8	–	1	–	2
HOUSTON, Chris	27	24	–	4	–	–	16
McKINNON, Alex	20	9	15	2	–	–	8
McMANUS, James	26	19	–	10	–	–	40
MASON, Willie	32	15	2	1	–	–	4
MATA'UTIA, Peter	21	1	–	–	–	–	–
MULLEN, Jarrod	25	24	–	8	–	–	32
NAIQAMA, Kevin	22	8	–	7	–	–	28
NAIQAMA, Wes	29	6	–	1	9	–	22
O'DONNELL, Kyle	21	–	1	–	–	–	–
ROBERTS, Tyrone	21	18	–	3	40	–	92
ROCHOW, Robbie	22	2	6	1	–	–	4
SA'U, Junior	25	8	–	2	–	–	8
SNOWDEN, Kade	25	19	–	–	–	–	–
TAHU, Timana	31	22	–	7	–	–	28
TAIA, Zeb	27	9	14	1	–	–	4
TETEVANO, Zane	21	5	8	–	–	–	–
TUIMAVAVE, Evarn	28	2	1	–	–	–	–
UATE, Akuila	24	22	–	18	–	–	72

COACH Wayne Bennett
CAPTAINS Danny Buderus (18), Kurt Gidley (4), Jarrod Mullen (1), Chris Houston (1)

New Zealand

	AGE	STARTS	BENCH	TRIES	GOALS	F-GOALS	POINTS
BROWN, Lewis	25	12	12	4	–	–	16
FISIIAHI, Glen	21	4	–	1	–	–	4
FRIEND, Nathan	31	17	–	2	–	–	8
GODINET, Pita	24	2	2	1	–	–	4
HENRY, Ben	20	23	1	8	2	–	36
HURRELL, Konrad	21	14	3	12	–	–	48
IKAHIHFO, Sebastine	21	3	1	–	–	–	–
INU, Krisnan	25	2	1	1	–	–	4
JOHNSON, Shaun	21	22	–	12	–	–	48
LILLYMAN, Jacob	28	4	12	2	–	–	8
LOCKE, Kevin	23	14	–	7	–	–	28
LOUSI, Sam	21	–	2	–	–	–	–
LOUSI, Sione	22	5	17	1	–	–	4
LUCK, Micheal	30	2	4	–	–	–	–
MALONEY, James	26	23	1	4	67	3	153
MANNERING, Simon	26	19	–	3	–	–	12
MARA, Alehana	22	6	–	–	–	–	–
MATEO, Feleti	28	18	6	3	–	–	12
MATULINO, Ben	23	18	4	3	–	–	12
PACKER, Russell	22	20	4	–	–	–	–
RAPIRA, Sam	25	–	7	–	–	–	–
RAPIRA, Steve	23	1	5	–	–	–	–
ROPATI, Jerome	27	8	–	2	–	–	8
SLAIMANKHEL, Omar	20	4	1	–	–	–	–
TA'AI, Ukuma	25	1	11	1	–	–	4
TAYLOR, Elijah	22	23	–	2	–	–	8
TUIMAVAVE, Carlos	20	3	2	1	–	–	4
TUPOU, Bill	22	24	–	7	–	–	28
VATUVEI, Manu	26	20	–	12	–	–	48

COACHES Brian McClennan (22), Tony Iro (2)
CAPTAINS Simon Mannering (19), **Manu Vatuvei** (5)

North Queensland

	AGE	STARTS	BENCH	TRIES	GOALS	FIELD GOALS	POINTS
BOLTON, Scott	25	–	14	1	–	–	4
BOWEN, Matthew	30	26	–	13	12	2	78
COOPER, Gavin	27	26	–	10	–	–	40
FAIFAI-LOA, Kalifa	22	6	–	2	–	–	8
GRAHAM, Ashley	28	24	–	21	–	–	84
HALL, Glenn	31	20	3	4	–	–	16
JOHNSON, Dallas	30	26	–	1	–	–	4
LEARY, Blake	21	–	1	–	–	–	–
LINNETT, Kane	23	24	–	12	–	–	48
LUI, Robert	22	–	1	–	–	–	–
MITCHELL, Anthony	23	2	6	1	–	–	4
MORGAN, Michael	20	10	3	4	–	–	16
PANGAI, Mosese	20	1	–	–	–	–	–
PATERSON, Cory	25	2	1	1	–	–	4
PAYNE, Aaron	29	25	–	1	–	–	4
RIETHMULLER, Joel	27	–	10	–	–	–	–
SCOTT, Matthew	27	18	–	1	–	–	4
SEGEYARO, James	22	1	13	3	–	–	12
SIMS, Ashton	27	8	17	1	–	–	4
SIMS, Tariq	22	5	2	1	–	–	4
TAMOU, James	23	23	1	2	–	–	8
TATE, Brent	30	23	–	9	–	–	36
TAUMALOLO, Jason	19	–	17	5	–	–	20
THOMPSON, Ray	22	16	2	5	–	–	20
THORBY, Ricky	26	2	13	–	–	–	–
THURSTON, Johnathan	29	24	–	3	90	–	192
WINTERSTEIN, Antonio	24	26	–	8	–	–	32

COACH Neil Henry
CAPTAINS Johnathan Thurston (24), Matthew Scott (20),
Matthew Bowen (1), Aaron Payne (1)

Parramatta

	AGE	STARTS	BENCH	TRIES	GOALS	F-GOALS	POINTS
ALLGOOD, Mitchell	23	7	10	–	–	–	–
BLAIR, Cheyse	20	22	–	5	–	–	20
BURT, Luke	31	20	–	7	53	–	134
HAYNE, Jarryd	24	12	–	8	–	–	32
HINDMARSH, Nathan	32	23	–	2	1	–	10
HORO, Justin	25	2	4	–	–	–	–
KEATING, Matthew	25	15	–	2	–	–	8
KELLY, Luke	21	4	–	–	–	–	–
LASALO, Taniela	22	4	8	1	–	–	4
McGUIRE, Casey	32	4	8	1	–	–	4
MAITUA, Reni	30	17	4	2	–	–	8
MANNAH, Tim	24	20	4	1	–	–	4
MOIMOI, Fuifui	32	12	10	1	–	–	4
MORGAN, Ryan	22	19	–	9	–	–	36
MULLANEY, Jake	22	7	–	3	–	–	12
O'HANLON, Pat	21	–	2	1	–	–	4
PAULO, Joseph	28	10	13	–	–	–	–
POORE, Justin	27	6	17	1	–	–	4
ROBERTS, Ben	27	18	1	1	–	–	4
RYAN, Matt	24	13	4	2	–	–	8
SANDOW, Chris	23	22	1	9	14	3	67
SIO, Ken	21	24	–	13	–	–	52
SMITH, Ben	27	7	1	1	–	–	4
SMITH, Nathan	29	9	–	1	–	–	4
TAUTAI, Taulima	24	–	9	1	–	–	4
TONGA, Esikeli	24	3	–	–	–	–	–
TONGA, Willie	29	12	–	1	–	–	4

COACHES Stephen Kearney (18), Brad Arthur (6)
CAPTAINS Nathan Hindmarsh (23), Tim Mannah (1)

Penrith

	AGE	STARTS	BENCH	TRIES	GOALS	F-GOALS	POINTS
ACHURCH, Mitch	24	–	11	–	–	–	–
ARMIT, Chris	28	–	11	–	–	–	–
AUSTIN, Blake	21	7	6	1	8	–	20
BURNS, Travis	28	13	2	5	1	1	23
CIRALDO, Cameron	27	20	1	1	–	–	4
COOTE, Lachlan	22	24	–	9	2	1	41
DANIELA, Geoff	25	8	–	2	–	–	8
DOCKER, Adam	21	–	3	–	–	–	–
EARL, Sandor	22	3	–	–	–	–	–
EISENHUTH, Tom	20	1	–	–	–	–	–
GALEA, Danny	28	2	12	–	–	–	–
GORDON, Michael	28	7	–	1	2	–	8
GRANT, Tim	24	15	1	–	–	–	–
JENNINGS, Michael	24	17	–	10	–	–	40
KINGSTON, Kevin	29	22	–	5	–	–	20
LEWIS, Luke	29	13	–	2	–	–	8
McKENDRY, Sam	23	20	1	1	–	–	4
MANSOUR, Josh	22	14	–	7	–	–	28
NEWTON, Clint	31	21	2	4	–	–	16
PLUM, Nigel	29	9	4	–	–	–	–
ROBINSON, Matt	22	1	11	3	–	–	12
ROBINSON, Travis	25	2	–	1	–	–	4
SEIJKA, Harry	20	2	–	–	–	–	–
SELUINI, Nafe	22	–	2	–	–	–	–
SHACKLETON, Shane	30	–	4	–	–	–	–
SIMMONS, David	27	16	–	2	–	–	8
SIMPKINS, Ryan	23	5	12	2	–	–	8
SMITH, Nathan	29	4	–	1	–	–	4
TAUMATA, Arana	23	–	2	1	–	–	4
TIGHE, Brad	28	21	–	8	–	–	32
UAISELE, Etuate	27	14	–	5	–	–	20
WALSH, Luke	25	21	–	1	46	1	97
WESTON, Dayne	25	10	11	–	–	–	–

COACH Ivan Cleary
CAPTAINS Luke Lewis (10), Kevin Kingston (10), Cameron Ciraldo (2)

St George Illawarra

	AGE	STARTS	BENCH	TRIES	GOALS	F-GOALS	POINTS
AH MAU, Leeson	22	2	9	–	–	–	–
COOPER, Matt	33	15	–	6	–	–	24
CREAGH, Ben	27	22	–	7	–	–	28
DE BELIN, Jack	21	11	8	–	–	–	–
FIEN, Nathan	33	6	9	1	–	–	4
GOODWIN, Bronx	28	3	–	2	–	–	8
GOWER, David	26	–	2	–	–	–	–
GREEN, Nathan	20	5	–	–	–	–	–
HORNBY, Ben	32	24	–	2	2	–	12
HUNT, Dan	25	22	–	3	–	–	12
KING, Cameron	20	–	5	–	–	–	–
LATIMORE, Jeremy	25	6	8	–	–	–	–
MARKETO, Jake	23	4	5	1	–	–	4
MATTHEWS, Will	24	3	3	1	–	–	4
MERRIN, Trent	22	10	13	2	–	–	8
MILLER, Josh	29	2	7	1	–	–	4
MORRIS, Brett	26	23	–	14	–	–	56
NIGHTINGALE, Jason	25	24	–	7	–	–	28
PRIOR, Matt	25	12	5	3	–	–	12
REIN, Mitch	22	22	2	7	–	–	28
SCOTT, Beau	28	14	–	2	–	–	8
SOWARD, Jamie	27	19	1	2	43	3	97
STANLEY, Chase	23	10	1	1	6	–	16
STANLEY, Kyle	21	14	–	5	2	–	24
STOCKWELL, Jack	20	–	3	–	–	–	–
VEA, Atelea	25	1	1	–	–	–	–
VIDOT, Daniel	22	20	–	5	–	–	20
WEYMAN, Michael	27	10	–	2	–	–	8
YOUNG, Dean	28	8	14	–	–	–	–

COACH Steve Price
CAPTAIN Ben Hornby (24)

South Sydney

	AGE	STARTS	BENCH	TRIES	GOALS	F-GOALS	POINTS
ASOTASI, Roy	30	12	1	2	–	–	8
BURGESS, George	20	–	3	–	–	–	–
BURGESS, Luke	30	12	6	–	–	–	–
BURGESS, Sam	23	21	1	5	–	–	20
CLARK, Jason	23	–	23	1	–	–	4
CORRIGAN, Shaune	24	7	1	–	–	–	–
CROCKER, Michael	32	27	–	2	–	–	8
EVERINGHAM, Andrew	25	25	–	17	–	–	68
FARRELL, Dylan	21	27	–	8	–	–	32
GEDDES, Scott	31	10	2	–	–	–	–
HUNT, Justin	24	10	–	5	–	–	20
INGLIS, Greg	25	22	–	12	–	1	49
KING, Matt	32	20	–	3	–	–	12
LOWE, Ben	27	–	18	1	–	–	4
LUKE, Issac	25	18	4	5	3	–	26
McQUEEN, Chris	25	14	9	5	–	–	20
MERRITT, Nathan	29	19	–	14	–	–	56
PEATS, Nathan	21	9	9	5	–	–	20
PETTYBOURNE, Eddy	24	13	10	1	–	–	4
REYNOLDS, Adam	22	27	–	3	97	2	208
STARLING, Josh	22	–	3	–	–	–	–
SUTTON, John	27	27	–	4	–	–	16
TALANOA, Fetuli	24	1	1	–	–	–	–
TAYLOR, Dave	24	25	1	9	–	–	36
TYRRELL, Dave	23	5	16	–	–	–	–

COACH **Michael Maguire**
CAPTAINS **John Sutton** (27), **Michael Crocker** (27), **Matt King** (10),
Roy Asotasi (7), **Sam Burgess** (5)

Sydney Roosters

	AGE	STARTS	BENCH	TRIES	GOALS	F-GOALS	POINTS
ANASTA, Braith	30	22	–	4	62	–	140
ARONA, Tinirau	23	4	16	3	–	–	12
AUBUSSON, Mitchell	24	22	2	3	–	–	12
BOSDEN, Jack	23	1	3	1	–	–	4
CARNEY, Justin	24	5	–	–	–	–	–
CORDNER, Boyd	20	15	7	4	–	–	16
FRIEND, Jake	22	20	4	2	–	–	8
GUERRA, Aidan	24	18	1	5	–	–	20
HENRY, Adam	21	4	–	1	–	–	4
KENNEDY, Martin	23	17	7	1	–	–	4
KENNY–DOWALL, Shaun	24	17	–	8	–	–	32
LEILUA, Joseph	20	19	–	6	–	–	24
MASOE, Mose	23	1	13	–	–	–	–
MINICHIELLO, Anthony	32	24	–	9	–	–	36
MITCHELL, Anthony	23	4	2	1	–	–	4
MOGA, Tautau	18	14	–	7	–	–	28
MORTIMER, Daniel	23	4	4	2	5	–	18
NU'UAUSALA, Frank–Paul	25	18	1	2	–	–	8
PEARCE, Mitchell	23	22	–	10	–	–	40
PERRETT, Sam	27	15	–	3	–	–	12
SELUINI, Nafe	22	–	7	–	–	–	–
SYMONDS, Tom	23	1	1	1	–	–	4
TAGIVE, Ratu	23	5	–	–	–	–	–
TAKAIRANGI, Brad	23	5	11	1	–	–	4
TASI, Lama	22	3	16	2	–	–	8
TUIVASA–SHECK, Roger	19	6	–	–	–	–	–
TUPOU, Daniel	21	3	–	3	–	–	12
WAEREA–HARGREAVES, Jared	23	23	–	3	–	–	12

COACH Brian Smith
CAPTAINS Braith Anasta (22), Mitchell Aubusson (1), Anthony Minichiello (1)

Wests Tigers

	AGE	STARTS	BENCH	TRIES	GOALS	F-GOALS	POINTS
AYSHFORD, Blake	24	20	3	4	–	–	16
BELL, Matthew	31	9	14	–	–	–	–
BLAIR, Adam	26	23	–	3	–	–	12
CASHMERE, Ray	32	–	10	1	–	–	4
ELLIS, Gareth	31	11	–	1	–	–	4
FARAH, Robbie	28	16	–	4	–	1	17
FULTON, Liam	28	18	2	6	–	–	24
GALLOWAY, Keith	26	18	–	1	–	–	4
GROAT, Matt	20	3	4	–	–	–	–
HEIGHINGTON, Chris	30	20	–	3	–	–	12
HUMBLE, Tom	23	9	6	2	–	–	8
IOSEFA, Masada	24	3	6	3	–	–	12
KOROIBETE, Marika	20	6	–	7	–	–	28
LAWRENCE, Chris	23	20	–	6	–	–	24
MARSHALL, Benji	27	24	–	5	72	3	167
MEANEY, Sean	26	–	4	–	–	–	–
MILLER, Jacob	20	1	–	1	–	–	4
MOLTZEN, Tim	23	20	–	12	1	–	50
MOORS, Junior	26	–	14	–	–	–	–
MURDOCH–MASILA, Ben	21	–	20	5	–	–	20
POLITONI, Pat	21	–	1	–	–	–	–
REDDY, Joel	26	9	5	3	–	–	12
RYAN, Beau	27	24	–	9	–	–	36
SIMONA, Tim	20	1	2	–	–	–	–
SIRONEN, Curtis	21	5	1	1	–	–	4
TEDESCO, James	19	1	–	–	–	–	–
TUQIRI, Lote	33	12	–	5	–	–	20
UTAI, Matt	31	15	1	6	–	–	24
WOODS, Aaron	21	24	–	1	–	–	4

COACH Tim Sheens
CAPTAINS Robbie Farah (16), Benji Marshall (8)

THE 2012 LADDER

		PLAYED	WINS	LOSSES	DRAWS	FOR	AGAINST	POINTS	DIFFERENTIAL
1	Canterbury	24	18	6	–	568	369	40	199
2	Melbourne	24	17	7	–	579	361	38	218
3	South Sydney	24	16	8	–	559	438	36	121
4	Manly Warringah	24	16	8	–	497	403	36	94
5	North Queensland	24	15	9	–	597	445	34	152
6	Canberra	24	13	11	–	545	536	30	9
7	Cronulla	24	12	11	1	445	441	29	4
8	Brisbane	24	12	12	–	481	447	28	34
9	St George Illawarra	24	11	13	–	405	438	26	–33
10	Wests Tigers	24	11	13	–	506	551	26	–45
11	Gold Coast Titans	24	10	14	–	449	477	24	–28
12	Newcastle	24	10	14	–	448	488	24	–40
13	Sydney	24	8	15	1	462	626	21	–164
14	Warriors	24	8	16	–	497	609	20	–112
15	Penrith	24	8	16	–	409	575	20	–166
16	Parramatta	24	6	18	–	431	674	16	–243

TOP TRYSCORERS

BARBA, Ben (Canterbury) 21
GRAHAM, Ashley (North Queensland) 21
UATE, Akuila (Newcastle) 18
MORRIS, Josh (Canterbury) 17
ROBINSON, Reece (Canberra)................. 17
CROKER, Jarrod (Canberra) 16
EVERINGHAM, Andrew (South Sydney)..... 15
MERRITT, Nathan (South Sydney)............. 14
MORRIS, Brett (St George Illawarra) 14
GLENN, Alex (Brisbane)........................... 13
SIO, Ken (Parramatta) 13
WRIGHT, Jonathan (Canterbury) 13
BOWEN, Matthew (North Queensland) 12
SLATER, Billy (Melbourne) 12
CHAMBERS, Will (Melbourne)................... 12
HURRELL, Konrad (Warriors) 12
JOHNSON, Shaun (Warriors)................... 12
LINNETT, Kane (North Queensland) 12
MOLTZEN, Tim (Wests Tigers)................. 12
VATUVEI, Manu (Warriors)....................... 12
WILLIAMS, David (Manly Warringah)........ 12
STEWART, Brett (Manly Warringah) 11
INGLIS, Greg (South Sydney).................. 11
FERGUSON, Blake (Canberra)................. 10
COOPER, Gavin (North Queensland)........ 10

DUFFIE, Matthew (Melbourne)................ 10
GORDON, Kevin (Gold Coast Titans) 10
JENNINGS, Michael (Penrith) 10
McMANUS, James (Newcastle).............. 10
MEAD, David (Gold Coast Titans) 10
O'NEILL, Justin (Melbourne)................... 10
PEARCE, Mitchell (Sydney).................... 10
REYNOLDS, Josh (Canterbury)................ 10
TE'O, Ben (Brisbane)............................. 10

TOP POINTSCORERS

	T	G	F-G	F
CROKER, Jarrod (Can))	16	78	–	220
REYNOLDS, Adam (Sou)	2	87	2	184
THURSTON, Johnathan (NQ)	3	82	–	176
LYON, Jamie (Man)	9	68	–	172
MARSHALL, Benji (Tig)	5	72	3	167
MALONEY, James (NZ)	4	67	3	153
SMITH, Cameron (Mel)	2	68	–	144
ANASTA, Braith (Roo)	4	62	–	140
CARNEY, Todd (Cro)	4	60	3	139
PRINCE, Scott (GC)	4	61	–	138
INU, Krisnan (Bul, NZ)	9	49	2	136
BURT, Luke (Par)	7	53	–	134

THE DALLY M MEDAL

PLAYER OF THE YEAR
Ben Barba

PROVAN–SUMMONS MEDAL
Ben Barba

ROOKIE OF THE YEAR
Adam Reynolds

CAPTAIN OF THE YEAR
Jamie Lyon and **Jason King**

REPRESENTATIVE PLAYER OF THE YEAR
Nate Myles

COACH OF THE YEAR
Des Hasler

TOP TRYSCORER
Ben Barba, Ashley Graham

TOP POINTSCORER
Jarrod Croker

PETER FRILINGOS MEMORIAL AWARD
Ben Barba – Barba's home-town
performance in Mackay

TOYOTA CUP PLAYER OF THE YEAR
David Klemmer

BEST FULLBACK
Ben Barba

BEST WINGER
Akuila Uate

BEST CENTRE
Josh Morris

BEST FIVE–EIGHTH
Johnathan Thurston

BEST HALFBACK
Cooper Cronk

BEST LOCK
Paul Gallen

BEST SECOND ROWER
Nate Myles

BEST PROP
Sam Kasiano

BEST HOOKER
Cameron Smith

THE HINDMARSH MEDAL TOP 10

THURSTON, Johnathan 33
BARBA, Ben.. 31
GALLEN, Paul 28
CRONK, Cooper 27
BOWEN, Matt 22
INGLIS, Greg 21
SLATER, Billy... 20
MYLES, Nate... 20
LYON, Jamie... 17
FARAH, Robbie 17

THE RUGBY LEAGUE ALMANAC TEAM OF THE YEAR

FULLBACK
Ben Barba, Canterbury

WING
Brett Morris, St George Illawarra

CENTRE
Brent Tate, North Queensland

CENTRE
Jamie Lyon, Manly

WING
Reece Robinson, Canberra

FIVE-EIGHTH
Johnathan Thurston, North Queensland

HALFBACK
Cooper Cronk, Melbourne

LOCK
Paul Gallen, Cronulla

SECOND ROW
Nate Myles, Gold Coast)

SECOND ROW
Nathan Hindmarsh, Parramatta

PROP
Aaron Woods, Wests Tigers

HOOKER
Robbie Farah, Wests Tigers

PROP
James Graham, Canterbury

THE HINDMARSH MEDAL
TOP VOTEGETTERS BY TEAM

BRISBANE
Corey Parker (11)

CANBERRA
Josh Dugan, Shaun Fensom (12)

CANTERBURY
Ben Barba (31)

CRONULLA
Paul Gallen (28)

GOLD COAST
Nate Myles (20)

MANLY
Jamie Lyon (17)

MELBOURNE
Cooper Cronk (27)

NEWCASTLE
Jarrod Mullen (12)

NEW ZEALAND
Ben Matulino (9)

NORTH QUEENSLAND
Johnathan Thurston (33)

PARRAMATTA
Chris Sandow, Nathan Hindmarsh (13)

PENRITH
Luke Walsh (15)

ST GEORGE ILLAWARRA
Jason Nightingale (13)

SOUTH SYDNEY
Greg Inglis (21)

SYDNEY ROOSTERS
Jake Friend (10)

WESTS TIGERS
Robbie Farah (17)

REFEREES

ARCHER, Tony	LYONS, Steve
ATKINS, Grant	MAXWELL, Jared
BADGER, Gavin	MORRIS, Gavin
CECCHIN, Matt	MUNRO, David
CUMMINS, Ben	PERENARA, Henry
DE LAS HERAS, Tony	REYNOLDS, Gavin
DEVCICH, Adam	ROBINSON, Jason
GEE, Adam	SHORTALL, Alan
HAINES, Phil	SUTTON, Bernard
HAYNE, Shayne	SUTTON, Gerard
JAMES, Chris	SUTTOR, Brett
KLEIN, Ashley	

Discover a new sportswriting community at

footyalmanac.com.au

THE ALMANACKERY

Pete Abela is a Panthers fan who lives for the once-in-a-decade premiership title. He thinks the next one must be due soon. He's also an author <PETEABELA.COM>.

Michael Adams' pathological devotion to sport has been described by more than one ex as "disturbing". A Dragons fan from the inner west of Sydney, his greatest moment was meeting Ricky Walford at Newtown McDonalds in 1991.

A huge Wally Lewis fan growing up, **Cliff Bingham**'s hopes of emulating his hero were dashed when he realised he had the turning circle of a Boeing 747. He now awaits the inaugural North Queensland premiership.

Andrew Bomm is a lobbyist, Rain God and family man. He is a jack-of-all-trades and master of none. A sporadic follower of the Raiders, he writes about rugby league to secure his wife's permission to watch it.

Daniel Boss is a Balmain and Wests Tigers supporter from the revered Boss family. He has a massive man crush on Benji Marshall and wishes that more players would have hair like Kevin Hardwick.

Nathan Boss is a Cronulla Sharks tragic whose rugby league career came to a dramatic halt when Jonathan Docking-style headgear was discontinued. He is now attempting to rekindle interest in rugby league-related board games.

Bruno Brayovic started barracking for Parramatta when he entered Guilford PS, where it was mandatory. When his family moved to Campsie he became quicker, stronger and more evasive as he dodged the baying Canterbury fans.

Peta Bryant is a sporting tramp. She holds no allegiance to any team or code. She follows rugby league from a distance because it is the faith practised most devoutly by her extended family.

THE ALMANACKERY

Too small for the forwards, too slow for the backs and devoid of physical courage, as a player **John Campbell** realised he had a great future behind him. His birthday, 16/10, is Souths' last Grand Final winning score.

Arianna Canato is a Dragons fan with a heart of Steel. She thinks WIN Stadium is an apt name for a home ground. She is still suffering from a premiership hangover.

Luke Charlton is a 20-something bloke who inherited his love of rugby league and the Rabbitohs from his father. Translated, their family motto is *Live in Hope*. Which he does.

A new Northern Territorian, **Niall Connolly** stares vacantly out of windows a lot and vaguely contemplates all that serenity. He thinks Steve Matai is misunderstood.

As a young boy **Paul Connolly** bought comics from the same Wollongong newsagency frequented by St George's dashing fullback Brian Johnston. This remains important to him.

Mark Courtney's moods during winter are defined entirely by the Rabbitohs. The author of *Moving the Goalposts* and Russell Crowe's *Book of Feuds*, he has complete faith that South Sydney will be premiers in his lifetime.

Lindsey Cuthbertson writes about music and sport while teaching the drums deep in Broncos' heartland. A Manly and New South Wales diehard, he is loving every minute of life behind enemy lines.

Paul Dalligan is an NRL fanatic living in AFL Central. He believes the Chinese got it wrong when they said 2011 was the Year of the Rabbit.

THE ALMANACKERY

Adam Donnelly is a Newcastle-based Tigers fanatic who believes rugby league is the best exemplar of all that is good and powerful in group ritual and folklore. He also hates the Rabbitohs.

Daniel Dwyer is a loyal supporter of the Knights and a legend of the fantasy football world. More commonly known as 'The People's Champion', he is also the champion of the Spider Cup for season 2012.

Will Evans has a head like Ben Kennedy but tackles like Jason Taylor. Which is why he is a writer. He recently committed rugby league sacrilege, switching allegiance from the Broncos to the Warriors.

Matt Fisk is a rugby league trainspotter. He is a Wests Magpie, loves his NSW Blues and dreams of visiting Lloyd Robson Oval for a sanctioned Test Match against the Kangaroos.

Dave Fletcher is a proud North Queenslander and passionate Cowboys and Maroons fan. He has survived in the belly of the beast that is Sydney for a decade. He enjoys tormenting his colleagues.

Breatharians claim they can be nourished by light with no need for food or drink. **Huw Fowles** claims he is a sportarian, a person nourished by sport with no need for musicals or non-alcoholic beer.

Michael Grosvenor loves the Sydney Roosters, the Swans, Tottenham, the Jets, the Mets and the Knicks. However, he'd rather watch re-runs of the Brady Bunch than suffer a game of rugby union.

Russel 'Rabbitoh' Hansen was born to follow Souths – he announced himself to the world in Kingaroy (home town of current Bunnies utility Chris McQueen) on Grand Final day 1967, the day of the famous McCarthy intercept.

THE ALMANACKERY

John Harms was a thinking boys' five-eighth for the Oakey JRLC. His side won one game in four seasons. He believes Darryl Brohman should be premier of Queensland.

Days before the 1989 Grand Final, **Michael Harrison-Ford** used orange hair dye to make his pet dog Basil a Tigers mascot. The Tigers lost that Grand Final in extra-time, while Basil was put down shortly after.

Ian Hauser is an about-to-retire teacher and Maroons diehard. He sees rugby league happiness as Sunday afternoon on the western mound at Redcliffe's Dolphin Oval watching the locals run around in the Queensland Cup.

Liam Hauser is a Queenslander. He bleeds maroon. He also supports the Broncos. His favourite sportspeople include Matthew Hayden and Allan Langer. A sports journalist, he is the author of *State of Origin: 30 Years*.

Peter Hulthen spent most of his adult life teaching young people. He believes sport can play a big part in putting kids on track. A Cowboys fan, he is married to Matt Bowen's aunt.

Glen Humphries has been a Dragons fan since back in 1977, when footballs were made of leather, players were obliged to grow moustaches and every kid longed to be a sandboy. He misses those days.

Brett Hutchins follows league religiously despite abhorring all forms of male violence, corporate excess and anything vaguely connected to Rupert Murdoch. These contradictions are caused by a quixotic dedication to the Parramatta Eels.

Hailing from the Snowy Mountains, former Cooma Stallions winger **Luke Jamieson** looks back fondly at a playing career entailing no footwork, no defence and a big thirst. Hard of hearing, he is an avid night-swimmer.

THE ALMANACKERY

Dan Keary is a lifelong Roosters supporter who, despite his doctor's advice, refuses to throw in his Roosters towel. He can sometimes be heard muttering: "I wish it could be 1975 again."

Michael Kennedy has followed the Eels for many years. His mind is caught in 1986. Hobbit-esque in nature, he's likely to be found savouring the delights of coffee, chocolate and cryptic crosswords.

Dara Lawlor is a muggle-blood Wests Tigers fan who's never seen them play at Leichhardt Oval. He does a mean Ray French impression and was at Wembley in 1999 when Graham Murray actually won something.

Titans fan **Alex Madge** has been a rugby league man ever since he was a rugby league child. He longs to see a field goal in the opening minutes of a match, preferably by a second rower.

Steve Mascord raced onto Dapto Showground to snatch the corner post after Illawarra's first trial match in 1982. This qualifies him perfectly for his role as chief writer at *Rugby League Week*.

As a Warriors fan living in AFL-land, **Samson McDougall** doesn't have many mates. If you have Foxtel and like rugby league, he's more than happy to bring the beer and the Twisties.

Tigers fan **Nick McGrath** was left devastated, and deaf in his left ear, when his boys' perfect finals record was broken in their extra-time loss to the Roosters in 2010.

Justin McIlveen wanted to be a professional footballer but was let down by his ability and work ethic. He turned his attention to writing but has been let down by his ability and work ethic.

THE ALMANACKERY

Jack Muir supports the Warriors. Currently living in Hong Kong, he spends most of his weekends in verbal altercations with rugby union fans. He has been labelled the David Koresh of rugby league.

Adam Muyt can't help it: he grew up in Manly. His favourite colour is maroon, except when worn by Queensland teams. Now living in Hobart, he has been writing for the *Almanac* since 2008.

Everything **Tim Napper** knows he learned from George Orwell, Kurt Vonnegut and Chuck Norris. When not watching the Raiders underachieve, surrender or miss crucial conversions, he writes on politics at <WWW.MAKINGTHENUT.COM>.

Boof Nichols claims he's not a one-eyed Sharks supporter. He is adamant Jonathan Docking should be the next Immortal and believes if Kiwi Luke Covell had pledged his allegiance to NSW, the Blues would be celebrating seven straight.

Lawyer **Brett Oaten** loves his family, his work, punk rock, country music, the beach and the Sydney Roosters – not necessarily in that order. He co-presents *Fire Up!* on FBI in Sydney, Australia's least popular rugby league show.

A Rugby league purist from the Northern Riverina, **Greg Oberscheidt** prefers the Les Boyd approach to Braith Anasta's. A Balmain tragic, he wanted to be Tim Brasher but performed more like Hassan Saleh.

With the O'Hanlon moniker, it's no wonder **Matt O'Hanlon** is waiting for the Commission's decision to put the mighty Brothers in the NRL so that the team in the blue and the white is again the cream of the state.

Chris Parkinson has baffled haematologists worldwide with his ability to bleed lime green. Some have theorised over links to reptilian heritage, but league aficionados understand it is purely a symptom of a deep-seated love of the Raiders.

THE ALMANACKERY

Brendan Pearson is a one-time Balmain supporter who defected to the Raiders in 1982 while at uni in the national capital. A very average prop, he combined the creativity of Graham Olling with the footwork of Victor the Viking.

Mick Pearson loves racing, rugby league and the punt, preferably combined. To date, his horses have won one race – the Swankys Turfing Class 1 Handicap at Ipswich on a Friday in 2010.

Paul Robertson is a corporate bean counter, avid reader and lover of all things rugby league. He is the leader of *League of Our Own*, a large and growing group of rugby league supporters based in Melbourne.

Doug Roweth was never meant to be a South Sydney fan. But like the *Titanic*, hip hop music and Ben Roberts' rugby league career, some things just happen.

Andrew Ryan – no relation to 'Bobcat' – is a long-suffering Souths supporter, whose highlights include meeting the Gobbledock and getting free Smiths Crisps, Eion Crosson's first try, the 1994 Tooheys Cup and Nathan Merrit's SCG field goal.

Mark 'The Professor' Seymour is a fanatical Canterbury supporter. He has been on medication since the Bulldogs secured the 2002 wooden spoon after having 37 points deducted for a mathematical miscalculation over player salaries.

Mark Shannon turned to writing about league after inept playing, coaching and administrative careers. Cruelly called 'Mini-bus' by his team (half a coach), the pen represents his last chance for success in rugby league.

After a decade of threatening to write a letter to the NRL decrying foul play every time his Warriors lost, **Andrew Smith** finally got off his arse and put pen to paper in 2012.

THE ALMANACKERY

Edwin Smith is a recent graduate of Sports Media at the University of Canberra. A diehard Parramatta fan, he made a delicious cake with the Eels' wooden spoon.

Joshua Smith is a Dragons fan (via the Sharks and the Bulldogs). A former NRL bean counter, he is now a podcaster. He craves world peace.

Marty Spencer is an aging Dragons supporter who enjoys a peppery shiraz on a cool evening and a frosty beer in a chilled glass on any given day. He is currently Back to School, Dangerfield style.

Matt Tedeschi is a Raider to the core. He continues to resent Albert Fulivai and Jason Bulgarelli. He once wore shorts to Bruce Stadium when the wind chill factor had conditions hovering around minus eight.

Nick Tedeschi is a Canterbury diehard. In physical appearance, he has been compared to both Mick Molloy and a young Francis Ford Coppola. He remains very much in love with both Winnie Cooper and Tony Grimaldi.

Grant Vickers jumped on the Panthers bandwagon in 1991 as a nine-year-old and has been stuck there ever since. With no athletic ability to speak of, his shoulder injury is a convenient excuse for his lack of sporting success.

Tasmania isn't exactly rugby league heartland, but that hasn't stopped **Stu Warren** watching as much of the game as the current free-to-air rights deal allows. His NRL views are greenish after a stint in the nation's capital.

Mike Wilson has been watching footy since birth and has been spreading his love of it like chicken pox ever since. A fair dinkum Sea Eagles tragic, he wishes Beaver Menzies a long and happy life.

ACKNOWLEDGEMENTS

The Rugby League Almanac is an enormous project which takes a lot of organisation. Many people have been involved.

Thanks especially to all the writers and contributors who have given so much and have made this all possible. Your enthusiasm for the game is here for all to see. You've been terrific.

Thanks to **Hannah Browne** for introducing us to each other.

Thanks to **Ian Hauser** who has been a key part of the process of compiling, editing, and proof-reading this book.

Thanks to **John Kingsmill** from Tabloid who has done such a magnificent job designing the book and helping oversee the whole process.

Thanks to artist **Martin Tighe** for his superb portrait of Ben Barba.

Thanks to **Carolyn Beddoes** at McPherson's Printing.

Thanks to **Dips O'Donnell** of Hillard O'Donnell, **Hap Hannan** at Friday Median **Neil Belford** for his IT advice, **John Stanley**, **Bruce Humphrys** and **Nick Livermore**.

Thanks to **Mark Branagan**, **Tony Collins** and **Paul Noonan** for legal advice.

Thanks to our sponsors and advertisers: **Brad Tamer** at TattsBet; **Lyle Meaney**, **Kane Miller** and **Gary Robb** at Dixon Advisory; **Nigel Clark** and **Natalie Davies** at Momentum, **Bill McVeigh** at Murrindindi Vineyards and **Marty McGrath** at **Brimar Electrical**.

Thanks to **Stephen Cooke**, **James Demetrie** at Diskman, and **Phil Dimitriadis** for their ongoing development of www.footyalmanac.com.au

Thanks to **Louise** and **Susan** for their support.

 Discover a new sportswriting community at

footyalmanac.com.au

Become a Friend of Murrindindi and enjoy our Family Reserve range of shiraz, cabernet and chardonnay.

The Penguin Good Australian Wine Guide rates the 2005 chardonnay as "the best white wine in Australia".

The exciting *Don't Tell Dad* range of riesling and cabernet is also available with huge discounts off retail prices.

Join now and receive the current six vintages for $100. (RRP $150)

DELIVERY IS FREE IN VIC, SA AND NSW FOR ALMANAC READERS.

Murrindindi Vineyards

NEAR YEA, IN THE FOOTHILLS OF VICTORIA'S HIGH COUNTRY

WINERY Cummins Lane, Murrindindi VIC 3717
SALES OFFICE 5A Northcote Avenue, Balwyn VIC 3103
TELEPHONE 0467 555 449 **FAX** 3 9836 6648
EMAIL billm@murrindindivineyards.com
WEBSITE www.murrindindivineyards.com
ABN 54 115 981 041

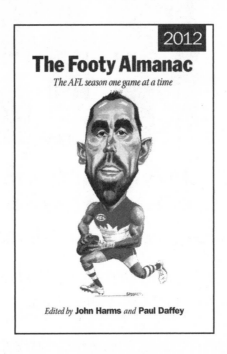

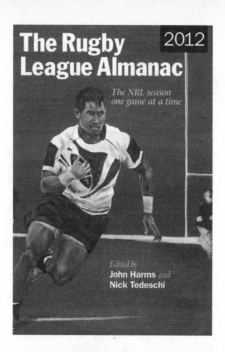

Write for us!

No doubt many of you are sitting there thinking you wouldn't mind having a go at this writing caper.

Well, we would love to publish your stories, especially on Rugby League, but across all sports. We are interested in fresh writing: match reports of the top level sport, stories of your own sport, memoir, historical pieces. Whatever you like, really.

footyalmanac.com.au has published over 6,000 articles by fans since 2009. So, have a go yourself.

If you show a bit of form on the website, then you're sure to thrust your name before the selectors and you'll be writing for one of our books in no time.

EMAIL footyalmanac@bigpond.com
MAIL PO Box 1402, Fitzroy North Vic 3068
Or contact john harms
j.t.h@bigpond.net.au

ST.GEORGE

THE CHARGE BEHIND THE DRAGONS.

We're proud to be a sponsor of St George Illawarra Dragons. And the power behind the 2013 premiership charge.

momentum.com.au

A Hydro Tasmania Business

momentum
energy